Something in Common—
An IWW Bibliography

The working class and the employing class have nothing in common. There can be no peace so long as hunger and want are found among millions of working people and the few, who make up the employing class, have all the good things of life.

—from the IWW Preamble

Something in Common—

An IWW Bibliography

compiled by

Dione Miles

Archives of Labor and Urban Affairs
Walter P. Reuther Library
Wayne State University

Wayne State University Press · Detroit, 1986

Library of Congress Cataloging-in-Publication Data

Miles, Dione, 1921–
Something in common.

Includes indexes.
1. Industrial Workers of the World—Bibliography.
2. Trade-unions—United States—Bibliography.
I. Title.
Z7164.T7M54 1986 016.33188′6 85-26586
[HD8055.I4]
ISBN 0-8143-1796-0

Mourn not the dead that in the cool earth lie,
Dust unto dust—
The calm sweet earth that mothers all who die,
As all men must;

Mourn not your captive comrades who must dwell
Too strong to strive—
Each in his steelbound coffin of a cell,
Buried alive;

But rather mourn the apathetic throng,
The cowed and meek
Who see the world's great anguish and its wrong,
And dare not speak.

—Ralph Chaplin
IWW Prisoner

Contents

Foreword

THE Industrial Workers of the World is one of the most interesting and important labor organizations to develop in the United States. Although its membership was never large compared to other international unions, few labor organizations have played such a significant role or had such an impact upon the American and international scene.

Founded in 1905, the Industrial Workers of the World, whose members were popularly called "Wobblies," attempted to organize workers into one great union embracing all industries. In the years that followed, the IWW was involved in historic strikes and events in McKees Rocks, Pennsylvania; Paterson, New Jersey; Lawrence, Massachusetts; Wheatland, California; Bisbee, Colorado; and Everett and Centralia, Washington.

Its leaders became national figures, and some, like Joe Hill, the composer of protest songs, even became martyrs. Others, like Vincent St. John, Bill Haywood, William Trautmann, Elizabeth Gurley Flynn, J. T. "Red" Doran, Walt Westman, Joseph Ettor, and Fred Thompson gained international reputations. Other Wobblies made important contributions to the new industrial unions, including the United Automobile Workers and the United Steel Workers.

In 1963 the IWW officially designated the Archives of Labor and Urban Affairs at the Reuther Library of Wayne State University in Detroit, Michigan, as the official depository of its inactive historical records. Although many IWW records were seized by the Federal Government in 1918 during the infamous Palmer Raids and later destroyed, large holdings of archival material had been saved and were given to the Archives. In addition, the official files of the IWW locals and the personal papers of many Wobblies have been collected and preserved. New collections of IWW material turn up constantly.

The IWW collections in the Archives have been used extensively by writers from a variety of humanistic disciplines. Hundreds of books, monographs, and journal articles have been based upon the Archives'

IWW collections. Graduate students from the United States, Canada, and other foreign countries have also selected research topics relating to the IWW. In addition to accounts of the IWW itself and of historic strikes and events, research topics have included the cartoons of Ernest Riebe, the originator of the famous Mr. Block illustrations, the protest songs of Joe Hill, and the IWW in the theater. The producers of the recent film *Reds* extensively utilized the IWW and related collections in the Archives.

In addition to archival material, extensive information about the IWW and its leaders is available in a variety of publications—books, monographs, magazine and periodical articles, newspaper accounts, films, dissertations and theses, and government documents. The IWW has also sponsored hundreds of publications, including the famous *Little Red Song Book.*

In order to assist researchers, Dione Miles, archivist on the staff of the Reuther Library, has prepared a comprehensive bibliography of published materials relating to the IWW, including many rare and obscure items. She is unusually well qualified for the task, having been actively involved with the Archives' IWW collections since she joined the staff in 1969. She was ably assisted by Stanley Mallach, bibliographer of the Fromkin Memorial Collection at the University of Wisconsin, Milwaukee.

The publication of this bibliography was made possible by grants from the Archives Memorial Fund and the University Stimulation and Development Fund.

Philip P. Mason
Director, Archives of Labor and Urban Affairs
Walter P. Reuther Library
Wayne State University

Acknowledgments

WORKING in the Archives of Labor and Urban Affairs of Wayne State University has given me access to many old published sources regarding the Industrial Workers of the World (IWW)—sources that are not easily found elsewhere. The official records of the IWW are deposited here also, in the Reuther Library. As archivist of the collection, I start with the world's greatest wealth of published and unpublished IWW material right at my elbow. Therefore, my first thanks go to the Director of the Archives, Professor Philip P. Mason, who gave me this opportunity and whose suggestion it was that I should compile a bibliography on the IWW.

If this book proves to be as clear and useful as I hope it will be, it is thanks to Stanley Mallach, bibliographer of the Fromkin Collection at the Golda Meir Library of the University of Wisconsin in Milwaukee. His keen and critical eye helped to discipline this mass of materials, and his high standards and erudition inspired me to aim for higher standards in a field to which I am a newcomer. His painstaking and patient editorial assistance was accompanied by a sense of humor that helped to make the hard work seem like fun.

I am especially grateful also for the help of Fred W. Thompson of the IWW, who provided both information and ideas. Over the years, he has sent us an assortment of papers written about the IWW that he has received from many friends around the country. He is himself a walking encyclopedia on the subject, so he makes a useful as well as a pleasant and inspiring friend.

I was not able to visit most of the other areas where good IWW material may be found, but I received no little assistance by mail. Joseph R. Conlin, whose recently published book, *At the Point of Production* (see no. 39) got me started (I compiled a much smaller local history bibliography for it), was another friend who encouraged me. Professor Alex Baskin sent many ideas from New York, and Genevieve Lawrence of Centralia, Washington, was my "agent" out West, sending me lists and getting others to do so. Gayle Palmer of Centralia Timberland Library sent some useful lists of Western materials.

The largest previous bibliography on the IWW is Paul J. Green and Siegfried A. Vogt's *Sources on the Industrial Workers of the World (IWW),* which was published in Pullman, Washington, in 1978 and is based mainly on Western sources. This excellent work (no. 4917 in this book) was especially useful in listing Western materials at Washington State that I could not go out to see. The copy of this book mailed me shows that scope and precision can be possible even with such a complex subject covering so many years. Other useful bibliographies are *American Working-Class History in Historical Journals, 1961–1972: A Bibliography,* by Andor and Julia Williams Skotnes (New Brunswick, NJ: Labor Education Center, Rutgers University—the State University of New Jersey, 1974), and its predecessor, *American Labor in Journals of History: A Bibliography,* compiled by Fred Duane Rose (Champaign, IL: Institute of Labor and Industrial Relations, University of Illinois, 1962). A further useful one is James C. McBrearty's *American Labor History and Comparative Labor Movements: A Bibliography* (Tucson, AZ: University of Arizona Press, 1973).

At Wayne State University's Purdy Library, interloan librarians were essential for my work in searching the rarer journals, and I thank Joan Martin, Hugh O'Connor, Robert Kunnath, and Don Forshey, as well as unknown librarians at the other end of this valuable book-borrowing service. Also thanks to Gary Boyer of Syracuse University, who gave suggestions on IWW fiction, and to Professor Robert Zieger of Wayne State University, who was helpful with the section on published histories. Finally, my husband, Richard Miles, gets my biggest thanks for his patient editorial work and encouraging support.

The illustrations throughout come from the files of the Archives of Labor and Urban Affairs at the Reuther Library.

Introduction

THE Industrial Workers of the World (IWW), first organized over eighty years ago, has been a popular subject for historical research for many years—just how popular, this book will show. Today, newly released materials are stimulating the interest of scholars, and the number of students—and possibly members—of the colorful IWW seems destined to increase.

The IWW held the attention of the whole nation from 1905 to 1921. The very name became a generic term for all radicals, whether they were members or not. Since then, the union has attracted much less popular attention, while receiving more scholarly interest. As a subject of study, the IWW has provided such rewarding features as revolutionary ideas, imaginative and daring actions, heroes or villains who aroused national love or hate, and artistic or romantic flair. Most of all, however, it was and is a serious union intent on organizing not only the organized but also the passive members of passive unions, hoping to galvanize them to action, hoping to revolutionize their thinking.

The chief distinguishing idea of the IWW has been that the workers should organize along industrial lines rather than into separate craft unions. This audacious idea, emphasized so strongly, frightened employers, citizens, and the government because of its implication of mass power. Although the CIO began to achieve success in horizontal unionism more than thirty years later, the IWW has maintained its own purpose separately and has followed its independent course right up to the present.

Other IWW beliefs have been that the worker and his employer have "nothing in common"—most outrageous to many, especially employers; that women, blacks, and immigrants should be equal co-workers with all other workers (even in 1905, the founding date); that strikes should be "on the job," "at the point of production," and preferably short; that signing a contract with an employer, however favorable, hobbles the worker and compromises his or her freedom of action; and, finally, that the most effective form of protest is a general strike of all the workers.

The beliefs of the union are stated fully in its famous Preamble, which is reprinted in nearly all IWW publications.

The IWW unions had a penchant for imaginative tactics, which brought them considerable publicity. Some unions promoted pageants, plays, children's marches, free speech fights, clever songs and sharp cartoons, chalk-talks, lantern-slide shows, public picnics, postal song cards, and poem and cartoon cards for mailing around. Also promoted were the famous small stickerettes, "the little organizers," which combined art with catchy mottoes and which were designed to be stuck on public walls and fence posts. All of this effort was to rouse the passive population, rile the authorities, and "fan the flames of discontent" among the people. The famous "little red song books," which anybody could get for a nickel and which featured new words to tunes everybody knew, were enjoyed from coast to coast, and not by IWW members alone.

In the first dozen years after its founding in 1905, the IWW grew among laborers who were the least shielded from the economic oppression of the times: miners, lumberworkers, migratory farmworkers, dock workers, railroad gangs, textile weavers, and many others. These were the people for whom the IWW Preamble had special appeal. Strikes at McKees Rocks, Goldfield, Lawrence, Paterson, and elsewhere; the Wheatland Hop Riot; the execution of Joe Hill; the Bisbee deportation; and the Centralia and Everett Massacres were events that provided the "Wobblies" with national causes and heroes. Free speech fights, the eight-hour-day struggle, and a few highly publicized strikes brought them some small success and much notoriety.

Colorful leaders emerged who attracted public interest: Big Bill Haywood, the crowd-pleaser; quiet Vincent St. John ("the Saint" to his friends); the skilled orators J. T. "Red" Doran, Elizabeth Gurley Flynn, Joseph Ettor, and James P. Thompson; the poets Ralph Chaplin and Arturo Giovannitti; the songmakers, especially Joe Hill; and, of course, the other martyrs whose killings evoked much sympathy and horror—Frank Little, Wesley Everest, and the other victims of hundreds of violent incidents.

Later leaders of the IWW—speakers, poets, great organizers, great sacrificers—were also talented and colorful. Although they worked as hard, during a period of continuing conservatism, as earlier leaders had, their timing in history was not so conducive to the appearance of insouciance and dash. They came to be seen not as social crusaders but as dangerous and annoying. Through all opposition, they continued working for their principles, and they still do.

In 1917, when this country joined World War I, a strong tide of patriotism worked against the success of any union group daring to suggest strikes or even sharing the new profits. The IWW was conspicuous in its denunciation of the war and of American participation in it. This made it a choice target of attack for being "disloyal" or even, to some, "traitorous" to the United States. Therefore, the IWW, with its large foreign membership and "anarchist" literature, was espeically subject to fierce scrutiny and criticism on patriotic grounds.

With the passage of laws on Criminal Syndicalism, the Federal Government was able to seize papers and records from all IWW headquarters, and did so promptly. Most of these records were destroyed, which explains the scarcity of IWW historical papers. Many IWW people were imprisoned just for being members, and those who were not operated under a continual threat of charges and arrest under laws that are still on the books. Not only were leaders jailed and records destroyed, but office equipment and funds of cash were seized and never returned. The full force of this government repression is still being discovered by researchers today. The IWW interpreted it as an effort of employers, using the government as the tool, to get rid of unionism altogether.

The organization survived through the twenties, and there was even a small increase in membership, but prospects were severely damaged by the Depression. Another period of some hope and increased membership was dashed in the forties by the Taft-Hartley Act and then in the early fifties by the Attorney General's "subversive list" (although the IWW is not pro-Communist). That list is gone for now.

A corps of believers carries on today, with membership varying from year to year. Some of the IWW's once-radical beliefs, such as industrial unionism, are now widely accepted. Besides creating a colorful chapter in labor history and adding to the spread of belief in industrial unionism, the IWW remains an example of a group that has stood up for its principles against nearly impossible odds. Lately, the Polish union Solidarność (once the name of an American Polish IWW newspaper) has been described, even by conservatives, as brave, daring, and dedicated to the rights of workers against heavy odds. So also has the IWW seen itself.

Research into the IWW has been greatly spurred by such publishers as Greenwood Press and Arno Press, whose reprints of old newspapers, pamphlets, and books have breathed life into many a forgotten work and brought material to readers and scholars that was formerly difficult or impossible to find. Archives from coast to coast are receiving primary materials on radicals and radicalism that were once hidden in attics. Recent changes in the policies of the National Archives (in some departments) have opened for inspection new research materials on the government's role in labor oppression that could not be seen five or ten years ago.

Many states have designated one library in the state to be a collection center that preserves all the newspapers of the state's smaller towns and cities. Local history societies are growing and collecting, and some of them have acquired estimable minor IWW collections. Therefore, the research possibilities are growing rather than drying up.

This book documents what has been written about the IWW over the many years of its existence. An attempt has been made to include representative viewpoints from every decade of this century and from as many published sources as possible.

IWW Chronology

A short chronology of events in IWW history has been placed near the front of this book. It may be useful in determining whether some items are relevant in a particular time span or possibly related to a particular event or issue. The chronology may be used as a supplement to the subject-author index at the back of the book or to an entry whose information may seem insufficient.

Books

The books selected include most monographs on the IWW and a number of histories that treat the IWW as part of labor history. Various decades are represented, even though the treatment in some periods was rather slight. This lack of interest is itself part of the IWW story, and it helps to show the historiographical trends. Some books provide background, some mere opinion. A few are, frankly, not really good. Nonetheless, a full understanding of attitudes toward the IWW is impossible without a few such inclusions, even if they seem dated. An attempt has been made to include the differing views of many years, as well as the current, possibly more accurate, views of recent scholarship. A selection of foreign-language books has been included, without annotation, because they may be useful to some readers and because they reveal a worldwide interest.

Articles

The collection of articles here is as inclusive as possible. Articles were selected from sources available at some libraries and from interlibrary loans. Because both popular and scholarly efforts are represented here, a special index, which follows the section of articles, lists all the articles by journal. Readers interested in special perspectives can find in this index the titles of appropriate journals (scholarly or popular, old or new); under those titles, entries will be listed by number. In addition, a comprehensive index at the end of the book includes subjects and authors.

Most articles are available at libraries or through library loan. A few journals (such as certain lumbering and manufacturing house organs) were merely sampled because their contribution to the study of the IWW is marginal, although they must not be overlooked because they too had a special viewpoint on the IWW.

Pamphlets about the IWW and Pamphlets and Leaflets Published by the IWW

Pamphlet literature was an important part of early twentieth-century propaganda. The pamphlets in this bibliography have been separated into those about the IWW, which were published by many different people and groups, and those published by the IWW itself. IWW pamphlets have become collectors' items, and many people are interested in lists of such publications. This list is as complete as I was able to make it. It includes some pamphlets that I was not able to examine because they are in distant archives. As the largest known collection of IWW pamphlets is part of the Archives of Labor and Urban Affairs at Wayne State University, where I work, I have been lucky in this respect.

I have listed at least one location for most of the hard-to-get pamphlets. The symbols used for the locations of the pamphlets are similar to the symbols used in the *Union List of Serials.* The key to these symbols is located near the front of this book. Not all pamphlets have a known location; information about them was garnered from old IWW literature lists, from scholarly bibliographies, or in some cases from microfilms. Some of the pamphlets, seized by the U.S. Post Office during the Red Scare, are at the National Archives in Washington, DC, and are still part of the old Post Office records. Many of these, however, can also be seen in archival collections. Some of the leaflets remain fugitive items.

As to authorship of the pamphlets, some writers preferred to remain anonymous—sometimes for safety's sake, to avoid arrest, sometimes to keep the words impersonal. Pamphlets were an important, conscious part of the IWW organizing effort, and successful pamphlets have been republished many times. Some have been in print for sixty years and are still selling. Many of the pamphlets and leaflets are not dated. This was to keep them "fresh" on the newstand. Occasionally other bibliographic data, such as publisher and city, are missing, a reminder of the days, 1917–1923, when the mere possession of a pamphlet was reason for arrest, trial, and possibly years in prison. All information available has been included with the pamphlet and leaflet list.

The IWW printed pamphlets in all major foreign languages and in lesser-known ones, such as Slovenian, Montenegrin, Bulgarian, Lithuanian, Greek, and Finnish. These were usually translations of the English pamphlets. Because of their bulk, and because their use is limited, foreign-language pamphlets have been omitted here. Persons interested in seeing them should inquire at the New York Public Library, the Tamiment Library of New York University, the Labadie Collection at the University of Michigan, and the Archives of Labor and Urban Affairs of Wayne State University. These institutions seem to have the largest collections of such pamphlets in all languages.

IWW Newspapers and Magazines

The many newspapers published by the IWW were sold at IWW bookstores and newstands and by all IWW delegates. The delegates received them in large bundles from headquarters. These papers were popular, forming the base of a real newspaper empire that stretched across the country. The chief IWW newspapers are now available in reprint or on microfilm, as are the most popular IWW magazines. A list of some of the foreign-language papers is added to show the scope of the IWW's publication ventures. Locations are given for as many items as possible. In some cases, in which no one place appears to have a full run, two or more locations are given. The location key is found near the front of the book.

A special effort was made to include some articles from other labor union journals, such as *Miners' Magazine* and *American Federationist,* and from concurrent publications of individual trade unions. These articles are usually inimical to the IWW, of course, but the authors were knowledgeable as to where to inflict damage, so their hostile views are part of the story, and these articles were probably powerful at the time. Other perspectives—Socialist, Socialist Labor, Communist, Anarchist, the popular middle-class magazines and the intellectual journals—are included as well. These specialized viewpoints will be most easily recognized in the journal index.

Dissertations and Theses

Compiling a list of dissertations written on the IWW or subjects closely related to it would have been even more difficult without *Dissertation Abstracts International* (Ann Arbor, MI: University Microfilms International) or *America: History and Life* (Santa Barbara, CA: American Bibliographic Center of ABC-Clio). The former, however, relies on title keywords that are sometimes less than useful in eliciting parts of the IWW story. Some works not often cited in footnotes (for many of these dissertations were found in such places) regrettably may have slipped through the net. Dissertations that later became books are sometimes included in this list, for such inclusions help fill in the picture of the development of scholarly interest in the IWW. Changes can be seen in kinds of subject and in patterns of research. Not all dissertations listed are concerned wholly with the IWW, but all have made a contribution to our knowledge of it.

The inclusion after the dissertations of a selection of master's essays and theses serves to round out the presentation of the ways in which the IWW has been used as an academic research subject and, of course, provides an additional body of information.

Government Documents and Publications

U.S. documents often cited in IWW studies are included in the bibliography, with a sampling as well of some material printed in the *Congressional Record* and some other government-published journals. Some pamphlets printed by the U.S. Government are also included. Following the U.S. Government material is a selection of state and local government documents. It was impossible to include the hundreds of legal papers, court cases, etc. They are important but too bulky for this finite listing. They can be found at some state archives and libraries, but many are still part of courthouse and local records. The documents included here are often lengthy, but they provide good detailed descriptions and testimony about IWW events.

Miscellaneous Historical Writings

Some of the miscellaneous historical writings included here are reminiscences intended for publication or historical views of the IWW by members of the union, such as Covington Hall and Ben Williams, both IWW editors. Essays and treatises whose purposes are not identified but which still may be of use and value are included. Some of the papers were sent to IWW historian Fred Thompson by their authors, and others have come into archives around the country. Probably most of these items were intended for future publication. Any of them may constitute interesting research material.

Miscellaneous Imaginative Views

A section that lists dramatic, poetic, and fictional writings about the IWW is included because it shows some further possibilities of IWW history. Several novels that use IWW incidents as part of their stories have been published in the last few years. They are added to a list of works from previous decades. Rather than diminishing, the appearances of the IWW in the more imaginative forms of writing have increased. In the IWW union itself, the use of songbooks, poem cards, plays, and good yarns has always been a part of the pleasure. A few poetic or dramatic items may appear in the Pamphlets or Articles sections of this bibliography if they were primarily written for a special purpose. For the most part, however, they will be found in this miscellaneous group of artistic writings, whose purpose was usually the expression of deeply felt emotions.

Not Included

Neither archival holdings nor oral histories were included in this book. There is currently a great increase in donations to archives of IWW collections all over the country. In only a few years, these collections will be more accurately listed and available. Oral histories are not yet well reported, but the oral-history groups are working on great improvements. In a few years these too will be ready for listing. For a preliminary list of archival holdings in many states and in Washington, DC, see my local-history bibliography, included in the book edited by Joseph R. Conlin, *At the Point of Production* (no. 39 in this bibliography).

Some other items, such as the fascinating cartoons and drawings of the IWW, can be seen in some of their published forms, as in Joyce Kornbluh's *Rebel Voices* (no. 132) and in Ernest Riebe's work (nos. 3827–29), which are included in this bibliographic listing. No discography of IWW songs is included here, but they can be found through the indexes of record and tape manufacturers. Proceedings, minutes, and minor newsletters and bulletins can be found at a number of archives, specifically at the Reuther Library at Wayne State University and at the Labadie Collection at the University of Michigan.

The Index

The subject-author index at the back of the book, in addition to the index of journals, is intended to help the researcher form special small bibliographies on any of the many incidents or individuals or subjects involved in eighty years of IWW history. Some materials could not be indexed in detail. They are the more general works that cover ranges of political and philosophical arguments or histories that encompass, or try to encompass, everything. The index should not be relied upon without a perusal of the bibliography, however, because many of the entries had multiple subjects and could not be indexed under every possible heading.

Annotations

At the beginning of the research for this bibliography, it was decided that there should be a minimum of annotation because of the need to save space in a listing of eighty years' worth of writings. However, many of the titles are not informative, so annotations have been added wherever possible for clarity. There were some items that I was unable to see, however, either because they are not available for library loan (such as the dissertations) or because no nearby library or archive had them, although they are known to exist. On entries for which it was deemed notes would be superfluous, the annotation was omitted; on others I tried to be as generous as possible.

Research on the IWW is a rewarding enterprise, and each facet of the IWW has its researcher "fans." Nevertheless, there are still many areas that have not been explored. It is my hope that this bibliography will help to point out some of the unexplored areas and to reveal long-lost or new views of the old familiar ones.

D. M.

Abbreviations

AFL	American Federation of Labor
BIR	Bureau of Industrial Research
BTW	Brotherhood of Timber Workers
CDC	California District Committee, sometimes California Defense Committee
CPC	Centralia Publicity Committee
GDC	General Defense Committee
NEB	National Executive Board
NEC	National Executive Committee
OBU	One Big Union, referring to either the IWW One Big Union or the Canadian One Big Union
WFM	Western Federation of Miners

IWW Unions

AWIU	Agricultural Workers Industrial Union
AWO	Agricultural Workers Organization
BCWIU	Building Construction Workers Industrial Union
CMWIU	Coal Mine Workers Industrial Union
CWIU	Construction Workers Industrial Union
FWIU	Food Workers Industrial Union
GCWIU	General Construction Workers Industrial Union
HRDWIU	Hotel, Restaurant, and Domestic Workers Industrial Union
LWIU	Lumber Workers Industrial Union
MMWIU	Metal Mine Workers Industrial Union
MTWIU	Marine Transport Workers Industrial Union
OWIU	Oil Workers Industrial Union
RRWIU	Railroad Workers Industrial Union

Key to Location Symbols

Arizona

AzTeS	Arizona State University Library, Tempe
AzTU-PH	Arizona Pioneer Historical Society, Tucson

California

CLU	University of California Library, Los Angeles
CSt	Stanford University Libraries, Stanford
CSt-H	Hoover Library, Stanford
CU	University of California Library, Berkeley
CU-B	Bancroft Library, University of California, Berkeley

Colorado

CoU	University of Colorado Library, Boulder

Connecticut

CtY	Yale University Library, New Haven

District of Columbia

DL	Department of Labor Library, Washington
DLC	Library of Congress, Washington

Hawaii

HU	University of Hawaii Library, Honolulu

Idaho

IdB	Boise Public Library
IdU	University of Idaho Library, Moscow

Illinois

ICJ-N	John Crerar Library, in Newberry Library
IU	University of Illinois Library, Urbana

Indiana

InU	Indiana University Library, Bloomington

Louisiana

LNHT	Tulane University Library, New Orleans

Maryland

MdBJ	Johns Hopkins University Library, Baltimore

Massachusetts

MH	Harvard University Library, Cambridge
MH-AH	Harvard University, Andover-Harvard Theological Library, Cambridge

MH-L	Harvard Law School Library
MH-Pu	Harvard University, Pusey Library
Michigan	
MiDW-A	Archives of Labor and Urban Affairs, Walter P. Reuther Library
MiU	Harlan Hatcher Library, University of Michigan, Ann Arbor (houses the Labadie Collection)
Minnesota	
MnHi	Minnesota Historical Society, St. Paul
MnU	University of Minnesota Library, Minneapolis
Montana	
MtBC	Montana State University Library, Bozeman
MtHC	Carroll College Library, Helena
MtHiLH	Montana Historical Library, Helena
MtU	University of Montana Library, Missoula
MtU-M	Mansfield Library, University of Montana, Missoula
New Jersey	
NjP	Princeton University Library, Princeton
New York	
N	New York State Library, Albany
NGHWS	Warren H. Smith Library, Hobart and William Smith Colleges, Geneva
NN	New York Public Library, New York
NNC	Columbia University Library, New York
NNU-T	Tamiment Library, New York University, New York
North Carolina	
NcD	Duke University Library, Durham
North Dakota	
NdFA	North Dakota State University Library, Fargo
Ohio	
OO	Oberlin College Library, Oberlin
Oregon	
Or	Oregon State Library, Salem
OrPR	Reed College Library, Portland
OrU	University of Oregon Library, Eugene
Pennsylvania	
PBm	Bryn Mawr Library, Bryn Mawr
PP	Free Library of Philadelphia
PU	University of Pennsylvania Library, Philadelphia
Rhode Island	
RPB	Brown University Library, Providence

Texas

TxU	University of Texas Library, Austin

Washington

WaU	University of Washington Libraries, Seattle
WaPS	Washington State Library, Pullman
WaE	Everett Public Library
WaHi	Washington State Historical Society, Tacoma

Wisconsin

WHi	State Historical Society of Wisconsin, Madison
WU	University of Wisconsin Library, Madison

Canada

CaOTU	University of Toronto Library, Toronto

IWW Chronology

1898	May	Western Labor Union is organized.
1899		Miners strike, Coeur d'Alene, ID.
1902		Western Labor Union becomes American Labor Union.
1903–4		Miners strike, Cripple Creek, CO.
1904	November	Preliminary meeting of industrial unionists, Chicago.
1905	April	Miners strike, Vivian, AZ.
1905	June–July	Industrial Workers of the World founded, Chicago.
1905		Frank Steunenberg, who had broken the Coeur d'Alene strike, is murdered in Idaho.
1905		Harry Orchard confesses to Steunenberg murder, implicating Haywood, Moyer, and Pettibone.
1906		Troubles begin in Goldfield, NV; interunion rivalries.
1906		Textile workers strike, Skowhegan, ME.
1906	January	Stogie workers strike, Cleveland, OH.
1906	February	Haywood, Moyer, and Pettibone kidnapped in Colorado and taken to Idaho; indicted for Steunenberg murder.
1906	September	Second IWW convention; Sherman deposed, office of president abolished; factionalism apparent.
1906	December	Silk workers strike, New Brighton, CT.
1906		Other smaller strikes include hotel and restaurant workers' strike, Goldfield, NV; window washers strike, Chicago, IL; marble workers' strike, Cincinnati, OH; silk workers' strike, Trenton, NJ, and Staten Island, NY; lumberworkers' strike, Lake Charles, LA.

1906	December	First U.S. sit-down strike: electrical workers' strike, Schenectady, NY.
1907	January	IWW demonstration, Goldfield, NV.
1907	February	Lumberworkers strike, Somers, MT.
1907	March	Lumberworkers strike, Portland, OR.
1907	April	Sawmill workers strike, Portland, OR.
1907	May	Loggers strike, Eureka, CA.
1907	May	Steunenberg, or first Haywood trial, begins.
1907	July	Machine workers strike, Bridgeport, CT. Significant numbers of foreign-born workers are involved.
1907	July	William Haywood acquitted at first trial, after inspiring speech by Clarence Darrow, sympathetic to the labor cause.
1907	October	Lumberworkers strike, Vancouver, B.C.
1907	October	Severe financial panic throughout the country.
1907	November	Silk workers strike, Lancaster, PA.
1907	November	Streetcar workers strike, Yonkers, NY.
1907	December	Troops sent to Goldfield, NV.
1907		Other smaller strikes include silk workers' strike, Paterson, NJ: piano workers' strike, Paterson, NJ; miners' strike, Tonopah, NV; sheet steel workers' strike, Youngstown, OH; foundry workers' strike, Detroit, MI; and smeltermen's strike, Tacoma, WA.
1908		Haywood resigns from WFM.
1908		WFM severs connection with IWW.
1908		De Leon leads Socialist Labor faction out of IWW and forms "Detroit IWW," which lasts until 1915.
1908		Unemployed march to City Hall, St. Louis, MO.
1908	April	Quarry workers strike, Marble, CO.
1908	April	IWW forms New York Propaganda League.
1908	August	Textile workers strike, Lawrence, MA (first of several).
1908	September	Overalls Brigade, from Western states, attends convention.
1908	September	Vincent St. John elected General Secretary-Treasurer; serves until 1915.
1908	September	IWW repudiates political action.

1908		Smaller strikes include farmworkers' strike, Waterville, WA; pressers' strike, St. Louis, MO; drygoods workers' strike, New York, NY.
1909		Free Speech Fights: Missoula, MT; Spokane, WA; and New Castle, PA.
1909	May	Lumberworkers strike, Prince Rupert, B.C.
1909	May	Lumberworkers strike, Kalispell, MT and Somers, MT.
1909	June	Steel workers strike, McKees Rocks, PA.
1909	July	Sheet and tin platers strike, New Castle, PA.
1909	August	Sheet and tin platers strike, Shenango, PA.
1909		First "little red songbook" published by the Spokane Branch.
1910		Words *passive resistance, sabotage,* and *direct action* appear in IWW press.
1910		Joe Hill joins IWW at San Pedro, CA.
1910	January	Metal workers strike, East Hammond, IN.
1910	March	Glass workers strike, Muncie, IN.
1910	April	Farmworkers strike, North Yamhill, OR.
1910	May	Textile workers strike, New Bedford, MA.
1910	June	Garment workers strike, St. Louis, MO.
1910	July	Auto workers strike, Reading, PA.
1910		Free Speech strikes, Wenatchee, WA; Walla Walla, WA; Fresno, CA.
1910	October	*Los Angeles Times* building is bombed; McNamara brothers arrested.
1910	November	Shoe workers strike, Brooklyn, NY.
1910		Smaller strikes include gas workers' strike, San Diego, CA; window cleaners' strike, Providence, RI; meat packers' strike, Pittsburgh, PA.
1911		IWW establishes Pacific Coast District Organization.
1911		William Z. Foster suggests dual unionism and the "boring from within" tactic; ideas greeted with argument.
1911	January	Boot and shoe workers strike, New York, NY.
1911	January	Miners strike, La Grande, WA.
1911	May	Western Federation of Miners joins AFL.
1911	May	MacNamara brothers' trial begins.
1911	May	Clothing workers organized, with interunion problems, Baltimore, MD.

1911	June	Brotherhood of Timber Workers organized by Arthur Emerson and Jay Smith in Louisiana.
1911	August	John Kirby, Louisiana lumberman, locks out BTW.
1911	September	Brotherhood of Timber Workers sends delegate to IWW convention.
1911		Free Speech Fights, Duluth, MN; Denver, CO; Kansas City, MO; and Aberdeen, WA.
1912	January	Textile workers strike, Lawrence, MA.
1912	January	IWW "army" takes Mexicali, supporting F. Magon in the Mexican civil war.
1912	January	Dynamite plot in Lawrence; school official convicted.
1912	January	Lawrence striker Annie LoPizza is killed by militia.
1912	January	Haywood-Hillquit debate, New York. Haywood endorses sabotage and direct action.
1912	February	Textile workers strike, Lowell, MA.
1912		Free Speech Fights, Aberdeen, WA; Vancouver, B.C.; San Diego, CA; New Bedford, MA; Minneapolis, MN.
1912	February	Lawrence strikers' children are taken to New York and Barre, VT, amidst much publicity.
1912	March	Lumberworkers strike, Hoquiam and Aberdeen, WA.
1912		Railroad workers strike, British Columbia.
1912	March	Paterson, NJ, strikers give up an unsuccessful strike called by Detroit faction IWW.
1912	April	Textile workers strike, Willimantic, CT.
1912	April	Street railroad workers strike, Kansas City, MO.
1912	April	Piano and organ workers strike, New York, NY.
1912	April	Harris Weinstock holds hearings on brutal San Diego Free Speech Fight.
1912	May	Streetcar workers strike, Portland, OR.
1912		Brotherhood of Timber Workers officially joins IWW.
1912	June	Construction workers strike, White Salmon, WA.
1912	June	Textile workers strike, Clinton, MA, and New Bedford, MA.
1912	July	Company guards shoot strikers in BTW strike, Grabow, LA.
1912	July	Dockworkers strike, San Pedro, CA.
1912	August	Syndicalist League founded by William Z. Foster.

1912	August	Lumberworkers strike, Merryville, LA; much violence.
1912	September	Lawrence strikers parade includes a "No God—No Master" sign, causing much notoriety.
1912	September	Seventh IWW convention agrees to principle of direct action.
1912	September	Lawrence strike leaders, J. Ettor and A. Giovannitti go on trial at Salem, MA; acquitted in November.
1912	October	Arthur Emerson acquitted after trial of BTW strike leaders.
1912	October	Textile workers strike, Little Falls, NY.
1912	November	Lumberworkers strike, Merryville, LA.
1912		H. Weinstock report on San Diego issued.
1912		Smaller strikes include lumberworkers' strike, Grays Harbor, WA; farmworkers' strike (the second), North Yamhill, OR; construction workers' strike, British Columbia; wire fence workers' strike, Cleveland, OH; and construction workers' strike, Portland, OR.
1912	December	Haywood's position defeated in Socialist Party convention.
1913		Marine Transport Workers Union is organized.
1913		Tom Mann visits from England; suggests "dual unionism."
1913		Barbers strike, New York, NY.
1913		Dockworkers strike, Duluth, MN.
1913	January	Construction workers strike, Big Creek, CA.
1913	January	Cannery workers strike, San Francisco, CA.
1913	February	Rubber workers strike, Akron, OH.
1913	February	Silk workers strike, Paterson, NJ.
1913	February	Silk workers strike, Hazleton, PA.
1913	February	Haywood is recalled from the NEC of the Socialist Party.
1913	March	Textile workers strike, Esmond, RI.
1913	March	Rubber workers strike, Cleveland, OH.
1913	March	Tailors strike, Seattle, WA.
1913	March	Matilda Rabinowitz arrested for organizing auto workers, Detroit, MI.
1913	March	Electrical workers strike, Stockton, CA.
1913	April	Sash and door workers strike, Rock Island, IL.

1913	April	Marine Firemen, Oilers, and Water Tenders Union affiliates with IWW, adding 25,000 members.
1913	April	Miners strike, Mount Hope, NJ.
1913	May	Lumberworkers strike, Marshfield, OR. Lynchings, police actions, kiss-the-flag incidents, and beatings ensue.
1913	June	Textile workers strike, Ipswich, MA.
1913	June	The Paterson pageant enacted in Madison Square Garden, under John Reed's direction.
1913	June	Auto workers strike, Detroit, MI, at Studebaker plant.
1913	July	Copper miners strike, Calumet, MI (Calumet-Hecla strike).
1913	July	Soldiers and sailors riot in Seattle, wrecking IWW and Socialist halls and, by mistake, Salvation Army, in the "Potlatch Days Riot."
1913	August	Paterson strikers give up in defeat.
1913	August	Wheatland Hop Riot, farmworker living conditions brought to national attention.
1913	September	Tobacco workers strike, Pittsburgh, PA.
1913	September	Lumberworkers strike, Sweet Home, LA.
1913	December	Fire in Italian Hall kills many children of Calumet-Hecla strikers and is blamed on company gunmen.
1913	December	Unemployed workers demonstrate in Los Angeles, meeting police violence.
1913		Free Speech Fights, Denver, CO; Minot, ND; Seattle, WA; and Kansas City, MO.
1913		Pat Quinlan, Paterson strike leader, put on trial.
1913–15		Nationwide depression and widespread unemployment.
1914		Cline and Rangel found guilty of violating Neutrality Act for Mexican civil war activities.
1914	January	Marysville, CA, trial: Ford and Suhr convicted for Wheatland activities.
1914	January	Ford Motor Company announces $5 wage for an eight-hour day; IWW takes credit, saying fear of their organizing led Ford to that step.
1914	January	Unemployed "army" marches from Portland to Eugene, OR.

1914	January	Unemployed workers are organized by IWW, West Coast.
1914	February	Frank Tannenbaum leads unemployed men into church, New York, NY.
1914	February	"Kelly's Army" of unemployed (many IWW) marches from San Francisco to Sacramento; greeted with beatings.
1914	February	Lumberworkers renew strike, Sweet Home, LA.
1914	April	Ludlow Massacre occurs, Ludlow, CO.
1914	June	Union hall is dynamited, Butte, MT, before and after which many fights occur between WFM and IWW.
1914	June	Joe Hill is convicted of murder in Utah.
1914	August	Unsuccessful general strike to protest imprisonment of Ford and Suhr is called by the IWW.
1914		Free Speech Fights in Aberdeen, SD, and Sioux City, IA.
1914		Chemical workers strike, Roosevelt Borough, NJ; some are shot by Sheriff Kinkead or his men.
1914		World War I starts in Europe; defense industries begin to tool up in the U.S.
1915		Worldwide appeals are made for the staying of Joe Hill's execution.
1915	January	The song "Solidarity Forever," by Ralph Chaplin, is first published in IWW newspaper, *Solidarity.*
1915	April	IWW organizes AWO and starts a big grainbelt organizing drive.
1915	July	Chemical workers strike, Bayonne, NJ. Armed guards attack strikers.
1915		William D. Haywood becomes General Secretary-Treasurer.
1915		Free Speech Fight, Paterson, NJ.
1915	November	Joe Hill is executed.
1915		Patriotic fervor; newspaper editorials start to charge IWW with disloyalty, especially during strikes.
1916		Longshoremen strike, Philadelphia, PA.
1916	June	Quarry workers strike, Red Granite, WI.
1916	June	Iron miners start long, bitter strike along the Mesabi Range, MN.

1916		IWW affiliates with Finnish Socialists and helps support Work Peoples College, Duluth, MN.
1916	June	IWW members refuse to register for draft, Rockford, IL.
1916	July	Bomb thrown at Preparedness Day parade, San Francisco. Tom Mooney is convicted.
1916	August	Miners strike, Scranton, PA.
1916		Free Speech Fights at Old Forge, PA, and Everett, WA.
1916	October	Charges made against IWW in Australia. In December the "Unlawful Associations Act" makes IWW membership a criminal offense in Australia.
1916	November	Everett Massacre occurs: a shooting of IWW members approaching Everett, WA, by boat.
1917	February	Tom Mooney is given long sentence.
1917	February	Sugar workers and loaders strike, Philadelphia, PA.
1917	February	Longshoremen strike, Philadelphia, PA.
1917	March	Idaho passes Criminal Syndicalism Act. Many other states follow suit within the next five years.
1917	March	E. B. Mercadier organizes Toilers of the World, a pseudo-IWW group of cannery workers in California, actually an AFL Federal union that appeared to be IWW.
1917	April	Irrigation workers strike, Exeter, CA.
1917	April	U.S. enters World War I; Espionage Act is passed, aimed at internal labor troubles. Patriotic spirit demanded of all.
1917	May	Tom Tracy, IWW defendant in Everett trial, is acquitted.
1917		IWW advises workers to "strike on the job," a phrase subject to various interpretations.
1917	July	IWW members and others are illegally kidnapped and deported from Bisbee, AZ.
1917	Summer	Lumberworkers' strikes abound in the Pacific Northwest, "on-the-job" style.
1917	June	Metal miners strike, Butte, MT.
1917	Summer	Non-Partisan League offers IWW one of the first farmworker contracts; IWW does not sign because contracts are against IWW principles.
1917	July	G. J. Bourg, AWIU secretary, is kidnapped and beaten.

1917	August	Frank Little, IWW leader, is lynched and murdered, Butte, MT.
1917	August	"Green Corn Rebellion," an insurrection of the Working Class Union, started by the IWW, erupts in rural Oklahoma but is swiftly stifled.
1917		Foreign administrations of the IWW are established in New Zealand, Australia, Great Britain, and South Africa.
1917		President's Mediation Commission is established to seek a way to mitigate labor problems.
1917	August	John Avila beaten, Franklin, NJ. Similar incidents follow throughout the country, as citizen vigilantes become active.
1917	September	Department of Justice raids all IWW offices seeking evidence of disloyalty.
1917	October	Globe-Miami and Clifton-Morenci, AZ, labor disputes are settled by government action.
1917	November	Seventeen IWW oilworker organizers are beaten, tarred, and feathered by citizen vigilantes, Tulsa, OK.
1917	November	Wobblies attending convention at Omaha, NB, are all arrested.
1917		Government sends U.S. Army, under Col. Bryce Disque, to see that spruce needed for planes is cut without interference.
1917		American Protective League, citizen secret service, is organized; in the following year, it works with the Department of Justice.
1918		A general strike is attempted, Butte, MT.
1918		Sedition Act (amendment to Espionage Act) is passed, making it illegal to speak against the flag, Army or Navy uniforms, or war production.
1918		Seventy miners kidnapped by company gunmen, Jerome, AZ.
1918	April	Chicago trial begins, with 166 IWW defendants charged under the Espionage Act.
1918	May	12,000 arrested, many for deportation, Detroit, MI.
1918	May	Nationwide arrests of IWW members on many different charges, arresting officers including local police, government agents, and citizen members of APL, often plant and mill officers.

1918	June	Eugene Debs is arrested.
1918	July	Workers Industrial Union of Australia is organized, using IWW Preamble.
1918		Tenant farmer-landlord dispute, called "race war," Elaine, AR.
1918	August	Jury convicts IWW members at Chicago trial.
1918	November	World War I ends; raids and imprisonments continue.
1918	December	Wichita Trial for Criminal Syndicalism begins, Wichita, KS.
1918	December	Sacramento, CA, trial for Criminal Syndicalism begins. "Silent defense" technique is used by the defense, which refuses to give testimony.
1919	February	Seattle General Strike, Seattle, WA, the first large-scale general strike attempted, involving many unions, including the IWW.
1919	May	Winnipeg General Strike, Winnipeg, Manitoba.
1919	Fall	Palmer Raids begin, under Attorney General's direction. Foreign-born radicals selected for deportation.
1919	September	Steel workers strike, Chicago, IL, Gary, IN, and across country; William Z. Foster a prominent leader.
1919		Many workers, including IWW members, are arrested for deportation. "Red Special" railway train, from Seattle to Ellis Island, makes stops across the country to add deportees.
1919	December	U.S. transport ship *Buford* sails with 249 deportees.
1920		IWW establishes Bureau of Research, under Howard Scott.
1920	January	Steel strike is called off.
1920		Local prosecutions of IWW continue.
1920	August	Some Philadelphia longshoremen expelled for loading munitions for Wrangel's army in Russia.
1921	April	Haywood, after last appeal is denied, skips bail and goes to Russia.
1921		Syndicalism arrests continue.
1921		Clemency debate between IWW prisoners divides them; some do not want conditional pardons.

1922	October	Marine transport workers strike, Philadelphia, PA, and Portland, OR.
1922		IWW colony including ex-Americans is established at Kuzbas, Siberia.
1922	November	Construction workers strike, Hetch Hetchy, CA.
1923	April	Marine transport workers attempt a general strike at many ports, principally Portland, OR, and New Orleans, LA.
1923		Some federal prisoners pardoned and released by President Harding.
1923		Free Speech Fights start again in Port Arthur, TX; Great Falls, CA; Fargo, ND; and San Pedro, CA.
1923	July	San Pedro seamen convicted on Criminal Syndicalism charges.
1924		Split occurs in IWW over decentralization of the union. Many leave with James Rowan and his "Emergency Program."
1924	June	San Pedro IWW Hall is raided by police, with beatings and violence toward children and wives present.
1925		IWW calls for nationwide boycott of California products because of severity of treatment of IWW in courts there.
1925	September	Richard Ford, Wheatlands prisoner, is released, then rearrested.
1926	January	Richard Ford is acquitted.
1926	October	Herman Suhr is released from prison. Gradually some, but not all, IWW prisoners are released.
1927		Protests against Sacco-Vanzetti conviction include unsuccessful attempt by IWW to call a general strike.
1927	August	Miners strike in Colorado, with IWW participation.
1927	November	Violence and death at the Columbine mine in Colorado.
1928	May	Haywood dies in Moscow.
1928		Police fire on IWW Hall in Walsenburg, CO.
1930		IWW foreign administrations established in many cities, including Liverpool, Antwerp, Sydney, Colón, Tampico, Buenos Aires, Valparaiso, and Rosario.

1930	May	Miners strike in Harlan County, KY, with IWW participation.
1930		Mary Harris ("Mother") Jones dies, aged 100. Many mention "the death of an era."
1931	April	Construction workers strike, Boulder Dam, CO.
1931		Unemployed unions formed in many cities.
1932	May	Construction workers strike, Cle Elum, WA.
1933	January	Auto workers strike, Detroit, MI; IWW active at Murray Body, Briggs, and Motor Products companies.
1933	May	Hop pickers strike, Yakima, WA.
1933	June	Metal workers strike, Cleveland, OH.
1933	August	All IWW members fired from Boulder Dam project, CO.
1933		Metal workers strike, Cleveland, OH, at Draper Steel.
1933		Technocracy becomes popular, led by ex-IWW Howard Scott.
1933		Meat packers strike, Omaha, NB, at Hormel plant.
1934	May	Truckers strike, Minneapolis, MN.
1935		Metal workers strike, Cleveland, OH; problems at National Screw Co. and Cleveland Brass end in arrests of some IWW members, including Mike Lindway and Bart Dudek.
1936	April	Lumberworkers strike, Camp L, ID, against Weyerhaeuser.
1936	August	AFL Timber Workers, assisted by IWW, strike, Fremont, ID.
1941		Metal mine workers organized by IWW, Bishop, CA.
1941		Harry Bridges, once an IWW, on trial.
1947	June	Taft-Hartley Act is passed over President's veto.
1948		Wallace Stegner writes that Joe Hill might have been guilty, evoking nationwide protests from Wobblies.
1949		IWW included on Attorney General's "subversive" list.
1950		Cleveland IWW members refuse to sign Taft-Hartley affidavits.
1964		Waiters strike, San Francisco, CA, at Cedar Alley Coffee House.
1968		IWW sees a revival; many campus branches open.

1971	Workers at Hip Products strike, Chicago, IL.
1971	Workers at Three Penny Cinema strike, Chicago, IL.
1970s, 1980s	Rise of scholarly interest in IWW, which becomes the topic of historical research and writing and of movies, novels, and poetry. IWW continues as a working union, with branches in many cities and headquarters in Chicago.

BEWARE

GOOD PAY OR BUM WORK

I.W.W

ONE BIG UNION

SABOTAGE

INFORMATION ADDRESS I W W CHICAGO U S A

Books

THE books selected for this list include some that are wholly about the IWW and its history, some that are about a part of that history, and some that contain material on the IWW along with other subjects. They were chosen as representative of the treatment given to the IWW over the eighty years since its founding. The books were not always selected for intrinsic excellence but sometimes to cover a point of view or a special aspect or attitude. A few biographies have been included, affording some personal historical perspective. Many hundreds of books mention the IWW briefly. Because of space limitations, these books were not included. The books in this listing represent significant works dealing with the IWW.

A few books in foreign languages are included. Most are not annotated, but they may be of importance to those familiar with the languages, and they demonstrate, as well, the worldwide interest aroused by the IWW for many years.

1. Adamic, Louis. *Dynamite: The Story of Class Violence in America.* New York: Viking, 1931. Reprint: Gloucester, MA: Peter Smith, 1959.

   The historical evolution of violence as it occurred in various labor and class struggles and the use of violence as "publicity for the underdog." Included are accounts of Centralia, the Haywood trial, the Lawrence strike, and sabotage. The book is somewhat dated.

2. Adams, Graham J. *Age of Industrial Violence, 1910–1915: The Activities and Findings of the United States Commission on Industrial Relations.* New York: Columbia University Press, 1966. Reissued, 1971.

   An even-handed history of the noted Commission whose findings created popular concern for working people and brought some of labor's first favorable publicity. The book touches on Paterson and Ludlow.

3. Ameringer, Oscar. *If You Don't Weaken: The Autobiography of Oscar Ameringer.* New York: H. Holt and Co., 1940. Reprint: Westport, CT: Greenwood Press, 1973.

   Autobiography of an active Socialist who comments on the political machinations and national events he saw and the people with whom he shared the radical experience.

4. Anderson, Nels. *The Hobo: The Sociology of the Homeless Man: A Study Prepared for the Chicago Council of Social Agencies under the Direction of the Committee on Homeless Men.* Chicago: University of Chicago Press, 1923. Reissued 1927, 1961, and in the Midway Reprint Series, 1975.

   Personal observation of a phenomenon once closely associated with the IWW, the casual migrant worker.

5. Archer, Jules. *Strikes, Bombs and Bullets: Big Bill Haywood and the IWW.* New York: J. Massner, 1972.

   Featuring the more sensational side of the IWW; intended for juvenile readers.

6. Baxandall, Rosalyn Fraad. *Dreams and Dilemmas: Elizabeth Gurley Flynn's Writing on Women.* New Brunswick, NJ: Rutgers University Press, 1986.

   A compilation of the writings of a prominent IWW speaker and organizer, who always encouraged women in particular to join in union activism.

7. Beal, Fred. *Proletarian Journey: New England, Gastonia, Moscow.* New York: Hillman-Curl, 1937. Reprint: New York: Da Capo Press, 1970 (Civil Liberties in American History Series).

   Autobiography of a man who started with the IWW but later took the Communist road.

8. Bedford, Henry F. *Socialism and the Workers in Massachusetts, 1889–1912.* Amherst: University of Massachusetts Press, 1966.

   Includes background and description of the Lawrence strike, emphasizing its political aspects.

9. Benedict, Harry C. *Red Metal: The Calumet and Hecla Story.* Ann Arbor, MI: University of Michigan Press, 1952.

   History of the mining company as written by one of its officers. One chapter describes the "one most unfortunate exception" to the company's "peaceful history of labor relations." The author sarcastically describes the forceful deportation of WFM leader Charles Moyer.

10. Bercuson, David J. *Confrontation at Winnipeg: Labour, Industrial Relations and the General Strike.* Montreal: McGill-Queen's University Press, 1974.
    Background and detailed account of the important six-week Winnipeg strike, involving some actions that reflected IWW ideas.

11. ———. *Fools and Wise Men: The Rise and Fall of the One Big Union.* Toronto: McGraw-Hill Ryerson, 1978.
    Story of the Canadian One Big Union, influenced at the start by the IWW.

12. Blaisdell, Lowell L. *The Desert Revolution: Baja California, 1911.* Madison: University of Wisconsin Press, 1962.
    Story of the Magon brothers. It includes some material on the support they sought and received from the IWW in this Mexican incident.

13. Bloomfield, Daniel, comp. *Selected Articles on Modern Industrial Movements.* New York: H. W. Wilson, 1919.
    Well-selected contemporary articles, including several on syndicalism, industrial unionism, and the IWW.

14. Bock, Gisela. *Die Andere Arbeiterbewegung in den USA von 1909–1922* (The other labor movement in the USA from 1909–1922). Munich: Trikont, 1976.
    Not translated from the German.

15. Bötcher, Hans. *Zur Revolutionaren Gewerksschaftsbewegung in America, Deutschland und England* (Toward revolutionary unionism in America, Germany, and England). Jena: G. Fisher, 1922.
    Not translated from the German.

16. Boyer, Richard O., and Herbert M. Morais. *Labor's Untold Story.* New York: Cameron Associates, 1955.
    Some chapters on the Wobblies in this light run-through of labor episodes.

17. Brecher, Jeremy. *Strike!* San Francisco: Straight Arrow Books, 1972. Reprint: Boston: South End Press, 1977.
    Describes some IWW strikes, among others. The accounts of the mining strikes and the Seattle strike of 1919 are especially interesting.

18. Brissenden, Paul F. *The I.W.W.: A Study of American Syndicalism.* Columbia University Studies in History, Economics, and Public Law No. 193. New York: Columbia University Press, 1919. Second edition: New York: Russell and Russell, 1957.

    Covers the first dozen years of the IWW comprehensively and soundly. Brissenden's *Justice and the I.W.W.* (see no. 3979) was printed as a pamphlet by the IWW.

19. Brommel, Bernard J. *Eugene V. Debs: Spokesman for Labor and Socialism.* Chicago: Charles H. Kerr, 1977.

    Analyzes Debs' attitudes toward the IWW and explains why he defended the IWW after he dissociated himself from it.

20. Brooks, John G. *American Syndicalism: The I.W.W.* New York: Macmillan, 1913. Reprints: New York: Arno Press, 1969 (American Labor, from Conspiracy to Collective Bargaining Series); New York: Da Capo Press, 1970 (Civil Liberties in American History Series); and New York: AMS Press, 1978.

    Based on 1911 university lectures, and somewhat hortatory in nature. The author suggests a strong connection between the IWW and European syndicalism and attempts to explain the psychology of the IWW's success.

21. ———. *Labor's Challenge to the Social Order: Democracy Its Own Critic and Educator.* New York: Macmillan, 1920. Reprint: Port Washington, NY: Kennikat Press, 1971 (Economic Thought, History and Challenge Series).

    IWW platform and preamble enlarged by quotations from Socrates; a philosophical exposition of the New Society as envisioned over sixty years ago.

22. Brooks, Thomas R. *Toil and Trouble: A History of American Labor.* New York: Delacorte Press, 1964. Revised edition, 1971.

    Labor history from an organizer's viewpoint. The author tries to evaluate the efforts and techniques of different unions to better the working person's life.

23. Bruns, Roger A. *Knights of the Road: A Hobo History.* New York: Methuen, 1980.

    Somewhat romantic, breezy account of hoboes, who are seen as a migratory labor force. Chapter 6, "Toward the 'One Big Union,'" relates the IWW's efforts to organize hoboes.

24. Budish, Jacob M., and George Soule. *New Unionism in the Clothing Industry.* New York: Harcourt, Brace, and Howe, 1920. Reprint: New York: Russell & Russell, 1968.

Includes some statistics and contemporary comment on the IWW.

25. Byrkit, James. *Forging the Copper Collar: Arizona's Labor-Management War, 1901–1921*. Tucson: University of Arizona Press, 1982.

Thorough and well-researched history of the Bisbee deportation, with other material about the IWW in the Southwest.

26. Cahn, William. *Lawrence Nineteen Twelve: The Bread and Roses Strike.* Phillipsburg, NJ: Pilgrim, 1980.

All about the famous IWW strike, which is described in colorful terms. A revision of *Mill Town* (see no. 27).

27. ———. *Mill Town: A Dramatic Pictorial Narrative of the Century-Old Fight To Unionize an Industrial Town.* New York: Cameron and Kahn, 1954.

A light pictorial account of the Lawrence strike. The last few pages bring the story up to date.

28. Cannon, James Patrick. *Notebook of an Agitator.* New York: Pioneer Press, 1958. Second edition: New York: Pathfinder Press, 1973.

A collection of Cannon's journalistic writings over the years, the book includes articles on Frank Little, William Haywood, and the Centralia Massacre. The author believes that any genuine proletarian movement in the future will need the spirit and the techniques of the IWW. For Cannon's short history of the IWW, see no. 3638.

29. Carlson, Peter. *Roughneck: The Life and Times of Big Bill Haywood.* New York: Norton, 1983.

A particularly good biography, as smooth and interesting as a novel. The work is backed by thorough research, including the use of many original materials that became available only recently.

30. Caughey, John W. *Their Majesties, the Mob.* Chicago: University of Chicago Press, 1960.

A study of vigilantism, including incidents against the IWW.

31. Chafee, Zechariah, Jr. *Freedom of Speech.* New York: Harcourt, Brace, and Howe, 1920. Rev. ed., Cambridge: Harvard University Press, 1941 (retitled *Free Speech in the United States*). Reprint: New York: Atheneum, 1969.

Legal cases and illegal actions against the IWW. Chafee's book is a classic work on civil liberties, especially civil liberties threatened during wartime.

32. Chaplin, Ralph. *Wobbly: The Rough and Tumble Story of an American Radical.* Chicago: University of Chicago Press, 1948. Reprint: New York: Da Capo Press, 1972 (Civil Liberties in American History Series).

Interesting account of Chaplin's life as an IWW member, organizer, artist, and poet. It includes good information on West Virginia strikes, the IWW trials, and the writing of "Solidarity Forever," the universal labor song.

33. Chaplin, Ralph; B. H. Lampman; the Federal Council of Churches of Christ in America; et al. *The Centralia Case: Three Views of the Armistice Day Tragedy at Centralia, Washington, November 11, 1919.* New York: Da Capo Press, 1971.

The Centralia story as seen from three different viewpoints: the American Legion, the IWW, and a church group. Reprinting of a selection of three earlier original pamphlets (see, in Pamphlet section, nos. 4009, 3764, and 3689).

34. Chiappetta, Giuseppe. *IWW, Industrial Workers of the World: Storia e Considerazioni Critiche* (The IWW, Industrial Workers of the World, history and analysis). Milan: Filorosso, 1978.

Not translated from the Italian.

35. Clark, Norman H. *Mill Town: A Social History of Everett, Washington from Its Earliest Beginnings on the Shores of Puget Sound to the Tragic and Infamous Event Known as the Everett Massacre.* Seattle: University of Washington Press, 1970. Reissued, 1979.

A complete account, vivid and descriptive, of the activities in Everett. The author uses local sources extensively.

36. Coben, Stanley. *A. Mitchell Palmer: Politician.* New York: Columbia University Press, 1963. Reprint: New York: Da Capo Press, 1972 (Civil Liberties in American History Series).

A biography providing good background and information on the Palmer Raids.

37. Cole, Donald B. *Immigrant City: Lawrence, Massachusetts, 1845–1921.* Chapel Hill, NC: University of North Carolina Press, 1963. Reissued in 1980.

A review of the Lawrence strike, with emphasis on the foreign-born strikers. It describes the working conditions there both before and after the strike.

38. Conlin, Joseph R., ed. *The American Radical Press: 1880–1960.* Vol. 1 of 2 vols. Westport, CT: Greenwood Press, 1974.

A compilation of descriptive articles on various early radical papers and journals, with a good introduction.

39. ———. *At the Point of Production: The Local History of the IWW.* Contributions in Labor History No. 10. Westport, CT: Greenwood Press, 1981.

A compilation of recent local studies of the IWW, covering many IWW strikes and incidents. A lengthy bibliography on IWW local history is included.

40. ———. *Big Bill Haywood and the Radical Labor Movement.* Syracuse, NY: Syracuse University Press, 1969. Reissued as part of the Men and Movement Series, 1979.

Examines the life, character, and especially the union work of the IWW leader. Each chapter describes a different role: Haywood as a worker, as a unionist, as a Wobbly, as a Socialist, and as a Communist.

41. ———. *Bread and Roses Too: Studies of the Wobblies.* Westport, CT: Greenwood Publishing Corp., 1970.

A series of analytic essays on aspects of the IWW, viewing the members as part of the American mainstream rather than as immigrants or outlaws.

42. Cook, Roy. *Leaders of Labor.* New York: J. B. Lippincott, 1966.

Contains a chapter on William D. Haywood.

43. Crook, Wilfrid Harris. *The General Strike; a Study of Labor's Tragic Weapon in Theory and Practice.* Chapel Hill, NC: University of North Carolina Press, 1931. Reissued in 1966.

Comparison of techniques of striking, in which the IWW ideas of the social general strike are considered to be "crudities" by the author. They take little space in this compendium of "real" general strikes.

44. Daniel, Cletus E. *Bitter Harvest: A History of California Farmworkers, 1870–1941.* Ithaca, NY: Cornell University Press, 1981.

A perceptive and scholarly examination of the historic problems of farmworkers in California. The author includes the story of the migrant IWW in that state, as well as details on the Wheatland episode.

45. *Daniel De Leon. The Man and His Work: A Symposium.* New York: National Executive Committee of the Socialist Labor Party, 1920. Reprint: Palo Alto, CA: New York Labor News, 1969.

A symposium called after De Leon's death, to which many surviving friends contribute. His role in the IWW is evaluated.

46. Darrow, Clarence S. *The Story of My Life.* New York: C. Scribner's Sons, 1932. Reissued in 1960. Reprint: New York: Grosset & Dunlap, 1957.

Autobiography that touches on the first Haywood trial, for which Darrow was the defense attorney. Among several other books describing Clarence Darrow and his experiences with William D. Haywood and the IWW are Irving Stone, *Clarence Darrow for the Defense* (Garden City, NY: Doubleday, Doran, & Company, 1941) and Kevin Tierney, *Darrow: A Biography* (New York: Crowell, 1979).

47. Daugherty, Carrol. *Labor Problems in American Industry.* Boston: Houghton Mifflin, 1933. Reprinted in 1948 (new title, *Labor Problems in American Industry, 1948–1949 Impression*).

Comprehensive textbook centering on "labor maladjustments" and attempts to gain harmony. It analyzes the history, structure, and function of the IWW, as one factor in the labor movement.

48. Debs, Eugene V. *Eugene V. Debs Speaks.* Edited by Jean Y. Tussey. New York: Pathfinder Press, 1970.

Earlier Debs essays and speeches on industrial unionism, and his defense of the IWW when it was under the pressure of the Red Scare.

49. De Caux, Len. *Labor Radical: From the Wobblies to the CIO, a Personal History.* Boston: Beacon Press, 1970.

Entertaining first-hand account of the IWW during the 1920s and the 1930s, by a spirited ex-Wobbly.

50. ———. *The Living Spirit of the Wobblies.* New York: International Publishers, 1978.

De Caux's history of the IWW as he saw it.

51. Dell, Floyd. *Homecoming: An Autobiography.* New York: Farrar and Rinehart, 1933. Reprint: Washington, NY: Kennikat Press, 1969.

The social side of the IWW as fondly remembered by an early member and supporter. He recalls the good old days in Greenwich Village, arguing the shades of radicalism, days of bread and roses and wine.

52. DeWitt, Howard A. *Images of Ethnic and Radical Violence in California Politics, 1917–1930: A Survey.* San Francisco: R. & E. Research Associates, 1975.

A historical explanation of various radical causes, including the IWW, and of the episodes in which they participated.

53. Dick, William M. *Labor and Socialism in America: The Gompers Era.* New York: National University Publications, 1972.

An analysis of the many shades of opinion of factions interested in labor, all centered around the strongly held trade union views of the man who led the AFL.

54. Dolgoff, Sam. *The American Labor Movement: A New Beginning.* Champaign, IL: Resurgence, 1981.

View of an ex-member of the IWW who sees the history of the labor movement as a changing balance between the conservative and the revolutionary forces of labor. There are frequent comments on the IWW throughout.

55. Dowell, Eldridge F. *A History of Criminal Syndicalism in the United States.* Johns Hopkins University Studies in the Social Sciences, 57th Series. Baltimore, MD: Johns Hopkins Press, 1939. Reprints: New York: Da Capo Press (American History, Politics, and Law Series), and New York: AMS Press, 1978.

Based on a more detailed dissertation. This summary is still useful for the legal study of labor repression. Details of the legislative indictments and of attempts to repeal the syndicalist laws are included.

56. Draper, Theodore. *The Roots of American Communism.* New York: Viking Press, 1957. Reprint: New York: Octagon Press, 1977.

Shows the relation between the early left wing of the Socialists, the IWW, and the Communists. It provides a viewpoint of the IWW as seen by those farther to the left.

57. Dreiser, Theodore, et al. *Harlan Miners Speak: Report of Terrorism in the Kentucky Coal Fields.* New York: Harcourt, Brace, 1932. Reprint: New York: Da Capo Press, 1970 (Civil Liberties in American History Series).

Some personal accounts of a struggle in which the IWW had some part, as told by participants and their families.

58. Dubofsky, Melvyn. *Industrialism and the American Worker, 1865–1920.* New York: Crowell, 1975, and Arlington Heights, IL: AHM, 1975.

A historiographical survey of the period that includes good background readings. Apparently it is intended for college students.

59. ———. *We Shall Be All: A History of the Industrial Workers of the World.* Chicago: Quadrangle Books, 1969.

A book that has become the standard account of the IWW. Despite some initial criticism of its somewhat Marxist viewpoint, this book is generally regarded as the most fair, reliable, and important IWW history.

60. Dunn, Robert F., ed. *The Palmer Raids.* New York: International Publishers, 1948.

One of the first historical accounts of the Palmer Raids and the Red Scare. The book includes selections from documents and press quotations.

61. Egbert, Donald D., and Stow Persons, eds. *Socialism and American Life.* 2 vols. Princeton Studies in American Civilization, No. 4. Princeton, NJ: Princeton University Press, 1952.

Briefly touches upon the place of the IWW in the Socialist sphere and on Socialist struggles with the IWW problem. The second volume contains an outstanding bibliography.

62. Estey, James A. *Revolutionary Syndicalism: An Exposition and a Criticism.* London: P. S. King & Son, 1913.

What syndicalists "propose to do" and some account of the evolution of syndicalism and its relation to socialism. Estey analyzes the European version of syndicalism.

63. Ficken, Robert E. *Lumber and Politics: The Career of Mark E. Reed.* Seattle: University of Washington Press, 1979.

Biography of one of the supporters of the Loyal Legion of Loggers and Lumbermen. It details the problems of the Northwest from the viewpoint of the mill owners and politicians.

64. Fine, Nathan. *Labor and Farmer Parties in the United States, 1828–1928.* New York: Rand School of Social Science, 1928. Reprints: Ann Arbor, MI: Ann Arbor Press, 1959, and New York: Russell & Russell, 1961.

Claims IWW "helped undermine faith in the system." This book does not give much room to the "rebel band of footloose fighters," as the author refers to the IWW. The IWW averred it was "not political." Fine provides valuable analysis of radical groups and their history.

65. Flynn, Elizabeth Gurley. *I Speak My Own Piece: Autobiography of "The Rebel Girl."* New York: Masses and Mainstream, 1955. Reprint: New York: International Publishers, 1973 (new title, *The Rebel Girl: An Autobiography*).

An account of Flynn's early days of speaking, organizing, and fundraising for the IWW, and for other groups shortly thereafter.

66. Foner, Philip S. *The Case of Joe Hill.* New York: International Publishers, 1965.

An account of the whole Joe Hill episode and of the famous trial.

67. Foner, Philip S., ed. *Fellow Workers and Friends: The I.W.W. Free Speech Fights as Told by Participants.* Contributions in American History Series, No. 92. Westport, CT: Greenwood Press, 1981.

Personal accounts and actual speeches of numerous well-known and lesser-known free speech participants.

68. ———. *History of the Labor Movement in the United States: Volume IV: The Industrial Workers of the World, 1905–1917.* vol. 4 of 6 vols. New York: International Publishers, 1965.

A competent and detailed historical account of the IWW.

69. Foster, James C., ed. *American Labor in the Southwest: The First One Hundred Years.* Tucson: University of Arizona Press, 1982.

Contains articles on several aspects of IWW history, including the oil workers, the Bisbee deportation, and the IWW in the Southwest.

70. Foster, William Zebulon. *American Trade Unionism: Strategy and Tactics.* New York: International Publishers, 1947. Reissued in 1970.

Some mention of the IWW (the "fanatic dualists" of the author's earlier years).

71. ———. *From Bryan to Stalin.* New York: International Publishers, 1937.

Includes memories of Foster's days as an IWW member.

72. ———. *The Great Steel Strike and Its Lessons.* New York: B. Huebsch, 1920. Reprints: New York: Da Capo Press, 1971 (Civil Liberties in American History Series) and New York: Arno Press, 1976 (Mass Violence in America Series).

Insider's account of the Steel Strike frustrations, in which the IWW played a minor part.

73. ———. *Pages from a Worker's Life.* New York: International Publishers, 1939. Reissued in 1970 and 1972.

Autobiography of a Communist once in the IWW. It is a sequel to *From Bryan to Stalin* (see no. 71).

74. Friedheim, Robert. *The Seattle General Strike.* Seattle: University of Washington, 1965.

Detailed account of what many believed would be the real revolution. There is perhaps some bias against the IWW.

75. Frost, Richard. *The Mooney Case.* Stanford, CA: Stanford University Press, 1968.

Scholarly account of the fate of Tom Mooney, once a member of the IWW.

76. Gambs, John S. *The Decline of the I.W.W.* Columbia University Studies in History, Economics, and Public Law, No. 361. New York: Columbia University Press, 1932. Reprint: New York: Russell & Russell, 1966.

IWW history that includes details of the IWW split in 1924. The book pictures the union as a dwindling anachronism.

77. Gentry, Curt. *Frame-Up: The Incredible Case of Tom Mooney and Warren Billings.* New York: Norton, 1967.

Well-written and lively history of the dramatic case of two men, once IWW members, who became labor's "martyrs."

78. George, Harrison. *The IWW Trial.* New York: Arno Press, 1970. (Mass Violence in America Series).

Reprint of a pamphlet about the IWW Chicago trial, published by the IWW in 1918. (See no. 4149.)

79. Ginger, Ray. *The Bending Cross: A Biography of Eugene V. Debs.* New Brunswick, NJ: Rutgers University Press, 1949. Reprints: New York: Collier Brothers, 1962 (new title, *Eugene V. Debs: A Biography*), and New York: Russell & Russell, 1969 (original title).

Still the definitive biography; includes knowledgeable comments on Debs' brief participation in the IWW.

80. Goldberg, Harvey, ed. *American Radicals: Some Problems and Personalities.* New York: Monthly Review Press, 1957. Second edition issued in 1969.

A collection of articles by several writers, some relevant to the IWW.

81. Goldman, Emma. *Living My Life.* Vol. 1 of 2 vols. New York: Knopf, 1931. Reprints: Garden City, NY: Garden City Publish-

ing Co., 1936; New York: AMS Press, 1971; New York: Da Capo Press, 1973 (Civil Liberties in American History Series); and New York: New American Library, 1977.

Autobiography that includes plenty of personal comment (often acerbic) on events, people, and sometimes the IWW. There are lengthy comments on the San Diego Free Speech Fight and the deportations.

82. Goldstein, Robert J. *Political Repression in Modern America: 1870 to the Present.* Cambridge, MA: Schenkman Publishers and Two Continents Publishing Group, 1978.

Explains why political repression was so much a part of IWW history. The earlier chapters recount in detail how the actions of the government affected the history and growth of the IWW, from its beginning to the present.

83. Gompers, Samuel. *Seventy Years of Life and Labor: An Autobiography.* Vol. 1 of 2 vols. New York: Dutton, 1925. Reissued in 1957. Reprint: Fairfield, NJ: A. M. Kelley, 1966.

Useful for learning the nature of the IWW's opposition. Gompers, though occasionally threatened by the IWW, chose to ignore it when possible ("now and then I encountered IWW's in my work") and dimisses the IWW with little mention in this first autobiographical volume.

84. Graham, H. D., and T. R. Gurr, eds. *The History of Violence in America: Historical and Comparative Perspectives. Report Submitted to the National Commission on the Causes and Prevention of Violence.* New York: Frederick A. Praeger, 1969.

Articles on the subject of revolutionary violence and rioting, including one by Philip Taft and Philip Ross on the IWW.

85. Grant, Percy Stickney. *Fair Play for the Workers: Some Sides of Their Maladjustments and the Causes.* New York: Moffat, Yard, 1918.

Contemporary work showing some aspects of workers' maladjustments, probing for the causes for their feelings of despair.

86. Greaves, C. Desmond. *The Life and Times of James Connolly.* London: Lawrence & Wishart, 1961. Reprint: New York: International Publishers, 1972.

About the early IWW organizer and later Irish martyr. The biography includes interesting material on the early IWW and comments and reminiscences about other IWWs, such as Patrick Quinlan and Frank Tannenbaum.

87. Green, James R. *Grassroots Socialism: Radical Movements in the Southwest, 1895–1943*. Baton Rouge, LA: Louisiana State University Press, 1977.

    Includes good information about, and frequent mention of, the IWW and the part it played in organizing workers in Louisiana and the Southwest.

88. Green, Marguerite. *The National Civic Federation and the American Labor Movement, 1900–1925*. Washington, DC: Catholic University Press, 1956. Reprint: New York: Greenwood Press, 1973.

    Sympathetic account of this organization, one of whose purposes was to combat the IWW. Much effort was spent over the years to accomplish the downfall of the IWW. Included is a long chapter on the Federation's struggle against "the radicals."

89. Grover, David H. *Debaters and Dynamiters: The Story of the Haywood Trial.* Studies in American History Series, No. 4. Corvallis, OR: Oregon State University Press, 1964.

    A detailed history of the first Haywood trial.

90. Gutfeld, Arnon. *Montana's Agony: Years of War and Hysteria, 1917–1921*. Gainesville: University Presses of Florida, 1979.

    A solidly documented tale with the IWW as a central protagonist and victim. It includes an excellent bibliography.

91. Gutman, Herbert G. *Work, Culture and Society in Industrializing America: Essays in American Working-Class and Social History.* New York: Random House, 1976.

    How workers have come to react to the difficult demands of modern industry; includes comment on IWW attitudes.

92. Hanson, Ole. *Americanism versus Bolshevism.* New York: Doubleday, Page, 1920.

    Demonstrates that although Hanson did not invent bias, he made a name for himself using it. The book is one of the results of the Seattle strike, which Hanson blames wholly on immigrants and the IWW. IWWs are Bolsheviks, and the "foreigners" and "Bolsheviks" caused most of the problems of the whole U.S.A.

93. Hapgood, Hutchins. *A Victorian in the Modern World.* New York: Harcourt, Brace, 1939. Reprint: Seattle: University of Washington Press, 1972.

    Autobiography of a liberal and IWW sympathizer, describing his times.

94. Hapgood, Norman, ed. *Professional Patriots.* New York: A. and C. Boni, 1927.

Interesting contemporary accounts of citizen organizations that took it upon themselves to defend America from radicals. Hapgood includes the history of such organizations as the Better American Federation, the National Civic Federation, and others less well known; he also describes some now nearly forgotten "causes."

95. Hardy, George. *Those Stormy Years: Memories of the Fight for Freedom on Five Continents.* London: Laurence and Wishart, 1956.

Autobiography of a quondam IWW member. Hardy was an IWW editor and activist who believed the IWW was not radical enough.

96. Harley, J. H. *Syndicalism.* London: T. C. and F. C. Jack, 1912, and New York: Dodge, 1912.

A short history of syndicalist thought, from a worldwide viewpoint and in beautiful rhetoric. The book provides a background on syndicalism without direct reference to the IWW, which, when this was written, was still only six or seven years old.

97. Hawley, Lowell S., and Ralph B. Potts. *Counsel for the Damned: A Biography of George Francis Vanderveer.* Philadelphia: Lippincott, 1953.

Biography of one of the IWW's staunchest legal defenders.

98. Hays, Arthur Garfield. *Trial by Prejudice.* New York: Covici Friede, 1933. Reprints: New York: Da Capo Press, 1970 (Civil Liberties in American History Series), and Westport, CT: Negro University Press, 1970.

Recalls the Mooney Case, Centralia, and the first Haywood trial for a popular audience of the 1930s. The noted civil rights lawyer points out the injustices in these cases.

99. Haywood, William Dudley. *Bill Haywood's Book: The Autobiography of William D. Haywood.* New York: International Publishers, 1929. Reissued in 1966 as *Autobiography of Big Bill Haywood.*

Haywood's own fascinating story and that of the IWW, from the WFM to the Kuzbas Colony.

100. Hennacy, Ammon. *Autobiography of a Catholic Anarchist.* New York: Catholic Worker Books, 1954. Reprint: Salt Lake City, by the author, 1965 (revised and retitled *The Book of Ammon*); reissued in 1970.

Reminiscences about the past of an ex-member of the IWW. This revision includes a chapter on the Joe Hill House of Salt Lake City.

101. Hicks, Granville. *John Reed: The Making of a Revolutionary.* New York: Macmillan, 1936. Reprints: Ann Arbor, MI: Ann Arbor Press, 1967, and New York: B. Blom, 1968.

A fascinating account of the man who created the Paterson Pageant and who enjoyed his adventures as a member of the IWW until he went to Russia.

102. Hidy, Ralph W.; Frank E. Hill; and Allan Nevins. *Timber and Men: The Weyerhaeuser Story.* New York: Macmillan, 1963.

The story of the LLLL (Loyal Legion of Loggers and Lumbermen) and the IWW, as told from the viewpoint of one of the biggest lumber-producing companies.

103. Hillstrom, Joseph. *The Letters of Joe Hill.* Compiled and edited by Philip S. Foner. New York: Oak Publications, 1965.

A short book of Joe Hill's 1914–1915 letters, with historical footnotes, illustrations, and poems.

104. Holbrook, Stewart H. *Holy Old Mackinaw: A Natural History of the American Lumberjack.* New York: Macmillan, 1938. New enlarged edition, 1956. Reprint: Eugene, OR: Comstock Editions, 1979.

A light and cheerful account of the lumbering days when the IWW was a strong force in the woods.

105. ———. *The Rocky Mountain Revolution.* New York: Henry Holt, 1956.

A popular account of the first Haywood trial, which is sympathetic toward the accusing witness, Harry Orchard.

106. Hough, Emerson. *The Web.* Chicago: Reilly and Lee, 1919. Reprint: New York: Arno Press, 1973 (Mass Violence in America Series).

Written in the bad temper of its own time, during the Red Scare. This collection of opinions and rumors views the IWW as a very dangerous conspiracy to be wiped out at all costs.

107. Hoxie, Robert F. *Trade Unionism in the United States.* New York: D. Appleton, 1926. Second edition issued, with supplement, in 1931. Reprint: New York: Russell & Russell, 1966.

Includes a chapter on the IWW's "revolutionary unionism."

108. Hoyt, Edwin P. *The Palmer Raids, 1919–1920: An Attempt To Suppress Dissent.* New York: Seabury Press, 1969.

The Red Scare revisited. The author uses many newspaper stories to demonstrate the feverish patriotism and fear of radicals.

109. Humon, George. *Uusi yhteisdkunta ja sen rakentajat* (History of American labor unions). Duluth: Workers Society Publishing Company, 1923.

Not translated from the Finnish. Shows the IWW as the final culmination of the workers' efforts to have a good union.

110. Hunter, Robert. *Violence and the Labor Movement.* New York: Macmillan, 1914. Reissued, 1919. Reprint: New York: Arno Press, 1969 (Mass Violence in America Series).

Includes a chapter on syndicalism as "the newest anarchism." The author sees the IWW as an American version of Syndicalism, but one lacking in real importance.

111. Hutchins, Grace. *Labor and Silk.* New York: International Publishers, 1929.

Emphasis on textile workers and their problems from a view sympathetic toward labor. Hutchins discusses the Paterson strike among others.

112. Hyman, Harold. *Soldiers and Spruce: Origins of the Loyal Legion of Loggers and Lumbermen.* Monograph Series No. 10. Los Angeles: University of California Institute of Industrial Relations, 1963.

Splendid story of the time the government avoided labor problems by sending in the Army to wield axes rather than guns. This is a scholarly history of a bizarre episode.

113. ———. *To Try Men's Souls: Loyalty Tests in American History.* Berkeley: University of California Press, 1960. Reissued in 1969.

Recounts the fierce and vengeful roles of the American Protective League and the Loyal Legion of Loggers and Lumbermen, as well as the U.S. Government, in opposition to the IWW and others with irregular opinions.

114. Interchurch World Movement of North America, Commission of Inquiry. *Report on the Steel Strike of 1919.* New York: Harcourt, Brace, and Howe, 1920; New York: Putnam, 1923. Reprint: New York: Da Capo Press, 1970 (Civil Liberties in American History Series).

Statistics, data, and personal testimony leading to an elaborate list of findings about the strike, in which the IWW played a minor role.

115. Jaffe, Julian F. *Crusade Against Radicalism: New York during the Red Scare, 1914–1924*. Port Washington, NY: Kennikat Press, 1972.
Based on the papers of the Lusk Committee. This is a good local review of bureaucratic repressions that analyzes the public fear of radicalism.

116. Janes, George Milton. *American Trade Unionism*. Chicago: A. C. McClurg & Co., 1922.
A contemporary view of the struggle between industrial unionism and trade unionism. The author describes the IWW and industrial unionist groups as the "antagonistic organizations" that may be trade unionism's greatest threat.

117. Jensen, Joan. *Price of Vigilance*. Chicago: Rand McNally, 1968.
Excellent and thorough study of the American Protective League and its power during the Red Scare. Jensen makes good use of government records of the government's employment of citizen vigilantes.

118. Jensen, Vernon H. *Heritage of Conflict: Labor Relations in the Nonferrous Metals Industry up to 1930*. Ithaca, NY: Cornell University Press, 1950. Reprint: New York: Greenwood Press, 1968 (Industrial and Labor Relations Series).
The story of the mining wars and especially the Western Federation of Miners. It is both meticulously documented and well told.

119. ———. *Lumber and Labor*. New York: Farrar and Rinehart, 1945. Reprint: New York: Arno Press, 1971 (American Labor from Conspiracy to Collective Bargaining Series).
Includes the Brotherhood of Timberworkers, other IWW unions, Centralia, the LLLL, and lumber strikes in a detailed account.

120. Johnson, Donald O. *Challenge to American Freedom: World War I and the Rise of the American Civil Liberties Union*. Lexington, KY: For the Mississippi Valley Historical Association, University of Kentucky Press, 1963.
Describes the important role of the ACLU in defending the IWW's activities during World War I.

121. Johnson, Frederick Ernest. *The New Spirit in Industry.* New York: Association Press, 1919.

A contemporary view of labor unionism that sees a more militant unionism, perhaps partly modeled on the IWW, for the future.

122. Jones, Mary Harris. *Autobiography of Mother Jones.* Chicago: Charles H. Kerr, 1925. Third revised edition, 1980.

A terse account of Mother Jones' life with militant labor. She makes no mention of the IWW to speak of, as she grew to dislike that group, which she helped to found, but the book is an important view of the times.

123. Kantorovitch, Haim. *Di geshikhte fun der amerikaner arbeyter bavegung* (History of an American labor union). New York: Poalei Zion, Branch Six, 1920.

Not translated from the Yiddish.

124. Karni, Michael G., ed. *The Finnish Experience in the Western Great Lakes Region: New Perspectives.* Institute for Migration, Turku, Finland, in cooperation with the Immigration History Research Center. Minneapolis: University of Minnesota Press, 1975.

Ethnic study, taking Finnish participation in the IWW into account.

125. Karson, Marc. *American Labor Unions and Politics, 1900–1918.* Carbondale, IL: Southern Illinois University Press, 1958.

Shows how the American environment worked against radicalism. The failure of the left and the success of the AFL are explained.

126. Kawashima, Shojiro. *IWW Sekai Sangyo Rodoshan* (History of the IWW). Japan, 1920.

Not translated from the Japanese. Japanese scholars are said to find this book particularly meritorious.

127. Keller, Helen. *Helen Keller: Her Socialist Years; Writings and Speeches.* Edited by P. S. Foner. New York: International Publishers, 1967.

Shows Helen Keller's great outspoken sympathy for the IWW and other victims of injustice.

128. Kirk, William. *National Labor Federations in the United States.* Johns Hopkins University Studies in Historical and Political Science,

Nos. 9–10. Baltimore, MD: Johns Hopkins Press, 1906. Reprint: New York: AMS Press, 1978.

Contains one of the earliest serious explications of the IWW.

129. Kirkaldy, Adam W. *Economics and Syndicalism.* New York: G. P. Putnam's Sons, 1914.

Examines and compares syndicalist philosophies, with most attention given to the European.

130. Kirkpatrick, George R. *War—What For?* West Lafayette, OH: by the author, 1910. Reprints: New York: Garland, 1978 (Library of War and Peace; Labor, Socialism, and War Series), and Brooklyn, NY: Revisionist Press, 1981.

The book that helped convict the IWW at the Chicago Trial of 1918. Mere possession of it was cause for conviction and jail. Kirkpatrick argues that peace is impossible under capitalism.

131. Kluger, James R. *The Clifton-Morenci Strike: Labor Difficulty in Arizona 1915–1916.* Tucson, AZ: University of Arizona Press, 1970.

About the "peaceful strike" of copper miners, who were heavily surrounded by U.S. Army troops.

132. Kornbluh, Joyce L., ed. *Rebel Voices, an I.W.W. Anthology.* Ann Arbor, MI: University of Michigan Press, 1964. Reprint: Chicago: Charles H. Kerr, 1985.

An outstanding and entertaining collection of writings, cartoons, verses, and reports from the IWW literature, with historical introductions.

133. Kraditor, Aileen S. *The Radical Persuasion, 1890–1917: Aspects of the Intellectual History and the Historiography of Three American Radical Organizations.* Baton Rouge, LA: Louisiana State University Press, 1981.

Compares the views of the Socialists, the Socialist Labor Party, and the IWW on nearly everything. It is an extraordinarily interesting and perceptive intellectual history that portrays the not-too-distant past without anachronistic overlay.

134. Lafargue, Paul. *The Right To Be Lazy and Other Studies.* Chicago: Charles H. Kerr, 1907. Reissued, 1975. Partly based on *The Right To Be Lazy: A Refutation* (New York: International Publishers, 1898), which was a translation of Lafargue's *Le Droit à la Paresse: Réfutation du "Droit au Travail" de 1848* (Paris: Siège du Conseil National, 1883).

This book was widely read and highly admired by the IWW and others. It played a strong part in the Chicago IWW trial of 1918, when prosecutors declared it treasonable.

135. Laidler, Harry W. *Boycotts and Labor Struggle: Economic and Legal Aspects.* New York: John Lane, 1914. Reprint: New York: Russell & Russell, 1968.

A contemporary history that points out how sabotage resulted from the suppression of the boycott. It details the IWW position on boycotts.

136. Lane, Roger, and John J. Turner, Jr. *Riot, Rout, and Tumult: Readings in American Social and Political Violence.* Contributions in American History, No. 69. Westport, CT: Greenwood Press, 1978.

A book of readings, of varying quality, some concerning violent episodes in IWW history.

137. Langdon, Emma F. *The Cripple Creek Strike: A History of Industrial Wars in Colorado, 1903–4–5.* Denver, CO: Great Western, 1905. Reprint: New York: Arno Press, 1975 (Mass Violence in America Series).

Stout defense of the Western Federation of Miners. The book includes a contemporary account of the Haywood-Moyer-Pettibone trial and gives a background understanding of the roots of the Western IWW.

138. ———. *Labor's Greatest Conflict: The Formation of the Western Federation of Miners: A Brief Account of the Rise of the United Mine Workers of America.* Denver, CO: Great Western, 1908.

Sympathetic history of the WFM.

139. Larkin, Emmet. *James Larkin, Irish Labour Leader, 1876–1947.* Cambridge: MIT Press, 1965. Reprint: Boston, MA: Routledge and Kegan Paul, 1977.

Contains an interesting though brief account of Larkin's days in America with the IWW.

140. Laslett, John H. M. *Labor and the Left: A Study of Socialist and Radical Influences in the American Labor Movement, 1881–1924.* New York: Basic Books, 1970.

Includes case studies, notably one on the WFM. The author gives reasons for the spread of radicalism and explains the failure of radicalism to dominate the labor movement in this country.

141. Leighton, George R. *Five Cities.* New York: Harper, 1937. Reprint: New York: Arno Press, 1979.

Includes a chapter on the city of Seattle, describing the Seattle General Strike and the regional IWW activities.

142. Leiserson, William M. *Adjusting Immigrant and Society.* New York: Harper & Brothers, 1924. Reprint: New York: Arno Press, 1973 (American Labor from Conspiracy to Collective Bargaining Series).

One chapter carefully analyzes the ways in which the IWW organizers failed the immigrant workers.

143. Lens, Sidney. *The Labor Wars: From the Molly Maguires to the Sit-Downs.* Garden City, NY: Doubleday, 1973.

Labor wars include "wars" involving the IWW against the state of Idaho in the Steunenberg trial, at McKees Rocks, in the Free Speech Fights, and in the Lawrence and Paterson strikes.

144. ———. *Left, Right and Center: Conflicting Forces in American Labor.* Hinsdale, IL: H. Regnery, 1949.

Includes some material on the role of the IWW as a force in the fight to achieve industrial unionism.

145. ———. *Radicalism in America.* New York: Crowell, 1966.

Contains a chapter on IWW radicalism and another on the Red Scare.

146. Levin, Murray B. *Political Hysteria in America: The Democratic Capacity for Repression.* New York: Basic Books, 1971.

Recalls the Red Scare and tries to explain the reasons for such occurrences in this country.

147. Lowenthal, Max. *The Federal Bureau of Investigation.* New York: Sloane, 1950. Reprint: Westport, CT: Greenwood Press, 1970.

A detailed account of the Red Scare days, from the investigators' side. One chapter tells about the General Intelligence Department of the government and its interest in the IWW.

148. Lynn, Mrs. Ethel. *The Adventures of a Woman Hobo.* New York: George H. Doran, 1917.

Contemporary account of a woman who crossed the country as a hobo and encountered interesting people along the way, including a few Wobblies.

149. McCormack, Andrew Ross. *Reformers, Rebels and Revolutionaries: The Western Canadian Radical Movement, 1899–1919.* Toronto: University of Toronto Press, 1977.

Includes a discussion of the part played by the IWW and militant industrial unionism in the history of Western Canada.

150. McGowan, Joseph A. *History of the Sacramento Valley.* Vol. 2 of 2. New York: Lewis Historical Publishing Co., 1961.

Contains information about the public's apprehension of the IWW and about migrant workers.

151. McWilliams, Carey. *Factories in the Field: The Story of Migratory Farm Labor in California.* Boston: Little, Brown, 1939. Reprint: Hamden, CT: Shoestring Press, 1969.

Includes a chapter on the Wheatlands Hop Riot and its aftermath.

152. ———. *Ill Fares the Land: Migrants and Migratory Labor in the United States.* Boston: Little, Brown, 1942. Reprint: New York: Arno Press, 1976 (Chicano Heritage Series).

Shows how progressive farmers were better able to tolerate the IWW than some others and explores the changes in migrant labor over the years.

153. Macy, John. *Socialism in America.* New York: Doubleday Page, 1916.

A contemporary account of Socialism and its difficult relationship with the IWW.

154. Madison, Charles. *American Labor Leaders: Personalities and Forces in the Labor Movement.* New York: Ungar, 1962.

Contains a chapter on William Haywood.

155. Malkov, Victor. *ТОМ МУНИ—узник Сан-Квентина* (Tom Mooney: San Quentin prisoner). Moscow: Mysl, 1976.

Not translated from the Russian. Biography by one of Russia's foremost historians. Malkov also wrote a biography of Haywood, not yet available.

156. Mann, Tom. *Tom Mann's Memoirs.* London: Labor Publishing Co., 1923.

Memories of the Australian rebel and IWW supporter who toured America and England assisting in the "rabble-rousing."

157. Markmann, Charles Lam. *The Noblest Cry: A History of the American Civil Liberties Union.* New York: St. Martin's, 1965.

Includes an account of the difficult defense of the IWW by the NCLB and the ACLU when they were among the few defenders of citizens' rights during World War I and the Red Scare.

158. Marot, Helen. *American Labor Unions, by a Member.* New York: Holt, 1914. Reprint: New York: Arno Press, 1970 (American Labor from Conspiracy to Collective Bargaining Series).

Includes interesting contemporary analysis of the IWW, viewed then as "a national force," not just another union.

159. Meltzer, Milton. *Bread and Roses: The Struggle of American Labor, 1865–1915.* New York: New American Library, 1977.

Simplified labor story depicting the courage and perseverance of the strikers during such times as the Lawrence and Paterson strikes and the Ludlow Massacre.

160. Mereto, Joseph. *The I.W.W.* Chicago: Iconoclast, 1919.

One of the extreme anti-IWW books published during the Red Scare.

161. Montgomery, David. *Workers' Control in America: Studies in the History of Work, Technology, and Labor Struggles.* New York: Cambridge University Press, 1979.

A volume of essays, one of which, on "The New Unionism and the Transformation of Workers' Consciousness in America, 1909–1922," discusses the effect of IWW militancy.

162. Morris, James O. *Conflict within the AFL: A Study of Craft versus Industrial Unionism, 1901–1938.* Cornell Studies in Industrial and Labor Relations, vol. 10. Ithaca, NY: State School of Industrial and Labor Relations, Cornell University Press, 1958. Reissued in 1974.

Some of the conflict provided by IWW unionists, who were considered dangerous enemies by the AFL.

163. Murdoch, Angus. *Boom Copper: The Story of the First U.S. Mining Boom.* New York: Macmillan, 1943.

An anecdotal popular history of Michigan's copper country from the 1840s, which includes some material on Calumet and Hecla.

164. Murray, Robert K. *Red Scare: A Study in National Hysteria.* Minneapolis: University of Minnesota Press, 1955. Reprint: Westport, CT: Greenwood Press, 1980.

One of the first thorough studies of the subject. The book describes the ordeal of IWWs and other citizens under repressive actions by the government and citizens' groups.

165. Musto, Renato. *Gli IWW e il Movimento Operaio Americano: Storia e Documenti, 1905–1914* (The IWW and the American labor

movement: history and documents, 1905–1914). Naples: Thélème, 1975.

Not translated from the Italian.

166. National Industrial Conference Board. *Strikes in American Industry in Wartime.* Research Report No. 3. Washington, DC: National Industrial Conference Board, 1918.

Statistical compilations useful for reference, including figures on the IWW strikes.

167. Nerman, Ture. *Arbetarsångaren Joe Hill, Mördare eller Martyr?* (Worksong writer Joe Hill: murderer or martyr?). Stockholm: Federatios Forlag, 1951.

Not translated from the Swedish.

168. Oakes, Edwin S. *The Law of Organized Labor and Industrial Conflicts.* Rochester, NY: Lawyers Co-operative Publishing Co., 1927.

Serious and scholarly book on labor strife and the laws pertaining to it. It deals with criminal anarchy, criminal syndicalism, and sabotage.

169. O'Connor, Harvey. *Revolution in Seattle: A Memoir.* New York: Monthly Review Press, 1964. Reprint: Seattle, WA: Left Bank Press, 1981.

Historical and personal account of the General Strike and other troubles in Washington. The author describes working conditions in the Pacific Northwest and explains the Everett Massacre and Centralia.

170. O'Connor, Richard, and Dale L. Walker. *The Lost Revolutionary: A Biography of John Reed.* New York: Harcourt, Brace and World, 1967.

Well-written romantic biography of Reed, including details of his early membership in the IWW and his enthusiasm for it.

171. Orchard, Harry (Albert E. Horsley). *The Confessions and Autobiography of Harry Orchard.* New York: S.S. McClure Co., 1907.

One version of the Steunenberg murder, by a criminal whose confession implicating Haywood and others astounded all America.

172. Orth, Samuel P. *The Armies of Labor.* New Haven, CT: Yale University Press, 1919.

Strong, virulent, and as anti-IWW as possible.

173. Panunzio, Constantine M. *The Deportation Cases of 1919–1920.* New York: Commission on Church and Social Service, Federal

Council of Churches of Christ in America, 1921. Reprint: New York: Da Capo Press, 1970 (Civil Liberties in American History Series).

About the Palmer Raids and the deportation of radicals.

174. Parker, Carleton H. *The Casual Laborer and Other Essays.* New York: Harcourt, Brace, and Howe, 1920. Reprints: New York: Russell & Russell, 1967, and Seattle: University of Washington Press, 1972 (American Library Series).

Parker's attempt to help people understand migrant workers and their relations with the IWW. He includes a report on conditions in the hop fields.

175. Parker, Cornelia S. *An American Idyll: The Life of Carleton H. Parker.* Boston: Atlantic Monthly Press, 1919.

Biography of an author (see no. 174) who was also a participant in California labor investigations, notably of Wheatland.

176. Perlman, Selig, and Philip Taft. *History of Labor in the United States, 1896–1932.* Vol. IV, *Labor Movements.* New York: Macmillan, 1935.

Classic work of labor history. The authors include a short history of the IWW up to the 1930s.

177. Perry, Louis B., and Richard S. Perry. *A History of the Los Angeles Labor Movement, 1911–1941.* Berkeley: University of California Press, 1963.

Contains a brief description of the maritime workers and of the San Pedro strike.

178. Peterson, H. C., and Gilbert C. Fite. *Opponents of War, 1917–1918.* Madison, WI: University of Wisconsin Press, 1957.

About pacifists, nonconformists, and extremists (under which heading the authors include the IWW) and their experiences in a time of high patriotism. The authors' account is descriptive, analytic, and thorough.

179. Post, Louis Freeland. *The Deportations Delirium of Nineteen-Twenty: A Personal Narrative of an Historic Official Experience.* Introduction by Moorfield Storey. Chicago: Charles H. Kerr and Co., 1923. Reprints: New York: Da Capo Press, 1970 (Civil Liberties in American History Series) and New York: Gordon Press, 1976 (Ethics of Democracy Series).

An almost cheerful account by the brave bureaucrat, an official in the Labor Department's Immigration Office, who dared to speak out. Post relates how the government ignored civil rights and due process to get rid of radicals.

180. Preston, William. *Aliens and Dissenters: Federal Suppression of Radicals, 1903–1933*. Cambridge, MA: Harvard University Press, 1963.

A study of the government's strong efforts to abet local leaders in quashing the IWW and other radicals. Preston's book is based on a meticulous review of government documents.

181. Radosh, Ronald, comp. *Debs*. Great Lives Observed Series. Englewood Cliffs, NJ: Prentice-Hall, 1971.

Contains many references to the IWW, which the author unfortunately calls "International" Workers of the World. The book is a collection of opinions on Eugene V. Debs.

182. Raisky, Leonid G. *Daniel De Leon: The Struggle against Opportunism in the American Labor Movement*. New York: New York Labor News Co., 1932.

Biography of an important early member of the IWW.

183. Ramirez, Bruno. *When Workers Fight: The Politics of Industrial Relations in the Progressive Era—1898–1916*. Westport, CT: Greenwood Press, 1978.

An unusual and perceptive three-part view of the relations among labor, government, and business, each explained historically. The author reviews the role of the National Civic Federation in resolving various labor-management problems. He also analyses IWW strategies concerning the organization of the unskilled and its attitude toward contracts. The book's concluding chapter is an analysis of the IWW through the examination of the "institutional mechanisms designed to regulate industrial conflict."

184. Rand School of Social Science. *American Labor Year Book*. Vols. 1–6. New York: Rand School, 1916–1925.

Useful reference tool for statistics on strikes and other labor actions.

185. Reeve, Carl. *The Life and Times of Daniel De Leon*. Historical Studies, No. 8. New York: American Institute for Marxist Studies, 1972.

Describes De Leon's part in the founding of the IWW and his faction's split from the organization.

186. Reeve, Carl, and Ann B. Reeve. *James Connolly and the United States: The Road to the 1916 Irish Rebellion.* Historical Studies, No. 10. Atlantic Highlands, NJ: Humanities Press, 1978.

Details Connolly's role in the IWW as a member and organizer.

187. Renshaw, Patrick. *The Wobblies: The Story of Syndicalism in the United States.* Garden City, NY: Doubleday, 1967; London: Eyre and Spottiswoode, 1967.

English history that includes good accounts of the foreign administrations, usually omitted from other IWW histories.

188. Reynolds, Lloyd G., and Charles C. Killingsworth. *Trade Union Publications, 1850–1941.* 3 vols. Baltimore, MD: Johns Hopkins Press, 1944–1945.

A reference work providing description and bibliography, with a subject index. The book covers official journals, convention proceedings, and constitutions.

189. Richmond, Alexander. *Native Daughter: The Story of Anita Whitney.* San Francisco: Anita Whitney 75th Anniversary Committee, 1942.

Biography of a radical who, with the IWW, was a defendant in the California Syndicalist trials.

190. Rosenblum, Gerald. *Immigrant Workers: Their Impact on American Labor Radicalism.* New York: Basic Books, 1973.

A sociological look at immigrants that explains how and why some of them were radicalized.

191. Rosenstone, Robert A. *Romantic Revolutionary: A Biography of John Reed.* New York: Alfred A. Knopf, 1975.

Biography of Reed that includes a chapter on the Paterson strike and the pageant.

192. Ross, Carl. *The Finn Factor in American Labor, Culture and Society.* New York Mills, MN: Parta Printers, 1977.

Includes material on the Finnish-Americans' involvement in the Mesabi and Michigan strikes and their radicalism during World War I.

193. Russell, Bertrand. *Proposed Roads to Freedom: Socialism, Anarchism and Syndicalism.* New York: H. Holt & Co., 1919. Reprint: Winchester, MA: Allan & Unwin, 1966 (new title, *Roads to Freedom*).

Includes comparison of the IWW with syndicalism, "pure syndicalism," and guild socialism.

194. Saposs, David J. *Left Wing Unionism: A Study of Radical Policies and Tactics.* New York: International Publishers, 1926. Reprint: New York: Russell & Russell, 1967.

An analysis of union strategies and methods, including those of the IWW. Saposs discusses dual unionism and the shades of difference among radicals.

195. Savage, Marion Dutton. *Industrial Unionism in America.* New York: Ronald Press, 1922. Reprint: New York: Arno Press, 1971 (American Labor Series No. 2).

Contemporary review of industrial unions, industry by industry. It discusses revolutionary industrial unionism; compares IWW and OBU.

196. Scheiber, Harry N. *The Wilson Administration and Civil Liberties, 1917–1921.* Cornell Studies in American History, Literature, and Folklore No. 6. Ithaca, NY: Cornell University Press, 1960.

A short study of federal legislation that "abridged traditional American liberties" and the government's official part in the Red Scare.

197. Schroeder, Theodore. *Free Speech for Radicals.* Riverside, CT: Hillacre Bookhouse, 1916. Reprint: New York: B. Franklin, 1970 (Research and Source Works Series No. 281).

Probes the problem of how far a radical may go. The author includes a chapter on the San Diego Free Speech Fight.

198. Schwantes, Carlos A. *Radical Heritage: Labor, Socialism and Reform in Washington and British Columbia, 1885–1917.* Emil and Kathleen Sick Lecture Book Series in Western History and Biography. Seattle: University of Washington Press, 1979.

A comparison of labor relations in the two similar Northwest areas. This book explains how and why Socialism was able to survive in one area and not the other. The two political cultures and their labor movements are described.

199. Scott, Jack. *Plunderbund and Proletariat: History of the I.W.W. in B.C.* Vancouver, BC: New Star Books, 1975.

A modern and somewhat idiosyncratic version of IWW history, by a Canadian member.

200. Seretan, L. Glen. *Daniel De Leon: The Odyssey of an American Marxist.* Cambridge: Harvard University Press, 1979.

Analysis of the thinking of De Leon, with great emphasis on the philosophic break from the IWW.

201. Shannon, David A. *The Socialist Party of America: A History.* New York: Macmillan, 1955. Reprint: Chicago: Quadrangle Books, 1967.

An excellent organizational history that points up the importance of the relationship between the IWW and the Socialist Party and how that relationship affected the party's history.

202. Siringo, Charles A. *A Cowboy Detective: A True Story of Twenty-Two Years With a World-Famous Detective Agency; Giving the Inside Facts of the Bloody Coeur d'Alene Labor Riots and the Many Ups and Downs of the Author throughout the U.S., Alaska, British Columbia and Old Mexico, Also Exciting Scenes Among the Moonshiners of Kentucky and Virginia.* Chicago: W. B. Conkey, 1912. Reprint: Lincoln, NE: University of Nebraska Press, 1966. A second and similar book is *Two Evil Isms: Pinkertonism and Anarchism, by a Cowboy Detective Who Knows, as He Spent 22 Years in the Inner Circle of Pinkerton's National Detective Agency.* Chicago: by the author, 1915.

Two books of local color and comment whose titles indicate their contents. They are highly individual accounts of what opposition some radicals faced.

203. Smith, Gibbs M. *Joe Hill.* Salt Lake City, UT: University of Utah Press, 1969.

Considered by many to be the definitive biography of the IWW martyr.

204. Soderstron, Ingvar. *Joe Hill Diktare och Agitare* (Joe Hill, leader and agitator). Stockholm, 1940.

Not translated from the Swedish.

205. Souchy, Agustin. *Schreckensherrschaft in Amerika* (The rule of terror in America). Berlin: E. Kater, 1927.

Not translated from the German. Emphasizes police brutality and government repression.

206. Spargo, John. *Syndicalism, Industrial Unionism and Socialism.* New York: B. W. Huebsch, 1913.

Collected lectures stating Spargo's views on various groups and their involvement in politics. It is a very early contemporary analysis of the IWW.

207. Steuben, John. *Labor in Wartime.* New York: International Publishers, 1949.

Reviews IWW and other labor actions during World War I.

208. Strong, Anna Louise. *I Change Worlds: The Remaking of an American.* Garden City, NY: Garden City Publishing Co., 1937. Reprints: Seattle, WA: Seal Press, 1979, and Seattle, WA: Madrona Press, 1979.

An eyewitness account of the Seattle strike and other IWW events by a journalist sympathetic to the IWW.

209. Suggs, George G., Jr. *Colorado's War on Militant Unionism: James H. Peabody and the Western Federation of Miners.* Detroit: Wayne State University Press, 1972.

A history of the Western Federation of Miners. The book provides a background for the Cripple Creek strike and the rise of William Haywood.

210. Symes, Lillian, and Clement Travers. *Rebel America: The Story of Social Revolt in the United States.* New York: Harper, 1934. Reprint: New York: Da Capo Press, 1972 (Civil Liberties in American History Series).

A panoramic view of American "rebels," including the IWW, Socialists, IWWs, and Communists, portrayed as an important part of social history.

211. Taft, Philip. *The A. F. of L. in the Time of Gompers.* New York: Harper, 1957. Reprint: New York: Octagon Books, 1970.

Relates the struggle of the AFL against antagonistic Socialist, IWW, and collectivist ideas. The author, a noted economist and historian, was once an IWW member.

212. Taylor, Paul S. *The Sailors Union of the Pacific.* New York: Ronald Press, 1923. Reprint: New York: Arno Press, 1971 (American Labor Series 2).

Includes the IWW as part of the SUP's "internal conflict" and as a strong union rival to the SUP.

213. Thompson, Fred. *The I.W.W., Its First Fifty Years, 1905–1955: The History of an Effort To Organize the Working Class.* Chicago: IWW, 1955.

Provides a sympathetic and detailed account of IWW history, including many minor incidents often overlooked. The author was a participant in much of the history.

214. Thompson, Fred, and Patrick Murfin. *The I.W.W., Its First Seventy Years, 1905–1975.* Chicago: IWW, 1977.

Attempts to bring the history of the IWW up to date. The

authors recapitulate the past in much detail. This volume is one of the few sources for very recent IWW history.

215. Todes, Charlotte. *Lumber and Labor.* New York: International Publishers, 1931. Reprint: New York: Arno Press, 1975 (American Farmers and the Rise of Agriculture Series).
A history of lumberworkers that includes the story of the IWW lumberjacks in the Northwest and the Brotherhood of Timber Workers in the South. Centralia and the Everett Massacre are described.

216. Toole, K. Ross. *Twentieth-Century Montana: A State of Extremes.* Norman, OK: University of Oklahoma Press, 1972. Reissued, 1979.
An evocative narrative that includes a colorful account of the astonishing anti-IWW hysteria during World War I.

217. Tridon, André. *The New Unionism.* New York: B. Huebsch, 1913.
A 1913 viewpoint on syndicalism's history and possibilities. An explanation of the IWW is included.

218. Turner, Ian. *Industrial Labor and Politics: The Dynamics of the Labour Movement in Eastern Australia, 1900–1921.* Canberra: Australian National University Press, 1965.

219. ———. *Sydney's Burning! (An Australian Political Conspiracy.)* London: Heinemann, 1967.

220. ———. *Tom Barker and the I.W.W.* Canberra: Center for the Study of Labour History, 1965.
Australian histories. The foremost historian of the Australian IWW relates the history, problems, trials, and philosophies of the organization and its leaders in Australia in these three volumes.

221. Tyler, Robert L. *Rebels of the Woods: The I.W.W. in the Pacific Northwest.* Eugene, OR: University of Oregon Press, 1967.
Well-written and carefully documented account of the IWW participation in the lumbering industry.

222. Van Tine, Warren R. *The Making of the Labor Bureaucrat: Union Leadership in the United States, 1870–1926.* Amherst, MA: University of Massachusetts Press, 1973.
A statistical and biographical study of 350 union leaders, with analysis of the apparent changes, or lack of changes, in the style of leadership and power of office. It is scholarly and evenhanded. IWW people are included in the study.

223. Vorse, Mary Heaton. *Footnote to Folly: Reminiscences of Mary Heaton Vorse.* New York: Farrar and Rinehart, 1935. Reprint: New York: Arno Press, 1980 (Signal Lives Series).

A journalist's memories of the Lawrence strike. The author's recollections include Frank Tannenbaum's arrest and the issue of the unemployed in New York City, the Mesabi Range strike, the steel strike of 1919, the Palmer Raids, and other events that she witnessed or covered as a reporter.

224. Weinberg, Arthur M., ed. *Attorney for the Damned.* New York: Simon and Schuster, 1957. Reprint: New York: Putnam, 1980 (revised, with coauthor Lila Weinberg, retitled *Clarence Darrow, the Sentimental Rebel*).

A biography of Clarence Darrow, defense attorney at the first Haywood trial.

225. Weinstein, James. *Ambiguous Legacy: The Left in American Politics.* New York: New Viewpoint, 1975.

Includes a thoughtful analysis of the IWW position in politics and history.

226. ———. *The Decline of Socialism in America, 1912–1925.* New York: Monthly Review Press, 1967.

Contains some interweaving of Socialist attitudes toward the IWW.

227. Werstein, Irving. *Pie in the Sky: An American Struggle, the Wobblies and Their Time.* New York: Delacorte Press, 1969.

A popular history of the IWW that includes a glossary of IWW slang and expressions.

228. Wertheimer, Barbara. *We Were There: The Story of Working Women in America.* New York: Pantheon Books, 1977.

IWW women are depicted in a chapter on the Lawrence strike and elsewhere in this book. Stressing the women's role, which is often overlooked in labor histories, the author points out that the IWW included more women organizers and speakers than any other union.

229. Woehlke, W. V. *Union Labor in Peace and War.* San Francisco: Sunset Publishing House, 1918.

Includes an essay on IWW wartime attitudes and the reaction of the public to those attitudes.

230. Wolman, Leo. *The Growth of American Trade Unions, 1880–1923.* New York: National Bureau of Economic Research, 1924. Re-

print: New York: Arno Press, 1975 (National Bureau of Economic Research Series).

Contemporary statistical studies useful for reference; also economic survey of unions including the IWW.

231. Wyman, Mark. *Hard Rock Epic: Western Miners and the Industrial Revolution, 1860–1910.* Berkeley: University of California Press, 1979.

The impact of technological change on miners and their reaction, which included unionization and radicalism. WFM and IWW dominate the story in the last decade.

232. Yellen, Samuel. *American Labor Struggles.* New York: Harcourt, Brace, 1936. Reprints: New York: Arno Press, 1969 (American Labor Series 1), and New York: Monad Press, 1974.

Includes a long description of the Lawrence strike, the steel strike of 1919, and the Ludlow Massacre.

233. Yoneda, Shotaro. *Bankin Shakai Shiso no Kenkyu* (History of the IWW). Japan, 1922.

Not translated from the Japanese. The second of two major IWW histories written by Japanese scholars (see also no. 126).

234. Young, Alfred F., ed. *Dissent: Explorations in the History of American Radicalism.* DeKalb, IL: Northern Illinois University Press, 1968.

Includes Melvyn Dubofsky's article, "The Radicalism of the Dispossessed: William D. Haywood and the IWW." See no. 955.

235. Young, Arthur H. *Art Young: His Life and Times.* New York: Sheridan House, 1939. Reprint: Westport, CT: Hyperion Press, 1975 (Radical Tradition in America Series).

Autobiography of the stalwart Socialist, whose life included a long-time association with the IWW and other radical groups. Young includes some of his great political cartoons and tells about the Chicago trial, which he covered as a reporter and as an artist.

ONE BIG UNION

OF ALL THE

WORKERS

THE I.W.W.

PRINTED IN U.S.A

Articles

THESE articles vary greatly: contemporary accounts, popular magazine features, newspaper stories, pieces from IWW publications, and especially scholarly and historical studies are all included here. Each type makes its special contribution. For the convenience of the person who wants only one type of article, a journal index, in which all entries are listed under serial titles, has been provided at the end of this section. This index could be especially useful for library research. Authors and subjects are listed in the general index at the end of the volume. From this second index it would be possible to compile quickly a smaller bibliography on a particular subject, for instance, on William D. Haywood or the Paterson strike.

A few newspaper articles are included. Some parts of IWW history have not been much emphasized, and some items are included here, otherwise short and not outstanding, because they were helpful in presenting a more complete and balanced view of the IWW. A few entries are from trade union journals that opposed industrial unionism. The IWW viewpoint is amply represented in the articles from IWW publications as well as others.

I was unable to examine every article, and therefore a number of entries lack annotation. As the size of this bibliography grew, space limitations had to be kept in mind. In some cases, newspaper stories and articles had been clipped and placed in scrapbooks, as at the Labadie Collection. Although these were dated, page numbers were often missing. Some entries gleaned from the footnotes and bibliographies of doctoral dissertations lacked details. Rather than discard a good entry because it was incomplete, I retained it if a reader could reasonably expect to locate it. As many historical and scholarly articles were included as could be found. Where the titles describe the contents adequately, no annotation was added.

236. Abbott, Mabel. "A Chicago Interlude." *New Republic* 15 (July 27, 1918):367–68.

Description of the Chicago IWW trial.

237. Abel, Herbert. “Gun Rule in Kentucky.” *Nation* 133 (September 23, 1931):306–8.
Kentucky’s long history of violent coal mine strikes.

238. “Acquittal of Haywood.” *Outlook* 86 (August 3, 1907):715–16.
The first, or Idaho, trial of Haywood.

239. “Acquittal of the IWW Leaders.” *Literary Digest* 45 (December 7, 1912):1049–50.
The Lawrence strike and the trials that followed it.

240. “Acquittal of William D. Haywood.” *Arena* 38 (September, 1907):332–33.
The verdict at Haywood’s first trial.

241. “Activities of the I.W.W. Enjoined in California: Membership Forbidden.” *Law and Labor* 5 (October, 1923):272–74.

242. “An Able Address.” *Miners Magazine* 7 (September 14, 1905):8.
Description of a speech by Lucy Parsons given at the IWW convention.

243. “Abolitionists and the IWW.” *Industrial Pioneer* 1 (April, 1924):27–28.
A comparison.

244. “About Haywood.” *Literary Digest* 46 (June 14, 1913):1352–54.
A. Tridon’s description of Haywood.

245. “The Acid Test.” *Garment Worker* 12 (August 29, 1913):6.
All organizations must be based upon correct principles. The author believes the IWW’s principles are incorrect.

246. “The Acid Test.” *Shoe Workers Journal* 14 (November, 1913):8–9.
Violence brings the IWW publicity, but can it increase membership?

247. Adamic, Louis. “Assassin of Wilson.” *American Mercury* 21 (October, 1930):138–46.
Explains the “folded-arms” technique of sabotage and discusses a coincidental connection with President Wilson.

248. Adams, Graham, Jr. “Radicalism and the American Ethos.” *Canadian Review of American Studies* 11 (No. 1, 1980):95–102.

249. ———. Review of *The Wobblies*, by Patrick Renshaw. *Labor History* 9 (Spring, 1968):285–87. See no. 187.

250. Adams, John D. “Clod or Brother.” *Survey* 27 (March 30, 1912):2014–15.
The Lawrence strike.

251. Addams, Jane, and Elizabeth Gurley Flynn. "What Is a Minimum Wage?" *Square Deal* 12 (February, 1913):33–35.

252. "Address of Judge O. N. Hilton before the Board." *Miners Magazine* 11 (January 13, 1910):4–7.
A plea for Preston and Smith before the Nevada Pardon Board, following the Goldfield affair.

253. "Address of Judge O. N. Hilton of Denver in Behalf of Preston and Smith." *Miners Magazine* 10 (January 14, 1909):6–11.
Address concerning the Goldfield affair.

254. "Address of President Moyer." *Miners Magazine* 15 (July 23, 1914):3–20.
Long address including statements on the IWW and the Michigan copper strike.

255. "Address to the Wage Workers." *Miners Magazine* 7 (September 28, 1905):9–11.
The desirability of industrial unionism.

256. "A. F. of L. Convention—Gompers Still Captain on the Drifting Ship." *One Big Union Monthly* 2 (July, 1920):52–53.

257. "Affairs in San Diego." *Public* 15 (May 31, 1912):512–13.
Describes the Harris Weinstock report on the San Diego Free Speech Fight and quotes from it extensively.

258. "Affidavits from 'Law and Order' Guards." *Miners Magazine* 15 (February 19, 1914):10–11.
Executive Board report on the Michigan copper strike. Affidavits were obtained from armed thugs proving they were hired to make trouble.

259. "Afraid of an Investigation." *Miners Magazine* 15 (February 5, 1914):10–11.
Claims Michigan copper barons and the Michigan governor do not want an investigation of the Michigan copper strike.

260. "Aftermath of a Strike." *Outlook* 100 (June 1, 1912):237–38.
The Lawrence strike.

261. "Aftermath of the Paterson Strike." *Outlook* 105 (November 29, 1913):679.

262. "Again, the Wobblies." *Time* 47 (April 1, 1946):24.
An IWW convention described in a mournful manner.

263. "Agents Provocateurs." *One Big Union Monthly* 1 (April, 1919):4.
Red Scare tactics described and deplored.

264. "Agricultural Workers." *International Socialist Review* 18 (November–December, 1917):307.
California migrant workers.

265. "Agricultural Workers Campaign." *One Big Union Monthly* 2 (August, 1920):5.

266. "Agricultural Workers Industrial Union." *One Big Union Monthly* 1 (April, 1919):53–54.

267. Ainsworth, C. L. "Letter to the Editor." *Survey* 39 (November 10, 1917):151.
Women and preachers are greatly offended by the dreadful pamphlets on scabbing.

268. "Akron Rubber Strike the Usual Noisy IWW Affair." *Square Deal* 12 (April, 1913):279–80.

269. "Alarums and Excursions." *Freeman* 8 (January 9, 1924):412–14.
The Palmer Raids.

270. "An Alaska OBU." *One Big Union Monthly* 1 (December, 1919):48.
History of a successful industrial union.

271. Alaskan Miner. "Shall We Unite?" *International Socialist Review* 12 (June, 1912):843–44.
Believes that unions should not fight one another.

272. Albers, Frank. "Center Shots." *Voice of the People* 2 (October 30, 1913):3.
A series of sayings, jokes, and aphorisms about the IWW and its beliefs.

273. "Alexander Scott Freed." *International Socialist Review* 14 (June, 1914):763.
Account of a writer who was jailed for his stories on the Paterson strike because they favored the strikers.

274. "Alien and Sedition Bills of 1920." *Literary Digest* 64 (February 7, 1920):11–13.
The raids and arrests of radicals.

275. "Alien and Sedition Laws of Today." *Review of Reviews* 62 (October, 1920):431–32.
The raids and arrests of radicals.

276. Allen, Edgar F. "Aftermath of Industrial War at Ipswich, Massachusetts." *Survey* 32 (May 23, 1914):216–17.
Dispassionate analysis by one of the arbitrators of the strike,

who says the immigrants come from undeveloped races and embrace an idealism they do not understand.

277. Allen, Harbor. "The Flynn." *American Mercury* 9 (December, 1926):426–33.

A reporter's personal story of how Elizabeth Gurley Flynn made her first speech, and an interview twenty years later.

278. Allinson, Brent Dow. "Leavenworth." *New Republic* 29 (October, 1920):21–23.

A plea for the release of Eugene Debs and the IWW prisoners.

279. ———. "Principles and Prisons." *One Big Union Monthly* 2 (October, 1920):21–23.

The treatment of political prisoners in a "corrupt" prison.

280. Altenbaugh, Richard J., and Rolland G. Paulston. "Work Peoples College: A Finnish Folk High School in the American Labor College Movement." *Paedagogica Historica* 18 (1978):237–56.

281. "American Bolsheviki." *Bellman* 23 (December 8, 1917):623.

Government raids on IWW headquarters.

282. "American Labor and Bolshevism." *Literary Digest* 61 (June 21, 1919):9–11.

283. "The 'American Legion' a Revolutionary Body." *One Big Union Monthly* 1 (December, 1919):9–10.

Claims that the Legion raids violate civil rights.

284. "American Syndicalism." Review of *American Syndicalism: The IWW,* by John G. Brooks. *Outlook* 24 (May, 1913):41–42. See no. 20.

285. "Americanization." *Outlook* 112 (March 1, 1916):482–84.

Events in East Youngstown, Ohio.

286. "America's Cancer Sore—the I.W.W." *Los Angeles Times Magazine Supplement* (December 9, 1917):4, 18.

287. Ameringer, Oscar. "From Boston to Calumet." *Miners Magazine* 15 (March 19, 1914):14.

Conditions in Calumet, Michigan, compared to conditions just before the American Revolution. Perhaps it is time for another rebellion.

288. Ami, Covington. "Another Letter to the Editor." *One Big Union Monthly* 2 (January, 1920):61.

Comments on current events. "Covington Ami" was a pseudonym frequently used by Covington Hall. See nos. 1379–94.

289. ———. "The Damned IWW." *Industrial Pioneer* 2 (March, 1925):28–30.

On the difficulty of organizing workers.

290. ———. "Dawn of the Industrial Age." *One Big Union Monthly* 2 (December, 1920):52.

Ami's belief that the determining factor in social evolution is economic.

291. ———. "The Fundamental Difference." *Industrial Pioneer* 3 (September, 1925):26.

Explores the difference between the IWW and other "isms," then states what the author thinks the IWW believes.

292. ———. "The Ghurkas of Democracy." *One Big Union Monthly* 1 (December, 1919):51.

Says American taxpayers' money is being spent to further conservative views. If there are ghurkas, they are the "ghurkas of Gompersism."

293. ———. "The Industrial Age." *One Big Union Monthly* 1 (September, 1919):32–33.

IWW philosophy.

294. ———. "A Letter to the Editor." *One Big Union Monthly* 1 (November, 1919):49.

The Elaine, Arkansas, "race war."

295. ———. "New Schools for New Workers." *Industrial Pioneer* 3 (July, 1925):29–30.

Work Peoples College in Duluth.

296. ———. "Problems Confronting Labor." *Industrial Pioneer* 3 (July, 1925):35–37.

Craft versus industrial unions.

297. ———. "Southern Conditions." *One Big Union Monthly* 1 (September, 1919):45–46.

298. ———. "The Three Mushyteers." *One Big Union Monthly* 1 (May, 1919):21–22.

Craft and industrial unions and Gompers.

299. ———. "Triumphant Industrial Democracy." *One Big Union Monthly* 1 (March, 1919):20.

Industrial unions will succeed over craft unions.

300. ———. "What Is the Economic Situation?" *Industrial Pioneer* 3 (August, 1925):36–38.

The great mass of workers is not sharing the current prosperity.

301. "Ammon and the Works of Peace." *Catholic Worker* 40 (January, 1974):3.

About Ammon Hennacy, the Catholic anarchist, once an IWW.

302. "Amnesty of Political Prisoners." *Labor Defender* 1 (March 18, 1918):3.

303. "Among the Persons Convicted." *New Republic* 36 (October 17, 1923):190–91.

Sacramento and Wichita prisoners are still in prison, while Coolidge "quibbles."

304. "Analysis of Labor Union Bureaucracy." *One Big Union Advocate* 1 (June, 1939):13–21.

305. "The Anarchist Deportations." *New Republic* 21 (December 24, 1919):96–98.

Due process and freedom of speech are American freedoms not being exercised in the deportation of IWWs and anarchists.

306. "Anarchistic Agitators Denounced." *American Lumberman* 2307 (August 2, 1919):40.

The IWW should be driven out of the country.

307. "Anarchy versus Unionism." *Square Deal* 11 (October, 1911):208–9.

Compares quotations from Jack Whyte, of the IWW, and Samuel Gompers to show their differing philosophies.

308. "Anarchy Run Mad in the Copper District of Michigan." *Miners Magazine* 14 (January 1, 1914):7.

The Michigan copper strike.

309. Anderson, Bryce W. "The Bomb at the Governor's Gate." *American West* 2 (Winter, 1965):12–21.

A popular detailed account of the Steunenberg murder and the first Haywood trial in Idaho.

310. Anderson, C. G. "Will the IWW Work To Fulfill Its Mission?" *One Big Union Monthly* 3 (January, 1921):45–47.

311. Anderson, C. W. "Oil Field Raids." *Defense News Bulletin* 9 (January 12, 1918):1.

U.S. government jails 50 IWW organizers in Kansas and Oklahoma.

312. ———. "Wichita Defendants Go Back to Dungeons." *Rebel Worker* 2 (April 15, 1919):1, 4.

Description of the terrible Sedgewick County jail that houses the IWW prisoners.

313. Anderson, Edward E. "Farm Workers, Organize!" *Industrial Pioneer* 3 (July, 1925):14–16.

314. Anderson, Evert. "Mr. Scissorbill Objects." *One Big Union Monthly* NS 1 (April, 1937):12–14.

The trouble with capitalism is that there is no plan for human welfare. The author gives his thoughts on the economy and the "simpleminded" worker.

315. Anderson, M. J. "The Oil Fields of Wyoming." *Industrial Pioneer* 1 (April, 1924):37.

Urges all oil workers to stay organized and fight Standard Oil.

316. Anderson, Raymond H. "Americans Played Role in Early Economic Development of the Soviet Union." *New York Times* (November 1, 1967):26.

In addition to helping the Soviet Union with the Kuzbas engineering project, Americans helped to launch the Russian auto industry.

317. Anderson, Rondo W. "Joe Hill—the Legend after Fifty Years." *Western Folklore* 25 (April, 1966):129–30.

318. Andrews, Clarence A. "Big Annie and the 1913 Michigan Copper Strike." *Michigan History* 57 (Spring, 1973):53–68.

Annie Clemenc is featured in a story about the strike, with good photos.

319. Andreytchine, George. "One More Renegade." *One Big Union Monthly* 2 (March, 1920):41.

Says Harold Lord Varney has been discovered to be a spy within the IWW. The author believes Varney has been helping the government set up the raids.

320. ———. "Towards an International of Action." *Industrial Pioneer* 1 (February, 1921):30–32.

The IWW must be revolutionary and join the Russians or it will not last much longer.

321. ———. "Where Are We Going?" *One Big Union Monthly* 2 (October, 1920):25–26.

Hope for support of the International and the Communist movement.

322. "Another Game of Swindle." *Miners Magazine* 13 (March 27, 1913):6.

The Denver Free Speech Fight.

323. "Another One Big Union." *Miners Magazine* 1 (July, 1920):1.

After a succession of four unsuccessful industrial unions (The Knights of Labor, the American Railway Union, the Workers Labor Union, and the IWW), an OBU of transportation workers is now proposed. The author says it is not yet time.

324. "Another Shady IWW Deal Uncovered." *Miners Magazine* 14 (June 5, 1913):5.

Discusses possible shortage in IWW strike funds. The author suspects that the IWW juggles all its funds.

325. "Anti-Bolshevik Laws." *Independent* 101 (January 17, 1920):100–101.

Agents-provocateurs in the Department of Justice? The possibility seems remote.

326. "The Anti-Syndicalist Laws." *One Big Union Monthly* 1 (April, 1919):9.

327. "An Appeal for War." *Square Deal* 15 (September, 1914):282–83.

The only war that the IWW will support is the war against capitalism.

328. "Appeal of Judge Hilton Is Denied." *Miners Magazine* 10 (January 21, 1909):5.

The Goldfield convictions were the result of troops sent there, for they started all the trouble.

329. "The Appeal to Murder." *Masses* 4 (March, 1913):5.

Joseph Ettor's words during the Lawrence strike were taken out of context by the U.S. press.

330. "Apples." *Industrial Pioneer* 1 (December, 1923):11.

A promise that next year the IWW will really organize in Washington.

331. Ardzrooni, Leon. "Syndicalism and the War." *The Public* 21 (June 1, 1918):693–96.

332. "Are You Prepared To Manage Industry?" *One Big Union Monthly* 1 (May, 1919):42.

If capitalism collapses the worker must be trained, educated, and ready to take over the textile industry.

333. "Armistice Day Parade." *Nation* 109 (November 29, 1919):673.

The Centralia affair was a godsend to the Republicans.

334. Aronowitz, Stanley. "Which Side Are You On? Trade Unions in America Today." *Liberation* 16 (December, 1971):20–41.
A discussion of modern unionism in the light of history, including the philosophical history of industrial unionism, radicalism, and violence.

335. Ashleigh, Charles. "Defense Fires Opening Guns." *International Socialist Review* 17 (May, 1917):673–74.
Detailed report of the Everett Massacre, the court cases that followed, and the special brutality that appeared in the courtroom.

336. ———. "Everett, November Fifth." *International Socialist Review* 17 (February, 1917):479.
A narrative poem.

337. ———. "Everett's Bloody Sunday." *Masses* 9 (February, 1917):18–19.
The Everett Massacre.

338. ———. "The Floater." *International Socialist Review* 15 (July, 1914):34–38.
About migrant workers.

339. ———. "From an IWW in Jail." *New Republic* 14 (March 23, 1918):234.
Letter about attempts of the Department of Justice to cripple IWW fund-raising efforts.

340. ———. "The Full Story of the Battle at Everett." *Blast* 1 (December 15, 1916):6.
Detailed account of the Everett massacre.

341. ———. "The Job War in Chicago." *International Socialist Review* 15 (November, 1914):262–68.
It is up to the unemployed to better their condition. One way is to follow the IWW program.

342. ———. "Labor in Prison: America, 1917." *International Socialist Review* 18 (February, 1918):397–98.
Descriptive poem.

343. ———. "The Lumber Trust and Its Victims." *International Socialist Review* 17 (March, 1917):536–38.
The lumber bosses are trying to stamp out the IWW.

344. ———. "Night in Prison." *Liberator* 1 (May, 1918):25.
Descriptive poem by an IWW prisoner.

345. ———. "To the Gentlemen of the Press—A Challenge." *Mother Earth* 12 (February, 1917):772–74.

The Everett Massacre was not fairly reported in the public press. The partiality shown is the basis for a drastic condemnation of American institutions.

346. "Automobile Industry." *International Socialist Review* 13 (September, 1912):255–58.

A strike may come in the auto industry because of unrest among workers in Detroit.

347. Avery, Donald H. "British-Born 'Radicals' in North America, 1900–1941: The Case of Sam Scarlett, 1918." *Canadian Ethnic Studies* 10 (2):65–85.

Story of an IWW from Great Britain.

348. "Awaiting Haywood's Answer." *Square Deal* 12 (February, 1913):94–95.

Expecting a witty retort from Haywood to Gompers' latest insult.

349. "The Awakening of the Negro." *One Big Union Monthly* 1 (December, 1919):23–25.

The National Brotherhood of Workers of America.

350. Babson, Roger W. "Sign of the Times." *Masses* 5 (December, 1913):20.

Reprint of Babson's article in the September, 1913, *Babson's Report.* This piece was considered by the IWW one of the few "fair" reports. Babson believed that poor working conditions would help the IWW movement to grow rapidly.

351. ———. "What of the I.W.W.'s?" *Masses* 5 (December, 1913):20.

Further comment on the IWW from Babson.

352. Bacon, Walter. "Slavery in Alaska." *Industrial Pioneer* 3 (January, 1926):12–14, 25.

About Fishermen's Industrial Union #130.

353. Bakeman, Robert A. "The Labor War at Little Falls, N.Y." *Public* 15 (November 29, 1912):1134–35.

The Little Falls strike.

354. ———. "Little Falls: A Capitalist City Stripped of Its Veneer." *New Review* 1 (February 8, 1913):167–74.

The Little Falls strike.

355. Baker, Ray Stannard. "Revolutionary Strike." *American Magazine* 74 (May, 1912):18–30.
Long article on the Lawrence strike, with good photographs.

356. Balch, E. "Songs for Labor." *Survey* 31 (January 3, 1914):408–12, 422–28.
Impressive history of labor songs, including a section on IWW songs.

357. Baldazzi, Giovanni. "Control of Industry." *One Big Union Monthly* 2 (November, 1920):17–20.
On the final aim of the IWW.

358. ———. "Ethics of Revolutionary Syndicalism." *Solidarity* 8 (January 27, 1917):3.

359. ———. "How an Industrial Union Works." *One Big Union Monthly* 2 (February, 1920):53–55.

360. ———. "Syndicalism as the Will to Power." *One Big Union Monthly* 2 (February, 1920):11–12.

361. Baldwin, Roger N. "What the IWW Is Up Against." *Socialist Review* 10 (January, 1921):2–3.
The states are taking up repression where the U.S. Government left off.

362. Ballinger, J. E. "Letters on Calumet-Hecla." *Miners Magazine* 15 (February 19, 1914):12–13; (March 12, 1914):10–12; (March 19, 1914):9–10.
Letters about the congressional committee investigating the Michigan strike.

363. ———. "Christmas Festivities End in Carnage." *Miners Magazine* 14 (January 1, 1914):13–14.
The Calumet-Hecla strike tragedy.

364. "Baltimore Situation." *Garment Worker* 12 (August 8, 1913):4.
The IWW is trying to lure members of the UGA into its union.

365. Bangs, John K. Review of *American Syndicalism: The IWW,* by John G. Brooks (see no. 20). *Literary Digest* 47 (August 2, 1913):179–80.

366. Barajemes. "The Harvest Message." *Industrial Pioneer* 2 (August, 1924):9–10, 23.
Predicts that there will be an oversupply of farmworkers this year.

367. ———. "Three Letters, Full of War." *Industrial Pioneer* 1 (February, 1924):5–6.
Oil companies are gearing up for war again.

368. Baranof, M. "Haywood as a Labor General." *Miners Magazine* 13 (January 16, 1913):5.
Haywood is a poor leader because of his tendency toward violence.

369. "Barbarous Spokane." *Independent* 68 (February 10, 1910):330.
Admits the crimes and cruelties against free speech, but says there was no other choice than to crack down on the radicals.

370. Barker, Tom. "The Future of the Marine Transport Industry." *One Big Union Monthly* 2 (December, 1920):29–30.

371. ———. "One Union for All of Us." *Industrial Pioneer* 1 (July, 1921):17–18.

372. ———. "Red Russia and the IWW." *Industrial Pioneer* 1 (April, 1921):3–5.

373. ———. "Story of the Sea." *One Big Union Monthly* 3 (January, 1921):17–25.
A history of IWW maritime workers, which was continued in *Industrial Pioneer* after the government suppressed *One Big Union Monthly*. See no. 374.

374. ———. "Story of the Sea." *Industrial Pioneer* 1 (February, 1921):52–58; (March, 1921):40–44; (April, 1921):49–52.

375. Barnes, Donald M. "The Everett Massacre: A Turning Point in IWW History." *Organon* 1 (1969):35–42.

376. "Barnett Corrects IWW." *Labor Defender* (September, 1929):184.
Barnett states that the IWW has not told his story quite accurately. He and most of the Centralia prisoners did not repudiate the ILD.

377. Barnett, Eugene. "From a Man in Prison to a Good Christian." *Industrial Pioneer* 2 (October, 1924):7–9.

378. ———. "No. 744 Missing in Action." *Industrial Pioneer* 2 (May, 1924):5–6, 29–32.
A fictional account of a coal miner's real working conditions.

379. ———. "An Open Letter to the President." *One Big Union Monthly* 2 (September, 1920):50.
It is time for amnesty for the prisoners.

380. ———. "A Rebel Worker's Life." *Labor Defender* 2 (January, 1927):12–13; (February, 1927):27–28; (March, 1927):43–44; (April, 1927):59–60; (May, 1927):59–60; (June, 1927):92–93; (July, 1927):109–10; (August, 1927):124–25; (September, 1927):141–42; (November, 1927):172–73; vol. 3 (January, 1928):18.

381. Barnett, George E. "Dominance of the National Union in American Labor Organization." *Quarterly Journal of Economics* 27 (May, 1913):455–81.
Membership in the IWW deemed insignificant.

382. ———. "Growth of Labor Organizations in the US, 1897–1914." *Quarterly Journal of Economics* 30 (August, 1916):780–95.
IWW membership figures in Appendix.

383. Barr, Albert. "Oil and Oil Workers." *Industrial Pioneer* 1 (September, 1921):11–12.

384. "Barren Record of the I.W.W. Movement." *New York Times Annalist* 1 (September 22, 1913):378.
The IWW has not yet proved itself.

385. Bassett, Michael. "The Socialist Party Dilemma, 1912–1914." *Mid-America* 47 (October, 1965):243–57.
The dilemma of conflicting beliefs among the Socialists.

386. "The Battle at Bayonne." *International Socialist Review* 16 (September, 1915):138–41.
The New Jersey oil workers' strike.

387. "Battlefields of Paterson." *Industrial Pioneer* 2 (November, 1924):15.

388. Bauer, Kaspar. "Bauer Replies." *International Socialist Review* 14 (September, 1913):188–89.
The San Diego Free Speech Fight.

389. Baxandall, Rosalyn Fraad. "Elizabeth Gurley Flynn: The Early Years." *Radical America* 8 (January–February, 1975):97–115.

390. Bayard, Charles J. "The 1927–1928 Colorado Coal Strike." *Pacific Historical Review* 32 (August, 1963):235–50.
Historical account of the IWW role in the strike.

391. Bean, Walter. "Ideas of Reform in California." *California Historical Quarterly* 51 (1972):213–26.

More violence was used against the IWW than the IWW itself ever used.

392. Beck, Bill. "Someone Yelled 'Fire' and 72 Died in the Panic." *Detroit Free Press Sunday Magazine* (April 8, 1979):8–12, 14.
The Calumet-Hecla strike.

393. Beck, William. "Law and Order during the 1913 Copper Strike." *Michigan History* 54 (Winter, 1970):257–92.

394. Becker, J. Carlos. "Labor Is Interdependent." *Voice of Labor* 3 (February, 1905):17.
Looking forward to an industrial union.

395. Beetee. "A Radical Is Made." *One Big Union Monthly* NS 2 (February, 1938):10–13.
Story of a young Canadian radical whose wandering work life convinced him that the IWW had the right answer to workers' problems.

396. Beffel, John N. "The Descending Knife." *Liberator* 5 (July, 1922):10.
The Centralia trial.

397. ———. "Fear in the Jury Box." *Liberator* 3 (April, 1920):13.
The Centralia trial.

398. ———. "Four Radicals." *American Mercury* 25 (April, 1932):441–47.
Debs, Haywood, Vanzetti, and Parsons.

399. ———. "Mr. Kyne Joins the Head-Hitters." *Industrial Pioneer* 1 (June, 1923):31.
California's fight against the IWW and other radicals.

400. "Before the Trial, Various Agencies of the Government Illegally Interfered with the Defense." *Messenger* 4 (July, 1922):451–52.
Governmental actions before the Chicago trial.

401. Belknap, Michael R. "The Mechanics of Repression: J. Edgar Hoover, the Bureau of Investigation, and the Radicals, 1912–1925." *Crime and Social Justice* 7 (Spring–Summer, 1978):49–58.

402. Bell, George L. "A California Labor Tragedy." *Literary Digest* 48 (May 23, 1914):1239–40.

403. ———. "Wheatland Hop Fields' Riot." *Outlook* 107 (May 16, 1914):118–23.

404. Bell, Leland. "Radicalism and Race: The IWW and the Black Worker." *Journal of Human Relations* 19 (January, 1971):48–56.

405. Bell, T. H. "An Industrial Unionized Conference." *Freedom* 1 (October, 1933):5–6.
Describes Joseph Ettor and Mortimer Downing and their actions at the conference.

406. "Ben Fletcher, Class, and Political Amnesty." *Messenger* 3 (July, 1921):213.
Describes the black waterfront union leader.

407. Benchley, Robert C. "Making of a Red." *Nation* 108 (March 15, 1919):399–400.
Excellent satire describing an IWW-like character.

408. "Benjamin J. Legere." *Voice of the People* 1 (April 23, 1913):2.
The progress of the Little Falls strike.

409. "Benjamin J. Legere." *New Review* 1 (July, 1913):656–57.
Legere and the Little Falls strike.

410. Bercowich, Henry. "Capitalist Dynamiters." *International Socialist Review* 14 (July, 1913):40.
The Lawrence strike.

411. Bercuson, David J. "Labour Radicalism and the Western Industrial Frontier, 1897–1919." *Canadian Historical Review* 68 (June, 1977):154–75.

412. ———. "The One Big Union in Washington." *Pacific Northwest Quarterly* 69 (July, 1978):127–34.
Compares the OBU and the IWW.

413. Berkman, Alexander. "The IWW Convention." *Mother Earth* 8 (October, 1913):232–34.
The IWW needs a larger vision.

414. ———. "Tannenbaum before Pilate." *Mother Earth* 9 (April, 1914):45–49.
Describes Tannenbaum's trial for his notorious demonstration on behalf of New York's unemployed.

415. Berner, Richard C. Review of *Mill Town,* by Norman H. Clark (see no. 35). *Labor History* 12 (Summer, 1971):461–63.

416. Best, J. M. "City Labor vs. Country Labor." *Industrial Pioneer* 1 (March, 1924):27–28.
The farmers' viewpoint.

417. Bethune, W. T. "The I.W.W.: Its Significance." *The Mediator* 6 (July, 1913):16–20.

418. Betton, Neil. "Riot, Revolution, Repression in the Iron Range Strike of 1916." *Minnesota History* 41 (Summer, 1968):82–94.
Account of the Mesabi strike, with good cartoons and photos.

419. ———. "Strike on the Mesabi—1907." *Minnesota History* 40 (Fall, 1967):340–47.
The WFM strike recounted in detail.

420. Beveridge, Albert J. "The Assault upon American Fundamentals." *Reports of the American Bar Association* 45 (1920):188.

421. Beyer, J. H. "Everett Memorial Address." *Labor Defender* 1 (May 1, 1918):7.

422. ———. "What We Want." *Labor Defender* 1 (April 1, 1918):3.

423. "Big All-Inclusive Labor Trust—the Aim of the I.W.W." *Review of Reviews* 46 (November, 1912):613–15.

424. "Big Annie." *International Socialist Review* 14 (December, 1913):342.
Annie Clemenc's role as morale-booster in the Calumet-Hecla strike.

425. "Big Bill Haywood." *Outlook* 149 (May 30, 1928):171.

426. "Big Copper Barons of Northern Michigan." *Miners Magazine* 15 (April 1, 1915):1.
The Calumet-Hecla strike's aftermath.

427. "Big News." *Masses* 5 (February, 1914):6.
A plea for responding seriously to the workers' demands. It was Henry Ford's plea and was similar to Roger Babson's (see no. 350).

428. "The Big Task before Us." *One Big Union Monthly* 1 (March, 1919):14–15.
Getting ready to take over industry.

429."Big Trial Is On." *Labor Defender* 1 (April 15, 1918):1.
The Chicago trial.

430. "Bills Drafted To Curb the I.W.W." *Survey* 38 (August 25, 1917):457–58.

431. "Billy Sunday and the I.W.W." *Labor Defender* 1 (February 16, 1918):5.
His advice: shoot them all.

432. Bindley, Barbara. "Helen Keller Would Be IWW's Joan of Arc." *New York Tribune* (January 16, 1916, Sec. 5):5.
Sarcastic view of Keller's pro-IWW sentiments.

433. "Birth of a Song Hit." *One Big Union Monthly* NS 2 (March, 1938):28, 31.
The origin of the song "Hallelujah, I'm a Bum."

434. "Bisbee." *Miners Magazine* 19 (August, 1918):6.
The strike at Bisbee and the President's Mediation Commission report.

435. "Bisbee Deportations." *Survey* 38 (July 21, 1917):353.
The deportation of IWW miners and others.

436. "The Bisbee Deportations Illegal." *Survey* 39 (December 8, 1917): 291–92.

437. Biscay, J. S. "The Ipswich Strike." *International Socialist Review* 14 (August, 1913):90–92.

438. ———. "Liberty or the Penitentiary? A Plot To Railroad Innocent Strikers of Little Falls Now on Trial." *International Socialist Review* 13 (April, 1913):750–54.
The trial of the leaders of the Little Falls strike.

439. ———. "Punished for Loyalty to Their Class." *Lumberjack* 1 (June 5, 1913):1.
The convictions of Fillipo Bocchino and Benjamin Legere were based on false evidence in the Little Falls strike cases.

440. ———. "The Timber Wolves." *Voice of the People* 3 (May 1, 1914):2.
A plea to IWW lumberjacks to maintain discipline in their camps and to increase membership and strengthen loyalty.

441. ———. "Two Jurors Disappeared." *International Socialist Review* 13 (May, 1913):822.
The court cases that followed the Little Falls strike.

442. Blaisdell, Lowell L. "Was It Revolution or Filibustering? The Mystery of the Flores Magon Revolt in Baja California." *Pacific Historical Review* 23 (May, 1954):147–64.

443. "Blind Who Will Not See." *Upton Sinclair's* 1 (December, 1918):16.
The persistence of Helen Keller's favorable view of the IWW.

444. "Blood Spilling in Colorado." *Literary Digest* 95 (December 3, 1927): 5–7.
The Colorado coal strike.

445. "Bloodshed at Everett." *Literary Digest* 53 (November 25, 1916): 1395.
Description of the Everett Massacre.

446. "Bloodshed in Labor-Wars." *Literary Digest* 51 (August 7, 1915): 237–38.
Bayonne, New Jersey, labor wars, with photographs.

447. "Bloody Colorado." *Nation* 125 (November 6, 1927):534.
The Colorado coal strike.

448. Bloor, Ella Reeve. "Michigan Strike Letter." *Bridgemen's Magazine* 14 (March, 1914):142.
The Calumet-Hecla strike.

449. ———. "Michigan Strike Letter." *Miners Magazine* 15 (March 5, 1914):10.
One of a series of reports on the Calumet-Hecla strike. See no. 448.

450. Blossom, Frederick A. "Iron Age Ahead." *Labor Defender* 1 (November 15, 1918):4–5.
How can the workingman make progress when so many are trying to check his progress?

451. ———. "IWW Dues." *Survey* 43 (January 17, 1920):440.
Denies that IWW dues were doubled.

452. ———. "Labor's Crucifixion." *New York Call* 10 (August 16, 1917):8.
The lynching of Frank Little in Butte, Montana.

453. ———. "Misconceptions of the I.W.W." *Industrial Worker* 1 (August 9, 1919):2.
Lists the true aims of the IWW, which differ from the misconceptions seen in the public press.

454. ———. "One Enemy—One Union." *One Big Union Monthly* 2 (February, 1920):42–44.

455. ———. "Strike on the Job." *One Big Union Monthly* 2 (August, 1920):46.
Appeals to workers to slow down while working or risk working themselves out of a job.

456. Blythe, Samuel G. "Our Imported Troubles and Troublemakers." *Saturday Evening Post* 190 (May 11, 1918):3–4.
Believes workers who do not appreciate this country are potential Bolsheviks. Bolshevik is a good term for all protesters.

457. "Boasting of their Shameless Vocation." *Miners Magazine* 14 (November 13, 1913):4.
Copper strike looming in Michigan at Calumet-Hecla.

458. Boas, R. P. "The Loyal Legion of Loggers and Lumbermen." *Atlantic Monthly* 127 (February, 1921):221–26.
A union approved by the lumber companies.

459. Bobspa, David. "Justice to the IWW." *New Justice* 1 (June 15, 1919):14–15.
Prosecutions of the IWW are unfair.

460. Bohn, Frank. "The Ballot." *International Socialist Review* 10 (June, 1910):1118–20.
A speculation on the worth of the ballot to labor, with examples of union experience with the ballot box since 1827.

461. ———. "The Bayonne Strike." *Masses* 9 (December, 1916):17.

462. ———. "Butte Number One." *Masses* 5 (August, 1914):9–11.
An account of the battle between the WFM and the IWW to organize Butte miners.

463. ———. "Concerning the Chicago Manifesto." *International Socialist Review* 5 (April, 1905):585–89.
A Socialist's analysis of the IWW manifesto.

464. ———. "Failure To Attain Socialist Unity." *International Socialist Review* 8 (June, 1908):752–55.
Fears the argumentation within the Socialist Party.

465. ———. "Is the IWW to Grow?" *International Socialist Review* 12 (July, 1911):42–44.

466. ———. "Mission and Functions of Industrial Unionism." *Industrial Union Bulletin* 2 (May 2, 1908):1.
Industrial unionism: the "developing form of future government."

467. ———. "The Mission of Industrial Unionism." *Miners Magazine* 6 (April 27, 1905):13.
The IWW is to be the "army" of the working class.

468. ———. "Some Definitions." *International Socialist Review* 12 (May, 1912):747–49.
Discusses the meaning of Socialism, anarchism, political action, direct action, and sabotage.

469. ———. "The Strike of the New York Hotel and Restaurant Workers." *International Socialist Review* 13 (February, 1913):620–21.

470. Bohn, William E. "The Industrial Workers of the World." *Survey* 28 (May 4, 1912):220–25.

The IWW is increasingly "a power in the land."

471. ———. "James Connolly." *International Socialist Review* 17 (July, 1916):41–42.

Recollects the slain Irish revolutionary who was once active in the IWW in America. Quotations from Connolly conclude the obituary.

472. "Bolsheviki Busy at Bogalusa." *American Lumberman* No. 2324 (November 29, 1919):1.

Expresses satisfaction that black and white agitators are being "taken care of."

473. "A Bolsheviki Crew Visits Seattle." *Survey* 39 (January 26, 1918):465.

Report of the Soviet ship *Shilka* arriving in Seattle, amidst rumors that it was carrying money for the IWW. After humorous mix-ups and misunderstandings, the crew (but not the IWW) was wined and dined by the Seattle Chamber of Commerce.

474. "Bolshevism Cowed in Seattle." *Modern City* 4 (February, 1919):25.

475. "Bomb Plots." *One Big Union Monthly* 1 (July, 1919):7.

Believes that the rumors about bomb plots were planted to discredit the IWW.

476. Boose, Arthur. "The Lumber Jack." *International Socialist Review* 16 (January, 1916):414–16.

477. Booth, E. T. "Wild West." *Atlantic Monthly* 126 (December, 1920): 785–88.

Working with men whose only hope is the program of the IWW.

478. "Born on the Waterfront." *One Big Union Advocate* 1 (October, 1939):19–20.

The history of the One Big Union Club.

479. Bossenberger, Florence. "Woman Suffrage." *One Big Union Monthly* 2 (October, 1920):13–14.

480. "Both IWW Groups in Los Angeles Meet." *New Unionist* 2 (February 14, 1931):1.

Centralists and decentralists might get together.

481. Botting, David C., Jr. "Bloody Sunday." *Pacific Northwest Quarterly* 49 (October, 1958):162–72.

Historical account of the Everett Massacre.

482. Bowden, Witt. "Two Alternatives in the Settlement of the Colorado Coal Strike." *Survey* 31 (December 20, 1913):320–22.

483. Bowerman, Fred W. "Is Industry Slowing Down?" *Industrial Pioneer* 2 (June, 1924):11–12.

The problems of metal workers.

484. ———. "Organizing in Steel." *Industrial Pioneer* 1 (October, 1923):15–16.

485. ———. "Steel Workers Awakening." *Industrial Pioneer* 1 (September, 1923):3–4.

486. Boyd, Frederick Sumner. "General Strike in the Silk Industry." In *Pageant of the Paterson Strike* (New York: Success Press, 1913), 3–8.

487. Boyle, James. "Fiendish Aims and Policies of the Industrial Workers of the World." (Canton, Ohio) *Union Reporter* (September, 1913):4.

488. ———. "Syndicalism, the Latest Manifestation of Labor's Unrest." *Forum* 48 (August, 1912):223–33.

Fears that Syndicalism and the IWW will be problems in the future.

489. Brady, Charles S. "A Birds-Eye View of Syndicalism." *Common Cause* 4 (July, 1913):43–46.

490. "Branding the IWW." *Literary Digest* 58 (August 31, 1918):14–16.

491. Brandon, Joseph. "The Organic Structure of Industrial Unionism." *Radical Review* 2 (July, 1918):49–53.

492. "The Brazen Conspiracy." *Miners Magazine* 8 (September 27, 1906):6–7.

The coal companies ordered Vincent St. John's arrest on a trumped-up charge because he was organizing so successfully.

493. Brazier, Richard. "Amazing Deportation Mania." Review of *The Deportations Delirium of Nineteen-Twenty,* by Louis F. Post (see no. 179). *Industrial Pioneer* 1 (February, 1924):43–44.

494. ———. "The Mass I.W.W. Trial of 1918: A Retrospect." *Labor History* 7 (Spring, 1966):178–92.

495. ———. "The Spokane Free Speech Fight, 1909." *Industrial Worker* 64 (December, 1966):6–7; (January, 1967):4–5; (February, 1967):4–5.

496. ———. "The Story of the I.W.W.'s 'Little Red Songbook.'" *Labor History* 9 (Winter, 1968):91–105.

497. ———. "Yakima Citizens 'Receive' IWW." *Solidarity* 7 (October 14, 1916):1, 4.

Police are closing halls and arresting IWWs.

498. Brewer, George D. "Children Murdered." *Worker's Chronicle* 4 (January 2, 1914):1.

A disaster during the Calumet-Hecla strike.

499. Brewster, Edwin T. "Free Speech in Lawrence." *Survey* 27 (March 30, 1912):215–16.

Aspects of the Lawrence strike.

500. "A Brief History of the Harlan Frame-ups." *Workers Defense* 2 (August, 1927):2.

How mine owners bought justice and prosecuted Kentucky strikers.

501. "Brief of Judge O. N. Hilton in the Preston and Smith Cases." *Miners Magazine* 11 (July 13, 1911):5–8.

New witnesses in the Preston and Smith case might sway the Pardon Board.

502. "A Brief Outline of the 1936–7 Maritime Strike." *One Big Union Advocate* 1 (May, 1939):15–18.

503. "Bring Portland Spruce Hearing to End." *American Lumberman* No. 2314 (September 20, 1919):47.

Thinks the hearing was held in part to help quell the IWW.

504. Brinley, John E., Jr. "Radicalism and the Western Federation of Miners." *Intermountain Review* 3 (Spring, 1972):51–58.

505. Brissenden, Paul. "Butte Miners and the Rustling Card." *American Economic Review* 10 (December, 1920):755–75.

The rustling-card system and the union troubles in Butte.

506. ———. "Free the IWW's, Mr. President." *Labor Age* 10 (December, 1921):26–28.

Eloquent plea for amnesty by the economic historian, who states that the trials were not really fair.

507. ———. "The Launching of the Industrial Workers of the World." *University of California Publications in Economics* 4 (November, 1913):1–82.

508. ———. "Lively Corpse." *New Republic* 8 (August 26, 1916):95.
If the IWW is dead, it makes a lively corpse.

509. "Brockton Shoe Workers Revolt." *Industrial Pioneer* 1 (August, 1923):18–19.
How some shoe workers decided to join the IWW.

510. Brook, Michael. Review of *Joe Hill,* by Gibbs Smith. *Minnesota History* 43 (Spring, 1972):36–37.

511. Brooks, John G. "The Challenge of Unemployment." *Independent* 81 (March 15, 1915):385.
Thanks the IWW for stinging us into some recognition of our duty.

512. ———. "The Real Trouble With the Industrial Workers of the World." *Survey* 31 (October 25, 1913):87–88.
Criticizes the IWW's outworn view of industry and politics.

513. ———. "The Shadow of Anarchy: The Industrial Workers of the World." *Survey* 28 (April 6, 1912):80–82.

514. "The Brotherhoods and the Crafts versus RWIU #600." *One Big Union Monthly* 2 (May, 1920):31–35.

515. Browder, E. R. "The IWW and the Communists." *Labor Monthly* 4 (February, 1923):100–104.

516. Brown, Giles T. "The West Coast Phase of the Maritime Strike of 1921." *Pacific Historical Review* 19 (November, 1950):385–96.
Historical account of the strike.

517. Brown, Joseph W. "Use of the Militia in Strikes, Principles on which State Military Establishments are Based; Their Employment in Aid of Police Power." *American Employer* 2 (November, 1913):223–26.

518. Brown, Ray. "High Spots of the Thirteenth IWW Convention." *Industrial Pioneer* 1 (June, 1921):50–56; (July, 1921):38–42.

519. Brown, William Thurston. "A Little Journey to Leavenworth." *One Big Union Monthly* 1 (May, 1919):22–23.
IWW prisoners.

520. ———. "The Tragedy of the Kenilworth Mine." *Solidarity* 2 (March 4, 1911):3; (March 11, 1911):3.
The disaster was not the fault of the Greek miners.

521. Browne, L. A. "Bolshevism in America." *Forum* 59 (June, 1918): 703–17.

Radicals are the excrescence of the political melting pot. American Bolshevism is inherent in most radical groups, especially in the IWW.

522. Broyles, Glen J. "The Spokane Free Speech Fight, 1909–1910: A Study in IWW Tactics." *Labor History* 19 (Spring, 1978):238–52.

523. Bruere, Robert W. "Copper Camp Patriotism." *Nation* 106 (February 21, 1918):202–3.

The Bisbee, Arizona, deportations.

524. ———. "Copper Camp Patriotism: An Interpretation." *Nation* 106 (February 28, 1918):235–36.

The Bisbee deportations and patriotism.

525. ———. "The Industrial Workers of the World, an Interpretation." *Harper's* 137 (July, 1918):250–57.

526. ———. "The I.W.W." *Labor Defender* 1 (July 15, 1918):11–12.

527. ———. "Notes on the IWW in Arizona and the Northwest." *Reconstruction after the War* (Journal of the National Institute of Social Sciences) 4 (April 1, 1918):99–108.

528. "Bruere Tells of IWW in West." *Labor Defender* 1 (February 16, 1918):3.

529. Bruner, Roberta. "The 11th Annual I.W.W. Convention." *One Big Union Monthly* 1 (June, 1919):46–49.

530. ———. "Get More Technical Knowledge." *One Big Union Monthly* 2 (June, 1920):48.

Common labor will not be much in demand in the future. The worker must be trained to perform skilled work and educated to understand who is his enemy.

531. ———. "A 'Gummy Goo' Story." *One Big Union Monthly* 2 (July, 1920):58–59.

Story demonstrating that the need for charity is one of the faults of the capitalist system.

532. ———. "The 11th Annual Convention—Last Seven Days." *One Big Union Monthly* 1 (July, 1919):18–19.

533. ———. "Righteous Harding." *Solidarity* NS 121 (February 26, 1921):1.

Harding's answers to the interviewer's question reveal his true thoughts.

534. ———. "Yesterday, Today, and Tomorrow." *One Big Union Monthly* 1 (May, 1919):33–35; (June, 1919):23–26.
History and future of the IWW.

535. Bubka, Tony. "Time To Organize: The IWW Stickerettes." *American West* 5 (January, 1968):21–22, 25–26.

536. Bucker, A. "The Right To Live." *Industrial Pioneer* 2 (October, 1924):22–23.
The problems of migrant workers.

537. Buhle, Paul. "The Meaning of Debsian Socialism." *Radical America* 2 (January–February, 1968):44–59.

538. "Building the I.W.W." *Industrial Pioneer* 1 (September, 1923):39–41.
Building the organization through more organizing.

539. "The Bummery in Denver." *Miners Magazine* 13 (April 3, 1913):6.
The Denver Free Speech Fight.

540. Buonfino, Giancarlo. "Il Mushio non Cresce sui Sassi Che Rotolano: Grafica e Propaganda IWW" (A rolling stone gathers no moss; IWW propaganda and graphics techniques). *Primo Maggio* 1 (September, 1973):57–88.

541. Burbank, Garin. "Agrarian Radicals and Their Opponents: Political Conflict in Southern Oklahoma 1910–1924." *Journal of American History* 58 (June, 1971):5–23.

542. ———. "Disruption and Decline of the Oklahoma Socialist Party." *Journal of American Studies* 7 (August, 1973):139–41.

543. Burki, Mary Ann Mason. "The California Progressives: Labor's Point of View." *Labor History* 17 (Winter, 1976):24–37.

544. Burnside, R. H. "The History and Aims of the Loyal Legion." *Timberman* (November, 1919):65–66.

545. "Busick Forces Connors' Conviction." *Industrial Worker* 7 (June 13, 1925):1.
How Judge C. O. Busick left the bench and became a volunteer witness for the prosecution during a Syndicalist case over which he was presiding in California. This is one of a number of similar court cases described in IWW papers in 1924 and 1925.

546. "Business Interests behind Deportations." *Rebel Worker* 2 (April 1, 1919):4.

547. “Butte Lynching: Industrial Workers of the World.” *Outlook* 116 (August 15, 1917):572.

548. “Butte Number One.” *Masses* 5 (August, 1914):9–11.
The WFM’s loss of a union and a union hall to the IWW.

549. Byers, J. C., Jr. “Harlan County—Act of God?” *Nation* 134 (June 15, 1932):672–74.
Strike activities in Evarts, Kentucky.

550. Bylin, James. “Union of Yesteryear, the Wobblies Make a Comeback of Sorts.” *Wall Street Journal* 175 (May 20, 1970):1, 31.

551. Byrkit, James. “The Bisbee Deportation.” In James Foster, ed., *American Labor in the Southwest* (Tucson: University of Arizona Press, 1982), 86–102.

552. ———. “The IWW in Wartime Arizona.” *Journal of Arizona History* 18 (Summer, 1977):149–70.
The Bisbee deportation.

553. ———. “Reply to Pamela Mayhall on Bisbee.” *American West* 9 (November, 1972):48. See no. 2073.

554. ———. “Walter Douglas and Labor Struggles in Early 20th Century Arizona.” *Southwest Economy and Society* 1 (Spring, 1976):14–25.
The Bisbee deportation.

555. Caldwell, H. “Evolution of the IWW.” *Miners Magazine* 15 (February 4, 1915):1, 3.

556. “California and Criminal Syndicalism.” *One Big Union Monthly* 2 (April, 1920):15.

557. “California as Seen by a Worker.” *Industrial Pioneer* 2 (January, 1925):35–37.
Westwood, a company-owned town, as an example of peonage in California.

558. “California Crime-Factory.” *Upton Sinclair’s* 1 (April, 1918):7–8.
IWW prisoners in literally lousy quarters: the Los Angeles County jail.

559. “California Holds the Key.” *Industrial Pioneer* 1 (January, 1924):7.
If the workers can stay strong throughout the period of persecution in California, they will gain enough organizational strength to survive.

560. "California Injunction against the IWW Sustained on the Ground That This Organization Is a Public Nuisance." *Law and Labor* 6 (September, 1924):240–43.

561. "California Justice." *Nation* 121 (August 12, 1925):182.
The Syndicalist case of Tom Connors, in which there were extreme judicial irregularities. Judge Busick voluntarily left the bench where he was presiding and took the stand for the prosecution.

562. "California Justice." *New Republic* 36 (September 19, 1923):97–100.
The injustices of the Sacramento Syndicalism trial.

563. "California Labor Tragedy." *Literary Digest* 48 (May 23, 1914): 1239–40.
The Wheatland Hops Riot.

564. "Californians Hit C.S. Law." *Industrial Solidarity* 5 (June 3, 1925):6.
Some Californians do not like the Syndicalist law.

565. "California's Anti-Red Law Upheld." *Literary Digest* 93 (May 28, 1927):9–10.
Discusses the Syndicalism law, which has now been upheld as constitutional.

566. "A Call to All A.F. of L. Union Men." *One Big Union Monthly* 2 (November, 1920):36–37.
AFL men should join the IWW because their own unions are doing nothing for them.

567. "Call to Justice." *Messenger* 4 (June, 1922):432.
Advises union leaders Walter Nef and E. F. Doree not to resist the war and the government.

568. Callahan, L. W. "How Long? Oh God! How Long." *Miners Magazine* 9 (December 5, 1907):7.
Predicts that another industrial union will be formed soon.

569. Callender, Harold. "New Unionism in Seattle." *Forward* 3 (May, 1919):72–75.
The Seattle General Strike.

570. ———. "The Truth about the IWW." *Masses* 10 (November-December, 1917):5–12.
Praises the IWW's motives and recounts the union's actions in Butte and Bisbee.

571. ———. "The Truth about the IWW." *International Socialist Review* 17 (January, 1918):332–42.
A reprint of no. 570.

572. ———. "War and the IWW." *National Conference of Social Work Proceedings* 1918 (1919):420–25.

573. Calmer, Alan. "The Wobbly in American Literature." *New Masses* 12 (September 18, 1934):21–22.
The IWW has appeared in poetry and fiction, but usually in a minor role.

574. "Calumet and Hecla." *Miners Magazine* 14 (November 6, 1913):4.
Attempts at strike-breaking at the Calumet-Hecla strike.

575. "Calumet Horrors and What Followed and the Calumet Disaster." *Miners Magazine* 14 (January 15, 1913):6–8.
The Calumet-Hecla strike and the disastrous fire that occurred.

576. "Calumet Investigation." *Life & Labor* 4 (March, 1914):74–77.
The Calumet-Hecla strike.

577. "Calumet Sacrifice and Story of the Outrage." *Miners Magazine* 14 (January 8, 1913):5–10.
The Calumet-Hecla strike and the mysterious fire.

578. "Calumet Strike." *Bridgemen's Magazine* 13 (November, 1913):825.
The Calumet-Hecla strike.

579. "Can Women Stop War?" *One Big Union Monthly* 2 (July, 1920):54–55.
The similarities between the WILPF and the IWW views of war.

580. "Canada's Labor War." *Literary Digest* 61 (June 14, 1919):18–19.
Labor rebellions in Canada will spread to the Pacific Northwest.

581. Candeloro, Dominic. "Louis F. Post and the Red Scare of 1920." *Prologue* 11 (Spring, 1979):40–55.
Historical account of Post and the reactions to his stand for civil liberty.

582. ———. "The *Public* of Louis F. Post and Progressivism." *Mid-America* 52 (April, 1974):109–23.

583. Cannata, G. "Technique and Revolution." *Industrial Pioneer* 1 (February, 1921):49–51; (March, 1921):27–30.
Workers should receive technical education.

584. Cannon, James P. "Frank Little, the Rebel, on the Ninth Anniversary of His Death." *Labor Defender* 1 (August, 1926):132–33.

585. ———. "The IWW." *Fourth International* 16 (Summer, 1955):75–86.
The "bold design" of the IWW and how it was carried out. The article was in honor of the IWW's fiftieth anniversary.

586. ———. "The Seventh IWW Convention." *International Socialist Review* 13 (November, 1912):424.

587. Cannon, Joseph D. "Eloquent Funeral Address." *Miners Magazine* 14 (September 11, 1913):5.
Calumet, Michigan, miners' funeral.

588. ———. "Familiar Though Insidious Game." *Miners Magazine* 17 (April 6, 1916):1.
Garment workers in New York affected by IWW.

589. Cannon, Laura G. "Notes from the Strike Zone." *Miners Magazine* 14 (August 28, 1913):5–6.
The cold-blooded murder of two strikers by hired thugs has horrified the Michigan copper strike area.

590. ———. "State Militia—Strike Breakers." *Miners Magazine* 14 (September 11, 1913):8–9.
The harsh use of the militia in the Calumet-Hecla strike.

591. "Capitalism Run Mad." *One Big Union Monthly* 1 (December, 1919):8–9.
The Centralia Massacre.

592. Carleton, Frank T. "Pedagogy and Syndicalism." *Public* 22 (February 8, 1919):133–34.

593. Carlysh, Jennie. "The Camouflage That Failed." *Labor Defender* 1 (March 5, 1918):3.
The raids and persecution of the IWW are instigated by big industry.

594. "Carolyn Lowe Leads Free Speech Fight." *Workers Chronicle* 4 (January 23, 1914):5.
Speakers at the Kansas City Free Speech Fight included the popular IWW lawyer Carolyn Lowe.

595. Carstens, C. C. "The Children's Exodus from Lawrence." *Survey* 28 (April 6, 1912):70–71.
The involvement of children in the Lawrence strike.

596. Carter, C. F. "West Virginia Coal Insurrection." *North American Review* 198 (October, 1913):457.

The general public cannot be expected to understand the difficulties that the authorities have encountered because of armed opposition to the right of an employer to select his employees.

597. Carter, David A. "The Industrial Workers of the World and the Rhetoric of Song." *Quarterly Journal of Speech* 66 (No. 4, 1980):365–74.

Singing was important to the IWW. The author shows that the lyrics characterized the IWW in a pleasant way, which made the union more acceptable to the public.

598. Carter, Paul J., Jr. "Mark Twain and the American Labor Movement." *New England Quarterly* 30 (September, 1957):382–88.

Analyzes Mark Twain's statement that workers' manifestos are as old as human despair.

599. Cartosio, Bruno. "L'IWW nel Sindicalismo Rivoluzionario Internazionale, 1904–1914" (The IWW as international revolutionary Syndicalism). *Ricerche Storiche* 11 (January–April, 1981): 167–240.

600. ———. "Mosca 1921: Una Intervista a "Big Bill" Haywood" (Moscow 1921: An interview with "Big Bill" Haywood). *Primo Maggio* 16 (Autumn–Winter, 1981–1982):11–20.

601. ———. "Note e Documenti sugli Industrial Workers of the World" (Comments and documents on the IWW). *Primo Maggio* 1 (September, 1973):43–56.

602. Cary, Lorin. "The Bureau of Investigation and Radicalism in Toledo, Ohio:1918–1920." *Labor History* 21 (Summer, 1980):430–40.

603. Cascaden, Gordon. "The 12th Annual Convention of the IWW." *One Big Union Monthly* 2 (June, 1920):5, 49–55.

604. "'Case against the Reds' Palmer." *Forum* 63 (February, 1920):173–85.

The Palmer Raids and Palmer's personal involvement.

605. "Case for Amnesty." *New Republic* 27 (July 20, 1921):203–5.

606. "The Case of Jim Larkin." *One Big Union Monthly* 2 (October, 1920):58.

Asks contributions for the defense of Larkin, who was prosecuted in New York for criminal anarchy.

607. "The Case of Joe Hill—Joe Hill: IWW Martyr." *New Republic* 119 (November 15, 1948):18–20.
"No unbiased person can read the record and not see travesty."

608. "Case of the Hop Pickers." *International Socialist Review* 14 (April, 1914):620–21.
The Wheatland Hops Riot.

609. Casillas, Mike, and Jennifer Pruett, eds. "Strike for Liberty! Songs, Poetry and Comments by the Workers of the Western Federation of Miners:1900–1907." *Southwest Economy and Society* 5 (Fall, 1979, and Winter, 1979–1980):3–136.

610. Castle, Victor. "Well, I Quit My Job at the Dam." *Nation* 133 (August 26, 1931):207–8.
Conditions and wages at the Boulder Dam construction project, as described by an IWW worker.

611. "Catholic View of the Copper Miners' Strike in Upper Michigan." *Survey* 31 (January 31, 1914):521–22.

612. Cedervall, Tor. "Has a Substitute for the I.W.W. Been Found?" *One Big Union Monthly* NS 1 (March, 1937):32–34.
Can the CIO take the place of the IWW?

613. "Centralia." *New Republic* 22 (April 14, 1920):217–20.
The various points of contention at the Centralia trial.

614. "Centralia before the Court." *Survey* 44 (April 3, 1920):13–15.
The Centralia trial.

615. "Centralia Case Again." *New Republic* 62 (May 14, 1930):340–41.
The Centralia prisoners.

616. "Centralia Murder Trial." *Review* 2 (April 3, 1920):321–22.
The Centralia trial.

617. "Centralia Prisoners." *New Republic* 61 (January 15, 1930):226.
The Centralia prisoners.

618. "Centralia Tragedy." *Outlook* 156 (October 22, 1930):287.
The Centralia prisoners.

619. "The Centralia Verdict." *One Big Union Monthly* 2 (April, 1920):10–11.

620. Chafee, Zechariah, Jr. "California Justice." *New Republic* 36 (September 19, 1923):97–100.

In California a person can be punished merely for saying something that someone might judge to be radical.

621. Chak, Hon Kee. "There Is No Reason or Justice." *Nation* 118 (January 23, 1924):90.

Protest from the Chinese Seamen's Union about the random imprisonment of members of the IWW.

622. "A Challenge—Joe Hill." *International Socialist Review* 16 (December, 1915):329–30.

623. "A Change in Looms." *Square Deal* 12 (March, 1913):190.

The causes and the beginning of the Paterson strike.

624. "Changes in the Industrial Relations Commission." *Survey* 33 (March 27, 1915):686.

625. Chaplin, Ralph. "The Background of Centralia." *One Big Union Monthly* 2 (May, 1920):17–19.

Contemporary article about Centralia.

626. ———. "The Bureau of Research and Its Work." *One Big Union Monthly* 2 (July, 1920):56–57.

The IWW's new bureau.

627. ———. "Casey Jones." *New Masses* (January, 1929):14.

628. ———. "The Centralia Conspiracy." *Industrial Pioneer* 1 (December, 1923):9–10, 60–62.

Contemporary analysis of the Centralia affair.

629. ———. "Centralia—1931." *Workers Defense* 1 (November, 1931):3.

Centralia and the lynching of Wesley Everest.

630. ———. "Frank Little and the War." *Workers Defense* 1 (August, 1926):135–36.

Little's opposition to the war led to his lynching.

631. ———. "A Hunger 'Riot' in Chicago." *International Socialist Review* 15 (March, 1915):518.

632. ———. "Joe Hill." *Industrial Pioneer* 2 (November, 1924):31.

A poem, with a drawing of the execution.

633. ———. "Joe Hill." *International Socialist Review* (December, 1915):325.

A poem and a cartoon about Joe Hill's arrest.

634. ———. "Joe Hill, a Biography." *Industrial Pioneer* 1 (November, 1923):23–25.

635. ———. "Joe Hill's Funeral." *International Socialist Review* 16 (January, 1916):400–405.

636. ———. "The Negro in the Sacramento Woodpile." *Industrial Pioneer* 1 (September, 1923):35–36.
Discussion of the Sacramento trial.

637. ———. "Notorious Centralia." *Workers Defense* 2 (November, 1932):2.

638. ———. "The Picket Line of Blood—Another Red Chapter of Labor History from Butte, Mont." *One Big Union Monthly* 2 (June, 1920):9–13.
A sheriff's testimony of how gunmen hired by the mill owners shot fifteen men who were peacefully picketing in Butte.

639. ———. "Violence in West Virginia." *International Socialist Review* 13 (April, 1913):729–36.
Description of Chaplin's days in the violent Kanawha strike region.

640. ———. "What the Movie Photographed." *Industrial Pioneer* 1 (March, 1924):33–35.
A newsreel made at Centralia was suppressed because it showed that the American Legion provoked the fighting.

641. ———. "Why I Wrote 'Solidarity Forever.'" *American West* 5 (January, 1968):18–27.
Chaplin's own story as quoted by Bruce Le Roy.

642. ———. "A Yellow Epidemic." *Socialist and Labor Star* (March 14, 1913):1.
The ouster of Haywood from the Socialist Party.

643. "Charge Misuse of Lawrence Strike Fund." *Garment Worker* 12 (July 25, 1913):5.
Describes the charge by William E. Trautmann that the Lawrence strike funds were mishandled.

644. "Chart of Industrial Communism." *One Big Union Monthly* 2 (October, 1920):32–33.

645. Charters, A. W. "Industrial Unionism." *Miners Magazine* 6 (April 13, 1905):11.
June 27, 1905, the date the IWW was founded, will mark "an

epoch in the history of America by the side of which the emancipation of chattel slaves will pale into insignificance."

646. Cheney, Charles B. "Labor Crisis and a Governor: An Averted Strike on the Mesaba Range." *Outlook* 89 (May 2, 1908):24–30.

647. Cheyney, E. Ralph. "The IWW." *Survey* 39 (November 10, 1917):150–51.
The arrests of Flynn, Tresca, Giovannitti, and Baldazzi are outrageous and the accusations are lies.

648. "Chicago Conference for Industrial Unionism." *International Socialist Review* 5 (February, 1905):496–99.
Describes the early conference of industrial unionists.

649. "The Chicago Conference for Industrial Unions." *Miners Magazine* 6 (March 2, 1905):8.
The AFL is only a clique of labor politicians. A real union is needed to improve the lives of workers.

650. "Chicago Convention." *Miners Magazine* 6 (June 15, 1905):8.
Editorial comments on the WFM joining the Socialists.

651. "Chicago: Hobo Capital of America." *Survey* 50 (June 1, 1923): 287–90, 303–5.

652. "Chicago Industrial Union Convention." *Miners Magazine* 6 (July 6, 1905):3–5; (July 13, 1905):3–5.
Detailed account of the convention.

653. Child, R. W. "Industrial Revolt at Lawrence." *Collier's* 48 (March 9, 1912):13–15.
An account of the Lawrence strike, with good cartoons.

654. ———. "Who's Violent?" *Collier's* 49 (June 29, 1912):12–13, 22.
An account of the Lawrence strike, with photographs showing the sources of violence.

655. "Children as Exhibits." *Independent* 72 (February 22, 1912):427.
Criticizes the using of children in strikes, as happened during the Lawrence strike.

656. "Children of a Strike." *Survey* 27 (February 24, 1912):1791.
An account of the Lawrence strike and the part played in it by children.

657. "The Chinese and the I.W.W." *One Big Union Monthly* 1 (March, 1919):6.
Meetings of Chinese IWWs have been made particular tar-

gets of government raids because of racist feelings. Chinese people are, unfortunately, more vulnerable because of the chance of deportation.

658. Christenson, Otto. "Invading Miners' Homes." *International Socialist Review* 17 (September, 1916):161–62.
The Mesabi strike and invasions of the strikers' homes.

659. "Christmas Conditions in Cleveland." *Industrial Pioneer* 1 (December, 1923):63–64.
Unemployment is affecting Ohio steelworkers. Only a good union can help them.

660. "The Church and the Unemployed." *Masses* 5 (April, 1914):10–11.
Explores the ethical questions raised by Frank Tannenbaum when he sheltered New York unemployed in a church and was arrested along with the whole group. A John Sloan drawing, "Calling the Xn Bluff," is featured.

661. "Churches' Plea Wins Parole." *Christian Century* 48 (July 29, 1931):980.
Some Centralia prisoners were freed because of the churches' plea.

662. "Churches Raided by the Jobless." *Literary Digest* 48 (March 14, 1914):556–57.
The Frank Tannenbaum incident.

663. "The Churches, the City, and the 'Army of the Unemployed' in New York." *Survey* 31 (March 28, 1914):792–95.
Frank Tannenbaum's effort to make the churches responsible for the homeless unemployed.

664. "The CIO in Lawrence." *One Big Union Monthly* NS 1 (December, 1937):25–26.
Reports that in September, 1937, the CIO was able to organize all the workers overnight by promising no spontaneous strikes and no dues until benefits were available. The article recalls an earlier Lawrence strike.

665. Claghorn, Kate H. "Alien and Sedition in the New Year." *Survey* 43 (January 17, 1920):422–23.
The raids, arrests, and deportations.

666. ———. "More about the Deportations." *Survey* 42 (May 3, 1919):196–98.

667. "Clarence Darrow and Conspiracy Trials." *Workers Defense* 2 (March, 1932):3.
Trials involving the Harlan miners.

668. Clark, Earl. "Wages in Cotton Mills at Home and Abroad." *Survey* 27 (March 23, 1912):1957–58.
The Lawrence strike was not political in nature and there is no evidence that the violence was caused by union rivalry.

669. Clark, H. F. "What I Learned from a Strike." *Survey* 31 (November 22, 1913):207.
The Lawrence strike.

670. Clark, J. "The Politics of Liberation: From Class to Culture." *Black Rose* 7 (December 4, 1981):4.
Traces modern libertarian ideas to IWW ideas, among others.

671. Clark, Norman. "Everett, 1916 and After." *Pacific Northwest Quarterly* 57 (April, 1966):57–64.
The Everett Massacre.

672. ———. Review of *Rebels of the Woods,* by Robert Tyler (see no. 221). *Labor History* 10 (Winter, 1969):136–39.

673. Clark, William. "Courts and Direct Action." *One Big Union Monthly* 1 (September, 1919):12–13.
Disagrees with W. I. Fisher (see no. 1128) and says that money should be spent for the prisoners' defense or they may rot forever in prison.

674. "The Clashing Branches of the IWW." *Survey* 39 (November 10, 1917):146.

675. "Class Murder in America." Review of *Centralia Conspiracy,* by Ralph Chaplin (see no. 33). *Liberator* 3 (August, 1920):30–31.

676. "Class War at San Diego." *Public* 15 (June 7, 1912):529–31.
The San Diego Free Speech Fight.

677. Clay, Samuel H. "The Man Who Heads the Spruce Drive." *Review of Reviews* 57 (June, 1918):633–35.
Colonel Disque and the Loyal Legion of Loggers and Lumbermen and Disque's way of modifying the effect of the IWW.

678. Clayton, Harry. "The IWW on a Full-Rigged Ship." *Industrial Pioneer* 4 (September, 1926):19–21.
An IWW's account of working conditions on one of the last sailing vessels.

679. "Clean Them Up Quickly." *Bellman* 23 (August 18, 1917):173–74.
Membership in the IWW is a kind of incipient treason.

680. Cleland, Hugh G. "The Effects of Radical Groups on the Labor Movement." *Pennsylvania History* 26 (April, 1959):119–32.
The Pressed Steel Car strike, 1909. "There were more IWW Locals in Pennsylvania than in any other state," the author says, and he adds that they were the forerunners of the CIO.

681. "The Close of the Industrial Convention." *Miners Magazine* 6 (July 20, 1905):6.
A description of the first IWW convention.

682. "Closed Mind of Mr. Bowers." *New Republic* 2 (May 1, 1915):316–18.
A criticism of how the Colorado coal strike was handled.

683. Cobb, Frank. "The Press and Public Opinion." *New Republic* 21 (December 31, 1919):144–47.
The public was either uninformed about the nature of the government raids or unable to express itself freely. Indirectly concerns the IWW.

684. Coben, Stanley. "A Study in Nativism: The American Red Scare of 1919–1920." *Political Science Quarterly* 79 (March, 1964):52–75.

685. Cochran, R. A. "Hogging the Propaganda." *One Big Union Monthly* 1 (June, 1919):26–27.
The IWW's use of the Russian Revolution for propaganda. The Red Scare persecutions will strengthen the organization in the long run.

686. Colbron, Grace I. "Bad Health and Big Business." *Public* 16 (January 3, 1913):6–7.
The Little Falls strike and Helen Schloss, a strike leader.

687. Colby, Elbridge. "The Industrial Workers of the World." *Bellman* 22 (March 3, 1917):233–35.

688. ———. "Syndicalism in the Light of History." *Sewanee Review* 22 (October, 1914):405–19.
The IWW is the latest and sanest of modern labor movements.

689. Cole, Donald B. "Lawrence, Massachusetts: Model Town to Immigrant City, 1845–1912." *Historical Collections of the Essex Institute* 92 (October, 1956):349–75.

690. Cole, John N. "The Issue at Lawrence." *Outlook* 100 (February 24, 1912):405–6.

691. Coleman, B. S. "IWW and the Law—the Result of Everett's Bloody Sunday." *Sunset* 39 (July, 1917):35, 68–70.
The trial after the Everett Massacre.

692. "Collective Bargaining and Colorado: Letters Exchanged by J. D. Rockefeller, Jr., W. L. M. King, and J. F. Welborn." *Survey* 33 (January 16, 1915):426–30.
The Colorado coal strike.

693. Collins, Peter W. "'The Disruptors' and 'Syndicalism.'" *Common Cause* 3 (March, 1913):287.
Explains Syndicalism and reflects on the new IWW.

694. "Colonel Disque and the IWW." *New Republic* 14 (April 6, 1918):284–85.
Northwest lumber problems as solved by the U.S. Army. What are Disque's reasons for seeking to commandeer property?

695. "Colorado a Year after the Coal Strike." *Survey* 36 (May 13, 1916):190.
The Colorado coal strike. See also nos. 696 and 698–703.

696. "Colorado and the Nation." *New Republic* 1 (January 9, 1915): 6–7.

697. "Colorado Coal Battle." *Outlook* 147 (December 7, 1927):422.
The series of coal strikes in Colorado in 1927.

698. "Colorado Coal Strike Report." *Journal of Political Economy* 23 (April, 1915):394–96.

699. "Colorado Invaded." *Miners Magazine* 13 (May 1, 1913):5.
Reports that the "Workless Willies" have moved into Denver.

700. "Colorado Situation." *Survey* 33 (December 5, 1914):261–62.

701. "Colorado Strike Commission." *Outlook* 108 (December 9, 1914):800–801.

702. "The Colorado War and Compulsory Arbitration." *New Review* 2 (June, 1914):357–61.

703. "Colorado's Labor War." *Independent* 80 (December 7, 1914):358–59.

704. "Colored and White Workers Solving the Race Problem for Philadelphia." *Messenger* 3 (July, 1921):214–15.

The Marine Transport Workers Union, which is and has been fully integrated.

705. "Coming into One Big Union." *Miners Magazine* 17 (April 6, 1916):3.
The AFL may eventually become an industrial union. While the IWW talks about one big union, it is the AFL that keeps growing.

706. "Comments on the Manifesto." *Miners Magazine* 6 (February 9, 1905):6–7.
The IWW manifesto.

707. "Common Sense and the I.W.W.: Programme for the Social and Economic Rehabilitation of Our National and Agricultural Lands." *New Republic* 14 (April 27, 1918):375–76.
Agricultural rehabilitation and better planning might improve the working conditions that have created the rebellion of the IWW.

708. "Commission on Industrial Relations." *Public* 17 (September 11, 1914):878–79.
Investigation of the Wheatland episode.

709. "Communication from Porcupine Miners." *Miners Magazine* 12 (April 11, 1912):7–9.
Miners are questioning the stories against the IWW and are asking for proof of wrongdoing.

710. "Communist International to the I.W.W." *One Big Union Monthly* 2 (September, 1920):26–30.
Zinoviev's letter to the IWW from the Red Trade Union International.

711. "Comparison of Recent Strikes Made by the Civic Federation." *Square Deal* 12 (February, 1913):57–61.
Deals in part with the IWW's New York hotel waiters' strike.

712. "A Comparison of the Two Big Unions." *Miners Magazine* 21 (April, 1920):4.
Compares the IWW with the Canadian One Big Union.

713. "Conciliation versus Strikes." *Outlook* 88 (January 4, 1908):8–9.
The Goldfield strike.

714. "Conditions at Lawrence." *Outlook* 100 (March 16, 1912):566.

715. "Conditions on the Pacific Coast, by a Wandering Wobbly." *One Big Union Monthly* 2 (August, 1920):42–43.

716. "Conferring the Double Cross on Rail Engineers and Firemen." *International Socialist Review* 16 (July, 1915):15–17.
Problems caused by craft unions. Perhaps now that the Arbitration Board has disappointed the railroad workers, they will join the one big union.

717. "Congress Asked To Look Into 'Bloody Sunday.'" *Survey* 37 (February 10, 1917):553.
A possible investigation of the Everett Massacre.

718. "Congress Grapples with the Question of Bolshevism and Anarchism." *Current Opinion* 68 (January, 1920):9–13.
Problems of definition of radicals in Congress.

719. "Congressional Report on Colorado." *Survey* 33 (March 20, 1915):664.
The Colorado coal strike.

720. Conlin, Joseph R. Review of *Bisbee '17: A Novel,* by Robert Houston (see no. 5001). *Labor History* 23 (Winter, 1982):105–9.

721. ———. "The Case of the Very American Militants: Notes on the IWW as a Product and a Reflection of Mainstream America." *American West* 7 (March, 1970):4–10.

722. ———. "The Haywood Case: An Enduring Riddle." *Pacific Northwest Quarterly* 59 (January, 1968):23–32.

723. ———. "The IWW and the Question of Violence." *Wisconsin Magazine of History* 51 (Summer, 1968):316–18.

724. ———. "The IWW and the Socialist Party." *Science and Society* 31 (Winter, 1967):22–36.

725. ———. "Old Boy, Did You Get Enough Pie?" *Journal of Forest History* 23 (October, 1979):165–85.
Life of the lumberjacks as sometimes pleasant and jolly.

726. ———. Review of *Colorado's War on Militant Unionism,* by George G. Suggs (see no. 209). *Labor History* 14 (Summer, 1973):448–51.

727. ———. Review of *Gli IWW e il Movimento Operaio Americano* (The IWW and the American labor movement), by Renato Musto (see no. 165). *Labor History* 20 (Winter, 1979):147–48.

728. ———. Review of *History of the Labor Movement, Volume IV, the Industrial Workers of the World, 1905–1917,* by Philip Foner (see no. 68). *Studies on the Left* 6 (March–April, 1966):81–91.

729. Conlon, P. J. "Went Up Like a Rocket; Came Down Like a Stick." *Machinists Monthly Journal* 18 (December, 1906):1108–11.
The new IWW will never survive. Its purpose is only to seize the Socialist Party.

730. Connell, Jim. "How I Wrote 'The Red Flag.'" *Sing* 2 (April, 1955):8.

731. Connolly, James. "Industrialism and the Trades Unions." *International Socialist Review* 10 (February, 1910):714–22.
Trade unionism is the most dispersive force and industrial unionism the most unifying. When poltical action is necessary, the worker will use it, whether or not he is in the IWW.

732. Connolly, Thomas G. "Courts and Labor Unions." *Twentieth Century* 5 (April, 1912):525–31; 6 (May, 1912):70–77.
Labor's greatest problem is that most judges are conservative and antiunion. Their discrimination is apparent everywhere.

733. Conolly, C. P. "The Fight of the Copper Kings." *McClure's* 29 (May–June, 1907):1–16.

734. ———. "Labor Fuss in Butte." *Everybody's Magazine* 31 (August, 1914):205–8.
The struggle between the IWW and the WFM.

735. ———. "Protest by Dynamite; Similarities and Contrasts between the McNamara Affair and the Moyer-Haywood-Pettibone Trial." *Collier's* 48 (January 13, 1912):9–10.

736. "Conspiracy & Street Speaking." *International Socialist Review* 14 (July, 1913):42.
The San Diego Free Speech Fight.

737. "Conspiracy to Murder." *International Socialist Review* 6 (March, 1906):558–61.
The first Haywood trial.

738. "Conspirators at Work in Goldfield, Nevada." *Miners Magazine* 8 (June 6, 1908):14.
The Vincent St. John trial.

739. "Constitution and the Police." *Survey* 29 (October 26, 1912):93–94.
The Little Falls strike and police violations of civil rights.

740. "Construction of the World on the Basis of Industrial Democracy." *One Big Union Monthly* 1 (September, 1919):27–31.

741. "Constructive Work before the Industrial Relations Commission: Symposium." *Survey* 30 (August 2, 1913):571–88.

742. "Contempt of Court." *Rebel Worker* 2 (February 1, 1919):4.
The "silent defense" at the Sacramento trial.

743. "Contempt of Government." *Square Deal* 13 (September, 1913): 191.
The Socialist Tom Mann and the IWW.

744. "The Convention of the Industrial Workers in Chicago." *Miners Magazine* 8 (October 4, 1906):6.
WFM troubled by reports from the IWW convention.

745. "Conversion of the Soap Box." *Outlook* 119 (August 14, 1918): 581–82.
Describes how a "flying squadron" of the National Security League is being trained to preach American patriotism from soapboxes on street corners, in the same way that the "Bolsheviks" try to teach peace and justice to the poor man.

746. "The Conviction of Alexander Scott." *International Socialist Review* 14 (July, 1913):10–11.
How Scott was convicted for printing stories about the Paterson strike that were sympathetic to the strikers.

747. "Conviction of John R. Lawson." *Survey* 34 (May 22, 1915):181.
Lawson's conviction for the murder of John Nimmo during the Colorado coal strike may help send other strike leaders to prison.

748. "Conviction of '28' Affirmed." *Industrial Solidarity* 5 (March 4, 1925):1.
The Criminal Syndicalism convictions in California.

749. "Conviction of 27 Starts General Strike in San Pedro." *Industrial Pioneer* 1 (August, 1923):3–4.
The attempted general strike in San Pedro.

750. Cook, Bernard A. "Covington Hall and Radical Rural Unionization in Louisiana." *Louisiana History* 18 (Spring, 1977):227–38.

751. Cook, Bernard A., and James A. Watson. "The Sailors and Marine Transport Workers' 1913 Strike in New Orleans: The AFL and the IWW." *Southern Studies* 18 (1979):111–22.
Historical account of the maritime strike.

752. Cook, Philip. "Red Scare in Denver." *Colorado Magazine* 43 (Fall, 1966):309–26.
Contains excellent contemporary cartoons.

753. Cooper, Charles. "Stogy Makers and the I.W.W. in Pittsburgh." *Survey* 31 (November 28, 1913):214.

754. Copeland, Tom. "Elmer Smith—Lumberjacks' Lawyer." *William Mitchell's Opinion* (November, 1976):9–10.
The lawyer for the IWW defendants at Centralia.

755. "The Copper Country Indictments." *Square Deal* 14 (February, 1914):88–89.
The Calumet-Hecla strike from the management viewpoint.

756. "The Copper Country Investigation." *Square Deal* 14 (March, 1914):185–86.
The Calumet-Hecla strike from the management viewpoint.

757. "Copper-Mine Owners' Side." *Outlook* 106 (February 21, 1914): 397–400.
The Calumet-Hecla strike. See also nos. 758–59, 761–65.

758. "Copper Mine Strike." *American Industries* 14 (November, 1913): 7–8.

759. "Copper-Miners' Strike." *Outlook* 106 (February 7, 1914):294–95.

760. "The Copper Settlement in Arizona." *Survey* 39 (November 3, 1917):128, 130.

761. "Copper Strike." *International Socialist Review* 14 (November, 1913):269–71.

762. "The Copper Strike." *Square Deal* 13 (November, 1913):377–78.

763. "The Copper Strike: A Socialist Battle." *Square Deal* 14 (February, 1914):86–87.

764. "Copper Strike Investigation." *American Industries* 14 (March, 1914):9–10.
The Calumet-Hecla strike from the management viewpoint.

765. "The Copper Strike Investigation." *Square Deal* 14 (June, 1914): 408–13.
The Calumet-Hecla strike from the management viewpoint.

766. Corbin, David A. "Betrayal in West Virginia Coal Fields: Eugene V. Debs and the Socialist Party of America, 1912–1914." *Journal*

of American History 64 (March, 1978):987–1009.
The West Virginia Socialists might really have been Wobblies.

767. ———. "*The Socialist and Labor Star;* Strike and Suppression in West Virginia 1912–1913." *West Virginia History* 34 (January, 1973):168–86.
Ralph Chaplin's role in the West Virginia miners' strike.

768. Corcoran, Sister Theresa. "Vida Scudder and the Lawrence Textile Strike." *Historical Collections of the Essex Institute* 115 (July, 1979):183–95.
The effect of Professor Scudder's Lawrence speech.

769. Corder, Raymond. "Angry Waters." *One Big Union Monthly* NS 1 (March, 1937):3–10.
Flood problems demonstrate that poor people are the prey of a predatory system.

770. ———. "Industrial Unionism in the IWW Job Branch." *One Big Union Monthly* NS 1 (July, 1937):9–11.
An explanation for new members of how the IWW operates as a union.

771. ———. "John Farmer All Washed Up." *One Big Union Monthly* NS 1 (April, 1937):15–18.

772. Cortner, Richard. "The Wobblies and *Fiske v. Kansas:* Victory amid Disintegration." *Kansas History* 4 (Spring, 1981):30–38.

773. "Cossack Regime." *The Blast* 1 (July 15, 1916):6–7.
The violence in the Mesabi strike in Minnesota.

774. "Cossack Regime in San Diego." *Mother Earth* 7 (June, 1912): 97–107.
The terrible experiences of Emma Goldman and Ben Reitman, as well as many IWWs, at the San Diego Free Speech Fight.

775. Cothren, Marion B. "When Strike-Breakers Strike." *Survey* 36 (August 26, 1916):535–36.
The Mesabi strike in Minnesota.

776. "Counting the Copper Strike's Cost." *Literary Digest* 48 (April 25, 1914):973–74.
The Calumet-Hecla strike.

777. "Country-Wide Free Speech Fight." *Mother Earth* 7 (April, 1912): 46–49.

778. "Courts Moving To Check Anarchy." *Square Deal* 13 (November, 1913):370–71.

The courts are taking care of the IWW problem by convicting so many IWWs.

779. Covert, Dr. W. C. "Story of a Six Weeks' Tour on the 'Spruce Front.'" *Monthly Bulletin* (of the Spruce Production Division, U.S. Army) (October, 1918):7–9.

The U.S. Government's spruce drive in the Pacific Northwest.

780. Cowan, Paul. "Dying Like a True Rebel." Review of *The Case of Joe Hill* and *Letters of Joe Hill,* by Philip S. Foner (see nos. 66 and 103). *Nation* 203 (September 26, 1966):291.

781. Cowart, B. T. "James McParland and the Haywood Case." *Idaho Yesterdays* 16 (Fall, 1972):24–29.

782. Cox, John H. "Trade Associations in the Lumber Industry of the Pacific Northwest, 1899–1914." *Pacific Northwest Quarterly* 41 (1950):285–311.

783. "Craft Form versus the I.W.W." *Industrial Pioneer* 3 (April, 1926):32–33.

784. Crawford, Archibald. "The Spectre of Industrial Unions." *International Socialist Review* 18 (August, 1917):80–83.

The IWW in South Africa.

785. Crawford, Ruth. "Piloting the Bomb Squad." Review of *The Immigrants' Day in Court,* by Kate Claghorn. *Survey* 49 (January 1, 1923):461–62.

786. Creel, George. "The American Newspaper." *Everybody's Magazine* 40 (1919):40–44.

Publicity about Bisbee and other IWW episodes has made the IWW seem worse than it is.

787. ———. "Feudal Towns of Texas." *Harper's Weekly* 60 (January 23, 1915):76.

The Kirby Lumber Company controls the timber workers' economic life by issuing company store "merchandise checks."

788. ———. "Guilty!" *Harper's Weekly* 60 (May 22, 1915):487–88.

The Colorado coal strike.

789. ———. "Harvesting the Harvest Hands." *Harper's Weekly* 59 (September 26, 1914):292.

Organizing the farmworkers.

790. ———. "The High Cost of Hate." *Everybody's Magazine* 30 (June, 1914):755–70.
The Cripple Creek strike, with good photographs.

791. Creel, H. G. "Pinemade Peonage: Or, on the Trail of the Timber Trust." *National Rip-Saw* 8 (February, 1912):26.

792. ———. "Timber Trust Answers the *Rip-Saw* with Bullets." *Rip-Saw* 9 (July, 1912):10.

793. ———. "Timber Trust Outlaws." *Rip-Saw* 9 (June, 1912):12.

794. "Crime at Butte, Montana." *Miners Magazine* 18 (September, 1917):1, 6.
The lynching of Frank Little.

795. "The Crime of July 12, 1917 and Obsolete Laws." *Rebel Worker* 2 (August 15, 1919):2.
The Bisbee deportation.

796. "Crime of Spokane." *Appeal to Reason* (January 8, 1910):2.
The Spokane Free Speech Fight.

797. "Criminal Syndicalism." *New Justice* 1 (November, 1919):1.
A sarcastic discussion of the Criminal Syndicalism prosecutions.

798. "Criminal Syndicalism Statutes before the Supreme Court." *University of Pennsylvania Law Review and American Law Register* 76 (December, 1927):198–203.

799. "Criticism and a Reply." *Miners Magazine* 20 (April, 1919):4.
The Seattle General Strike.

800. Crocker, Donald M. "The IWW after the War." *Rebel Worker* 2 (March 1, 1919):2.
The raids and arrests of many IWW members.

801. Crocker, William. "Luxuries and the Labor Shortage." *New Republic* 13 (December 22, 1917):215.
Ex-Wobbly speaking in defense of the IWW states that with the depression and unemployment, prices are raised so that the rich have luxuries while the poor get poorer.

802. Crowell, M. "Whirlwind Sheriff: E. F. Kinkead and the Bayonne Strike." *American Magazine* 80 (December, 1915):51.
The New Jersey oil strikes and the harsh actions of Kinkead.

803. Crowley, Din. "Cast Misery Aside by Joining the Industrial Workers of the World." *New Unionist* 1 (January 5, 1929):3.

804. Crowley, Louise. "On the Unwholesomeness of Honest Toil." *Rebel Worker* 5 [1966?]:10–13.
It is bad to work too hard.

805. Crowther, Samuel. "Radical Propaganda—How It Works." *World's Work* 39 (April, 1920):618–24.

806. Cumberland, William H. "Plain Honesty: Wallace Short and the IWW." *Palimpsest* 61 (No. 5, 1980):146–60.

807. Cunliffe, William. "Industrial Organization." *Miners Magazine* 14 (June 19, 1913):10.
The Akron strike.

808. "Current Comment." *Debs Magazine* 1 (June, 1922):6–7.
The Centralia conspiracy against the IWW.

809. "Current Lessons from the Experience of Labor, by Card No. X–22063." *One Big Union Monthly* NS 1 (June, 1937):16–20.
A comparative history of unions, including the IWW.

810. Currie, B. W. "How the West Dealt with One Labor Union." *Harper's Weekly* 51 (June 22, 1907):908–10.
Particularly interesting account of the Goldfield strike.

811. "The Curse of California." *Industrial Pioneer* 4 (May, 1926):33–38.
The San Pedro police raid.

812. "Cutting Down the Corpse." *Review* 1 (November 22, 1919):596–97.
The Centralia Massacre and the lynching of Wesley Everest.

813. Dada, A. "Aspetti del Sindicalismo Rivoluzionario Statunitense: 'l' Industrial Workers of the World'" (An American variety of revolutionary Syndicalism: "The Industrial Workers of the World"). *Ricerche-Storiche* 11 (January–April, 1981):131–65.

814. Dallas, Onofre. "Anarcho-Syndicalism and the General Strike." *Freedom* 1 (May, 1933):6.

815. ———. "The I.W.W. and Anarcho-Syndicalism." *Freedom* 1 (January, 1933):5–6.
Philosophical differences between IWW and anarcho-Syndicalist ideas.

816. Daly, W. M. "Labor's New Phases and Phrases." *Everybody's Magazine* 27 (September, 1912):351–52.

817. Damon, Allen L. "The Great Red Scare." *American Heritage* 19 (February, 1968):22–27.

818. "Danger Ahead!" *New Review* 1 (August, 1913):673.
The Socialist party began to decline after it rejected the IWW.

819. Daniel, Cletus E. "In Defense of the Wheatland Wobblies: A Critical Analysis of the IWW in California." *Labor History* 19 (Fall, 1978):485–509.

820. ———. "Radicals on the Farm in California." *Agricultural History* 49 (October, 1975):629–46.

821. ———. "Wobblies on the Farm: The IWW in the Yakima Valley." *Pacific Northwest Quarterly* 65 (October, 1974):166–75.

822. Darby. "Winnipeg's Revolution." *New Republic* 19 (July 9, 1919): 310–12.
The Winnipeg strike.

823. Darcy, Jim. "The Battle of Passaic." *Industrial Pioneer* 3 (April, 1926):2–4.
The Passaic textile strike.

824. "Darrow Now the Main Target for a Broadside of I.W.W. Wrath." *Square Deal* 12 (February, 1913):43–44.
How Darrow missed a speech date with the IWW. The author speculates about a possible IWW reprisal.

825. Davenport, F. M. "Light Ahead in Colorado." *Outlook* 110 (June 2, 1915):273–77.
The Colorado coal strike and prospects after the hearings.

826. ———. "Treating Men White in Akron Town." *Outlook* 126 (November 3, 1920):407–11.
Industrial patronage in Akron.

827. Davis, Horace B. "American Labor and Imperialism prior to World War I." *Science and Society* 27 (Winter, 1963):70–76.

828. Davis, L. E. "Strike-Riot in Pennsylvania." *Independent* 67 (September 2, 1909):533–37.
Strike at McKees Rocks described as a veritable battle.

829. Davis, Mike. "The Stop Watch and the Wooden Shoe: Scientific Management and the IWW." *Radical America* 9 (January–February, 1975):69–95.

830. Davis, W. T. "Southern Colorado Coal Strike." *Outlook* 106 (January 3, 1914):24–26.
The Colorado coal strike from the viewpoint of one of the soldiers sent in to "keep order."

831. ———. "Strike War in Colorado." *Outlook* 107 (May 9, 1914):67–73.

832. Dawson, Frank. "St. Mary's Fighting Mayor." *International Socialist Review* 13 (June, 1913):874–76.
An Ohio mayor's problems with labor disruption.

833. "Dead-Line of Sedition." *Literary Digest* 64 (March 6, 1920):17–19.
The problems of sedition and treason.

834. "The Deadly Parallel." *International Socialist Review* 17 (April, 1917):618.
The high cost of war.

835. "Dealing with Red Agitators." *Current History* 12 (July, 1920):698–703.
The spate of raids and arrests.

836. Debs, Eugene V. "The Butte Affair Reviewed." *Miners Magazine* 15 (July 30, 1914):7–8.
The fight between IWW and WFM over the union and the union hall.

837. ———. "The Coming Labor Union." *Miners Magazine* 7 (October 26, 1905):13.
The strong tide of the new IWW will be difficult to stem.

838. ———. "Debs and Moyer: A Page of American Labor History." *Revolutionary Age* 1 (December 7, 1918):7.
Letter of protest about Moyer's friendly attitude toward the AFL.

839. ———. "Debs on Industrial Unionism." *Miners Magazine*. 7 (December 14, 1905):10–11.
The weaknesses of craft unionism. Debs states that the year 1905 will be remembered as the year the IWW began.

840. ———. "Debs on Industrial Unionism." *Miners Magazine* 7 (January 25, 1906):8–12.

841. ———. "The Industrial Convention." *International Socialist Review* 6 (August, 1905):85–86.
Vociferous praise for the new industrial organization.

842. ———. "Industrial Unionism." *International Socialist Review* 11 (August, 1910):11.
Debs' hopes for a better organization.

843. ———. "Stripping and Searching." *Miners Magazine* 7 (January 25, 1906).

Deplores the searching of miners at Goldfield to see if they have taken gold ore.

844. ———. "Industrial Unionism." *Miners Magazine* 6 (June 22, 1905):5–6.
The prospects of the new union.

845. ———. "Investigation by Congress of Moyer, Haywood, and Pettibone." *Miners Magazine* 8 (March 28, 1907):13–14.
Senator Carmack may hold hearings on the Haywood-Moyer-Pettibone case.

846. ———. "The IWW Bogey." *International Socialist Review* 18 (February, 1918):395–96.

847. ———. "Lessons in Capitalism." *Debs Magazine* 2 (March, 1923):1.

848. ———. "Lower Mortal Beings Never Sank." *Miners Magazine* 15 (July 1, 1915):3.
The violence and hiring of gunmen in the Calumet-Hecla strike.

849. ———. "May Day and the Working Class." *Industrial Pioneer* 3 (May, 1925):3–4.
A salute to the IWW and industrial unionism.

850. ———. "Murder in the First Degree." *International Socialist Review* 17 (October, 1916):203–5.
Comments on the Mesabi crimes.

851. ———. "A Plea for Solidarity." *International Socialist Review* 14 (March, 1914):534–38.

852. ———. "Sound Socialist Tactics." *International Socialist Review* 12 (February, 1912):481–86.
The split in the Socialist party between those who agree with Haywood about direct action and those who would oust him.

853. ———. "Unionism and Socialism." *Wayland's Monthly* 52 (August, 1904):2–44.

854. ———. "To the Rescue." *Miners Magazine* 7 (May 3, 1906):7–8.
The Haywood-Moyer-Pettibone trial in Idaho.

855. ———. "Why They Are in Jail." *Labor Defender* 1 (March 18, 1918):1.
The IWWs and other radical prisoners.

856. "Debs and the IWW." *Garment Worker* 12 (July 4, 1915):4.
Debs' remarks on IWW tactics, such as sabotage and direct action, which he finds dangerous.

857. "Debs Denounces Critics." *International Socialist Review* 14 (August, 1913):104–6.
Denounces the IWW for disrupting the organizing of the UMW. Would they dare to object to Mother Jones?

858. "Debs, Haywood, and Mooney." *Revolutionary Age* 1 (April 19, 1919):1.

859. "Debs in Minneapolis." *Socialist World* 4 (May, 1923):10.
Pleads for fifty-two IWW members who are still in prison.

860. "Debs Working for Industrial Unionism." *Voice of Labor* 3 (June, 1905):7.

861. De Caux, Len. "The Great Lakes Are Open Shop." *Industrial Pioneer* 2 (October, 1924):32–33.
Problems of the Great Lakes seamen.

862. "Decentralization." *Voice of the People* 2 (October 9, 1913):2.

863. "Decentralized Localism." *Voice of the People* 2 (October 9, 1913):2.

864. "Decided Action Taken in Baltimore." *Garment Worker* 12 (September, 1913):1.
UGA assurance to the owners of textile mills that they are peaceful and law-abiding unionists and that their members should not be dismissed as though they were IWWs.

865. "Decision of Judge O'Brien." *Miners Magazine* 14 (December 25, 1913):5.
The Calumet-Hecla strike.

866. "Defenders of the Despised." *Nation* 110 (February 14, 1920):202.
Lawyers are ostracized if they defend the IWW; will Eastern lawyers come West and help defend the "despised"?

867. "Defense and *Worker* Office Raided." *Industrial Worker* 2 (December 29, 1917):1.
Deplores the fact that government raiders took everything in the Spokane office, including Mrs. Kate McDonald, the editor's wife.

868. "Defense Fires Opening Guns—Everett Brutality Revealed in Court." *International Socialist Review* 17 (May, 1917):673–74.

869. "Defense Situation." *One Big Union Monthly* 2 (December, 1920): 60, 63.
The many IWW defendants all over the country and the need to help.

870. "Defining Vagrancy." *Survey* 42 (September 13, 1919):850–51.
IWWs are being arrested for vagrancy even when they have jobs.

871. De Ford, Miriam Allen. "Injury to All: Criminal Syndicalism Law in California." *Overland* 82 (December, 1924):536–37, 575–76.

872. ———. "Vacation at San Quentin." *Nation* 117 (August 1, 1923):114–15.
Conditions of the Sacramento prisoners, none of whom had committed a crime.

873. ———. "Wheatland—1921." *Liberator* 4 (September, 1921):24.
Poem on Wheatland.

874. Deland, L. F. "The Lawrence Strike: A Study." *Atlantic Monthly* 109 (May, 1912):694–705.

875. Delaney, Ed. "Wheatland: The Bloody Hop Field." *Industrial Pioneer* 2 (February, 1925):34–36.

876. De Leon, Daniel. "As to Trautmann's Reply." *Weekly People* (September 13, 1913):4.

877. ———. "The Intellectual against the Worker." *Industrial Union Bulletin* 2 (October 10, 1908):1–2.
A newspaper "debate" with Vincent St. John. See no. 2619.

878. ———. "The IWW Convention." *Industrial Union Bulletin* 2 (September 19, 1908):1.
The "overalls brigade."

879. ———. "The Preamble of the Industrial Workers of the World." *Miners Magazine* 7 (October 19, 1905):9–10; (October 26, 1905):11–12; (November 2, 1905):11–13; (November 9, 1905):9–11.

880. De Leon, Solon. "Daniel De Leon Bibliography." *Tamiment Institute Library Bulletin* 23 (September–October, 1959).

881. ———. "Personals." *Survey* 28 (August 28, 1912):677.
Short note about Rudolf Katz, an early IWW member.

882. Dell, Floyd. "Carleton Parker." Review of *The Casual Laborer and Other Essays,* by Carleton Parker (see no. 174). *Liberator* 4 (August, 1920):32.

883. ———. "The Invincible IWW." *Liberator* 2 (May, 1918):9–11.
The deportations of aliens.

884. ———. "What Are You Doing out There?" *Liberator* 1 (January, 1919):14–15.
About the radicals who have been imprisoned.

885. "Demand for Amnesty." *Nation* 115 (July 19, 1922):59–60.
Many are asking that the political prisoners receive amnesty now that it is four years after the war.

886. Demeter, John. "Independent Film and Working Class History: A Review of 'Northern Lights' and 'The Wobblies.'" *Radical America* 14 (January–February, 1980):17–26.

887. Deming, Seymour. "Message to the Middle Class." *Atlantic Monthly* 114 (July, 1914):1–14.
Middle-class people must learn that immigrants and common workers will not endure bad factory conditions forever.

888. "Democracy and Deportation." *Rebel Worker* 2 (February 1, 1919):1.
The AFL had a hand in the troubles of the IWW.

889. Dennett, Tyler. "The Mining Strike in Minnesota: The Other Side." *Outlook* 113 (August 30, 1916):1046–48.

890. "Deportation of IWW Members." *One Big Union Monthly* 1 (March, 1919):9.

891. "Deportation of Undesirables." *Public* 22 (February 22, 1919):177.
Deplores the deportation of people who have committed no crime.

892. "Deportation Report." *Survey* 45 (January 22, 1921):592–93.

893. "The Deportations." *Survey* 41 (February 22, 1919):722–24.

894. "Deporting a Political Party." *New Republic* 21 (January 14, 1920):186.
Why are only radicals deported? Who will be next?

895. Derber, Milton. "The Idea of Industrial Democracy in America, 1898–1915." *Labor History* 7 (Fall, 1966):259–86.

896. ———. "The Idea of Industrial Democracy in America, 1915–1935." *Labor History* 8 (Winter, 1967):3–29.

897. De Silver, Albert. "The Great Battle for Amnesty." *Nation* 118 (January 2, 1924):10–11.
A history of efforts for amnesty for wartime political prisoners.

898. ———. "Mr. Palmer Shudders." *World Tomorrow* 3 (March, 1920): 74–75.

Because Palmer fears radicals, it seems the whole country must.

899. "Destruction Denounced." *Shoe Workers Journal* 14 (August, 1913): 1–2.

Gompers' views on Pouget's ideas of sabotage and destruction.

900. "Developments in the Conspiracy." *Miners Magazine* 6 (March 15, 1906):10–15.

The progress of the Haywood-Moyer-Pettibone trial.

901. Devine, Edward T. "The Bisbee Deportations." *Survey* 38 (July 21, 1917):353.

902. ———. "Social Forces." *Survey* 28 (April 6, 1912):1–2.

The different radicals involved in the Lawrence strike.

903. ———. "Winnipeg and Seattle." *Survey* 43 (October 4, 1919):5–8.

Compares the two general strikes.

904. Devlin, Charles. "Help Organize H. R. & D. Workers." *One Big Union Monthly* 2 (February, 1920):49.

The Hotel, Restaurant, and Domestic Workers Industrial Union of the IWW.

905. ———. "The Immediate Aims of the Lumber Workers Industrial Union." *One Big Union Monthly* 2 (February, 1920):13–14.

906. ———. "Who Does Not Work Neither Shall He Eat." *One Big Union Monthly* 2 (August, 1920):56–57.

The Hotel, Restaurant, and Domestic Workers Industrial Union.

907. ———. "Who Will Feed Us When Capitalism Breaks Down?" *One Big Union Monthly* 2 (November, 1920):40–42.

Foodstuff workers can join to run the industry themselves after capitalism breaks down.

908. De Wal, Martin. "Deportation Is a Howling Farce." *New Solidarity* 99 (October 18, 1919):3.

A Washington lumberjack who was put on the deportation train, the "Red Special," and sent to Ellis Island, describes in detail his difficulties and adventures in the hands of the U.S. Government.

909. Dietz, D. D. "As to Some Present Time Controversies." *One Big Union Monthly* 2 (October, 1920):38.
The Zinoviev appeal, which was rejected by the IWW, made the important point that the radicals should present a "solid front."

910. ———. "Job Talks." *One Big Union Monthly* 1 (October, 1919): 45–47.
Agrees with Vanderveer that the IWW has too many philosophers and not enough organizers. All members should organize while on the job.

911. ———. "The Lumberjack." *One Big Union Monthly* 1 (November, 1919):48.

912. Dimmit, William. "An Organized Harvest." *Industrial Pioneer* 1 (September, 1921):3–7.
Believes that organization of farmworkers is especially important this year.

913. ———. "Splitting the Big Drive." *Industrial Pioneer* 1 (December, 1921):9–11.

914. Dimnet, E. "Syndicalism and Its Philosophy." *Atlantic* 111 (January, 1913):17–30.

915. "Direct Action." *One Big Union Monthly* NS 1 (February, 1937): 23–26.
Examples of direct action ranging from Goldfield in 1907 to Cle Elum in 1932.

916. "'Direct Action' and 'Sabotage.'" *Miners Magazine* 12 (July 11, 1912):10–12.
Explaining the 1912 Socialist Party's decision to abjure sabotage and direct action.

917. "Direct Action and the Public." *Review* 1 (August 16, 1919):292–93.
The Seattle General Strike and the public reaction to it.

918. "Direct Action as a Weapon." *Independent* 74 (January 9, 1913): 70–71.
Comment on the views of A. Tridon. The editorial opposes direct action as a weapon for workers.

919. "A Direct Appeal to the American People." *One Big Union Monthly* 1 (March, 1919):32–34.
Appeal from one of the "silent defense" prisoners at the Sac-

ramento Criminal Syndicalism trial for public support and understanding.

920. Disque, Bryce P. "How We Found a Cure for Strikes in the Lumber Industry of the Pacific Northwest." *System* 36 (September, 1919):379–84.
How Disque brought the Army in to cut lumber.

921. ———. "Open Letter." *Four L Bulletin* 1 (March, 1919):3–5.
How happy the lumberworkers are with the new LLLL union.

922. "Dividing War Profits with Copper Miners." *Survey* 34 (June 12, 1915):239.
The Calumet-Hecla Company will share some of its profits with the workers.

923. "Documents in the Case: Positions on the Raids." *Survey* 43 (January 31, 1920):500–503.
The detailed and official positions on the IWW raids and the deportations taken by Secretary of Labor William Wilson, U.S. Attorney F. F. Kane, and Attorney General A. Mitchell Palmer.

924. Dodd, J. Stephen. "The Forerunner of Industrial Democracy." *Solidarity* 7 (December 30, 1916):3.
The IWW will be the forerunner of true industrial democracy.

925. "Does the IWW Spell Social Revolution?" *Current Literature* 52 (April, 1912):380–84.
About the Lawrence strike, with good photographs.

926. Dogan, Con. "Songs of the Struggle." *One Big Union Monthly* NS 1 (July, 1937):21–22, 34.
Reviews songs of different countries and groups, including the IWW, and says that they all reflect the movement they come from exactly.

927. Doherty, Robert E. "Thomas J. Hagerty, the Church, and Socialism." *Labor History* 3 (Winter, 1962):39–56.

928. "Don't Like the IWW." *International Socialist Review* 16 (June, 1916):762.
A humorous filler telling how a Chicago boss conceded to all the strikers' demands on condition that he would sign with the Chicago Federation of Labor rather than the IWW.

929. Doran, J. T. "Industrial Unionism Clearly Explained to Electrical Workers and Incidentally to the Rest of the Working Class." *Solidarity* 4 (September 6, 1913):1, 4.

930. ———. "Murder in Centralia." *Liberator* 3 (February, 1920):16–18.
The Centralia affair.

931. Doree, E. F. "Gathering the Grain." *International Socialist Review* 15 (June, 1915):740–43.
An IWW farmworker organizer on the year's prospects for labor in the farm belt.

932. ———. "Ham-stringing the Philadelphia Sugar Hogs." *International Socialist Review* 17 (April, 1917):615–17.
The longshoremen and the wartime "sugar wars."

933. ———. "I.W.W. Longshoremen Tie Up Water Front in Philadelphia." *One Big Union Monthly* 2 (July, 1920):5–9.

934.———. "Stomach Equality." *Lumberjack* 1 (February 6, 1913):3.
The IWW must work even harder to bring the Negroes into the IWW.

935. Dosch, Arno. "What the IWW Is." *World's Work* 26 (August, 1913):406–20.
Excellent article describing the IWW's ability to organize, with details on the Lawrence and Paterson strikes and many excellent photographs.

936. "A Double Labor War at Paterson." *Outlook* 104 (May 3, 1913):11.
The recent textile strikes at Lawrence and elsewhere show that the war is not only between the strikers and the owners but also between the AFL and the IWW.

937. Dougherty, T. G. F. "IWW Seeks To Organize All Wage Workers." *Labor Defender* 1 (April 1, 1918):3.
The IWW, unlike other unions, wishes to organize the unskilled workers.

938. Douglas, J. "Syndicalism or Cooperation—the Latest and Greatest Labor Problem." *Engineering Magazine* 44 (March, 1913):833–41.

939. Downing, Mortimer. "California Agriculture Demands Industrial Tactics." *Industrial Pioneer* 1 (August, 1921):26–30.

940. ———. "The Case of the Hop Pickers." *International Socialist Review* 14 (October, 1913):210–13.

Graphic description of the conditions at the Durst Hop Ranch and of the shootings.

941. ———. "The Ghastly Frame-Up in the Mooney Case." *Solidarity* 8 (March 17, 1917):1.

Describes some of the irregularities at the trial and reasons for calling it a frame-up.

942. ———. "The Historic Mission of the I.W.W." *One Big Union Monthly* NS 2 (March, 1938):9.

943. ———. "Wage Workers Unite." *One Big Union Monthly* NS 2 (June, 1938):32–33.

944. ———. "Workers Are Staked Out Cattle." *One Big Union Monthly* NS 2 (May, 1938):23.

Explains how helpless workers are without strong organization.

945. ———. "Workers and Welfare." *New Unionist* 2 (July, 1929):3.

946. "Dr. Babson and His IWW Nightmare." *National Civic Federation Review* 4 (March, 1914):13.

The stir caused when economist Roger Babson wrote favorably of the IWW. See nos. 350–51.

947. "Dramatizing the Paterson Strike." *Survey* 30 (May 31, 1913):316.

The Paterson pageant.

948. "Drastic Sedition Laws." *Literary Digest* 64 (January 24, 1920):18.

Even conservatives find the sedition legislation to be extreme.

949. "Drifting to Peonage in California." *Industrial Pioneer* 2 (April, 1925):39–40.

The worsening of California farmworkers' situation.

950. Dubofsky, Melvyn. "Film as History: History as Drama: Some Comments on 'The Wobblies,' a Play by Stewart Bird and Peter Robilotta, and 'The Wobblies,' a Film by Stewart Bird and Deborah Shaffer." *Labor History* 22 (Winter, 1981):136–40.

951. ———. "The *Industrial Union Bulletin*: An Introduction and Appraisal." *Labor History* 12 (Spring, 1971):289–92.

952. ———. "James H. Hawley and the Origins of the Haywood Case, 1892–1899." *Pacific Northwest Quarterly* 58 (January, 1967): 23–32.

953. ———. "The Origins of Western Working Class Radicalism, 1890–1905." *Labor History* 7 (Spring, 1966):131–54.

954. ———. "The Radical Goad." *Nation* 209 (September 8, 1969):218–21.

Economic power and direct action can substitute for political action.

955. ———. "Radicalism of the Dispossessed: William D. Haywood and the IWW." In Alfred F. Young, ed., *Dissent: Explorations in the History of American Radicalism* (De Kalb, IL: Northern Illinois University Press, 1968), 175–213.

956. ———. Review of *The Case of Joe Hill* and *Letters of Joe Hill*, by Philip S. Foner (see nos. 66 and 103). *Labor History* 7 (Fall, 1966):354–58.

957. ———. Review of *The Seattle General Strike*, by Robert Friedheim (see no. 74). *Labor History* 6 (Fall, 1965):264–66.

958. ———. "Socialism and Syndicalism" and "Reply." In Laslett, John H. M., and Seymour M. Lipset, eds., *Failure of a Dream? Essays in the History of American Socialism* (Garden City, NY: Anchor Press, 1974), 252–85 and 295–99.

959. ———. "The IWW: An Exchange of Views." *Labor History* 11 (Summer, 1970):364–72.

Comments on Jensen's review of Dubofsky's *We Shall Be All* (see no. 1717).

960. Du Bois, W. E. B. "I.W.W." *Crisis* 18 (June, 1919):60.

Does not believe IWW methods are advisable because of possible violence.

961. Duchez, Louis. "Class War in New Castle." *International Socialist Review* 10 (April, 1910):876–77.

A Pennsylvania town is upset by the presence of the IWW.

962. ———. "The Passive Resistance Strike." *International Socialist Review* 10 (November, 1909):409–12.

963. ———. "Revolutionary Psychology." *Wilshire's Magazine* 14 (May, 1910):14–15.

During its brief history, the IWW has succeeded in making the country pay attention to it.

964. ———. "The Strikes in Pennsylvania." *International Socialist Review* 10 (September, 1909):203.

The McKees Rocks strike.

965. ———. "Victory at McKees Rocks." *International Socialist Review* 10 (October, 1909):289–300.

966. Dueberg, Helmuth. "I.W.W.'s Attempt To Organize Discontent." *Los Angeles Times* (August 16, 1914): Part 6, 4.
The IWW takes advantage of bad conditions and tries to make workers discontented.

967. Duff, Hezekiah N. "The IWW's—What They Are and What They Are Trying To Do." *Square Deal* 10 (May, 1912):297–310.
The IWW has played a large part in all the recent industrial disputes.

968. Duke, David C. "Anna Louise Strong and the Search for a Good Cause." *Pacific Northwest* 66 (July, 1975):123–37.

969. Dukes, H. N. "Centralia Case, Ten Years Afterward." *World Tomorrow* 12 (June, 1929):277–79.

970. Duncan, Don. "The Centralia Massacre: Shots across the Gulf." *Seattle Times* (November 12, 1969): n.p.

971. Dunn, Arthur W. "The 'Reds' in America." *Review of Reviews* 61 (February, 1920):161–66.
The arrests of radicals.

972. Dunn, R. W. "Red Raids." *Nation* 123 (September 22, 1926): 267–68.

973. Dunne, William F. "August, 1917, in Butte—the Murder of Frank Little." *Labor Defender* 1 (August, 1926):123–24.

974. ———. "Centralia's Red Armistice Day." *Labor Defender* 1 (November, 1926):191–92.
Historical comments on the Centralia Massacre.

975. Dunnigan, J. S. "Doings in Boise, Idaho." *Miners Magazine* 8 (May 16, 1907):7–12.
The first Haywood trial.

976. Dunning, J. J. "The Lumber Industry—Will Its Workers Waken?" *Industrial Pioneer* 3 (February, 1926):6–8, 20–21.
Only by organizing will the workers improve bad working conditions.

977. Dyer, Francis John. "The Truth about the Copper Strike." *National Magazine* 40 (May, 1914):235–51.
The Calumet-Hecla and Arizona copper strikes.

978. "Dynamite in the Lawrence Strike." *Literary Digest* 45 (September 14, 1912):407.

William Wood and the dynamite explosion in Lawrence.

979. Easley, Ralph M. "Radicals Mislead Churches about Labor." *National Civic Federation Review* 4 (March 25, 1919):3–4, 7.

Churches err in their investigation of incidents such as Centralia.

980. ———. "Survey of IWW Activities during the War." *New York Times* (July 7, 1918): Sec. 3, p. 3, cols. 1–6.

981. ———. "Samuel Gompers: The Flag and McNamara Incidents." *National Civic Federation Review* 3 (February 15, 1912):13–15, 25.

982. Eastman, Crystal. "The Mooney Congress." *Liberator* 1 (March, 1919):19–24.

Describes the congress of radicals who met in January, 1919, to vote on a general strike for the liberation of Tom Mooney, their arguments and differences.

983. Eastman, Max. "Editorial." *Liberator* 4 (April, 1921):5–6.

Compares William Haywood and William Z. Foster as labor leaders.

984. ———. "Examples of 'Americanism.'" *Liberator* 3 (February, 1920):12–16.

The word *Americanism* does not describe the Palmer Raids and the imprisonment of radicals because of their beliefs.

985. ———. "Bill Haywood, Communist: An Interview." *Liberator* 4 (April, 1921):13–14.

986. ———. "I.W.W.: The Great American Scapegoat." *New Review* 2 (August, 1914):465–70.

The Tannenbaum church incident was the perfect morality play, having shown up the churches' "Christianity" for what it was worth.

987. ———. "Revolutionary Progress—The Uses of Dictatorship." *Masses* 9 (October, 1917):12–13.

One of the most admirable examples of labor progress was the IWW under James Rowan, when the lumberworkers obtained better conditions and shorter hours.

988. ———. "The Tannenbaum Crime." *Masses* 5 (May, 1914):6–8.

How Frank Tannenbaum sheltered the unemployed in a church.

989. ———. "Why Not Send Them to Siberia?" *Masses* 5 (March, 1914):5.
Comments on the Wheatland episode; would the authorities like to exile the discontented workers?

990. Eastman, Phineas. "The Southern Negro and the One Big Union." *International Socialist Review* 13 (June, 1913):890–91.
The first integration of union members in the South.

991. ———. "To Political Pleaders." *Voice of the People* 2 (October 16, 1913):3.
Defends the IWW and direct action and asserts that "yellow" Socialists have misrepresented the IWW.

992. ———. "Organization Opportunities in Kansas Oil Fields." *Industrial Worker* (April 7, 1917):4.

993. "Easy Thinkers on Hard Questions." *Nation* 101 (September 16, 1915):350.
A sermon on the IWW is quoted, with comments on the Industrial Relations Commission.

994. Ebert, Justus. "A Commendable Spirit." *Labor Defender* 1 (August 15, 1918):11–12.
Comments on the lithographers union, which has given some support to the currently beleaguered IWW.

995. ———. "The Ideal of Complete Social Regeneration." *Industrial Worker* 26 (July 21, 1945):1.

996. ———. "The Ideals of the I.W.W." *One Big Union Monthly* 2 (July, 1920):39–44.

997. ———. "Industrial Democracy." *Industrial Pioneer* 1 (September, 1921):36–38.

998. ———. "Imperialism or Industrial Unionism—Which?" *One Big Union Monthly* 1 (April, 1919):34–35.

999. ———. "Is Machinery Destroying Organization?" *One Big Union Monthly* NS 1 (February, 1937):3.

1000. ———. "The IWW in Theory and Practice." *One Big Union Monthly* NS 1 (April, 1937):3–4.
A revision of the author's pamphlet by the same name (see no. 4082).

1001. ———. "The Most Important Question." *One Big Union Monthly* 1 (March, 1919):22–23.

The most important question is the one with the most important answer: "What is industrial unionism?"

1002. ———. "Reconstruction: A Workingclass Presentation of Its Problems." *One Big Union Monthly* 1 (September, 1919):22–25.

1003. ———. "Roll of Honor of the First Convention." *Industrial Worker* 26 (July 7, 1945):1, 4.

Names and discusses the earliest delegates.

1004. ———. "Suppressing the IWW in New York." *Solidarity* 5 (February 14, 1914):2.

Direct shop agitation would be better than public agitation.

1005. Elbert, Justus, and Covington Hall. "Decentralization or Cooperation, Which?" *Voice of the People* 2 (November 13, 1913):2.

Debate in which Hall argues for a decentralized union, while Ebert pleads for cooperation.

1006. Ebner, Michael H. "I Never Died: The Case of Joe Hill v. the Historians." *Labor History* 12 (Winter, 1971):139–43.

1007. ———. "The Passaic Strike of 1912 and the Two I.W.W.'s." *Labor History* 11 (Fall, 1970):452–66.

1008. ———. "Strikes and Society: Civil Behavior in Passaic, 1875–1914." *New Jersey History* 97 (Spring, 1979):7–24.

1009. "An Echo from Lawrence." *Miners Magazine* 12 (May 9, 1912):15.

The use of children for liberal causes.

1010. "An Echo of the Famous Haywood Trial." *Life* 28 (March 13, 1950):113–16.

Pictorial review of the first Haywood trial, featuring Harry Orchard's current life and good photographs.

1011. "Echoes of Centralia at Yakima." *Western Worker* (September 18, 1933).

Persecution of farm workers at Yakima.

1012. "Editorial." *International Socialist Review* 12 (February, 1912):505–6.

The idea of direct action as opposed to parliamentary action.

1013. "Editorial Comment from the Press." *Miners Magazine* 7 (March 8, 1906):4–7.

Press opinion on the Haywood-Moyer-Pettibone trial.

1014. "Editorial Comments from the Labor Press on the Vindication of WFM." *Miners Magazine* 9 (January 23, 1908):7–10.

1015. "Editorial Notes." *Garment Worker* 8 (June 19, 1914):4.
The struggle between the WFM and the IWW.

1016. Edwards, Forrest. "Average Americans." *Labor Defender* 1 (September 15, 1918):6.
Did the Chicago trial jury really consist of "average citizens"?

1017. ———. "The Class War in Harvest Country." *Solidarity* 7 (August 19, 1916):1.
The AWO is getting stronger, from Kansas to the Dakotas.

1018. ———. "Gompers and Deportation." *Industrial Pioneer* 1 (December, 1923):59–60.

1019. ———. "Merits of Legal Defense." *One Big Union Monthly* 1 (September, 1919):10–11.

1020. ———. "Minneapolis' Big Amnesty Meetings." *Industrial Pioneer* 1 (November, 1923):11.

1021. ———. "Shingle Weavers Called." *Voice of the People* 3 (February 12, 1914):2.
Fears that the shingle weavers, who are on piece work, may not support the eight-hour-day drive because they will make less money.

1022. Edwards, George. "Free Speech in San Diego." *Mother Earth* 10 (July, 1915):182–85.

1023. "Eight Books on Syndicalism." *Survey* 31 (November 8, 1913):166–68.

1024. "An Eight Hour Day on the Pacific Coast." *Agitator* 1 (February 1, 1911):1.
The agitation for a shorter work day among the Pacific Northwest lumbermen.

1025. Eldridge, Maurice E. "Preston and Smith." *International Socialist Review* 10 (April, 1910):894–98.
Deplores the fact that Preston and Smith are still being held in prison for the Goldfield shooting.

1026. Eldridge, P. W. "The Wheatland Hop Riot and the Ford and Suhr Case." *Industrial and Labor Relations Forum* 10 (May, 1974):165–95.

1027. "The Elections and the I.W.W." *One Big Union Monthly* 2 (December, 1920):5–7.

1028. "Elizabeth Gurley Flynn's Contest with Paterson." *Survey* 35 (December 11, 1915):283.

1029. "Elizabeth Gurley Flynn: Labor Leader." *Outlook* 111 (December 15, 1915):905.

1030. Ellae, Enness [Nicolaas Steelink]. "Musings of a Wobbly." *Industrial Worker* 26 (August 4, 1945):2.

Explains what the IWW is and how it is organized. Steelink's column appeared regularly in IWW publications for many years.

1031. Elliott, Russell R. "Labor Troubles in the Mining Camp at Goldfield, Nevada, 1906–1908." *Pacific Historical Review* 19 (November, 1950):369–84.

1032. Elliott, W. Y. "Political Application of Romanticism." *Political Science Quarterly* 34 (June, 1924):234–64.

The IWW's ideas of direct action caused the repression by the government.

1033. Ellis, Clifford B. "What Life Means to a Worker." *Industrial Pioneer* 4 (May, 1926):14–18.

Experiences at the Work Peoples College.

1034. Ellis, William T. "The 'Fighting Quaker' of the Cabinet." *American Review of Reviews* 61 (January, 1920):35–38.

A profile of A. Mitchell Palmer that describes his activities against radicals.

1035. "Embargo on the Strike Children." *Survey* 27 (March 2, 1912): 1822.

The use of children as part of the Lawrence strike tactics drew great criticism.

1036. Embree, A. S. "Bingham Strike." *Solidarity* 3 (November 9, 1912):3.

The failing Bingham Canyon strike is compared to the Homestake and Lawrence strikes.

1037. ———. "Butte Employers in Secret Conclave." *Industrial Pioneer* 4 (August, 1926):7–8, 43–46.

Describes and quotes the secret minutes of the Anaconda and other mine employers and Butte businessmen at a meeting held during a 1919 strike. Their plot was to bring in the military and by violence get rid of the strike leaders. Embree says it was the same group that "got rid" of Frank Little.

1038. ———. "General Defense Committee." *Labor Defender* 1 (September 15, 1918):5.
The "bomb threat" in Chicago, probably put out by the government and undoubtedly phony, has caused great problems for the IWW, as it was intended to do.

1039. ———. "Ludlow." *Industrial Pioneer* 4 (July, 1926):13–19.
An eyewitness account of the Ludlow Massacre.

1040. ———. "Hold the Fort." *Labor Defender* 1 (September 1, 1918):10.
The Chicago trial.

1041. ———. "Story of the Great Colorado Coal Strike." *Industrial Solidarity* 7 (December 28, 1927):3.

1042. Emery, Henry. "Under Which King, Bezonian?" *Yale Review* 8 (July, 1919):680–93.
The "American Bolsheviks" should state where their loyalties lie.

1043. Emery, James A. "Shall the Decalogue Be Repealed?" *American Industries* 13 (June, 1913):15–17.
A call to make labor unions illegal.

1044. ———. "Union Labor's Demand for Exemption from the Law." *American Industries* 1 (December, 1913):8–10.
Labor leaders think they can get away with strikes and other property violations.

1045. "Emphasis." *Industrial Pioneer* 1 (October, 1921):17–19.
The IWW should always focus on education, emancipation, and organization.

1046. Emrich, Duncan. "Casey Jones, Union Scab." *California Folklore Quarterly* 1 (1942):293.

1047. "End of the Colorado Coal Strike." *Literary Digest* 49 (December 19, 1914):1210–11.

1048. "End of the Colorado Coal Strike." *Survey* 33 (December 19, 1914):308.

1049. "End of a Great Strike at McKee's Rocks." *Outlook* 93 (September 18, 1909):84.

1050. "The End of Leadership." *One Big Union Monthly* NS 2 (June, 1938):24–27.
Union leaders are no longer what they used to be.

1051. "End of the Mesaba Range Strike." *Survey* 37 (January 6, 1917):411–12.

1052. "End of the Paterson Strike." *Outlook* 104 (August 9, 1913):780.

1053. "End of the Strike at Lawrence." *American Review of Reviews* 45 (April, 1912):402.

1054. "Enemy within Our Midst." *Gateway* 29 (December, 1917):13–16.

Radicals are seditious and constitute a great danger to the war effort and to domestic peace as well.

1055. Engdahl, J. Louis. "William D. Haywood—'Undesirable Citizen.'" *Communist* 7 (July, 1928):434–41.

An obituary that praises Haywood by listing and describing his enemies.

1056. ———. "The Strike of the Copper Miners." *Miners Magazine* 14 (September 4, 1913):12.

The violence of the Calumet-Hecla strike comes from the militia and hired thugs, not from the strikers.

1057. Engdahl, John. "Gruesome Story of American Terrorism." *One Big Union Monthly* 2 (April, 1920):12–14.

America is holding hundreds of prisoners only because of their political and economic beliefs. The author includes a complete list of Centralia prisoners.

1058. Engle, Phil. *International Socialist Review* 11 (November, 1910):315.

Letter about Western meetings of the IWW, including one at Salt Lake City.

1059. Englemann, Larry D. "We Were the Poor People—The Hormel Strike of 1933." *Labor History* 15 (Fall, 1974):483–510.

1060. Enright, L. J. "On the Anniversary of Centralia." *Industrial Pioneer* 3 (November, 1925):12, 28.

1061. "Enslaved by Gunmen." *One Big Union Monthly* 2 (March, 1920):33–35.

Some of the famous Chicago gangsters carry on union-busting as a regular practice.

1062. "Episcopal View of the Calumet Copper Miners Strike." *Survey* 32 (August 15, 1914):502–4.

1063. Esmond, Leone. "Harding's 'Lettre Du Cachet.'" *Industrial Pioneer* 1 (August, 1923):8–9.

The commutations of some prisoners' sentences.

1064. "Espionage in Peace Times." *Survey* 43 (January 31, 1920):493.
Even though the war is over, the hunt for "spies" increases.

1065. "Ethics of a General Strike." *Independent* 68 (March 17, 1910):588–89.
The failed Philadelphia General Strike shows that most people disapprove of such strikes.

1066. Ettor, Joseph. "The English Novel and IWW Songs." Review of *The Development of the English Novel,* by Wilbur R. Cross. *Solidarity* 6 (February 13, 1915):4.
Old minstrel songs were the forerunners of IWW songs. Both puncture the world's romantic views.

1067. ———. "The I.W.W. versus the A.F.L." *New Review* 2 (May, 1914):275–85.

1068. ———. "The Light of the Past." *Industrial Worker* 26 (June 30, 1945):5; (July 14, 1945):3; (July 21, 1945):2.
History of the IWW.

1069. ———. "A Retrospect on Ten Years of the IWW." *Solidarity* 6 (August 14, 1915):2.

1070. ———. "Why a World of Anathemas on Our Heads?" *Lumberjack* 1 (March 20, 1913):3.
Criticism from many quarters will not deter the IWW.

1071. Ettor, Joseph, and Arturo Giovannitti. "Appeal from Lawrence." *Mother Earth* 7 (May, 1912):92–94.
The Lawrence strike. See nos. 1073, 1074.

1072. Ettor, Joseph J., and W. D. Haywood. "What the I.W.W. Intends To Do to the U.S.A." (NY) *World* (June 14, 1914): Sec. E, p. 1.

1073. "Ettor in Jail: Strike Goes On." *Survey* 27 (February 10, 1912):1726.

1074. "Ettor the Irresponsible." *Square Deal* 12 (February, 1913):95.

1075. Evans, Walter. "The Centralia Massacre." *Seattle Post-Intelligencer* (October 26, 1975):7.

1076. "Everybody Is Agreed." *Review* 1 (June 21, 1919):113.
Most people think lumberjacks are not worth more than $5 a day.

1077. Ewer, W. N. "League of Secret Police." *Dial* 67 (September 6, 1919):209–10.

Even though the war is over, the repression of radicals will continue.

1078. "The Execution of the I.W.W. Poet." *Survey* 35 (November 27, 1915):200.
The execution of Joe Hill.

1079. "An Exhibition of Solidarity." *International Socialist Review* 6 (April, 1906):623–24.
Threatened conspiracies against Vincent St. John and the Idaho defendants have brought a new solidarity among all unions.

1080. "Exoneration of William M. Wood." *Outlook* 104 (June 21, 1913):351–52.
The man who planted the dynamite in order to make people think the IWW did it was exonerated in the local courts.

1081. "Expelling Bill Haywood." *Common Cause* 1 (February, 1912):94–95.
Haywood's expulsion from the Socialist Party.

1082. "The Exposure." *Mother Earth* 12 (May, 1917):71–72.
The Mooney Case and the Washington trials of the IWW.

1083. "Extracts from Committee on Industrial Relations on Conditions in Minnesota." *Miners Magazine* 17 (October, 1916):5.
A report of the Mesabi strike investigation.

1084. "Extracts from the Press Relative to the Colorado and Michigan Strikes." *Miners Magazine* 14 (October 23, 1913):6–10.

1085. Fabrick, Susan. "Rebel Wedding." *Industrial Worker* 73 (September, 1981):2.
The IWW wedding of Frank and Jenny Cedervall.

1086. "Facts in Connection with the Second Riot at Butte." *Miners Magazine* 15 (July 2, 1914):5–6.

1087. Faegre, Torwald. "Organizing Blueberries." *Rebel Worker* 2 (Summer, 1964):6–9.
The attempt to organize Michigan fruit pickers.

1088. Fagin, Sophie. "November: Golden-Brown or Bloody Red?" *Workers Defense* 2 (November, 1932):4.
Notable Novembers in IWW history.

1089. Fahey, John. "Coeur d'Alene Confederacy." *Idaho Yesterdays* 12 (Spring, 1968):2–7.
The Coeur d'Alene strike from the mine-owners' viewpoint.

1090. ———. "Ed Boyce and the Western Federation of Miners." *Idaho Yesterdays* 25 (Fall, 1981):18–30.
The first Haywood trial.

1091. Fair, Agnes T. *International Socialist Review* 10 (December, 1909): 558.
A telegram from an "agitator" regarding organizing in the Pacific Northwest.

1092. Faires, Clifford C. "I.W.W. Patriotism in Globe." *Nation* 106 (March 21, 1918):319–20.
The Globe miners wanted grievance committees and a little more money. For these demands they were called "unpatriotic."

1093. "The Fall of Kansas City." *Agitator* 2 (December 1, 1911):1.
The Kansas City Free Speech Fight.

1094. "Fall of the American Bastille." *Wilshire's Magazine* 17 (May, 1913):1.
Some IWWs have been exonerated in a few of the courts.

1095. "Farm Workers and Farm Jobs." *One Big Union Monthly* NS 2 (June, 1938):10–13.

1096. "The Farmer and the War." *New Republic* 13 (November 3, 1917):8–9.

1097. Fasce, Ferdinando. "Gli Industrial Workers of the World e Il Movimento Socialista Americano" (The IWW and the American socialist movement). *Movimento Operaio e Socialista* 22 (1975):23–50.

1098. ———. "Gli 'Industrial Workers of the World': La Classe Operaia Americana tra Spontaneita e Organizazione" (The IWW: Spontaneity and organization in the American working class). *Università di Genova Istituto di Storia Moderna e Contemporanea* 6 (Nos. 1–2, 1974).

1099. "Fear Not, Organize!" *Industrial Pioneer* 1 (February, 1921):42–43.
Organizers should not be daunted by the government harassment.

1100. "Federal Commission on Industrial Relations." *International Socialist Review* 15 (June, 1915):714–17.
Haywood testimony before the Industrial Commission, with good photographs.

1101. "Federal Commission To Study Calumet and Colorado." *Survey* 31 (January 24, 1914):486.

1102. "Federal Investigation of Strike Region." *Survey* 31 (February 7, 1914):541.

Colorado and Michigan will be included in the strike investigation.

1103. Feinberg, Harry. "When the Master's Pocketbook Is Hit." *Industrial Pioneer* 1 (May, 1923):19–20.

Imprisoning the IWW is a way of fending off labor's power.

1104. ———. "Yakima Valley Hop News." *Voice of the People* 2 (September 17, 1914):4.

1105. Fenton, Edwin. "Italians and the Labor Movement." *Pennsylvania History* 26 (April, 1959):133–48.

1106. Ferguson, L. E. "The IWW Convention." *Revolutionary Age* (June 14, 1919):6, 8.

1107. ———. "The Life of Democracy—A Reply." *One Big Union Monthly* 1 (April, 1919):19–20.

Takes issue with Varney's description of Socialism and the Socialists. See no. 3099.

1108. "The Ferris Investigation." *Miners Bulletin* 51 (January 9, 1914):1.

Questions the Michigan governor's actions during the Calumet-Hecla strike.

1109. Ficken, Robert E. "The Wobbly Horrors: Pacific Northwest Lumbermen and the Industrial Workers of the World." *Labor History* 24 (Summer, 1983):325–41.

1110. Fickle, James E. "The Louisiana–Texas Lumber War of 1911–1912." *Louisiana History* 16 (Winter, 1975):59–85.

1111. ———. "Race, Class, and Radicalism: The Wobblies in the Southern Lumber Industry, 1900–1916." In Joseph Conlin, ed., *At the Point of Production* (Westport, CT: Greenwood Press, 1981), 97–113 (see no. 39).

1112. "Fiendish Persecution in Kansas." *One Big Union Monthly* 1 (July, 1919):12.

IWW prisoners have languished for more than a year without trial in a dreadful jail.

1113. "Fight for Free Speech." *Appeal to Reason* 729 (November 20, 1909):5.

The Spokane Free Speech Fight.

1114. "Fight to the Death in Kansas City! Free Speech at All Costs!" *Voice of the People* 3 (February 26, 1914):2.

1115. "Fighting Germany's Spies—(VIII) The American Protective League." *World's Work* 36 (August, 1918):393–401.
Profile of a citizen vigilante group that attacks radicals under the guise of patriotism.

1116. "Fights Industrial Workers of the World." *Miners Magazine* 14 (July 31, 1913):5.
The struggle between the AFL and the IWW.

1117. Filigno, C. "Another One, and They Call It Justice." *Voice of the People* 3 (January 8, 1914):2.
Marine workers arrested in Philadelphia.

1118. ———. "The Power of the General Strike." *Lumberjack* 1 (May 22, 1913):2.

1119."Final Hearings on Industrial Relations." *Outlook* 109 (February 17, 1915):358–59.

1120. "The Finest Answer to IWW-ism." *Square Deal* 17 (December, 1915):139–41.
Description of Amoskeag Mills parade in Manchester, NH, where there was a great show of patriotism and flag-waving.

1121. Finger, Charles J. "A Social Ill." Review of *The IWW*, by Paul Brissenden (see no. 18). *Public* 22 (May 17, 1919):522.

1122. Fink, Gary M. "Introduction." In Philip Taft, *Organizing Dixie* (Westport, CT: Greenwood Press, 1981), xvii–xxv.
Includes interesting biographical information about Professor Taft, with information on his years as a member of the IWW.

1123. "First Aid to Patriotism." *Nation* 109 (July 26, 1919):101.
Patriotism can be proved by a display of flags as well as by government raids.

1124. "The First Sit-Down," *Industrial Worker* 26 (August 18, 1945):5.
The IWW sit-down in Schenectady in 1906 at the General Electric plant.

1125. Fishbein, Meyer. "The President's Mediation Commission and the Arizona Copper Strike, 1917." *Southwestern Social Science Quarterly* 30 (December, 1949):175–82.

1126. Fisher, Harry. "Ku Klux Klan Tries Intimidation." *Industrial Pioneer* 1 (April, 1924):30–31.
A Ku Klux Klan parade that encircled the block on which an IWW meeting was being held.

1127. ———. "Over Eight Hundred Hear Geo. Speed Expose the Truth about the San Pedro Raid." *Industrial Pioneer* 2 (August, 1924):3–6, 43–44.

1128. Fisher, W. I. "Justice through the Courts or through Direct Action?" *One Big Union Monthly* 1 (July, 1919):31–33.
Spending a lot of money on lawyers and defense is a mistake. The IWW should continue with organizing and direct action.

1129. Fitch, John A. "Arson and Citizenship; East Youngstown and the Aliens Who Set It on Fire." *Survey* 35 (January 22, 1916):477–80.

1130. ———. "Baiting the IWW." *Survey* 33 (March 6, 1915):634–35.
The IWW meets particular opposition in Oregon.

1131. ———. "Colorado Strike." *Survey* 31 (December 20, 1913):333–34.

1132. ———. "The IWW: An Outlaw Organization." *Survey* 30 (June 7, 1913):355–62.
The IWW is clearly unwanted in Lawrence, Paterson, San Diego, and Akron.

1133. ———. "Law and Order." *Survey* 33 (December 5, 1914):241–58.
The Colorado coal strike.

1134. ———. "Lawrence—a Strike for Wages or for Bolshevism?" *Survey* 42 (April 5, 1919):42–46.

1135. ———. "Sabotage and Disloyalty." *Survey* 39 (October 13, 1917): 35–36.
Reports of the IWW's lack of patriotism and enthusiasm for the war.

1136. ———. "The Paterson Silk Strike: A Year After." *Survey* 32 (June 27, 1914):339–40.

1137. ———. "When a Sheriff Breaks a Strike." *Survey* 34 (August 7, 1915):414–16.
How Sheriff Eugene Kinkead broke the Bayonne strike.

1138. Fitch, John A., et al. "Probing the Causes of Unrest." *Survey* 32, 33, 34, and 35. Parts 1–8: John A. Fitch (April 18, 1914, to July 11, 1914). Part 9: C. Merriman (August 8, 1914). Parts 10–21: John A. Fitch (August 29, 1914, to February 27, 1915). Part 22: C. W. Holman (April 17, 1915). Part 23: O. McFeely (May 8, 1915). Parts 24–25: G. R. Taylor (May 22, 1915, and May 29,

1915). Part 26: John A. Fitch (June 5, 1915). See also Fitch, "Review of Reports." *Survey* 35, Part 1 (December 18, 1915):317–33; Part 2 (January 1, 1916):395–402; Part 3 (January 8, 1916):432–34.

Analysis of the Industrial Commission reports.

1139. "510's Fresh Water Campaign." *Industrial Pioneer* 1 (April, 1924):9–10.

The IWW drive to organize the Great Lakes seamen.

1140. "Fix the Responsibility for Seattle Outrage." *Miners Magazine* 13 (August 7, 1913):9.

The Free Speech Fights are useless annoyances.

1141. "Flare-up among Pittsburgh Steel Workers." *Survey* 28 (July 6, 1912):487–88.

1142. Fleming, John H. "The Janitors." *Industrial Pioneer* 1 (December, 1921):18–19.

The AFL is having a hard time finding a craft union to which janitors can belong, whereas the IWW is ready for any kind of worker.

1143. Fletcher, Ben. "Negro and Organized Labor." *Messenger* 5 (July, 1923):759–60.

The Philadelphia IWW unions are well integrated.

1144. ———. "Philadelphia Waterfront's Unionism." *Messenger* 5 (June, 1923):740–41.

1145. Flynn, Elizabeth G. "And Don't Wait Till the Sunrise." *Labor Defender* (March, 1937):4–5.

The history of Criminal Syndicalist laws and cases.

1146. ———. "Contract Slavery in Paterson Silk Mills." In *Pageant of the Paterson Strike* (New York: Success Press, 1913), 29–31.

1147. ———. "Figures and Facts." In *Pageant of the Paterson Strike* (New York: Success Press, 1913), 15.

1148. ———. "Free Speech Fight at Spokane." *International Socialist Review* 10 (December, 1909):483–89.

1149. ———. "I Have No Regrets: A Chapter from American Labor History." *Woman Today* 2 (April, 1937):11, 26.

Her years with the IWW.

1150. ———. "The IWW—Its Place in History." *Political Affairs* 43 (September, 1964):27–31.

1151. ———. "Latest News from Spokane." *International Socialist Review* 10 (March, 1910):828–34.
The Spokane Free Speech Fight.

1152. ———. "One Boss Less: The Minersville Strike." *International Socialist Review* 12 (July, 1911):8.
The miners' living and working conditions in Pottsville, Tremont, and Mahoney City, Pennsylvania.

1153. ———. "Problems Organizing Women." *Solidarity* 5 (July 15, 1916):3.

1154. ———. "Shall This Man Serve Ten Years in Sing Sing?" *International Socialist Review* 11 (May, 1911):685–88.
Vincent Buccafori was unfairly convicted of murder.

1155. ———. "The Shame of Spokane." *International Socialist Review* 10 (January, 1910):610–19.
The Spokane Free Speech Fight.

1156. ———. "Sister Kathie Says: Our Mother Was a Born Rebel!" *Daily Worker* 10 (May 13, 1945):11.
The mother of Elizabeth G. and Kathie Flynn has been neglected by history.

1157. ———. "A Visit to Joe Hill." *Solidarity* 6 (May 22, 1915):1, 4.

1158. ———. "The Weavers." *Survey* 35 (February 26, 1916):648.
Seeing Hauptmann's play *The Weavers* reminds Flynn strongly of the Lawrence strike. The lot of the textile workers is still not what it should be.

1159. Flynn, Tom. "Bill Haywood." *International Socialist Review* 10 (January, 1910):610–19.

1160. Flynt, Wayne. "Florida Labor and Political Radicalism 1919–1920." *Labor History* 9 (Winter, 1968):73–90.

1161. Fogelson, Nancy. "They Paved the Streets with Silk: Paterson, New Jersey Silk Workers." *New Jersey History* 7 (Autumn, 1979): 133–48.

1162. "The Following Appeared." *Miners Magazine* 12 (January 4, 1912):6.
Discusses the AFL and the tactic of "boring from within" in view of the fact that the WFM might possibly join the AFL.

1163. "Following the Trail of the IWW; A First-Hand Investigation into Labor Troubles of the West." *New York Evening Post* (November

14, 17, 24; December 1, 8, 12, 15, 1917; February 13, 16, 23; March 2, 9, 16, 23, 30; April 6, 13, 20, 1918).

1164. Foner, Philip S. "The IWW and the Black Worker." *Journal of Negro History* 55 (January, 1970):45–64.

1165. ———. "Professor Foner Replies." *Labor History* 12 (Winter, 1971):109–14.

A reply to James O. Morris about alleged plagiarism. See no. 2149.

1166. ———. "*United States of America vs. Wm. D. Haywood et al.*: The IWW Indictment." *Labor History* 11 (Fall, 1970):500–530.

1167. Foote, E. J. "The Ethics of Industrial Unionism." *Industrial Union Bulletin* 3 (February 20, 1909):4.

The most important ethic of the IWW is "an injury to one is an injury to all."

1168. ———. "The Positive of Industrialism." *Industrial Union Bulletin* 1 (May 4, 1907):2.

The positive reasons for organizing along industrial lines.

1169. "For Fair Trials." *Public* 15 (July 5, 1912):626.

The indictments of the strike leaders after the Lawrence strike.

1170. "For the Study of Industrial Welfare." *Outlook* 110 (June 2, 1915):242.

Comments on the Industrial Commission reports.

1171. Forain, René. "Toward a Renewal of Libertarian Researches." *Rebel Worker* 4 [1965?]:8–9.

1172. Forcey, Charles B. "Walter Weyl and the Class War." In Harvey Goldberg, ed., *American Radicals: Some Problems and Personalities* (New York: Monthly Review Press, 1957), 265–76.

1173. Ford, Grace. "For Life." *International Socialist Review* 15 (December, 1914):342–43.

The Wheatland Hop Riot and the injustice done to those prosecuted.

1174. Ford, James. "The Cooperative Franco-Belge of Lawrence." *Survey* 28 (April 6, 1912):68–70.

The Lawrence strikers.

1175. Ford, Lynn. "The Growing Menace of the I.W.W." *Forum* 61 (January, 1919):62–70.

The Bolsheviks and the IWWs are the same.

1176. "Ford and Suhr." *International Socialist Review* 15 (October, 1914):256.
The Wheatland convictions.

1177. "Ford Is Free." *Industrial Pioneer* 3 (March, 1926):4–5.
Richard Ford's release from prison.

1178. "Forgiving War-Offenders." *Literary Digest* 67 (October 2, 1920): 18–19.
European nations have declared amnesties, but the U.S. war offenders, such as Eugene Debs, Kate O'Hare, and the IWW members, are still imprisoned.

1179. Forster, Arnold. "Violence on the Fanatical Left and Right." *Annals of the American Academy of Political and Social Science* 364 (March, 1966):141–48.
Discusses IWW incidents of violence, among many others.

1180. Forster, C. H. "Despised and Rejected of Men: Hoboes of the Pacific Coast." *Survey* 33 (March 20, 1915):671–72.

1181. Fortney, Glenn B. "For Unity in the Metal Industry." *Industrial Pioneer* 1 (July, 1921):37.

1182. Fosdick, Harry E. "After the Strike in Lawrence." *Outlook* 101 (January 15, 1912):340–46.

1183. "Foster Homes Investigated." *Survey* 27 (February 24, 1912): 1791–92.
The Lawrence strikers' children and their welfare is a concern to the public. Who knows where they are being sent?

1184. Foster, James C. "AFL, IWW, and Nome, 1905–1908." *Alaska Journal* 5 (No. 2, 1975):66–77.

1185. ———. "Syndicalism Northern Style: The Life and Death of WFM No. 193." *Alaska Journal* 4 (No. 2, 1974):130–41.

1186. ———. "The Treadwell Strikes; 1907 and 1908." *Alaska Journal* 6 (No. 1, 1976):2–11.
Western Federation of Miners striking in Alaska.

1187. ———. "The Western Federation Comes to Alaska." *Pacific Northwest Quarterly* 66 (October, 1975):161–73.

1188. ———. "The Western Wobblies." In James Foster, ed., *American Labor in the Southwest* (Tucson: University of Arizona Press, 1982), 59–64.

1189. Foster, Warren D. "New Bedford Textile Strike." *Survey* 28 (August 24, 1912):658–59.

1190. Foster, William Z. "The IWW Convention." *Agitator* 2 (October 15, 1912):2–3.

1191. ———. "The Miners' Revolt in Butte." *Mother Earth* 9 (September, 1914):216–20.

1192. ———. "Revolutionary Tactics." *Agitator* 2 (April 15, 1912):2–3; (May 1, 1912):4; (May 15, 1912):2; (June 1, 1912):2; (June 15, 1912):2, 15; (July 1, 1912):2.
Criticism of the IWW's tactics.

1193. ———. "Syndicalism Distinct from IWW." *Agitator* 2 (September 15, 1912):1.

1194. ———. "Syndicalism in Germany." *Industrial Worker* 4 (September 14, 1911):4.

1195. "Foul Deeds of Hop King's Hellions." *Voice of the People* 3 (January 8, 1914):3.
The Wheatland Hop Riot.

1196. "Four Objections to Syndicalism." *Common Cause* 3 (March, 1913):278.
Catholic objections to the ideas of Syndicalism.

1197. Fowler, James H., II. "Creating an Atmosphere of Suppression, 1914–1917." *Chronicles of Oklahoma* 59 (Summer, 1981):202–23.

1198. ———. "Tar and Feather Patriotism: The Suppression of Dissent in Oklahoma during World War One." *Chronicles of Oklahoma* 56 (Winter, 1978–79):409–30.

1199. Fox, Jay. "Attention IWW." *Syndicalist* 3 (August 1–15, 1913):2.
Criticism of the IWW by a member is printed in the *Syndicalist* because it was refused by an IWW paper.

1200. ———. "A General Strike." *Agitator* 1 (June 1, 1911):1.
A general strike over the McNamara incident might deter McNamara's indictment.

1201. ———. "The Fall of Kansas City." *Agitator* 2 (December 1, 1911):1.
The Kansas City Free Speech Fight.

1202. ———. "Fanaticism and the IWW." *Agitator* 1 (August 1, 1911):1.
Direct rather than political action is the IWW's technique.

1203. ———. "An I.W.W. Report." *Agitator* 2 (November 1, 1912):1.
Criticism of IWW tactics.

1204. ———. "The Lawrence Leaders." *Agitator* 2 (October 1, 1912):1.

1205. ———. "The Lawrence Strike." *Agitator* 2 (February 15, 1912):1.

1206. ———. "The Lawrence Strike." *Agitator* 2 (March 15, 1912):1.

1207. ———. "Organizing the Woodsmen." *Syndicalist* 3 (March 1, 1913):2.
The effort to organize lumberworkers was not strong enough.

1208. ———. "Our Attitude towards IWW." *Agitator* 2 (October 15, 1912):1.
IWW views conflict with real Syndicalism.

1209. ———. "The Paterson Strike: Its Lesson." *Syndicalist* 3 (September 1–15, 1913):54.
The IWW kept the workers out on strike too long and did not have enough experienced organizers.

1210. ———. "Railroad Construction Strike." *Agitator* 2 (April 15, 1912):1.
The British Columbia strike.

1211. ———. "Thugs Rule in Aberdeen." *Agitator* 2 (December 15, 1911):1.
The lumber kings of the Northwest are trying to drive out the IWW.

1212. ———. "Trial of the Lawrence Leaders." *Agitator* 2 (June 1, 1912):1.

1213. Fox, Matthew K. "Agricultural Workers Industrial Union." *Labor Defender* 1 (July 15, 1918):14; (July 30, 1918):7; (August 15, 1918):7.
The organizer of AWO #400 reports that working conditions are improving and membership is increasing.

1214. ———. "The Story of No. 400." *One Big Union Monthly* 1 (September, 1919):49–50.

1215. Foy, James. "A Migratory Worker's Diary." *Industrial Pioneer* 1 (February, 1924):29.

1216. Fraina, L. C. "Daniel De Leon." *New Review* 2 (July, 1914):390–99.

1217. ———. "The I.W.W. Trial." *The Class Struggle* 1 (November–December, 1917):1–5.
Revolutionary unionism is on trial at the Chicago trial.

1218. ———. "Syndicalism and Industrial Unionism." *International Socialist Review* 14 (July, 1913):25–28.

1219. "Framed Up." *Rebel Worker* 2 (June 15, 1919):1.
Standard Oil Company officials framed the Oklahoma IWW.

1220. "Frank Cedervall." *Cleveland Magazine* 9 (February, 1980):17.

1221. Frank, Waldo. "The Lesson of Daniel De Leon." *Commentary* 4 (July, 1947):43–51.
De Leon was too political.

1222. Frazer, George F. "Organizer's Report." *Bulletin* 3 (January, 1909):124–25.

1223. "Free Love and the IWW." *Labor Defender* 1 (July 15, 1918):9–10.

1224. "Free Press Fight at Boulder Dam." *Workers Defense* 2 (September, 1932):4.
Gunmen have attempted to run the IWW out of the camp.

1225. "Free Press of New Castle." *Miners Magazine* 12 (October 10, 1912):4.
Blames the IWW members because their presence alone tempts the police.

1226. "Free Speech, a Precious Right: Quoting Senator LaFollette." *Life and Labor* 3 (September, 1913):282.

1227. "Free Speech and Jailed Speakers." *Literary Digest* 77 (June 16, 1923):10–12.

1228. "Free Speech Fight." *International Socialist Review* 10 (January, 1910):642–43.
Reports on the jailing of Elizabeth Gurley Flynn for speaking in Spokane. She should not have been jailed while pregnant.

1229. "The Free Speech Fight." *Agitator* 1 (December 15, 1910):1.
The Fresno Free Speech Fight.

1230. "Free Speech Fight in Kansas City." *International Socialist Review* 14 (February, 1914):510.

1231. "Free Speech in Paterson." *Outlook* 111 (November 24, 1915):692–93.

1232. "Free Speech in San Diego." *Agitator* 1 (December 1, 1910):1.

1233. "A Free Speech Victory." *Public* 20 (May 11, 1917):451.
Thomas Tracy's acquittal after the Everett Massacre.

1234. "Freedom of Press at Issue in Paterson." *Survey* 30 (June 14, 1913):368.

1235. "Freedom with a String." *Survey* 50 (July 15, 1923):425.
Commutations of IWW sentences were conditional on promises of future good behavior.

1236. Freeman, Irving. "Lenine and the IWW." *Rebel Worker* 2 (October 15, 1919):4.

1237. Freyr, Fred. "The Man on the Job." *Voice of the People* 2 (December 11, 1913):3.
There should be a system to keep track of new migratory members so that they can be retained in the union after they move to a new job.

1238. Friedberg, Gerald. "The Socialist Party of America: Decline and Fall, 1914–1918." *Studies on the Left* 4 (Summer, 1964): 79–96.
Discusses the IWW and William D. Haywood, with a comment by James Weinstein.

1239. Friedheim, Robert L. "Prologue to a General Strike: The Seattle Shipyard Strike of 1919." *Labor History* 6 (Winter, 1965):121–42.

1240. ———. "The Seattle General Strike of 1919." *Pacific Northwest Quarterly* 52 (July, 1961):81–98.

1241. Friends of Joe Hill Committee. "Joe Hill: IWW Martyr." *New Republic* 119 (November 15, 1948):18–20.
Answer to Stegner's conclusions that Joe Hill might have been guilty. See no. 2817.

1242. "From a Centralia Prisoner." *Christian Century* 46 (May 8, 1929):619.

1243. "From the I.W.W. Indictments." *International Socialist Review* 17 (November–December, 1917):271–78.
Detailed discussion of the indictments of IWWs all over the country.

1244. "From the Railroad Workers." *International Socialist Review* 14 (May, 1914):687–88.
The railroad union seems unable to publicize the railroad workers' problems.

1245. Fruit, W. I. "A General Strike or a General Lockout?" *Freedom* 1 (May, 1933):5.
More workers have been locked out by unemployment than have walked out on strikes.

1246. Fry, C. Luther. "Migratory Workers of Our Industries." *World's Work* (October, 1920):600–611.

1247. ———. "The Under Dog—'and They Wonder Why We're Red.'" *Outlook* 126 (September 1, 1920):18–19.

1248. Fuller, Leon W. "Colorado's Revolt against Capitalism." *Mississippi Valley Historical Review* 21 (December, 1934):343–60.
A history of Colorado's strike problems.

1249. "Furniture Strike Ends in Defeat in Grand Rapids." *Solidarity* 2 (August 26, 1911):1, 4.
The furniture strike failed because of craft union tactics.

1250. "The Future and the IWW, by a Washington Official." *Public* 22 (February 8, 1919):134–36.
The lumber industry owners felt that the repressions of the IWW were a necessity.

1251. "Future of the IWW." *One Big Union Monthly* 2 (December, 1920):59.
The IWW is being repressed on a worldwide basis.

1252. "The Future and the I.W.W." *Public* 22 (February 8, 1919):134–36.

1253. Gaffield, Chad. "Big Business, the Working-Class, and Socialism in Schenectady." *Labor History* 19 (Summer, 1978):350–72.
Material on the early IWW activities in Schenectady.

1254. Gahan, John. "Twelve Years after Ludlow." *Industrial Pioneer* 3 (February, 1926):17–20.

1255. Galambos, Louis. "AFL's Concept of Big Business: A Quantitative Study of Attitudes toward the Large Corporation, 1894–1931." *Journal of American History* 57 (March, 1971):847–63.
Comparison of the *American Federationist* and *Solidarity* reports of the labor news.

1256. "The Gandy Dancers, by One of Them." *One Big Union Monthly* NS 1 (February, 1937):27–29.
A railroad worker's story.

1257. Gannett, Lewis S. "Americans in Russia." *Nation* 113 (August 17, 1921):167–68.
Letter from ex-IWW Karl Senntag from Novgorod.

1258. ———. "Bill Haywood in Moscow." *Liberator* 4 (September, 1921):11–12.

1259. ———. "The IWW." *Nation* 111 (October 20, 1920):448–49.
The government raids and the IWW trials.

1260. Garretson, Thomas P., III. "Criminal Syndicalism." *University of Kansas Law Review* 19 (Summer, 1971):809–19.

1261. Gates, David, and David Gonzales. "The Union That Never Died." *Newsweek* (September 24, 1984):16, 18.
Provides a short sketch of the current IWW, with statements by Jon Bekken and Fred Thompson.

1262. Gaveel, Jack. "At the Parting of the Ways." *One Big Union Monthly* 1 (May, 1919):24–26.
People are adjusting their personal philosophies since the raids, and some are far less radical in their beliefs than before.

1263. ———. "The Awakening: A History of the Child Slaves, the IWW and the Migratory Workers." *One Big Union Monthly* 2 (July, 1920):33–37.

1264. ———. "Sunny California, Land of Romance and Unemployment." *Industrial Pioneer* 1 (February, 1921):6–10.
California migrant workers.

1265. ———. "Things That Count in the Proletarian Revolution." *One Big Union Monthly* 2 (December, 1920):17–21.
Analyzes radical doctrines and compares them with IWW beliefs.

1266. ———. "With 400 through the Harvest Fields." *One Big Union Monthly* 2 (October, 1920):17–20.
The success of the AWO among farmworkers.

1267. Gearity, Jack B. "New Castle Free Speech Fight." *International Socialist Review* 12 (August, 1911):97–99.
The first indictments of IWW members for seditious libel.

1268. Gedicks, Al. "Ethnicity, Class Solidarity, and Labor Radicalism among Finnish Immigrants in Michigan Copper Country." *Politics and Society* 7 (1977):127–56.

1269. ———. "The Social Origins of Radicalism among Finnish Immigrants in Midwestern Mining Communities." *Review of Radical Political Economies* 8 (Fall, 1976):1–31.

1270. Gendel, Martin. "Criminal Law: Criminal Syndicalism, Red Flag Law: History of Enforcement in California." *California Law Review* 19 (November, 1930):64–69.

1271. "General Convention Most Important Yet." *Industrial Pioneer* 1 (January, 1924):41–42.

Believes the convention is important because of the split which is becoming apparent.

1272. "The General Defense Committee of the IWW." *International Socialist Review* 18 (February, 1918):408–9.

Describes the work of the IWW General Defense Committee, with good photographs.

1273. "The General Defense Committee: 20 Years of Activity." *One Big Union Monthly* NS 1 (October, 1937):20–21.

1274. "General Industrial Conditions: Wheeling." *Square Deal* 15 (August, 1914):79–81.

Joseph Ettor and the IWW are agitating among the workers around Wheeling, West Virginia.

1275. "General Industrial Conditions." *Square Deal* 16 (April, 1915): 272–73.

Frank Tannenbaum's solution to the unemployment problem—taking some of the unemployed into a church.

1276. "General Strike in Philadelphia." *Current Literature* 48 (April, 1910):361–65.

1277. "The General Strike in Seattle." *One Big Union Monthly* 1 (March, 1919):38–39.

1278. "General Strike of Lumber Workers." *International Socialist Review* 18 (August, 1917):113.

1279. Gengarelly, W. Anthony. "Secretary of Labor William B. Wilson and the Red Scare, 1919–1920." *Pennsylvania History* 46 (October, 1980):311–30.

1280. Genini, Ronald. "Industrial Workers of the World and Their Fresno Free Speech Fight, 1910–1911." *California Historical Quarterly* 53 (Summer, 1974):100–114.

1281. "Genteel Tradition." Review of *The Dwelling Place of Light,* by Winston Churchill (see no. 4982). *New Republic* 12 (October 13, 1917):306–7.

1282. "George Andreytchine." *International Socialist Review* 17 (September, 1916):170.

About the Minnesota deportations, with good photographs.

1283. "George Hardy's Report to the Convention." *Industrial Pioneer* 1 (June, 1921):3–9.

1284. George, Harrison. "The Can Opener." *Liberator* 7 (January, 1924):16–17.

The IWW prisoners' lives in the "Cook County Can" in Chicago and their prison newspaper.

1285. ———. "The Cow-Boy." *International Socialist Review* 15 (May, 1915):663–65.

The cowboy needs IWW direct action. As he breaks in a horse, so he is broken in by industrial evolution.

1286. ———. "A Grave of Liberty." *Labor Defender* 1 (April 1, 1918):1.

Conditions in the Cook County jail in Chicago, where many IWWs are incarcerated.

1287. ———. "Hitting the Trail in the Lumber Camps." *International Socialist Review* 17 (February, 1917):454–57.

1288. ———. "The Mesaba Iron Range." *International Socialist Review* 17 (December, 1916):328–32.

The Minnesota mine strike.

1289. ———. "Victory on the Mesaba Range." *International Socialist Review* 17 (January, 1917):429–31.

1290. ———. "Will the IWW Fight Decadence?" *Liberator* 7 (August, 1924):26–28.

The IWW's response to the Red Trade Union International.

1291. Gerhard, Peter. "The Socialist Invasion of Baja California, 1911." *Pacific Historical Review* 15 (September, 1946):295–304.

1292. "German Plotters Fear Him." *Literary Digest* 55 (September 29, 1917):61–64.

Government agent A. Bielaski and the raids on the IWW.

1293. Germer, Adolph. "A Near View of 'Bill' Haywood." *Miners Magazine* 13 (February 6, 1913):5.

Haywood mishandled funds of the Steve Adams defense committee.

1294. ———. "Nuts for Haywood To Crack." *Miners Magazine* 13 (March 20, 1913):5–6.

Questions how Haywood handled the Lawrence strike funds.

1295. Gerould, James T. Review of *The Dwelling Place of Light,* by Winston Churchill (see no. 4982). *Bellman* 23 (October 27, 1917):468–69.

1296. "Getting into Business." *American Industries* 13 (July, 1913):9.
The financial aspects of the Paterson pageant.

1297. Ghent, W. J. "The Devotees of Syndicalism." *Miners Magazine* 12 (August 29, 1912):13.
Syndicalism is not proletarian.

1298. Ghetti, Sandra. "Gli IWW e la ristrutturazione del capitale negli anniventi" (The IWW and its rebuilding in the twenties). *Primo Maggio* 16 (Autumn–Winter, 1981–1982):21–26.

1299. "Ghosts of 1919 Massacre Still Haunt Centralia." *Tacoma New Tribune* (November 8, 1970): sec. A, 6.

1300. Gill, Robert S. "The Four L's in Lumber." *Survey* 44 (May 1, 1920):165–70.
The Loyal Legion of Loggers and Lumbermen, the union that "includes the employer." The workers felt it was a pleasure and a duty to belong to it. See no. 3280.

1301. Gillmore, Inez Haynes. "At the Industrial Hearing." *Masses* 6 (March, 1915):8–9.
Describes the work of the Industrial Commission.

1302. ———. "Marysville Strike." *Harper's Weekly* 58 (April 4, 1914):18–20.
The Wheatland episode.

1303. ———. "Shadows of Revolt." *Masses* 6 (July, 1915):7–8.
Some good reasons for revolt being discovered by the Industrial Commission.

1304. Giovannitti, Arturo. "Fighting Steel." *Masses* 8 (September, 1916):18.
Only the IWW is strong enough to organize the steel industry.

1305. ———. "Selecting a Perfect Jury." *Liberator* 1 (July, 1918):8.

1306. ———. "Syndicalism—the Creed of Force." *Independent* 76 (October 30, 1913):209–11.
An analysis of Syndicalism, with photographs of violent strike actions.

1307. ———. "When the Cock Crows—to the Memory of Frank Little, Hanged at Midnight." *Masses* 9 (October, 1917):18–20.
Narrative poem about Little's lynching.

1308. Glazer, Sidney. "The Michigan Labor Movement." *Michigan History* 29 (Michigan History) 29 (January–March, 1945):73–82.
The IWW Studebaker strike of 1913.

1309. Gold, Michael. "Wanted: Pioneers for Siberia!" *Liberator* 5 (March, 1922):5–8.
Tells about the IWW colony of Americans in Kuzbas, Siberia, and invites those interested to join them.

1310. Goldberg, David J. Review of *At the Point of Production,* edited by Joseph R. Conlin (see no. 39), and *Fellow Workers and Friends,* edited by Philip Foner (see no. 67). *International Labor and Working Class History* 23 (Spring, 1983):104–8.

1311. Goldbloom, Maurice J. "Communists and Wobblies." Review of *Roots of American Communism,* by Theodore Draper (see no. 56), and *The I.W.W.,* by Paul Brissenden (see no. 18). *Commentary* 24 (August, 1957):177–80.

1312. Goldman, Emma. "The Outrage of San Diego." *Mother Earth* 7 (June, 1912):115–22.
A personal account of the San Diego Free Speech Fight.

1313. ———. "Power of the Ideal." *Mother Earth* 7 (June, 1912):125–31.
The San Diego Free Speech Fight.

1314. Golin, Steve. "Defeat Becomes Disaster: The Paterson Strike of 1913 and the Decline of the IWW." *Labor History* 24 (Spring, 1983):223–48.

1315. Gomez, Joseph A. "History, Documentary, and Audience Manipulation: A View of 'The Wobblies.'" *Labor History* 22 (Winter, 1981):141–45.
Gomez believes the film is manipulative and criticizes its historical coverage. See no. 4943.

1316. Gompers, Samuel. "Bisbee's Autocrats Indicted." *American Federationist* 25 (July, 1918):597–98.
The Bisbee deportation.

1317. ———. "Destruction the Avowed Purpose of the I.W.W." *Garment Worker* 12 (August 8, 1913):5–6.

1318. ———. "The Industrial Workers of the World." *Mediator* 5 (September, 1912):5–9.
Criticizes the IWW for interference with AFL unions.

1319. ———. "The I.W.W. Strikes." *American Federationist* 20 (August, 1913):622–24.

Critizes the Lawrence and Paterson strikes, saying that the IWW was really trying to attack the AFL.

1320. ———. "Justice Grossly Outraged." *American Federationist* 13 (April, 1906):233–35.

The kidnapping of William D. Haywood before the first Haywood trial.

1321. ———. "Lawrence Dynamite Conspiracy." *American Federationist* 19 (October, 1912):815–23.

1322. ———. "The Lawrence Dynamite Conspiracy." *Miners Magazine* 12 (October 31, 1912):11.

Reprint of no. 1321.

1323. ———. "Lawrence Strike." *American Federationist* 19 (April, 1912): 281–93.

1324. ———. "Socialist Methods versus Trade Union Methods." *American Federationist* 19 (February, 1912):135–41.

1325. ———. "Syndicalism, 'Partyism,' and Unionism." *American Federationist* 19 (May, 1912):361–71.

1326. ———. "Those 'World Redeemers' at Chicago, Their Plight." *American Federationist* 12 (August, 1905):514–16.

AFL reaction to the industrial unionists' convention.

1327. ———. "The Trade Unions To Be Smashed Again." *American Federationist* 12 (March, 1905):139–41; (April, 1905):214–17; (May, 1905):277.

William Haywood is calling a congress of industrial unionists.

1328. ———. "Unemployment: An Illusive and a Real Way Out." *American Federationist* 21 (April, 1914):310–12.

1329. ———. "Upton Sinclair's Mental Marksmanship." *American Federationist* 21 (April, 1914):293–302.

Sinclair should join the true reformers in the AFL.

1330. "Gompers on the IWW." *Garment Worker* 12 (July 11, 1913):2.

Gompers says that the IWW is destructive in theory and practice.

1331. Good, J. E. "Akron and the IWW." *Collier's* 51 (June 21, 1913):31.

The Akron rubber strike.

1332. ———. "How Akron Was Vindicated." *Leslie's Illustrated Weekly* 116 (May 22, 1913):558.

About the Akron rubber strike.

1333. Goodwyn, Lawrence. "The Cooperative Commonwealth and Other Abstractions: In Search of a Democratic Premise." *Marxist Perspectives* 3 (No. 2, 1980):8–42.

1334. Goodyear, De Mont. "The Lawrence Textile Strike." *Independent* 72 (February 8, 1912):299–300.

1335. Gordon, F. G. R. "A Labor Man's Story of the Paterson Strike. Aftermath of the IWW Reign of Violence, Intimidation, and Graft." *National Civic Federation Review* 2 (December 1, 1913):16, 17.

The Paterson strike provided a pattern for later strikes at Hopedale and Ipswich, Massachusetts.

1336. "The Government and the Industrial Workers of the World." *Outlook* 117 (September 26, 1917):114.

The government raids on the IWW.

1337. "The Government at Test in Copper Zone Issue." *Square Deal* 14 (March, 1914):143–46.

Discusses Milo D. Campbell's statement that nowhere on earth are miners so well off as in America.

1338. "Governor Ferris and Trade Councils." *Square Deal* 13 (September, 1913):188.

The local trade council views the Calumet-Hecla strike.

1339. Graham, John. "Upton Sinclair and the Ludlow Massacre." *Colorado Quarterly* 21 (Summer, 1972):55–67.

1340. Granich, Irwin. "Mr. Spargo." *One Big Union Monthly* 2 (February, 1920):36–37.

Discussion of John Spargo's ideas and character. Granich says he is just another politician climbing a ladder of words.

1341. Grant, Luke. "The Haywood Trial: A Review." *Outlook* 86 (August 24, 1907):855–62.

1342. ———. "The Idaho Murder Trial." *Outlook* 85 (April 6, 1907): 805–11.

1343. ———. "Orchard's Testimony." *Outlook* 86 (June 15, 1907):303–4.

1344. Grant, Percy S. "Brains versus Bayonets." *North American Review* 196 (August, 1912):183–93.

The Lawrence strikers outwitted the National Guard.

1345. Gray, Charles. "The Everett Massacre." *Labor Defender* 1 (November, 1926):193–95.

1346. ———. "Work." *Industrial Pioneer* 1 (December, 1921):27.
The IWW is the only organization with the answer to unemployment.

1347. Grayson, Robert. "An Appeal for Spokesmen." *Industrial Pioneer* 1 (October, 1921):41.
The IWW would be stronger if it had more members belonging to the "home guard," workers who do not migrate.

1348. ———. "Industrial Unionism and the Strike in Steel." *Industrial Pioneer* 1 (August, 1921):33–34.

1349. "The Great Agricultural Workers' Drive." *Industrial Pioneer* 1 (July, 1923):3–5.

1350. "Great Builders, These General Construction Workers." *Industrial Pioneer* 4 (August, 1926):24–28.

1351. "Great Labor Trial: Astounding Verdict." *Labor Defender* 1 (September 1, 1918):3–6.
The Chicago trial.

1352. Green, Archie. "American Labor Lore: Its Meanings and Uses." *Industrial Relations* 4 (February, 1965):51–68.
Origin of the word *scissorbill.*

1353. ———. "John Neuhaus, Wobbly Folklorist." *Journal of American Folklore* 73 (No. 3, 1960):189–217.

1354. Green, B. A. "Portland's Mayor-made Revolution." *Nation* 115 (December 6, 1922):605–6.
A strike was turned into a revolution by the actions of public officials.

1355. ———. "Sedition Run Riot." *Nation* 116 (April 25, 1923):495.
Defends the IWW and lists its "reasonable" demands.

1356. Green, James R. "Brotherhood of Timberworkers 1910–1913: A Radical Response to Industrial Capitalism in the Southern USA." *Past and Present* (August, 1973):161–200.

1357. ———. "Tenant Farmer Discontent and Socialist Protest in Texas, 1901–1917." *Southwestern Historical Quarterly* 81 (October, 1977):133–54.

1358. Grey, G. "One Big Union." *Nation* 108 (May 10, 1919):733–34.

1359. Griffin, C. R. "The Short Log Country." *International Socialist Review* 17 (January, 1917):422–23.

Describes the sawmills of Idaho, working conditions there, and the thriving IWW.

1360. Griffiths, John. "The General Strike." *Industrial Pioneer* 1 (September, 1923):26–27.
General strikes are not planned but born of bad working and living conditions and wrong public policies.

1361. Grob, Gerald N. Review of *Bread and Roses Too,* by Joseph R. Conlin (see no. 41). *Journal of American History* 57 (December, 1970):733–34.

1362. Grout, Louise Adams. "Giacomo and Jonathan." *Twentieth Century* 5 (March, 1912):11–13.
The Lawrence strike and its ethnic mix.

1363. Grover, David H. "Borah and the Haywood Trial." *Pacific Historical Review* 32 (February, 1963):65–77.

1364. "The Gruesome Story of American Terrorism—Lest We Forget." *One Big Union Monthly* 2 (March, 1920):5–21.
Includes a list of prisoners and prosecutions.

1365. "Gun Thugs Kill Another Miner." *Workers Defense* 2 (June, 1932):3.
IWW miner Jack Vanetter shot at Evarts, Kentucky.

1366. Gunns, Albert F. "Ray Becker, the Last Centralia Prisoner." *Pacific Northwest Quarterly* 59 (April, 1968):88–99.

1367. Gutfeld, Arnon. "The Murder of Frank Little: Radical Labor Agitation in Butte, Montana, 1917." *Labor History* 10 (Spring, 1969):177–92.

1368. ———. "The Speculator Disaster in 1917: Labor Resurgence at Butte, Montana." *Arizona and the West* 11 (Spring, 1969):27–38.

1369. ———. "The Ves Hall Case, Judge Bourquin and the Sedition Act of 1918." *Pacific Historical Review* 37 (May, 1968):163–78.

1370. Gutman, Herbert G. "Work, Culture and Society in Industrializing America, 1815–1919." *American Historical Review* 78 (June, 1973):567–69.
Immigrant workers and their responses to the new necessities of factory life.

1371. Hadcock, Editha. "Labor Problems in the Rhode Island Cotton Mills—1790–1940." *Rhode Island History* 4 (July, 1955):82–85.

1372. Hader, John J. "Honk Honk Hobo." *Survey* 60 (August 1, 1928): 453–55.
Hoboes in Chicago.

1373. Hagerty, Thomas J. "Economic Determinism." *Voice of Labor* 3 (February, 1905):6.
A theoretical discussion.

1374. ———. "Function of Industrial Unionism." *Voice of Labor* 3 (March, 1905):5.
A theoretical discussion.

1375. ———. "Reasons for Industrial Unionism." *Voice of Labor* 3 (March, 1905):7–8.
Craft unionism has totally failed.

1376. "Hagerty in Montana." *Miners Magazine* 6 (April 13, 1905):8.
The IWW is perfecting unionism.

1377. Hale, Swinburne. "Act-of-Hate Palmer." *Nation* 110 (June 12, 1920): 789–91.
The Palmer raids.

1378. ———. "The 'Force and Violence' Joker." *New Republic* 21 (January 21, 1920):231–33.
Recent abridgments of freedom of speech by Congress as well as by the other agents of government.

1379. Hall, Covington. "Associated Press and IWW." *New Republic* 13 (December 1, 1917):126–27.

1380. ———. "Direct Action." *Voice of the People* 2 (October 30, 1913):2.

1381. ———. "I Am Here for Labor." *International Socialist Review* 13 (September, 1912):223–26.
A description of Arthur Emerson, president of the Brotherhood of Timber Workers and a leader of the Louisiana lumber strikes. The brutality of the employers is also discussed.

1382. ———. "Industrial Unionism: Its Power and Promise." *One Big Union Monthly* NS 1 (November, 1937):6–8.

1383. ———. "IWW vs. Bastard Industrialism." *Voice of the People* 3 (April 23, 1914):2.

1384. ———. "The Job." *Voice of the People* 2 (September 25, 1913):3.
The IWW is interested in more than just "the job."

1385. ———. "Louisiana Lumber." *Industrial Worker* 26 (July 14, 1945):1; (July 21, 1945):3; (July 28, 1945):3.
Historical account of the Southern lumber strikes of 1912–1913.

1386. ———. "Negroes against Whites." *International Socialist Review* 13 (October, 1912):349–50.
The IWW has been accused of organizing Negroes against whites, but such changes are only attempts to divide and conquer.

1387. ———. "The New Woman of the Old South." *Progressive Woman* 6 (October, 1912):6.
The wives of the Louisiana timber workers were active and courageous in their support of the strike.

1388. ———. "Revolt of the Brotherhood." *One Big Union Monthly* NS 2 (April, 1938):18–22.
A recollection of the strike of the Brotherhood of Timber Workers.

1389. ———. "Revolt of the Southern Timber Workers." *International Socialist Review* 13 (July, 1912):51–52.
The Southern strike of timberworkers.

1390. ———. "Sabotage." *Voice of the People* 3 (January 22, 1914):1.
Sabotage, to the IWW, is a fair form of guerrilla warfare.

1391. ———. "The Southern Lumber War." *Coming Nation* (June 22, 1912):2.

1392. ———. "Unskilled Workers Doomed?" *One Big Union Monthly* NS 2 (June, 1938):8–9.
Technological progress will make unskilled workers anachronistic.

1393. ———. "The Victory of the Lumber Jacks." *International Socialist Review* 13 (December, 1912):470–71.
The organizing successes of the Brotherhood of Timber Workers.

1394. ———. "With the Southern Timber Workers." *International Socialist Review* 13 (May, 1913):805–6.

1395. Hall, Henry N. "Two Wings of Labor's Big Army Warring on Each Other." (New York) *World* (July 27, 1913):1.
The IWW and the AFL are fighting each other in the Eastern strikes.

1396. Halverson, Guy, and William E. Ames. "The *Butte Bulletin*: Beginnings of a Labor Daily." *Journalism Quarterly* 46 (Summer, 1969):260–66.

A Socialist paper printed in Butte, Montana.

1397. Ham, W. T. "*Seattle Union Record* Suppressed for Condoning the Centralia Outrage." *New Republic* 21 (December 17, 1919):78–79.

1398. Hammer, John. "Copper Smelting." *Industrial Pioneer* 1 (October, 1921):20–27.

The history of copper smelting from the ancient world to the present. What is needed now is not thrilling revolt but day-to-day organizing.

1399. Hand, Wayland D. "Folklore, Customs, and Traditions of the Butte Miner." *California Folklore Quarterly* 5 (January, 1946):1–25; (April, 1946):153–76.

1400. Hanson, Nils H. "Among the Harvesters." *International Socialist Review* 16 (August, 1915):75–78.

1401. ———. "Texas Justice! 99 Years!" *International Socialist Review* 16 (February, 1916):476–78.

The sentencing of labor radicals to such long terms is outrageous: Rangel and Cline were the victims of injustice and prejudice.

1402. ———. "Threshing Wheat." *International Socialist Review* 16 (December, 1915):344–47.

Hanson's personal experiences threshing in the grain belt. Workers must force employers to come through with what they need.

1403. Hanson, Ole. "Fighting the Reds in Their Home Town": *World's Work* 39 (December, 1919 to March, 1920); "Why and How I Became Mayor of Seattle" (December, 1919):123–26; "Smashing the Soviet in Seattle" (January, 1920):202–7; "Seattle's Red Revolution" (February, 1920):401–8; "The Victory over Seattle Reds" (March, 1920):484–87.

An account of the Seattle General Strike by the mayor.

1404. Hard, William. "After the Strike." *New Republic* 21 (January 28, 1920):259–62.

The role of Catholic priests, the IWW, and others in the U.S. Steel strike.

1405. ———. "Moments in the Steel Strike: Mr. Brown Is Talking about the IWW." *New Republic* 21 (December 3, 1919):23.

Quoting a desperate AFL member: "IWW don't have to eat. He don't have to sleep. He leaks through a brick wall."

1406. ———. "Perhaps the Turn of the Tide." *New Republic* 21 (February 11, 1920):313–16.

The defeat of the Graham anti-free-speech bill may turn back the tide now sweeping over civil liberties.

1407. ———. "Western Federation of Miners." *Outlook* 83 (May 19, 1906):125–33.

The WFM's radicalism prevents it from joining with the AFL, but, in any case, WFM members are just adventurous native-born Americans.

1408. ———. "William Z. Foster." *New Republic* 21 (January 7, 1920): 163–66.

Foster was jailed for his connections with the IWW.

1409. "Hard to Draw to." *Miners Magazine* 12 (November 7, 1912):5.

Criticism of William Haywood and Fred Heslewood for seeking to involve the Socialist Party in violence.

1410. Hardoen, Robert H. "The Negro Worker Falls into Line." *Industrial Pioneer* 1 (October, 1921):13–15.

Details the various ideological groups with which Negro workers have banded. Hardoen, however, believes that only class justice will free them.

1411. Hardy, George. "As to the Third International." *One Big Union Monthly* 2 (October, 1920):24.

Hopes that the IWW will support the Third International.

1412. ———. "George Hardy on the I.W.W." *Industrial Pioneer* 1 (May, 1921):12–13.

Report from ex-member George Hardy, who went to Russia. Europeans are rigidly Syndicalist, compared to the flexible Americans.

1413. ———. "International Class Unionism." *Industrial Pioneer* 1 (August, 1921):5–8.

1414. ———. "Shop Organization the Base of the IWW." *One Big Union Monthly* 2 (June, 1920):30–36.

1415. Harn, Harry. "An American Trade Unionist in Ruined Russia." *American Federationist* 30 (May, 1923):369–70.
An unfavorable account of Kemerovo and Haywood.

1416. "Harold Lord Varney 'Exposes' the I.W.W." *One Big Union Monthly* 2 (March, 1920):35–39.
Varney was a spy and is a turncoat.

1417. Harriman, Job. "The Class War in Idaho." *Miners Magazine* 5 (October 8, 1903):8.
One of a series of articles on Idaho labor history taken from a pamphlet, no. 3718.

1418. Harris, Ellis B. "Annie Clemenc." *Miners Magazine* 15 (March 19, 1914):14.
"Big Annie"'s role in the Calumet-Hecla strike.

1419. Hartman, Fred H. "The I.W.W.: A Scapegoat." *Radical Review* 2 (July, 1918):54–61.
A WIIU viewpoint.

1420. *Harvard Lampoon* 78 (January 16, 1920).
The entire issue is devoted to humorous comment and satire on the Red Scare, Bolsheviks, and the IWW.

1421. Haug, Charles J. "The Industrial Workers of the World in North Dakota, 1913–1917." *North Dakota Quarterly* 39 (Winter, 1971):85–102.

1422. "Have They Lost?" *Square Deal* 13 (September, 1913):190–91.
The Paterson strike.

1423. Hawley, James H. "Steve Adam's Confession and the State's Case against Bill Haywood." *Idaho Yesterdays* 7 (Winter, 1963–64):16–27.
The first Haywood trial.

1424. Hayes, John. "Scabs Again." *International Socialist Review* 14 (May, 1914):688.
St. Louis Bag and Trunk Workers experienced intolerable scabbing.

1425. Hayes, Max. "World of Labor." *International Socialist Review* 5 (February, 1905):500–502; (June, 1905):753–55; (September, 1905):181–82.
The IWW's development as a union.

1426. ———. "World of Labor." *International Socialist Review* 6 (January, 1906):434–36.
Comments on IWW activities.

1427. ———. "World of Labor." *International Socialist Review* 7 (July, 1906):54–57.
Comments on IWW activities.

1428. ———. "World of Labor." *Miners Magazine* 7 (January 25, 1906): 12–13.
IWW is gaining strength in Chicago and Schenectady.

1429. ———. "World of Labor." *Miners Magazine* 11 (January 13, 1909):11–12; (October 21, 1909):7.
The New Castle and McKees Rocks strikes.

1430. Hayhand, John. "Following the Trail of Industry." *Industrial Pioneer* 2 (August, 1924):13–14.
The industrialization of farm work and workers.

1431. Hayner, N. S. "Taming the Lumber Jack." *American Sociological Review* 10 (April, 1945):217–25.
Domestication is beginning to tame the "bindlestiffs," or migrant workers.

1432. Haynes, John E. "Revolt of the Timberbeasts: IWW Strike in Minnesota." *Minnesota History* 42 (Spring, 1971):160–74.

1433. Hays, Arthur G. "The Right To Get Shot." *Nation* 134 (June 1, 1932):619.
How the IWW forced out the UMW and in turn was forced out by the NMU.

1434. Haywood, William D. "An Appeal for Industrial Solidarity." *International Socialist Review* 14 (March, 1914):544–46.

1435. ———. "The Battle at Butte." *International Socialist Review* 15 (October, 1914):223–26.
The IWW's battle with the WFM over Miner's Union No. 1.

1436. ———. "Blanket Stiff Philosophy." *International Socialist Review* 12 (December, 1911):320.
Slogans and aphoristic sayings pertaining to migrant workers.

1437. ———. "Blanket Stiff Philosophy." *International Socialist Review* 13 (September, 1912):258.
Sayings and slogans.

1438. ———. "Break the Conspiracy." *One Big Union Monthly* 1 (December, 1919):6–7.
A plea for moral and financial support for the political prisoners.

1439. ———. "Butte Better." *International Socialist Review* 15 (February, 1915):473–75.
Butte is recovering from a period of martial law.

1440. ———. "A Detective." *International Socialist Review* 12 (December, 1911):345.
Aphorisms and sayings about industrial spies.

1441. ———. "The Fighting IWW." *International Socialist Review* 13 (September, 1912):247.

1442. ———. "The General Defense." *One Big Union Monthly* 2 (July, 1920):16.
Asks support for the IWW prisoners.

1443. ———. "The General Defense." *One Big Union Monthly* 2 (August, 1920):16.
Asks support for the IWW prisoners.

1444. ———. "General Defense." *One Big Union Monthly* 2 (September, 1920):58–59.
Asks support for the IWW prisoners.

1445. ———. "General Defense." *One Big Union Monthly* 2 (October, 1920):15.
Asks support for the IWW prisoners.

1446. ———. "The General Strike." *International Socialist Review* 11 (May, 1911):680–84.
The meaning and techniques of a general strike.

1447. ———. "Haywood Demands Proof from Mr. Simons." *International Socialist Review* 12 (May, 1912):785.
Haywood's philosophical differences with A. M. Simons of the Socialist Party. Haywood believes that Simons does not understand his position.

1448. ———. "Industrial Unionism." *Miners Magazine* 6 (May 11, 1905):6.

1449. ———. "Industrial Unionism." *Voice of Labor* 3 (June, 1905):3–4.

1450. ———. "Insurance against Agitation." *Masses* 5 (February, 1914):22.
Henry Ford's philanthropy is a form of insurance.

1451. ———. "The IWW Prisoners." *One Big Union Monthly* 2 (May, 1920):9–11.

1452. ———. "Jim Larkin's Call for Solidarity." *International Socialist Review* 14 (1913–1914):469–74.

1453. ———. "A Letter from Bill Haywood." *Labor Defender* 3 (June, 1928):129.
Letter received from Haywood shortly before news of his death in Russia arrived, in which he tells a little about his life and asks after friends.

1454. ———. "A Message from Bill Haywood." *Labor Defender* 1 (June, 1926):86.
A letter from Moscow recalling the many IWW prisoners still in jail and asking support for the ILD.

1455. ———. "Message to the Deportees." *One Big Union Monthly* 1 (May, 1919):41.
Message from the imprisoned Haywood, wishing the deportees a happier and freer life than they had in America.

1456. ———. "On the Inside." *Liberator* 1 (May, 1918):15–16.
Life at the Cook County jail during the Chicago trial.

1457. ———. "On the Paterson Picket Line." *International Socialist Review* 13 (June, 1913):847–51.

1458. ———. "On the Picket Line at Little Falls, New York." *International Socialist Review* 13 (January, 1913):519–23.

1459. ———. "Open Letter to the American Congress." *One Big Union Monthly* 1 (December, 1919):17–18.
Demands a Congressional investigation of the Centralia Massacre.

1460. ———. "Organize—Organize Right!" *International Socialist Review* 17 (November, 1916):291–92.

1461. ———. "Pick and Shovel Pointers." *International Socialist Review* 12 (July, 1911):7.
Humorous little sayings related to labor.

1462. ———. "'Reasonable' Crime." *International Socialist Review* 12 (August, 1911):84–85.
Incidents of mine owners covering up criminal negligence.

1463. ———. "Revolt at Butte." *International Socialist Review* 15 (August, 1914):89–96.

Detailed account of the WFM-IWW fight to control Butte Miners Union No. 1.

1464. ———. "The Rip in the Silk Industry." *International Socialist Review* 13 (May, 1913):783–88.

Analysis of the Paterson strike.

1465. ———. "Sentenced To Be Shot—Act Quick." *International Socialist Review* 16 (August, 1915):110.

Plea for funds for the defense of Joe Hill.

1466. ———. "Shots for the Workshop." *International Socialist Review* 11 (April, 1911):588.

Humorous sayings for the working man.

1467. ———. "Smoothing Out the Wrinkles in Silk." In *Pageant of the Paterson Strike*. (New York: Success Press, 1913), 22–27.

1468. ———. "Socialism: The Hope of the Working Class." *International Socialist Review* 12 (February, 1912):461–71.

1469. ———. "Solidarity in Prison." *International Socialist Review* 10 (June, 1910):1065.

Plea for the moral and financial support of IWW and Socialist prisoners in jail in New Castle, Pennsylvania, and in Milwaukee, humiliating punishment for editors who are just trying to print the truth.

1470. ———. "Timber Workers and Timber Wolves." *International Socialist Review* 13 (August, 1912):105–10.

Explains the Southern lumber strikes and describes charismatic Brotherhood of Timber Workers leader Arthur Emerson. Strike activities at Grabow are reported.

1471. ———. "To the Membership." *International Socialist Review* 13 (October, 1912):372.

The dissension in the Socialist Party.

1472. ———. "When the Kiddies Came Home." *International Socialist Review* 12 (May, 1912):716–17.

The use of children in the Lawrence strike.

1473. ———. "With Drops of Blood the History of the Industrial Workers of the World Has Been Written." *One Big Union Monthly* 1 (October, 1919):5–8.

1474. ———. "With the Copper Miners of Michigan." *International Socialist Review* 11 (August, 1910):65–68.

1475. Haywood, William D.; Frank Bohn; John Moody; and George K. Turner. "The Problem and Its Solution." *International Socialist Review* 12 (December, 1911):368.
Juxtaposes quotations from Turner and Moody with those of Haywood and Bohn, showing their totally contrasting viewpoints.

1476. Haywood, William D., and Joseph Ettor. "What the IWW Intends to Do to the USA." *Solidarity* 5 (June 27, 1914):3.
The general strike is the primary tool of the IWW.

1477. Haywood, William D., and William E. Trautmann. "Important Information." *Miners Magazine* 6 (June 8, 1905):5.
How to attend the first IWW convention.

1478. "Haywood Accepts the Socialist Nomination for Governor." *Miners Magazine* 8 (July 26, 1906):8–9.
Haywood's program and platform in his run for the Colorado governorship.

1479. "Haywood an Anarchist? So Debs Infers." *Wilshires Magazine* 17 (May, 1913):6–7.

1480. "Haywood and Direct Action." *Common Cause* 2 (August, 1912): 201–2.

1481. "Haywood and the IWW." *International Socialist Review* 14 (November, 1913):277.

1482. "Haywood at Uniontown, Pa." *International Socialist Review* 13 (October, 1912):374.
A detailed description of the occasion of a Haywood speech. Thousands gathered to hear him even though the papers all refused to print a notice of it.

1483. "Haywood Demands an Investigation." *International Socialist Review* 13 (April, 1913):769.
Moyer and the WFM called to task for printing Germer's article, which accuses Haywood of mishandling funds. He denies it and challenges them to make an audit. See no. 1293.

1484. "Haywood Home Again." *Miners Magazine* 9 (August 8, 1907):4.
Haywood and his family are greeted by cheering thousands after the Idaho trial.

1485. "The Haywood Meetings." *International Socialist Review* 11 (March, 1911):557.
Meetings at which Haywood spoke.

1486. "Haywood Not Guilty." *Miners Magazine* 9 (August 1, 1907):3, 8.
Verdict of the first Haywood trial.

1487. "Haywood in Europe." *International Socialist Review* 11 (November, 1910):286–88.

1488. "Haywood on Stand." *Labor Defender* 1 (September 1, 1918):7.
Haywood's testimony at the Chicago trial.

1489. "Haywood on the Flag." *Common Cause* 3 (March, 1913):272.
Haywood on patriotism and its uses.

1490. "Haywood Speaks in Allentown." *Nome Industrial Worker* 2 (May 1, 1908):3.
Speech is reported in great detail and is admired for its epigrams, style, and spirit.

1491. "The Haywood Trial." *Idaho Yesterdays* 25 (Spring, 1981):68.

1492. "The Haywood Trial." *Outlook* 86 (June 22, 1907):350–53.

1493. "Haywood Tries To Explain." *Common Cause* 2 (November, 1912):660.
Haywood's explanation for the "No God—No Master" sign carried in the Lawrence strikers' parade.

1494. "Haywood's Acquittal." *Nation* 85 (August 1, 1907):92.
The "murderous" character of the IWW is not alleviated by Haywood's acquittal.

1495. "Haywood's Arrest." *Literary Digest* 45 (September 28, 1912): 502–3.
Haywood's arrest during the Lawrence strike, with good photographs.

1496. "Haywood's Battle in Paterson." *Literary Digest* 46 (May 10, 1913): 1043–44.

1497. "Haywood's Conviction Upheld: Documents of an Association May Be Used in Evidence To Convict Its Members." *Law and Labor* 2 (November, 1920):252–55.

1498. "Haywood's Impudence." *Square Deal* 11 (October, 1911):284–85.
Criticizes Haywood's comments about "paralyzing industry."

1499. "Haywood's Letter to Moyer and Moyer's Answer." *Miners Magazine* 13 (March 13, 1913):8.

1500. "Haywood's Luminous Thought." *Miners Magazine* 7 (September 7, 1905):10.
Envisages a federal system of unions. If industrial unions were states, craft unions would fit in as counties.

1501. Hazard, Henry. "A Modern General Strike." *Industrial Pioneer* 1 (October, 1923):3–4, 26.
The short general strike in the Pacific Northwest in 1923.

1502. "He Died with His Boots On." *Miners Magazine* 11 (September 9, 1909):7–10.
Chief witness against Preston and Smith at Goldfield is murdered and then discovered to have been a member of the Butch Cassidy gang.

1503. "He Is Wiser Now." *Miners Magazine* 21 (October, 1920):1–2.
Raymond Fanning, released IWW prisoner, recants.

1504. "He Knows 'Big Bill.'" *Miners Magazine* 21 (August, 1920):1–2.
Harold Lord Varney's description of William Haywood as an opportunist and mediocrity.

1505. "He Strikes from the Shoulder." *Miners Magazine* 12 (June 20, 1912):8–9.
The ouster of Haywood from the Socialist Party.

1506. "Heart to Heart Talk with Railway Workers." *Industrial Pioneer* 1 (June, 1921):40–44.
Says craft unionism spoiled railway workers' strike in 1920 and will continue to fail them.

1507. Heaton, James P. "The Legal Aftermath of the Lawrence Strike." *Survey* 28 (July 6, 1912):503–10.
States that Lawrence is the first time since Haymarket that labor leaders have been prosecuted as accessories to murder.

1508. ———. "The Salem Trial." *Survey* 29 (December 7, 1912):301–4.
The Lawrence strike trial.

1509. Hedrick, P. C. "The I.W.W. and Mayor Hanson." *Unpartizan Review* 12 (July, 1919):35–45.
Spokane's police chief, a former friend of Bat Masterson and Wyatt Earp, applies frontier techniques he learned from them to the IWW.

1510. Hein, Carl. "William Haywood and the Syndicalist Faith." In Harvey Goldberg, ed., *American Radicals: Some Problems and Personalities* (New York: Monthly Review Press, 1957), 179–97.

1511. Heitzman, Jim. "Wasted Union Blues: Centralia 1919 Legacy of Guilt." *Klipsun* 6 (Spring, 1972):32–37 (publication of Western Washington State College).

1512. "Helen Keller Scores IWW Persecutions." *Labor Defender* 1 (February 16, 1918):1.

1513. "Help Cleanse the Labor Movement." *Miners Magazine* 19 (April, 1918):4.

The IWW should be "demolished."

1514. Henry, W. G. "Bingham Canyon." *International Socialist Review* 13 (October, 1912):341–43.

Organizing the copper miners in Utah.

1515. "A Hero—for Lucre." *Square Deal* 11 (December, 1911):478–79.

Money contributed to Joseph Ettor after the Lawrence strike was more important to him than the praise he received.

1516. "A Heroine Whose Name Is Not Found in the Society Columns." *Miners Magazine* 14 (October 23, 1913):4–5.

Essay on Annie Clemenc, parade leader at the Michigan copper strike.

1517. Herreshoff, David. "Daniel De Leon: The Rise of Marxist Politics." In Harvey Goldberg, ed., *American Radicals: Some Problems and Personalities* (New York: Monthly Review Press, 1957), 199–215.

1518. Heslewood, Fred. "Barbarous Spokane." *International Socialist Review* 10 (February, 1910):705–13.

Police treated the IWWs brutally during and after the Spokane Free Speech Fight.

1519. ———. "Relations of Trade-Unions and the Political Party." *Industrial Union Bulletin* (September 14, 1907):1, 5.

Report from the International Trade Union Congress.

1520. Hibschman, Harry. "The IWW Menace Self-Revealed." *Current History* 16 (August, 1922):761–68.

American Legion attorney discussing Centralia. See no. 2821.

1521. Higgins, E. J. "Direct Action *versus* Impossibilism." *Mother Earth* 7 (April, 1912):39–45.

1522. Hill, Eli. "Attack and Counter-Attack." *One Big Union Monthly* NS 1 (April, 1938):9–13.

A historical listing of IWW strategies and tactics in the class struggle.

1523. Hill, Joe. "How To Make Work for the Unemployed." *International Socialist Review* 15 (December, 1914):335–36.

By working more slowly, a form of sabotage, workers create more jobs for the unemployed.

1524. ———. "Scissor Bill." *International Socialist Review* 16 (December, 1915):326–27.

Chumley's drawing, with Joe Hill's famous verse about scissorbills.

1525. ———. "To the People of Utah." *International Socialist Review* 16 (October, 1915):222–23.

Joe's letter saying he did not kill Morrison, but because he had lived like an artist he would die like an artist.

1526. Hill, Mary A. "The Free Speech Fight at San Diego." *Survey* 28 (May 4, 1912):192–94.

1527. Hillier, Alfred J. "Albert Johnson, Congressman." *Pacific Northwest Quarterly* 36 (July, 1945):193–211.

Describes the effect of the IWW on Johnson's political career.

1528. Hilton, Judge O. N. "A Challenge: Open Letter to the Board of Pardons of the State of Utah." *International Socialist Review* 16 (December, 1915):328.

Asks to discuss Joe Hill's case in person with the Board of Pardons, so that a judicial murder may be avoided.

1529. ———. "Judge O. N. Hilton on the Joe Hill Case." *International Socialist Review* 16 (September, 1915):171–72.

Defense argument for Joe Hill.

1530. Hilton, O. A. "Oklahoma Council of Defense and the First World War." *Chronicles of Oklahoma* 20 (March, 1942):18–42.

1531. "Hired Detective Chief Apostle of Anarchy." *Miners Magazine* 15 (April 1, 1915):1, 4.

The fight between the IWW and the WFM over the Butte Miners Union.

1532. "A History-Making Convention." *International Socialist Review* 12 (June, 1912):873–75.

The Socialist Party convention that ousted Haywood.

1533. "History Repeats Itself." *Miners Magazine* 7 (March 1, 1906):3–15.

The Steunenberg story, in detail, with a description of the kidnapping of Haywood and Moyer.

1534. Hitch, Marcus. "Violence in Class Struggles." *International Socialist Review* 12 (February, 1912):491–93.

1535. "Hoarse." *New Yorker* 22 (October 26, 1946):25.
Recollections of Elizabeth Gurley Flynn.

1536. Hobby, Daniel T., ed. "We Have Got Results: A Document on the Organization of Domestics in the Progressive Era." *Labor History* 17 (Winter, 1976):103–8.
How the IWW organized domestic workers in Colorado in 1917.

1537. "Hoboes' Convention." *Solidarity* 2 (February 18, 1911):1, 4.
A big convention of the unemployed in Milwaukee to which the IWW sent a delegate.

1538. Hodges, Leroy. "Immigrant Life in the Ore Region of Northern Minnesota." *Survey* 28 (September 7, 1912):703–9.

1539. Hofteling, Catherine. "Arbuckle and the IWW." *Nation* 116 (February 14, 1923):170–71.
Sacramento Syndicalist prisoners did not get the kind of publicity Fatty Arbuckle did.

1540. ———. "The IWW to Warren G. Harding." *Nation* 117 (August 29, 1923):217.
The request for a pardon or commutation for the IWW prisoners.

1541. ———. "Sunkist Prisoners." *Nation* 113 (September 21, 1921):316.
The IWW was convicted on false evidence in the Syndicalist trials.

1542. Hogaboom, W. "Last Stand at Goldfield: Trouble between the Western Federation of Miners and the Goldfield Mine Operators Association." *Overland* 51 (February, 1908):111–19.

1543. Hokanson, Nels. "Swedes and the I.W.W." *Swedish Pioneer Historical Quarterly* 23 (January, 1972):25–35.

1544. Holbrook, Stewart. "Daylight in the Swamp." *American Heritage* 9 (October, 1958):1–19, 77–80.
Logging and unionism.

1545. ———. "Last of the Wobblies." *American Mercury* 62 (April, 1946):462–68.
About Arthur Boose, a beloved old-time Wobbly.

1546. ———. "Wobbly Talk." *American Mercury* 7 (January, 1926):62–65.
Slang from the IWW.

1547. "Hold the Fort: Grand Entertainment." *International Socialist Review* 18 (November–December, 1917):279.
The program of Cook County jail's IWW prisoners' entertainment.

1548. Hold, Upton. "Salting Down the Marine Workers." *Industrial Pioneer* 1 (October, 1921):34–38.
Sailors all over the world are becoming interested in the IWW.

1549. ———. "Tieing the Shot on the Corpse." *Industrial Pioneer* 1 (November, 1921):6.
Describes the effect of declared open shop policy on the ISU and invites all marine workers to join the IWW.

1550. Holmen, Ernest. "Has the I.W.W. a Monopoly of Industrial Organization?" *One Big Union Monthly* 2 (January, 1920):51–52.
The IWW is not an enemy of the AFL or of the International Federation of Workers, but rather an enemy of craft unionism.

1551. Holmes, John Haynes. "Tannenbaum in the Large." *Survey* 32 (April 25, 1914):94–96.
Frank Tannenbaum and his handling of the unemployed in New York.

1552. "The Homeless Pacifists." *Bellman* 23 (September 8, 1917):259.
Opposition to People's Councils.

1553. Hooper, Charles. "A Seattle Shepherd." *Survey* 39 (December 8, 1917):299.
Defends the IWWs against those who call them damnable, asserting that it is society that is sick.

1554. "The Hop-Pickers' Strike." *Life and Labor* 4 (May, 1914):151–52.

1555. Hopkins, Ernest J. "San Diego Fight." *Coming Nation* (May 4, 1912):7–9.
The San Diego Free Speech Fight.

1556. Hough, Merrill. "Leadville and the Western Federation of Miners." *Colorado Magazine* 49 (Winter, 1972):19–34.

1557. House, A. E. "The IWW: An Outlaw Organization." *Survey* 30 (September 13, 1913):723.

1558. "How about Those Bombs? The Intelligence of Our Senators." *Voice in the Wilderness* 2 (July, 1919):39–41.
There is something suspicious about the bomb rumors and scares, probably a government frame-up.

1559. "How Does the Public?" *New Republic* 13 (January 5, 1918):262.
The President's Commission's report on the Bisbee deportations does not get much newspaper coverage because many people do not like its findings.

1560. "How Governors Would Cope with Proposed General Strike." *Square Deal* 8 (July, 1911):506.
The idea of a general strike was proposed in America by Haywood.

1561. "How It's Done in California." *Industrial Pioneer* 2 (July, 1924):35–36.
The California Syndicalist trials.

1562. "How the Capitalists Solve the Problem of the Unemployed." *International Socialist Review* 14 (May, 1914):648–50.
The Unemployed March to Sacramento was greeted with fire-hoses and arrests; readers are invited to the San Diego Free Speech Fight.

1563. "How the IWW Looks at Close Range." *Miners Magazine* 14 (July 17, 1913):15.
The shingle weavers in the Pacific Northwest.

1564. "How the Spruce Production Investigation Is Progressing." *American Lumberman* 2311 (August 30, 1919):47–48.
The government's spruce drive and the Four Ls union.

1565. "How To Fight on the Job." *International Socialist Review* 16 (April, 1916):619–21.

1566. Howard, Joseph K. "Butte Remembers Big Bill Haywood." *Nation* 141 (October 30, 1935):514–15.

1567. Howard, Sidney. "Our Professional Patriots." *New Republic* 40 (October 8, 1924):143.
The Red Scare in California.

1568. Howe, F. C. "Where Are the Pre-War Radicals—Reply." *Survey* 56 (April 1, 1926):33–34.
Pre-war radicals are digging turnips and going intellectual,

but there are plenty of evangelists who want to change people rather than institutions. See no. 3226.

1569. "Howl, Slaves, Howl." *Miners Magazine* 11 (September 30, 1909): 7–8.
Mounted police chase strikers during the McKees Rocks strike.

1570. Hoxie, Robert F. "American Economist on Syndicalism." *New Review* 2 (May, 1914):308–9.

1571. ———. "The Truth about the Industrial Workers of the World." *Journal of Political Economy* 21 (November, 1913):785–97.
The IWW is not really a union.

1572. ———. "The Truth about the I.W.W." *International Molders Journal* 50 (January, 1914):6–13.
Reprint of no. 1571.

1573. Hull, Ernest D. "Shall We Recall the Recall?" *New Review* 1 (May, 1913):543–44.
Haywood's ouster from the Socialist Party.

1574. "Human Vermin." *American Law Review* 53 (May, 1919):430–32.
On the IWW and other war dissenters.

1575. Hunter, Robert. "The General Strike: Is It a Disease of Infancy?" *Miners Magazine* 13 (January 9, 1913):9–10.
Haywood and the General Strike.

1576. ———. "Socialists and Syndicalism: Violence and the Labor Movement." *Nation* 98 (April 16, 1914):434–35.
The antagonism between Syndicalism and Socialism.

1577. ———. "The Trade Union and the Socialist Party: IV, the Industrial Union." *Miners Magazine* 12 (March 14, 1912):11–12.
Describes the IWW "impossibilists."

1578. "I Decide to Become a Wobbly." *One Big Union Monthly* NS 1 (September, 1937):5–7.
The Marine Transport Workers.

1579. "If I Had My Way." *New Republic* 35 (August 22, 1923):342–43.
W. M. Smelzer, chairman of the Board of Review, U.S. Department of Labor, believes that each and every IWW member should be hanged.

1580. "Ill Weeds Grow Apace." *Living Age* 295 (November 24, 1917): 492–93.
The IWW is not large, but its power for mischief is.

1581. Illinois Manufacturers' Association. "I W of W at Work in Illinois." *International Socialist Review* 14 (September, 1913):76.
A warning about the IWW's power to make trouble.

1582. "In Memoriam—Fred Moore." *Freedom* 1 (September, 1933):4.
Tribute to the well-liked IWW defense lawyer.

1583. "In the Best Tradition." *New Republic* 20 (November 26, 1919):363.
Only two newspapers spoke out against the Red Scare hysteria over the IWW and Bolshevism.

1584. "In the Copper Country." *American Industries* 14 (February, 1913):10.
Michigan miners are being exploited by their unions.

1585. "An Incident in a Sailor's Life." *Industrial Pioneer* 2 (October, 1924):13–14.
The Marine Transport Workers Union.

1586. "Indict Bisbee Deporters." *Miners Magazine* 19 (June, 1918):1.

1587. "The Indomitable Spirit of Mother Jones." *Current Opinion* 55 (July, 1913):19–20.
Describes Mother Jones.

1588. "Industrial Action News." *International Socialist Review* 17 (June, 1917):727–28.
Describes the trial of Tom Tracy after the Everett Massacre, at which he was acquitted.

1589. "Industrial Conditions: Baltimore." *Square Deal* 14 (June, 1914):461–62.
An attempt to agitate the masses in Baltimore on May Day.

1590. "The Industrial Encyclopedia." *One Big Union Monthly* 1 (December, 1919):15.
The IWW is planning to compile an encyclopedia.

1591. "An Industrial International." *One Big Union Monthly* 2 (April, 1920):5–7.
International possibilities for the IWW.

1592. "Industrial Organization of the Workers." *Miners Magazine* 6 (March 23, 1905):15.
Includes an early copy of Hagerty's chart.

1593. "Industrial Organization of the Workers." *Voice of Labor* 3 (May, 1905):2.

Explains the new union and includes a chart.

1594. "Industrial Relations Commission." *Survey* 33 (December 12, 1914):303–4.

Letters of G. P. West and Basil Manby.

1595. "Industrial Relations Committee Reports." *Outlook* 111 (September, 1915):7–9.

1596. "Industrial Relations; Report of the Industrial Commission." *Century* 92 (May, 1916):153–54.

Negative opinion of the findings of the Industrial Commission.

1597. "Industrial Science and Organization." *Industrial Pioneer* 1 (August, 1921):16.

1598. "The Industrial Union Convention." *Voice of Labor* 3 (April, 1905):14.

The call for an industrial union convention may be spurious.

1599. "Industrial Union Convention—a Discussion." *Voice of Labor* 3 (May, 1905):3–11.

Other opinions on the first industrial union convention.

1600. "Industrial Union Manifesto." *Voice of Labor* 3 (March, 1905):3–5.

1601. "Industrial Unionism." *International Socialist Review* 17 (October, 1916):222–23.

1602. "Industrial Unionism." *Miners Magazine* 6 (February 2, 1905):8.

A pressing need for a unifying union rather than a divisive one.

1603. "Industrial Unionism." *Socialist* 1 (May 6, 1919):6.

1604. "Industrial Unionism and Its Ideals." *Review of Reviews* 45 (June, 1912):744–46.

1605. "Industrial Unionism and the Building Trades." *Industrial Pioneer* 3 (October, 1925):10–14.

1606. "Industrial Unionism in Building Industry." *Industrial Pioneer* 2 (July, 1924):27–28.

1607. "Industrial Unionism: Labor's Only Answer to Imperialized Capital, by J.M.G." *International Socialist Review* 18 (July, 1917):26–27.

1608. "Industrial Unionism or Destruction—The Industrial Railroad Workers." *International Socialist Review* 14 (June, 1914):761–63.
Industrial unions in Pennsylvania.

1609. "Industrial War." *Locomotive Engineers' Monthly Journal* 47 (August, 1913):702–3.

1610. "Industrial War at McKees Rocks." *Outlook* 93 (September 4, 1909):1–3.

1611. "Industrial War in Colorado." *Review of Reviews* 49 (June, 1914): 732–34.
The Colorado coal strike.

1612. "Industrial Workers." *Miners Magazine* 8 (August 9, 1906):9.
The growth of industrial unionism.

1613. "Industrial Workers." *Independent* 72 (May 9, 1912):1020–21.
The IWW and IWW techniques.

1614. "Industrial Workers' Mass Meeting in New York." *Miners Magazine* 7 (September 14, 1905):7.
A meeting called to try to unite all unions.

1615. "Industrial Workers of the World." *Miners Magazine* 7 (September 14, 1905):6.
The new union that the WFM will join.

1616. "Industrial Workers of the World." *Survey* 28 (May 4, 1912):222.
The IWW and the Lawrence strike.

1617. "The Industrial Workers of the World." *Miners Magazine* 12 (August 22, 1912):4–5.
Description and unfavorable opinion.

1618. "The Industrial Workers of the World." (Detroit) *Motorman and Conductor* 21 (August, 1913):4–5.
Description and opinion.

1619. "The Industrial Workers of the World." *Miners Magazine* 14 (October 2, 1913):6.
Description and opinion.

1620. "The Industrial Workers of the World." *One Big Union Monthly* NS 2 (February, 1938):32–33.
The chief aim of the IWW is to abolish wage slavery.

1621. "Industrial Workers of the World and the New York Waiters." *Square Deal* 12 (February, 1913):29–32.
The IWW attempt to organize New York restaurant workers.

1622. "The Industrial Workers of the World Make Confession." *Square Deal* 13 (October, 1913):236–38.
Derides comments in the IWW newspaper *Solidarity*.

1623. "Industrial Workers of the World: Their French Progenitors." *Steam Shovel Magazine* (September, 1914):9–10.
French Syndicalism as the source of the IWW.

1624. "Industrial Workers Who Won't Work." *Literary Digest* 55 (July 28, 1917):20–21.
About the Bisbee deportation and the many lumber strikes.

1625. "Industrialism." *Miners Magazine* 6 (February 23, 1905):6.
As offer by Haywood to send the new chart of industrial unionism to all subscribers.

1626. "Industrialism." *Miners Magazine* 7 (February 1, 1906):9.
IWW declines any relationship with the UMW.

1627. "An Infamous Circular." *Shoe Workers Journal* 13 (July, 1912):5–7.
The Socialists have always tried to split established unions as a recent circular proves. The IWW must be involved, as it claims that the Shoe Workers Union is working with the employers.

1628. "Infant Revolutionists." *Independent* 78 (April 13, 1914):80–81.
A recent "IWW revolutionary riot" turned out to be a prank of children. The real revolution will come when we have electronic communication and people can be aroused faster and in greater numbers.

1629. Ingham, John M. "A Strike in the Progressive Era: McKees Rocks, 1909." *Pennsylvania Magazine of History and Biography* 90 (July, 1966):353–77.

1630. "Inside." *International Socialist Review* 18 (November–December, 1917):268–70.
On the arrests and imprisonment of many radicals.

1631. "An Interesting Infant." *Miners Magazine* 12 (October 17, 1912): 8–9.
The IWW will end up in the potter's field of history.

1632. "An Interesting Revelation of IWW Methods." *Law and Labor* 4 (December, 1922):340–42.

1633. "Internal Warfare To Disrupt I.W.W." *Garment Worker* 12 (September 26, 1913):2.

The Detroit faction of the IWW and possible decentralist activities in the IWW.

1634. "International Relations of the I.W.W." *Industrial Relations* 1 (July, 1921):24–25.
The growing international connections of the IWW.

1635. "Investigation of the Strike in the Michigan Copper Region." *Square Deal* 14 (March, 1914):121–26.

1636. Irwin, Will. "Patriotism That Pays." *Nation* 119 (November 12, 1924):513–16.
Discusses the Bolshevik scare and the currently popular "spider web" charts that seek to prove conspiratorial radical connections.

1637. "Is Civil Liberty Dead?" *Liberator* 1 (November, 1918):43.
Criticizes government raids and the IWW trials.

1638. "Is Haywood a Traitor?" *Wilshire's Magazine* 17 (January, 1913):4.
Has Haywood betrayed the Socialist Party?

1639. "Is Justice Dead in Tonopah?" *Voice of the People* 2 (October 1, 1914):1.
A report about John Pancner, who organized the hotel and restaurant workers and helped them win an eight-hour day. With police watching, a mob of people attacked Pancner, who shot a man in the leg. It was Pancner they arrested.

1640. "Is There Any Justification for Violent Methods in Industrial Struggles?" *Current Opinion* 54 (June, 1913):484–85.

1641. "Is Violence Their Only Answer?" *Appeal to Reason* 1223 (May 10, 1919):1.

1642. "Is Your Job 100% I.W.W.?" *One Big Union Monthly* NS 1 (April, 1937):11.
The Marine Transport Workers union.

1643. "Issue at Lawrence: The Manufacturers' Point of View." *Outlook* 100 (February 24, 1912):405–6.

1644. "The Issue before the Membership." *Miners Magazine* 12 (May 30, 1912):5–6.
No affiliation with the IWW.

1645. "Issue in Colorado." *Literary Digest* 48 (May 9, 1914):1099–1101.
The Colorado coal strike.

1646. "Issue in Colorado." *Independent* 78 (May 11, 1914):248–49.
The Colorado coal strike.

1647. "It Happened to a Direct Actionist." *Miners Magazine* 12 (December 12, 1912):6–7.
Sarcastic account of a physical attack on Haywood and the fisticuffs that followed.

1648. "It's Getting So Big Bill Haywood—" *Miners Magazine* 12 (October 3, 1912):4.
Criticism of Haywood's organizing tactics.

1649. Ivey, Paul W. "Economic Significance of the Calumet Strike Situation." *Review of Reviews* 49 (April, 1914):445–46.

1650. "IW of W Followers Are Now Object of the A.F. of L. Agitators." *Square Deal* 11 (October, 1911):245–49.
The AFL will eventually recognize and wish to organize unskilled foreign labor.

1651."The I.W.W." *Miners Magazine* 12 (August 1, 1912):5.
The IWW is an enemy of labor because of its fights against other unions.

1652. "IWW." *Survey* 31 (December 13, 1913):312.
André Tridon, Louis Levine, and T. Proctor Hall on the IWW.

1653. "The IWW." Review of *The IWW*, by Paul Brissenden (see no. 18). *Nation* 109 (October 4, 1919):468–69.

1654. "IWW Activity in Illinois." *International Socialist Review* 14 (January, 1914):76.

1655. "IWW Acts for Centralia Victims." *Industrial Unionist* 1 (September 16, 1925):1.
The Centralia Defense Committee believes that it has finally convinced the governor to act on releasing the prisoners. This is one of a series of stories about prisoner release in this paper.

1656. "IWW Acts vs. Critical Theories." *Rebel Worker* 2 (June 1, 1919):3.
Ultra-left Socialists severely criticize the IWW.

1657. "IWW Alive in Boston." *Industrial Worker* 78 (January 1, 1981):2.
The Boston branch of the IWW and its many activities.

1658. "The I.W.W.: An Inside View of Its Methods." (Pittsburgh) *Industrial Worker* (December 22, 1913):1526–27.

1659. "I.W.W. and Politics." *One Big Union Monthly* 2 (August, 1920):9–10.

Restates the IWW position that members do not subscribe to any particular political view.

1660. "IWW and Revolution." *Review of Reviews* 48 (September, 1913): 370–71.

1661. "IWW and the Shingle Weavers." *International Socialist Review* 14 (April, 1914):620.

The shingle weavers, who belong to a craft union, began to take in all loggers and mill workers to avoid the IWW. They are becoming radicalized, however, because there has been some boring from within.

1662. "The IWW and the Socialist Party." *International Socialist Review* 18 (October, 1917):205–9.

On the many raids on and arrests of IWWs and Socialists.

1663. "The IWW and Why the Workers Should Join It." *Industrial Pioneer* 3 (June, 1925):46–47.

Article on organizing activities written by a Vancouver logger.

1664. "IWW as an Agent of Pan-Germanism." *World's Work* 36 (October, 1918):581–82.

Rumors that there is a connection between the Germans and the IWW.

1665. "The I.W.W. as Prison Reformers." *Survey* 37 (January 20, 1917): 461–62.

Thanks to Frederick Sumner Boyd, who was convicted after the Paterson strike, an investigation of the New Jersey state prison was made. Among other heinous discoveries, it was found that prisoners were chained to cell walls for months, one prisoner was forced to wear a ball and chain for four and a half years, and consumptives were crowded together with the other prisoners.

1666. "IWW Barred." *Common Cause* 2 (October, 1912):444.

Why the IWW was barred from the New York Labor Day parade.

1667. "The I.W.W. Boys." *International Socialist Review* 18 (November-December, 1917):278–79.

The many raids on the IWW.

1668. "IWW Cause of Strike, Says Tighe." *Rebel Worker* 2 (October 15, 1919):1.

M. F. Tighe, president of the Amalgamated Association, told a Senate committee that the steel strike should be blamed on the IWW, especially on its Russian and Hungarian members.

1669. "The IWW Closes the Saloons." *Nation* 116 (May 23, 1923):588.

The IWW did not allow its members to drink alcoholic beverages during the Seattle strike.

1670. "IWW Comes Back in New England." *Industrial Pioneer* 2 (June, 1924):18–20.

The recent textile strikes have attracted the IWW, and they are back again.

1671. "The IWW Defense." *New Justice* 1 (April 1, 1919):15–16.

1672. "IWW Demands Presented." *American Lumberman* 2309 (August 6, 1919):67.

IWW demands include the right to determine company policy.

1673. "IWW Develops into a National Menace." *Current Opinion* 63 (September, 1917):153–54.

The militant Western IWW is a national menace.

1674. "IWW Exonerated." *Public* 20 (May 11, 1917):459.

The acquittal of Tom Tracy after the Everett Massacre trial indicates that other IWW prisoners will go free.

1675. "IWW Harvest Organizers Jailed." *Workers Defense* 2 (September, 1932):4.

North Dakota jury convicts organizers.

1676. "I.W.W. in California." *One Big Union Monthly* 2 (August, 1920): 25–30.

A Stanford University investigator reports on the IWW.

1677. "The IWW in Convention Assembled." *Industrial Pioneer* 1 (December, 1923):16, 50.

1678. "IWW in the Prison Camps." *One Big Union Monthly* 1 (December, 1919):39–41.

1679. "IWW in the World of Cartoons." *One Big Union Monthly* 1 (December, 1919):43–44.

1680. "IWW is Down and Out in Baltimore." *Garment Worker* 12 (August 15, 1913):1.

The IWW did not succeed in luring garment workers away from the UGA.

1681. "I.W.W. Leaders in Pennsylvania." *Miners Magazine* 17 (March 2, 1916):1.
Joseph Ettor is demanding $5 a day for the IWW workers at the Greenwood colliery.

1682. "IWW Leaders Must Disgorge." *Square Deal* 15 (November, 1914):376–77.
There may have been mishandling of IWW strike funds.

1683. "The I.W.W. 'Machine' and the Industrial Worker." *Social War* (August 16, 1913): n.p.

1684. "IWW, 1919." *One Big Union Monthly* 2 (January, 1920):5–11.
Review of the nationwide raids and persecutions of the IWW, with photographs.

1685 "The IWW: A Non-Political Labor Union." *One Big Union Monthly* NS 2 (June, 1938):34.

1686. "The IWW: Not Criminals But Political Prisoners." *Industrial Worker* 1 (October 16, 1920):1.
The Chicago trial proved no criminal activity by the IWW.

1687. "The IWW on Trial." *Outlook* 119 (July 17, 1918):448–50.
The Chicago trial.

1688. "The IWW Pageant." *Outlook* 104 (June 21, 1913):352–53.
Describes the Paterson strike pageant.

1689. "The IWW Puts One Over on the Tonopah Bosses." *Voice of the People* 2 (October 1, 1914):2.
IWW leader Henry McGucken.

1690. "IWW Raids." *Defense News Bulletin* 1 (November 3, 1917):2.
The U.S. Department of Justice raids on IWW offices from coast to coast.

1691. "The IWW Raids and Others." *New Republic* 12 (September 15, 1917):175–77.
Sinister reasons for all the labor strikes.

1692. "The IWW Reigns Supreme in Butte, Montana." *Miners Magazine* 15 (July 9, 1914):7–8.
The IWW won the fight over the Butte union hall.

1693. "IWW Release Asked on Coast." *Labor's News* 17 (July 27, 1929):8.
A plea for release of IWW prisoners.

1694. "IWW Revives." *Business Week* 801 (January 6, 1945):96–98.
The war may unite the radicals.

1695. "IWW Scare in Salt Lake City: Conviction of Joseph Hillstrom for Murder." *Sunset* 35 (November, 1915):854–55.

1696. "IWW Steel Drive." *Industrial Pioneer* 1 (September, 1923):4–5, 32.
IWW activities in the steel industry in Toledo.

1697. "The IWW Strike." *Miners Magazine* 19 (October, 1918):6.
The Butte copper strike is curtailing copper output.

1698. "IWW Strike in Colorado." *United Mine Worker* 38 (November 1, 1927):7.
Colorado coal strikers are demanding a minimum wage.

1699. "I.W.W. Strikes." *American Federationist* 20 (August, 1913):622–24.
Paterson repeats the pattern of other IWW strikes.

1700. "The IWW Sufferers." *Square Deal* 12 (May, 1913):382–83.
The suffering of citizens of Akron and Paterson as a result of IWW-led strikes.

1701. "I.W.W. Tactics." *International Molders Journal* 50 (August, 1914): 652–53.

1702. "IWW the Bugaboo in Extreme Northwest." *Square Deal* 12 (April, 1913):210–12.

1703. "I.W.W. Try Trouble Making." *Miners Magazine* 17 (July 6, 1916):3.
Frank Little's activities in Joplin, Missouri.

1704. "IWW vs. AFL at Butte." *New Review* 2 (September, 1914):550–53.
Controversy between the IWW and the WFM is intensifying.

1705. "IWW Wins in Jerome, Arizona." *Solidarity* 8 (June 9, 1917):1.
The IWW outnumbered the WFM in the strike and won a pay increase.

1706. "IWW's Beaten Up, Says Stanley Clark." *New Appeal* 1208 (January 25, 1919):2.
Beatings of radicals by people who looked like ordinary citizens.

1707. "IWW's Convicted *en Masse*." *Nation* 119 (November 5, 1924):483.
The deportation hearings of Mahler, Moran, Negra, and Oates.

1708. "I.W.W's Invade the Minnesota Ore Range." *Miners Magazine* 17 (August 17, 1916):1.

1709. "Jack Whyte Dead." *International Socialist Review* 15 (March, 1915):571.
The shooting of Jack Whyte.

1710. "Jacob Silverman, a Poor Junkman." *Nation* 115 (September 13, 1922):239.
Letter to President Harding from IWW prisoners asking how he can pardon a junk man's dog but refuse a pardon to organizer E. F. Doree.

1711. Jacobson, Pauline. "Parker, Social Diagnostician." *Miners Magazine* 15 (April 2, 1914):6–8.
Carleton Parker put the blame for the Wheatland Hop Riot on the inhuman working conditions.

1712. "Jailed for Labor! Rowan and Many Fellow Workers Arrested by Soldiers." *Solidarity* 8 (September 1, 1917):1.
Describes the raid by military officers on the Spokane office and the harsh arrests of James Rowan and others, one of many such descriptions.

1713. "The Jailing of IWW Members in Kansas." *Public* 22 (September 13, 1919):972–73.

1714. "James Ford Report." *Miners Magazine* 15 (December 3, 1914):1, 3; (January 7, 1915):1, 3.
Butte Miners Union No. 1 and the fight between the WFM and the IWW.

1715. Jeffreys-Jones, Rhodri. "Profit over Class: A Study in American Industrial Espionage." *Journal of American Studies* 6 (December, 1972):233–48.

1716. Jensen, Vernon H. "The Legend of Joe Hill." *Industrial and Labor Relations Review* 4 (April, 1951):356–66.

1717. ———. "The IWW—an Exchange of Views." Review of *We Shall Be All*, by Melvyn Dubofsky (see no. 59). *Labor History* 11 (Summer, 1970):355–64.
Dubofsky's reply in same issue.

1718. "Jerome Settlement." *Miners Magazine* 18 (July, 1917):1.
The IWW is interfering with organizers of the IUMMSW in Jerome, Arizona.

1719. Jewell, Gary. "The History of the IWW in Canada." *Our Generation* 11 (Summer, 1976):35–45.

1720. "Joe Hill." *International Socialist Review* 16 (December, 1915):329–36.

Describes the execution of Joe Hill, with a drawing of the prison.

1721. "Joe Hill Letter." *Revolt* 5 (December, 1915):7.

1722. Johanson, S. G. "The One Big Union." *One Big Union Monthly* 2 (February, 1920):9–11.

1723. "John Lawson a Free Man Again." *Survey* 38 (April 21, 1917):72–73.

The release of a strike leader.

1724. "John M. O'Neill Scores Red Radicals." *Miners Magazine* 21 (February, 1920):1, 6.

IUMMSW official's attack on the IWW.

1725. "John Walker of U.M.W.A." *Miners Magazine* 14 (July 31, 1913):4.

Opinions about the IWW.

1726. Johnpoll, Bernard. "A Note on Daniel De Leon." *Labor History* 17 (Fall, 1976):606–12.

1727. Johnson, Aili K. "Finnish Labor Songs from Northern Michigan." *Michigan History* 31 (September, 1947):331–43.

Reminiscences of IWW lumberjacks. The IWW songs in the text are translated from the Finnish.

1728. Johnson, Bruce C. "Taking Care of Labor: The Police in American Politics." *Theory and Society* 3 (Spring, 1976):89–118.

1729. Johnson, Donald. "The Political Career of A. Mitchell Palmer." *Pennsylvania History* 25 (October, 1958):345–70.

1730. ———. "Wilson, Burleson, and Censorship in the First World War." *Journal of Southern History* 28 (February, 1962):46–58.

1731. Johnson, Frank and Lou Ludwig. "Scandinavian Labor Parties and the IWW." *Nation* 145 (October 23, 1937):459.

Controversy over Ragmar Johansen's role in the IWW and in Europe.

1732. Johnson, Harold. "The Conviction: A Presage." *Labor Defender* 1 (October 15, 1918):3.

The Chicago trial.

1733. ———. "Joe Hill, Song Writer." *Industrial Pioneer* 2 (June, 1924):44.

1734. Johnson, Michael. "Albert R. Parsons: An American Architect of Syndicalism." *Midwest Quarterly* 9, no. 2 (1968):195–206.

1735. ———. "The IWW and Wilsonian Democracy." *Science and Society* 28 (Summer, 1964):257–74.

1736. Johnson, Oakley. "Starvation and the 'Reds' in Kentucky." *Nation* 134 (February 5, 1932):140–42.

Johnson's conversations with mine operators and police officials in Bell and Harlan counties, showing their ignorance and prejudice.

1737. Johnson, Rudolph. "Work People's College." *North County Anvil* 19 (July–August, 1976):17.

The Duluth, Minnesota, college for radicals.

1738. Johnstone, J. W. "Report of the I.W.W. Convention." *Agitator* 2 (December 1, 1911):3.

1739. "Joint Meeting Denounces the Wobblies," *Four L Bulletin* 1 (December, 1919):16.

The LLLL does not want the IWW in the woods.

1740. Jones, Hayden. "On the Firing Line When Labor Resorts to Riot." *Square Deal* 10 (March, 1912):161–69.

The Lawrence strike compared with other strikes.

1741. Jones, Mary Harris. "Mother Jones Makes a Plea." *Miners Magazine* 15 (August 20, 1914):8.

Mother Jones' opinion that the fighting should stop and the IWW should get out.

1742. Jordan, J. "Massachusetts Textile Strike Remembered." *Guardian* 32 (June 21, 1980):8.

The Lawrence strike.

1743. "Joseph D. Cannon Pulls the Mask off the IWW." *Miners Magazine* 15 (November 5, 1914):1, 3.

The altercations in Butte between the IWW and the WFM.

1744. "Judge Gary's Indictment." *Literary Digest* 52 (March 25, 1916): 808.

"Class use" of indictments in the East Youngstown strike by Gary, the "steel dictator."

1745. "Judicious Estimate of the Centralia Case." *Christian Century* 47 (October 24, 1930):1299–1300.

The Federal Council of Churches' investigation of Centralia.

1746. Julius, Emanuel. "The IWW and Ownership." *Miners Magazine* 14 (September 4, 1913):13.
Statements by Walter Lippmann and William Haywood that Julius believes show the IWW as antisocial.

1747. "Juries Uphold Free Speech." *Public* 17 (November 6, 1914):1069.
The acquittal of Becky Edelson in Tarrytown, New York.

1748. "Justice Triumphant: The Story of the Second Ford Trial." *Industrial Pioneer* 3 (March, 1926):6–8, 28–30.
The story of Richard Ford, a Wheatland prisoner, and his acquittal after many years in prison.

1749. "Kaiser's Secret Army Here." *Literary Digest* 55 (December 1, 1917):15–16.
The IWW accused of working for the Germans.

1750. Kanarek, Harold K. "Pennsylvania Anthracite Strike of 1922." *Pennsylvania Magazine of History and Biography* 99 (April, 1975):207–25.
The IWW's failure to organize the anthracite miners.

1751. Kane, Frances F. "The Communist Deportations." *Survey* 44 (April 24, 1920):141–44.

1752. Kane, H. F. "What Shall Be the Verdict?" *Labor Defender* 1 (March 18, 1918):4.
Description of what the IWW prisoners are feeling, written by one of those prisoners.

1753. Kanka, Mabel. "The Foodstuff Workers." *One Big Union Monthly* 2 (December, 1920):58.
What the union can do and who is eligible for membership.

1754. ———. "Woman's Struggle for Emancipation." *One Big Union Monthly* 2 (December, 1920):22–23.
The place of women in the IWW.

1755. Karson, Marc. "The Catholic Church and the Political Development of American Trade Unionism (1900–1918)." *Industrial and Labor Relations Review* 4 (July, 1951):527–42.

1756. Katayama, Sen. "Workers and Law in Japan." *Labor Defender* 1 (April 15, 1918):4.
In Japan police are much harder on Socialists and other radicals than they are in America.

1757. "Keep Your Eyes on Everett!" *International Socialist Review* 17 (April, 1917):608–9.

1758. Keister, Jack. "Why the Socialists Won at Butte." *International Socialist Review* 11 (June, 1911):733.

1759. Kekkonen, T. "Education as a Social and Class Problem." *Industrial Pioneer* 2 (November, 1924):42.
The work of the Work Peoples College in Duluth.

1760. Keller, Helen. "A Call for Harmony." *International Socialist Review* 13 (February, 1913):606.
The harsh attacks on Haywood by the Socialists are disrupting the Socialist Party.

1761. ———. "Helen Keller Scores IWW Persecutions." *Labor Defender* 1 (February 16, 1918):1.
A speech in which Keller deplores the un-American persecutions.

1762. ———. "Little Falls." *International Socialist Review* 13 (January, 1913):518.
Letter to John Macy about the Little Falls strike.

1763. ———. "In Behalf of the I.W.W." *Liberator* 1 (March, 1918):13.
The raids and persecutions of the IWW are unfair and illegal.

1764. Kellogg, Paul U. "The McKees Rocks Strike." *Survey* 22 (August 7, 1909):656–65.

1765. ———. "McKees Rocks Strike." *Review of Reviews* 40 (September, 1909):353–55.

1766. Kelly, H. "The Moyer, Haywood and Pettibone Case." *Voice of Labor* 1 (March 30, 1907):76.

1767. Kennedy, James. "Evolution of the Lumber Industry." *Industrial Pioneer* 1 (February, 1921):38–42.
The technological changes in the lumber industry and how they affected the lumberman's work.

1768. ———. "How the IWW Is Organized." *Industrial Pioneer* 1 (May, 1921):17–22.
An explanation of how the IWW is organized and an appeal for readers to join.

1769. ———. "Organization." *Industrial Pioneer* 1 (April, 1921):22–25.
Industrial unionism in the lumber camps.

1770. Kennell, Ruth E. "Kuzbas: A New Pennsylvania." *Nation* 116 (May 2, 1923):511–12.
Problems at the IWW colony in Siberia.

1771. ———. "A Kuzbas Chronicle." *Nation* 116 (January 3, 1923):7–10.
William Haywood's role at the Kuzbas colony.

1772. ———. "Kuzbas in 1924." *Nation* 117 (November 26, 1924):566–68.
The IWW colony in Russia.

1773. ———. "The New Innocents Abroad." *American Mercury* 17 (May, 1929):11.
The IWW colony in Russia.

1774. "The Kept Press and the Ku Klux Klan." *One Big Union Monthly* 1 (June, 1919):13.
Klan raids on the IWW unreported or misreported.

1775. Kerr, Charles H. "Free Speech Fight." *International Socialist Review* 10 (January, 1910):642–43.
The arrest of Elizabeth Gurley Flynn at the Spokane Free Speech Fight and the tough sentences received by some IWW members.

1776. ———. "The Industrial Workers of the World." *International Socialist Review* 10 (October, 1909):359–60.
Admiring description of the coming union.

1777. ———. "Violence and the I.W.W." *Public* 15 (July 12, 1912):655–56.
The Lawrence strike.

1778. ———. "Will Prosecute Mill Owners." *International Socialist Review* 13 (March, 1913):676.
The "riot" at the Little Falls strike a police frame-up; readers asked to send donations and get up petitions.

1779. "Kidnapping and Justice in Merryville." *Lumberjack* 1 (January 16, 1913):3.
A Negro IWW arrested and jailed for asking a worker not to scab.

1780. "Killed on the Way to Spokane!" *International Socialist Review* 10 (December, 1909):557–58.
The death of IWW poet James Kelly Cole.

1781. Kinkead, W. L. "Paterson Silk Strike." *Survey* 30 (May 31, 1913): 315–16.

1782. Kinnear, Peter. "Rubber Workers Rebel." *International Socialist Review* 13 (March, 1913):654.
The IWW in Akron.

1783. Kirk, E. E., and Harry M. McKee. "Propaganda in Jails and Prisons." *International Socialist Review* 14 (October, 1913):250–51.
The speaking and singing continue in prison.

1784. Kissane, Leedice. "The Haywood Trial: Steve Adams, the Speechless Witness." *Idaho Yesterdays* 4 (Fall, 1960):18–21.

1785. Kizer, B. H. "Elizabeth Gurley Flynn." *Pacific Northwest Quarterly* 57 (July, 1966):110–12.

1786. Klemanski, John S., and Alan DiGaetano. "Wobblies and Auto Workers: The Industrial Workers of the World in Detroit." *Detroit in Perspective* 6 (Spring, 1982):22–39.

1787. Koettgen, Ewald. "IWW Convention." *International Socialist Review* 14 (November, 1913):275–76.

1788. ———. "Making Silk." *International Socialist Review* 14 (March, 1914):551–55.
Detailed description of the silk industry and the IWW's plans to organize it.

1789. ———. "No Grievances at All!" In *Pageant of the Paterson Strike* (New York: Success Press, 1913), 9–11.

1790. Kolb, Harold H. "Industrial Millstone." *Idaho Yesterdays* 16 (Summer, 1972):28–32.
The greatest problem of the WFM was the IWW.

1791. Kolinsky, Paul. "No One Shall Go Hungry." *One Big Union Monthly* NS 1 (June, 1937):12–14.
The hobo life.

1792. Kolko, Gabriel. "The Decline of American Radicalism in the Twentieth Century." *Studies on the Left* 6 (September, 1966):9–26.

1793. Koppes, Clayton R. "The Industrial Workers of the World and County-Jail Reform in Kansas, 1915–20." *Kansas Historical Quarterly* 41 (Spring, 1975):63–86.

1794. ———. "The Kansas Trial of the IWW, 1917–1919." *Labor History* 16 (Summer, 1975):338–58.

1795. Korman, Gerd. Review of *The Wobblies,* by Patrick Renshaw (see no. 187). *Journal of American History* 54 (March, 1968):908–9.

1796. Krieger, Nancy. "Queen of the Bolsheviks: The Hidden History of Dr. Marie Equi." *Radical America* 17 (No. 5, 1983):53–73.
A fascinating account of the woman, once an active member

of the IWW, who went to jail for pacifist views during World War I.

1797. "Kuzbas." *Nation* 114 (June 14, 1922):730–32.
The complete text of the Kuzbas workers' agreement and the workers' "pledge."

1798. "Labor Agitators." *Bellman* 23 (July 21, 1917):80.
A middle-class view of the IWW.

1799. "Labor and the Law." *Nation* 96 (May 22, 1913):515–16.
Quinlan's conviction after the Paterson strike.

1800. "Labor and Wealth." *Industrial Union Bulletin* 1 (March 23, 1907):2.
Typical arguments in the Preamble controversy, during the year that some changes were made in the Preamble.

1801. "Labor Conditions: Portland." *Square Deal* 12 (September, 1913): 131–33.
A cannery strike and a Free Speech Fight.

1802. "Labor Conditions: Portland." *Square Deal* 13 (December, 1913): 422–23.
Police unduly handicapped by IWW acquittals.

1803. "Labor Conditions: Portland." *Square Deal* 14 (February, 1914):19.
The unemployment problem may be caused by the IWW.

1804. "Labor Conditions: Seattle." *Square Deal* 13 (November, 1913): 330–31.
IWW oratory is ribald.

1805. "Labor Fight at Everett." *Outlook* 114 (November, 1915):583–84.

1806. "A Labor Law That Caused a Strike." *Literary Digest* 44 (January 27, 1912):148–49.
The Lawrence strike and its causes.

1807. "Labor Leaders Charged with Murder of Governor Steunenberg." *Outlook* 82 (March 10, 1906):532–33.
The arrests of Moyer, Haywood, and Pettibone.

1808. "Labor Melts a Link with Its Fiery Past: Smelter Workers Merger into the USW Ends an Era." *Business Week* No. 1952 (January 28, 1967):109–10.
The smelter workers, who formerly had strong ties to the IWW, now are merging with the USW. Oscar N. Peterson recalls episodes in their history.

1809. "The Labor Movement Must Crucify the Traitors." *Miners Magazine* 12 (August 1, 1912):6.
Criticism of the IWW.

1810. "Labor Movement Must Win this Battle." *Miners Magazine* 14 (December 4, 1913):6.
The Calumet-Hecla strike.

1811. "Labor News throughout the Country: Seattle." *Square Deal* 12 (May, 1913):324–25.
Labor controversy in Seattle.

1812. "Labor Notes: After Youngstown What?" *International Socialist Review* 16 (April, 1916):621–22.
The IWW and its techniques, which do not always work.

1813. "Labor Theories and a Labor War." *Outlook* 104 (June 7, 1913): 275–78.
Speculations about Syndicalist thought.

1814. "Labor Troubles at Home." *Independent* 72 (March 14, 1912):544–45.
Investigation of the Lawrence strike.

1815. "Labor Union Struggle Menaces Coast." *American Lumberman* 2308 (August 9, 1919):53.
Owners feel threatened.

1816. "Labor Unrest in the Southwest." *Survey* 38 (August 11, 1917): 428–29.
Allegations of connections between the IWW and the Germans have threatened all unions.

1817. "Labor War." *Public* 17 (February 27, 1914):204.
The violence in the Calumet-Hecla strike.

1818. "Labor War." *Public* 17 (March 20, 1914):276–77.
Charles Moyer's deportation from Michigan and Frank Tannenbaum's indictment in New York.

1819. "Labor War." *Public* 17 (April 17, 1914):372–73.
An IWW riot at Rutgers Square in New York City and a protest by Lincoln Steffens about police handling of it.

1820. "Labor Wars in the West." *Square Deal* 14 (December, 1914):431.
The Wheatland episode.

1821. "Labor Wars in the West." *Sunset* 33 (October, 1914):651–52.
The conviction of the Wheatland labor leaders.

1822. "Labor's Attitude toward the 'Red' Agitators." *Literary Digest* 64 (March 20, 1920):21–23.

The reactions of conservative and liberal labor people.

1823. "Labor's New Davy Crockett." *Square Deal* 12 (February, 1913):86–87.

Joseph Ettor and the New York waiters' strike.

1824. "Lads on the Lakes." *Industrial Pioneer* 1 (October, 1923):23–24.

The drive to organize Great Lakes seamen.

1825. La Monte, Robert Rives. "Industrial Unionism and Syndicalism." *New Review* 1 (May, 1913):527–29.

1826. ———. "Socialist Respect for Capitalist Law." *International Socialist Review* 12 (February, 1912):500–504.

Disputes the claim that no Socialist can be a law-abiding citizen. La Monte credits Haywood for daring to discuss unpopular questions.

1827. ———. "Syndicalism as It Is." Review essay on *The New Unionism,* by André Tridon (see no. 217). *New Review* 2 (February, 1914):111–14.

1828. Lamson, Warren. "The Essence of Industrialism." *Industrial Pioneer* 3 (October, 1925):39–43.

The future will set women free, and at that point men will also be more free. An industrial society will have no superior-inferior relations.

1829. ———. "These Twenty Years." *Industrial Pioneer* 3 (August, 1925):16–18, 47; (September, 1925):37–40.

The first tumultuous twenty years of the IWW.

1830. Lance, James. "Labor under Industrialised Agriculture." *Industrial Pioneer* 2 (May, 1924):13–15.

Trends in agriculture toward enormous company-owned farms make industrial unionism all the more necessary.

1831. "Land of Sunshine and Serfdom." *Industrial Pioneer* 2 (June, 1924):23, 26.

The California trials in various cities and their lack of fairness.

1832. Landis, Kennesaw Mountain. "Address to the Jury." *Defense News Bulletin* No. 41 (August 24, 1918):3–4.

Judge Landis' charge to the Chicago trial jury.

1833. Lane, Winthrop. "The Buford Widows." *Survey* 43 (January 10, 1920):391–92.

Women left behind in the United States by the deportees are without help or support.

1834. ———. "Presumption of Innocence in Kansas." *Liberator* 3 (January, 1920):39.

How thirty-four IWWs were held for more than two years without trial.

1835. ———. "Strike at Fort Leavenworth." *Survey* 41 (February 15, 1919):687–93.

1836. ———. "Uncle Sam, Jailor." *Survey* 42 (September 6, 1919):806–12, 834.

The terrible jails of Kansas, particularly the Sedgewick County jail, in which the IWW prisoners were held without trial for nearly two years.

1837. Langerock, Hubert. "The Road to Autocracy." *Industrial Pioneer* 3 (August, 1925):22–24; (September, 1925):28–29.

The U.S. is turning into a capitalist oligarchy.

1838. Lanier, Alexander S. "IWW's Didn't Violate Espionage Act, Asserts Intelligence Officer." *Appeal to Reason* 1222 (May 3, 1919):2.

1839. ———. "To the President: An Open Letter in Regard to the Case of *United States versus Wm. D. Haywood et al.*" *New Republic* 18 (April 19, 1919):383–84.

A lawyer's appeal for executive clemency for the IWW.

1840. La Piere, Richard T. "The General Strike in San Francisco: A Study of the Revolutionary Pattern." *Sociology & Social Research* 19 (March–April, 1935):355–63.

1841. "Large Scale Mining Makes Robots." *Industrial Pioneer* 1 (April, 1924):25–26.

New technologies are changing the work of miners.

1842. "Larger Bearings of the McNamara Case: Symposium." *Survey* 27 (December 30, 1911):1413–29.

1843. Larkin, Jim. "Murder Most Foul." *International Socialist Review* 16 (December, 1915):330–31.

The Joe Hill case and his execution.

1844. Larrowe, Charles P. "Maritime Strike of 1934." *Labor History* 11 (Fall, 1970):403–51.

1845. Lasker, L. D. "America and Her Political Prisoners." *Survey* 44 (August 2, 1920):578–82.

1846. "The Last Letters of Joe Hill." *Industrial Pioneer* 1 (December, 1923):53–56.

1847. Latchem, E. W. "The Agricultural Workers Convention" and "Aftermath." *One Big Union Monthly* 2 (November, 1920):56–58.
The farmworkers' demands include payment by the day instead of by the hour and the choice of job stewards.

1848. ———. "The Coming Industrial International." *One Big Union Monthly* 2 (December, 1920):50–51.
The planned Third International and the IWW's place in it.

1849. ———. "First of May in Minneapolis." *One Big Union Monthly* 2 (June, 1920):6–8.
The police repeatedly tried to break up the IWW May Day parade.

1850. ———. "Modern Agricultural Slave." *One Big Union Monthly* 2 (August, 1920):54–56.
The grain belt farmers will make trouble for the IWW this year.

1851. ———. "Where Do We Belong?" *One Big Union Monthly* 2 (October, 1920):28–30.
Where the IWW might fit into various radical groups. The Russian Communists are too political for the IWW.

1852. "Late News of the Battle." *Appeal to Reason* No. 731 (December 4, 1909):3.
The Spokane Free Speech Fight.

1853. "The Latest Group." *New Republic* 12 (October 27, 1917):339.
The Anti-Suffrage Association is trying to connect the IWW to the women's suffrage movement.

1854. Lauck, W. Jett. "The Lawrence Strike: A Review." *Outlook* 100 (March 9, 1912):531–36.
The riot police caused at Lawrence when they forcefully prevented the strikers' children from boarding a train while being evacuated. Lauck finds three evils at Lawrence: the lawlessness of the strikers, the evils of their working conditions, and the wrongs done by the manufacturers.

1855. ———. "Lesson from Lawrence." *North American Review* 195 (May, 1912):665–72.

The lesson we have not learned is that the terrible conditions of the immigrant workers in Lawrence exist all over the country.

1856. ———. "The Significance of the Situation at Lawrence." *Survey* 27 (February 17, 1912):1772–74.

How the textile manufacturers benefit by cheap labor and a protective tariff. The strike shows that unrestricted immigration is an advantage to them and that the protective tariff is a necessity.

1857. "The Laundry Workers: They Can Be Organized." *One Big Union Monthly* NS 1 (August, 1937):9, 21–22.

1858. Laut, Agnes C. "Revolution Yawns!" *Technical World* 18 (September, 1912):134–44.

Describes the powerful IWW in the Pacific Northwest, with good photographs.

1859. "'Law and Order' In Disgrace." *Miners Magazine* 9 (January 23, 1908):5.

The Goldfield authorities are flaunting law and order themselves.

1860. "Lawlessness and Labor Unions." *Outlook* 83 (May 19, 1906):108–9.

No lawlessness is justified: Moyer and Haywood should not be freed without a trial and an acquittal despite their illegal kidnapping.

1861. "Lawlessness and Sabotage." *Century* 81 (March, 1911):791–92.

Sabotage was imported to America from France by the IWW.

1862. "Lawlessness in Support of a Cause." *Century* 81 (February, 1911):632–33.

Strikes in Philadelphia and Columbus, Ohio.

1863. "Lawrence and Indianapolis." *Independent* 72 (February 1, 1912): 220–21.

The influence of the Lawrence strike on subsequent strikes.

1864. "Lawrence and the Industrial Workers of the World." *Survey* 28 (April 6, 1912):79–80.

The Lawrence strike committee states that benefits are not conferred on workers but that workers themselves must take what they need, shorter hours and progressively increasing wages.

1865. "Lawrence Demonstration Strike." *Survey* 29 (October 12, 1912): 53.
The Lawrence strike.

1866. "Lawrence Dynamite Conspiracy." *Square Deal* 12 (July, 1913):571.
The unsuccessful attempt to blame the IWW for violence.

1867. "The Lawrence Incident." *Weekly Bulletin of the Clothing Trade* (UGWA) 11 (March 8, 1912):4.
Use of children in the Lawrence strike.

1868. "The Lawrence Labor Victory." *Literary Digest* 44 (March 23, 1912):575–76.

1869. "The Lawrence Leaders." *Agitator* 2 (October 1, 1912):1.
Although Ettor and Giovannitti are praised for their leadership in the Lawrence strike, the real leader was the man who refused a smaller paycheck.

1870. "Lawrence Once More in the Foreground." *Survey* 28 (September 7, 1912):693–94.
The Lawrence dynamite plot.

1871. "The Lawrence Settlement." *Survey* 27 (March 23, 1912):1949–50.
The strike victory analyzed by examining the settlement.

1872. "The Lawrence Strike." *Agitator* 2 (February 15, 1912):1. See also (March 15, 1912):1.
The strike was a class war.

1873. "The Lawrence Strike." *Commercial Telegraphers' Journal* 10 (March, 1912):78.
Mill owners whose forefathers fought slavery are now engaging in industrial slavery, according to Senator Ben Tillman.

1874. "The Lawrence Strike." *Independent* 72 (February 8, 1912):280–81.
The rioting.

1875. "The Lawrence Strike." *Life and Labor* 2 (April, 1922):124.
Joseph Fels' contribution to the Lawrence children's fund.

1876. "The Lawrence Strike." *Shoe Workers' Journal* 13 (February, 1912): 12–14.
The strikers at Lawrence are at fault for joining the IWW. AFL unions should not be expected to contribute to the IWW strike fund because the IWWs betrayed craft unionism.

1877. "The Lawrence Strike: A Poll of the Press." *Outlook* 100 (February 17, 1912):356–58.

1878. "The Lawrence Strike: A Review." *Outlook* 100 (March 9, 1912): 531–36.
Exhaustive account of the strike and the use of the children.

1879. "The Lawrence Strike Children." *Literary Digest* 44 (March 9, 1912):471–72.
The police action against the children was brutal.

1880. "Lawrence Strike From Various Angles: A Symposium." *Survey* 28 (April 6, 1912):65–80.

1881. "Lawrence Strike Made Difference in Figures on the Unemployed." *Square Deal* 12 (April, 1913):241–43.
Statistical study of the strike.

1882. "Lawrence Strike Raises a Big Question in Immigration—What Would Happen If All Foreign Unskilled Labor Would Join the Independent [*sic*] Workers of the World?" *Square Deal* 10 (April, 1912):263–68.

1883. "Lawrence Strikers." *Independent* 72 (February 22, 1912):382.

1884. "Lawrence Strikers Win." *Weekly Bulletin of the Clothing Trade* (UGWA) 11 (March 15, 1912):4.

1885. "Lay Australian Arson Plot to IWW." *New York Times* (April 14, 1917):p. 6, col. 1–3.
The Australian IWW.

1886. "Leaning Tower of Capitalism Is Swaying the Rail and Coal Situation." *One Big Union Monthly* 2 (August, 1920):6–8.
Surpluses this year will mean unemployment. Capitalists in the coal and railroad industries are about to go under.

1887. "Learning from Henry Ford." *Industrial Pioneer* 2 (May, 1924):39–41.
Organizing at the Ford Motor Company.

1888. Lee, William. "Industrial Masses: The Builders of Freedom." *One Big Union Monthly* 2 (February, 1920):41–42.
Historical summary of economies in which the working man builds the fortunes of a few.

1889. Leeds, John B. "Industrial Opportunities for Negroes in Philadelphia." *Southern Workman* 40 (July, 1914):417–22.

1890. "Left Wing and IWW." *Revolutionary Age* 1 (April 19, 1919):3.
Analysis and comparison of radical views.

1891. "The 'Left Wingers' and Mass Action." *One Big Union Monthly* 1 (May, 1919):9–11.
Different definitions of "mass action."

1892. "'Left-Wingers' and the I.W.W." *One Big Union Monthly* 1 (July, 1919):14–15.
The expulsion of left-wingers from the Socialist Party.

1893. "Legal Persecution Starts in the West." *One Big Union Monthly* 1 (July, 1919):9, 16.
The Criminal Syndicalism trials in California and the Seattle General Strike trial.

1894. Legere, Benjamin J. "The Red Flag in the Auburn Prison." *International Socialist Review* 15 (December, 1914):337–41.
Life in jail after Legere's Little Falls trial.

1895. "Legere Sentenced to One Year." *International Socialist Review* 14 (July, 1913):41.
The Little Falls strike.

1896. "Legion's War on Disloyalty." *Literary Digest* 63 (November 29, 1919):19–20.
The many raids of Legionnaires on groups they deem "unpatriotic."

1897. "Legionnaires Rout the Wobblies." *American Lumberman* 2319 (October 25, 1919):64.
The American Legion fights the IWW at Centralia and elsewhere.

1898. Lehman, Ed. "Why the Working Class Should Not Use Sabotage." *Lumberjack* 1 (March 13, 1913):2.
A tongue-in-cheek article advocating the use of sabotage.

1899. Leighton, G. R. "Seattle, Washington, the Edge of the Last Frontier." *Harpers* 178 (March, 1939):422–40.

1900. Leinenweber, Charles. "The American Socialist Party and 'New Immigrants.'" *Science and Society* 32 (Winter, 1968):1–25.

1901. Lemon, W. J. "American Railway Industry and Its Workers." *Industrial Pioneer* 1 (September, 1921):13–15.
Railroad workers should realize the futility of craft unions, particularly in their industry.

1902. ———. "The Brotherhoods and the Crafts versus Railroad Workers Industrial Union No. 600, or Revolutionary Industrial Unionism." *One Big Union Monthly* 2 (May, 1920):31–35.

The crafts and brotherhoods believe in a fair day's wage for a fair day's pay, but who decides what's fair?

1903. ———. "Union Strikebreakers." *One Big Union Monthly* 2 (February, 1920):22–24.

The IWW shows more solidarity than other unions.

1904. Lens, Sidney. "The Wobblies 50 Years Later." *Progressive* 19 (August, 1955):20–21.

1905. Lenz, Hugo. "Action—Direct or Indirect?" *Machinists' Monthly Journal* 24 (November, 1912):1010–12.

1906. Lepschutz, Celia. "Pittsburgh Traitors." *International Socialist Review* 13 (May, 1913):821.

Some unionists betrayed others at the Oliver Company.

1907. Lescohier, D. D. "With the I.W.W. in the Wheatlands." *Harpers* 147 (August, 1923):371–80.

1908. Le Sueur, Arthur. "Legal Side Lights on Murder." *International Socialist Review* 17 (November, 1916):298–300.

The Mesabi strike violence and the arrests of strikers.

1909. Le Sueur, Meridel. "Notes on North Country Folkways." *Minnesota History* 25 (September, 1944):215–23.

IWW "folkways."

1910. "A Lesson for Socialists." *International Socialist Review* 12 (February, 1912):486–87.

The Socialist Party cannot confine itself to political action.

1911. "A Lesson in Handling Strikes." *Square Deal* 14 (June, 1914):453.

The Michigan and Colorado strikes were handled well by the companies, the police, and the military.

1912. "The Lesson of Paterson." *Common Cause* 4 (July, 1913):35–42.

There was too much fighting between unions.

1913. "The Lesson of Lawrence." *Masses* 3 (April, 1912):3.

A Socialist view of the Lawrence strike.

1914. "Lessons from the Past." *One Big Union Advocate* 1 (October, 1939):11–14.

The IWW's "400," the agricultural unit.

1915. "Let's Make 'Em Go with Us." *Industrial Pioneer* 2 (September, 1924):22–23.

Answer to an article by Whiting Williams about railroad workers "cooperating" with Baltimore and Ohio officials rather than being militant.

1916. "A Letter and Its Answer." *Square Deal* 13 (October, 1913):279–81.

Protests that the journal is always unfair to the IWW are answered by the editors, who see little good in that organization.

1917. "Letter from a Butte Miner." *International Socialist Review* 15 (October, 1914):227–28.

An account of Butte under martial law and of the fight between IWW and WFM.

1918. "Letter to the President, from Local 8." *Messenger* 4 (March, 1922):377.

The Marine Transport Workers of Philadelphia.

1919. "Letter of Trautmann to Haywood." *Miners Magazine* 14 (June 5, 1913):7–8.

Provocative "letter to Haywood" by one of his enemies.

1920. "Letters to Joe Bradley." *Miners Magazine* 15 (November 5, 1914):1, 4.

The Butte Miners Union.

1921. Leupp, Constance D. "The Lawrence Strike Hearings." *Survey* 27 (March 23, 1912):1953–54.

1922. Levenstein, Harvey. "Samuel Gompers and the Mexican Labor Movement." *Wisconsin Magazine of History* 51 (Winter, 1967–1968):155–63.

1923. Levin, Howard. "The Paterson Silk Weavers' Strike of 1913." *King's Crown Essays* 9 (Winter, 1961–1962):44–64.

1924. Levine, Louis. "The Development of Syndicalism in America." *Political Science Quarterly* 28 (September, 1913):451–79.

Although it is a new union, the IWW seems ready to exert influence and strength.

1925. ———. "Direct Action: Its Interpretation." *Wilshire's Magazine* 16 (October, 1912):2; (November, 1912):2–3.

1926. ———. "Direct Action: The Philosophy of the Labor Struggles of Today." *Forum* 47 (May, 1912):577–88.

1927. ———. "Standpoint of Syndicalism." *Annals of the American Academy of Political and Social Science* 44 (November, 1912):114–18.

1928. ———. "Syndicalism." *North American Review* 196 (July, 1912):9–19.

1929. Le Warne, Charles P. "The Aberdeen, Washington, Free Speech Fight of 1911–1912." *Pacific Northwest Quarterly* 66 (January, 1975):1–12.

1930. ———. "The Bolsheviks Land in Seattle: The Shilka Incident of 1917." *Arizona and the West* 20 (Summer, 1978):107–22.

1931. ———. "On the Wobbly Train to Fresno." *Labor History* 14 (Spring, 1973):264–89.

The recollections of E. M. Clyde, an old Wobbly who was on the train.

1932. Lewis, Austin. "The Basis of Solidarity." *New Review* 3 (August 15, 1915):185–88.

A craft union parade that refused room for the unemployed as an example of why craft unionism will never win; reports on the aftermath of the Wheatland episode.

1933. ———. "The Drift in California." *International Socialist Review* 12 (November, 1911):272–74.

The problems of organizing unskilled workers.

1934. ———. "Movements of Migratory Unskilled Labor in California." *New Review* 2 (August, 1914):458–65.

Wheatland and the Fresno Free Speech Fight.

1935. ———. "The New Labor Movement of the West." *Class Struggle* 1 (September–October, 1917):1–10.

1936. ———. "Organization of the Unskilled." *New Review* 1 (November, 1913):873–82; (December, 1913):956–63.

Comparison of the AFL's and Syndicalists' approach to the problem of organizing migrant and unskilled workers.

1937. ———. "Solidarity: Merely a Word?" *New Review* 3 (July 15, 1915):125–28.

Defense of the IWWs after the Wheatland episode.

1938. Lewis, Howard T. "The I.W.W." *The Mediator* 6 (February, 1914):21–30.

1939. Lewis, Lena Morrow. "The Seattle General Strike." *New Justice* 1 (March 1, 1919):10–11.

1940. Lewis, Tom J. "Spokane." *International Socialist Review* 10 (December, 1909):558.
The situation in Spokane during and after the Free Speech Fight.

1941. "Lexington Explosion: Repudiation of Our Dead Comrades by the IWW." *Mother Earth* 9 (July, 1914):132–33.
An unexplained bomb explosion at a Lexington Avenue address, disclaimed by the IWW although one of the persons involved was a member.

1942. "The Life of the Gandy Dancer." *One Big Union Monthly* NS 1 (May, 1937):14–17.
A personal view of the growing difficulties of railroad employees at a time when railroads are beginning to fail.

1943. "The Limits of Free Speech." *Outlook* 146 (June 1, 1927):145–46.
The Supreme Court decision upholding the states' right to limit freedom of speech may indicate that the pendulum has swung too far and liberties are endangered.

1944. Lind, John. "Johnny Comes Home." *One Big Union Monthly* NS 1 (January, 1937):23–27.
Life story of two brothers, lumberworkers, experiencing problems from Centralia up through the 1936 strikes.

1945. ———. "This Really Was the Initial Labor School." *Railway Clerk* (September, 1963):16.
The Work Peoples College.

1946. Lindquist, John H. "Jerome Deportation of 1917." *Arizona and the West* 11 (Autumn, 1969):233–46.

1947. Lindquist, John H., and James Fraser. "A Sociological Interpretation of the Bisbee Deportation." *Pacific Historical Review* 37 (November, 1968):401–22.

1948. Lippmann, Walter. "The IWW: Insurrection or Revolution?" Review of *American Syndicalism: The IWW*, by John G. Brooks (see no. 20). *New Review* 1 (August, 1913):701–6.

1949. "Literary Illusions about the IWW." *One Big Union Monthly* NS 1 (February, 1937):33–34.
Questions Gilbert Seldes' views of the IWW, as expressed in his book *Mainland.*

1950. "Little Falls Strike Settled." *Review of Reviews* 47 (February, 1913): 148.

1951. Little, Frank; Frank Watts; and G. J. Bourg. "Free Speech and Police Brutality in K. C." *Voice of the People* 3 (January 8, 1914):2.

1952. Lively, D. O. "Agricultural Labor Problems during the Past Season." *Monthly Bulletin* (California State Commission of Horticulture) (January–February, 1918):70–73.

1953. Llewellyn, Thomas. "A Scathing Letter." *Miners Magazine* 7 (October 5, 1905):8.

Letter from early union organizer to Haywood complaining that poor leadership in the UMW caused its failure to organize miners sufficiently.

1954. Lloyd, Edward. "1924 Is Beginning." *Industrial Pioneer* 1 (January, 1924):3–4, 10.

Prospects for the IWW look bleak.

1955. Lloyd, Harry, and Harry F. War. "Amnesty and the Civil Liberties Union." *Nation* 118 (March 26, 1924):346.

1956. "Local 8 of IWW on Firing Line." *Messenger* 4 (February, 1922): 355–56.

The Philadelphia longshoremen and their recent strike.

1957. Lockhart, J. W. "The IWW Raid at Centralia." *Current History* 17 (October, 1922):55–57.

See no. 1520.

1958. "Lockout in Kansas City." *Syndicalist* 3 (August 1–15, 1913):52.

1959. Lopez, Frank R. "This Happened in Good Old 'Mass.'" *Labor Defender* 1 (April 15, 1918):3.

A raid on the IWW in Dedham, Massachusetts.

1960. Lore, Ludwig. "The IWW Trial." *Class Struggle* 2 (September–October, 1918):377–83.

The Chicago trial.

1961. ———. "Scandinavia's 'New Democracy.'" *Nation* 145 (September 25, 1937):315–18.

Ragmar Johansen's successes in Sweden: "IWW may be a thing of the past, but the seed it scattered is growing and bearing abundant fruit."

1962. Lorwin, Lewis L. "The Development of Syndicalism in America." *Political Science Quarterly* 28 (1913):451–97.

1963. "The Louis F. Post Case." *New Republic* 22 (May 26, 1920):411.

The attempted prosecution of Post because of his book, *The Deportations Delirium* (see no. 179).

1964. Lovejoy, Owen R. "Right of Free Speech in Lawrence." *Survey* 27 (March 9, 1912):1904–5.
Eyewitness account of the strike by a leader of the National Child Labor Committee.

1965. ———. "The Right of Free Speech in Lawrence." *Weekly Bulletin of the Clothing Trades* (UGWA) 11 (March 15, 1912):5.
A reprint of no. 1964.

1966. Lovin, Hugh T. "Idaho and the 'Reds,' 1919–1926." *Pacific Northwest Quarterly* 69 (July, 1978):107–15.

1967. ———. "Moses Alexander and the Idaho Lumber Strike of 1917—The Wartime Ordeal of a Progressive." *Pacific Northwest Quarterly* 66 (July, 1975):115–22.

1968. ———. "Red Scare in Idaho, 1916–1918." *Idaho Yesterdays* 17 (Fall, 1973):2–13.

1969. Lowe, Caroline. "Letter from Our Attorney on the Wichita Case." *One Big Union Monthly* 1 (September, 1919):9.
The progress of the Wichita cases.

1970. Lowney, J. C. "Lowney's Letter from the Strike Zone." *Miners Magazine* 14 (November 27, 1913):9.
Violence at the Calumet-Hecla strike.

1971. ———. "Lowney Sums Up the Situation in Michigan." *Miners Magazine* 14 (November 6, 1913):6–7.
The Calumet-Hecla strike.

1972. ———. "The Michigan Strike." *Miners Magazine* 14 (September 11, 1913):12–13.

1973. ———. "Report from Montana." *Miners Magazine* 21 (November, 1920):1.
The confusion left after the struggle between the IWW and the WFM and other unions.

1974. "Lumber Strike." *International Socialist Review* 18 (November–December, 1917):308–9.

1975. "Lumber War News." *Lumberjack* 1 (June 19, 1913):1, 4.

1976. "Lumber Workers' Conference." *Industrial Pioneer* 3 (April, 1926):29.
A Pacific Northwest conference.

1977. "Lumberman Calls for Militant Americanism." *American Lumberman* 2319 (October 25, 1919):40.

Lumber company spokesman says that the only solution to the IWW problem is to kill its members.

1978. "Lumbermen Aroused by Assassinations." *American Lumberman* 2322 (November 15, 1919):45.
The Centralia Massacre from the lumber companies' point of view.

1979. Lusk, Clayton R. "Radicalism under Inquiry." *Review of Reviews* 61 (February, 1920):167–71.
The Lusk Committee actions explained by a New York State senator.

1980. Lusk, Hugh H. "The Australian Strike for National Control." *Bellman* 24 (June 22, 1918):685–89.

1981. Lynch, Patrick. "Pittsburgh, the IWW, and the Stogie Workers." In Joseph R. Conlin, ed., *At the Point of Production* (Westport, CT: Greenwood Press, 1981), 79–94 (see no. 39).

1982. "Lynch-Law and Treason; Lynching of Frank Little in Butte." *Literary Digest* 55 (August 18, 1917):12–13.

1983. Lyons, Eugene. "Tulsa: A Study in Oil." *One Big Union Monthly* 1 (December, 1919):35–37.
The flimsy indictment and trial of Charles Krieger, an IWW victim of the Carter Oil Company frame-up.

1984. McClelland, John M., Jr. "Terror on Tower Avenue." *Pacific Northwest Quarterly* 57 (April, 1966):65–72.
The Centralia affair.

1985. McClurg, Donald J. "The Colorado Coal Strike of 1927—Tactical Leadership of the IWW." *Labor History* 4 (Winter, 1963):68–92.

1986. ———. Review of *Debaters and Dynamiters,* by David H. Grover (see no. 89). *Labor History* 6 (Fall, 1965):262–63.

1987. McCormack, A. Ross. "Industrial Workers of the World in Western Canada, 1905–1914." *Historical Papers of the Canadian Historical Association, 1975,* 167–90.

1988. McCormick, Kyle. "The National Guard of West Virginia during the Strike Period of 1912–1913." *West Virginia History* 22 (October, 1960):34–35.

1989. McDonald, E. E. "An Injury to One Is the Concern of All." *One Big Union Monthly* 1 (May, 1919):46.
Report from Ellis Island of a radical deportee.

1990. MacDonald, J. A. "Building the New Society Now." *Industrial Pioneer* 4 (July, 1926):7–9.

1991. ———. "From Butte to Bisbee." *International Socialist Review* 18 (August, 1917):69–71.

The demands of striking copper miners who faced troops, gunmen, deportation, and perjured witnesses.

1992. ———. "A New Chapter in Industrial Revolution." *International Socialist Review* 16 (December, 1915):347–49.

Organizing Midwestern agricultural workers.

1993. ———. "Paving, Slaving, and Saving." *Industrial Pioneer* 4 (May, 1926):4–9.

Arguments for joining a union.

1994. ———. "Training for Freedom." *Industrial Pioneer* 1 (March, 1924):29–30, 36.

Experiences of IWW lumberworkers in the Canadian Rockies, showing that the IWW was a moral force.

1995. ———. "Training for Freedom." *Industrial Pioneer* 3 (March, 1926):11–12.

The Finnish IWW cooperative in Port Arthur, Ontario, its outstanding restaurant, and artistic groups that train the workers for a better world.

1996. McDonald, P. B. "Michigan Copper-Miners." *Outlook* 106 (February 7, 1914):297–98.

The Calumet-Hecla strike.

1997. MacDonald, William. "Seattle Strike and Afterwards." *Nation* 108 (March 29, 1919):469–70.

1998. ———. "Where Labor Points the Way." *Nation* 108 (April 5, 1919):499–501.

The government raids and arrests an insufficient response to the problem.

1999. Macfarlane, P. C. "Issues at Calumet." *Collier's* 52 (February 7, 1914):5–6, 22–25.

2000. McGowan, Kenneth. "Giovannitti—Poet of the Wop." *Forum* 52 (October, 1914):609–11.

The IWW gave, through Giovannitti and others, "illiterates" and "scum" a realization of their dignity and rights.

2001. McGregor. "The Way Rockefeller Looks at It." *Harper's Weekly* 58 (May 23, 1914):12–13.

Rockefeller disclaims any responsibility for mine conditions, working conditions, or the Ludlow Massacre.

2002. ———. "Wreckers of Peace—Industrial Workers of the World Are Railroad Strike Advocates All Over the World. An Illustration of the Fact from New Zealand." *Labor World* 22 (February 12, 1914):4, 13.

2003. McGurty, Edward J. "The Copper Miners' Strike." *International Socialist Review* 14 (September, 1913):150–53.
The Calumet-Hecla strike.

2004. McKee, Don K. "Daniel De Leon: A Reappraisal." *Labor History* 1 (Fall, 1960):264–97.

2005. ———. "The Influence of Syndicalism on Daniel De Leon." *Historian* 20 (May, 1958):275–89.

2006. McKee, Harry M., and E. E. Kirk. "Review Vindicated." *International Socialist Review* 14 (October, 1913):231.
The San Diego Free Speech Fight.

2007. "McKees Rocks Strikers Win." *Survey* 22 (September 11, 1909):795.

2008. McKenna, William E. "The Tariff and the Worker." *Public* 16 (July 4, 1913):631.
The investigations after the Little Falls strike proved how bad the working conditions were.

2009. McKinley, F. "The Railway Situation." *Industrial Pioneer* 1 (November, 1921):3–4.
Railroad workers should get out of craft unions.

2010. McMahan, Ronald L. "Rang-U-Tang; The IWW and the 1927 Colorado Coal Strike." In Joseph R. Conlin, ed., *At the Point of Production* (Westport, CT: Greenwood Press, 1981), 191–212 (see no. 39).

2011. McMahon, Theresa S. "Centralia and the IWW." *Survey* 43 (November 29, 1919):173–74.

2012. ———. "Strike in Seattle." *Survey* 41 (March 8, 1919):821–23.

2013. McMurray, Donald L. Review of *The Decline of the I.W.W.*, by John S. Gambs (see no. 76). *Mississippi Valley Historical Review* 19 (September, 1932):313.

2014. MacPhee, Donald A. "The Centralia Incident and the Pamphleteers." *Pacific Northwest Quarterly* 62 (July, 1971):110–16.

2015. McPherson, John B. "The Lawrence Strike of 1912." *Bulletin of the National Association of Wool Manufacturers* (September, 1912):219–65.
Excellent analysis of the strike.

2016. McWhiney, Grady. "Louisiana Socialists in the Early Twentieth Century: A Study of Rustic Radicalism." *Journal of Southern History* 20 (August, 1954):315–36.

2017. Madison, Charles A. "Out of Labor's Past: The Insurgent I.W.W." *Labor and Nation* 5 (July, 1949):35–38.
A brief scholarly account of the IWW.

2018. Mahoney, C. E., Haywood, W. D., et al. "To Believers in Industrial Unionism." *Miners Magazine* 9 (January 9, 1908):5.
Defense of the IWW against growing dissent among the WFM.

2019. Maitland, F. "Bolshevism Testing Canadian Common Sense." *Outlook* 122 (June 18, 1919):282–83.
Winnipeg's general strike will not be tolerated by Canadians.

2020. Malkov, V. L. "Dva Neizvestnykh Pis'ma Villiama D. Kheivuda" (Two letters by William D. Haywood). *Amerikanskii Eghegodnik* (1980):301–11.
Describes two letters written from Moscow by William D. Haywood.

2021. "The Man that Was Hung." *International Socialist Review* 18 (September, 1917):135–38.
Frank Little's lynching.

2022. "The Man Who Made a Hero of Himself and His Comrades." *Square Deal* 11 (December, 1912):410–12.
Derogatory article about Joseph Ettor.

2023. "The Man with the Gun." *Bellman* 24 (February 16, 1918):174–75.
The IWW is a force for evil.

2024. "Manifesto and Call for a Convention." *Miners Magazine* 6 (February 2, 1905):13.
Reprinted in later issues.

2025. "Manifesto of Industrial Unionists." *International Socialist Review* 5 (February, 1905):476–79.
The IWW manifesto.

2026. "Manifesto on Deportation." *One Big Union Monthly* 1 (May, 1919):29–30.
Manifesto prepared by the IWW's New York Defense Committee declares that Gompers and the AFL are behind the deportations of radical unionists.

2027. Mann, Fred. "The Harvest Drive Is On Again." *Industrial Pioneer* 3 (July, 1925):3–7.

2028. ———. "The Old 400." *Industrial Pioneer* 4 (July, 1926):10–12.
The Agricultural Workers Union, a special unit of the IWW.

2029. ———. "Revolution to the Front!" *Industrial Pioneer* 2 (December, 1924):28–30.
Interpretation of the 1924 convention.

2030. Mann, Tom. "A Plea for Solidarity." *International Socialist Review* 14 (January, 1914):392–94.
Mann's twenty-week tour through the U.S.; he believes that the IWW has not organized well enough and that all unions seem to be in conflict.

2031. Mannheimer, Leo. "Darkest New Jersey—How the Paterson Strike Looks to One in the Thick of the Conflict." *Independent* 74 (May 29, 1913):1190–92.
Discussion of the strike, during which several unions were in contention.

2032. "March of Industrial Unionism—The Giant Stirs." *Messenger* 2 (September, 1919):6–7.
Man's inexorable desire to organize.

2033. Marcus, I. M. "Benjamin Fletcher: Black Labor Leader." *Negro History Bulletin* 35 (October, 1972):138–40.
A well-known IWW leader.

2034. Marcy, Leslie H. "Calumet." *International Socialist Review* 14 (February, 1914):453–61.
The Calumet strike.

2035. ———. "800 Per Cent and the Akron Strike." *International Socialist Review* 13 (April, 1913):711–24.
Thorough examination of the rubber workers' working conditions and strike.

2036. ———. "The Eleven Hundred Exiled Copper Miners." *International Socialist Review* 18 (September, 1917):160–62.
The Bisbee deportation.

2037. ———. “The Iron Heel on the Mesabi Range.” *International Socialist Review* 17 (August, 1916):74–80.
The force used against strikers during the Mesabi Range strike.

2038. ———. “More ‘Law and Order.’” *International Socialist Review* 17 (November, 1916):269–70.
The brutality of the police and military toward the strikers.

2039. ———. “On the Strike Field—the Fight in the Mountains.” *International Socialist Review* 13 (March, 1913):647–49.
The West Virginia coal strike.

2040. ———. “Tenth Annual I.W.W. Convention.” *International Socialist Review* 17 (January, 1917):406–9.
Account of the convention with sketches of the leaders.

2041. Marcy, Leslie H., and Frederick S. Boyd. “One Big Union Wins.” *International Socialist Review* 12 (April, 1912):613–30.
The Lawrence strike is “the greatest victory in labor history.”

2042. Marcy, Mary. “The Battle for Bread in Lawrence.” *International Socialist Review* 12 (March, 1912):533–43.

2043. ———. “The IWW Convention.” *Liberator* 2 (July, 1919):10–12.

2044. ———. “Killed without Warning by the American Capitalist Class.” *International Socialist Review* 17 (March, 1917):519–22.
Ludlow proved that death without warning can come to workers in unsafe factories and mines, as well as at the hands of police and governments.

2045. ———. “A Month of Lawlessness.” *International Socialist Review* 18 (September, 1917):154–57.
The lynching of Frank Little.

2046. ———. “The Passing of Cripple Creek.” *One Big Union Monthly* 2 (April, 1920):25.
The long and violent history of Cripple Creek, Colorado.

2047. ———. “The Spendthrift Workers.” *One Big Union Monthly* 2 (August, 1920):58–59.
Economic projection of a bleak and materialistic future.

2048. Margolis, Jacob. “The Orthodox Wobbly and the Borer from Within.” *One Big Union Monthly* 1 (October, 1919):27–29.
The “boring-from-within” technique of European Syndicalism will never work in America.

2049. ———. "The Streets of Pittsburgh." *International Socialist Review* 13 (October, 1912):313–20.
The Pittsburgh Free Speech Fight.

2050. "Marine Transport Industry." *Industrial Pioneer* 1 (June, 1923): 29–30.
The MTWIU #510.

2051. "Marine Transport Workers Close Up New York." *Rebel Worker* 2 (October 15, 1919):1.
The New York harbor strike.

2052. "Marine Worker." *One Big Union Advocate* 1 (July, 1939):16–20.
The activities and success of the Marine Transport Workers Union.

2053. Markus, Rosa. "The Case of Ettor and Giovannitti." *Agitator* 2 (July 1, 1912):4.

2054. Marriott, J. A. R. "Political Syndicalism." *Fortnightly Review* 111 (March, 1919):331–40.

2055. Martin, Frederick Roy. "From the Associated Press." *New Republic* 12 (October 6, 1917):275.
The connection between the Associated Press and the mine owners.

2056. Martin, John. "Defense News." *Industrial Pioneer* 1 (March, 1921): 45.
The IWW prisoners, considered as political prisoners.

2057. ———. "Defense News." *One Big Union Monthly* 2 (November, 1920):54–55.
The sudden great numbers of prisoners and the help that will be needed.

2058. ———. "Defense Situation." *Industrial Pioneer* 1 (February, 1921): 58–60.
The need for moral and financial support of the prisoners.

2059. ———. "Industrial Revolt at Lawrence." *Independent* 72 (March 7, 1912):491–95.
A legal minimum wage might help avoid strikes such as the Lawrence strike.

2060. ———. "News from the Lumber Workers' Strike." *International Socialist Review* 18 (September, 1917):144–48.
Strikers are being arrested by the hundreds.

2061. "Mary Konovsky's Wage—Little Falls Investigation Causes Interesting Letter." *Square Deal* 12 (February, 1913):49–50.
Employer believes that the wages for some "stupid" immigrants are already too high.

2062. Mason, Gregory. "Industrial War in Paterson." *Outlook* 104 (June 7, 1913):283–87.

2063. Mason, Philip P. "Notes and Documents: Joe Hill, Cartoonist." *Labor History* 25 (Fall, 1984):533–57.
Describes hand-drawn postcards sent by Joe Hill to his friends and the circumstances in which they were sketched.

2064. "Mass Action—Where We Stand." *International Socialist Review* 17 (December, 1916):367–69.
A Socialist view of the IWW, direct action, sabotage, and other concerns.

2065. "Master in Chancery Report." *Industrial Workers of the World Bulletin No. 5* (January 10, 1907):2.
Legal report after the first IWW split, when Socialist Labor and WFM members left.

2066. "Mass and Craft Unions." *Survey* 27 (February, 1912):1792–94.
The Lawrence strike was a controversy between two kinds of unions.

2067. Mathews, M. A. "I.W.W." *Survey* 39 (October 20, 1917):75.
Typical expression of hate and fear of the IWW during the Red Scare, in a letter to the editor.

2068. Matthews, Franklin. "Murder as a Labor Weapon." *Harper's Weekly* 50 (June 2, 1906):766–68.
The Steunenberg murder.

2069. "May Day and the Six Hour Day." *Industrial Worker* 47 (May 2, 1955):2.

2070. "May Day in Ft. Leavenworth." *Liberator* 2 (June, 1919):10.
IWW prisoners celebrate May Day.

2071. "May First." *Industrial Pioneer* 4 (May, 1926):26–27.
The worker and employer still have "nothing in common."

2072. May, Henry F. "The End of American Radicalism." *American Quarterly* 2 (Winter, 1950):291–302.
The IWWs may have been the last real rebels.

2073. Mayhall, Pamela. "Bisbee's Response to Civil Disorder—A Matter of Circumstance." *American West* 9 (May, 1972):22–31.
Article answered by James Byrkit. See no. 553.

2074. "Mayor Gill Says IWW Did Not Start Everett Riot." *Solidarity* 7 (November 25, 1916):1.
The Everett citizens who fired on the IWW were to blame for the massacre.

2075. "Mayor Ole Hanson, Who Sat Tight at Seattle." *Literary Digest* 60 (March 8, 1919):47–50.
The Seattle General Strike.

2076. Meader, John R. "Industrial Socialism: A New Peril." *Common Cause* 1 (February, 1912):33–37.
A discussion of Haywood and Bohn's *Industrial Socialism.*

2077. "The Meaning of the Western Strikes." *Literary Digest* 60 (March 1, 1919):14–15.

2078. "The Meeting of the General Executive Board." *Industrial Union Bulletin* 1 (February 1, 1908):1–2.
A crucial IWW meeting described in detail.

2079. Melis, Louis. "Hotel, Restaurant and Domestic Workers." *One Big Union Monthly* 1 (April, 1919):59–62.
Presents the union and its advantages to waiters and domestic workers.

2080. "Membership Criminal in California." *Nation* 114 (April 19, 1922):456.
Membership in the IWW without any overt act is a crime.

2081. "The Men Whom We Are Deporting." *American Review of Reviews* 61 (February, 1920):123–30.

2082. Menchen, L. "Is Religion a Handicap to the Labor Movement?" *One Big Union Monthly* 1 (April, 1919):40.
Mind control is unnecessary to the labor movement.

2083. Merz, Charles. "The Issue in Butte." *New Republic* 12 (September 22, 1917):215–17.
Control of industry should be put on a democratic basis.

2084. ———. "Tying Up Western Lumber." *New Republic* 12 (September 29, 1917):242–44.
The rash of lumber strikes in the Pacific Northwest, many of them IWW strikes for the eight-hour day.

2085. "Methods of Sabotage." *Outlook* 103 (February 1, 1913):255–57.
Methods and types of sabotage.

2086. Meyer, E. F. "Six Killed, Twenty Wounded: A Case Study of Industrial Conflict." *Survey* 59 (February 15, 1928):644–46.
The Colorado coal strike.

2087. Meyerhuber, Carl, Jr. "The Alle-Kiski Coal Wars, 1913–1919." *Western Pennsylvania Historical Magazine* 63 (July, 1980):197–213.

2088. Meyers, Rex C. "Vigilante Numbers: A Re-Examination." *Montana, Magazine of Western History* 24 (Autumn, 1974):67–70.
About "3–7–77," the mystery number left by the lynchers of Frank Little.

2089. Michaelis, G. V. S. "The Westinghouse Strike." *Survey* 32 (August 1, 1914):463–65.
The strike of electrical workers in Pittsburgh.

2090. Michelson, M. "Feudalism and Civil War in the United States." *Everybody's Magazine* 28 (May, 1913):615–28.
A description of the emotions of Mother Jones during labor controversies, with a good photograph of her.

2091. "The Michigan Copper Miners' Strike; Fight of the Western Federation of Miners to Unionize Calumet and Hecla and Other Peninsula Properties." *American Employer* 2 (November, 1913): 227–30.

2092. "The Michigan Copper Strike." *Literary Digest* 47 (December 6, 1913):1097–98.

2093. "The Michigan Copper Strike." *Outlook* 106 (January 31, 1914):237–39.

2094. "The Michigan Defeat and Its Lesson." *Miners Magazine* 15 (May 7, 1914):4.
The cost of the Calumet-Hecla strike.

2095. "The Michigan Press on the Copper War." *Literary Digest* 48 (January 10, 1914):47–49.
The Calumet-Hecla strike.

2096. "Michigan Strike a Victory and Merely a Skirmish." *Miners Magazine* 15 (April 30, 1914):8.

2097. Miles, Dione. "Agnes Inglis." *The Dandelion* 3 (Winter, 1979):7–15.
The former curator of the Labadie Collection at the University of Michigan, an active member of the IWW.

2098. ———. "Sources for the Local History of the IWW." In Joseph R. Conlin, ed., *At the Point of Production* (Westport, CT: Greenwood Press, 1981), 237–318 (see no. 39).
Extensive bibliography of IWW sources, limited to local history.

2099. "A Militia Man's Experiences." *Survey* 28 (April 6, 1912):76–77.
A personal recollection of the Lawrence strike.

2100. "Mill Murderers of Massachusetts." *Miners Magazine* 12 (March 7, 1912):7–8.
About the Lawrence strike, showing great bias against the IWW.

2101. "A Mill Overseer's View." *Survey* 28 (April 6, 1912):75–76.
The Lawrence strike from the employers' side.

2102. Miller, Charles H. "Our Great Neglected Wobbly." *Michigan Quarterly Review* 6 (Winter, 1967):57–61.
About the author B. Traven. See nos. 5017–18.

2103. Miller, Charles J. "Lawrence, 1912." *Industrial Worker* 26 (July 14, 1945):3; (July 21, 1945):3.
An IWW history of the strike.

2104. Miller, Francis. "Some Criticism of the IWW." *Solidarity* 4 (September 13, 1913):2.
The IWW answer to criticism in the magazine *Social War.* See no. 1683.

2105. Miller, Grace. "The IWW Free Speech Fight: San Diego 1912." *South California Historical Society Quarterly* 54 (Fall, 1972):211–38.

2106. Miller, Guy E. "Lesson of the Michigan Strike." *Miners Magazine* 15 (March 19, 1914):7–8.

2107. ———. "That Manifesto." *Miners Magazine* 6 (February 23, 1905):7–8.
Proposed new American Labor Union, which might be better than the last American Labor Union.

2108. Miller, H. A. "Joe Ettor's Socialism." *Survey* 27 (March 16, 1912):1943–44.
A letter and an editorial answer regarding the Lawrence strike and the IWW.

2109. "Millions Made on the Mesaba." *International Socialist Review* 17 (October, 1916):230.
The Mesabi Range made millions for a few but little for the miners.

2110. Mills, Edward L. "The Centralia Report." *Christian Century* 47 (November 26, 1930): 1461.
The Federal Council of Churches' report on Centralia. See no. 33.

2111. ———. "Churches' Plea Wins Parole." *Christian Century* 48 (July 29, 1931):980.
Some of the Centralia prisoners were released thanks to the plea of the churches.

2112. Mills, James. "Comes the Revolution." *San Diego Magazine* (October, 1959):67.
The earlier days of the IWW.

2113. "Miners Strike." *Life and Labor* 3 (November, 1913):346–47.
The Calumet-Hecla strike.

2114. "Miners' Strike at Goldfield." *Outlook* 87 (December 21, 1907): 833–39.
A long and detailed description of the Goldfield strike.

2115. "The Miners' Strikes." *Life and Labor* 4 (February, 1914):52–54.
Strikes in Michigan and West Virginia.

2116. "Mining War in Colorado." *Outlook* 107 (May 9, 1914):49.
The Colorado coal strike.

2117. "Minnesota Workers Strike." *Miners Magazine* 17 (July 6, 1916):1.
The IWW strike in the Mesabi region and strike leaders Sam Scarlett and Bill Haywood.

2118. "Minnesota's Striking Iron Miners." *Literary Digest* 53 (September 23, 1916):732–33.

2119. Minor, Robert. "The Great Flop." *Liberator* 3 (May, 1920):20–22.
Harold Lord Varney, once an IWW member, resigned and worked against the union when the raids and arrests began.

2120. ———. "In the Anthracite Hills." *International Socialist Review* 16 (April, 1916):589–94.
Dissatisfaction and unrest among Pennsylvania coal miners.

2121. "Misconceptions of the IWW." *Labor Defender* 1 (December 1, 1918):4–5.

2122. "Miss Scudder's Misreported Speech." *Outlook* 100 (April 20, 1912):846–47.
The Lawrence strike speech that caused trouble for Vida Scudder.

2123. Mittleman, Edward B. "Gyppo System." *Journal of Political Economy* 31 (December, 1923):840–51.
An unusual system of remuneration in the Pacific Northwest lumber mills.

2124. ———. "Loyal Legion of Loggers and Lumbermen." *Journal of Political Economy* 31 (June, 1923):313–41.
The new union sponsored by the lumbermen's employers and the U.S. Government.

2125. "Mobs Cannot Kill the Revolutionary Spirit." *Lumber Jack* 3 (May 4, 1918):1.
Raids and arrests will not stop the IWW.

2126. "Modern Judas." *Miners Magazine* 22 (May, 1921):1.
The IWW is the Judas of labor.

2127. Modesto, Zapata. "The Death of Joe Hill." *Masses and Mainstream* (September, 1962):3–16.

2128. ———. "In Salt Lake City a Living Memorial to Joe Hill." *Sing Out* 12 (October–November, 1962):14–16.

2129. Moe, Fred. "The Fresno Mob." *Agitator* 1 (January 1, 1911):4.
The Fresno Free Speech Fight.

2130. ———. "Industrialism Coming." *Agitator* 1 (February, 1911):4.
Unionism is growing with the advent of industrial unions.

2131. Monaco, F. "San Francisco Shoe Workers Strike." *International Socialist Review* 13 (May, 1913):818–19.

2132. Monoldi, Peo. "The Construction Worker." *One Big Union Monthly* NS 1 (July, 1937):3–6.
The Construction Workers Industrial Union.

2133. Monroy, Douglas. "Anarquismo y Comunismo: Mexican Radicalism and the Communist Party in Los Angeles during the 1930's." *Labor History* 24 (Winter, 1983):34–59.

2134. "Montana IWW's Arrested." *Miners Magazine* 19 (October, 1918):2.

One of several stories in the issue expressing satisfaction at the IWW's troubles.

2135. "Montesano—Is the IWW on Trial?" *Survey* 43 (March 13, 1920):734–35.

The fairness of the Centralia trial.

2136. Montgomery, David. "The Conventional Wisdom." *Labor History* 13 (1972):107–36.

Bibliographic review of a sixty-volume series of books on American labor.

2137. ———. "The New Unionism and the Transformation of Workers' Consciousness in America, 1909–1922." *Journal of Social History* 7 (Summer, 1974):509–29.

Radicals' contribution to industrial unionism and consciousness of rights.

2138. Montgomery, James. "The Lawrence Strike and the Literacy Test." *New Review* 1 (March 22, 1913):376–81.

Fear engendered by the Lawrence strike's show of power by the workers led to restrictive laws against immigrants.

2139. "The Mooney General Strike and the I.W.W." *One Big Union Monthly* 1 (July, 1919):11.

Part of an attempt to call a general strike to free Mooney.

2140. "More Centralia Case Letters." *New Republic* 64 (September 17, 1930):129.

2141. Moresby, George. "Centralia in 1925." *Industrial Pioneer* 2 (February, 1925):9–12.

Review of the evidence of various witnesses shows the unfairness of the Centralia trial.

2142. Morgan, George T., Jr. "The Gospel of Wealth Goes South: John Henry Kirby and Labor's Struggle for Self-Determination, 1901–1916." *Southwestern Historical Quarterly* 75 (October, 1971):186–97.

The (IWW) Brotherhood of Timber Workers' strike.

2143. ———. "No Compromise—No Recognition: John Kirby, the Southern Lumber Operators' Association and Unionism in the Piney Woods 1906–1916." *Labor History* 10 (Spring, 1969):193–204.

The (IWW) Brotherhood of Timber Workers' losing fight in the South.

2144. Morgan, J. Edward. "The Living Dead in San Francisco." *Everyman* (April–May, 1914):13–26.

Bad conditions will create more radicals.

2145. ———. "The Unemployed in San Francisco." *New Review* 2 (April, 1914):193–99.

The march of the army of unemployed to the governor's house.

2146. Morgan, John S. "The IWW on High Seas and Waterfront." *One Big Uniion Monthly* NS 1 (December, 1937):7–9.

Recent successes in organizing marine workers and seamen.

2147. Morris, James. "The Labor Movement and the I.W.W." *Industrial Pioneer* 1 (November, 1923):45–46.

The ebb and flow of IWW fortunes in organizing and defending itself.

2148. ———. "Tired Radicals." *Industrial Pioneer* 1 (January, 1924):37–38.

Settling down in everyday life, a radical often becomes an ex-radical. How can ex-Wobblies be revived?

2149. Morris, James O. "Philip Foner and the Writing of the Joe Hill Case: An Exchange." *Labor History* 12 (Winter, 1971):81–114.

See no. 1165.

2150. Morton, Jack. "Trial of the Timber Workers." *International Socialist Review* 13 (November, 1912):407.

The Louisiana lumber strike and its aftermath.

2151. Morton, Michael. "No Time To Quibble: The Jones Conspiracy Trial of 1917." *Chronicles of Oklahoma* 59 (Summer, 1981):224–36.

The Green Corn rebellion, in which the IWW, which originated the Working Class Union in Oklahoma, had a peripheral part.

2152. "Moses and the IWW." *Lumberjack* 1 (June 5, 1913):4.

Could Moses have been the first Wobbly?

2153. Moss, William R. "Your Country and Mine—the Danger Facing It." *American Lumberman* 2318 (October 18, 1919):46–47, 76.
The danger of Syndicalism.

2154. Most, Mel. "Further Light on the 1913 Silk Strike." (Hackensack, NJ) *Sunday Record Magazine* (November 11, 1973):6–8.

2155. ———. "Going Back." (Hackensack, NJ) *Sunday Record Magazine* (September 30, 1973):8, 20.
Former striker Sophie Cohen and *Record* editor visiting the site of the Paterson strike.

2156. ———. "A Modest Place in History." (Hackensack, NJ) *Record* (September 29, 1974):n.p.
The Pietro Botto house, a National Historic Landmark and an important site in the Paterson strike.

2157. ———. "The Silk Strike Terror of 1913." (Hackensack, NJ) *Sunday Record Magazine* (September 30, 1973):6–7, 11–13.
Eye-witness accounts of the Paterson strike.

2158. "The Motion To Recall Haywood." *International Socialist Review* 13 (February, 1913):625.
The ouster of Haywood and the split in the Socialist Party.

2159. "Moving Mountains for Molehill Wages." *Industrial Pioneer* 2 (September, 1924):5, 37.
The overworked and underpaid workers of Bingham, Utah.

2160. Moyer, Charles. "Letter to the Membership." *Miners Magazine* 18 (August, 1917):3.
The trouble and hatred as well as the rivalry between the WFM and the IWW.

2161. Moyer, Charles H., and W. D. Haywood. "Discuss the Manifesto." *Miners Magazine* 6 (April 13, 1905):3
The manifesto and the launching of the IWW.

2162. ———. "Open Letter to All WFM Members, April 10, 1905." *Miners Magazine* 6 (April 13, 1905).
The WFM should support the IWW.

2163. "Moyer and Haywood Have Forgotten Their Old Companionship." *Square Deal* 12 (April, 1913):263–65.
The WFM says that the IWW mishandled the Lawrence strike funds.

2164. "Moyer, Haywood and Pettibone Arrested—A Kidnapping Conspiracy." *Miners Magazine* 7 (February 22, 1906):4–5.

2165. "Moyer, Haywood Trial." *Miners Magazine* 8 (March 28, 1907):4–5.

2166. "Mr. D'Olier's Warning to the American Legion." *New Republic* 21 (December 31, 1919):129.
American Legion officer's warning to the Legion that civil liberties should not be violated.

2167. "Mr. Kent on the I.W.W." *Public* 21 (July 13, 1918):878–79.
Reasons to support the IWW defense in the Chicago trial and elsewhere.

2168. "Mrs. Avery and a Lawrence Mill Worker." *Common Cause* 1 (April, 1912):98–99.
Differing views on the Lawrence strike.

2169. Mueller, J. R. "Food in the Lumber Camps." *Journal of Home Economics* 13 (June, 1921):241–45.
Lumberworkers' food, a subject of dispute between them and their employers.

2170. Mundell, Charles. "The Socialist and Communist Conventions." *One Big Union Monthly* 1 (October, 1919):17–19.
Socialist and Communist attitudes toward the IWW.

2171. "Municipal Plans for the Unemployed." *Survey* 31 (February 21, 1914):633–35.
Kansas City and St. Louis plans for unemployed workers disputed.

2172. "Murder Charge at a Labor Union's Door." *Harper's Weekly* 51 (May 25, 1907):762–65.
The first Haywood trial.

2173. "Murder Is Murder." *Outlook* 109 (January 27, 1915):151.
Labor trouble at a fertilizer works in New Jersey; Roosevelt's famous words about the shooting of a striker.

2174. Murphy, Paul L. "The Sources and Nature of Intolerance in the 1920s." *Journal of American History* 51 (June, 1964):60–76.

2175. Murray, Keith. "Issues and Personalities of Pacific Northwest Politics." *Pacific Northwest Quarterly* 41 (July, 1950):213–33.
A broad view of politics and people, including a statement that the IWW destroyed itself by its own excesses.

2176. Murray, Robert K. "Centralia: An Unfinished American Tragedy." *Northwest Review* 6 (Spring, 1963):7–18.

2177. ———. "Communism and the Great Steel Strike of 1919." *Mississippi Valley Historical Review* 38 (December, 1951):445–66.
The IWW had a place in the strike.

2178. ———. "Review of *Rebels of the Woods,* by Robert Tyler (see no. 221). *Journal of American History* 55 (December, 1968):674–75.

2179. ———. Review of *We Shall Be All,* by Melvyn Dubofsky (see no. 59). *Journal of American History* 57 (December, 1970):183–85.

2180. "A Musical Auxiliary." *Bulletin* 1 (November 15, 1907):93–94.
New York musicians join the IWW.

2181. "Musicians and Evolution." *Bulletin* (IMTIU) 2 (May 5, 1908):97–99.
The International Music and Theater Industrial Union disappointed in the IWW.

2182. Mussey, Henry R. "Louis F. Post—American." *Nation* 110 (June 12, 1920):192–93.
Post's support of civil rights and opposition to the deportations.

2183. Myers, Gustavus. "Bolshevik 'Industrial Government.'" *National Civic Federation Review* 4 (December 20, 1918):8–9, 18–19.
Boleshevik ideas of industrial government compared with those of the IWW.

2184. "Mysterious Journey of State Police." *Miners Magazine* 9 (February 27, 1908):11.
State policemen headed for Goldfield are in such comic and extreme disguise that they may be spotted instantly.

2185. Nafe, Gertrude. "The School Teacher and the IWW." *Labor Defender* 1 (July 30, 1918):6.
Teachers do not teach justice, liberty, or democracy because they do not understand it. They should ask the IWW what the words mean.

2186. Nagel, Charles. "Why Are These Men in Jail?" *Collier's* 72 (October 13, 1923):33.
The sentences being given the IWWs are far too harsh.

2187. "Nailing a Lie." *Shoe Workers' Journal* 13 (May, 1912):8–12.
Those who call the Shoe Workers' union label "tainted" are lying.

2188. "National Socialist." *Miners Magazine* 12 (December 26, 1912):5.
Bill Haywood's ouster from the Socialist Party.

2189. "National Socialist Convention of 1912." *International Socialist Review* 12 (June, 1912):807–31.
Bill Haywood's ouster from the Socialist Party.

2190. Nearing, Scott. "On the Trail of the Pittsburgh Stogies." *Independent* 65 (July, 1908):22–24.
Child labor among the Pittsburgh cigar workers.

2191. ———. "Those Who Own and Those Who Work." In Austin Lewis, ed., *Proletarian and Petit-Bourgeois* (Chicago: IWW, 1911), 35–47.
America's chief economic contrast is between those with property income and those with service income. Pay should go only to those who work.

2192. "The Need for One Big Union." *One Big Union Advocate* 1 (May, 1939):5–9.

2193. "A Needless Labor War." *Outlook* 100 (January 27, 1912):151–52.
A disapproving view of the Lawrence strike.

2194. Nef, W. T. "Job Control in the Harvest Fields." *International Socialist Review* 17 (September, 1916):141–43.
The astonishing increase in the number of organized farmworkers.

2195. ———. "The Militant Harvest Workers." *International Socialist Review* 17 (October, 1916):229–30.
The successful drive to organize farmworkers.

2196. ———. "A Miscarriage of Justice." *Messenger* 3 (September, 1921):252–53.
The AFL does not really accept the Negro equally.

2197. ———. "A Miscarriage of Justice—Continued." *Messenger* 3 (November, 1921):282–83.
A continuation of no. 2196.

2198. "Negro and the American Federation of Labor." *Messenger* 2 (August, 1919):10–12.

2199. "Negro at Work." *Review of Reviews* 59 (April, 1919):387–93.

2200. "Negro Workers: The AFL or IWW." *Messenger* 2 (July, 1917):14–15.
Only the IWW is without prejudice.

2201. "Negro's Best Weapon." *Challenge* (November, 1919):164–65.
If Negroes organize and achieve solidarity they will move ahead.

2202. Nelles, W. "In the Wake of the Espionage Act." *Nation* 111 (December 15, 1920):684–86.
The raids and the arrests of radicals all over the country.

2203. "New Alien and Sedition Law." *New Republic* 20 (November 26, 1919):366.
Attorney General Palmer and the ethics of the Palmer Raids.

2204. "A New and Better Wheatland." *Outlook* 111 (October 15, 1915):348–49.
Conditions for farmworkers have improved since the Wheatland episode.

2205. "A New Element in Strikes." *World's Work* 24 (May, 1912):13–14.
In the Lawrence strike, the IWW wanted job control rather than agreement.

2206. "New Jersey Needs the Recall." *Public* 17 (June 16, 1914):605.
Pat Quinlan's sentence after the Paterson strike.

2207. "A New Jersey Weaver, a Budget and a Gospel of Revolution." *Survey* 28 (May 18, 1912):289–91.
A personalized story of the Paterson strike.

2208. "New Jersey's Journalistic Perils." *Literary Digest* 46 (June 21, 1913): 1366–67.
Alexander Scott was indicted for publishing unfavorable news stories about the role of the police at the Paterson strike.

2209. "The New Labor Movement." *Literary Digest* 44 (April 6, 1912):677–78.
The strikes at the textile mills of New Jersey and Massachusetts are part of a new style of unions and a new style of striking.

2210. "New One-Man Drill Likely To Cause Big Copper Mine Strike." *Square Deal* 12 (February, 1913):69–70.
Haywood's prediction that a labor-saving technological innovation will cause strikes in the copper industry.

2211. "New Philosophy of the Labor Movement." *Nation* 94 (March 28, 1912):304–6.
Syndicalism was introduced in America by the Lawrence strike.

2212. "A New Program." *One Big Union Monthly* 1 (March, 1919):5.
The American Social Democratic League.

2213. "New Proof in the Centralia Case." *Industrial Pioneer* 2 (September, 1924):34.

Some witnesses and some jurors have changed their minds.

2214. "New Republic Is Being Picketed." *Nation* 166 (April 17, 1948): 407.

Protests over Stegner's Joe Hill article. See no. 2817.

2215. "The New Scabbery." *One Big Union Monthly* 3 (January, 1921):38–40.

Says the "gypo system," or piece-work system, is a new kind of scabbing.

2216. "New Song Book." *Industrial Worker* 78 (February 3, 1981):4.

2217. "The New Unionism." *Miners Magazine* 11 (September 30, 1909):11.

The McKees Rocks strike demonstrates a new kind of union militance.

2218. "The New Unionism." Review of *The New Unionism,* by André Tridon (see no. 217). *Journal of Political Economy* 21 (December, 1913):970–72.

2219. "The New Wild West." *Liberator* 3 (January, 1920):21–23.

The Legion assault on the IWW hall was like the old West with its shoot-outs and posses.

2220. "New York a Prey to Strikes." *Outlook* 103 (January 18, 1913): 102–3.

2221. "New York IWW." *Industrial Worker* 73 (January 8, 1981):9.

2222. Newbill, James G. "Farmers and Wobblies in the Yakima Valley, 1933." *Pacific Northwest Quarterly* 68 (April, 1977):80–87.

2223. ———. "Yakima and the Wobblies, 1910–1936." In Joseph R. Conlin, ed., *At the Point of Production* (Westport, CT: Greenwood Press, 1981), 167–90 (see no. 39).

2224. Newman, Philip. "The First IWW Invasion of New Jersey." *New Jersey Historical Society Proceedings* 58 (October, 1940):268–83.

The Paterson strike.

2225. "News from Lawrence." *Independent* 72 (March 7, 1912):484–85.

A contemporary account of the Lawrence strike.

2226. Newton, E. E. "The Ant and the Grasshopper."' *Survey* 38 (September 15, 1917):522–23.

On the current disapproval of the IWW by many types of

citizens. Why do those who despise the "lawless" IWW members treat them so lawlessly?

2227. Nichols, Barry. "Joe Hill: Some Notes on an American Culture Hero." *Wobbly* 3 (October, 1963):2–11.

2228. "No IWW Delegate at Moscow." *One Big Union Monthly* 2 (December, 1920):57.

The IWW did not send a delegate to the Third International.

2229. "No More Work for Wobblies." *American Lumberman* 2320 (November 1, 1919):55.

Lumbermen will hire LLLL rather than IWW members.

2230. "No Section of the Country." *New Republic* 13 (December 15, 1917):160–61.

The President's Mediation Commission found that many of labor's grievances were genuine.

2231. Nochlin, Linda. "The Paterson Strike Pageant of 1913." *Art in America* 62 (May–June, 1974):64–68.

2232. Nomura, Tatsuro. "The American Labor Radicalism and Violence: The Case of the IWW." *Monthly Journal of the Japanese Institute of Labor* 16 (September, 1974):45–53.

2233. ———. "The Brotherhood of the Timber Workers." *American Review* (March, 1975):n.p.

2234. ———. "The McKees Rocks Strike and the IWW Activities in the Pittsburgh Steel Industry." (Aichi Prefectural University, Nagoya) *Journal of the Faculty of Foreign Studies* (1975):n.p.

2235. ———. "Partisan Politics in and around the IWW: The Earliest Phase." (Aichi Prefectural University, Nagoya) *Journal of the Faculty of Foreign Studies* (1977):n.p.

2236. "The Non-Partisan League." *Bellman* 24 (March 23, 1918):314.

Rural populations are using harsh methods to deal with "seditious" utterances from groups such as the Non-Partisan League and the IWW.

2237. North, Cedric. "Brotherhood of Man and the Wobblies." *North American Review* 227 (April, 1929):487–92.

The IWW in South Dakota.

2238. "Not a Labor War." *Outlook* 83 (July 7, 1906):544–46.

Haywood and Moyer deserve a fair trial despite their radicalism.

2239. "Notes and Comments on the Recent Convention." *Bulletin* 1 (January, 1907):26–28.
About the IWW convention, at which there was factional dissension.

2240. "Notes from the Strike Zone in Michigan." *Miners Magazine* 14 (August 21, 1913):8.
The Calumet-Hecla strike.

2241. "Now . . . the Judicial." *Bridgemen's Magazine* 13 (February, 1913): 85–87.
The dynamite plot in Lawrence, an attempt to disgrace the IWW.

2242. Nyland, W. "Western Mining Town: The Copper Camp of the Early 1900's." *Scribner's Magazine* 95 (May, 1934):365–69.
The camps in which the IWW was active.

2243. "O For Mark Twain!" *Nation* 112 (June 29, 1921):905.
Ed Garman organized a branch of the IWW in prison and received an additional sentence of seven months for his efforts.

2244. Oates, J. "Globe-Miami District." *International Socialist Review* 18 (August, 1917):72–74.
The demands of the workers at Bisbee.

2245. O'Brian, John L. "Uncle Sam's Spy Policies: Safeguarding American Liberty during the War." *Forum* 61 (April, 1919):407–16.

2246. O'Brien, James. "Wobblies and Draftees: The IWW's Wartime Dilemma, 1917–1918." *Radical America* 1 (September–October, 1967):6–18.

2247. O'Connell, Lucille. "The Lawrence Textile Strike of 1912: The Testimony of Two Polish Women." *Polish American Studies* 36 (Autumn, 1979):44–62.

2248. O'Connor, Harvey. Review of *The IWW: Its First Fifty Years,* by Fred Thompson (see no. 213). *Nation* 183 (August 25, 1956):165.

2249. Oehler, Hugo. "The Fight in Berwind Canyon." *Labor Defender* 2 (December, 1927):180–81.
The IWW Colorado coal strike, with good photographs.

2250. "Of a Similar Character." *Nation* 110 (January 3, 1920):843.
The city of Spokane and its treatment of the IWW.

2251. O'Flaherty, Thomas J. "Recollections of Bill Haywood." *Labor Defender* 3 (July, 1928):153, 159.
Haywood's role in the Lawrence strike.

2252. O'Hare, Kate. "Mother Jones of the Revolution." *Miners Magazine* 14 (September 11, 1913):7–8.

2253. "Ol' Rags an' Bottles." *Nation* 108 (January 25, 1919):114–16.
The Sacramento indictments.

2254. Older, C. "Last Day of the Paint Creek Court Martial." *Independent* 74 (May 15, 1913):1085–88.
Mother Jones and the activities of the Paint Creek miners in West Virginia.

2255. "Ole Hanson Six Months Late." *Rebel Worker* 2 (September 15, 1919):4
The controversial Seattle Mayor resigned from the AFL well after the Seattle General Strike was over.

2256. Olin and Dvorak, translators. "William D. Haywood in Europe." *International Socialist Review* 11 (November, 1910):286–88.

2257. Oliver, Amy. "The Sacramento 'Trial.'" *One Big Union Monthly* 1 (March, 1919):41–43.

2258. Oliver, Egbert S. "Sawmilling on Grays Harbor in the Twenties: A Personal Reminiscence." *Pacific Northwest Quarterly* 69 (January, 1978):1–18.
Reminiscences, including some about the IWW in the woods.

2259. "On Numerous Occasions." *New Republic* 39 (July 9, 1924):169–70.
The brutal police action at San Pedro.

2260. "On Saturday." *New Republic* 39 (July 2, 1924):144.
The IWW deliberately spread hoof-and-mouth disease the same week the government declared that it was eradicated.

2261. "On the Iron Range." *The Blast* 1 (September 1, 1916):7.
The Minnesota iron range strike.

2262. "On the Job." *International Socialist Review* 13 (October, 1912):375.
The construction workers of Prince Rupert, British Columbia.

2263. "On the Walsh Bill." *Labor Defender* 1 (June 15, 1918):2–4.
This is a bill to destroy the IWW.

2264. "On Their Way to Jail." *Survey* 49 (October 15, 1922):75.
The many raids, arrests, and convictions of IWWs.

2265. "The One Big Union." *Garment Worker* 12 (June 27, 1913):4.
Other unionists might mistakenly be attracted to the objectionable IWW.

2266. "One Big Union—Western Labor Paper Exposes Fallacies." *Garment Worker* 12 (September 5, 1913):5.
Despite IWW claims, it is the AFL that is getting new members.

2267. "The One Big Union Wreckers Are Getting Busy in Arizona." *Miners Magazine* 18 (April, 1917):1, 7.
The copper miners will strike.

2268. "One Hundred American Labor Leaders Sent to Prison." *Public* 21 (August 24, 1918):1068–69.
The Chicago trial.

2269. "110's Best Drive Ever." *Industrial Pioneer* 1 (August, 1923):5–6.
Despite the national troubles, the IWW is gaining membership.

2270. "One Hundred and Twenty-One Men." *International Socialist Review* 18 (August, 1917):96–98.
Most of the pacifists jailed during the war were Socialists or IWWs.

2271. "One Measure for All." *Class Struggle* 2 (December, 1918):628–30.
The Bisbee deportation.

2272. O'Neal, James. "Catholicism and Socialism." *Wayland's Monthly* 2 (April, 1915).
The dilemma of religious liberals who are considering supporting Socialism and the IWW.

2273. ———. "The Passing of the IWW." *Current History* 21 (January, 1925):528–34.
The social significance of the IWW, with a photograph of Haywood in Russia.

2274. O'Neill, John M. "Editor Refuses To Be Gagged." *Miners Magazine* 9 (December 12, 1907):4–5.
The WFM withdrawal from affiliation with the IWW.

2275. ———. "No Apologies To Offer." *Miners Magazine* 9 (March 26, 1908):6–7.
Controversial letters on fund-raising between WFM, IWW, and SLP.

2276. ———. "Our Comment on the Various Reports of the IWW Convention." *Miners Magazine* 8 (November 8, 1906):6–9.

2277. ———. "There Is No Room for Anarchy." *Miners Magazine* 17 (October, 1916):4.
Unrest among workers in Yakima.

2278. O'Neill, William. "Labor Radicalism and *The Masses.*" *Labor History* 7 (Spring, 1966):197–208.

2279. "Only a Damn Chink." *Rebel Worker* 2 (February 15, 1919):1.
A brutal raid on a Chinese IWW meeting in New York.

2280. "Open Letter to President Wilson." *One Big Union Monthly* 1 (May, 1919):27–28.
A letter to the president asking for release of IWWs from prison now that the war is over.

2281. "Open Shop at Boulder Dam." *New Republic* 47 (June 24, 1931):147–48.
Labor troubles are being deliberately aggravated.

2282. "Open the Prison Gates!" *Revolutionary Age* 1 (December 14, 1918):1
Plea for the prisoners who criticized society.

2283. Oppenheimer, Moses. "Direct Action and Sabotage." *New Review* 1 (January 25, 1913):113–15.
A Socialist viewpoint.

2284. "Opportunity of Negro Labor." *Crisis* 18 (September, 1919):236–38.
The IWW has never rejected Negroes.

2285. Orchard, Harry. "The Confession and Biography of Harry Orchard." *McClure's Magazine* 29 (July, 1907):294–306; (August, 1907):367–79; (September, 1907):507–23; (October, 1907):658–72; (November, 1907):113–29.
Confessions of a witness who lied at the first Haywood trial.

2286. An Oregonian. "Busting a Boost!" *Industrial Pioneer* 2 (June, 1924):15–16, 29.
Working conditions in Oregon are bad, and the circulars and ads sent out calling for workers are misleading.

2287. "Organization Cannot Be Suppressed—Will Conquer World." *Rebel Worker* 2 (May 1, 1919):1–2.

2288. "Organization or Anarchy." *New Republic* 11 (July 21, 1917):320–22.

The influence of the IWW depends on sensational press accounts of its activities.

2289. "Organization That Destroys Organization." *Miners Magazine* 15 (July 16, 1914):7.

The fights between the IWW and the WFM to organize miners, particularly in Butte, Montana.

2290. "The Organized Mob in Michigan." *Miners Magazine* 14 (November 27, 1913):8.

A Citizen's Alliance has been formed at Calumet-Hecla, which means that there will be illegal violence against the strikers.

2291. Orson, Dick. "The Wobblies Raid the Seaman's Union." *Liberator* 5 (June, 1922):12–14.

The rivalry in organizing seamen and the IWW struggle with the SUP for their loyalty.

2292. Orth, S. P. "Battle Line of Labor—II, the Warfare." *World's Work* 25 (December, 1912):197–205.

A description of several strikes, with an anti-labor and anti-IWW bias.

2293. Osborn, Chase S. "Is Deportation the Cure?" *North American Review* 211 (February, 1920):179–81.

Advocates internment of radicals at reservations or camps.

2294. Osborne, James D. "Paterson: Immigrant Strikers and the War of 1913." In Joseph R. Conlin, ed., *At the Point of Production* (Westport, CT: Greenwood Press, 1981), 61–78 (see no. 39).

2295. O'Sullivan, Mary K. "Labor War at Lawrence." *Survey* 28 (April 6, 1912):72–74.

2296. "Our Attitude towards IWW." *Agitator* 2 (October 15, 1912):1.

Why various left-wing factions criticize the IWW.

2297. "Our Chief Danger." *Nation* 109 (November 22, 1919):653.

Denounces the American Legion raid on the IWW at Centralia.

2298. "Our Explanation." *Miners Magazine* 9 (November 14, 1907):7–8.

Reviews the increasing controversies with the IWW and explains why the WFM is withdrawing its support.

2299. "Our Ferocious Sentences." *Nation* 107 (November 2, 1918):504.
Radicals are getting longer sentences than real criminals.

2300. "Our Heritage." *Industrial Pioneer* 1 (November, 1921):16–17.
November is the month to mourn the IWW martyrs, as so many of them met death in that month over the years.

2301. "Our Social and Industrial System Blamed for the IWW." *Bankers Magazine* 98 (November, 1917):544–46.

2302. Overstreet, Daphne. "On Strike—The 1917 Walkout at Globe, Arizona." *Journal of Arizona History* 18 (Summer, 1977):197–218.

2303. Overstreet, H. A. "Casual Laborer." *Nation* 3 (October 20, 1920): 455.

2304. Ovington, Mary White. "Bogalusa." *Liberator* 3 (January, 1920): 31–33.
Atrocities are being committed by the Southern lumber companies against the workers.

2305. ———. "The Status of the Negro in the United States." *New Review* 1 (September, 1913):744–49.
Philadelphia and Southern timberworkers set an example of true brotherhood in integrating their unions.

2306. Owen, William C. "Economic Revolution and the I.W.W." *Social War* (September, 1913).
The IWW may create an economic revolution.

2307. "Pageant as a Form of Propaganda." *Current Opinion* 55 (July, 1913):32.
The impact of the Paterson pageant.

2308. "Pageant of the Paterson Strike." *Survey* 30 (June 28, 1913):428.

2309. Palmer, A. Mitchell. "Three Strikes and Out." *Independent* 102 (May 22, 1920):267.
The government has dealt fairly with dissidents.

2310. Palmer, Bryan D. "'Big Bill' Haywood's Defection to Russia and the IWW: Two Letters." *Labor History* 17 (Spring, 1976):271–78.

2311. ———. "Class Conception and Conflict: The Thrust for Efficiency, Managerial Views of Labor and the Working Class Rebellion, 1903–22." *Review of Radical Political Economics* 7 (Summer, 1975):31–49.

2312. Palmer, Frank L. "The Massacre at the Columbine." *Labor Defender* 3 (January, 1928):11–15.
The murders during an IWW strike in Colorado coal mines, with good photographs.

2313. ———. "Solidarity in Colorado." *Nation* 126 (February 1, 1928): 118–20.
The IWW caused the coal miners' strike.

2314. ———. "War in Colorado." *Nation* 125 (December 7, 1927):623–24.
A newspaper campaign to connect the IWW with the violence in the Colorado coal strikes.

2315. Palmer, James. "What the IWW Offers to the Farmer and the Farm Hand." *One Big Union Monthly* 2 (December, 1920):34.
Envisions a time when all farms would be cooperative and farmers and farmworkers could have city conveniences.

2316. Palmer, Lewis E. "A Strike for Four Loaves of Bread at Lawrence." *Survey* 27 (February 3, 1912):1690–97.

2317. Palmer, R. "Degrees of Redness." *Independent* 76 (December 4, 1913):460–61.
The decent (IWW) delegates now have headquarters in Detroit. The "Detroit faction" is superior to the main body of the IWW.

2318. "Panic and Death—The Copper Strike in Michigan." *Outlook* 106 (January 3, 1914):6.

2319. Pankratz, Herbert. "The Suppression of Alleged Disloyalty in Kansas during World War I." *Kansas Historical Quarterly* 42 (Autumn, 1976):277–307.

2320. Papanikolas, Helen Z. "The Great Bingham Strike of 1912 and the Expulsion of the Padrone." *Utah Historical Quarterly* 38 (Spring, 1970):121–33.

2321. ———. "Life and Labor among the Immigrants of Bingham Canyon." *Utah Historical Quarterly* 33 (1965):289–315.

2322. Parker, Carleton H. "The California Casual and His Revolt." *Quarterly Journal of Economics* 30 (November, 1915):110–26.
Migrant laborers are products of their environment, and the conditions under which they live in California will force them to rebel.

2323. ———. "The IWW." *Atlantic Monthly* 120 (November, 1917):651–62.

A detailed description of the IWW, its history, and its purpose.

2324. ———. "The Wheatland Riot and What Lay Back of It." *Survey* 31 (March 14, 1914):768–70.

2325. "The Parlor Provocateur." Review of *The Parlor Provocateur, or From Salon to Soap-Box,* by Kate C. Gartz. *Industrial Pioneer* 1 (September, 1923):21–23.

A compilation (by M. C. Sinclair) of Gartz's many written protests on behalf of the Criminal Syndicalist prisoners.

2326. Parsons, Geoffrey. "Wichita's Way with a Wave of IWW Bolshevism." *New York Tribune* (March 2, 1919):Sec. 7, p. 3.

The Wichita Syndicalist cases and the treatment of the prisoners.

2327. Pasewalk, Walter. "Nolo-Contendere." *Labor Defender* 1 (September 1, 1918):14.

Reports that 26 IWW delegates who went to Omaha for a convention were arrested and have been in jail for nearly a year without trial. They refused to plead *nolo contendere.*

2328. "The Passing Show." *Agitator* 1 (March 15, 1911):1, 4.

The Fresno Free Speech Fight.

2329. "The Passing Show—An IWW Report." *Agitator* 2 (November 1, 1912):1.

Criticism of the General Executive Board Report.

2330. "Pat Quinlan." *Masses* 6 (April, 1915):16.

The prosecution of Quinlan after the Paterson strike.

2331. "Paterson." *Miners Magazine* 14 (September 4, 1913):4.

The strategy and tactics of the IWW in the Paterson strike.

2332. "Paterson Conditions." *Miners Magazine* 14 (June 26, 1913):5–6.

About the Paterson strike, noting signs of failure.

2333. "Paterson Convictions Again Set Aside." *Survey* 31 (November 22, 1913):191–92.

The trial of strike leaders after the Paterson strike.

2334. "Paterson Strike." *Independent* 74 (May 29, 1913):1172.

Disapproves of the IWW's principles, but praises the imagination of the IWW leaders.

2335. "Paterson Strike." *International Socialist Review* 14 (September, 1913):177–78.

2336. "Paterson Strike Is Leaderless." *Square Deal* 13 (August, 1913):94.
The IWW made false promises to the strikers.

2337. "Paterson Strike Leaders in Jersey Prison." *Survey* 34 (April 3, 1915):3.
F. Sumner Boyd's appeal for justice. Boyd, an English intellectual and Socialist, made speeches supporting the IWW and was arrested.

2338. "Paterson Strike Pageant." *Independent* 74 (June 19, 1913):1406–7.
On the pageant; contains an interesting photograph of the performance.

2339. "Paterson—West Virginia—California." *New Review* 1 (June, 1913):545–47.
The IWW is provoking strikes all over.

2340. "Paterson's Authorities." *New Republic* 4 (September 18, 1915):164.
The *New York Times* says authorities may justifiably repress free speech if the speakers are routers, vultures, or rattlesnakes.

2341. "Patriotic Citizens Crush Radicalism." *American Lumberman* 2323 (November 22, 1919):54.
Lynchings and beatings in the Pacific Northwest to suppress labor and radicalism.

2342. "Patriotism and the I.W.W." *Labor Defender* 1 (July 15, 1918):9.
Offers many definitions of patriotism and says they do not in fact fit the IWW. Working people do not like soldiers, for good reasons and from long experience.

2343. "Patriotism in the Middle West." *Masses* 9 (June, 1917):19–21.
Mobilization Week in Kansas City. Some workers seem reluctant about the war, especially the IWWs.

2344. Patterson, Keith. "The Lion and the Fox." *American History Illustrated* 13 (April, 1978):12–21.
The first Haywood trial and the attorneys' differing personalities.

2345. Paulsen, Paul I., and James Lord. "The Strike in Michigan." *Bridgeman's Magazine* 14 (February, 1914):75–79.
The Calumet-Hecla strike.

2346. Pawa, J. M. "The Search for Black Radicals: American and British Documents Relative to the 1919 Red Scare." *Labor History* 16 (Spring, 1975):272–84.

2347. Pawar, Sheelwant B. "The Structure and Nature of Labor Unions in Utah: Historical Perspective, 1890–1920." *Utah Historical Quarterly* 35 (Summer, 1967):236–55.

On L. J. Trujillo, organizer of the Building Employees' I.U. #262, who was an IWW member.

2348. Payne, C. E. "Captain Coll, Legionnaire." *Nation* 129 (July 10, 1929):38–39.

After ten years Centralia is still upset about the Centralia affair; Captain Coll, who defended the IWW's position, was ostracized.

2349. ———. "The Fundamental Principles of the IWW." *One Big Union Monthly* 1 (November, 1919):38–39.

2350. ———. "The Mainspring of Action." *One Big Union Monthly* 1 (April, 1919):29–30.

The Aberdeen, Washington, Free Speech Fight.

2351. ———. "Our Press." *Industrial Pioneer* 4 (July, 1926):20–21.

The importance of the IWW press cannot be exaggerated, as it strengthens the organization.

2352. ———. "Proudly, Defiantly, the IWW Marches to Its Final Goal." *Industrial Worker* 26 (June 30, 1945):1.

The IWW has moved the nation closer to the abolition of wage slavery.

2353. ———. "The Spring Drive of the Lumber Jacks." *International Socialist Review* 17 (June, 1917):729–30.

2354. ———. "Stumping the Stump Ranches." *Industrial Pioneer* 1 (November, 1921):4–5.

Lumberworkers who buy cut-over land from the lumber companies are in for some arduous work. Can they be organized?

2355. Payne, C. E.; W. J. Fisher; and J. T. McCarthy. "History of the Aberdeen Free Speech Fight." *Industrial Worker* 4 (February 1, 1912):1.

2356. "Peace or War." *Outlook* 103 (February 8, 1913):296–98.

Middle-class attitudes toward industrial strikes.

2357. Pease, Frank. "Boring from Within." *Agitator* 2 (February 15, 1912):2.
There is "Fosterism" in the IWW.

2358. ———. "The IWW and Revolution." *Forum* 50 (August, 1913):153–68.
The IWW is the only proletarian organization with a potential for success.

2359. "Pedagogy and Syndicalism." *Public* 22 (February 8, 1919):133–34.
The IWW trials may be inadvisable, as they could lead to excesses.

2360. "The Peerless Ingrate." *Miners Magazine* 13 (January 16, 1913):6.
William D. Haywood is ungrateful for all that the WFM did for him.

2361. "Pennsylvania Cossacks." *Miners Magazine* 11 (September 16, 1909):8.
The McKees Rocks strike and police brutality.

2362. Perkins, Jacob R. "Remember San Diego!" *Masses* 5 (May, 1914):9–10.
Police brutality in the San Diego Free Speech Fight.

2363. Perry, Grover H. "Metal Miners Blast." *International Socialist Review* 17 (June, 1917):730–31.
Labor problems in Arizona.

2364. ———. "Transport Workers Join IWW." *International Socialist Review* 13 (May, 1913):812.
There is an influx of marine workers in the IWW.

2365. "Persecution against the I.W.W." *One Big Union Monthly* 1 (April, 1919):11.
The government raids on radicals.

2366. Person, Carl E. "Blazing the Way." *Voice of the People* 3 (May 1, 1914):1.
Workers could, and should, take over the world, as they have the power.

2367. ———. "Carl Person." *Voice of the People* 3 (May 7, 1914):1.
Person's trial for a shooting during a railroad strike.

2368. "Perspective of Tonopah, Nevada." *Industrial Pioneer* 2 (December, 1924):9–12.

The deplorable conditions in the silver mines; miners should join the IWW.

2369. "Pertinent Questions." *Miners Magazine* 20 (September, 1919):1, 3.
An angry response to publishers of a circular against Charles Moyer and the IUMMSW. IWW organizer A. S. Embree was one of the circular's signers.

2370. Peterson, Richard H. "Conflict and Consensus: Labor Relations in Western Mining." *Journal of the West* 12 (January, 1973):1–17.

2371. Petrus. "What Freedom Means to Us." *Industrial Pioneer* 2 (February, 1925):13–14, 37–39.
Details the thoughts and writings of imprisoned IWW members.

2372. Pfeffer, C. Whit. "From Bohunks to Finns." *Survey* 36 (April 1, 1916):8–14.
The striking Mesabi miners and their ethnic backgrounds.

2373. Pfeffer, Walter. "It Can Happen Here." *One Big Union Monthly* NS 1 (May, 1937):20–24, 25.
False reports about the IWW are sweeping the country and causing unjust arrests.

2374. ———. "A Little Economics for the Home." *One Big Union Monthly* NS 1 (October, 1937):29–30.
A little money spent for IWW dues will be paid back in increased income; a story-drama.

2375. "Philadelphia Marine Transport Workers Charter Revoked." *One Big Union Monthly* 2 (September, 1920):6–7.
The union's charter was revoked by the IWW when it was learned that the members had loaded ammunition to be used by Wrangel's White Army fighting the Bolsheviks.

2376. "Philadelphia Strike Is Over." *One Big Union Monthly* 2 (August, 1920):53.
The settlement terms of the bitter strike.

2377. "Philadelphia Waterfront Unionism." *Messenger* 5 (June, 1923): 740.
The integrated waterfront union.

2378. "Philadelphia's Sugar Strike." *Survey* 37 (March 17, 1917):696.

2379. Phillips, Jack. "Haywood of the IWW." *International Socialist Review* 18 (January, 1918):343.

Haywood and Civil War martyr John Brown both fought for social justice and suffered at the hands of the Federal Government.

2380. ———. "Speaking of the Department of Justice." *International Socialist Review* 18 (February, 1918):406–7.
The attorney who will prosecute the IWW for the government has close ties to the big copper companies.

2381. "Philosophy of Syndicalism." *Independent* 72 (April 18, 1912):850–52.
French and American Syndicalist ideas compared.

2382. "Philosophy of Syndicalism." *Nation* 99 (September 17, 1914):350.

2383. Pickering, Ruth. "The Lawrence Strike." *Liberator* 2 (May, 1919): 35–36.
The current Lawrence strike compared to the 1912 strike.

2384. "Pickers Pinching Apples." *Outlook* 116 (August 29, 1917):639–40.
Washington farmers are afraid of sabotage in the orchard.

2385. Pinchot, A. "Why Violence in Bayonne?" *Harper's Weekly* 61 (August 7, 1915):126.
The violence and shooting in the chemical workers' strike at Bayonne, New Jersey.

2386. Pingree, C. L. "The Ipswich Strike." *Lumberjack* 1 (July 3, 1913):4.
The textile strike in Ipswich, Massachusetts.

2387. "The Pinkerton Agency at Work Again." *Miners Magazine* 10 (July 2, 1908):5.
A letter from Detective James McParland, who played a part in the first Haywood trial.

2388. "Pioneers in Solidarity." *One Big Union Monthly* NS 1 (April, 1937): 23–24, 34.
The AFL, the CIO, and the IWW compared; one big union is what is needed, regardless of name.

2389. "Pittsburgh Strike." *Miners Magazine* 10 (September 2, 1909):7.
The McKees Rocks strike.

2390. "Pittsburgh's Morning After." *Everybody's Magazine* 23 (October, 1910):570–71.
The McKees Rocks strike and its consequences.

2391. "The Pity of It." *Independent* 74 (June 12, 1913):1317.
The eight-hour day proposed by Haywood will overthrow all industrial society.

2392. Plahn, Charles. "Isolation at Leavenworth." *One Big Union Monthly* 1 (December, 1919):38–39.
Some IWW prisoners have been put into solitary confinement at Leavenworth.

2393. "Plans of the IWW in Baltimore." *Garment Worker* 12 (September 19, 1913):1.
The IWW is devising new methods to harm other unions.

2394. "Playing the Same Old Game." *Miners Magazine* 13 (February 27, 1913):5–6.
The Denver Free Speech Fight.

2395. "Playing with Dynamite." *Public* 20 (November 16, 1917):1102–4.
The Department of Justice should not be given a free hand, as civil rights are being violated.

2396. "A Plea for Preparedness by Pacific Coast Business Men's Preparedness League." *International Socialist Review* 17 (August, 1916):80–81.
An anti-labor and anti-IWW view of handling labor problems.

2397. "A Plot To Murder Wage-Workers." *International Socialist Review* 12 (June, 1912):873.
Ettor and Giovannitti defended against the charge that as strike leaders they incited violence that resulted in the death of a striker.

2398. "The Plumb Plan." *One Big Union Monthly* 2 (January, 1920):12–14.
A plan for government ownership of the railroads.

2399. "Plutocracy Gone Mad." *One Big Union Monthly* 2 (February, 1920):7–8.
The Palmer Raids and the possibility of *agents provocateurs* making trouble.

2400. "Poems by IWW Prisoners." *Liberator* 5 (March, 1922):9.
Poems expressing grief and rebellion.

2401. "Poet of the I.W.W." *Outlook* 104 (July 5, 1913):504–6.
The role of Arturo Giovannitti in the Lawrence strike and his expressive poetry of rebellion.

2402. "Poetry of Syndicalism." *Atlantic* 111 (June, 1913):853–54.
An appreciation of Giovannitti's poetry.

2403. "Poison the Women Gently." *Industrial Pioneer* 3 (December, 1925):8–10.
Plans to use chemical gases on strikers and mobs, as outlined by Major General Amos A. Fries of the Army's Chemical Warfare Division.

2404. "Policy of Editor Repudiated." *Miners Magazine* 12 (November 30, 1911):8.
Some WFM members defend A. S. Embree, an IWW organizer, and the IWW, both of whom are persistently attacked by the magazine.

2405. "Political Prisoners' Reply." *New Republic* 36 (August 29, 1923):21.
Eleven IWW prisoners refuse a conditional pardon.

2406. "Politics and the American Legion." *World's Work* 38 (July, 1919): 242–44.
There is more to the American Legion raids than we know.

2407. Pollok, Theodora. "The Tragedy of the Hop Fields." *Everyman* (April–May, 1914):12–13.
The Durst Ranch Hop Riot at Wheatland.

2408. ———. "Will Labor Stand for Another Haymarket?" *International Socialist Review* 17 (December, 1916):360–63.
Mooney and Billings are martyrs of the drive against the open shop; the first Mooney trial reeked of prejudice.

2409. Pontius, James. "Who Are the 100 Per Cent Patriots?" *One Big Union Monthly* 2 (May, 1920):47–49.
Abrogation of civil rights is not patriotic.

2410. "Poor Big Bill Haywood." *Square Deal* 12 (March, 1913):173–74.
Haywood's expulsion from the Socialist Party.

2411. "Poor Mr. Dooley." *Nation* 108 (January 25, 1919):126.
Mr. Dooley quoted at the Sacramento trial.

2412. Portenar, A. J. "The Perversion of the Ideal: A Reply to the Doctrine of Syndicalism as Advocated by the I.W.W." *International Molders' Journal* 49 (August, 1913):635–38.

2413. "Position on the Raids." *Survey* 43 (January 31, 1920):501–2.

2414. "Possible Paterson." *Outlook* 104 (June 14, 1913):318–21.

2415. Potter, Bob. "Thoughts on Bureaucracy." *Rebel Worker* 2 (Summer, 1964):11–16.

2416. Pratt, W. M. "The Lawrence Revolution." *New England Magazine* 44 (March, 1912):7–16.
The Lawrence strike.

2417. "Preaching Sabotage." *Square Deal* 13 (November, 1913):382.
The harsh sentence of F. Sumner Boyd, the English Socialist who advocated sabotage at the Paterson strike.

2418. "Preamble and Constitution of the Industrial Workers of the World." *Miners Magazine* 6 (July 20, 1905):12–14.
Repeated in many later issues.

2419. "Present Labor Conditions: Seattle." *Square Deal* 13 (August, 1913):35–37.

2420. "President Moyer's Report on the Strike in Michigan." *Miners Magazine* 15 (April 16, 1914):5.

2421. "President Roosevelt and the Moyer-Haywood Trial." *Outlook* 86 (May 4, 1907):1–2.
Defends Theodore Roosevelt's characterization of Haywood, Debs, and Harriman as "undesirable citizens."

2422. "President Sherman's Report to 1906 Convention." *Miners Magazine* 8 (October 11, 1906):8–10.

2423. "President's Commission at Bisbee." *New Republic* 13 (December 8, 1917):140–41.
The Commission's investigation.

2424. "Press Reports of the Pettibone Trial at Boise, Idaho." *Miners Magazine* 9 (January 2, 1908):8–9; (January 9, 1908):9–10.
Newspaper reports about the Steunenberg trial.

2425. "Press Reports of the Situation in Goldfield, Nevada." *Miners Magazine* 9 (January 2, 1908):9–11; (January 9, 1908):10; (January 16, 1908):8–10.
Newspaper reports about Goldfield.

2426. Preston, William. "The Ideology and Techniques of Repression, 1903–1933." In Harvey Goldberg, ed., *American Radicals: Some Problems and Personalities* (New York: Monthly Review Press, 1957), 239–64.
The deliberate repression of the IWW.

2427. ———. "Shall This Be All? US Historians versus William D. Haywood et al."

Review of *We Shall Be All,* by Melvyn Dubofsky (see no. 59). *Labor History* 12 (Summer, 1971):435–53.

2428. "The Pretorium Must Be Destroyed." *The Lumberjack* 1 (January 30, 1913):3.

Interview with Gompers on the IWW.

2429. Price, A. H. "How the I.W.W. Men Brought About the 8-Hour Day in the Lumber Industry." *One Big Union Monthly* 1 (March, 1919):16–18.

2430. Price, Lucien. "Witchcraft: Then and Now." *Nation* 115 (October 4, 1922):331–33.

The conspiracy trials compared with the Salem witchcraft trials.

2431. "The Price of Strikes." *Current Literature* 53 (November 19, 1912):535–36.

A Boston paper states that strikes in one year have cost the world a billion dollars. A list of the strikes is appended.

2432. Price, W. D. "Greasy Olivers of Pittsburgh." *Technical World* 20 (September, 1913):8–19.

Conditions at the Oliver mill in Pittsburgh.

2433. Priddy, Al. "Controlling the Passions of Men in Lawrence." *Outlook* 102 (October 19, 1912):343–45.

A personal account of the strike, emphasizing the tactics of the militia, contrasting Lawrence with the New Bedford strike, at which there was no trouble at all because police were friendly and handled all strikers gently.

2434. "The Principle of Industrial Unionism." In Daniel Bloomfield, comp., *Selected Articles on Modern Industrial Movements* (New York: H. W. Wilson, 1919), 39–40.

2435. "Prison Life of Ettor and Giovannitti." *Literary Digest* 45 (September 14, 1912):441–43.

2436. "Prisoner's Letter." *Voice of the People* 2 (November 5, 1914):2.

A jailor is trying to sell drugs to the IWW prisoners in Butte.

2437. "Prisoners of War." *Sunset* 39 (September, 1917):6.

The Bisbee deportations.

2438. "Private War at the Mount Hope Mine." *Outlook* 104 (May 10, 1913):44–45.
The Empire Steel and Iron Company owners refuse to recognize the union and have hired professional strike breakers. Labor disputes should be settled by law, not by private wars.

2439. "Private War in Colorado." *Outlook* 107 (May 9, 1914):61–62.
The Colorado coal strike.

2440. "The Problems of Organization and Economic Equality." *One Big Union Advocate* 1 (May, 1939):5–7.

2441. "A Proclamation." *Miners Magazine* 12 (August 29, 1912):6–7.
The IWW is composed only of rascals, on the basis of a Pittsburgh leaflet.

2442. "'Proclamation' by Ole Hanson." *One Big Union Monthly* 1 (June, 1919):35.
The Seattle General Strike.

2443. "A Professional Assassin: Orchard's Testimony." *Outlook* 86 (June 15, 1907):303.
The testimony of Harry Orchard at the first Haywood trial is unbelievable.

2444. "The Progress of the Idaho Battle." *International Socialist Review* 7 (June, 1907):750–52.
The first Haywood trial. Roosevelt's "undesirable citizens" letter aroused so much interest in the case that the trial will have to proceed cautiously.

2445. "Progress of the World—Concerning 'Reds' in America." *American Review of Reviews* 61 (February, 1920):119–23.
The Palmer Raids and how America is dealing with the problem of "Reds."

2446. "The Proposed Communist Congress." *One Big Union Monthly* 1 (April, 1919):5–6.
The call from the Communist Party will probably be rejected by the IWW.

2447. "The Proposed New Labor Movement." *Miners Magazine* 6 (February 2, 1905):6.
Prospective support for the announced convention of industrial unionists.

2448. "Proposed Truce in Colorado." *Outlook* 108 (September 30, 1914):237.

2449. "Public Which Has a Short Memory—New Light on the Centralia Trial in 1919." *Nation* 114 (June 7, 1922):662.

2450. Putnam, S. "Red Days in Chicago." *American Mercury* 30 (September, 1933):64–71.
Remembrances of Charles Ashleigh and other notable IWW members.

2451. "Queer Actions of WFM Officials." *Miners Magazine* 13 (April 10, 1913):7–8.
The IWW may be undermining the WFM.

2452. "A Question of Justice." *Garment Worker* 12 (June 13, 1913):4.
The Lawrence dynamite plot, in which men were paid by the mill owner to plant dynamite and lay the blame on the IWW for doing it. The culprits were unpunished.

2453. Quinlan, Patrick. "Glorious Paterson." *International Socialist Review* 14 (December, 1913):355–57.
The Paterson strike.

2454. ———. "The Paterson Strike and After." *New Review* 2 (January, 1914):26–33.

2455. "Quinlan's Conviction." *Solidarity* 4 (May 31, 1913):3.
Pat Quinlan's trial and conviction after the Paterson strike.

2456. Quinnan, Thomas. "Labor Conditions in the Far West." *Miners Magazine* 20 (March, 1919):6.
The IWW uses labor spies.

2457. Rab, I. "Can Unions End Exploitation?" *Western Socialist* (March, 1948):17–22.
Unions will be unable to end exploitation of the workers.

2458. Rabinowitz, Matilda. "The Automobile Industry and the IWW in Detroit." *Solidarity* 4 (June 14, 1913):3.

2459. ———. "The Short Strike in the Automobile Industry." *Solidarity* 4 (July 12, 1913):4.
The earliest auto strikes in Detroit.

2460. Rader, Benjamin G. "The Montana Lumber Strike of 1917." *Pacific Historical Review* 36 (May, 1967):189–207.

2461. "Raiding the IWW." *Literary Digest* 55 (September 22, 1917):17.
The nationwide government raids on IWW halls.

2462. "Raids on IWW." *New Justice* 1 (April 15, 1919):11.

2463. "The Raids on the Reds." *Outlook* 123 (November 12, 1919):284.

2464. "The Railroad Boys." *International Socialist Review* 15 (July, 1914):62.
The problems of railroad workers in Pennsylvania.

2465. Rainey, George. "Why We Struck at Concrete." *Industrial Pioneer* 2 (January, 1925):5–7.
A strike at a hydroelectric dam project in Concrete, Washington.

2466. "Rallying Call to All I.W.W. Members." *Industrial Pioneer* 1 (June, 1921):17–18.
The raids must not discourage the IWW.

2467. Randolph, A. Philip, and Chandler Owen. "The Negro and the New Social Order." *Messenger* 2 (March, 1919):1–11.
Blacks can and should participate in unions with whites.

2468. Randolph, H. S. "Down with the Stars and Stripes—How Socialism Insults the Flag." *Common Cause* 1 (March, 1912):45–49.
On Haywood's famous Cooper Union speech.

2469. ———. "The I.W.W." *Common Cause* 1 (May, 1912):1–9.

2470. "A Rap at Industrial Unionism." *Miners Magazine* 6 (June 15, 1905):7–8.
On Wisconsin craft union circular opposing a new industrial union.

2471. "Rapid Developments in 'One Big Union.'" *Miners Magazine* 18 (October, 1917):1–2.
IWW arrests and indictments under the Espionage Act.

2472. "Ray Becker, Last Remaining Centralia Case Prisoner, Relates Inside Story to the ILD." *Western Worker* 3 (January 22, 1934).
Becker's problems with his defense committees.

2473. "R. D. Ginther, Working Man Artist and Historian of Skid Row." *California Historical Quarterly* 54 (Fall, 1975):263–71.
A self-taught artist who painted Skid Row scenes.

2474. Reading, A. B. "California Syndicalist Act, Strong or Wobbly?" *Overland* 83 (March, 1925):117–18.

2475. "The Real Haywood." *Shoe Workers Journal* 14 (April, 1913):7–8.
All the "free advertising" for Haywood has obscured the fact that he is not honest.

2476. "The Real Question." *Outlook* 100 (February 24, 1912):385–86.
The Lawrence strike.

2477. "Reasons for Industrial Unionism." *Voice of Labor* 3 (March, 1905):7–8.

2478. "Rebel Girls Help the Fight for Solidarity." *Industrial Pioneer* 2 (May, 1924):20, 41.
IWW women doing their part in the fight to keep the union strong.

2479. "*Rebel Worker*'s Office Razed by Cossacks." *Rebel Worker* 2 (July 1, 1919):1.
The Department of Justice raid on the *Rebel Worker* office.

2480. "Rebellion in Colorado." *Nation* 126 (January 11, 1928):33.
A strike like the Colorado coal strike should be declared unlawful.

2481. "Recall of Haywood." *Independent* 74 (March 6, 1913):490.
Haywood's ouster from the Socialist Party.

2482. "Recall of Haywood." *Literary Digest* 46 (March 15, 1913):562.
Haywood's ouster from the Socialist Party.

2483. "A Red Brigade—How the IWW of Columbus, Ohio Collected $40 for the Little Falls Strikers." *International Socialist Review* 13 (February, 1913):599–600.

2484. "Red Forces Disrupting American Labor." *Literary Digest* 63 (October 25, 1919):11–14.
The IWW is deliberately causing mischief.

2485. "Reds' Influence Wanes on the Coast." *American Lumberman* 2324 (November 29, 1919):48.
The lumber owners and the government have quelled the IWW.

2486. "The 'Reds' Riddled." *Miners Magazine* 21 (August, 1920):5.
A WFM official pleased by the government assaults on the IWW.

2487. Reed, John. "The IWW and Labor." *Communist* 1 (May 31, 1919):n.p.

2488. ———. "One Solid Month of Liberty." *Masses* 9 (September, 1917): 5–6.
This month saw only bad news for liberty: Emma Goldman, Tom Mooney, East St. Louis, the Bisbee deportations, and suppression of the press.

2489. ———. "Sheriff Radcliff's Hotel." *Metropolitan* 7 (July, 1913):14–16, 59–60.

Conditions in the Passaic County jail, where Reed and other IWWs were jailed for Paterson strike activities.

2490. ———. "War in Paterson." *International Socialist Review* 14 (July, 1913):43–48.
A good detailed account of the Paterson strike.

2491. ———. "War in Paterson." *Masses* 4 (June, 1913):14–17.
The Paterson strike.

2492. Reed, John, and Art Young. "The Social Revolution in Court." *Liberator* 1 (September, 1918):20–28.

2493. Reed, Mary. "San Pedro." *Nation* 119 (July 9, 1924):45–46.
The violent raid on the San Pedro IWW members.

2494. Reed, Merl. "IWW and Individual Freedom in Western Louisiana, 1913." *Louisiana History* 10 (Winter, 1969):61–69.
The government and the lumber kings robbed the Brotherhood of Timber Workers of their lives and civil rights.

2495. ———. "Lumberjacks and Longshoremen: The IWW in Louisiana." *Labor History* 13 (Winter, 1972):41–59.

2496. Reely, Mary Katharine. "Solidarity." *One Big Union Monthly* 2 (August, 1920):31–36.
The IWW is needed by the workers after the raids even more than before.

2497. Reeve, Karl. "Bill Haywood Comes Home." *Labor Defender* 3 (December, 1928):270–71.
The death of Haywood in Russia.

2498. Reimen, Jacqueline. "Radical Intellectuals and Repression of Radicalism during the First World War." *Revue Française d'Études Américaines* 1 (October, 1976):63–76.

2499. Reitman, Ben L. "Impressions of the Chicago Convention." *Mother Earth* 8 (October, 1913):239–42.
The IWW convention.

2500. ———. "The Respectable Mob." *Mother Earth* 7 (June, 1912):109–14.
First-hand account of the San Diego Free Speech Fight attacks.

2501. "Rejuvenation of the IWW." *Rebel Worker* 2 (September 15, 1919):4.
The IWW will fight harder to organize the workers, despite the raids.

2502. "A Release in Sight?" *Industrial Pioneer* 3 (March, 1926):5.

Hopes for an early release of the California Syndicalist prisoners.

2503. "Release Political Prisoners." *Dial* 66 (January 11, 1919):5–6.

2504. "Religious Press on the I.W.W. Invaders." *Literary Digest* 48 (April 4, 1914):760.

Reaction of the religious press to Tannenbaum's church invasion.

2505. "Remember Centralia." *Four L Bulletin* 1 (December, 1919):13.

2506. Renshaw, Patrick. "The IWW and the Red Scare, 1917–1924." *Journal of Contemporary History* 3 (October, 1968):63–72.

2507. ———. "The Lost Leader, 'Big Bill' Haywood." *History Today* 20 (No. 9, 1970):610–19.

2508. "A Reply to Congressman James F. Byrnes of South Carolina." *Messenger* 2 (October, 1919):11–14.

Blacks will achieve equality despite detractors like Byrnes.

2509. "A Reply to the Mine Owners." *Miners Magazine* 9 (January 2, 1908):8.

The Goldfield strike.

2510. "Report of President Moyer." *Miners Magazine* 10 (July 23, 1908):3–8.

The IWW-WFM split, the strike at Goldfield, and the Idaho trial.

2511. "Report of President Moyer." *Miners Magazine* 12 (July 18, 1912):4–11.

The IWW is an insidious force in the labor movement.

2512. "Report of the Executive Board, WFM." *Miners Magazine* 9 (December 26, 1907):6–8.

Allegiance to industrial unionism, but not to the IWW, affirmed in a report written after the split.

2513. "Report of the Industrial Workers of the World to the International Labor Congress at Stuttgart." *Industrial Union Bulletin* 1 (August 10, 1907):3–4.

2514. "Report on Conditions Existing in the Copper Mining District." *Square Deal* 13 (December, 1913):397–99.

A report that appears to favor the mine owners' and the Calumet Commercial Club's point of view.

2515. Repplier, A. "Beloved Sinner." *Century* 100 (June, 1920):145–49.
Showing good will to prisoners only encourages them to go out and break laws again, as seen in the IWW food strike at the Tacoma jail.

2516. "Resolution from Globe, Arizona." *Miners Magazine* 11 (December 9, 1909):9.
Globe miners complain that their union journal is unfair to the IWW.

2517. "A Resolution from Nome Miners Union." *Miners Magazine* 12 (October 19, 1911):7.
Miners Union in Nome, Alaska, sent an IWW delegate to the WFM convention, upsetting the WFM.

2518. "Retrenchment—Its Extent and Meaning Shown by a Railroad Worker." *Solidarity* 2 (March 18, 1911):1.
Retrenchment means unemployment, and the railroad cares nothing for its slaves.

2519. Reuss, Carl F. "The Farm Labor Problem in Washington, 1917–1918." *Pacific Northwest Quarterly* 34 (October, 1943):339–52.

2520. Reuss, Richard A. "The Roots of American Left-Wing Interest in Folk Song." *Labor History* 12 (Spring, 1971):259–79.
Popularity of IWW songs played a strong role.

2521. "Revelations of the Copper Investigation—What Will the Committee Report?" *Square Deal* 14 (April, 1914):201–8.
The coming report of the Calumet-Hecla strike.

2522. "Review of the Michigan Copper Strike." *American Industries* 14 (April, 1914):13–14.
A view from the owners' side.

2523. "The Revolutionary Kernel of the I.W.W." *Revolution* 4 (September, 1979):8–21.
The IWWs were the first real rebels in the labor movement.

2524. "Revolutionary Mass Action." *Socialist* 1 (May 13, 1919):1, 7.

2525. Rhea, M. "Revolt in Butte." *New Review* 2 (September, 1914):538–42.
The IWW-WFM fight in Butte over the union hall.

2526. ———. "The Trouble in Butte." *Masses* 5 (September, 1914):10–11.
The IWW-WFM fight in Butte.

2527. Rice, A. A. "Sweet Home Strike or Men vs. Decoys." *Voice of the People* 3 (January 29, 1914):1.
The IWW Forest and Lumber Workers Industrial Union #275 in Louisiana.

2528. Rice, Claude. "Unionism, Socialism and Syndicalism." *Miners Magazine* 18 (October, 1917):6.

2529. Rice, M. M. "Bloody Monday Again in Colorado." *Independent* 119 (December 31, 1927):655–56.
Colorado strike leaders, including Adam Bell of the IWW, and the violence they faced during the strikes.

2530. Richardson, C. H., et al. "Report of the Situation in Butte." *Miners Magazine* 15 (October 1, 1914):1–2.
The fight between the WFM and the IWW over Butte Miners Union No. 1.

2531. Richardson, N. A. "The Situation at San Diego." *Miners Magazine* 12 (May 30, 1912):11–12.
The San Diego Free Speech Fight.

2532. Richter, H. "The I.W.W.: Retrospect and Prospects." *Industrial Union News* 1 (January, 1912):1.

2533. Riddle, Claude. "Now a Few Words." *Miners Magazine* 7 (November 30, 1905):11.
The Socialists and the IWW.

2534. Riell, Robert B. "The 1917 Copper Strike at Globe, Arizona." *Journal of Arizona History* 18 (Summer, 1977):185–96.

2535. "Rioting at McKees Rocks." *Survey* 22 (August 28, 1909):719.

2536. "Riots and Race Wars, Lynchings and Massacres, Military Law, Terrorism and Giant Strikes." *One Big Union Monthly* 1 (November, 1919):9–10.
Countrywide events influencing the IWW.

2537. Robbins, Matilda. "A Near Industrial Union." *One Big Union Monthly* 2 (August, 1920):44–45.
Amalgamated Clothing Workers of America is only in part an industrial union.

2538. Roberts, William. "Upward and Onward: A Call to Servility." *One Big Union Monthly* 1 (June, 1919):22.
People feel they have gained virtue by attacking the IWW.

2539. Robertson, J. M. "The Dogma of 'Direct Action.'" *Everyman* 14 (August 16, 1919):445–46.

2540. Robinson, William J. "A Letter to the Lusk Committee." *Voice in the Wilderness* 3 (January–February, 1920):7–9.
A protest against the persecution of radicals.

2541. Rocha, Guy Louis. "The IWW and the Boulder Canyon Project: The Final Death Throes of American Syndicalism." *Nevada Historical Quarterly* 21 (Spring, 1978):3–24.

2542. ———. "The IWW and the Boulder Canyon Project: The Death Throes of American Syndicalism." In Joseph R. Conlin, ed., *At the Point of Production* (Westport, CT: Greenwood Press, 1981), 213–34 (see no. 39).

2543. ———. "Radical Labor Struggles in the Tonapah-Goldfield Mining District, 1901–1922." *Nevada Historical Society Quarterly* 20 (Spring, 1977):2–45.

2544. Rodnitzky, Jerome L. "The Evolution of the American Protest Song." *Journal of Popular Culture* 3 (Summer, 1969):35–45.
Protest songs, which used to be gloomy, were given a funny, clever twist by the IWW that made them popular.

2545. Roe, Gilbert E. "Repeal the Espionage Law." *Dial* 66 (January 11, 1919):8–11.

2546. Rogers, Bruce. "Labor Castes and the Unskilled." *New Review* 3 (March, 1915):160–63.

2547. ———. "Mutiny of the Lumber Army." *Coming Nation* (May 11, 1912):5–6.

2548. ———. "The War of Gray's Harbor." *International Socialist Review* 12 (May, 1912):750–53.

2549. Rooney, Eugene. "We Find That Labor." *Voice of Labor* 3 (May, 1905):8.
The prospects for a new industrial union (to be the IWW).

2550. "Roosevelt on Strikes." *Century* 81 (November, 1910):154.
Cheers Theodore Roosevelt's denunciation of the street car strike in Columbus, Ohio. Labor leaders must follow the law.

2551. "Roosevelt the Hun." *Labor Defender* 1 (July 30, 1918):10.
Roosevelt's attack on the IWW.
Roosevelt's attack on the IWW.

2552. Roosevelt, Theodore. "Murder Is Murder." *Outlook* 98 (May 6, 1911):12–13; *Outlook* 99 (December 16, 1911):901–2.
In the McNamara case and elsewhere, there is no excuse for murder.

2553. "Rooting Out the Reds." *Literary Digest* 58 (November 22, 1919): 14–15.
The Department of Justice raids on the IWW.

2554. Roscoe, Willson. "Sheriff's Aide Tells of the Bisbee Deportation." *Arizona Days and Ways* (November 8, 1964):42–43.

2555. Rose, Gerald A. "The Westwood Lumber Strike." *Labor History* 13 (Spring, 1972):171–99.
A 1937 Northern California lumber strike.

2556. Rosebury, A. "Industrialism: the Bugbear of Society. The IWW and its Poverty of Philosophy." *Leather Workers' Journal* 15 (October, 1912):42–43.

2557. Rosemont, Franklin. "On the Job." *Rebel Worker* 2 (Summer, 1964):3–5.
On unemployment.

2558. ———. "'The Wobblies Return' in Chicago." *Rebel Worker* 1 (Spring, 1964):5–7.
The convention of the now-changing IWW.

2559. Rosenthal, Star. "Union Maids: Organized Women Workers in Vancouver, 1900–1915." *B.C. Studies* 41 (Spring, 1979):36–55.
One Big Union women affected by the IWW idea.

2560. Ross, Edward A. "Freedom of Communication and the Struggle for Right." *Survey* 33 (January 9, 1915):405.
The president of the University of Wisconsin stating that employers are flouting civil rights with lavish use of club and cell. IWW workers have real grievances.

2561. Roth, H. "American Influences on the New Zealand Labour Movement." *Historical Studies, Australia and New Zealand* 9 (No. 36, 1961):413–20.
The New Zealand IWW.

2562. Rowan, James. "The Imprisoned IWW at Leavenworth." *Nation* 113 (August 3, 1921):123.

2563. Rowell, Wilbur E. "The Lawrence Strike." *Survey* 27 (March 23, 1912):1958–60.

Views of a judge involved in the legal side of the strike.

2564. "Rubber Companies Have Queer Schemes To Keep the Workers Down." *Industrial Solidarity* No. 289 (May 7, 1924):6.

2565. "Rubber Slavery at Akron." *Industrial Pioneer* 3 (August, 1925):3–5.

An industrial union at Goodyear Tire that is actually a company union.

2566. Rubin, W. B. "Concerning Bolshevism Here." *Miners Magazine* 20 (March, 1919):1, 6.

Apprehension over the Seattle General Strike.

2567. Rubinow, I. M. "Three Books on Socialism." Review of *American Syndicalism: The IWW,* by John G. Brooks (see no. 20); *Syndicalism, Industrial Unionism, and Socialism,* by John Spargo (see no. 206); and *The New Unionism,* by André Tridon (see no. 217). *Intercollegiate Socialist Review* 2 (October–November, 1913):20–22.

2568. Ruetten, Richard. "Anaconda Journalism: The End of an Era." *Journalism Quarterly* 37 (Winter, 1960):3–12.

The reporting of the all-powerful Anaconda company's strikes.

2569. "Rumored Split in the Rival Branches of the Workers of the World Organization in Chicago and Detroit, Apparently at Each Others' Throats." *Square Deal* 11 (August, 1912):65–68.

2570. Rus, Jan. "The Class War on the Railroads and West Virginia." *Industrial Pioneer* 1 (July, 1921):3–7.

Describes how the railroad unions scab in miners' strikes; if they were in one industrial union such things would never happen.

2571. Russell, Bert. "The General Strike." *One Big Union Monthly* NS 2 (January, 1938):3–6.

The possibility of a general strike.

2572. ———. "On Boring from Within." *One Big Union Monthly* NS 2 (February, 1938):20–22.

The CIO cannot achieve what the IWW might because of its adherence to that capitalistic tool collective bargaining.

2573. ———. "Royalty Is Out of a Job." *One Big Union Monthly* NS 1 (December, 1937):9–11.

As royalty seems an anachronism to Americans, craft unionism seems out of date to the IWW.

2574. ———. "In the Name of the Working Class." *One Big Union Monthly* NS 1 (July, 1937):17–20.

A comparison of the CIO and the IWW, with a warning that, unlike the IWW, the CIO may talk about unity but practices divisiveness.

2575. Russell, Bertrand. "Democracy and Direct Action." *Dial* 66 (May 3, 1919):445–48.

When it might be right to use direct action.

2576. Russell, Charles E. "The Radical Press in America." *Bookman* 49 (July, 1919):513–18.

Believes that there are fewer radical magazines partly because of the good work done by the Industrial Commission.

2577. ———. "What Comes of Playing the Game." In Austin Lewis, ed., *Proletarian and Petit-Bourgeois* (Chicago: IWW, 1911), 22–35 (see no. 4294).

The proletarian movement should have no place in politics.

2578. Russell, Francis. "The Last of the American Anarchists: The Strange Story of Carlo Tresca." *Modern Age* 8 (Winter, 1963–64):61–76.

2579. Russell, Phillips. "Acquittal of Ettor and Giovannitti." *International Socialist Review* 13 (January, 1913):556–57.

2580. ———. "The Arrest of Haywood and Lessig." *International Socialist Review* 13 (May, 1913):789–92.

The arrests during the Paterson strike were made to prevent Haywood and Lessig from making any more rousing speeches.

2581. ———. "Arrest of Haywood and Lessig," in *Pageant of the Paterson Strike* (New York: Success Press, 1913):11–14.

Reprint of no. 2580.

2582. ———. "The Class Struggle on the Pacific Coast: An Interview with O. A. Tveitmoe." *International Socialist Review* 13 (September, 1912):236–38.

The California building trades unionist supported the San Diego Free Speech Fight and hopes that the AFL will develop into a fighting union some day.

2583. ———. "Deportation and Political Policy." *Dial* 67 (August 23, 1919):147–49.

2584. ———. "The Dynamite Job at Lawrence." *International Socialist Review* 13 (October, 1912):308–11.

The $500 fined John Breen, a relative of the textile employers at Lawrence, for his dynamite plot compared to the life term given the McNamaras for theirs. There is one law for the rich and another for the poor.

2585. ———. "The Fourteen in Jail." *International Socialist Review* 13 (February, 1913):598–99.

Some interesting incidents during and after the Little Falls strike.

2586. ———. "Living on Determination in Paterson." *International Socialist Review* 14 (August, 1913):100–101.

The growing difficulties of the Paterson strike.

2587. ———. "The New Disease: Protocolic." *International Socialist Review* 13 (March, 1913):650–52.

The New York Garment Workers' protocol, or contract, achieved after a strike. Capitalists are no longer holding out for an open shop because they are afraid of the IWW.

2588. ———. "The Second Battle of Lawrence." *International Socialist Review* 13 (November, 1912):417–23.

The "second strike," a protest against the trial of Ettor and Giovannitti, with parades and other protest actions in Lawrence.

2589. ———. "The Strike at Little Falls." *International Socialist Review* 13 (December, 1912):455–60.

The New York textile strike now in progress and the brutal treatment of the strikers.

2590. ———. "Strike Tactics." *New Review* 1 (March 29, 1913):405–9.

Lawrence and Little Falls.

2591. ———. "To Frank Little." *International Socialist Review* 18 (September, 1917):132–33.

Poetic tribute memorializing Frank Little, the IWW leader who was lynched.

2592. ———. "What Is a Riot Anyhow?" *New Review* 1 (February 1, 1913):145–47.

2593. ———. "The World's Greatest Labor Play: The Paterson Strike Pageant." *International Socialist Review* 14 (July, 1913):6–9.

2594. Russell, Phillips, et al. "On the Strike Field." *International Socialist Review* 13 (March, 1913):647–54.
Strike news from West Virginia and New York.

2595. "Russian Methods in Spokane." *Progressive Woman* 3 (January, 1910):2.
The rough treatment and jailing of Elizabeth Gurley Flynn and others.

2596. "Russianism in the Little Falls Strike." *Syndicalist* 3 (January 1, 1913):2.
Both leaders and participants were jailed.

2597. Russo, Pasquale. "The Cossacks and the Workers." *Industrial Pioneer* 3 (July, 1925):21–24.
A historical account of rough treatment of workers, ending with some harsh examples from recent IWW history.

2598. ———. "From the Hell of Wage Slavery to Industrial Heaven." *Industrial Pioneer* 2 (June, 1924):21–22, 27–28.
Class exploitation and wage slavery are what the IWW is fighting. Religion is preaching the wrong message, the one demanded by the capitalists.

2599. ———. "Tony the Immigrant." *Industrial Pioneer* 1 (August, 1923):31–35.
A typical IWW member.

2600. Ryan, John A. "Good and Bad Labor Unions." *Survey* 31 (January 10, 1914):451.
Describes and evaluates labor unions in Philadelphia, including the IWW.

2601. ———. "The Unemployed and the Churches: A Reply." *Survey* 32 (June 27, 1914):342–43.
New York's problem with the unemployed.

2602. Ryder, David W. "California Ashamed and Repentant." *New Republic* 51 (June 1, 1927):41–44.
The Anita Whitney case compared with the IWW Syndicalist trials.

2603. "Sabotage." *Outlook* 98 (August 26, 1911):915–16.
Various kinds of sabotage.

2604. "Sabotage." *Square Deal* 13 (November, 1913):376.
Various kinds of sabotage.

2605. "Sabotage and Its Advocates." *Shoe Workers Journal* 14 (March, 1913):7–8.

2606. "Sabotage Illustrated." *Independent* 74 (February 6, 1913):276–77.

2607. "Sabotage 'Jackass Tactics' Indeed!" *Miners Magazine* 12 (August 29, 1912):6.
Decries IWW activities and the idea of sabotage.

2608. "Sacramento Grand Jury Brings in Unique Indictment." *Labor Defender* 1 (March 5, 1918):1.
The California Syndicalist trial at Sacramento.

2609. "Sacramento Prisoners Gagged; Silent Defense Is Unshaken." *Solidarity* No. 7 (December 28, 1918):1, 4.
Fully describes the famous "silent defense" trial, one of a series of accounts running weekly in *Solidarity.*

2610. St. Clair. "Job Control Is Most Effective." *One Big Union Monthly* 2 (November, 1920):48–49.
IWW ideas of a union functioning chiefly on the job, as done in Australia.

2611. St. John, Vincent. "The Brotherhood of Capital and Labor: Its Effect on Labor." *International Socialist Review* 10 (January, 1910):587–93.
The UMWA and the employers are working together. The disaster at the Cherry mines in Illinois proves that the "harmony of interest" theory of employer-worker relations, as opposed to the "nothing in common" theory, is dead wrong.

2612. ———. "The Economic Argument for Industrial Unionism." *International Socialist Review* 9 (September, 1908):172–79.

2613. ———. "Fake Industrial Union versus Real Industrial Union." *Industrial Worker* 3 (April 6, 1911):1.

2614. ———. "The Fight for Free Speech at San Diego." *International Socialist Review* 12 (April, 1912):649.

2615. ———. "The IWW's Defiance." *Solidarity* 3 (March 9, 1912):1.
The doughty and purposeful spirit of the IWW at the Lawrence strike.

2616. ———. "On the IWW Convention." *Miners Magazine* 8 (November 8, 1906):4–6.

2617. ———. "Vincent St. John on the Goldfield Strike." *Nome Industrial Worker* 2 (March 20, 1908):6.

2618. ———. "Vincent St. John on the IWW Convention." *Miners Magazine* 8 (November 1, 1906):8.

2619. ———. "The Worker against the Intellectual." *Industrial Union Bulletin* 2 (October 10, 1908):1–2.

An answer and challenge to Daniel De Leon, whose article "The Intellectual against the Worker" appears juxtaposed. See no. 877.

2620. ———. "The Working Class and War." *International Socialist Review* 15 (August, 1914):117–18.

The working class has nothing to gain from fighting its brothers in another country. A properly organized working class could abolish war.

2621. ———. "St. John's Letter." *Miners Magazine* 12 (August 29, 1912):9.

Letter printed within union proceedings to demonstrate that St. John was trying to disrupt the WFM.

2622. "The Salem Trial of the Lawrence Case." *Outlook* 102 (December 7, 1912):739–40.

The trial of Ettor, Giovannitti, and Caruso.

2623. "San Diego Free Speech Facts Made Public." *Miners Magazine* 13 (May 1, 1913):8.

2624. "The San Diego Outrage." *Weekly Bulletin of the Clothing Trades* 11 (May 24, 1912):4.

2625. "The *San Diego Union*'s Challenge." *Nation* 115 (November 22, 1922):539.

The testimony at the San Diego trial is unreliable. It was proved totally untrue that the IWW poisoned meat intended for soldiers.

2626. "San Diego's Free Speech Troubles." *Literary Digest* 44 (June 1, 1912):1146.

2627. "San Diego's Only Hope." *Wilshire's Magazine* 16 (June–July, 1912):3.

The San Diego Free Speech Fight shows that the workers need to be better organized.

2628. Sandburg, Carl. "Haywood Longs for 'Other Boys' in Jail." *International Socialist Review* 18 (November–December, 1917):277–78.

Haywood misses his IWW friends. If they were in jail with him it would be "home-like."

2629. ———. "Prosecution Stupid, Says Sandburg." *Labor Defender* 1 (April 1, 1918):2.

The Chicago trial.

2630. Sanders, H. F. "Butte: The Heart of the Copper Industry." *Overland* 48 (November, 1906):367–84.

Labor unrest among the Butte miners.

2631. Sandgren, John. "The Exodus from Egypt, Moses and the I.W.W." *One Big Union Monthly* 1 (September, 1919):17–25.

Historical comparison between the persecution of the IWW and of the Jews.

2632. ———. "Industrial Unionism *vs.* Bolshevism." *Industrial Worker* 1 (November 8, 1919):2.

2633. ———. "The Inside Story of American Bolshevism." *One Big Union Monthly* 2 (October, 1920):39–41.

Louis C. Fraina and the Zinoviev appeal.

2634. ———. "International Impostors." *One Big Union Monthly* 2 (July, 1920):45–48.

Louis C. Fraina and the Communist Party.

2635. ———. "The IWW—a Statement of Its Principles, Objectives and Methods." *One Big Union Monthly* 2 (May, 1920):36–41.

2636. ———. "The IWW Needs an Industrial Encyclopedia." *One Big Union Monthly* 1 (November, 1919):42–44.

Suggests a complete labor encyclopedia and explains the new IWW handbook.

2637. ———. "The Labor Party and the IWW." *One Big Union Monthly* 2 (January, 1920):43–44.

The IWW's policy of staying strictly out of politics.

2638. ———. "Man Overboard." *One Big Union Monthly* 2 (March, 1920):41–43.

Varney's defection and the current condition of the IWW.

2639. ———. "The 'Patriotic' Terrorist Caught with the Goods." *One Big Union Monthly* 1 (October, 1919):24–26.

On the question of profiteering by Senator McAdoo and Colonel Disque.

2640. ———. "Solving the Social Problem through Economic Direct Action." *One Big Union Monthly* 2 (October, 1920):30–31, 34–37.
Describes what Sandgren calls "industrial communism" and illustrates it with a chart.

2641. ———. "Sowing the Wind and Reaping the Whirlwind." *One Big Union Monthly* 2 (July, 1920):10–13.
The IWW accused of instigating many mob actions with which it had nothing to do. Accusers are looking for a scapegoat.

2642. ———. "Under the Spell of Terrorism." *One Big Union Monthly* 2 (March, 1920):23–28.
The secret U.S. Government has its seat in Wall Street and is ordering our government to recruit agents to commit violence against the radicals. Good photographs.

2643. ———. "The Vindication of the Utopians." *One Big Union Monthly* 2 (May, 1920):42–45.
How German Syndicalists operate. The IWW must try harder to educate the worker, as German Syndicalists have done.

2644. ———. "Wobbly Editor Helps the University Student with His Thesis." *One Big Union Monthly* 2 (July, 1920):49–51.
University of Michigan student poses hard questions about labor issues.

2645. Sang, Elias. "The Destroyers of Idols." *The Blast* 1 (January 1, 1917):6.
Migratory workers and hoboes are great fighters for freedom. Their organization, the IWW, deserves respect.

2646. Sanger, Margaret. "Let Us Have the Truth." *Labor Defender* 1 (August 15, 1918):16.
The IWW trial at Chicago.

2647. "Sanitation in the Hop Fields." *Life and Labor* 4 (October, 1914):318.
The conditions at the Durst hop ranch that led to the Wheatland riot.

2648. Santee, J. F. "The Oregon Military Police of World War I." *Oregon Historical Quarterly* 45 (June, 1944):124–32.

A firsthand account of the use of mobile state police to deal with the "IWW element."

2649. Sanville, Florence L. "Silk Workers in Pennsylvania and New Jersey." *Survey* 28 (May 18, 1912):307–12.
The rash of strikes at silk mills, chiefly in Paterson but also in other states.

2650. Saul, George. "The Colorado Battle Line." *Labor Defender* 2 (December, 1927):179–80.
The Colorado coal strikes.

2651. Sawyer, Rev. Roland D. "The Socialist Situation in Massachusetts." *New Review* 1 (January 25, 1913):117–18.
The Lawrence strike.

2652. ———. "What Threatens Ettor and Giovannitti." *International Socialist Review* 13 (August, 1912):114–15.
The Salem trial will be unfair to the strikers.

2653. Sayre, Francis B. "Criminal Conspiracy." *Harvard Law Review* 35 (February, 1922):394–427.
The new conspiracy laws are an uncomfortable problem where civil rights are concerned.

2654. Sayre, John. "Political Prisoners in America." *Dial* 65 (December 28, 1918):623–24.

2655. Scanlon, Michael A. "What Lawrence Really Did." *Square Deal* 11 (December, 1912):437–40.
The Lawrence mayor describes his handling of the strike.

2656. Schamehorn, H. Lee. "In the Shadow of Cripple Creek: Florence from 1885 to 1910." *Colorado Magazine* 55 (1978):205–29.

2657. Scharrenberg, Paul. "Sanitary Conditions in Labor Camps." *American Federationist* 25 (October, 1918):891–93.
The IWW should not take credit for the improved conditions because the managers would probably have improved them anyway.

2658. "Scenes from a Rank-and-File Convention." *Industrial Pioneer* 1 (June, 1921):26–28.
The 1921 convention described by a delegate who finds the IWW still undaunted by all the raids and troubles.

2659. Scheinberg, Stephen. "The Haywood Trial: Theodore Roosevelt's 'Undesirable Citizens.'" *Idaho Yesterdays* 4 (Fall, 1960):10–15.

2660. Schwantes, Carlos A. "Leftward Tilt on the Pacific Slope." *Pacific Northwest Quarterly* 70 (January, 1979):24–34.

Examines the early twentieth-century labor situation in the Pacific Northwest, where the strong influence of dual unionism, industrial unionism, and Socialism complicated the problem for AFL organizers, who were not very successful there.

2661.———. "Making the World Unsafe for Democracy: Vigilantes, Grangers, and the Walla Walla Outrages of June, 1918." *Montana, The Magazine of Western History* 31 (January, 1981):18–29.

2662. ———. Review of *At the Point of Production,* ed. by Joseph Conlin (see no. 39). *American Historical Review* 87 (June, 1982):869.

2663. ———. "Washington State's Pioneer Labor-Reform Press: A Bibliographical Essay and Annotated Checklist." *Pacific Northwest Quarterly* 71 (1980):112–26.

2664. Schwartz, Harvey. "Harry Bridges and the Scholars Looking at History's Verdict." *California History* 59 (Spring, 1980):66–79.

2665. Schwoegler, Steve. "Frank Little." *Industrial Worker* 79 (July, 1982):5.

A retrospective look at the martyred IWW leader.

2666. "Scotch the IWW Snake." *American Lumberman* No. 2322 (November 15, 1919):45.

Centralia will teach the IWW a lesson.

2667. Scott, Alexander. "What the Reds Are Doing in Paterson." *International Socialist Review* 13 (June, 1913):852–56.

The progress of the Paterson strike.

2668. "Scott Indicted Again." *International Socialist Review* 14 (August, 1913):101–2.

The jailing of pro-labor journalist Alexander Scott for his stories and editorials on the Paterson strike.

2669. Scudder, Vida. "For Justice Sake. Address Delivered at Lawrence." *Survey* 28 (April 6, 1912):77–79.

The speech delivered by an Ivy League professor that prompted many repercussions from her colleagues.

2670. Seagle, William. "The Technique of Suppression." *American Mercury* 1 (January, 1926):35–42.

California is operating a "convicting machine," and the Syndicalist laws are intended to suppress labor.

2671. "Seattle General Strike." *Rebel Worker* 2 (March 1, 1919):1–2.

2672. "Seattle General Strike, 1919: Can We Do Better Next Time?" *Progressive Labor* 9 (July, 1973):32–44.

2673. "Seattle's Red Flag Incident." *Literary Digest* 47 (August 2, 1913): 160–61.
How the IWW was raided by a group of sailors.

2674. "Second Installment from Porcupine Miners." *Miners Magazine* 12 (May 23, 1912):5–8.
The persisting desire of some WFM miners to reaffiliate with the IWW.

2675. "Secret Service Stunts That Spoiled Some Wily Hunish Plans." *Literary Digest* 62 (August 16, 1919):62–70.
Rejoices at the government's success in quelling the IWW.

2676. "Sedition Plank for the Republicans." *New Republic* 23 (June 16, 1920):75–76.
Mere membership in the IWW is sufficient grounds for deportation under the new law.

2677. Selavan, Ida C. "Jewish Wage Earners in Pittsburgh, 1890–1930." *American Jewish Historical Quarterly* 65 (March, 1976):274.

2678. "Selections from the Works of T-Bone Slim." *Rebel Worker* 1 (Spring, 1964):17–24.

2679. "Senator George W. Pepper—a Courageous Defender." *New Republic* 36 (September 5, 1923):31.
Pepper recommends release of the twenty-two Sacramento prisoners.

2680. Sennefelder, Alois. "The Workers' Press: How To Develop It." *Industrial Pioneer* 1 (January, 1924):40.

2681. "Sentence Pronounced by Judge Landis upon the IWW." *Survey* 40 (September 7, 1918):682.
The Chicago trial.

2682. Seraile, William. "Ben Fletcher, IWW Organizer." *Pennsylvania History* 46 (July, 1979):213–32.
The black IWW leader and organizer of Philadelphia longshoremen.

2683. Seretan, L. Glen. "Daniel De Leon as American." *Wisconsin Magazine of History* 61 (Spring, 1978):210–23.

2684. ———. "The Personal Style and Political Methods of Daniel De Leon: A Reconsideration." *Labor History* 14 (Spring, 1973): 163–201.

2685. ———. Review of *The Life and Times of Daniel De Leon,* by Carl Reeve (see no. 185). *Labor History* 14 (Spring, 1973):163–201.

2686. Seretan, L. G.; M. H. Ebner; L. Harrington. "Correspondence." *Labor History* 15 (Winter, 1974):147–53.

Daniel De Leon and the "two IWWs."

2687. "The Servant Girl Rediscovered." *One Big Union Monthly* 2 (January, 1920):53–54.

On formation of the Hotel, Restaurant, and Domestic Workers Industrial Union, IWW, in 1918. No other union can so well protect the working girl.

2688. Sessions, Alansom. "Blind Leaders of the Blind." *Rebel Worker* 2 (August 15, 1919):2.

The AFL does not work for the good of labor because it is divisive.

2689. "Shall America Go Hungry?" *One Big Union Monthly* NS 1 (January, 1937):28–29.

The lay-offs of WPA workers and the desperation of the unemployed.

2690. "Shall Haywood Be Sacrificed to Satisfy the Vengeance of the Politicians?" *Socialist and Labor Star* 1 (December 27, 1912):1.

Haywood's ouster from the Socialist Party.

2691. "Shame of Texas." *International Socialist Review* 16 (December, 1915):383.

Charles Cline's arrest.

2692. Shanks, Rosalie. "The IWW Free Speech Movement, San Diego, 1912." *Journal of San Diego History* 19, No. 1 (1973):25–33.

2693. Shannon, David A. "The Socialist Party before the First World War: An Analysis." *Mississippi Valley Historical Review* 38 (September, 1951):279–88.

The relations between the IWW and the Socialist Party.

2694. Shepard, Harvey N. "The Financial Downfall of Lawrence, Mass." *National Municipal Review* 1 (January, 1912):125–26.

The Lawrence strike and its cost to the city.

2695. ———. "The Thralldom of Massachusetts Cities." *National Municipal Review* 1 (January, 1912):182–94.
The effect of strikes on the cities where they take place.

2696. Sheridan, Donald. "Our Next Step." *Voice of the People* 3 (June 4, 1914):3.
It is time for a new approach to organizing in the Northwest.

2697. "Sheriff Kinkead's Busy Day." *Literary Digest* 51 (August 7, 1915): 256–61.
The rough and illegal force used against the striking chemical workers in Bayonne, New Jersey.

2698. "Sherlock Holmes' Successor Discovered by Eminent News." *Industrial Solidarity* 1 (January 5, 1927):1
A San Francisco newspaper discovers that one of William Haywood's trusted friends was a government spy.

2699. "Sherman Service, Inc." *One Big Union Monthly* 1 (December, 1919):11.
A detective confesses to some of the depredations blamed on labor.

2700. Shields, Arthur. "For the Silent Defenders." *Liberator* 5 (September, 1922):22–23.
The Sacramento trial.

2701. ———. "New Turn of the I.W.W." *Socialist Review* 10 (April, 1921):69–72.
The "builder" is replacing the "agitator."

2702. ———. "Recollections of the Paterson Silk Strike." *Political Affairs* 61 (January, 1982):32–35.

2703. ———. "The San Pedro Strike." *Industrial Pioneer* 1 (June, 1923):14–18.

2704. ———. "War in West Virginia." *Industrial Pioneer* 1 (October, 1921):3–9.
The hired thugs and frequent murders in the West Virginia coal strike country.

2705. Shippey, Hartwell S. "The Shame of San Diego." *International Socialist Review* 12 (May, 1912):718–23.
The San Diego Free Speech Fight disaster.

2706. "Shipping Lenine's Friends to Him." *Literary Digest* 64 (January 3, 1920):14–15.
The deportations of radical immigrants.

2707. Shirley, Steve. "Wobblies and Eureka Seldom Found Peace." *Missoulian* (August 30, 1973):n.p.
The constant labor problems in the Pacific Northwest.

2708. "Shop Organization in the Metal and Machinery Industry." *One Big Union Monthly* 2 (December, 1920):31–34.
Details of the city-wide system of IWW organizing, with a 1920 chart showing how it was done.

2709. Short, Wallace M. "How One Town Learned a Lesson in Free Speech." *Survey* 35 (October 30, 1915):106–8.
A free-speech episode in Sioux City, Iowa.

2710. "Should the Radical Stay in the A. F. of L.?" *Labor Age* 11 (January, 1922):14–16.
The IWW answer must be "no."

2711. Shurtleff, Wade. "One Big Union." *International Socialist Review* 15 (July, 1914):29–30.
The need for railroad workers to abandon craft unionism and join the IWW.

2712. ———. "Report of International Secretary." *Bulletin* 2 (May 5, 1908):n.p.
There may be a split between the Socialists and the IWW because of their differences over direct action and sabotage.

2713. "Shut Off the Fodder." *Miners Magazine* 15 (July 30, 1914):9.
John Pancner's arrest in Tonopah.

2714. "Shut Off the Revenue." *Miners Magazine* 13 (January 23, 1913):23.
The IWW will die out when it stops getting Socialist Party funds.

2715. Siantific, Woodby. "My Interpretation." *New Unionist* 1 (January 5, 1929):4.
An IWW method of redressing an unpaid waitress' wrongs.

2716. Sigrosser, Carl. "Sunday at Haledon." *New York Call* 6 (June 11, 1913):n.p.
The speech-making at strikers' rallies in a Paterson suburb.

2717. Silbert, Jacob. "What Is Industrial Unionism?" *Industrial Pioneer* 1 (June, 1923):11–13.

2718. "Silencing Industrial Workers." *Literary Digest* 44 (April 20, 1912):800.
The Free Speech Fights.

2719. "Silk Weavers on the Right Track." *Why* 1 (July, 1913):4–5.
The tactics of the Paterson strikers.

2720. Sima, Jonas. "Joe Hill: The Man Who Never Died." *American Swedish Historical Foundation Yearbook* (1965):59–64.

2721. Simon, A. F. "Anarchism and Anarcho-Syndicalism in South America." *Hispanic-American Historical Review* 26 (February, 1946):38–59.

2722. Simons, A. M. "The Chicago Conference for Industrial Unions." *International Socialist Review* 5 (February, 1905):496–99.

2723. ———. "The Industrial Workers of the World." *International Socialist Review* 6 (August, 1905):65–77.
The purpose and the promise of the new union. The convention in Chicago is a turning point in American working-class history.

2724. ———. "Industrial Workers of the World." *Miners Magazine* 6 (August 24, 1905):13–15.
The convention and the new universal label.

2725. ———. "Plain Words to Socialists." *Industrial Worker* 1 (March, 1906):5.
"Boring from within" has failed. The Civic Federations are corrupting the country.

2726. ———. "A Reply." *International Socialist Review* 5 (April, 1905):590–91.
Replies to Bohn's article about the Chicago Manifesto (see no. 463). Believes Socialism is growing fastest in the AFL.

2727. ———. "Some Matters of Tactics." *International Socialist Review* 5 (April, 1905):623–27.
The compatibility of De Leon, the SLP, and the IWW.

2728. Simony, Austin H. "The American Freedom Convention and the One Big Union." *One Big Union Monthly* 1 (December, 1919): 46–47.

2729. Sims, Robert C. "Idaho's Criminal Syndicalism Act: One State's Response to Radical Labor." *Labor History* 15 (Fall, 1974):511–27.

2730. Sinclair, Archie. "Hypocritical California." *Industrial Pioneer* 1 (December, 1923):7–8.
California products should be boycotted because of the trials.

2731. ———. "The Meaning of Revolution." *Industrial Pioneer* 2 (May, 1924):11–12.
The Criminal Syndicalist trials and prisoners.

2732. ———. "Now That the Storm Is Subsiding." *Industrial Pioneer* 1 (March, 1924):11–12.
The Criminal Syndicalist trials and prisoners.

2733. ———. "Vision of a New Day in California." *Industrial Pioneer* 1 (January, 1924):5–6.
The Criminal Syndicalist trials and prisoners.

2734. ———. "A Visit to San Quentin Prison." *Industrial Pioneer* 1 (October, 1923):27–29.
A visit to the prison where the IWW prisoners are held.

2735. ———. "Woe to the Cause that Hath Not Passed through a Prison." *Industrial Pioneer* 1 (February, 1924):7–8.
The IWW prisoners.

2736. Sinclair, Upton. "Civil Liberties in Los Angeles." *Industrial Pioneer* 1 (August, 1923):27–29.
California's Syndicalism laws have caused civil liberties to disappear in Los Angeles. The IWW should stop dual unionism and start sounding more American.

2737. ———. "Fooling America." *Appeal to Reason* 1289 (August 14, 1920):3.
Conflicting views on the Centralia Massacre.

2738. ———. "Labor's Crimes." *New Appeal* 1212 (February 22, 1919):4.
Is the IWW "criminal" for wanting a shorter work day?

2739. ———. "A Rebel in Jail." *New Appeal* 1211 (February 15, 1919):11.
Poetic description of life in jail.

2740. ———. "Revolt in Seattle." *Appeal to Reason* 1256 (December 27, 1919):3.
The Seattle General Strike.

2741. ———. "Russia: A Challenge." *New Appeal* 1218 (April 5, 1919):1.
The Russian revolution was a gigantic IWW strike.

2742. ———. "We Get Arrested a Little." *Liberator* 7 (July, 1923):16–22.
Sinclair's own arrest.

2743. Sirola, George. "Finnish Working Peoples' College." *International Socialist Review* 14 (August, 1913):102–4.
The Work Peoples College in Duluth, Minnesota.

2744. "Situation as Seen by a Manufacturer." *Survey* 28 (April 6, 1912):75.
The Lawrence and Paterson strikes as seen by a mill owner.

2745. "The Situation at Goldfield." *Outlook* 88 (January 11, 1908):57–58.
The Goldfield strike.

2746. "Situation in Balitmore Now Well in Hand." *Garment Worker* 12 (August 29, 1913):1.
Union workers were blamed for striking, when in fact they were only holding a shop meeting.

2747. "Situation in Lawrence." *Outlook* 102 (October 12, 1912):286–87.
The Lawrence strike.

2748. "Situation in Michigan." *Miners Magazine* 14 (October 2, 1913): 8–9.
The Calumet-Hecla strike.

2749. "Situation in the Copper District of Michigan." *Miners Magazine* 14 (August 7, 1913):6–7.

2750. "Situation Must Be Met." *Miners Magazine* 9 (November 14, 1907):5.

2751. Skakkeback, Mette. "Agrarian Radicalism after the Populists." *American Studies in Scandinavia* 1 (1979):1–3.
Mentions the IWW.

2752. "Skimming the Melting Pot." *Literary Digest* 60 (March 1, 1919):16.
The deportations of radical immigrants.

2753. "Slaughter at Roosevelt." *Outlook* 109 (February 3, 1915):241–42.
The shooting of striking chemical workers in Roosevelt, New Jersey.

2754. "Slime of the Slanderers." *Miners Magazine* 13 (April 3, 1913):5.
The Syndicalist has slandered the UMW in its discussions of West Virginia miners.

2755. Sloss, R. "Our New Industrial Conservation." *Harper's* 57 (January 25, 1913):13–14.
It is poor business practice to ignore the workers' problems.

2756. "Smash the IWW!" *Labor Defender* 1 (May 1, 1918):1.
Description of the raids.

2757. Smith, Charles J. "Scum of Industry." *Industrial Pioneer* 2 (December, 1924):47.
An answer to no. 2988.

2758. Smith, Elmer. "On the Centralia Front." *Labor Defender* 3 (August, 1928):168.
Memories of the Centralia trial and concern for those still in prison.

2759. Smith, Rufus. "Some Phases of the McKees Rocks Strike." *Survey* 23 (October 2, 1909):38–45.

2760. Smith, Vera. "Work Peoples College." *One Big Union Monthly* NS 2 (April, 1938):14–15.

2761. Smith, Vern. "Indications of International Solidarity." *Industrial Pioneer* 3 (November, 1925):19–25.
The IWW in relation to world labor and radical movements.

2762. ———. "The Negro—A Subject Race." *Industrial Pioneer* 1 (April, 1924):5–6.
Black workers urged to join the IWW.

2763. ———. "Smashing the Chains of Slavery." *Industrial Pioneer* 1 (June, 1923):3–9.
IWW strikes in the Northwest from 1917 to 1923.

2764. Smith, Walker C. "Remember the Fifth of November." *International Socialist Review* 17 (January, 1917):396–99.
The Everett Massacre.

2765. ———. "The Spirit of Revolt." *Mother Earth* 12 (April, 1917):46–48.
The Everett Massacre.

2766. ———. "The Voyage of the Verona." *International Socialist Review* 17 (December, 1916):340–46.
The Everett Massacre, with excellent photographs.

2767. Snell, Viola G. "In Memory of Frank Little." *Industrial Pioneer* 4 (August, 1926):6.

2768. Snow, Richard F. "Joe Hill." *American Heritage* 27 (October, 1976):78–79.

2769. Snyder, Robert E. "Women, Wobblies, and Workers' Rights: The 1912 Textile Strike in Little Falls, New York." *New York History* 60 (January, 1979):29–57. Also appears in Joseph R. Conlin, ed., *At the Point of Production* (Westport, CT: Greenwood Press, 1981), 27–48 (see no. 39).

2770. "The So-called American Wage-Earner and the Strike at Lawrence." *Review of Reviews* 45 (June, 1912):746–47.

2771. "Social Significance of Arturo Giovannitti." *Current Opinion* 54 (January, 1913):24–26.

Giovannitti is a real social portent because, despite his IWW connections, he is intellectual, poetic, and of good family. Does this mean there may be a real reason for revolution?

2772. "Social War in New Jersey." *Current Opinion* 55 (August, 1913):80–81.

The Paterson strike.

2773. "Socialism and 'Industrialism.'" *Public* 13 (October 21, 1910):985–87.

Can Socialism and industrialism be combined?

2774. "Socialism and Labor." Review of *American Syndicalism: The I.W.W.,* by John G. Brooks (see no. 20). *Nation* 97 (October 21, 1910): 80–81.

2775. "Socialism and Syndicalism." *Nation* 94 (May 30, 1912):533–34.

The first trial of Syndicalism was the Lawrence strike.

2776. "Socialism and the IWW." *Common Cause* 2 (December, 1912):770–71.

Can Haywood be both a Socialist and an IWW?

2777. "Socialism and Unionism." *Common Cause* 2 (July, 1912):95.

The possibility of combining Socialism and unionism.

2778. "Socialism Rebuking Violence." *Literary Digest* 44 (June 1, 1912): 1144–45.

Haywood's ouster from the Socialist Party.

2779. "Socialist Press and Industrial Unionism." *Common Cause* 2 (December, 1912):771–72.

How the press views industrial unionism.

2780. "Socialist Unity in America." *International Socialist Review* 12 (July, 1911):47–48.

Socialism may be drifting into "IWWism."

2781. "Socialists and the Old Line Unionist." *Survey* 29 (December 7, 1912):271–73.

There may be a split between Socialists and old unionists.

2782. Sofchalk, Donald G. "Organized Labor and the Iron Ore Miners of Minnesota, 1907–1936." *Labor History* 12 (Spring, 1971): 214–42.

2783. "Solidarity in Fargo." *Industrial Pioneer* 3 (September, 1925):3, 41.
Some jailed IWW farmworkers refuse to leave jail until all are released.

2784. "Solidarity Wins in Fresno." *International Socialist Review* 11 (April, 1911):634–36.
The Fresno Free Speech Fight.

2785. Solow, Herbert. "Class War in Minnesota." *Nation* 139 (December 26, 1934):743–44.
The current strikes in Minnesota.

2786. Soltis, John G. "The Bolsheviki in America." *One Big Union Monthly* 1 (May, 1919):19–20.
Intellectual Socialists do not understand that the IWW represents industrial democracy.

2787. ———. "Concerning Education." *One Big Union Monthly* 1 (July, 1919):49.
Action is more important than book-learning; emphasis should be on organization, not education.

2788. ———. "Psychology of Persecution in War Time." *One Big Union Monthly* 1 (June, 1919):34–35.

2789. "Some Comments on the I.W.W." *Typographical Journal* (February, 1913):149–50.
The AFL views the IWW strikes.

2790. "Some Facts about the Harlan Frame-ups." *Workers Defense* 2 (October, 1932):2.
IWW activities in Evarts, Kentucky.

2791. "Some History and Comments That May Be Interesting to the Miners of Butte, Montana." *Miners Magazine* 15 (July 16, 1914):7–10.
The fight between the IWW and the WFM over the union hall and Butte Miners Union No. 1.

2792. "Some Interesting Data." *Miners Magazine* 15 (February 12, 1914):6.
The Calumet-Hecla strike.

2793. "Some IWW Anniversaries." *One Big Union Monthly* 2 (November, 1920):59–60.
November is the month of many IWW tragedies.

2794. Somerville, H. "Successors to Socialism." *Catholic World* 99 (May, 1914):173–80.
On Criminal Syndicalism.

2795. Sonnischen, C. L. "Book News." *Journal of Arizona History* 18 (Summer, 1977):230–32.
Review of a number of recent articles on historic Arizona strikes, especially the Globe strike.

2796. Spargo, John. "Fight Bolshevism with Democracy." *McClure's* 51 (September, 1919):10.
Civil rights should not be violated, as in the government raids.

2797. ———. "The Psychology of the Parlor Bolsheviki." *World's Work* 39 (December, 1919):127–31.
Why Socialists like the IWW.

2798. ———. "Why the IWW Flourishes." *World's Work* 39 (January, 1920):243–47.
The IWW is strong because it believes so strongly that it is right.

2799. Speakman, T. R. "More about Communism." *One Big Union Monthly* 2 (June, 1920):17–19.
How Communism and the IWW differ.

2800. Speed, George. "A.F. of L. and I.W.W.—The Difference." *One Big Union Monthly* 2 (June, 1920):36.

2801. ———. "Industrial Organization." *Industrial Worker* 7 (June 26, 1926):3.
Theoretical discussion.

2802. ———. "Industrial Organization." *One Big Union Monthly* NS 2 (June, 1938):20–21.
Theoretical discussion.

2803. Spero, S. D., and J. B. Aronoff. "War in the Kentucky Mountains." *American Mercury* 25 (February, 1932):226–33.
Saome Harlan strikers join the IWW.

2804. Spielman, Jean E. "Are the IWW Still Revolutionary?" *Mother Earth* 2 (December, 1907):457–60.

The IWWs are not anarchists, but maybe they could be called revolutionaries.

2805. "The Spokane Cases." *Lumberjack Bulletin* (April 27, 1918):2.
The raid on the IWW Defense Committee headquarters in Spokane, in which more than 100 men and women were arrested.

2806. "Spruce and the IWW." *New Republic* 14 (February 23, 1918):99–100.
The IWW in the spruce industry.

2807. "Spruce Inquiry Methods Bring Retorts." *American Lumberman* 2313 (September 13, 1919):42.
The government's spruce drive.

2808. Stanter, I. N. "Is the IWW to Grow?" *Agitator* 1 (September 15, 1911):2–3.

2809. Stanwood, Edward B. "The Marysville Case." *Harper's Weekly* 58 (June 20, 1914):23.
The Wheatland Hop Riot.

2810. "State Investigation of the Little Falls Strike." *Survey* 29 (January 4, 1913):414.

2811. "State Police Raid New York Unions." *Rebel Worker* 2 (July 1, 1919):1.
The New York raids to obtain evidence for the Lusk Committee.

2812. "Statement from the I.W.W." *International Socialist Review* 18 (October, 1917):206–9.
The raids on the headquarters of the IWW in Chicago, as well as those in Seattle, Minneapolis, and other cities.

2813. Stavis, Barrie. "Joe Hill: Poet and Organizer." *Folk Music* (June–August, 1964):3.

2814. Steffens, Lincoln. "The Labor Contract of the I.W.W." *Solidarity* 3 (April 6, 1912):3.
Detailed description of IWW organizing techniques.

2815. Stegner, S. Page. "Protest Songs from the Butte Mines." *Western Folklore* 26 (1967):157–67.

2816. Stegner, Wallace. "I Dreamed I Saw Joe Hill Last Night." *Pacific Spectator* 1 (Spring, 1947):184–87.

2817. ———. "Joe Hill, the Wobbly Troubadour." *New Republic* 118 (January 5, 1948):20–24, 38.
An analysis of the Joe Hill trial that suggests Joe might have been guilty. This article caused many repercussions.

2818. Stelzle, Charles. "An East Side American." *Outlook* 142 (April 14, 1926):563–66.
Haywood and the miners of Cripple Creek.

2819. "Stemming the Tide." In *Labor Scrap-Book.* (Chicago: Charles H. Kerr, n.d.), 49–51.
Techniques for trying to crush revolutionary ideas and actions. See no. 3762.

2820. "Stenographic Report of the Hillquit-Haywood Debate." (New York) *Call* (January 14, 1912).
A debate that shows the incompatibility of Socialism and the IWW.

2821. Stephens, D. "Fair Play for the IWW: A Reply to H. Hibschman." *Current History* 17 (October, 1922):58.
A retrospective view of the Centralia episode. See no. 1520.

2822. Stephens, S. I. "So You Need a Maid!" *One Big Union Monthly* NS 1 (April, 1937):5–9, 27.
A lesson on employment agencies, in the form of a play.

2823. Stephenson, R. P. "What Were They Sentenced For?" *New Republic* 18 (February 8, 1919):59.
Radicals should be held responsible for intentions, not just deeds.

2824. Sterling, Jean. "The Silent Defense in Sacramento." *The Liberator* 1 (February, 1919):15–17.
The IWW defendants refused to talk during their trial.

2825. Stern, Max. "Many Objections." *Voice of Labor* 3 (May, 1905):7–8.
Objections to industrial unionism.

2826. Stevens, F. B. "The IWW—A World Menace to Civilization." *Brooklyn Eagle* Magazine Section (April 28, 1912):1–2.
The IWW is becoming too powerful and may be a threat to society.

2827. Stevens, James. "The Last of the Shanty Boys." *American Mercury* 60 (June, 1945):725–31.
Interesting story about migratory workers.

2828. Stevens, John D. "Wobblies in Milwaukee." *Historical Messenger of the Milwaukee County Historical Society* 24 (March, 1968):23–27.

2829. Stevens, Vincent S. "The Strike." *Survey* 30 (August 9, 1913):613–14.

Comments on the Akron strike.

2830. Stevenson, J. "Daniel De Leon and European Socialism." *Science and Society* 44 (Summer, 1980):199.

2831. Stewart, Oliver D. "West Virginia Coal Strike." *American Employer* 2 (November, 1913):195–202; (December, 1913):259–69.

Strikes at Paint Creek, Cabin Creek, and other areas.

2832. Stieber, Jack. "Forces Influencing the American Labor Movement: Past, Present, and Future." *Relations Industrielles* 23 (1968):591–604.

2833. Stirton, A. M. "Getting Collective Possession of Industries." *International Socialist Review* 10 (January, 1910):636–40.

2834. Stocker, Joseph. "Incident at Bisbee." *American History Illustrated* 15 (June, 1980):34–39.

A historical description of the Bisbee deportation.

2835. "Stools and Fools." *One Big Union Monthly* 2 (August, 1920):12.

Attorney General Palmer and 133,000 Secret Service men and their devious activities against the IWW.

2836. Strangeland, E. "Preliminaries to the Labor War in Colorado." *Political Science Quarterly* 23 (March, 1908):1–17.

2837. Stratton, G. F. "Ca' canny and Speeding Up." *Outlook* 99 (September 16, 1911):120–25.

A viable sabotage method, *ca' canny,* a slowdown that damages nothing but makes its point.

2838. Street, Jane. "Does Labor Prevent Thought?" *Industrial Pioneer* 2 (September, 1924):14–17.

The IWW is not only for the unskilled.

2839. "A Strike and Its Remedies." *Outlook* 103 (February 1, 1913):253–58.

Two ways to deal with bad conditions that cause strikes: sabotage, as advocated by Ettor and Giovannitti, or arbitration, which hurts nobody.

2840. "Strike at Jerome, Arizona." *Miners Magazine* 18 (June, 1917):1, 6.
The IWW is preventing the IUMMSW from organizing miners.

2841. "Strike at Little Falls." *Outlook* 103 (March 22, 1913):695.
The Little Falls textile strike.

2842. "Strike at Merryville." *Lumberjack* 2 (January 9, 1913):1.
The lumber strike in Merryville, Louisiana.

2843. "The Strike at the Woolen Mills." *Independent* 72 (February 29, 1912):433–34.
Immigrant workers who now have the nerve to go on strike in Lawrence were only recently nothing but pauper labor from Europe.

2844. "Strike Failures Are a Joy to the IWW Leaders." *Current Opinion* 68 (June, 1920):835–36.
The IWW leaders are satisfied with lost strikes because they are against peace and want the worker to be angry and dissatisfied.

2845. "Strike in Michigan." *Miners Magazine* 15 (January 22, 1914):8–9.
The Calumet-Hecla strike.

2846. "Strike of the Copper Miners." *Life & Labor* 3 (December, 1913):375–77.
The Calumet-Hecla strike.

2847. "Strike of the Jersey Silk Weavers." *Survey* 30 (May 31, 1913):300.
The Paterson strike.

2848. "Strike of the Jersey Silk Workers." *Survey* 30 (April 19, 1913):81–83.
The Paterson strike.

2849. "Strike of the Jersey Silk Workers—Reply." *Survey* 30 (May 31, 1913):316.
A reply to no. 2848.

2850. "Strike Riot in Pennsylvania." *Independent* 67 (September 2, 1909):533–37.
The McKees Rocks strike.

2851. "Strike That Oiled Its Own Troubled Waters; Seattle Strike." *Literary Digest* 61 (April 12, 1919):90–92.
The Seattle General Strike.

2852. "Strikers Standing Firm." *Miners Magazine* 14 (October 16, 1913):6.
The Calumet-Hecla strike.

2853. "Strikes and Rumors of Strikes." *Outlook* 110 (August 4, 1915):776–77.
The New Jersey chemical workers' strikes.

2854. "Strikes by Proclamation." *Agitator* 2 (October 1, 1912):1.
The IWW strike activities in Pittsburgh.

2855. "Strikes in Steel Industry Already Started and More Are Coming." *Square Deal* 12 (April, 1913):254–56.
The IWW strike at the Oliver Mill in Pittsburgh.

2856. "Strikes in the Steel District." *Survey* 28 (July 27, 1912):595–96.
The Socialists and the IWW are active in the Pittsburgh steel strike; description of their parade.

2857. Stromquist, J. A. "California Oranges." *Industrial Pioneer* 1 (March, 1921):23–26.
The problems of organizing farmworkers in California.

2858. Strong, Anna Louise. "Centralia: An Unfinished Story." *Nation* 110 (April 17, 1920):508–10.
The Centralia episode and the trial.

2859. ———. "Everett's Bloody Sunday." *Survey* 37 (January 27, 1917):475–76.
The Everett Massacre.

2860. ———. "Newspaper Confiscated—and Returned." *Nation* 109 (December 13, 1919):738–40.
The Centralia Massacre, the suppression of the *Seattle Union Record,* and the loss of civil rights.

2861. ———. "The Verdict at Everett." *Survey* 38 (May 19, 1917):160–62.

2862. Strong, Sidney. "Personal Experiences with the IWW, as told by a Congregational Minister." *Labor Defender* 1 (May 1, 1918):7.

2863. "The Struggle for Bread—and Law." *Miners Magazine* 12 (March 14, 1912):5–6.
The Lawrence strike.

2864. "The Struggle for Unity in the Marine Industry." *One Big Union Advocate* 1 (April, 1939):10–14.

An anonymous seaman describes the rivalry between unions in organizing seamen.

2865. "The Struggle for Unity in the Marine Industry." *One Big Union Advocate* 1 (May, 1939):15–18.
The problems of organizing marine workers.

2866. "Struggle in Nome, Alaska." *Miners Magazine* 15 (February 4, 1915):1.
An unusual WFM union in Alaska.

2867. "Struggles of Textile Workers Depicted by Labor Cartoonists." *Textile Labor* 34 (February, 1913):5.
Cartoons about the Lawrence and Paterson strikes.

2868. Stuart, Jack. Review of *Labor Radical: From the Wobblies to the CIO*, by Len DeCaux (see no. 49). *Labor History* 13 (Winter, 1972):137–39.

2869. "The Stuff They Fight About." *Industrial Pioneer* 2 (May, 1924):26–28.
The difficulties of organizing oil workers.

2870. "Stupendous Influence of the I.W.W." *One Big Union Monthly* 1 (December, 1919):13–15.

2871. "Subversive Wobblies." *Fortune* 40 (July, 1949):156.
The Attorney General's subversive list and its inclusion of the IWW.

2872. Suggs, George G., Jr. "Catalyst for Industrial Change: The WFM, 1893–1903." *Colorado Magazine* 45 (Fall, 1968):322–39.

2873. Suhr, Matilda. "A Mother's Appeal." *International Socialist Review* 15 (January, 1915):416–17.
An appeal for the release of the Wheatland prisoners, by the mother of one of them.

2874. Sullivan, James. "Reviewing the 1925 Harvest Drive." *Industrial Pioneer* 3 (November, 1925):5–7, 29–30.

2875. Sullivan, T. P. "Revolution in the Marine Industry." *Industrial Pioneer* 2 (March, 1925):3–5.
New technologies in sea transport must be matched with stronger efforts to organize the seamen.

2876. Sullivan, William A. "The 1913 Revolt of the Michigan Copper Miners." *Michigan History* 43 (September, 1959):294–314.

2877. Sumner, Charles G. "Vincent St. John." *Miners Magazine* 7 (April 5, 1906):13–14.

Vincent St. John's extraordinary bravery in saving lives during a mine disaster at Telluride, Colorado.

2878. Sumner, Mary B. "Arturo Giovannitti." *Survey* 29 (November 2, 1912):163–66.

The lyrical poetry of the Lawrence strike leader.

2879. ———. "Broad Silk Weavers of Paterson." *Survey* 27 (March 16, 1912):1932–35.

The Paterson strike and how it all started.

2880. ———. "Parting of the Ways in American Socialism." *Survey* 29 (February 1, 1913):623–30.

The Socialist Party's recall of Haywood.

2881. "Supreme Court Denies Petition of I.W.W. Prisoners." *Industrial Pioneer* 1 (May, 1921):4.

The rejection of the Syndicalist prisoners' appeal.

2882. "A Survey Article and the Recall." *Survey* 40 (April 6, 1918):21–22.

The American Legion must stamp out IWW disloyalty.

2883. "Survivor of the Ludlow Massacre." *United Mine Workers Journal* 89 (May, 1978):4–7.

The Colorado coal strike.

2884. Svanum, Kristen. "Industrial Research." *Industrial Pioneer* 3 (May, 1925):10–11, 36.

Methods of worker education.

2885. ———. "Work Peoples College." *Industrial Pioneer* 2 (February, 1925):47–48.

The IWW college in Duluth.

2886. ———. "Work Peoples College." *Industrial Pioneer* 3 (October, 1925):15–16.

The IWW college in Duluth.

2887. Swados, Harvey. Review of *Rebel Voices,* by Joyce Kornbluh (see no. 132). *Labor History* 6 (Fall, 1965):254–57.

2888. "Switchtender and His Job." *Industrial Pioneer* 1 (February, 1924):11–12.

The difficulties of organizing railroad unions.

2889. Sykes, W. H. "Business Successes from Small Beginnings." *Industrial Pioneer* 2 (November, 1924):7–8.

A Leonardsville, Kansas, merchant's answer to a request for an article on business opportunities, suggesting that the IWW is a good organization that the country needs.

2890. "Syndicalism: A Policy of Ruin." *Engineering Magazine* 44 (March, 1913):929–31.

2891. "Syndicalism: A Working Ethic for Barbarians." *Current Literature* 52 (May, 1912):555–58.

2892. "Syndicalism and Sabotage." *Shoe Workers Journal* 13 (October, 1912):7–8.

There is no room for such destructive unions as the IWW.

2893. "Syndicalism and the General Strike." Review of *The New Unionism,* by André Tridon (see no. 217). *Contemporary* 102 (September, 1912):450–52.

2894. "Syndicalism and the Supreme Court." *Outlook* 146 (May 25, 1927):100.

The Court decision upholding the constitutionality of the anti-Syndicalist laws.

2895. "Syndicalism Distinct from IWW." *Agitator* 2 (September 15, 1912):1.

The IWW is not Syndicalist in nature.

2896. "Syndicalism, Industrial Unionism and Socialism." Review of *Syndicalism, Industrial Unionism and Socialism,* by John Spargo (see no. 206). *Conservator* 24 (May, 1913):43–44.

2897. "Syndicalism, Sabotage, Socialism and the Industrial Workers of the World." *Labor World* (December 28, 1912):2

Theoretical comparisons.

2898. "Syndicalism, the New Labor Force." *Chautauqua* 69 (January, 1913):131–35.

The Lawrence and Paterson strikes, considered as Syndicalist.

2899. "Syndicalism versus IWW-ism." *Syndicalist* 3 (February 1, 1913):1.

The IWW is insufficiently Syndicalist.

2900. "Syndicalism—What It Is and What Its Aims Are." *Review of Reviews* 46 (August, 1912):228–30.

The San Diego Free Speech Fight.

2901. "The Syndicalists and the War." *New Review* 3 (April, 1915):230–32.

Syndicalists should be cautious about standing for peace at any price.

2902. "The Syndicalists' Double Standard of Ethics." *Garment Worker* 12 (September 26, 1913):3.

A critical AFL view of Syndicalism.

2903. "The Tactics of the Unemployed." *International Socialist Review* 15 (November, 1914):266–68.

Discusses Haywood's idea that if you need essentials you should take them. The unemployed should be organized; any of us could join that army next week.

2904. Taft, Clinton J. "California Justice." *New Republic* 40 (October 29, 1924):228.

The jailing of Professor Leo Gallagher for holding an IWW songbook in his hands.

2905. Taft, Philip. "The Bisbee Deportation." *Labor History* 13 (Winter, 1972):3–40.

2906. ———. "The Federal Trials of the IWW." *Labor History* 3 (Winter, 1962):57–91.

2907. ———. "The Harvest Hand Passes: Ushering Out Labor Color." *Labor History* 19 (Winter, 1978):76–81.

The work life of itinerant "hands" and the attempts to organize them. This is one of Taft's earlier articles, reprinted from a 1930 newspaper.

2908. ———. "Ideologies and Industrial Conflict." In Kornhauser, Arthur; Robert Dubin; and Arthur M. Ross, eds., *Industrial Conflict* (New York: McGraw-Hill, 1954. Reprint: New York: Arno, 1965), 257–65.

Traces from Marx and Engels the use of ideologies to influence social development. Ideology is used particularly in industrial disputes when injustice is perceived; the IWW is viewed as a revolutionary propaganda league combined with an embryonic industrial union.

2909. ———. "The I.W.W. in the Grain Belt." *Labor History* 1 (Winter, 1960):53–67.

Description of IWW harvest workers by a professor who was once one of them.

2910. ———. "Mayor Short and the I.W.W. Agricultural Workers." *Labor History* 7 (Spring, 1966):173–77.

A mayor of Sioux City whose defense of free speech principles contrasts with other mayors' denial of such rights to the IWW.

2911. ———. "A Note on General Mosby." *Labor History* 13 (Fall, 1972):552–54.

IWW participation in Mexican revolutionary actions.

2912. ———. "Strife in the Maritime Industry." *Political Science Quarterly* 54 (June, 1939):216–36.

The historic rivalries among maritime unions.

2913. ———. "Substituting Sewing Machines for Bake-Shops." Review of *Shall a Labor Party Be Formed in America. A Debate,* by Morris Hilquit and Edward F. Keating. *Labor History* 19 (Winter, 1978):74–75.

Defends the classic stance of the IWW against political action and disagrees with Hilquit and Keating. A reprint, along with other early articles, commemorating the death of the noted historian, formerly an IWW member.

2914. ———. "Violence in American Labor Disputes." *Annals of the American Academy of Political and Social Science* 364 (March, 1966):127–40.

2915. Taft, Philip, and Philip Ross. "American Labor Violence: Its Causes, Character, and Outcome." In H. D. Graham and T. R. Gurr, eds., *The History of Violence in America: Historical and Comparative Perspectives.* Report Submitted to the National Commission on the Causes and Prevention of Violence (New York: Frederick A. Praeger, 1969), 187–241.

2916. Takman, John. "Joe Hill's Sister: An Interview." *Masses and Mainstream* (March, 1956):24–30.

2917. Talbott, E. G. "Armies of the Unemployed in California." *Survey* 32 (August 23, 1914):523–24.

A protest march to the state capitol that included IWWs.

2918. "Talking American." *Industrial Pioneer* 1 (August, 1923):42.

Answer to Upton Sinclair; see no. 2736.

2919. "Tannenbaum Case To Be Appealed." *Public* 17 (August 21, 1914):806–7.

Frank Tannenbaum led a group of unemployed into a church in New York City.

2920. "The Tannenbaum Crime." *Masses* 5 (May, 1914):6–8.
New York unemployment and Tannenbaum's dramatic demonstration.

2921. "Tannenbaum's Speech." *Masses* 5 (May, 1914):3.
Frank Tannenbaum's explanation of his gesture.

2922. Tanner, Charles H. "Charles H. Tanner Reviews the Smith and Preston Cases." *Miners Magazine* 11 (April 13, 1911):9, 11–12.
The prosecutions of strike leaders at Goldfield.

2923. Tanner, Jack. "Flashlights on Labor and Revolution." *Industrial Pioneer* 1 (June, 1921):10–14.
British unionist's observations on American unions, the Red Trade Union International, the British Trade Union Congress, and the Workers' Committee Movement, and his conversations with Lenin in Moscow.

2924. Tarpey, M. F. "New Labor during War—IWW Activities." *Pacific Rural Press* (November 24, 1917):528.
We should import labor from China because there is a severe shortage of farm laborers. The IWW seems to be pressuring all farm hands to demand higher wages.

2925. ———. "Some Possibilities of the Development of New Labor during the War." Fiftieth State Fruit-Growers' Convention, *Proceedings* (Sacramento, November 21–23, 1917):74–79.
The IWW is causing farmworkers to demand too much. We should import coolies.

2926. "The Task of Local 8—The Marine Transport Workers of Philadelphia." *Messenger* 3 (October, 1921):262–63.
The integrated Philadelphia union.

2927. Taussig, F. W. "Copper Strike and Copper Dividends." *Survey* 31 (February 14, 1914):612–13.
An interesting discussion of whether it matters that a company cannot afford to pay workers a higher wage, using the Calumet-Hecla strike as an example.

2928. Taylor, G. R. "The Clash in the Copper Country: The First Big Strike in Fifty Years in the Industrial Backwoods of Upper Michigan." *Survey* 31 (November 1, 1913):127–35; 145–49.

2929. ———. "Moyer's Story of Why He Left the Copper Country." *Survey* 31 (January 10, 1914):433–35.
Moyer's expulsion from the Michigan copper country.

2930. ———. "Shifting the Blame for the Shooting in New Jersey." *Survey* 33 (January 30, 1915):457–58.
Sheriff Kinkead, who shot striking chemical workers in Roosevelt Borough, New Jersey, is now looking for a scapegoat. Industrial control is becoming aloof and hostile.

2931. Taylor, P. S., and N. L. Gold. "San Francisco and the General Strike." *Survey Graphic* 23 (September, 1934):405–11.

2932. Taylor, Paul S., and Tom Vasey. "Historical Background of California Farm Labor." *Rural Sociology* 1 (September, 1936):281–95.

2933. "Telling It to Wilson." *Labor Defender* 1 (October 15, 1918):4–5.
The IWW was wronged by Wilson when he encouraged or assented to the wartime raids under the Espionage Act.

2934. Terry, Sidney. "The Great New Orleans Strike." *Industrial Pioneer* 1 (November, 1923):5–6.
The marine transport workers.

2935. "Textile Worker's Strike." *Weekly Bulletin of the Clothing Trades* (UGWA) 11 (March, 1912):4.
The Lawrence strike.

2936. "Textile Workers Winning Uphill Fight." *Rebel Worker* 2 (September 1, 1919):2.
The Paterson strike of 1919.

2937. "Textiles—First Capitalized and Most Capitalized." *Industrial Pioneer* 2 (December, 1924):5–7.
A historical account of textile strikes in America, predicting that the new automatic looms will bring more problems for the textile workers, who will be losing employment.

2938. "That Proposed Unity." *Miners Magazine* 9 (February 27, 1908):6.
The "fanaticism" of the Socialist Labor Party will prevent union with the Socialist Party.

2939. "That Siberian Concession." *Survey* 48 (April 1, 1922):8–9.
The IWW's Kuzbas colony in Russia.

2940. "That Permanent Injunction." *Nation* 110 (January 24, 1920):95.
An injunction prohibiting IWW membership and activities.

2941. "They Are Nearing the Finish." *Miners Magazine* 14 (July 31, 1913):6.
The Hopedale, Akron, and even Paterson strikes are collapsing.

2942. "They Who Save the Republic." *Nation* 116 (May 20, 1923):618.
The arrest of 400 striking longshoremen.

2943. "A Third Broadside." *Miners Magazine* 14 (July 17, 1913):4.
Accuses the IWW of mishandling of funds.

2944. "Thirteenth Convention." *Industrial Pioneer* 1 (May, 1921):14.

2945. "The Thirteenth Convention of the I.W.W." *Industrial Pioneer* 1 (July, 1921):20–22.

2946. Thomas, A. E. "Goldfield: The New Eldorado." *Putnam's* 1 (March, 1907):658–72.
Outstanding description of Goldfield, Nevada.

2947. Thomas, Horace E. "Bone and Sinew for Our Aircraft." *Scientific American* 118 (June 22, 1918):564–65, 577–79.
How the government spruce production authorities attempted to stop the IWW organizing drive among lumberworkers.

2948. Thomas, Norman. "Political Prisoners in the United States." *Intercollegiate Socialist* 7 (February–March, 1919):11–12.
Why are so many political prisoners still in jail? It is time for amnesty.

2949. ———. "War's Heretics." *Survey* 41 (December 7, 1918):319–23.
Why are so many political prisoners still in jail, suffering outrageous prison conditions? They are not cowards or anarchists.

2950. Thompson, Charles W. "The New Socialism That Threatens the Social System." *New York Times* (March 17, 1912):part v., 1–2.
The Lawrence strike showed a face of Socialism that may threaten the social system in the future.

2951. Thompson, Daniel R. "Starvation Army, 1964." *Rebel Worker* 2 (Summer, 1964):17–22.

2952. Thompson, E. Bigelow. "The Case of the Lumberjack." *World Outlook* 6 (June, 1920):22–37.

2953. Thompson, Fred W. "Ben Fletcher Remembered." *Industrial Worker* 73 (May 8, 1981):9.
Recollection of the long-time Philadelphia union leader who led an integrated IWW union for many years and was also a defendant at the Chicago trial.

2954. ———. "A Brief Story of the Union Based on Strength, Sense, Ideals and Aims." *Industrial Worker* 26 (June 30, 1945):1, 6; (July 7, 1945):1, 4.

2955. ———. "The First Forty Years." *Industrial Worker* 26 (July 14, 1945):1, 4; (July 21, 1945):1, 4; (July 28, 1945):1, 4; (August 4, 1945):1, 4; (August 11, 1945):1, 4; (August 18, 1945):1, 4; (August 25, 1945):1, 4.

A continuation of "A Brief Story" (no. 2954). The two constitute a history of the IWW.

2956. ———. "Letter." *Labor History* 18 (Summer, 1977):467–70.

Comments on no. 2310.

2957. ———. "Lumber Strike, 1917." *Industrial Worker* 81, (January, 1984):4.

Comments on no. 1109.

2958. ———. "Rank-and-File Rule: What It Is and What It Isn't." *One Big Union Monthly* NS 2 (March, 1938):29–30.

2959. ———. Review of *At the Point of Production,* ed. by Joseph R. Conlin (see no. 39). *Industrial Worker* 79 (January, 1982):6.

2960. ———. "Rebel Voice: Fred Thompson Remembers Halifax, 1919–1920." *This Magazine* 12 (March, 1978):7–11.

Interesting reminiscences of the author, a rebel at age 19.

2961. ———. "School Days at Work Peoples College." *One Big Union Monthly* NS 1 (September, 1937):18–20.

Reminiscences of a professor at Work Peoples College.

2962. ———. "They Didn't Suppress the Wobblies." *Radical America* 1 (October, 1967):1–5.

Denies that the government or the employers suppressed the Wobblies during the Red Scare. Membership reached its peak in 1923, and although the 1924 split did disable the organization, the IWW has survived up to the present.

2963. ———. "What Excuse for Capitalism?" *One Big Union Monthly* NS 1 (June, 1937):21–26.

Capitalism has outworn its usefulness; it is time for industrial government.

2964. ———. "Why Rebel?" *Rebel Worker* 1 (Spring, 1964):3–4.

2965. Thompson, Fred, et al. "Some Facts To Correct." *New Republic* 118 (February 9, 1948):38–39; (November 15, 1948):38.

Correspondence on no. 2817, which implied Joe Hill was guilty.

2966. Thompson, James P. "Attempt To Kill Thompson." *Solidarity* 3 (March 9, 1912):1.
The violence used in trying to repress the Lawrence strike.

2967. ———. "Industrial Unionism: What It Is." *International Socialist Review* 18 (January, 1918):366–73.
Thompson's testimony before the Industrial Relations Commission defining and explaining industrial unionism.

2968. Thompson, W. H. "A Reply to Debs." *International Socialist Review* 14 (August, 1913):106–8.
Replies to Debs' charge that enemies of Socialism and the IWW condemned his report on the Socialist Party. Many good Socialists also condemned it.

2969. ———. "The Shadow of the Future." *Socialist and Labor Star* 1 (October 11, 1912):1.
The past and the gloomy outlook for West Virginia miners.

2970. Thorpe, Frank. "All Together for a Banner Drive." *Industrial Pioneer* 4 (June, 1926):2–4.
Predicts the best year ever for the IWW to organize farmworkers.

2971. ———. "The Harvest Isn't Over Yet." *Industrial Pioneer* 4 (September, 1926):4–8.
Organizers must work unceasingly to increase IWW membership among farmworkers.

2972. "Thorstein Veblen and the One Big Union." *One Big Union Advocate* 1 (April, 1939):3–4.
The encouraging statements of Veblen on the importance of the IWW and the success of the IWW's "400" harvest drive.

2973. "Those Were the Days." *Idaho Yesterdays* 4 (Fall, 1960):16–17.
The 1906 Haywood trial in Idaho, with good photographs.

2974. "Three Clippings." *Nation* 115 (October 4, 1922):320.
The political prisoners still held without amnesty.

2975. "Three Stars Union—Indianapolis." *Square Deal* 13 (September, 1913):133.
IWW activity in Indianapolis.

2976. "Thru the IWW to One Big Union." *One Big Union Advocate* 1 (November, 1939):9–18.
A history of the IWW, with a hope that it will develop into a larger movement toward "One Big Union."

2977. Thurner, Arthur W. "The Western Federation of Miners in Two Copper Camps: The Impact of the Michigan Copper Miners' Strike on Butte Local No. 1." *Montana, The Magazine of Western History* 33 (1983):30–45.
Butte miners felt the strike contributions were too burdensome.

2978. "Timber Workers Are Busy in the State of Louisiana." *Square Deal* 12 (February, 1913):32.
The Southern lumber strikes of the Brotherhood of Timber Workers.

2979. "The Timber Workers of the South." *Miners Magazine* 12 (August 15, 1912):4.
The Southern lumber strikes of the Brotherhood of Timber Workers.

2980. "Time for Action Is Here." *Miners Magazine* 15 (July 30, 1914):9.
Joseph Ettor is trying to convert WFM members to the IWW.

2981. "Tipping Over the Chair." *Agitator* 2 (July 15, 1912):1.
Joseph Ettor's advocacy of direct action.

2982. "To Investigate Centralia Convictions." *Christian Century* 45 (October 25, 1928):1279.
The Federal Council of Churches' plan to investigate the Centralia tragedy.

2983. "To Marine Workers of the World." *Industrial Pioneer* 1 (August, 1921):62–63.
Letter from a committee in Russia urging that an international seamen's union be established.

2984. "To the Old Question." *Nation* 109 (September 13, 1919):359.
The indictments of the IWW in Wichita.

2985. "To the Rescue." *International Socialist Review* 14 (June, 1914):763.
The arrest of Joe Hill and the need for an active defense committee.

2986. "To the Silk Workers of Paterson." *Rebel Worker* 2 (March 15, 1919):2.
The 1919 Paterson strike.

2987. Tobin, Eugene M. "Direct Action and Conscience: The 1913 Paterson Strike as Example of the Relationship between Labor Radicals and Liberals." *Labor History* 20 (Winter, 1979):73–88.

2988. Tobriner, Mathew O. "California and Syndicalism." *Machinists' Monthly Journal* 36 (August, 1924):371–72.
Believes that the California Syndicalist laws are wrong, even though they are aimed at the IWWs, the scum of the earth, interested only in organizing the dregs of society.

2989. "Tom Mann in N.Y. City." *International Socialist Review* 14 (September, 1913):145–46.
The lecture tour of the British Socialist.

2990. "Tom Mann's Doctrine." *Garment Worker* 12 (October 10, 1913):1.
Tom Mann's attack on the American Federation of Labor as a labor trust without any understanding of unskilled labor.

2991. "Tom Mooney." *Labor Defender* 1 (June 30, 1918):1, 3.
Tom Mooney as an active unionist before his imprisonment.

2992. "Torpedoed Seamen To Rally to Defense of Workers." *Labor Defender* 1 (April 15, 1918):1.
Seamen, who know what danger means, should support and testify for the Chicago trial defendants.

2993. "Tour Sparks Growth of the IWW." *Industrial Worker* 78 (January 2, 1981):3.
Frank Cedervall's speaking tour.

2994. "Toward Labor's Powers." *New Republic* 8 (August 5, 1916):7–8.
Most of the IWWs are merely orators.

2995. "Towards a Definite Syndicalist Policy." *Industrial Pioneer* 1 (April, 1921):6–7.

2996. Trackman, A. "Who Are the Agitators?" *One Big Union Monthly* 2 (April, 1920):39–40.
Dishonest bosses and companies he has known whose actions would turn any worker into a radical.

2997. "Trade Unions and Social Radicalism." *Chautauqua* 69 (January, 1913):136–38.

2998. "Tragedy of the Redwoods." *Industrial Pioneer* 1 (April, 1924):19–21.
Criminal Syndicalism in California.

2999. "Transportation Workers." *Bulletin* 1 (September, 1906):8–9.
Musical and theatrical union's paper discusses problems of the transportation workers.

3000. Trautmann, William E. "A Brief History of the Industrial Union Manifesto." *Industrial Union Bulletin* 1 (December 14, 1907):3; (January 4, 1908):3.

3001. ———. "A Bummery Trick That Failed." *Miners Magazine* 14 (July 17, 1913):10–11.
The IWW mishandled the Lawrence strike funds.

3002. ———. "Cat Out of the Bag." *Miners Magazine* 13 (May 15, 1913):5–6.
The IWW mishandled the Lawrence strike funds.

3003. ———. "Free Graft Fights." (New York) *Call* 6 (May 2, 1913):n.p.
The Free Speech Fights are just another way to drum up money.

3004. ———. "Power of Folded Arms." *One Big Union Monthly* NS 1 (October, 1937):3–7.
A history of radicalism, including the IWW.

3005. ———. "The Smashing Process against Industrial Unionism and Socialism." *Weekly People* (June 17, 1905):1–3.
The possibilities of a new industrial union (the IWW).

3006. "The Trautmann Case." *Voice of Labor* 3 (June, 1905):6.
An argument for a new industrial union.

3007. "Trautmann Makes Serious Charges and I.W.W. Answers." *Syndicalist* 3 (August 1–15, 1913):52.
Trautmann's insistent accusations that the IWW mishandled the Lawrence strike funds.

3008. "Trautmann, St. John et al. to IWW Members." *Miners Magazine* 8 (October 18, 1906):11–12.
Report from the General Executive Board of IWW activities.

3009. "Trautmann's Little Hatchet." *Garment Worker* 7 (June 13, 1913):5.
The IWW is only after money—the workers' money. This is a reprint of no. 3010.

3010. "Trautmann's Little Hatchet." *Miners Magazine* 14 (September 11, 1913):8–9.
The IWW is only after the workers' money.

3011. "A Traveler Makes Camp." *One Big Union Monthly* NS 1 (June, 1937):9–11.

The lumberworkers' "walking delegate," an organizer who covers more than one local territory.

3012. "Treading on Dangerous Ground." *Miners Magazine* 9 (January 16, 1908):6–7.

The Goldfield strike.

3013. "Treason!" *International Socialist Review* 15 (March, 1915):560.

The arraignment of Joseph Ettor for making an antiwar speech.

3014. "Treason Must Be Made Odious." *North American Review* 206 (October, 1917):513–17.

Harsh punishment for anyone who is against the war.

3015. Tresca, Carlo. "God and Country: Why They Are Used to Attack the IWW." *Voice of the People* 2 (September 11, 1913):4.

3016. ———. "The Unemployed and the I.W.W." *Retort* 2 (June, 1944):23–24.

The Frank Tannenbaum story.

3017. "Trial of the IWW." *Labor Defender* 1 (May 15, 1918):3.

The Chicago trial begins.

3018. "Tribute to Jack Whyte." *Mother Earth* 10 (April, 1915):90–91.

The IWW leader who was shot to death by an unknown assailant.

3019. Tridon, André. "Haywood." *New Review* 1 (May, 1913):502–6.

Describes Haywood's personality and charm, power and simplicity. In comparing Haywood with Teddy Roosevelt, Tridon assigns Roosevelt to yesterday and Haywood to tomorrow.

3020. ———. "Russian-Baiting in Our Ports." *Public* 21 (June 1, 1918): 698–700.

The "*Shilka*" incident in the port of Seattle. Rumors that a Russian ship was in port carrying money and arms to the IWW were met with alarms and arrests, then smoothed over with a Chamber of Commerce dinner.

3021. ———. "Syndicalism and 'Sabotage' and How They Were Originated." *Square Deal* 10 (June, 1912):407–14.

3022. ———. "The Workers' Only Hope: Direct Action." *Independent* 74 (January 9, 1913):79–83.
The IWW techniques, Syndicalism, sabotage, and strikes of short duration.

3023. "Tridon's *New Unionism.*" Review of *The New Unionism,* by André Tridon (see no. 217). *Journal of Political Economy* 21 (December, 1913):970–72.

3024. "Trouble Breeders." *Bellman* 23 (October 13, 1917):397–98.
The IWW may be treasonous.

3025. "Trouble in Baltimore." *Garment Worker* 12 (August 8, 1913):1.
The IWW is trying to disrupt the garment workers' union.

3026. "Troubles of the W.F.M." *Square Deal* 14 (July, 1914):567–68.
The IWW may be the WFM's biggest threat.

3027. "A True Story of the Michigan Copper Strike—Organization Politics the Cause." *Square Deal* 13 (January, 1914):487–89.

3028. "The Truth about Rockford." *Labor Defender* 1 (July 30, 1918):14.
The Rockford strike prisoners suffer from particularly unhealthy jail conditions.

3029. "The Truth about the Seattle Riots." *Square Deal* 13 (September, 1913):151–53.
Secretary of the Navy Josephus Daniels' speech against radicals may have sparked the dastardly attack on the IWW hall by U.S. sailors.

3030. Tucker, Irwin. "The Church and the I.W.W." *Churchman* 108 (August 30, 1913):278, 290.
The IWW always comes up with new ideas, as seen in the Paterson strike.

3031. Tugwell, Rexford G. "The Casual of the Woods." *Survey* 44 (July 3, 1920):472–74.
Migrant workers.

3032. ———. "The Outlaw." *Survey* 44 (August 16, 1920):641–42.
The raids and the public fear of the IWW.

3033. Tulin, Lee. "The Copper Situation." *Industrial Pioneer* 2 (September, 1924):10–11.
New mines in South America and Africa mean that the

American mines will see hard times. The worker will feel it first.

3034. "Tulsa, November 9th." *Liberator* 1 (April, 1918):15–17.
The tarring and feathering of IWW organizers.

3035. "Tulsa City Officials Led Mob That Perpetrated Outrage." *Labor Defender* 1 (March 5, 1918):1.
The brutal kidnapping of an IWW organizer. The writer believes that half of the "Knights of Liberty" mob that did it were city officials and businessmen.

3036. Turner, G. K. "The Actors and Victims in the Tragedies." *McClure's Magazine* 29 (September, 1907):524–29.
The real-life cast of characters in the first Haywood trial.

3037. Turner, John I. "Why the I.W.W. Will Not Die." *Industrial Pioneer* 3 (April, 1926):5–9.
Despite the raids, the prisoners, and now the split, the true believers in the IWW will carry on.

3038. "Twenty Members Still Held at Fresno." *Industrial Worker* 2 (December 8, 1917):4.
The 1917 government raids on the IWW.

3039. "Twenty Years Ago." *One Big Union Monthly* NS 1 (August, 1937): 24.
IWW leader Frank Little and his lynching in Butte.

3040. "25 to 40 Years." *One Big Union Monthly* 2 (May, 1920):11–13.
The unfairness of the Centralia trial and the sentences received by defendants who were only victims of assault.

3041. "Two Adverse Reports on the Colorado Militia." *Survey* 34 (July 17, 1915):344.
A report on the conduct and condition of the state militia used in the Colorado coal strike, deploring everything about it except the medical department and the band, was suppressed by the government.

3042. "Two Church Views of the Colorado Strike." *Literary Digest* 95 (December 17, 1927):31–32.
Both Methodist and Roman Catholic church newspapers plead for a living wage, as well as the right to organize, for the miners. They also demand that civil rights be observed.

3043. "Two Divergent Views of the Big Strike at Lawrence." *Square Deal* 10 (April, 1912):217–28.

How the IWW and the strike were reported by *The Register* (a Catholic weekly) and by the *New York Tribune*.

3044. "Two Infamous Measures: The Graham and Sterling Sedition Bills." *Nation* 110 (January 31, 1920):132.

3045. "Two Kinds of Unionism." *Independent* 75 (September 25, 1913):711–12.

The differences between trade unionism and Syndicalism.

3046. "Two Mayors—Which One Is a Real American?" *One Big Union Monthly* 1 (June, 1919):7.

How Mayor Short of Sioux City and Mayor Hanson of Seattle handled strike problems in their cities, with approval for Short's respect for civil rights.

3047. "Two Reports on the Little Falls Strike." *Survey* 29 (March 29, 1913):899.

The New York Department of Labor issued two reports: a wage and cost of living study and an arbitration report stating that there was a wage reduction of ten cents an hour. The wage study showed how poorly paid the workers were.

3048. "Two Ways To Speak of the Trial of the IWW." *Nation* 110 (March 27, 1920):385–86.

The Centralia trial at Montesano, Washington.

3049. Tyler, Robert L. "The Everett Free Speech Fight." *Pacific Historical Review* 23 (February, 1954):19–30.

3050. ———. "The IWW and the Brainworkers." *American Quarterly* 15 (Spring, 1963):41–51.

Howard Scott and the IWW Bureau of Research.

3051. ———. "The IWW and the West." *American Quarterly* 12 (Summer, 1960):175–87.

3052. ———. "I.W.W. in the Pacific Northwest: Rebels of the Woods." *Oregon Historical Quarterly* 55 (March, 1954):3–44.

3053. ———. Review of *Rocky Mountain Revolution,* by Stewart H. Holbrook (see no. 105). *Pacific Historical Review* 26 (May, 1957): 189–90.

3054. ———. Review of *Joe Hill,* by Gibbs Smith (see no. 203). *Journal of American History* 57 (September, 1970):465–66.

3055. ———. "The Rise and Fall of an American Radicalism: The I.W.W." *Historian* 19 (November, 1956):48–65.

3056. ———. "Socialism and Syndicalism—Comments." In John H. M. Laslett and Seymour M. Lipset, eds., *Failure of a Dream? Essays in the History of American Socialism* (Garden City, NY: Anchor Press, 1974), 286–94.

3057. ———. "The Strike in Lawrence, Mass. A View of Textiles and Labor Fifty Years Ago." *Cotton History Review* 2 (July, 1961): 123–31.

3058. ———. "The United States Government as Union Organizer: The Loyal Legion of Loggers and Lumbermen." *Mississippi Valley Historical Review* 47 (December, 1960):434–51.

3059. ———. "Violence at Centralia, 1919." *Pacific Northwest Quarterly* 45 (October, 1954):116–24.

3060. "Typical 'Chicago' IWW Songs." *Common Cause* 3 (February, 1913): 216–17.

3061. "Uncovers the I.W.W." *Miners Magazine* 21 (September, 1920):1–2.

Harold Lord Varney's sudden turn against the IWW.

3062. "Under the Big Tops by a Ballahoo Wobbly." *International Socialist Review* 17 (February, 1917):486–88.

A Wobbly circus worker on the wages and working conditions of circus people, who, he believes, are ready for the IWW.

3063. "An 'Undesirable Citizen' Departs." *Outlook* 128 (May 11, 1921):48.

Haywood's departure for Russia.

3064. "Unemployment and the IWW." *Rebel Worker* 2 (June 1, 1919):1–2.

Industrial unionism not a brainstorm in the minds of bad men but a historical truth.

3065. "The Union of Slackers." *Bellman* 24 (May 18, 1918):539.

The Germans may be paying the IWWs to be slackers.

3066. "Unionism at the Crossroads." *One Big Union Monthly* NS 2 (February, 1938):3–8.

Questions the success of the CIO. Will it last?

3067. "Unionism Face to Face with Facts." *Miners Magazine* 6 (June 1, 1905):8.

We must have industrial unionism.

3068. "Unionizing the Negro Workers." *Messenger* 2 (October, 1919): 8–9.

3069. "Unite Industrially and Politically." *Miners Magazine* 12 (February 15, 1912):8.
The Lawrence strike.

3070. "United Fruit Co. Riot." *Lumberjack* 1 (June 19, 1913):1, 3.
Marine Transport Workers Union at United Fruit loading docks.

3071. "Unity." *One Big Union Monthly* 2 (November, 1920):14–16.
No expectation of mercy or justice for the political prisoners at the Chicago trial.

3072. "Unjustifiable Strike at Akron." *American Industries* 13 (April, 1913):13.
The failing rubber workers' strike.

3073. "Unskilled Labor Problem." *Public* 21 (January 11, 1918):41–42.
Hopes the Chicago trial will expose bad working conditions.

3074. Untermann, Ernest. "No Sooner Had the Chicago Conference." *Voice of Labor* 3 (May, 1905):8–10.

3075. "Untold History of the IWW." *One Big Union Advocate* 1 (December, 1939):10–19; (January, 1940):12–13, 31–100.

3076. "Upton Sinclair's Arrest." *New Republic* 25 (June 13, 1923):180.
How Upton Sinclair and friends were arrested for reading the U.S. Constitution aloud on private property where they had obtained permission to do so.

3077. Urban, W. M. "Tubal Cain." *Atlantic* 110 (December, 1912):786–94.
The legendary figure of Tubal Cain as representative of labor and the common workman, the new strength of the laboring man, and the deeper meaning of Syndicalism and the General Strike.

3078. "Using the IWW against the Left Wing." *New York Communist* 1 (May 24, 1919):8.

3079. "A Valuable Dog." *Miners Magazine* 14 (October 30, 1913):7; (November 6, 1913):8.
A dog helps the Calumet-Hecla strikers by wearing a coat warning scabs to stay away, with a good photograph.

3080. Vanderleith, E. W. "The Mormon Brand of Justice." *Voice of the People* 3 (July 7, 1914):2.
Describes the Joe Hill trial.

3081. Vanderveer, G. F. "Winning Out in Idaho." *International Socialist Review* 18 (January, 1918):344.
The IWW lawyer describes a test case on the raids in Idaho, ending in a "not guilty" verdict for the IWW.

3082. "Vanderveer Opens for the Defense." *Labor Defender* 1 (July 15, 1918):3–4.
The opening days of the Chicago trial.

3083. Van Dorn, Henry. "Can Labor Unions Function as Revolutionary Organizations?" *Industrial Pioneer* 1 (July, 1921):17–19.
The union situation in other countries proves that all really large unions are conservative.

3084. ———. "For a Concerted Plan of Action." *Industrial Pioneer* 1 (April, 1921):17–21.
The IWW needs a clear plan for its organizational work, emphasizing greater efficiency and discipline.

3085. ———. "The Future of the American Working Class and the I.W.W." *One Big Union Monthly* 2 (August, 1920):37–39.
The working class is worse off than ever before because while the IWW is persecuted, the AFL has lost all of its strikes and the Socialist Party is breaking up. Solidarity is the only salvation.

3086. ———. "Lord Varney: A Warning." *One Big Union Monthly* 3 (January, 1921):14–15.
Varney was only looking for romance and supermen, was never a worker, but was an intellectual impostor.

3087. ———. "Meditations of a Wage Slave." *One Big Union Monthly* 1 (October, 1919):22–23.
There are many craven slaves since the time clock, the Taylor system of scientific management, and the massacres of Everett and Ludlow. Only rebels like the IWWs are really free.

3088. ———. "Organize the Unorganized!" *Industrial Pioneer* 1 (May, 1923):10–13.
Automobile workers and oil workers, who are largely unorganized, should be the next targets for the organizers, then the textile workers.

3089. ———. "Shall We Join the Communist International?" *One Big Union Monthly* 2 (November, 1920):50–51.
We should not join because we cannot endorse its program and would be putting ourselves under political control.

3090. Van Tine, Warren R. Review of *Big Bill Haywood,* ed. by Joseph R. Conlin (see no. 40). *Labor History* 11 (Winter, 1977):98–99.

3091. Van Valen, Nelson. "Bolsheviki and the Orange Growers." *Pacific Historical Review* 22 (February, 1953):39–50.

Questions the belief that the Wobblies were "the American arm of the Bolsheviki."

3092. Van Valkenburgh, W. S. "The Murder of Joseph Hillstrom." *Mother Earth* 10 (December, 1915):326–28.

Joe Hill will be more dangerous dead than he was alive.

3093. Van Wingerden, L. M. "Are We Radicals?" *One Big Union Monthly* 2 (March, 1920):51.

The IWW may be a symptom of overdeveloped capitalism.

3094. ———. "The Evolutionary IWW." *One Big Union Monthly* 2 (April, 1920):37–38.

The IWW must keep educating the worker to be ready to take over industry after capitalism fails.

3095. Varney, Harold Lord. "Battle for the Lakes." *International Socialist Review* 17 (June, 1917):731–32.

The organization of Great Lakes seamen.

3096. ———. "Butte in the Hands of the IWW." *One Big Union Monthly* 1 (March, 1919):34–35.

A personal account of the copper strike in Butte.

3097. ———. "The IWW Exposed by Its Chief Propagandist." *One Big Union Monthly* 2 (March, 1920):35–39.

How Varney left the "timorous dilettantism" of the Socialist Party for the daring IWW, became its "foremost lecturer" and leading writer, then decided that it would not achieve the revolution because its members do not want one.

3098. ———. "The IWW Exposed by Its Chief Propagandist." (New York) *World* (February 8, 1920):Sec. E, 1.

First and earliest version of no. 3097, Varney's article renouncing the IWW.

3099. ———. "The Life of Democracy." *One Big Union Monthly* 1 (March, 1919):21–22.

The difference between the IWW and Socialism is democracy.

3100. ———. "Reply to a Reply." *One Big Union Monthly* 1 (April, 1919): 21–23.

Left-wingers are too obsessed with Russia; the IWW will not turn Bolshevist (an answer to no. 1107).

3101. ———. "The Story of the I.W.W." *One Big Union Monthly* 1 (March, 1919):50–52; (April, 1919):26–28; (May, 1919):47–53; (June, 1919):39–41.

A history of the IWW.

3102. ———. "The Truth about the Steel Strike." *One Big Union Monthly* 1 (November, 1919):17–20.

Rumors that Foster was organizing the steel workers along industrial lines were untrue.

3103. ———. "Was Butte a Defeat?" *One Big Union Monthly* 1 (March, 1919):27, 39.

The strike served as a national protest; the miners are in good spirits.

3104. Veblen, Thorstein. "On the Nature and Uses of Sabotage." *Dial* 66 (April 5, 1919):341–46.

3105. ———. "Using the IWW To Harvest Grain: An Unpublished Paper on the IWW." *Journal of Political Economy* 40 (December, 1932):796–807.

A lost memo to Hoover from Veblen concerning the IWW and its organization of farmworkers.

3106. "Veblen on Sabotage." *Public* 20 (December 14, 1917):1215–16.

3107. Vecoli, Rudolph J. "Emigrati Italiani e Movimento Operaio Negli USA" (Italian immigrants and the US labor movement). *Movimento Operaio e Socialista* 22 (1976):153–67.

3108. Velsek, Charles. "Labor Is on the Move: An Analysis of the Labor Struggles of 1936." *One Big Union Monthly* NS 1 (January, 1937):16–22.

A splendid fighting spirit animates labor this year.

3109. Venn, George W. "The Wobblies and Montana's Garden City." *Montana, the Magazine of the West* 21 (October, 1971):18–30.

3110. Verlaine, Ralph. "Soybeans." *One Big Union Monthly* NS 1 (December, 1937):12–16.

Low pay and hard work in the Georgia fields educated this worker in economics.

3111. "The Victory at Lawrence." *International Socialist Review* 12 (April, 1912):679.

The Lawrence strike vindicates Haywood's tactics of direct action. Industrial unionism is sure to succeed.

3112. "A Victory Gained." *International Socialist Review* 8 (August, 1907):109–12.

The acquittal of Haywood is an epochal event in the history of the working class. Theodore Roosevelt is denounced for his "murder is murder" and "undesirable citizens" comments, which show his contempt for labor.

3113. Vincent, Fred W. "Getting Out Airplane Spruce." *Scientific American* 119 (November 30, 1918):438–39.

The Army's use of soldiers as lumberworkers.

3114. ———. "Wing-Bones of Victory." *Sunset* 30 (June, 1918):30–69.

The government's spruce drive and the IWW.

3115. "Violence and Democracy." *Outlook* 100 (February 17, 1912):352–53.

The Lawrence strike.

3116. Vlag, Piet. "The IWW or the Socialist Party." *Miners Magazine* 12 (May 23, 1912):12.

The IWW is not the only group that believes in industrial unionism. The Socialist Party does also.

3117. Vogler, Theodore K. "Centralia's Prisoners Stay Behind Bars." *Christian Century* 46 (April 4, 1929):450–51.

There will be no parole, despite the appeal of the Federal Council of Churches.

3118. Vorse, Mary Heaton. "Accessories before the Fact." *Masses* 9 (November, 1916):6–7, 22.

The Mesabi miners' strike in Minnesota.

3119. ———. "Children's Crusade for Amnesty." *Nation* 114 (May 10, 1922):559–61.

A parade of children in New York to protest the lack of amnesty for political prisoners.

3120. ———. "The Case of Adolf." *Outlook* 107 (May 2, 1914):27–31.

The story of one of the unemployed IWWs imprisoned with Tannenbaum for invading a New York church.

3121. ———. "Elizabeth Gurley Flynn." *Nation* 122 (February 17, 1926): 175–76.

Flynn's indomitable spirit in fighting for workers' rights.

3122. ———. "In Bayonne." *The Blast* 1 (November 1, 1916):3.

The strike of chemical workers in Bayonne, New Jersey.

3123. ———. "Mary Heaton Vorse Wants Fair Play for IWW." *Labor Defender* 1 (March 5, 1918):3.

3124. ———. "The Mining Strike in Minnesota—From the Miners' Point of View." *Outlook* 113 (August 30, 1916):1036, 1045–46.

3125. ———. "The Police and the Unemployed." *New Review* 2 (September, 1914):530–38.

Unemployed demonstrators in California are beaten by the police.

3126. ———. "The Trouble at Lawrence." *Harper's Weekly* 56 (March 16, 1912):10.

3127. ———. "Twenty Years." *Liberator* 4 (January, 1921):10–13.

The long sentences at the Chicago trial were unconscionable.

3128. Wagaman, David G. "The Industrial Workers of the World in Nebraska." *Nebraska History* 56 (Fall, 1975):295–337.

3129. ———. "'Rausch Mit': The IWW in Nebraska During World War I." In Joseph R. Conlin, ed., *At the Point of Production* (Westport, CT: Greenwood Press, 1981), 115–42 (see no. 39).

3130. Wagner, Joseph. "The Lost International." *One Big Union Monthly* NS 2 (May, 1938):20–23.

Under the present Russian leadership the Red Trade Union International seems to have disappeared.

3131. Wahmann, Russell. "Railroading in the Verde Valley 1894–1951." *Journal of Arizona History* 12 (Autumn, 1971):153–66.

History of the railroad, including the deportation of the Bisbee miners.

3132. "Waiting To Be Bailed Out." *One Big Union Monthly* 2 (April, 1920):11–12.

Everyone who can should put up bail for a jailed IWW member.

3133. Wakefield, Dan. "The Haunted Hall: The IWW at Fifty." *Dissent* 3 (Fall, 1956):414–19.

A hopeless and disintegrated IWW organization described.

3134. Walker, John H. "Revolt of the Copper Miners." *Syndicalist* 3 (September 1–15, 1913):55.
The Calumet-Hecla strike.

3135. "Wall Street Man and I.W.W. Leader on Same Platform." *Square Deal* 13 (August, 1913):55–58.
A panel on "The Workers' Fair Share," with Arturo Giovannitti and a Wall Street businessman.

3136. "Wall Street Wolves and the Wobs." *Industrial Pioneer* 1 (January, 1924):43–44.
The IWW will prevail when Wall Street fails.

3137. Wallace, Andrew. "Colonel McClintock and the 1917 Copper Strike." *Arizoniana* 3 (Spring, 1962):24–26.
New sources for information on the copper strike in Col. McClintock's papers.

3138. Walling, Anna S. "Giovannitti's Poems." Review of *Arrows in the Gale,* by Arturo Giovannitti. *New Review* 2 (May, 1914):288–92.

3139. Walling, William E. "Industrial or Revolutionary Unionism." *New Review* 1 (January 11, 1913):45–51.
Discussion of Syndicalism in which the author says the Lawrence strike was revolutionary because it was a struggle of unskilled workers.

3140. Walsh, John. "Chicago Trial Enters Last Month." *Labor Defender* 1 (August 15, 1918):3–5.

3141. ———. "Jack Walsh on the Trial." *Labor Defender* 1 (June 30, 1918):1, 4.
The progress of the Chicago trial.

3142. ———. "The Trial from Inside." *Labor Defender* 1 (June 15, 1918):1.
The Chicago trial.

3143. ———. "Two Days at the Chicago Trial." *Labor Defender* 1 (July 30, 1918):3–5.
The Chicago trial.

3144. Walters, Alonzo. "Hellish Conditions in Eastern Kentucky." *Industrial Pioneer* 2 (May, 1924):21–23.
The coal strikes in Kentucky.

3145. "Wanted—One Big Union." *One Big Union Monthly* NS 1 (May, 1937):9–10.
What the CIO may do to the IWW.

3146. "War Boom for Whom?" *One Big Union Advocate* 1 (December, 1939):4–5.
Workers will not profit from the war in Europe and Asia.

3147. "War in Colorado." *Outlook* 107 (May 2, 1914):6–7.
The Colorado coal strike.

3148. "The War Is On." *Miners Magazine* 14 (September 4, 1913):7–8.
Comments unfavorably about the IWW, especially the IWW's own press statements praising its strike activities.

3149. "A Warm Debate in Omaha." *Miners Magazine* 7 (December 28, 1905):11–12.
A well-attended debate between IWW and AFL representatives.

3150. Warren, Fred D. "The Free Speech Fight at New Castle, Pa." *International Socialist Review* 11 (July, 1910):34–36.

3151. Warren, W. H. "Treason by the Wholesale: An Exposé of IWW Methods." *Oregon Voter* 12 (March 9, 1918):310–11.

3152. Warrick, Sherry. "Radical Labor in Oklahoma: The Working Class Union." *Chronicles of Oklahoma* 52 (Summer, 1974):180–95.
The Working Class Union, which the IWW helped to organize.

3153. Warner, Austin. "White Guards in America: Truth about the American Legion: A Warning to Parliamentary Democrats." *Communist Review* 2 (January, 1922):184–91.
Believes that on occasion the Legion has engaged in violent activities.

3154. "War-Time Prisoners Let Out of Jail." *Literary Digest* 78 (July 7, 1923):16.

3155. "Washington, Bolsheviki, and IWW." *Survey* 39 (March 9, 1918):633.

3156. Watkins, C. S. "Present Status of Socialism in the United States." *Atlantic* 124 (December, 1919):821–30.

3157. Watkins, T. H. "Requiem for the Federation." *American West* 3 (Winter, 1966):4–12, 91–95.
The Western Federation of Miners.

3158. Watne, Joel. "Public Opinion toward Non-Conformists and Aliens during 1917." *North Dakota History* 34 (Winter, 1967):6–29.

3159. Watson, Fred. "Still on Strike: Recollections of a Bisbee Deportee." *Journal of Arizona History* 18 (Summer, 1977):171–84.

3160. Wax, Anthony. "Calumet and Hecla Copper Mines: An Episode in the Economic Development of Michigan." *Michigan History* 16 (Spring, 1932):218–24.

Praise for a "benevolent, meritorious company" that contributed to the growth of Michigan's economy.

3161. "Way of Syndicalism." *Independent* 73 (October 17, 1912):912–13.

Syndicalism instigated the reign of terror in place of the reign of law.

3162. "The Way They 'Organize.'" *Garment Worker* 12 (November 22, 1912):1.

IWW organizing in Philadelphia disrupts AFL organizing.

3163. "W. D. Haywood as We Saw Him in Chicago." *Socialist Woman* 1 (September, 1907):3.

3164. "W. D. Haywood in London." *International Socialist Review* 11 (December, 1910):352.

3165. "We Are not Gandhis." *Industrial Pioneer* 3 (September, 1925):2–3.

Members of the IWW may be pacifists but they are also fighters.

3166. "We Told You So." *One Big Union Monthly* 2 (May, 1920):15–16, 50.

The ouster of five New York assemblymen from the statehouse because they were Socialists proves the IWW's long-held belief in the futility of politics.

3167. Weber, Aaron. "Detroit, 1919." *Industrial Worker* 26 (July 14, 1945):3.

IWW meetings in Detroit always included a large contingent of police and American Legionnaires, ready to make trouble.

3168. Weed, C. "Maritime Merry-Go-Round." *One Big Union Monthly* NS 2 (February, 1938):9–10.

A confusing array of seamen's unions: the NMU, the ISU, the IWW, the SUP, and the CIO.

3169. Weed, Inis. "Reasons Why the Copper Miners Struck." *Outlook* 106 (January 31, 1914):247–51.

The Calumet-Hecla strike.

3170. Weinstein, James. "The IWW and American Socialism." *Socialist Revolution* 1 (September–October, 1970):3–42.

3171. ———. "The Left, Old and New." *Socialist Revolution* 2 (July–August, 1972):7–60.

3172. Weintraub, Hyman. Review of *Rebels of the Woods,* by Robert Tyler (see no. 221). *Pacific Historical Review* 37 (November, 1968):482–83.

3173. Weisberger, Bernard A. "Here Come the Wobblies!" *American Heritage* 18 (June, 1967):31–35, 87–93.
Popular account of the IWW, with photographs.

3174. Welch, N. L. "Under the Iron Heel." *Rebel Worker* 2 (March 15, 1919):1, 4.
IWW prisoners' fate worse than Jack London conceived in *The Iron Heel.*

3175. Welinder, P. J. "A New Society in Its Making." *Industrial Pioneer* 3 (June, 1925):12–14, 43–45.
A worker's attempt to explain the philosophy of the IWW in historical terms, emphasizing the need for on-the-job action at all times.

3176. ———. "The Sixteenth General Convention." *Industrial Pioneer* 2 (December, 1924):24–27.
The convention that had to deal with the split among members in 1924.

3177. ———. "What Shall We Do Now?" *Industrial Pioneer* 2 (October, 1924):37–38.
IWW tactics changed to emphasize education, but it should get back to organizing instead.

3178. Wells, Merl W. "The Western Federation of Miners." *Journal of the West* 12 (January, 1973):18–35.

3179. Wells, Nick. "As to Lubrication." *Industrial Pioneer* 1 (November, 1921):22–23.
Organizing the oil workers.

3180. ———. "Tactics in Oil." *Industrial Pioneer* 1 (December, 1921):26.
Organizing the oil workers.

3181. "We're in an Opera!" *Industrial Worker* 78 (February 3, 1981):4.
A new opera about the IWW's Columbine strike. See no. 4945.

3182. "West Coast Chaos: The CIO-AFL Inter-Union War." *One Big Union Monthly* NS 1 (October, 1937):27–28, 33.

An IWW view of the fighting between the AFL Teamsters and the ILA for control of the coastal and maritime unions. The article also discusses the failure of some of the CIO strikes.

3183. West, George P. "After Liberalism Had Failed: The Imprisonment of the Striking Longshoremen in Los Angeles." *Nation* 116 (May 30, 1923):629.

3184. ———. "Andrew Furuseth Stands Pat." *Survey* 51 (October 15, 1923):86–90.

The IWW threatens the Sailors Union of the Pacific and craft unionism.

3185. ———. "The Mesaba Range Strike." *New Republic* 8 (September 2, 1916):108–9.

The Mesabi Range strike.

3186. ———. "Mesabi Strike." *International Socialist Review* 17 (September, 1916):158–61.

The Mesabi Range strike.

3187. West, Harold E. "Civil War in West Virginia Coal Mines." *Survey* 30 (April, 1913):37–50.

The long history of the coal miners' troubles, working under peonage conditions; the work of Mother Jones described; good photographs.

3188. "The Western Federation and the Industrial Principle." *Agitator* 1 (January 1, 1911):1.

The WFM has applied to the AFL but wants to retain industrial union status.

3189. "The Western Federation of Miners." *Outlook* 82 (March 31, 1906):724–25.

WFM officers interviewed believe in admitting all types of miners into the union regardless of skill. They are theoretical Socialists.

3190. "The Western Federation of Miners in Alaska." *Miners Magazine* 9 (December 12, 1907):8.

The gratifying increase in WFM membership and imaginative organizing practices in Alaska.

3191. Westman, Walter H. "Modern America Was Built on the Sweat of the Shovel Stiff." *Industrial Worker* 26 (July 7, 1945):1, 4.

The IWW construction worker has left his mark from coast to coast, wherever dirt is moved.

3192. Weston, E. "Some Principles of the I.W.W." *Miners Magazine* 14 (September 4, 1913):7.

3193. Wetter, Pierce C. "The Men I Left at Leavenworth." *Survey* 49 (October 1, 1922):29–31.
The prisoners' sentiments as described by one of them.

3194. Wetzel, Kurt. "The Defeat of Bill Dunne: An Episode in the Montana Red Scare." *Pacific Northwest Quarterly* 64 (1973):12–20.

3195. Weyl, Walter. "It Is Time To Know." *Survey* 28 (April 6, 1912):65–67.
A plea to readers to try to understand the bad working conditions and problems of the Lawrence workers.

3196. ———. "The Lesson of Lawrence—It Is Time To Know." *Life & Labor* 2 (July, 1912):196–97.
The Lawrence strike, the interunion struggles, and the bad working conditions.

3197. ———. "The Strikers at Lawrence." *Outlook* 100 (February 10, 1912):309–12.
A description of the Lawrence strikers.

3198. "WFM as Seen by Their Opponents." *Outlook* 83 (July 7, 1906):551–55.
A hostile account of the miners' union in an unsigned article ("his life would be imperiled," the author says, if he were known to oppose the WFM).

3199. "What Churchmen Say about Kentucky Mine War." *Workers Defense* 1 (October, 1931):3.

3200. "What Has Been Proved at the IWW Trial: Review of Evidence Introduced at Chicago." *New York Times* (August 4, 1918): Section 4, p. 4, cols. 1–6.

3201. "What Haywood Says of the IWW." *Survey* 38 (August 11, 1917):429–30.
Haywood denies that the IWW is connected with Germany and states that Frank Little was lynched and murdered because of his strike activities.

3202. "What Haywood Says on Political Action." *International Socialist Review* 13 (February, 1913):622–24.

In hundreds of speeches Haywood has never wavered from his opinion that political action is fine for some but that class unionism is necessary in the economic field.

3203. "What I Learned from a Strike." *Survey* 31 (October 4, 1913):14–15.

The workers and employers in the garment industry do not know anything about each others' problems, according to a manufacturer. The workers who have been working a fifty-four-hour week demanded forty-eight hours but were willing to accept the fifty-two-hour week, which shows and proves that their conditions are tolerable.

3204. "What Is a Scissorbill?" *Labor Defender* 1 (May 15, 1918):2.

A *scissorbill* is a worker whose servility increases at the same rate as his delusions, a wage slave who believes everything he is told by those interested in his enslavement.

3205. "What Is Attorney General Palmer Doing?" *Nation* 110 (February 14, 1920):190–91.

The Palmer Raids.

3206. "What Is Bolshevism?" *One Big Union Monthly* 2 (September, 1920):8–9.

The Russian revolution was a great achievement, but the IWW must not be involved in the political Third International.

3207. "What Is Criminal Syndicalism?" *Outlook* 133 (May 2, 1923):786.

3208. "What Is Hostility to Government?" *Outlook* 104 (June 21, 1913):351.

The arrest of editor Alexander Scott for publishing stories favorable to the strikers at Paterson.

3209. "What Is the I.W.W. and What Does It Want?" *One Big Union Monthly* 1 (March, 1919):24–25.

The IWW is a labor union that wants to organize workers along industrial lines rather than by crafts and hopes to be the structure of a new society.

3210. "What Is the Matter with Minnesota?" *Nation* 85 (August 1, 1907):92–93.

A tongue-in-cheek description of how citizens in Minnesota are deporting strike leaders and condemning strikes. If this movement spreads nationwide, there will no longer be strikes and riots.

3211. "What of the Year 1913? The IWW May Be the Chief Factor in Labor Circles in the Coming Years." *Square Deal* 11 (January, 1913):485–89.

The Lawrence strike and other activities have made the IWW a union to reckon with.

3212. "What Shall Be Done with the I.W.W.?" *Seattle Municipal News* 7 (May 4, 1918):1–2.

3213. "What the IWW Black Cat and Wooden Shoe Emblems Mean." *Literary Digest* 61 (April 19, 1919):70–75.

The symbols of sabotage.

3214. "What the *Industrial Worker* Thinks about International Affiliation." *One Big Union Monthly* 2 (October, 1920):27.

Opposition to any political affiliation: the IWW must not become the tail of the kite of any political organization.

3215. "What the I.W.W. Is: A History of the Organization." *Boiler Makers Journal* (August, 1912):675–76.

3216. "What Was Done with the $7,000?" *Miners Magazine* 14 (July 24, 1913):4–5.

The IWW's handling of the Paterson strike funds.

3217. "What's the Difference?" *One Big Union Monthly* NS 1 (April, 1937):33.

The IWW, the AFL, and the CIO compared as to structure, method, people with power, and purposes.

3218. "What's Wrong with Labor? Federation Threatened with IWW Control from the Inside." *New York Times* (October 26, 1919): Sec. 4, pp. 1–2, col. 12.

IWW "boring-from-within" tactics.

3219. "Wheatland Boys." *International Socialist Review* 14 (January, 1914):442–43.

Nels Nelson, his arm shot off, "hanged himself" in jail, and 16-year-old Eddie Gleason has disappeared. Prisoners are not allowed to see their counsel.

3220. "Wheatland Boys." *International Socialist Review* 14 (March, 1914):522.

Suhr has been tortured. Austin Lewis gave the boys a good defense, but it was a crooked and brutal case.

3221. "Wheatland Riot and What Lay Back of It." *Survey* 31 (March 21, 1914):768–70.
The Wheatland riot and the bad conditions that started it.

3222. Wheeler, Robert J. "The Allentown Silk Dyers Stike." *International Socialist Review* 13 (May, 1913):820–21.
A remote IWW strike not often mentioned.

3223. "When Is a Revolution Not a Revolution?" *Liberator* 2 (April, 1918):23–25.
The Seattle General Strike.

3224. "When You Couldn't Talk at Fifth and E." *San Diego Magazine* (September, 1950):18.
A historical account of the San Diego Free Speech Fight.

3225. "When Work Women Organize." *Industrial Pioneer* 1 (September, 1923):7–8.
In the future women will be in regular unions, not just auxiliaries.

3226. "Where Are the Pre-War Radicals? Symposium." *Survey* 55 (February 1, 1926):556–66. See no. 1568.

3227. Whitaker, Robert. "Centralia and the Churches." *Christian Century* 47 (December 3, 1930):1478–80.
The Federal Council of Churches' investigation of the Centralia Massacre.

3228. ———. "Where Are the Radicals of Yesterday?" *Industrial Pioneer* 4 (May, 1926):11–13.
People seem indifferent to the suffering of class-war prisoners such as Tom Mooney and the Centralia victims. The radicals were preachers too much and scientists too little, but mostly just preachers after all. See no. 1568.

3229. White, Earl Bruce. "The IWW and the Midcontinental Oil Fields." In James C. Foster, ed., *American Labor in the Southwest* (Tucson: University of Arizona Press, 1982), 65–85.

3230. ———. "Might Is Right: Unionism and Goldfield, Nevada, 1904 to 1908." *Journal of the West* 16 (July, 1977):75–84.

3231. ———. "Communications." *Labor History* 18 (Winter, 1977):153–55.
Criticism of some footnotes in Clayton Koppes' article on the Kansas Syndicalism trials (see no. 1794). White believes the footnotes were attributed to the wrong person.

3232. ———. "A Note on the Archives of the Western Federation of Miners and International Union of Mine, Mill and Smelter Workers." *Labor History* 17 (Fall, 1976):613–17.

3233. ———. "*The United States v. C. W. Anderson et al.:* The Wichita Case, 1917–1919." In Joseph R. Conlin, ed., *At the Point of Production* (Westport, CT: Greenwood Press, 1981), 143–64 (see no. 39).

3234. "Whither Are We Drifting?" *Miners Magazine* 14 (October 30, 1913):5.
About the Calumet-Hecla and Colorado strikes.

3235. Whitten, Woodrow C. "The Wheatland Episode." *Pacific Historical Review* 17 (February, 1948):37–42.

3236. "Whom the I.W.W. Imitates." *Public* 17 (March 27, 1914):290.
Is the IWW injurious?

3237. "Who So Shall Offend." *Nation* 108 (January 25, 1919):113.
A national school newspaper that viciously maligns all radicals in its definition of a Bolshevik.

3238. "Why a Union Contract?" *One Big Union Advocate* 1 (September, 1939):4–8.
A long and serious discussion of why the IWW does not like contracts. Closed-shop contracts give great power to union officials.

3239. "Why All Automobile Workers Should Join." *Rebel Worker* 2 (July 15, 1919):4.
The IWW was the first union to try to organize the auto worker.

3240. "Why Amnesty Matters." *Nation* 114 (January 25, 1922):87–88.
The critic of war is the critic of the social order, and that is why amnesty for political prisoners is opposed.

3241. "Why Haywood Went to Russia." *Solidarity* NS 130 (April 30, 1921):1.
According to a Communist Party agent, he was ordered to go. He did not break faith with his friends and has never shown cowardice.

3242. "Why I Quit the IWW." *Sunset* 53 (November, 1924):15, 92–96.
Personal story of a disillusioned Wobbly.

3243. "Why Negroes Should Join the I.W.W." *Messenger* 2 (July, 1919):8.
The Negro must learn to engage in direct action and defend

his rights. He should stand for industrial unionism in the only union that is really integrated.

3244. "Why Not Send Them to Siberia?" *Masses* 5 (March, 1914):5.
The Wheatland prisoners.

3245. "Why Should These Men Be Released?" *Messenger* 4 (May, 1922):404–5.

3246. "Why the I.W.W. Is Dangerous." *San Francisco Labor Clarion* (April 5, 1912):n.p.

3247. "Why the Silent Defense?" *One Big Union Monthly* 1 (March, 1919):8–9.
The defendants were silent as a philosophical expression of their belief that there is no equal justice before the law.

3248. "Why the Textile Workers Must Eventually Join the I.W.W." *Rebel Worker* 2 (July 15, 1919):2.
The United Textile Workers are ignorant and the Amalgamated Textile Workers are inexperienced; the IWW hopes to step in and give the workers the kind of union that can be successful.

3249. "Why We Hate the Bolsheviki." *Public* 22 (February 8, 1919):126–27.
Reasons for fear and mistrust of American radicals.

3250. Whyte, Jack. "Speech before Judge Sloan." *International Socialist Review* 13 (October, 1912):320.
The speech of the IWW leader after his arrest at the San Diego Free Speech Fight.

3251. "The Wichita Cases." *Labor Defender* 1 (April 1, 1918):3.
Lists the prisoners and reminds readers of the strong connection between the Standard Oil Company's fight against unions and the Wichita arrests.

3252. "The Wicked IWW." *New Review* 2 (March, 1914):186–87.
A Socialist is quoted as believing that the IWW is less patriotic than the Socialist Party.

3253. Wieck, A. B. "Deportation and the Aftermath." *New Republic* 31 (August 2, 1922):278–79.
The Yecob deportation case as an example of how immigrant workmen are being deported for no real reason.

3254. Wildes, H. E. "Making Rebels in Philadelphia." *Forward* 3 (May, 1919):71–72.

3255. Wilkins, Bertha S. "The Old Unionism and the New." *Miners Magazine* 6 (July 20, 1905):9.
The first IWW convention and the rivalry between the new union and the old.

3256. Wilkins, Violet Clarke. "Yes, We Have a Labor Government." *One Big Union Monthly* NS 2 (January, 1938):7–8.
A prominent Australian member describes the IWW organization in her country under a Labour government.

3257. "Will Syndicalism Supplant Socialism?" *Current Literature* 53 (September, 1912):317–19.
If the government effectively cooperated with unions, Syndicalism could be avoided and Socialism achieved; if employers and unions combined, national control by the people would be impossible.

3258. Willard, Bert. "Farmer Jones on Party Problems." *International Socialist Review* 13 (August, 1912):129–32.
A dialect tale to make the point that although sabotage makes the Socialists uneasy, it is a necessary part of the class struggle.

3259. "William D. Haywood, Obituary." *Nation* 126 (May 30, 1928):601.
Haywood was as American as Bret Harte or Mark Twain.

3260. Williams, Ben H. "Class Unionism." *International Socialist Review* 14 (May, 1914):668–69.
Organization means power, and real class unionism would strike terror into employers.

3261. ———. "The Constructive Program of the I.W.W." *Solidarity* 4 (June 7, 1913):2.
How the IWW operates.

3262. ———. "A Lesson in Logic: The Physical Force Fallacy." *Industrial Union Bulletin* 2 (February 20, 1909):2.
Repudiates charges that the IWW incites violence and explains opposition to the ballot.

3263. ———. "Sixth IWW Convention." *International Socialist Review* 12 (November, 1911):300–302.
Personal description of the IWW convention.

3264. ———. "What Is the Matter with the IWW." *Solidarity* NS 130 (April 30, 1921):2.
Cites problems of mixed locals and job delegates; recommends emphasizing revolution.

3265. ———. "What Kind of a World Does the IWW Want?—The Trend toward Industrial Freedom." *American Journal of Sociology* 20 (March, 1915):626–28.

Thoughtful expression of the workers' need for a better government.

3266. Williams, David. "The Bureau of Investigation and Its Critics, 1919–1921: The Origins of Federal Political Surveillance." *Journal of American History* 68 (December, 1981):560–79.

3267. Williams, Frances. "The Winnipeg Strike." *Liberator* 2 (July, 1919):39–44.

The Winnipeg Strike a critical test of whether returned soldiers will be strike-breakers. Questions of scabbing and union recognition must also be dealt with.

3268. Williams, G. O. "The History of the Seattle Police Department." *Sheriff and Police Reporter* 12 (November, 1950):8–9, 18–21.

A retrospective look at police problems.

3269. Williams, George. "Defense News." *Industrial Pioneer* 1 (June, 1921):59.

Though $65,000 worth of bonds have been forfeited, the IWW, with voluntary assessments, will pay it off.

3270. Williams, J. C. "Acting President Williams' Report." *Miners Magazine* 7 (June 7, 1906):7–10.

The first Haywood trial and the illegal arrest of Vincent St. John.

3271. Williams, William J. "Bloody Sunday Revisited." *Pacific Northwest Quarterly* 71 (April, 1980):50–62.

The Everett Massacre.

3272. Williamson, J. "Sweet Home Strike Standing Solid." *Voice of the People* 3 (March 5, 1914):1.

Thugs, gunmen, and armed private detectives complicate the picture of the Louisiana lumber strike, with a crew striking, a crew working, a crew leaving for good, a crew coming to work, and a large crew of armed thugs hired by the employer.

3273. "Wilson and the Copper Strike." *Square Deal* 13 (December, 1913):475.

The Calumet-Hecla copper strike.

3274. Wilson, James. "The Value of Music in I.W.W. Meetings." *Industrial Union Bulletin* 4 (May 16, 1908):1.

Crowds come to hear the music at the Spokane IWW meetings. "Hallelujah, I'm a Bum" has already spread to other cities. A good song is worth ten men.

3275. Wilson, Marjorie H. "Governor Hunt, the 'Beast' and the Miners." *Journal of Arizona History* 15 (Summer, 1974):119–38.

3276. Wilson, William B. "The False Theories of the I.W.W." In Daniel Bloomfield, comp., *Selected Articles on Modern Industrial Movements* (New York: H. W. Wilson, 1919), 82–86.

3277. Wing, M. T. C. "The Flag at McKees Rocks." *Survey* 23 (October 2, 1909):45–46.
Some strikers go back to work in a parade carrying an American flag. They do not get all they asked, but many company abuses are publicized.

3278. Wingerden, L. M. V. "The Evolutionary IWW." *One Big Union Monthly* 2 (April, 1920):37–38.
Thoughts written in a Portland, Oregon, county jail about a workers' commonwealth in the future.

3279. Winslow, B. "The Struggle of the Lumber Workers." *Socialist Worker* 49 (May, 1981):11.
Historical review of lumber strikes.

3280. Winstead, Ralph. "Enter a Logger: An IWW Reply to the Four L's." *Survey* 44 (July 3, 1920):474–77.
Robert Gill's article about the loggers, the IWW, and the eight-hour day (see no. 1300) is wrong: the Four L is a joke even to its members.

3281. ———. "Evolution of Logging Conditions on the Northwest Coast." *One Big Union Monthly* 2 (May, 1920):20–30.

3282. ———. "Instinct and Better Organization." *One Big Union Monthly* 2 (August, 1920):40.
A system of delegate selection that would be preferable to the lumberworkers and would make better communication possible.

3283. ———. "Organization and the Lumber Industry." *Industrial Pioneer* 1 (August, 1921):23–24.
New tactics needed to consolidate the success of the 1917 lumber strikes, with coordination of the rank-and-file members.

3284. ———. "Organizing the Harvest Workers: With the I.W.W. in the Grain Fields." *Labor Age* 11 (June, 1922):18–20.
Organizing harvest workers.

3285. ———. "Social Structures." *One Big Union Monthly* 2 (November, 1920):38–39.
Historical examples of political groups that failed. Social ownership of the tools of production is the only way to true democracy.

3286. ———. "Spirit of Centralia Victims." *Industrial Pioneer* 1 (August, 1921):31–32.
The prisoners are brave, earnest, calm, and self-controlled.

3287. "Winstead's 'Enter a Logger' Reply." *Survey* 44 (August 16, 1920):640
A response to no. 3280, an opinion on the Four L's.

3288. Wiprud, Theodore. "Butte: A Troubled Labor Paradise." *Montana, the Magazine of Western History* 21 (October, 1971):31–38.
The suppression of the IWW as recollected by a member of the National Guard.

3289. "With Drops of Blood: Patriots Trafficking in the I.W.W. Scare." *One Big Union Monthly* 2 (May, 1920):46–47.
A phony version of Haywood's pamphlet (no. 4181) was published to damage the IWW.

3290. "With the Railroad Boys." *International Socialist Review* 15 (June, 1915):764–65.
Among letters stimulated by Carl Sandburg's interest in the railroad workers, this one proposes one big industrial union for all transportation workers.

3291. Withington, Anne. "The Lawrence Strike." *Life and Labor* 2 (March, 1912):73–77.
A somewhat dubious trade union (UTW) view of the strike.

3292. Witt, W. M. "When Will the I.W.W. Go Out of Business?" *Voice of the People* 2 (August 28, 1913):4.
Humorous listing of many seemingly impossible contingencies, including the day that equal rights will be enjoyed by all and special privileges by none.

3293. "Wm. E. Trautmann, Formerly General Secretary." *Miners Magazine* 14 (June 5, 1913):4–5.
Trautmann resigns from the IWW.

3294. "Wobblies in the Northwest." *Nation* 145 (November 13, 1937):543.
An IWW strike in the Potlatch forests of Idaho in 1936.

3295. "Wobblies March Again." *Time* 51 (April 19, 1948):26.
Picketing the *New Republic* for its publication of Stegner's article on Joe Hill (no. 2817).

3296. "The Wobblies' Expectation." *Four L Bulletin* 1 (November, 1919): 14.
Derogatory article on the IWW.

3297. "Wobs Are Psyched Again." Review of *Social Psychology*, by Floyd H. Allport. *Industrial Pioneer* 2 (November, 1924):45–57.
The IWW and other radicals mentioned in a psychology textbook.

3298. Woehlke, Walter V. "Bolshevikis of the West." *Sunset* 40 (January, 1918):14–16, 70–72.
The western IWW and the trouble it is having.

3299. ———. "The End of the Dynamite Case—'Guilty.'" *Outlook* 99 (December 16, 1911):903–8.
The McNamara case and its implications for labor.

3300. ———. "IWW." *Outlook* 101 (July 6, 1912):531–36.
The victimization of the IWW at San Diego and elsewhere.

3301. ———. "The I.W.W. and the Golden Rule—Why Everett Used the Club and Gun on the Red Apostles of Direct Action." *Sunset* 38 (February, 1917):16–18, 62–65.

3302. ———. "Porterhouse Heaven and the Hobo." *Technical World* 21 (August, 1914):808–18, 938.
The hoboes who favor the West; some thoughts on Wheatland and the Ford and Suhr case.

3303. ———. "Red Rebels Declare War." *Sunset* 39 (September, 1917): 20–21.
Attempts to organize the fruit pickers of the Yakima valley.

3304. ———. "Revolution in America; Seattle Crushes the First Soviet Uprising." *Sunset* 42 (April, 1919):13–16.
The Seattle General Strike.

3305. ———. "San Diego IWW." *Outlook* (July 6, 1912):531–36.
The troubles after the Free Speech Fight in San Diego.

3306. Wolff, W. A. "The Northwestern Front." *Collier's Weekly* 61 (April 20, 1918):10–11, 31–32.
Colonel Disque, who headed the spruce drive for the government, and his handling of the IWW problem.

3307. Wolman, Leo. "Extent of Labor Organization." *Quarterly Journal of Economics* 30 (May, 1916):486–518, 601–24.
Statistics on the IWW.

3308. "Women and the IWW." *Industrial Pioneer* 1 (April, 1924):7–8.
Favorable opinions of the IWW by a Buffalo stenographer and a mother who wishes her son to be a rebel.

3309. "Women in the Labor Movement." *One Big Union Monthly* NS 1 (March, 1937):19–20.
The actions of Mother Jones and the Women's Brigade in Flint, Michigan.

3310. "Women Wage Workers! Join the One Big Union!" *Rebel Worker* 2 (August 1, 1919):2.
Women should see that their men pay their dues and should acquaint themselves with the union's philosophy and possibly even join it themselves.

3311. Wood, C. W. "IWW's Plan To Strike." *Collier's* 70 (September 23, 1922):5–6, 28–29.
Rumors of a general strike.

3312. ———. "Revolution in Industrial Countries." *Industrial Pioneer* 1 (September, 1921):19–22.
A real revolution occurred in 1917, when the country pushed for greater production.

3313. Wood, Jack. "Two Surprises." *Agitator* 1 (October 15, 1911):4.
The IWW organization at Home, Washington.

3314. Woodruff, Abner E. "Ethics of the Producers in an Industrial Democracy." *One Big Union Monthly* 1 (July, 1919):40–45.
Some of Georges Sorel's ideas on work and efficiency adapted to America.

3315. ———. "Evolution of Industrial Democracy." *Solidarity* 7 (November 4, 1916):3; (November 11, 1916):3; (November 18, 1916):3; (November 25, 1916):3; (December 2, 1916):3; (December 9, 1916):3.

3316. ———. "The Law of Increasing Dependence." *One Big Union Monthly* 1 (June, 1919):28–32.
Believes that true industrial democracy can be achieved only

when workers have been organized along industrial lines. Then they will realize that their interdependence requires the exchange of mutual services.

3317. Woods, R. A. "The Breadth and Depth of the Lawrence Outcome." *Survey* 28 (April 6, 1912):67–68.

Higher wages will have to be paid in many places and prices will have to be raised, thanks to the Lawrence strike. The worst result of the strike is the prestige of the strike leaders; we must reeducate the public about them.

3318. ———. "The Clod Stirs." *Survey* 27 (March 16, 1912):1929–32.

A serious analysis of the Lawrence strike and a prediction that low-paid workers will not long be willing to put up with their wages.

3319. "Work and the Police, Mortal Foes of the I.W.W." *New York Tribune* (April 12, 1914):part 5, n.p.

3320. "Work of the IWW in Paterson." *Literary Digest* 47 (August 9, 1913):197–98.

3321. "Work Peoples College." *Industrial Pioneer* 3 (September, 1925):20.

The IWW-Socialist college in Duluth, Minnesota.

3322. "Work Peoples College." *One Big Union Monthly* 2 (September, 1920):61.

The IWW-Socialist college in Duluth, Minnesota.

3323. "*Worker* Suppressed: Printer Yields to Threats of Terrorists." *Labor Defender* 1 (May 30, 1918):1.

The printer of the IWW newspaper threatened with death and the destruction of his plant if he continues publishing; other plants also threatened by citizen vigilantes.

3324. "The Workers' International Educational Society." *Industrial Pioneer* 4 (July, 1926):35.

The group organized in 1925 to educate workers.

3325. "Workers of the World Now Run Affairs for New York Waiters." *Square Deal* 12 (February, 1913):29–31.

The organizing activities of Joseph Ettor and Elizabeth Gurley Flynn among the waiters and restaurant workers of New York.

3326. "A Worker's View." *One Big Union Monthly* 2 (June, 1920):46–47.

Workers want freedom and a chance to use their own ingenuity.

3327. "World War To Create Markets." *One Big Union Monthly* NS 2 (March, 1938):25–26.

There will soon be a war because there is no other way to get rid of the surplus goods being produced.

3328. Worth, Cedric. "The Brotherhood of Man." *North American Review* 227 (April, 1929):487–92.

The life of migrant workers and hoboes.

3329. Wortman, Roy. "The IWW and the Akron Rubber Strike of 1913." In Joseph R. Conlin, ed., *At the Point of Production* (Westport, CT: Greenwood Press, 1981), 49–60 (see no. 39).

3330. ———. "The Resurgence of the IWW in Cleveland: A Neglected Aspect of Labor History." *Northwest Ohio Quarterly* 47 (Winter, 1974–75):20–29.

3331. Wortman, Roy, ed. "An IWW Document on the 1919 Rossford Strike." *Northwest Ohio Quarterly* 43 (Summer, 1971):20–29.

A little-remembered strike at the Ford Plate Glass Company in Ohio.

3332. "The WPA Strike and Relief." *One Big Union Advocate* 1 (August, 1939):1–5.

WPA workers should receive pay equal to everyone else.

3333. "Wrangel and the Bolsheviki." *One Big Union Monthly* 2 (December, 1920):8–10.

Applauds the defeat of Wrangel's army in Russia but not the "Red Terror" that is being reported. Bolsheviks have no right to ram their ideas down the throats of the workers.

3334. Wright, Ralph D. "How Things Will 'Work Out': A Frank Statement of the Purposes of the Syndicalist Movement." *Common Cause* 3 (January, 1913):79–83.

A gloomy picture of what we may expect next from Syndicalism.

3335. "Wrong Way Out." *Public* 20 (1917):1235–36.

Everything about the government raids, the Syndicalist trials, and ideas of sabotage and direct action is all wrong.

3336. "Yakima Valley Hop and Fruit Growers Sabotage Workers!" *Voice of the People* 2 (September 10, 1914):2.

The growers are advertising too much and plan to hire too many workers so they can pay them less.

3337. Yarros, Victor S. "The IWW Judgment." *Survey* 45 (October 16, 1920):87.

The appeal judgment on the IWW trial. Many were surprised that the decision was not reversed because the jury deliberated for only forty minutes.

3338. ———. "The IWW Trial." *Nation* 107 (August 31, 1918):220–23.

The techniques of the lawyers for both sides. Yarros believes that the defense should not have cut short its chance to argue.

3339. ———. "Recent Assaults on Democracy." *Public* 21 (September 7, 1918):1144–48.

The Red Scare.

3340. ———. "Social Science and What Labor Wants." *American Journal of Sociology* 19 (November, 1913):308–22.

What labor wants is what everyone ought to want, says Yarros, in a long and interesting article comparing American and British workers' aspirations. A social scientist attempts to predict coming trends.

3341. ———. "The Story of the IWW Trial: The Atmosphere of the Trial." *Survey* 40 (August 31, 1918):603–4; "The Case for the Prosecution." (September 7, 1918):630–32; and "The Nature and Pith of the Defense." (September 14, 1918):660–63.

Complete coverage of the IWW trial at Chicago.

3342. Young, James D. "Daniel De Leon and Anglo-American Socialism." *Labor History* 17 (Summer, 1976):329–50.

3343. "Youngstown and Americanization." *Outlook* 112 (January 26, 1916):168.

The city school board refuses to open night schools or spend a cent on "foreigners." Their disbelief in Americanization will insure future strikes and riots.

3344. "Youngstown: The Riot." *Outlook* 112 (January 19, 1916):121–23.

During the strike riot eight were killed and twenty wounded, all by the employers' private detectives. The strikers only wanted a share in the enormous profits being made.

3345. Zanger, Martin. "The Politics of Confrontation: Upton Sinclair and the Launching of the ACLU in Southern California." *Pacific Historical Review* 38 (November, 1969):383–406.

Some Red Scare activities.

3346. Zellick, Anna. "Patriots on the Rampage: Mob Action in Lewistown, 1917–1918." *Montana, the Magazine of Western History* 31 (January, 1981):30–43.

3347. Zieger, Robert H. Review of *Bread and Roses Too,* ed. by Joseph R. Conlin (see no. 41). *Labor History* 11 (Fall, 1970):564–69.

3348. ———. "Robin Hood in Silk City: The IWW and the Paterson Silk Strike of 1913." *Proceedings of the New Jersey Historical Society* 84 (July, 1966):182–95.

3349. ———. "Workers and Scholars: Recent Trends in American Labor Historiography." *Labor History* 13 (Spring, 1972):245–66.

I WILL WIN

Index of Journals

Note: The journal articles below are indexed by subject and author in the General Index at the end of this book. Some articles are taken from books, and some of these sources can be found in the book section. Numbers are those of items in this bibliography.

IWW
ONE BIG UNION
OF ALL THE WORKERS
THE
GREATEST THING
ON EARTH

Dissertations, Theses, and Essays

THIS compilation of dissertations, theses, and essays has been gleaned from reference works, footnotes, bibliographic notes, and articles in scholarly journals. The list reveals which parts of IWW history have been given the most and which the least attention and at which colleges and universities such work has been done.

Because most dissertations are no longer available through Interlibrary Loan, there has been no attempt at annotation in this section. Summaries of many of the dissertations may be found in *Dissertation Abstracts International* (Ann Arbor, MI: University Microfilms International, 1938–.) A group of masters' theses and essays follows the listing of doctoral dissertations, but such works are not as well reported nationally as dissertations, and this section is doubtless incomplete.

The availability to a borrower of many works in this section may be questionable: an inquiry to the individual institution is advisable. Most can be purchased through University Microfilms International.

Universities and colleges may have changed names and added locations; I have listed campuses as I saw them in my sources.

Dissertations

3350. Adams, Graham. "Age of Industrial Violence: Social Conflict in America as Revealed by the US Commission on Industrial Relations." Columbia University, 1963.

3351. Allen, Winfred G., Jr. "Spokesman for the 'Dispossessed'; A Content Analysis of the Public Addresses of Eugene Debs, Daniel De Leon and William Haywood." University of California, Los Angeles, 1977.

3352. Altenbaugh, Richard J. "Forming the Structures of a New Society within the Shell of the Old: A Study of Three Labor Colleges and Their Contributions to the American Labor Movement." University of Pittsburgh, 1980

3353. Applen, Allen G. "Migratory Harvest Labor in the Midwestern Wheat Belt, 1870–1940." Kansas State University, 1974.

3354. Bailey, Kenneth R. "A Search for Identity: The West Virginia National Guard." Ohio State University, 1976

3355. Barnes, Donald M. "The Ideology of the Industrial Workers of the World, 1905–1921." Washington State University, 1962.

3356. Bates, James L. "Senator Walsh of Montana, 1918–1924: A Liberal under Pressure." University of North Carolina, 1952.

3357. Bedford, Henry F. "Socialism and Workers in Massachusetts, 1886–1912." University of Massachusetts, 1966.

3358. Bercuson, David J. "Labour in Winnipeg: The Great War and the General Strike." University of Toronto, 1971.

3359. Boyer, Gary. "The I.W.W. in Fiction and Drama." Syracuse University, forthcoming.

3360. Brinley, John E. "The Western Federation of Miners." University of Utah, 1972.

3361. Brooks, Robert R. "The United Textile Workers of America." Yale University, 1935.

3362. Brown, Myland. "The IWW and the Negro Worker." Ball State University, 1969.

3363. Brown, Roland C. "Hard-Rock Miners of the Great Basin and Rocky Mountain West, 1860–1920." University of Illinois, 1975.

3364. Burki, Mary Ann. "Paul Scharrenberg: White Shirt Sailor." University of Rochester, 1971.

3365. Byrkit, James W. "Life and Labor in Arizona, 1901–1921: With Particular Reference to the Deportations of 1917." Claremont Graduate School, 1972.

3366. Calvert, Jerry W. "A Changing Radical Political Organization: The Wobblies Today." Washington State University, 1972.

3367. Cash, Joseph H. "Labor in the West: The Homestake Mining Camp and Its Workers, 1877–1942. University of Iowa, 1966.

3368. Christopoulos, Diana. "American Radicals and the Mexican Revolution, 1900–1925." State University of New York, Binghamton, 1980.

3369. Close, J. A. "Some Phases of the History of the Anaconda Copper Mining Company." University of Minnesota, 1946.

3370. Coben, Stanley. "The Political Career of A. Mitchell Palmer." Columbia University, 1961.

3371. Cole, Donald B. "Lawrence, Massachusetts: Immigrant City, 1845–1912." Harvard University, 1957.

3372. Cole, Terry W. "Labor's Radical Alternative: The Rhetoric of the Industrial Workers of the World." University of Oregon, 1974.

3373. Conlin, Joseph R. "The Wobblies: A Study of the Industrial Workers of the World before World War I." University of Wisconsin, Madison, 1966.

3374. Cox, John H. "Organizations of the Lumber Industry in the Pacific Northwest, to 1917." University of California, Berkeley, 1937.

3375. Cullison, Frederick. "Western Federation of Miners." Columbia University, 1979.

3376. Daniel, Cletus E. "Labor Radicalism in Pacific Coast Agriculture." University of Washington, 1972.

3377. Dembo, Jonathan. "A History of the Washington State Labor Movement, 1885–1935." University of Washington, 1978.

3378. Dowell, Eldridge F. "A History of the Enactment of Criminal Syndicalism Legislation in the United States." Johns Hopkins University, 1933.

3379. Dunkel, William P. "Between Two Worlds: Max Eastman, Floyd Dell, John Reed, Randolph Bourne, and the Revolt against the Genteel Tradition." Lehigh University, 1976.

3380. Engberg, George B. "Labor in the Lake States Lumber Industry, 1830–1930." University of Minnesota, 1950.

3381. Fenton, Edwin. "Immigrants and Unions: A Case Study: Italians and American Labor, 1870–1920." Harvard University, 1958.

3382. Finney, John D., Jr. "A Study of Negro Labor during and after World War I." Georgetown University, 1957.

3383. Francis, Robert C. "A History of Labor on the San Francisco Waterfront." University of California, 1934.

3384. Frost, Richard H. "The Mooney Case." University of California, Berkeley, 1961.

3385. Fuller, Levi V. "The Supply of Agricultural Labor as a Factor in the Evolution of Farm Organizations in California." University of California, Berkeley, 1939.

3386. Gaboury, William J. "Dissension in the Rockies: A History of Idaho Populism." University of Idaho, 1966.

3387. Garber, Morris W. "The Silk Industry of Paterson, New Jersey, 1840–1913: Technology and the Origins, Development, and Changes in an Industry." Rutgers, The State University of New Jersey, 1968.

3388. Gedicks, Al. "Working Class Radicalism among Finnish Immigrants in Minnesota and Michigan." University of Wisconsin, Madison, 1979.

3389. Gengarelly, William A. "Resistance Spokesmen: Opponents of the Red Scare, 1919–1921." Boston University, 1972.

3390. Goldberg, Barry H. "Beyond Free Labor: Labor, Socialism, and the Idea of Wage Slavery." Columbia University, 1979.

3391. Goodstein, Phil H. "The Theory of the General Strike: From the French Revolution until World War I." University of Colorado, Boulder, 1981.

3392. Green, James R. "Socialism and the Southwestern Class Struggle, 1898–1918: A Study of Radical Movements in Oklahoma, Texas, Louisiana, and Arkansas." Yale University, 1972.

3393. Greenberg, Irving. "Theodore Roosevelt and Labor: 1900–1918." Harvard University, 1960.

3394. Gronquist, Ray E. "The Ideology of the Industrial Workers of the World as Represented in the Discursive Acts of William D. Haywood." Washington State University, 1975.

3395. Grover, David H. "Debaters and Dynamiters: The Rhetoric of the Haywood Trial." University of Oregon, 1962.

3396. Grubbs, Frank L. "The Struggle for the Mind of American Labor, 1917–1919." University of Virginia, 1963.

3397. Gunns, Albert F. "Civil Liberties and Crisis: The Status of Civil Liberties in the Pacific Northwest, 1917–1940." University of Washington, 1971.

3398. Gutfeld, Arnon. "Years of Hysteria: Montana, 1917–1921: A Study of Local Intolerance." University of California, Los Angeles, 1971.

3399. Helmes, Winfred O. "The People's Governor, John A. Johnson: A Political Biography." University of Minnesota, 1948.

3400. Hoffman, Dennis E. "An Exploratory Analysis of the Response of Urban Police to Labor Radicalism." Portland State University, 1979.

3401. Hoglund, Arthur W. "Paradise Rebuilt: Finnish Immigrants and Their America, 1880–1920." University of Wisconsin, 1957.

3402. Howard, Perry H. "Political Tendencies in Louisiana, 1812–1952." Louisiana State University, Baton Rouge, 1954.

3403. Jaffe, Julian F. "Anti-Radical Crusade in New York, 1914–1924: A Case Study of the Red Scare." New York University, 1971.

3404. Jamieson, Stuart M. "Labor Unionism in American Agriculture." University of California, Berkeley, 1943.

3405. Jensen, Joan M. "The American Protective League, 1917–1919." University of California, Los Angeles, 1962.

3406. Jensen, Vernon. "Labor Relations in the Northwest Lumber Industry." University of California, 1939.

3407. Jones, Dallas Lee. "The Wilson Administration and Organized Labor, 1912–1919." Cornell University, 1954.

3408. Kluger, James R. "Elwood Mead: Irrigation Engineer and Social Planner." University of Arizona, 1970.

3409. Knight, Robert E. L. "A History of Industrial Relations in the San Francisco Bay Area, 1900–1918." University of California, Berkeley, 1958.

3410. Krivy, Leonard P. "American Organized Labor and the First World War, 1917–1918: A History of Labor Problems and the Development of a Government War Labor Program." New York University, 1965.

3411. Larkin, Emmet. "James Larkin, Irish Labour Leader, 1876–1947." Columbia University, 1957.

3412. Loosbrock, Richard J. "The History of the Kansas Department of the American Legion, 1919–1968." University of Kansas, 1968.

3413. Mabon, David White. "The West Coast Waterfront and Sympathy Strikes of 1934." University of California, Berkeley. 1966.

3414. McClurg, Donald J. "Labor Organization in the Coal Mines of Colorado, 1878–1933." University of California, 1959.

3415. McCormack, Andrew R. "The Origins and Extent of Western Labour Radicalism, 1896–1919." University of Western Ontario, 1973.

3416. McEnroe, Thomas. "IWW Theories, Organization Problems, and Appeals as Revealed in the *Industrial Worker.*" University of Minnesota, 1960.

3417. McGovern, George S. "The Colorado Coal Strike, 1913–1914." Northwestern University, 1953.

3418. McKee, Donald K. "The Intellectual and Historical Influence Shaping the Political Theory of Daniel De Leon." Columbia University, 1955.

3419. Makarewicz, Joseph T. "The Impact of World War I on Pennsylvania Politics, with Emphasis on the Election of 1920." University of Pittsburgh, 1972.

3420. Maroney, James C. "Organized Labor in Texas, 1900–1929." University of Houston, 1975.

3421. Mason, Alpheus T. "Organized Labor and the Law, with Special Reference to the Sherman and Clayton Acts." Princeton University, 1923.

3422. Meany, Edmond S. "The History of the Lumber Industry in the Pacific Northwest to 1917." Harvard University, 1936.

3423. Meehan, (Sister) Maria E. "Frank P. Walsh and the American Labor Movement, 1864–1939." New York University, 1962.

3424. Mellinger, Philip A. "The Beginnings of Modern Industrial Unionism in the Southwest: Labor Trouble among Unskilled Copper Workers, 1903–1917." University of Chicago, 1978.

3425. Miller, Richard C. "Otis and His *Times:* The Career of Harrison Gray Otis of Los Angeles." University of California, Berkeley, 1961.

3426. Murray, Robert K. "The Great Red Scare of 1919–1920." Ohio State University, 1950.

3427. Myers, Howard B. "The Policing of Labor Disputes in Chicago." University of Chicago, 1929.

3428. Nash, Michael H. "Conflict and Accommodation: Some Aspects of the Political Behavior of America's Coal Miners and Steel Workers, 1890–1920." State University of New York, Binghamton, 1975.

3429. Nichols, Claude W., Jr. "Brotherhood in the Woods: A Twenty Year Attempt at 'Industrial Cooperation.'" University of Oregon, 1959.

3430. Olson, Richard E. "Some Economic Aspects of Agricultural Development in Nebraska, 1854–1920." University of Nebraska, 1965.

3431. Osborne, James D. "Italian Immigrants and the Working Class Community, Paterson, New Jersey, 1890–1915." Warwick University, England, 1979.

3432. Pawar, Sheelwant B. "An Environmental Study of the Development of the Utah Labor Movement, 1860–1935." University of Utah, 1968.

3433. Pinola, Rudolph. "Labor and Politics on the Iron Range of Northern Minnesota." University of Wisconsin, 1957.

3434. Powell, Allen K. "A History of Labor Union Activity in the Eastern Utah Coal Fields, 1900–1934." University of Utah, 1976.

3435. Prago, Albert. "The Organization of the Unemployed and the Role of the Radicals, 1929–1935." Union Graduate School, Ohio, 1976.

3436. Preston, William. "The Ideology and Techniques of Repression: Government and the Radicals, 1903–1933." University of Wisconsin, Madison, 1957.

3437. Ragan, Fred D. "The *New Republic:* Red Hysteria and Civil Liberties." University of Georgia, 1965.

3438. Randall, John H. "The Problem of Group Responsibility to Society: An Interpretation of the History of American Labor." Columbia University, 1922.

3439. Robinson, Leland W. "Social Movement Organizations in Decline: A Case Study of the IWW." Northwestern University, 1974.

3440. Scheinberg, Stephen J. "The Development of Corporation Labor Policy, 1900–1940." University of Wisconsin, Madison, 1966.

3441. Schofield, Ann. "The Rise of the Pig-Headed Girl: An Analysis of the American Labor Press for Their Attitudes toward Women, 1877–1920." State University of New York, Binghamton, 1980.

3442. Scholten, Pat. "Militant Women for Economic Justice: The Persuasion of Mary Harris Jones, Ella Reeve Bloor, Rose Pastor Stokes, Rose Schneiderman, and Elizabeth Gurley Flynn." Indiana University, 1979.

3443. Schwantes, Carlos A. "Left-Wing Unionism in the Pacific Northwest: A Comparative History of Organized Labor and Socialist

Politics in Washington and British Columbia, 1885–1917." University of Michigan, 1976.

3444. Seretan, L. Glen. "The Life and Career of Daniel De Leon, 1852–1914: An Interpretation." University of Toronto, 1975.

3445. Shaffer, Ralph E. "Radicalism in California, 1869–1929." University of California, Berkeley, 1962.

3446. Sharp, Kathleen A. "Rose Pastor Stokes, Radical Champion of the American Working Class, 1879–1933." Duke University, 1979.

3447. Simon, Jean-Claude G. "Textile Workers, Trade Unions, and Politics: Comparative Case Studies, France and the United States, 1885–1914." Tufts University, 1980.

3448. Smith, Robert W. "The Idaho Antecedents of the Western Federation of Miners, 1890 to 1893." University of California, Berkeley, 1938.

3449. Smith, William T. "The Kuzbas Colony: Soviet Russia 1921–1926, An American Contribution to the Building of a Communist State." University of Miami, 1978.

3450. Sperry, James R. "Organized Labor and Its Fight against Military and Industrial Conscription, 1917–1945." University of Arizona, 1969.

3451. Stevenson, Billie Jean Hackley. "The Ideology of American Anarchism, 1880–1910." University of Iowa, 1972.

3452. Stokes, George A. "Lumbering in Southwest Louisiana: A Study of the Industry." Louisiana State University, 1954.

3453. Suggs, George G., Jr. "Colorado Conservatives and Organized Labor: A Study of the James Hamilton Peabody Administration, 1901–1903." University of Colorado, 1964.

3454. Syrjamaki, John. "The Development of Mesabi Communities." Yale University, 1940.

3455. Tobie, Harvey E. "Oregon Labor Disputes, 1919–1923: A Study of Representative Controversies and Current Thought." University of Oregon, 1936.

3456. Toole, Kenneth R. "A History of the Anaconda Copper Mining Company: A Study in the Relationship between a State and Its People and a Corporation, 1880–1950." University of California, 1955.

3457. Tyler, Robert L. "Rebels of the Woods and Fields: A Study of the IWW in the Pacific Northwest." University of Oregon, 1953.

3458. Villere, Maurice F. "The Theme of Alienation in the Popular Twentieth Century American Industrial and Organizational Novel." University of Illinois at Urbana-Champaign, 1971.

3459. Westergard-Thorpe, Wayne L. "Revolutionary Syndicalist Internationalism, 1913–1923: The Origins of the International Working Men's Association." University of British Columbia, 1979.

3460. White, Earl Bruce. "The Wichita Indictments and the Trial of the IWW, 1917–1919, and the Aftermath." University of Colorado, Boulder, 1982.

3461. Whitten, Woodrow C. "Criminal Syndicalism and the Law in California, 1919–1927." University of California, Berkeley, 1946.

3462. Winters, Donald E. "The Soul of Solidarity: The Relationship between the IWW and American Religion in the Progressive Era." University of Minnesota, 1979.

3463. Wood, James E. "History of Labor in the Broad-Silk Industry of Paterson, N. J., 1872–1940." University of California, Berkeley, 1942.

3464. Wood, Samuel E. "The California State Commission of Immigration and Housing: A Study of Administrative Organization and the Growth of Function." University of California, Berkeley, 1942.

3465. Wortman, Roy T. "The IWW in Ohio, 1905–1950." University of Ohio, 1972.

3466. Youngdale, James. "Populism in a New Perspective: An Analysis of Political Radicalism in the Upper Midwest." University of Minnesota, 1972.

3467. Zappia, Charles. "Italian Workers and the Labor Movement in the United States, 1890–1950." University of California, 1984.

Theses and Essays

3468. Abramson, Paul. "The Industrial Workers of the World in the Northwest Lumber Industry." Reed College, 1952.

3469. Allison, Theodore F. "History of the Northwest Mining Unions through 1920." State College of Washington, 1943.

3470. Ascarelli, Maria. "Italian Immigrants and the IWW." University of Illinois, n.d.

3471. Bernhardt, Debra. "We Knew Different: The Michigan Timber Workers Strike of 1937." Wayne State University, 1977.

3472. Biagi, Robert. "Rip in the Silk: The 1912 and 1913 Paterson Textile Strikes." Wayne State University, 1971.

3473. Buechel, Henry T. "Labor Relations in the West Coast Lumber Industry." State College of Washington, 1936.

3474. Burns, John J. "The IWW in Illinois during World War I." Western Illinois University, 1972.

3475. Bush, Charles C. "The Green Corn Rebellion." University of Oklahoma, 1932.

3476. Clark, Douglas M. "Wheatland Hop Fields Riot." Ohio State University, 1963.

3477. Clark, Joseph C., Jr. "A History of Strikes in Utah." University of Utah, 1953.

3478. Cline, Mildred. "A Study of Criminal Syndicalism in Oregon." Reed College, 1932.

3479. Comstock, A. P. "History of the Industrial Workers of the World in the United States." Columbia University, 1913.

3480. Conlin, J. H. "The Industrial Workers of the World and the Lawrence Strike." Dartmouth College, 1948.

3481. Cook, D. G. "Western Radicalism and the Winnipeg Strike." McMaster University, Hamilton, Ontario, 1921.

3482. Cox, Annie M. "History of Bisbee, 1877 to 1937." University of Arizona, 1938.

3483. Crow, John E. "Ideology and Organization: A Case Study of the Industrial Workers of the World." University of Chicago, 1958.

3484. Delli Quadri, Carmen L. "Labor Relations on the Mesabi Range." University of Colorado, 1944.

3485. Denn, Harold B. "The History of the Silk Workers in Paterson, New Jersey, with Special Emphasis on Strikes, 1910–1920." New York University, 1947.

3486. De Shazo, Melvin Gardner. "Radical Tendencies in the Seattle Labor Movement." University of Washington, 1925.

3487. De Shazo, Peter. "The Industrial Workers of the World in Chile." University of Wisconsin, Madison, 1973.

3488. Diehl, Robert W. "San Diego Free Speech Fight." University of San Diego, 1977.

3489. Eckberg, Robert C. "The Free Speech Fight of the Industrial Workers of the World, Spokane, Washington, 1909–1910." Washington State University, 1967.

3490. Eichholz, Duane W. "Virginia and Rainy Lake Logging Company." University of Minnesota, Duluth, n.d.

3491. Elling, Karl A. "History of Organized Labor in Utah, 1910–1920." University of Utah, 1962.

3492. Ensign, John D., II. "Two Unions in the Utah Copper Industry: The Effect of Ideology upon Their Dealings with Management." University of Utah, 1957.

3493. Evanko, J. "The Anaconda Copper Mining Company: Its Influence in Montana." University of Colorado, 1939.

3494. Evans, Robert E. "Montana's Role in Enactment of Legislation to Suppress the IWW." University of Minnesota, 1964.

3495. Faigin, Henry. "Industrial Workers of the World in Detroit and Michigan from the Period of Beginning through the World War." Wayne State University, 1937.

3496. Fast, Stanley P. "The A.W.O. and the Harvest Stiff in the Mid-Western Wheat Belt, 1915–1920." University of Minnesota, Mankato, 1974.

3497. Fowler, James H. "Extralegal Suppression of Civil Liberties in Oklahoma during the First World War, and Its Causes." Oklahoma State University, 1974.

3498. Goode, Helen M. "Agricultural Labor in the State of Washington during World War I." University of Washington, n.d.

3499. Griesel, George H. "Study of the Personnel of the IWW Movement." University of Nebraska, 1920.

3500. Haller, Douglas M. "I.W.W. Cartoonist Ernest Riebe: Originator of the 'Mr. Block' Series." Wayne State University, 1982.

3501. Halonen, Arne. "The Role of Finnish Americans in the Political Labor Movement." University of Minnesota, 1945.

3502. Harris, Abram L., Jr. "The Negro Worker in Pittsburgh." University of Pittsburgh, 1924.

3503. Herrin, Robert. "Great Lumber Strikes in Northern Idaho." Northern Illinois University, 1967.

3504. Hull, Robert E. "IWW Activity in Everett, Washington, from May, 1916 to June, 1917." Washington State University, 1938.

3505. Johnson, Clarence H. "Origins, Population, Locations, Occupations, and Activities of the Swedes in Detroit." Wayne State University, 1940.

3506. Johnson, Michael R. "The Federal Judiciary and Radical Unionism: A Study of *The United States v. W. D. Haywood, et al.*" Northern Illinois University, n.d.

3507. Jokinen, Walfrid. "The Finns of Minnesota." Louisiana State University, 1953.

3508. Katz, Louis. "Free Speech and the I.W.W." Wayne State University, 1973.

3509. Kimber, Catherine. "History of Cripple Creek, Colorado, 1891–1971." University of Colorado, n.d.

3510. Koppes, Clayton R. "The Kansas Trial of the I.W.W., 1917–1919." University of Kansas, 1972.

3511. Landis, Paul H. "Three Iron Mining Towns: A Study in Cultural Change." University of Michigan, 1930.

3512. Lawson, Harry O. "The Colorado Coal Strike of 1927–1928." University of Colorado, 1950.

3513. Lehman, Ted. "Fresno Free Speech Fight." Fresno State College, 1971.

3514. Levin, Edward B. "The Seattle Labor Movement and the General Strike of 1919." Princeton University, 1962.

3515. Levine, Irving J. "The Lawrence Strike." Columbia University, 1936.

3516. Lynch, Patrick. "Pennsylvania Anthracite: A Forgotten IWW Venture, 1906–1916." Bloomsburg State University, 1974.

3517. McCord, Charles. "A Brief Survey of the Brotherhood of Timber Workers." University of Texas, 1959.

3518. Macpherson, James L. "Butte Miners Union: An Analysis of Its Development and Economic Bargaining Position." Montana State University, 1949.

3519. McWhiney, H. Grady. "The Socialist Vote in Louisiana, 1912: An Historical Interpretation of Radical Sources." Louisiana State University, 1951.

3520. Mooney, Martin C. "The Industrial Workers of the World and the Immigrants of Paterson and Passaic, N.J., 1907–1913." Seton Hall University, 1965.

3521. Morland, Robert. "Political Prairie Fire: The Non-Partisan League, 1915–1922." University of Minnesota, 1955.

3522. Nettleton, Allan L. "Persuasive Techniques Utilized in the IWW Free Speech Fight in Everett, Washington, 1916." Washington State University, 1968.

3523. Newman, Philip C. "The IWW in New Jersey." Columbia University, 1940.

3524. Notarianni, Philip F. "Italian Immigrants in Utah: Nativism, 1900–1925." University of Utah, n.d.

3525. Osborne, James D. "The Paterson Strike of 1913: Immigrant Silkworkers and the IWW Response to the Problem of Stable Unionism." University of Warwick, England, 1973.

3526. Perrin, Robert A., Jr. "Two Decades of Turbulence: A Study of the Great Lumber Strikes in Northern Idaho, 1916–1936." University of Idaho, 1961.

3527. Pittler, Alexander. "The Hill District of Pittsburgh: A Study in Succession." University of Pittsburgh, 1930.

3528. Pope, Virginia C. "The Green Corn Rebellion: A Case Study of Newspaper Censorship." Oklahoma State University, Stillwater, 1940.

3529. Remington, John A. "Violence in Labor Disputes: The Haywood Trial." University of Wyoming, 1965.

3530. Sain, Wilma Gray. "A History of the Miami Area, Arizona." University of Arizona, 1944.

3531. Samuels, Elliot. "Red Scare in Ontario: The Reaction of the Ontario Press to the Internal and External Threat of Bolshevism, 1917–1919." Queens University, 1971.

3532. Schleef, Margaret L. "Rival Unionism in the Lumber Industry." University of California, Berkeley, 1950.

3533. Schmidt, Dorothy B. "Sedition and Criminal Syndicalism in the State of Washington, 1917–1919." Washington State College, 1940.

3534. Scorup, D. A. "A History of Organized Labor in Utah." University of Utah, 1935.

3535. Scruggs, Joseph C. "Labor Problems in the Fruit Industry of the Yakima Valley." University of Washington, 1937.

3536. Sideman, Michael S. "The Agricultural Labor Market and Organizing Activities of the IWW, 1910–1935." University of Illinois, 1965.

3537. Smill, Eva. "The Stogy Industry on the Hill in Pittsburgh, Pa." Carnegie Institute, Pittsburgh, 1920.

3538. Smith, Norma. "The Rise and Fall of the Butte Miners' Union, 1878–1914." Montana State College, 1961.

3539. Smith, Sharon C. "Intellectuals and the Industrial Workers of the World, 1905–1920." University of Wisconsin, 1956.

3540. Souers, Ralph E. "The Industrial Workers of the World." University of Chicago, 1913.

3541. Tierney, Ruth. "The Decline of the Silk Industry in Paterson, N.J." Cornell University, 1938.

3542. Van Tine, Warren R. "Ben H. Williams: Wobbly Editor." Northern Illinois University, 1967.

3543. Villalobos, Charlotte B. "Civil Liberties in San Diego: The Free Speech Fight of 1912." San Diego State College, 1966.

3544. Wakefield, Richard R. "A Study of Seasonal Farm Labor in Yakima County, Washington." State College of Washington, 1937.

3545. Weintraub, Hyman. "The IWW in California, 1905–1931." University of California, Los Angeles, 1947.

3546. White, Laura. "Rise of the Industrial Workers of the World in Goldfield, Nevada." University of Nebraska, 1912.

3547. Wilkinson, Charles A. "Anti-German Reaction and Suppression of Dissent in Illinois during World War I." Western Illinois University, 1969.

3548. Wilson, Ione E. "IWW in California with Special Reference to Migratory Labor, 1910–1913." University of California, 1941.

3549. Youngman, W. S. "The Anaconda Copper Mining Company and Some Phases of Its Influence in the Politics of Montana, 1880–1929." Harvard University, 1929.

PRISON SACKS

IF THEY ARE ON THE RANCH

STRIKE!

**UNION MEN ARE
IN SAN QUENTIN
PRISON FOR FROM
ONE TO FOURTEEN
YEARS FOR BEING
LOYAL TO THE WORKING
CLASS**

Pamphlets about the IWW

THERE is always an ulterior motive behind the publishing of a pamphlet. A pamphlet is an opinion given muscle and permanence. The IWW published pamphlets in order to help workers realize where their advantages lay—to show them how an industrial union would serve them better than a craft union. Sometimes a pamphlet would explain an apparent misunderstanding on the part of either the public or the potential member. The usual IWW pamphlet was written to make workers of various kinds realize that their needs as workers might best be met if they joined one powerful union that would, with their help, create a new and better society within the shell of the old. Some pamphlets, it was hoped, would arouse protest from the public over injustices and illegalities that undoubtedly occurred. Already there are collectors of IWW pamphlets, and many on the following lists have become collectors' items.

Pamphlets published by groups other than the IWW are represented in the first section. These are pamphlets supporting, opposing, or commenting on IWW-related matters. They represent other viewpoints, by no means all inimical to the IWW, but not emanating from that organization. The second section is comprised of pamphlets published by the IWW. For the most part, they were written by members of the IWW, or at least by people whose views the IWW espoused.

There are enormous bibliographic difficulties in compiling these two lists. These problems have to do with ordinarily simple features such as author, date, and even publisher. In many cases the pamphlets were intentionally published without dates, in order to give them a greater permanence and a longer bookstall life. Sometimes no publisher was listed. This happened often during the Red Scare, for between 1917 and 1923 many persons were hurled into prison merely for owning some of these pamphlets, to say nothing of publishing, writing, or selling them. It is therefore not surprising that occasionally no author's name was given or that pseudonyms were used. Under the Criminal

Syndicalist laws, writing or publishing certain materials was a crime with severe penalty. Which one of us would not hesitate to face years in a state or federal penitentiary?

Sometimes the author's name might be included in an early edition of a pamphlet but omitted in later ones. The author may have become antagonistic, reactionary, inactive, or irrelevant; thus, his name was left out of later printings. An example of this is the work of William E. Trautmann, who went over to the Detroit faction but left some pamphlets that seemed to go on without him.

Often pamphlets were reissued with different covers, different illustrations, or different titles, but were the same or partly the same within. In this listing, some pamphlets appear twice in different ways of listing; not every edition is so noted.

Foreign-language pamphlets have been omitted from this list. In most cases they were simply translations of the most popular pamphlets, especially IWW-published pamphlets. There are important collections of foreign-language pamphlets at the New York Public Library, at New York University's Tamiment Library, at the U. S. Department of Labor Library, and at the Walter P. Reuther Library, to mention only the places known to me.

Annotations in this two-part section have been kept to a minimum. They are used to point out the contents of items that may be of interest or to explain the contents of pamphlets with unrevealing titles. Pamphlets that I have seen listed and that I know exist, but that I have not been able to read or read about, are simply listed without further comment. I hope that the IWW chronology included in this volume may be helpful in some of these cases.

I was sometimes unable to give the number of pages in a pamphlet or leaflet. Sources do not always tell the number of pages, and there are apparently some that count the actual text and others that count the advertising and the covers; there is a lot of room for variations, so a pamphlet cannot be known for its pages any more than for its cover.

When either the publisher or the place of publication is missing (in some cases, both are unavailable), the notation "n.p." is used. The notation "n.d." means that no date appears on the pamphlet. Some dates are my approximations, based on evidence in the pamphlets. These appear in parentheses with a question mark.

Because some pamphlets are particularly hard to find (often they are in archives rather than libraries) a location symbol appears at the far right-hand side of the entry. These symbols represent libraries or archives where the particular pamphlet may be found, although not necessarily the only place. The key to the locations is at the front of this book. Some pamphlets can be found in microfilmed collections. An example of such a source is:

Pamphlets in American History, Group II. A Bibliographic Guide to the Microfilm Collection. Edited by Lisa A. Derfler and Duane R. Bogenschneider. Sanford, NC: Microfilm Corporation of America, 1982.

As in most catalogs, entries for the National Civil Liberties Board and the American Civil Liberties Union are combined under the latter name. They are historically the same organization.

Pamphlets Not Published by the IWW

3550. *An Address Setting Forth the Objectives of the Citizen's Alliance of Helena.* Helena, MT: n.p., 1903, n.p.
A plan to combat any kind of labor unionism that might appear in Helena.

3551. *Address to International Labor Organizations.* n.p., 1914, n.p.
WFM spokesman urges all unionists to combat the encroaching IWW organizers.

3552. Allen, E. J. B. *Revolutionary Unionism.* London: Industrialist League, 1909, n.p.
An English view of the new kind of unionism. NcD

3553. American Civil Liberties Union. *American Deportation and Exclusion Laws: Report Submitted by Charles Recht, Counsel, to the New York Bureau of Legal Advice.* New York: NCLB, 1919, 33 p. NN

3554. ———. *Another Police Outrage.* Los Angeles: ACLU, n.d. (1924?), 4 p.
Police brutality against IWW members and their children at San Pedro. MiDW-A

3555. ———. *California Attacked by One of Her Own Laws!* San Francisco: California Committee, ACLU, n.d. (1925?), 8 p.
Quotations from dozens of respected citizens opposing California's Criminal Syndicalist law. MiDW-A

3556. ———. *California Justice.* Los Angeles: ACLU, 1923, 4 p.
Deplores the Syndicalist law and the trials. MiDW-A

3557. ———. *Civil Liberty Issues before Congress.* New York: ACLU, 1926, 4 p.
A list of bills that should be killed or amended. MiDW-A

3558. ———. *Civil Liberty Since the Armistice.* New York: ACLU, 1926, 4 p.
Attacks on civil liberties from 1918 to 1926.

3559. ———. *The Conviction of Mrs. Kate O'Hare and North Dakota Politics.* New York: NCLB, 1918, 12 p.
Spite over politics between the Democrats and the Non-Partisan League was a factor in O'Hare's conviction. MiDW-A

3560. ———. *Do We Need More Sedition Laws? Testimony of Alfred Bettman and Swinburne Hale.* New York: ACLU, 1920, 22 p.
Testimony before a House committee by two respected ex-officers of the government, who oppose harsher laws. MiDW-A

3561. ———. *Education! Organization!* Centralia, WA: ACLU, 1923, 4 p.
Call to a mass meeting supporting freedom of speech at Centralia. MiDW-A

3562. ———. *Federal Political Prisoners Still in Prison.* New York: ACLU, 1922, n.p.
Even four years after the war, there are still many political prisoners. MiU

3563. ———. *The Fight for Civil Liberty, 1927–1928.* New York: ACLU, 1928, 72 p.
All instruments of oppression have been strengthened. Many strikes have been dealt with by these instruments. MiDW-A

3564. ———. *The Fight for Civil Liberty, 1928–1929.* New York: ACLU, 1929, 48 p.
Strikers, radicals, and Negroes have been the chief victims of repression. MiDW-A

3565. ———. *The Fight for Free Speech.* New York: ACLU, 1921. 31 p.
Review of the travail of civil liberties during an especially difficult year. IU

3566. ———. *Free Speech in 1924.* New York: ACLU, 1925. 46 p.
Most prosecutions in 1924 were against IWW members, and most took place in California. MiDW-A

3567. ———. *Free Speech, 1925–1926.* New York: ACLU, 1926, 47 p.
Intolerance is still significant, and many cases were brought against strikers. Many petty prosecutions against the IWW were discovered. MiDW-A

3568. ———. *"Good and Religious Men"; Statements of Army Officers, Religious Organizations, Labor Organizations, and Statement Regarding Conscientious Objectors.* New York: NCLB, 1919, 3 p. OO

3569. ———. *A History of the Miners' Struggle in Harlan and Bell Counties.* New York: ACLU, 1932, 19 p. MiU

3570. ———. *Hysteria or Common Sense.* New York: ACLU, 1919, n.p.
Red Scare violations of civil liberties.

3571. ———. *In Defense of Our Liberties.* New York: ACLU, 1944, 79 p.
Freedom during wartime. MiDW-A

3572. ———. *The Individual and the State; The Problem as Presented by the Sentencing of Roger W. Baldwin.* New York: NCLB, 1918, 14 p. Or

3573. ———. *The Issues in the Centralia Murder Trial.* New York: ACLU, 1920, 8 p. MiU

3574. ———. *The Kentucky Miners' Struggle: The Record of a Year of Lawless Violence, the Only Complete Picture of Events Briefly Told.* New York: ACLU, 1932, 23 p. NN

3575. ———. *The "Knights of Liberty" Mob and the IWW Prisoners at Tulsa, Oklahoma, November 9, 1917.* New York: NCLB, February, 1918, 16 p.
How seventeen IWWs were lynched, whipped, tarred, and feathered by vigilantes with an apparent oil-company connection. MiDW-A

3576. ———. *The Law of the Debs Case. Constitutional Construction by the Supreme Court.* New York: ACLU, n.d. (1919?), n.p. OO

3577. ———. *Memorandum Concerning Political Prisoners within the Jurisdiction of the Department of Justice in 1919.* New York: ACLU, 1919, n.p. MH-L

3578. ———. *Memorandum Regarding the Persecution of the Radical Labor Movement in the United States.* New York: NCLB, 1919, 8 p.
Attacks on the IWW were not so much "patriotic" as anti-labor. MiDW-A

3579. ———. *Mob Violence in the United States: The Striking Facts in Brief Presented by the American Civil Liberties Union.* New York: ACLU, 1923, 4 p.
Government actions during and after the Palmer Raids. OO

3580. ———. *Mob Violence on the Rampage.* Los Angeles: ACLU, n.d. (1924?), 4 p.
The lynching of IWWs and police brutality in San Pedro.

3581. ———. *The Nation-Wide Spy System, Centering in the Department of Justice: Facts Showing the Enormous Recent Growth of a Government Secret Police System Engaged in Espionage, Intimidation, Propaganda and Provocative Acts.* New York: ACLU, n.d. (1920?), 15 p. NN

3582. ———. *Ol' Rags an' Bottles.* New York: NCLB, 1919, 8 p.
The IWW trial at Sacramento, California, and the unusual "silent defense." MiDW-A

3583. ———. *Open Letter to the President, Together with Memorandum Showing Interference by Federal Agents with the Operation of the General Defense Committee of the Industrial Workers of the World.* New York: ACLU, 1918, 3 p. NN

3584. ———. *The Operation of the Criminal Syndicalism and Sedition Laws, with Arguments for Their Repeal.* New York: ACLU, 1933, 14 p. Or

3585. ———. *Outrage on Rev. Herbert S. Bigelow of Cincinnati, Ohio (October 28, 1917.)* New York: NCLB, 1918, 16 p.
The brutal beating of the Reverend Bigelow was the result of his fight against the big utility companies, not his alleged pacifism. MiDW-A

3586. ———. *Persecution of the I.W.W.* New York: ACLU, 1921, n.p. NNU-T

3587. ———. *The Police and the Radicals: What 88 Police Chiefs Think and Do about Radical Meetings.* New York: ACLU, 1921, 11 p. MH

3588. ———. *Political Prisoners by States.* New York: ACLU, 1924, 3 p. OO

3589. ———. *Political Prisoners in Federal Military Prisons.* New York: NCLB, 1918, 21 p.
Conditions and treatment of prisoners. DLC, MiDW-A

3590. ———. *Railroading Workers to the Penitentiary.* Los Angeles: ACLU, n.d. (1925?), 4 p.
How some Syndicalist law prisoners won their appeals. MiDW-A

3591. ———. *The Record of the Fight for Free Speech in 1923.* New York: ACLU, 1924, 39 p. MiDW-A

3592. ———. *Report upon the Illegal Practices of the United States Department of Justice.* New York: ACLU, 1920, 67 p. NN

3593. ———. *Restore the Rights of Citizenship to the 1500 Espionage Act Victims!* New York: ACLU, 1928, 12 p.
Plea for political prisoners ten years after the war. MH

3594. ———. *The Right to His Day in Court: Shall Lawyers Defend Those Deemed to be Adversaries of Our Government?* New York: NCLB, 1918, 11 p.

3595. ———. *The Shame of Pennsylvania: The Story of How Pennsylvania Leads the States in Police Violence and Brutality, Prosecutions for Opinions and War on Strikers and Radicals.* New York: ACLU, 1928, 24 p. PU, Or

3596. ———. *Since the Buford Sailed: A Summary of the Developments in the Deportations Situation.* New York: ACLU, 1920, 14 p. NcD

3597. ———. *State Political Prisoners.* New York: ACLU, 1924, 8 p.
Nearly all state political prisoners are members of the IWW. Many prosecutions were instigated by local business interests. MiDW-A

3598. ———. *The Story of the Ford Case.* New York: ACLU, 1925, n.p. MH

3599. ———. *A Strike Is Criminal Syndicalism in California.* New York: ACLU, 1931, 12 p. MH

3600. ———. *The Truth about the I.W.W., Facts in Relation to the Trial at Chicago.* New York: NCLB, 1918, 55 p. DLC

3601. ———. *The Truth about the I.W.W. Prisoners.* New York; ACLU, 1922, 47 p.
There was no evidence that the IWW obstructed the war. NN

3602. ———. *Under the Shadow of Liberty.* New York: NCLB, n.d., 1 p. IU

3603. ———. *War on the Colorado Miners: Militia, State Police, Mine Guards, and Courts: All Attack the Rights to Meet, Parade, and Picket.* New York: ACLU, 1928, 11 p. NcD

3604. ———. *War-Time Prosecutions and Violence Involving the Rights of Free Speech and Peaceful Assemblage from April 1, 1917 to May 1, 1918.* New York: NCLB, 1918, 24 p. DLC

3605. ———. *Who Are the Traitors?* New York: NCLB, 1918, 4 p.
Those who incite mob action and vigilantes are hurting America. MiDW-A

3606. ———. *Who May Safely Advocate Force and Violence?* New York: ACLU, 1922, n.p. CU

3607. ———. *Why Should There Be an Amnesty?* New York: 1918, 2 p. NN

3608. ———. *Why Two Governors Freed Political Prisoners.* New York: ACLU, 1923, n.p. NN

3609. ———. *A Year's Fight for Free Speech.* New York: ACLU, 1923, 53 p.
The chief struggles were between the unions and the employers' open-shop drive, and court decisions have impaired the strikers' civil liberties. California alone continues the wholesale prosecution of radicals. MH

3610. American Federation of Labor. *Industrial Unionism in Its Relation to Trades Unionism: Being a Report of the Executive Council of the A F of L to the Rochester, N.Y. Convention, in Which the Subject Is Fairly Presented.* Washington, DC: AFL, 1912, 7 p. NN

3611. American Fund for Public Service. *Report for the Three Years, 1925–1928.* New York: AFPS, 1929, 98 p.
Enumeration of financial aid to various groups, including beleaguered radicals. PBm

3612. Amnesty League. *Free Political Prisoners by Christmas.* Chicago: AL, n.d., 2 p. MiU

3613. Angell, Norman. *Why Freedom Matters.* Chicago: W. B. Lloyd, n.d. (1916?), 62 p.
The importance of preserving civil liberties. The author, a noted British libertarian, thinks political heretics may be the "saviours of society."

3614. Associated Industries of Seattle. *The American Plan: Seattle's Answer to the Challenge of Bolshevism.* Seattle: AIS, 1919, 12 p.
How Seattle's employers deal with their labor problems. Or

3615. ———. *Revolution—Wholesale Strikes; Boycotts; Two Years of Attacks on Seattle Business and Industry Institutes by a Certain Radical Element.* Seattle: AIS, 1920, 16 p.
The only answer is extermination of the IWW. OrU

3616. Association of Unemployed on Direct and Work Relief. *Toward Solving Unemployment.* Cleveland, OH: AUDWR, n.d., 30 p.
A fifteen-point plan to establish workers' control and end the profit system. MiDW-A

3617. Atkinson, Henry A. *The Church and Industrial Warfare: A Report on the Labor Troubles in Colorado and Michigan.* New York: Federal Council of Churches of Christ in America, 1914, 62 p.
Report on the copper and coal strikes, including Calumet-Hecla. NN

3618. Bartholomew, H. E. *Anarchy in Colorado, Who Is to Blame?* Colorado: Bartholomew Publishing Company, 1905, 136 p.
Opinions on the Cripple Creek strike and its causes. DLC

3619. Batdorf, J. W. *The Menace of the I. W. W.; The Remedy through Cooperation and Government Ownership.* New York: Anti-Socialist Press, 1917, 31 p.
State socialism and Batdorf's own "geometric tax plan" as solutions to the problems of concentrated wealth and the IWW. DLC

3620. Batt, Dennis, and Karl Dannenberg. *The Batt-Dannenberg Debate: "Resolved That by Political Action Alone, without the Assistance of the Socialist Industrial Union, the Workers Can Emancipate Themselves."* Detroit, WIIU, 1919, 58 p. WHi

3621. Bellanca, Frank. *Scabs and Scab Agencies: Proven Facts of the Scandalous Scabbism of the I.W.W.* New York: Società Italiana Tipografica, 1916, 39 p.
Accuses IWW members of scabbing during AFL-IWW interunion jurisdictional disputes. NNU-T

3622. Better America Federation of California. *Behind the Veil.* Los Angeles: BAFC, n.d. (1921?), 8 p.
The IWW is a special "department" of Communism. CU

3623. Bittleman, Alex. *From Left-Socialism to Communism.* New York: Workers Library Publishers, 1933, 24 p.
Left-wing Socialists and Musteites are the chief stumbling-blocks in the progress toward communism. MiDW-A

3624. Boote, H. E. *Guilty or Not Guilty?* Sydney, Australia: The Worker Print, n.d., 52 p.
The cases against the IWW in Australia. MiDW-A

3625. Borah, William E. *Address at the Funeral Services of Frank Steunenberg; Delivered by W. E. Borah, Caldwell, Idaho, January 3, 1906.* Caldwell, ID: n.p., n.d., 9 p. NN

3626. ———. *Closing Arguments.* Boise, ID: Statesman Shop, n.d., 49 p.
Excerpt from Borah's closing argument at the first Haywood trial for Steunenberg's murder. IdB

3627. ———. *Political Prisoners: Speech of Hon. Wm. E. Borah, Lexington Theatre. N.Y., March 11, 1923.* Washington, DC: Joint Amnesty Committee, 1923, 11 p.
A plea for amnesty for the many political prisoners. NN

3628. Brotherhood of Railroad Trainmen. *The Truth about the Railroad Strike!* San Jose: BRT, n.d. (1946?), 1 p.
President Truman betrayed the union when he denounced the (IWW-supported) strike. MiDW-A

3629. Brown, Tom. *The British General Strike.* London: Freedom Press, 1943, 16 p.
Ideas of a noted British radical whose writings influenced the IWW. MiDW-A

3630. ———. *The Social General Strike.* London: C.A. Brock, n.d., 15 p. MiDW-A

3631. ———. *Trade Unionism or Syndicalism?* London: Freedom Press, 1942, 23 p.

3632. Bruere, Robert W. *Following the Trail of the I.W.W.* New York: New York Evening Post, 1918, 39 p.
Unusually favorable short history of the IWW. NNU-T

3633. Budgen, F. S., and L. Cotton. *Craft Unionism versus Industrial Unionism.* New York: National Executive Committee, Socialist Labor Party, 1922, 32 p. NN

3634. Bureau of Industrial Research. *Syndicalism and Industrial Unionism: A Bibliography Compiled by the Bureau of Industrial Research.* New York: BIR, 1920, 18 p. NN

3635. Callender, Harold. *The Truth about the IWW.* New York: Masses Publishing Company, 1917, 16 p.
The powerful and vengeful forces arrayed against the IWW and a portrayal of the character and family life of some IWW leaders. NN

3636. Campbell, T. E. *The Industrial Battles of 1917.* n.p., 1918, n.p.

3637. Cannon, James P. *The I.W.W.: The Great Anticipation.* Pioneer Pocket Library No. 4. New York: Pioneer Publishers, 1956, 33 p.
Fiftieth anniversary review of the IWW from a Communist viewpoint. MiDW-A

3638. Carmichael, N. *Some Factors Bearing on the Wage Question in the Clifton-Morenci-Metcalfe District.* Clifton, AZ: n.p., 1917, n.p.

3639. Carney, Jack. *Mary Marcy.* n.p, n.d. (1923?), 15 p.
Memorial tribute to the liberal activist. MiDW-A

3640. Cascaden, Gordon. *Crimes of Capital.* Detroit: Workers Defense League, n.d. (1919?), 4 p.
Efforts to halt the progress of the labor movement, citing the Everett Massacre as an example. Similar to no. 4001.

3641. ———. *Shall Unionism Die? "Red" Union International Congress Meeting in Moscow, Russia, Plans Division of Workers of Canada and the United States and Destruction of World Wide Labor Movement: Report by G. Cascaden.* Windsor, Ont.: n.p., 1922, 96 p.
An answer to the plea of the RTUI. NN, DLC

3642. Chafee, Zechariah. *California Justice.* Los Angeles: California Branch, ACLU, 1923, 4 p.
Criminal Syndicalist laws as real threat to civil liberties.

3643. Cheyenne. *Here I Go Again: Another Statement by Cheyenne.* Chicago: published by the author, n.d. (1971?), 4 p.
IWW policies have led to its decline, with little hope for its revitalization. MiDW-A

3644. *Citizens of Pennsylvania! Free Speech! Free Assemblage! The Right of the Workers To Organize, To Strike, and To Picket! This Is Your Fight!* Pittsburgh, PA: National Committee for Organizing Iron and Steel Workers, n.d., 2 p.
The steel trust is behind the arrests of union workers, and the rights of workers are being violated.

3645. Collins, Peter W. *The Truth about Socialism.* n.p., 1919, n.p.
Socialism and IWWism seen as unpatriotic. NN

3646. ———. *Triplets of Destruction: Bolshevism, IWWism, Socialism.* n.p., 1919, 16 p. NN

3647. Colorado Mine Operators Association. *The Criminal Record of the Western Federation of Miners: Coeur d'Alene to Cripple Creek.* Colorado Springs, CO: CMOA, 1904, 32 p. NjP

3648. A Colorado Wage Slave. *Behind the Scenes, Where Passes and Strike-Breaking Militia Kiss: A Scathing and Documentary Indictment of the Capitalist Class and Its Officials from Government Down.* New York: Labor News Press, 1904, 61 p. InU

3649. Communist Labor Party. *Communist Labor Party of Ohio: Letter to Comrades.* n.p., CLPO, 1919, n.p.

3650. ———. *Platform and Program: Communist Labor Party.* n.p., CLPO, n.d., 2 p.

Propaganda partly aimed at the Detroit Branch IWW.

3651. Communist International. *To the IWW: A Special Message from the Communist International (Moscow).* Melbourne, Australia: Proletarian Publishing Assn., 1920, 12 p.

Invites the IWW to join the Communist International. See no. 3931.

3652. Congress of Industrial Organizations. *The Case for Industrial Organization.* Washington, DC: CIO, 1936, 48 p.

An older plan with new arguments. MiDW-A

3653. ———. *Industrial Unionism; The Vital Problem of Organized Labor.* Washington, DC: CIO, 1935, 32 p. IU

3654. Connolly, James. *Socialism Made Easy.* Chicago: Charles H. Kerr, 1909, 61 p.

Written by the famous Irish rebel while a member of the IWW. Socialism and industrial unionism will solve labor's problems. MiDW-A

3655. Copper Country Commercial Club. *Strike Investigation by the Committee of the Copper Country Commercial Club of Michigan, 1913.* Chicago: M.A. Donohue & Co., 1913, 85 p.

Commercial Club finds militant unionism the cause of the troubles. DLC

3656. Council of Workers, Soliders and Sailors. *America for the Americans: The American Kaisers Must Go. An Appeal to All Discharged Soldiers, Sailors and Workingmen.* n.p.: CWSS, n.d. (1919?), 4 p.

Urges veterans to help the workers fight for control of the government by workers rather than by big business. MiDW-A

3657. Crosswaith, Frank R., and Alfred Baker Lewis. *True Freedom for Negro and White Labor.* New York: Negro Labor News Service, n.d., 60 p.

The prejudice faced by Negroes in the 1920s, with a historical summary of black labor history. MiDW-A

3658. Curran, Joseph. *Open Letter to All Seamen: Just One Big Union for Two.* New York: NMU, n.d. (1938?), 4 p.

The conflict between the CIO and AFL maritime workers, similar to earlier AFL-IWW disputes.

3659. Dannenberg, Karl. *The Road to Power, or the Constructive Elements of Socialism.* Detroit: Literature Bureau of the WIIU, 1919, 33 p.
Classic old Socialist tract admired by many IWWs. NN

3660. Darrow, Clarence. *Crime and Criminals. Address Delivered to Prisoners in the Chicago County Jail.* Chicago: Charles H. Kerr, 1919, 32 p. MiDW-A

3661. Debs, Eugene V. *Class Unionism.* Chicago: Charles H. Kerr, 1909, 32 p. NNU-T

3662. ———. *Craft Unionism.* n.p., n.d., 29 p. NNU-T

3663. ———. *Industrial Unionism.* Chicago: Charles H. Kerr, 1909, 32 p.
A speech given by Debs, December 10, 1905. CSt

3664. ———. *Industrial Unionism.* New York: New York Labor News, 1911, 22 p.
Same speech as in no. 3663. NN

3665. ———. *Revolutionary Unionism.* Chicago: Charles H. Kerr, 1909, 27 p. NN

3666. ———. *Unionism and Socialism: A Plea for Both.* Terre Haute, IN: Standard Pub. Co., 1904, 44 p. IU

3667. Debs, Eugene V., and C. E. Russell. *Danger Ahead for the Socialist Party in Playing the Game of Politics.* Chicago: Charles H. Kerr, n.d., 32 p. MH

3668. Debs, Eugene V., et al. *Unionism, Industrial and Political.* Chicago: Charles H. Kerr, 1909, n.p. NNC

3669. Debs Centennial Committee. *Eugene Victor Debs (1855–1955). The Centennial Year.* New York: DCC, 1956, 53 p.
Tributes to Debs from many individuals. MiDW-A

3670. De Leon, Daniel. *As to Politics.* New York: Socialist Labor Party National Executive Committee, 1915, 78 p. NNU-T

3671. ———. *Industrial Unionism.* New York: New York Labor News Co., 1918, 22 p. CST-H

3672. ———. *Industrial Unionism. Selected Editorials.* New York: New York Labor News Co., 1944, 79 p. CSt-H

3673. ———. *The Preamble of the Industrial Workers of the World; Address at Minneapolis, July 10, 1905.* New York: New York Labor News Co., n.d., 48 p. NNU-T

3674. ———. *Reform or Revolution.* New York: Industrial Union Party, 1934, 32 p. MiDW-A

3675. ———. *Socialist Reconstruction of Society. The Industrial Worker.* New York: New York Labor News Co., 1947, 66 p. MiDW-A

3676. ———. *Unity. An Address Delivered by Daniel De Leon at New Pythagoras Hall, N.Y., February 21, 1908.* New York: New York Labor News Co., 1914, 28 p. MiDW-A

3677. Doherty, Robert E. *Thomas J. Hagerty, the Church and Socialism.* Ithaca, NY: New York State School of Industrial Relations, Cornell University, n.d., 17 p. Reprint of a 1962 article. See no. 927.

3678. Dunn, W. C. *The Crime of Centralia.* Butte, MT: published by the author, n.d. (1920?), 16 p.

The handling of this incident was a crime, especially the victimization of Elmer Smith. MiDW-A

3679. Easley, Ralph M. *After the War Problems. No Bolshevik Revolution in America after War; Overwhelming and Sane Forces of Organized Labor Will Prevent Revolutionary Overturning of Order.* New York: n.p., 1918, 21 p. NN

3680. Ebert, Justus. *American Industrial Evolution—From the Frontier to the Factory, Its Social and Political Effects.* New York: New York Labor News Co., 1907, 88 p. DLC

3681. ———. *Trades Unionism in the United States—1742–1905, Bulwark of Capitalism or Framework of Socialism?* New York: New York Labor News Co., n.d., 26 p. MiDW-A

3682. Edgerton, Alice. *Liberty in Wartime: The Issue in the United States Today in the Light of England's Experience.* New York: Evening Post, 1917, 8 p.

An ironic comparison in which the U.S. comes second to England in civil freedoms. MiDW-A

3683. Edwards, Robert. *Economic Revolution.* Yellow Springs, OH: Institute for the Solution to Social Problems, n.d. (1967?), 4 p.

Control of the economy possible for workers who support one another. MiDW-A

3684. Ernest, Gifford. *William Z. Foster—Fool or Faker?* Chicago: Gifford Ernest, 1923, 16 p.

Fears that Foster cannot be trusted. MiDW-A

3685. *Ettor-Giovannitti Jury to be Drawn from a Hostile Class.* Lawrence, MA: Defense Committee, n.d. (1914?), 4 p. MiU

3686. Evans, L. O. *Butte Troubles, 1917. Address before the Chamber of Commerce at Missoula, Montana, Wednesday, August 29, 1917.* Butte, MT: McKee Prtg. Co., 1917, 29 p.
Most troubles caused by the IWW. NN

3687. Executive Committee of the General Labor Union. *Unity in Action.* New York: GLU, 1932, 16 p. NNU-T

3688. Executive Committee of the New England Civil Liberties Committee, John S. Codman, Chairman. *Facts about the Haywood Meeting.* n.p., n.d., 1 p.

3689. Federal Council of Churches of Christ in America. Dept. of the Church and Social Service. *The Centralia Case: A Joint Report on the Armistice Day Tragedy at Centralia, Washington, November 11, 1919.* New York: Brooklyn Eagle Press, 1938, 48 p. NN

3690. ———. *Labor Sunday Message, 1923, of the Commission on the Church and Social Service, and Review of the Year, 1922–1923.* New York: FCCCA, 1923, 47 p.
Review of court decisions, injunctions, and boycotts. MiDW-A

3691. ———. *Report on the Industrial Situation Revealed by the Lawrence Strike.* New York: FCCCA, 1914, 7 p. MH-AH

3692. ———. *Report on the Strike in the Textile Mills of Lawrence, Massachusetts.* New York: FCCCA, 1920, 24 p. DL

3693. Ferrero-Sallitto Defense Committee. *Fight against Deportation; Free Ferrero and Sallitto. Demand the Right of Political Asylum; Deportation Is a Weapon against Liberty.* New York: FSDC, 1936, 16 p.
A cause in which the IWW was active. Ferrero and Sallitto were Italian anti-Fascists being deported to Italy, where they could expect to be victimized by the Mussolini government.

3694. Fisher, Mark. *Evolution and Revolution.* Chicago: Chas. H. Kerr, n.d., 61 p. OO

3695. Flynn, Elizabeth Gurley. *Debs, Haywood and Ruthenberg.* New York: Workers Library Publishers, 1939, 48 p.
Flynn's recollections of three radicals who were her personal friends. MiU

3696. ———. *Memories of the Industrial Workers of the World.* Occasional Paper No. 24. New York: American Institute for Marxist Studies, 1977, 40 p. NN

3697. *For Labor's Martyrs.* n.p., n.d., 1 p. NNU-T

3698. Ford, Earl C., and William Z. Foster. *Syndicalism.* Chicago: W. Z. Foster, 1912, 47 p.
Syndicalism and Socialism cannot ever coincide; a call for political action. MiDW-A

3699. Ford Employees Committee. *From the Ford Men to the Ford Motor Company.* Detroit: FEC, 1921, 1 p.
A call for serious collective bargaining.

3700. Foster, William Z. *Industrial Unionism.* New York: Workers Library, 1936, 46 p. DLC

3701. ———. *Organize the Unorganized.* Chicago: Trade Union Education League, 1925, 20 p. NN

3702. Foster, William Z., and Herman F. Titus. *Insurgency: The Economic Power of the Middle Class. A Discussion between Wm. Z. Foster, Member of the IWW, Now in Europe, Former Spokane Correspondent of "The Workingman's Paper," and the Editor, Herman F. Titus.* Seattle: Trustee Pub. Co., 1910, 14 p. DL

3703. *Four Hour Day—Fourteen Reasons.* New York: Franklin Titus, 1919, 4 p.
Reasons for shortening the work day, notably to relieve unemployment. MiDW-A

3704. Freeman, A. A. *Bolsheviki, IWWs, Labor Unions, Strikes, et id genus omne.* Victoria, BC: published by the author, 1920, 11 p.
No government employee should belong to a labor union, nor should he go on strike. MiDW-A

3705. Fry, E. C. *Tom Barker and the IWW.* Canberra: Australian Society for the Study of Labour History, 1965, 39 p.
A historical summary of Barker's life as an IWW. MiDW-A

3706. Furuseth, Andrew. *The Shipowners and the IWW.* San Francisco: Pacific District Unions, ISUA, n.d., 15 p.
Includes an analysis of the IWW Preamble, which the author characterizes as "birdlime." MiDW-A

3707. Fusfeld, Daniel R. *The Repression of Radical Labor, 1877–1918.* Chicago: Charles H. Kerr, 1979, 64 p.

A historical summary of how labor has been repressed by big business in cooperation with the government. MiDW-A

3708. Gannes, Harry. *Kentucky Miners Fight.* New York: Workers International Relief, 1932, 32 p.
Describes the poverty-stricken condition of miners in 1931–1932 and many occurrences of violence by company-paid thugs. MiDW-A

3709. General Relief Committee, Textile Strikers. *The Textile Strike of 1926: Passaic, Clifton, Garfield, Lodi, New Jersey.* n.p., n.d. (1926?), 16 p.
The circumstances of the strike and the many factions participating in it, as well as the companies' responses to the strike. MiDW-A

3710. George, Alex. *Why the AWU Cannot Become an Industrial Union.* Sydney, Australia: n.p., n.d., n.p.
The fight for industrial unionism in Australia.

3711. Giovannitti, Arturo. *Giovannitti's Address to the Jury.* Boston: Boston School of Social Science, 1913, 12 p.
Giovannitti's famous impassioned speech, his first in English, in which he denies any violent activities and declares that workers' progress cannot be prevented. MiU

3712. Goldman, Emma. *Patriotism: A Menace to Liberty.* New York: Mother Earth, 1908; 16 p.
The process of demanding lip service to patriotism deprives some citizens of their civil liberties. DLC

3713. ———. *Syndicalism, the Modern Menace to Capitalism.* New York: Mother Earth, 1913, 14 p. NjP

3714. Goldman, Emma, and Alexander Berkman. *Deportation, Its Meaning and Menace; Last Message to the People of America.* New York: M. Fitzgerald, 1919, 31 p.
Deported dissenters will be leaving a country that has, not more freedom, but less. DLC

3715. Goodwin, Ginger; Frank Rogers, and Romeo Alba. *They Died for Their Class! Labor Martyrs and B.C. History.* Vancouver, BC: M. E. Publishers, n.d. (1965?), n.p.
The many occasions when strikers became martyrs because of persecution by government and big business. MiU

3716. Haldemann-Julius, Marcet. *The Amazing Frame-Up of Mooney and Billings.* Girard, KA: Haldemann-Julius, 1931, 113 p. DLC

3717. Harré, T. Everett. *The I.W.W. an Auxiliary of the German Espionage System: History of IWW Wartime Activities, Showing How the IWW Program of Sabotage Inspired the Kaiser's Agents in America.* New York: n.p., 1918, 64 p.

An answer to the pamphlet, *Truth about the IWW,* no. 3600. The author seeks to prove that the IWW and the Socialists are a part of and in the pay of the German government. MiDW-A

3718. Harriman, Job. *Class War in Idaho: The Horrors of the Bull Pen. An Indictment of Combined Capital in Conspiracy with President McKinley, General Merriam and Governor Steunenberg, for Their Crimes against the Miners of the Coeur d'Alenes.* New York: n.p., 1900, 32 p.

Defense of the WFM strikers. ICJ MiU

3719. Hass, Eric. *Socialist Industrial Unionism: The Workers' Power.* New York: New York Labor News Co., 1940, 62 p. DLC

3720. Havel, Hippolyte. *What's Anarchism?* Chicago: Free Society Group, 1932, 20 p. NN

3721. Haywood, William D. *Is Colorado in America?* n.p., published by the author, n.d. (1907?), 1 p.

Question stimulated by his illegal kidnapping. MiU

3722. Haywood, William D., and Frank Bohn. *Industrial Socialism.* Chicago: Charles H. Kerr, 1911, 64 p.

Industrial organization can eventually achieve an industrial republic. MiDW-A

3723. Hillis, Newell D. *A Straight Sermon to Young Men. A Remarkable Statement Showing the Real Issue of the War in Colorado.* n.p., n.d. (1914?), 16 p. Cover note: "Sent out from the office of the Cadillac Motor Company, Detroit, but printed elsewhere."

The 1914 miners' strikes. WHi

3724. *History of Activities of Seattle Labor Movement and the Conspiracy of Employers to Destroy It; and Attempted Suppression of Labor's Daily Newspaper, the Seattle Union Record.* Seattle: Seattle Union Record, 1919, n.p.

Similar to no. 3845.

3725. *History of the American Labor Movement, 1700–1943.* San Francisco: Tom Mooney Labor School, n.d. (1943?), 34 p.

3726. Holmes, John Haynes. *Freedom of Speech and of the Press.* New York: National Civil Liberties Bureau, 1918, 30 p. MiDW-A

3727. *Hot Shots from "The Gateway."* Detroit: John F. Hagan, 1914, 43 p.
Aphorisms about labor and radicals. MiU

3728. Independent Labour Party. *Resistance Shall Grow.* London: ILP, 1964, 34 p.
Citizens will tire of the economic burden under which they have suffered and will revolt. MiDW-A

3729. Industrial Union League. *Industrial Union League Manifesto: Declaration of Principles and Tactics.* Detroit: IUL, n.d., 2 p. MiDW-A

3730. *Industrial Workers: A Clear and Forcible Expose of the Crimes and Policies of the IWW.* Chicago: Bureau American, n.d., n.p.

3731. International Seamen's Union. *Attention, Please!* Philadelphia: ISU, n.d., 8 p.
Warns seamen against joining the IWW.

3732. ———. *Historical Fact. Circ. No. 3.* Philadelphia: Port Committee, ISU, n.d., 1 p. MiDW-A

3733. International Workers Defense League. *Justice and Labor in the Mooney Case.* San Francisco: IWDL, 1919, 31 p. CtY

3734. ———. *Labor Declares War on the California Frame-Up; No Peace until Mooney and Billings Are Granted a New Trial.* New York: IWDL, 1919, 4 p.
Urges a general strike of all labor until Mooney gets a new trial. MiDW-A

3735. ———. *Rank and File Will Strike.* San Francisco: IWDL, 1919, 1 p.
The Mooney case. MiDW-A

3736. International Working Men's Association. *IWMA, Its Policy, Its Aim, Its Principles.* n.p., IWMA, 1933, 18 p.
The workers can gain power by organizing. TxU

3737. Interracial Council of New York. *The Bolshevist Movement in America.* New York: ICNY, 1919, 5 p. NN

3738. Irwin, Inez Haynes. *The Story of the Ford Case: Are Strike Leaders Responsible for Whatever Violence Occurs in a Strike?* New York: American Civil Liberties Union, 1925, 11 p.

3739. *Jersey Justice at Work: First Decision on the Advocacy of Sabotage in the United States Courts.* New York: n.p., 1913, 12 p.
About the case of Frederick Sumner Boyd. WHi

3740. Joint Amnesty Committee. *Free the Political Prisoners.* Washington, DC: JAC, 1922, 4 p. MiDW-A

3741. ———. *Set the Political Prisoners Free.* Washington, DC: JAC, 1922, 4 p. OrU

3742. Jones, W. B. *Appeal from a Kentucky Prison Cell.* New York: n.p., 1931, 1 p.
Asks for clothes and food for the families of imprisoned miners. MiDW-A

3743. Kane, H. F. *Why Eleven Members of the IWW, Imprisoned at Leavenworth, Refused Conditional Pardon.* Reading, PA: published by the author, 1923, 2 p. MiDW-A

3744. Karsner, David. *The I.W.W. Trial.* New York: Irving Kay Davis, 1919, n.p.
The Chicago Trial.

3745. Kavanagh, J. *The Vancouver Island Strike.* Vancouver, BC: BC Miners Liberation League, n.d. (1914?), 16 p.
The 1912–1913 strike on the island and the part played by the provincial government in quelling it and arresting the strikers. CaOTU

3746. Kentucky Miners Defense. *A. F. of L. Convention Urges Pardons for Harlan Miners.* New York: KMD, 1940, n.p. MiU

3747. ———. *Bloody Harlan: The Story of Four Miners Serving Life for Daring to Organize a Union, Daring to Strike, Daring to Picket.* New York: KMD, 1937, 36 p. MiDW-A

3748. ———. *Christmas Pardons for the Harlan Miners.* New York: KMD, n.d., 4 p. MiU

3749. ———. *Free the Harlan Miners by Christmas 1936!* New York: KMD, 1936, 8 p. MiU

3750. ———. *How Much Longer Their Living Death? Four Harlan Miners Serving Life for Loyalty to Labor.* New York: KMD, 1938, n.p. MiU

3751. ———. *Pardon the Harlan Miners.* New York: KMD, 1939, 4 p. MiU

3752. ———. *Seven Harlan Miners Serving Life for Loyalty to Labor!* New York: KMD, n.d., 4 p. MiDW-A

3753. Keracher, John. *Labor-Saving Devices.* Chicago: Proletarian Party, n.d., 15 p.
Labor-saving devices should be called wage-saving devices because they help only the employer and promote unemployment. MiDW-A

3754. King, Carol W. *Deportations: Suggestions to Attorneys Handling Deportations Involving Political or Economic Views and Activities.* New York: American Civil Liberties Union, 1936, 14 p. CtY

3755. Kirchwey, George W. *A Survey of the Workings of the Criminal Syndicalism Laws of California.* New York: American Civil Liberties Union, 1926, 46 p. CU

3756. Kirkpatrick, George R. *Mental Dynamite.* New York, n.p., 1906, 16 p.
Writings against war and for Socialism. MiDW-A

3757. Koelsch, C. F. *Haywood Case.* Boise: Idaho Mining Association, 1946, n.p.
The first Haywood case, in which he was accused of murder.

3758. Kurinsky, Philip. *Industrial Unionism and Revolution.* New York: Modern Press, 1920, 47 p. NN

3759. Labor Defense Council. *The Burns' and Daugherty's Attack upon Labor and Liberty.* Chicago: LDC, 1923, 24 p.
How the U.S. Department of Justice has fought against labor. MH

3760. Labor Defense League of California. *Criminal Syndicalism Law of California.* San Francisco: LDLC, n.d., 2 p. MiDW-A

3761. ———. *Citizens of California.* San Francisco: LDLC, 1921, n.p.
Deplores the California Syndicalist law.

3762. *Labor Scrap Book.* Chicago: Charles H. Kerr, 1918, 31 p.
Various authors on strikes and labor questions.

3763. *Labor Scrap Book—Out of the Shell Hole of War!* Chicago: Charles H. Kerr, n.d. (1917?), 64 p.
Includes many short articles, notably Helen Keller's "On Behalf of the IWW" and James P. Thompson's "Capitalism Breaking Down." MiDW-A

3764. Lampman, Ben Hur. *Centralia—Tragedy and Trial.* Tacoma and Centralia: Joint publication of Grant Hodge Post No. 17, Centralia, and Edward B. Rhodes Post No. 2, Tacoma, WA: American Legion, 1920, 79 p.
The Legion viewpoint on the Centralia affair. MnU

3765. Lane, Winthrop. *Strike at Fort Leavenworth.* New York: National Civil Liberties Bureau, 1919, 8 p.
Participants included IWWs. NjP

3766. ———. *Uncle Sam, Jailor.* New York: National Civil Liberties Bureau, 1919, 8 p.
The Kansas jails in which IWWs were held for nearly two years. One Wichita jail was a revolving metal cage. See no. 4286. MiDW-A

3767. Lanier, A. S. *Justice to the I.W.W.* Chicago: American Freedom Foundation, 1920, 7 p.
Open letter of a former military intelligence officer to the President, deploring the injustices at the Chicago IWW trial. MiDW-A

3768. Lawrence Citizens Association. *Reign of Terror in an American City.* Lawrence, MA: LCA, 1912, n.p.
The Lawrence strike. NN

3769. ———. *Telling the Truth about the Ettor-Giovannitti Case: Taking Exceptions to a Magazine Article Lauding the United Press at the Expense of Lawrence and the Truth.* Lawrence, KS: LCA, 1912, n.p.
Dislikes the publicity Lawrence is getting. NN

3770. League for the Amnesty of Political Prisoners. *Free Our Political Prisoners!* New York: LAPP, n.d., 8 p. MiU

3771. Legere, Ben. *The Futility of Fosterism.* Winnipeg, Manitoba: OBU Bulletin, n.d. (1924?), 31 p. MiU

3772. Leland, Henry. *Industry and Labor Unionism.* Detroit: Round Table Club, 1917, 80 p. MiU

3773. *Letter from Colonel Roosevelt to Felix Frankfurter, Counsel for President Wilson's Mediation Commission in the Mooney Case.* n.p., December 19, 1917, 4 p.
Denies that Fickert should be recalled because of a possibly unjust trial because those demanding the recall are the radical element. "Murder is murder," no matter the cause. The IWW is a criminal organization. MiDW-A

3774. Leval, Gaston. *Social Reconstruction in Spain.* London: Spain and the World, 1938, 36 p.

The collectivization of the textile workers, transport workers, agricultural workers, and others in Spain under the anarchists, of interest to all those looking forward to an industrial workers' government. MiDW-A

3775. Lewis, Austin. *The People of the State of California, Plaintiff and Respondent, vs. Richard Ford, alias "Blackie" Ford, Defendant and Appellant.* n.p., 1914, 63 p.

Ford's trial after the Wheatland Riot. CU-B,DL

3776. Lewis, Austin, and Tom Mann. *Debate: Resolved That Economic Organization Is Sufficient, and Political Action Unnecessary to the Emancipation of the Working Class.* Chicago: Charles H. Kerr, 1914, 80 p. MiDW-A

3777. Lewis, John L. *Industrial Democracy in Steel.* Washington, DC: CIO, 1936, 16 p.

Industrial unionism as the answer to constant labor strife. MiDW-A

3778. Lipzig, James. *Sedition, Criminal Syndicalism, Criminal Anarchy Laws, Their Nature and Operation; the Arguments against Them.* New York: American Civil Liberties Union, 1937, 74 p. IU

3779. ———. *Summary of Arguments against Sedition, Criminal Syndicalism, Criminal Anarchy Laws.* New York: American Civil Liberties Union, 1939, n.p. NN

3780. McEwen, Alan. *Bill to Repeal Syndicalism Law Offered.* San Francisco: American Women's Independent Committee, 1923, 1 p. MiDW-A

3781. McDaniels, Julius, and Dorice McDaniels. *The Unknown Soldier.* Inglewood, CA: published by the authors, n.d., 40 p. Later published by the IWW (see no. 4310).

Short articles and poems by two IWWs, reflecting on revolution and Vietnam. MiDW-A

3782. McPherson, John B. *The Lawrence Strike of 1912.* Boston: Rockwell and Churchill Press, 1912, 46 p. WHi

3783. Magnes, Judah L. *Amnesty for Political Prisoners. Address, April 17, 1919.* New York: National Civil Liberties Bureau, 1919, 23 p. MiDW-A

3784. ———. *The "Raids on Reds" and Our Civil Liberty.* Chicago: American Freedom Foundation, n.d. (1920?), n.p.

3785. Marcy, Mary. *How the Farmer Can Get His.* Chicago: Charles H. Kerr, 1916, 32 p.

Advocates industrial organization for farmers, to help them achieve technological capabilities. MiDW-A

3786. ———. *Industrial Autocracy.* Chicago: Charles H. Kerr and Company Cooperative, 1919, 58 p.

Profit-sharing seen as a scheme to keep workers in line. MiDW-A

3787. ———. *Open the Factories.* Chicago: Charles H. Kerr and Co., n.d. (1920?), 28 p.

In an industrial democracy there would be no unemployment. MiDW-A

3788. Marine Workers Defense Committee. *The Case of Soderbert, Bunker, and Trajer.* New York: MWDC, n.d. (1932?), 4 p.

The marine workers on trial for plotting to dynamite a barge are victims of a spy in the pay of management. It is an attempt to destroy the union.

3789. *Merchant Marines! Heroes! We Salute You! C.N.T.: To Seamen of All Countries. Health.* n.p., National Syndicate of Maritime Transport of Spain, n.d. (1937?), 4 p.

All seamen should boycott and even sabotage Fascist products. MiDW-A

3790. Milwaukee Defense League. *Shall Eleven Innocent Workingmen Perish in Prison?* Chicago: MDL, n.d., 8 p.

3791. *Misconceptions of the IWW.* New York: Labor Defender, 1918, 4 p.

People misunderstand the IWW because they do not distinguish between a political and an industrial system of government. MiDW-A

3792. Minnesota Iron Range Strikers Defense Committee. *The Startling Story of the Minnesota Miners Strike on the Mesaba Range, 1916.* New York: MIRSDC, 1916, n.p. MiU

3793. Mooney Defense of Southern California. *Justice Is Waiting.* San Francisco, MDSC, 1930, 30 p.

Excerpts from newspapers showing popular sentiment that Mooney should be freed. MiDW-A

3794. National Council on Freedom from Censorship. *An Outline History of Post Office Censorship Including 12 Brief Case Histories and 20 Conflicting Types of Court Decisions.* New York: NCFC, 1932, 29 p.

3795. National Popular Government League. *To the American People: Report upon the Illegal Practices of the United States Department of Justice.* Washington, DC: NPGL, 1920, 67 p. DLC

3796. Nearing, Scott. *The One Big Union of Business.* New York: Rand School of Social Science, 1920, 32 p.

The wholesale arrests are an effort to destroy the labor movement. MiU

3797. ———. *Scott Nearing's Address to the Jury.* New York: Rand School, n.d. (1919?), 34 p.

In the United States a tiny minority controls economic affairs, and until this changes the majority will not secure justice. MiDW-A

3798. Nelles, Walter, ed. *Espionage Act Cases with Certain Others on Related Points.* New York: National Civil Liberties Bureau, 1918, 92 p. DLC

3799. ———. *Seeing Red: Civil Liberty and Law in the Period following the War.* New York: American Civil Liberties Union, 1920, 11 p. NN

3800. New England Civic Federation. *Were the Lawrence Strike Funds Honestly Managed?* Boston: NECF, 1913, 16 p. NNC

3801. New York Defense Committee. *The Persecution of the Radical Labor Movement in the United States.* New York: NYDC, 1919, 8 p.

Reprint from a 1918 NCLB pamphlet, *Memorandum Regarding The Persecution of the Radical Movement in the United States.*

3802. ———. *Workers Jailed in Hell Hole; IWW Men 16 Months in Medieval Dungeon without a Trial; Five Die in Prison.* New York: NYDC, 1918, 1 p.

Wichita's Sedgewick County jail and its conditions. MiDW-A

3803. Newbold, J. T. Walton. *The Gang behind the Government: or, Capital's Case for Industrial Unionism.* Glasgow, Scotland: Reformers Bookstall, n.d., 15 p. MiDW-A

3804. Nilsson, B. E. *Political Socialism: Capturing the Government.* Portland, OR: n.p., n.d., 32 p.

3805. Noyes, Alfred. *Beyond the Desert: A Tale of Death Valley.* New York: F. A. Stokes, 1920, 85 p. NN

3806. O'Hare, Kate Richards. *In Prison.* St. Louis, MO: Frank O'Hare, 1920, 64 p.
Her experiences as a political prisoner. MiDW-A

3807. ———. *Kuzbasing in Dixie.* Newllano, LA: n.p., 1923, 24 p.
The Newllano colony commune in Louisiana compared to the IWW colony in Russia. MiDW-A

3808. Olin, J. M. *Review of the Mooney Case: Its Relations to the Conduct in This Country of Anarchists, IWW, and Bolsheviki: Facts That Every True American Should Know.* Madison, WI: J. M. Olin, 1919, 104 p. WHi

3809. *One Big Union—An Outline of a Possible Industrial Organization (with Chart).* Chicago: Charles H. Kerr and Co., 1911, 32 p.

3810. *One Big Union of All the Workers—The Industrial Workers of the World.* Glasgow, Scotland: Wm. Johnston, 1946, 18 p.
Explains the IWW, its organization, and its plans. MiDW-A

3811. Oneal, James. *Sabotage; or Socialism versus Syndicalism: A Critical Study of Theories and Methods.* St. Louis, MO: National Rip-Saw Publishing Company, 1913, 34 p. MiDW-A

3812. *Open Letter from John Golden, President of the UTWA to Striking Employees of the Marston Worsted Mills, Skowhegan, Me.* n.p., n.d., 1 p. MiU

3813. *Pageant of the Paterson Strike, Madison Square Garden, Saturday, June 7, 8:30 P.M.* New York: Success Press, 1913, 30 p. MiDW-A

3814. Palmer, Frank. *Spies in Steel: An Expose of the Industrial War.* Denver: Labor Press, 1928, 62 p. MiDW-A

3815. Passaic General Relief Committee. *Hell in New Jersey: Story of the Passaic Textile Strike Told in Pictures.* Passaic: PGRC, n.d. (1927?), 46 p. MiDW-A

3816. Payne, C. E. *Industrial Government.* Usk, WA: published by the author, 1945, 10 p.
A plan for workers' control of the government. MiDW-A

3817. Peabody, J. H. *Governor Peabody to the Voters: The Colorado Situation Discussed and Misstatement Refuted.* Denver, CO: n.p., 1904, 8 p. WHi

3818. Pegler, Westbrook. *Who Were the Wobblies?* n.p., 1961, 4 p. NNU-T

3819. Petersen, J. C. *Solution of the Labor Problem: How the Workers May Organize and Take Off the Market the Unemployed; How to Get Control of the Jobs.* Butte, MT: Butte Mine Publishing Co., 1912, 46 p.

3820. Petriella, Teofilo. *The Western Federation of Miners on the Mesaba Range: An Address Delivered November 26, 1906, at a Social Entertainment of the Hibbing Mine Workers by Teofilo Petriella, Industrial Workers of the World.* Hibbing, MN: Miners Union No. 155, WFM, 1906, n.p.

3821. Pinto, Vincent. *Soliders and Strikers: Counterinsurgency on the Labor Front, 1877–1970.* San Francisco: United Front Press, 1974, 48 p.
A history of strikes, including McKees Rocks, Lawrence, and others in which the IWW participated, showing how the military has been used to suppress them. MiDW-A

3822. *Plotting To Convict Wheatland Hop Pickers.* Oakland, CA: International Press, 1914, 28 p. CLU, DL

3823. Pouget, Emile. *Sabotage.* Chicago: Chas. H. Kerr, 1913, 128 p.
A history of sabotage and its methods. MiDW-A

3824. Quin, Michael. *The CS Case against Labor: The Story of the Sacramento Criminal Syndicalism Railroading.* San Francisco: ILD, n.d. (1936?), 31 p.
The later Criminal Syndicalism cases in California. CSt-H

3825. *The Red Labor International: Resolutions and Decisions.* Chicago: Voice of Labor, 1921, 96 p. MiDW-A

3826. Republican State Central Committee of Colorado. *Facts as to the Moyer and Other Decisions of the Supreme Court of Colorado.* Denver: RSCCC, 1906, n.p.

3827. Riebe, Ernest. *Crimes of the Bolsheviki.* Chicago: published by the author, 1919, 48 p.
Defends the Russian Bolsheviks and IWW workers, with cartoons and text. MiDW-A

3828. ———. *Mr. Block and the Profiteers.* Chicago: All-American Publishing Company, 1919, 45 p.
Cartoons about Mr. Block, who was reluctant to join the union. MiDW-A

3829. ———. *Twenty-four Cartoons of Mr. Block.* Minneapolis: Block Supply Company, 1912, 27 p. DLC

3830. Ringsdorf, Anna Maley. *Women, a World to Win.* n.p., Socialist Party, n.d., 2 p.

Women may find a place as complete citizens under a Socialist or industrial government. MiDW-A

3831. *Robert Minor, Anarchist and Disloyalist, and His Tender Treatment by the Administration.* n.p., 1919, 4 p.

Objects to the assistance Minor received from the U.S. Government when he was in France. Radicals should not be helped in any way. Probably by the author of nos. 3898 and 3899. MiDW-A

3832. Robertson, James. *Labor Unionism Based upon the American Shop System.* Portland, OR: Keystone Press, 1919, 15 p.

Shop stewards and the One Big Union. DLC

3833. Ross, Charles G. *Sacramento Political Prisoners Not Guilty of Overt Acts.* Washington: Joint Amnesty Committee, 1923, 8 p. MiDW-A

3834. Russell, Bertrand. *Democracy and Direct Action.* London: Independent Labour Party, 1919, 4 p.

This appeared later as an article in *Dial* 66 (May 3, 1919): 445–48.

3835. Sacco-Vanzetti Defense Committee. *The Awakening of America's Conscience.* Boston: SVDC, n.d. (1926?), 4 p.

Many editorial opinions show that many people believe Sacco and Vanzetti are innocent. MiDW-A

3836. Sage of La Jolla [Pseud., Henry Austin Adams]. *History versus Histerics* [sic]: *An Open Letter to the Vigilantes and the IWW.* La Jolla, CA: published by the author, n.d., 8 p. WHi

3837. San Francisco Labor Council. *San Diego's Free Speech Controversy.* San Francisco: SFLC, 1912. 12 p.

The San Diego Free Speech Fight. CLU

3838. Sansom, Philip. *Syndicalism: The Workers' Next Step.* London: Freedom Press, 1951, 45 p.

Because either capitalists or politicians control the means of production, the workers are wage slaves. When they achieve Syndicalism they will be free. MiDW-A

3839. *The Scandal of Mooney and Billings: The Decisions of the California Supreme Court, the Advisory Board, and Governor Young, in Denying*

Pardons to Mooney and Billings. New York: National Mooney-Billings Committee, 1931, 62 p.

3840. Scott, Jack. *Martyrs and Militia.* Vancouver, BC: M.E. Publications, n.d., 36 p.
Strike actions in Western Canada. MiU

3841. Seattle General Strike Committee. *The Seattle General Strike: An Account of What Happened in Seattle, February 6 to 11, 1919.* Seattle: Seattle Union Record, 1919, 63 p. Wa, CSt-H

3842. *The Seattle General Strike.* Charlestown, MA: Bum Press, 1972. Root and Branch Pamphlet No. 5, 76 p.
A reprint, with additions, of no. 3841. MiDW-A

3843. *The Shame of Spokane—Mass Meeting.* Detroit: n.p., 1912, 1 p.
A call to protest the Spokane Free Speech Fight. MiU

3844. Sheils, A. J. *Industrial Unrest: Cause and a Deterrent.* Newark: NJ: Cosgrove's Detective Agency, 1919, 24 p.
Warning against bloody revolution and industrial unrest, such as the IWW causes, and suggestion that good industrial detectives can help the worried businessmen. MiDW-A

3845. Short, William. *History of the Activities of the Seattle Labor Movement and the Conspiracy of Employers To Destroy It, and Attempted Suppression of Labor's Daily Newspaper, the "Seattle Union Record."* Seattle: Washington Federation of Labor, 1919, 69 p.
See no. 3724.

3846. Simons, A. M. *Class Struggles in America.* Chicago: Charles H. Kerr, 1905, 64 p.
A history of the American working class, its difficult legal and social development. MiDW-A

3847. Sinclair, Archie. *Open the Prison Gates.* n.p., n.d., 4 p.
A plea for the release of political prisoners. MiU

3848. Socialist Labor Party. *Debs' Address Supporting IWW, New York, December, 1905.* New York: SLP, n.d. (1908?), 21 p.

3849. ———. *Two Enemies of Labor. The Complaints of the Anarchists.* New York: SLP, n.d., n.p.

3850. Socialist Party of Washington. *Hot Stuff.* Everett, WA: SPW, n.d. (1917?), 4 p.
Urges workers to protest the war and the violence against workers. MiDW-A

3851. Solow, Herbert. *Union-Smashing in Sacramento; The Truth about the Criminal Syndicalism Trial.* New York: National Sacramento Appeal Committee, 1935, 28 p.
The 1935 California Syndicalist trials are, like the earlier ones, an employers' attempt to destroy unions. MiDW-A

3852. Southern California Councils for Constitutional Rights. *On to Sacramento.* n.p.: SCCCR, 1936, 1 p.

3853. Sparks, Nemmy. *The Struggle of the Marine Workers.* New York: International Pamphlets, 1930, 63 p. DLC, OrU

3854. Spector, Frank. *Story of the Imperial Valley.* Pamphlet No. 3. New York: ILD, n.d., 30 p. NN

3855. Steiger, J. H. *Memoirs of a Silk Striker: An Exposure of the Principles and Tactics of the I.W.W.* Paterson, NJ: published by the author, 1914, 128 p. WHi, DLC

3856. *Technocracy and the IWW.* Philadelphia: n.p., n.d., 2 p.
The IWW is "practical technocracy." MiDW-A

3857. Thomas, Norman M. *War's Heretics: A Plea for the Conscientious Objector.* New York: Civil Liberties Bureau of the American Union against Militarism, 1917, 12 p.
Why it is possible that some people are against the war. MiDW-A

3858. *Three Criminal Syndicalism Laws.* n.p., 1919, 1 p.
A comparison of America's Syndicalist laws with those of Russia and Germany, showing America's to be the harshest. MiDW-A

3859. *Throw Them Out!* n.p., 1919, 1 p. MiU

3860. *To All District Organizers, June 17, 1920.* n.p., n.d., 1 p.

3861. Tom Mooney Molders' Defense Committee. *Free Mooney, Labor's Champion, a Class War Prisoner for 18 Years on July 27, 1934: The Victim of a Monstrous Capital Class Frame-Up.* San Francisco: TMMDC, 1934, 1 p. NN

3862. ———. *Governor Young, Pardon Tom Mooney. He Is Innocent.* San Francisco: TMMDC, n.d., 32 p.

3863. ———. *Justice for Tom Mooney, Who Cries Out from His Tomb for Help.* San Francisco: TMMDC, 1932, 6 p. NN

3864. ———. *Labor Leaders Betray Tom Mooney.* San Francisco: TMMDC, 1931, 50 p.

Paul Scharrenberg and the AFL have turned their backs on Mooney and Billings and even worked against their release. MiDW-A

3865. ———. *Workers of America! Free Your Working Class Leaders Rotting in the Bosses' Prisons. Demand Amnesty for Mooney and Billings and the Imperial Valley Organizers.* San Francisco: TMMDC, n.d., 6 p. CU-B

3866. Tompkins, George R. *The Truth about Butte: A Little History for Thoughtful People.* Butte, MT: Century Printing, 1917, 47 p.
A history of Butte's labor problems from the nineteenth century, including an account of the struggle of Miners Union No. 1, the blowing up of the union hall, and the strife between WFM and IWW. MiDW-A

3867. Trainor, Charles E. *A Message to the Membership of the Industrial Workers of the World and the Working Class in General.* Hamtramck, MI: n.p., n.d. (1905?), 4 p.

3868. Trautmann, William E. *Direct Action and Sabotage.* Pittsburgh: Socialist News Co., 1912, 43 p. NcD

3869. ———. *Industrial Union Methods.* Chicago: Charles H. Kerr, 1912, 27 p.
Published in several editions, sometimes with different titles. NN

3870. ———. *Industrial Unionism.* Chicago: Charles H. Kerr, 1909, 29 p. NN

3871. ———. *Industrial Unionism, the Hope of the Workers.* Pittsburgh: Socialist News Co., 1913, 64 p.
Published in several editions, sometimes with different titles. NN

3872. ———. *One Big Union: An Outline of a Possible Industrial Organization.* Chicago: Charles H. Kerr, 1912, 31 p. NN

3873. ———. *One Great Union: The Wage Workers' Means of Education and Defense.* Detroit: WIIU, n.d., 34 p.
Some editions entitled *One Big Union.* MiU

3874. Trautmann, William E., and A. M. Rovin. *War against War.* Los Angeles: n.p., 1915, 46 p. OrU

3875. Trautmann, William E., and A. Schlecweis. *Industrial Combinations.* New York: Industrial Literature Bureau, 1909, 32 p.
The need for industrial unionism. DLC

3876. *The Truth about Lawrence.* Boston: Forward Press, 1919, 32 p. MiU

3877. *The Truth about the Lawrence Police.* Boston: Forward Press, 1919, n.p. MiU

3878. Turner, C. *San Diego Free Speech Fight: A Threat to Property.* n.p., n.d., n.p.

3879. Turner, John Kenneth. *Story of a New Labor Union.* Leaflet No. 16. Portland, OR: Portland Mill Workers Industrial Union, n.d. (1907?), n.p.
About the IWW.

3880. United Cloth Hat, Cap and Millinery Workers' International Union. *Deceit of the I.W.W.: A Year's Record of the Activity of the Industrial Workers of the World in the Cloth Hat and Cap Trade.* New York: UCHCMWIU, 1906, 31 p.
The IWW will destroy the other unions. WHi

3881. ———. *Rule or Ruin Policy of the Industrial Workers. Official Statement of the Capmakers' Union on a Matter of Vital Importance to the American Labor Movement.* New York: UCHCMWIU, n.d., n.p.
The IWW will destroy the Capmakers' Union.

3882. United Mine Workers of America. District 14. *Here is the Resolution of the United Mine Workers Demanding Fair Play for the IWW.* n.p., 1919, n.p.
The IWW is persecuted for organizing, not for radicalism.

3883. United Textile Workers of America. *Bread, Milk, at This Critical Period.* Passaic, NJ: UTWA, n.d. (1925?), 4 p.
The travails of the workers during the Passaic strike. MiDW-A

3884. Varney, Harold L. *Industrial Communism—the I.W.W.* Butte: The Bulletin Print, 1919, 24 p. NN

3885. Veblen, Thorstein. *On the Nature and Uses of Sabotage.* New York: Dial, 1919, 21 p. MH

3886. *Veritas.* Denver: Smith Brooks Press for the Republican Party, 1906, n.p.

3887. Vorse, Mary Heaton. *Passaic.* Chicago: ILD, n.d. (1927?), 24 p.
The 1926 Passaic textile strike. MiDW-A

3888. ———. *The Passaic Textile Strike, 1926–1927.* Passaic: General Relief Committee of the Textile Strikers, 1927, 125 p. MiU

3889. *A Wage and Price Freeze for Canada? Why the IWW Says No!* Vancouver, BC: Mother Earth Publications, 1972, n.p. MiU

3890. Walklin, Frank. *A Fair Trial? A Record of the Prejudice and Passion That Dominated the Legal Profession and the Press in the Famous Centralia Labor Case.* n.p., 1920, 15 p. OrU

3891. Warbasse, James Peter. *The Effects of War on a Nation.* Brooklyn, NY: n.p., 1915, 2 p.
The danger of violating civil rights. NN

3892. ———. *The Ethics of Sabotage.* New York: NY Call, 1913. 12 p. DLC

3893. Warren, Fred D., comp. *People's College Edition of the Report of the Industrial Relations Commission.* Fort Scott, KA: People's College, n.d., 64 p.
A condensed version of the report showing the wrongs done to labor. MiDW-A

3894. *Watch for a Call of General Strike To Free All Class War Prisoners.* Klamath Falls, OR: n.p., 1923, 1 p.

3895. Wedge, Frederick R. *Inside the IWW, by a Former Member and Official: A Study of the Behavior of the IWW with Reference to Primary Causes.* Berkeley: F. R. Wedge, 1924, 48 p.
An extremely unfavorable report of IWW activities. DLC

3896. Weinstock, Harris. *Shall Free Speech Be Restricted?* Berkeley, CA: n.p., 1912, 12 p. PP

3897. *Wellman's Indictment of Moyer, Haywood, and the Western Federation of Miners.* New York: Herald, 1904, 15 p.

3898. Welsh, Francis Ralston. *An Illustrative Crime of the American Federation of Labor, and Notes on the Interrelations of Anarchists and the United States and AFL Officials.* n.p., n.d. (1922?), 64 p. NN

3899. ———. *Some Camouflaged IWW and Their Political Friends.* n.p., n.d., 2 p.
Anyone who defends the IWW must be a Wobbly himself. See also no. 3831. MiDW-A

3900. Western Federation of Miners. *Their Only Crime, Loyalty to the Working Class.* Denver: WFM, 1906, 1 p. CU-B

3901. Whitaker, Robert. *Radio Address of Reverend Robert Whitaker, Nov. 21, 1934.* San Francisco: International Labor Defense, n.d. (1934?), n.p. MiU

3902. Willock, Harry H. *Unused Democracy.* Portland, OR: Oregon Labor Press, 1919, 10 p.

Industrial democracy can be achieved by political democracy and public ownership of all excess land. NN

3903. Wilson, Walter. *The American Legion and Civil Liberty.* New York: American Civil Liberties Union, 1936, 32 p.

3904. Woehlke, W. V. *I.W.W.: A Sketch of the Industrial Workers of the World.* Cleveland: National Metal Trades Assn., 1912, 16 p. NN

3905. Wolfson, Theresa, and Abraham Weiss. *Industrial Unionism in the American Labor Movement.* New York: League for Industrial Democracy, 1937, 51 p. NN

3906. Wood, F. *Introductory Chapter to the History of the Trials of Moyer, Haywood, and Pettibone.* Caldwell, ID: Caxton Printers, 1931, n.p.

3907. Woodcock, George. *Syndicalism: The Industrial Expression of Anarchism.* San Francisco: Bay Area Anarchists, n.d. (1973?), 2 p.

Modern view of Syndicalism still holding that the means of production should be the property of society, held in common. MiDW-A

3908. Workers' Council of Butte, Montana. *Resolutions on Intervention in Russia.* Butte: WCB, 1919, n.p.

3909. Workers Defense League, Detroit. *Crimes of Capital.* Detroit: WDL, 1917, 4 p. MiU

3910. Workers Defense Union. *Dumb Submission or Deportation?* New York: WDU, 1919, n.p. NN

3911. ———. *Free Your Fellow Workers: Russian Pogroms in America.* New York: WDU, 1919, n.p. NN

3912. ———. *Lumber vs. Labor: Workers! Judge for Yourselves about Centralia.* New York: WDU, 1919, 4 p.

3913. ———. *To the American People: Report upon the Illegal Practices of the United States Department of Justice.* New York: WDU, 1920, 67 p. NN

3914. ———. *Using the Espionage Act To Terrorize Labor: Some Judicial Atrocities.* New York: WDU, 1920, 2 p. MiDW-A, NN

Note: the Detroit Branch, or Detroit Faction, sometimes called the De Leon faction, of the IWW was not the same as the

Industrial Workers of the World, which was the "real" IWW and also had its own Detroit branch. The Detroit Faction changed its name to Workers International Industrial Union in 1916. Some of its earlier publications are included below.

3915. Workers International Industrial Union. *The Cause of Unemployment. How To Remove This Social Crime.* Detroit: WIIU, n.d., 4 p. MiU

3916. ———. *Industrial Unionism: Form, Tactics, and Goals.* Detroit: Detroit IWW, n.d., 4 p. MiU

3917. ———. *Industrial Unionism versus Anarchy and Reform: How the Working Class Can Abolish Wage Slavery.* Hamtramck, MI: H. Richter for Detroit Branch, IWW, n.d., n.p. MiU

3918. ———. *Industrial Workers of the World: One Big Union for All Wage Workers.* Detroit: Detroit Branch, IWW, n.d., n.p. MiU

3919. ———. *Manifesto of Socialist Industrial Unionism, Principles of the Workers' International Industrial Union, Leaflet No. 1.* Detroit: GEB, 1916, 4 p.

The principles and philosophy of the group and how to join it. MiDW-A

3920. ———. *Metal Workers of America!* Detroit: Detroit Branch, IWW, n.d., 4 p. MiU

3921. ———. *The Mines to the Control of the Miners!* Detroit: WIIU, n.d. (1919?), n.p. MiU

3922. ———. *Organize Right To Have Might.* Detroit: WIIU, n.d. (1919?), 4 p.

3923. ———. *Preamble of the Workers International Industrial Union.* Detroit: WIIU, n.d. (1916?), 1 p. MiDW-A

3924. ———. *So-Called Socialist versus Capitalist Industrial Unionism.* Detroit: WIIU, n.d., n.p. WHi

3925. ———. *The Textile Industry Controlled by the Textile Workers.* Detroit: IWW, n.d., 2 p. WHi

3926. ———. *The Two IWW's.* Detroit: Detroit Branch, IWW, n.d., n.p.

3927. ———. *We Need the WIIU, the New Union.* Detroit: WIIU, n.d. (1916?), n.p. WHi

3928. *Workers of the World Unite! Comrades and Fellow Workers.* n.p., 1919, 1 p.

3929. Workers Prison Relief Committee of Paterson, New Jersey. *Financial Statement of the Workers Prison Relief Committee of Paterson, N.J., 1922–1923.* Paterson, NJ: WPRCP, 1923, 16 p. MiU

3930. Wright, Morris. *Takes More Than Guns: A Brief History of the International Union of Mine, Mill and Smelter Workers, CIO.* Denver: Press and Education Department, UMMSW, 1944, 18 p.

3931. Zinoviev, G. *Appeal by the Central Executive Board of the Communist International to the I.W.W.* n.p.: GEC of the CPA, 1920, 12 p.
An appeal for the IWW to join the Communists. This is one of many leaflets containing this appeal. MiDW-A

Pamphlets Published by the IWW

3932. *Abajo Franco! A Bas De Gaulle!* Chicago: Spanish Workers Defense Fund, IWW, n.d. (1937?), 1 p.
Franco's repression of trade unionists and De Gaulle's "connivance" with it (in English). MiDW-A

3933. *Address of the Defendant Arturo M. Giovannitti to the Jury.* Chicago: IWW, n.d. (1913?), 12 p.
Giovannitti's famous impassioned speech, in which he denies any violence done by the IWW. Same speech as printed in no. 3711. MiDW-A

3934. *Address of the Defendant Ettor to the Jury.* Chicago: IWW, n.d. (1913?), 12 p.
Heartfelt speech of a leader of the Lawrence strike at his trial. MiDW-A

3935. *Address to Hotel and Restaurant Workers.* New York: IWW, Local 130, 1908, 4 p.
Organizing leaflet describing bad working conditions. MiDW-A

3936. *Address to Colored Workingmen and Women.* Chicago: IWW, n.d., 4 p.
The working conditions of colored workers and the attitude of the IWW toward all workers.

3937. *Address to Railroad Workers.* Chicago: RWIU #520, IWW, n.d. (1919?), 8 p.
Organizing leaflet urging complete racial integration of the union, with an explanation of industrial unionism. MiDW-A

3938. *Address to Wage Workers, by the Industrial Workers of the World.* Industrial Leaflet No. 18. Chicago: IWW, n.d., 4 p.
Organizing leaflet pointing out the disadvantages of craft unionism. MiDW-A

3939. *The A. F. of L. and Industrial Unionism, an Analysis of Raymond Moley's Criticism of Craft Unions, by an Industrial Unionist.* Chicago: GRU, n.d., 8 p.
Predicts that the Wagner Act will bring Fascism and quotes Raymond Moley's arguments against craft unionism. MiDW-A

3940. *After the War.* Chicago: IWW, n.d., 2 p.
Post-World War I pamphlet describing hopes of the IWW to get back to organizing without interference.

3941. *The Age Long Struggle.* San Francisco: CBGDC, 1923, 4 p.
The struggle of right versus wrong continues in California, where Syndicalist prisoners are victims of injustice. MiDW-A

3942. *Agricultural Workers—Attention. Organization. Solidarity. Shorter Hours, More Wages, and Better Conditions.* Chicago: IWW Pub. Bureau, 1918, 4 p.
Organizing leaflet for the AWIU 400 drive. DLC

3943. *Agricultural Workers I.U. #110, Minutes of Convention, New Rockford, N.D.* Chicago: IWW, n.d., n.p.
A portion of the minutes of the union used as an organizing leaflet.

3944. *Agriculture: The Mother of Industry.* Chicago: AWIU #110, IWW, n.d., 4 p.
Farmers are either capitalists or wage workers. Where once they produced "use" values, now they produce "exchange" values. MiDW-A

3945. *Agriculture: The World's Basic Industry and Its Workers.* Chicago: BIR, IWW, n.d. (1921?), 64 p.
History of farming from ancient days to present, describing tenant farming as modern serfdom. MiDW-A

3946. *All Centralia Members of the Industrial Workers of the World: Mass Meeting.* Centralia: IWW, 1919, 1 p. Reprinted by Berkeley Stage Co.
Reproduction of an old Centralia leaflet as part of a stage production in the 1970s. MiDW-A

3947. *American Legion and the Centralia Case.* Chicago: GDC, 1924, 4 p.
Accuses Legionnaires of pocketing some of the Centralia Memorial Fund money. The pamphlet describes how some Centralia jurors changed their minds after the trial. MiDW-A

3948. *American Railway Industry and Its Workers.* Chicago: IWW, 1924, 4 p.
Organizing leaflet discussing the wage cuts after the war and the increased need for industrial organization. MiDW-A

3949. Ameringer, Oscar. *Union Scabs and Others.* New Castle, PA: IWW Pub. Bureau, 1912, 4 p.
Famous and often-quoted characterization of the scab worker. MiDW-A

3950. *Anarchy and Who's To Blame?—Statement of the IWW, October 5, 1912.* Lawrence, MA: City Central Committee #20, IWW, 1912, 1 p.
Lawrence strike leaflet.

3951. *And in the United States Liberty Lies Crushed.* Chicago: GDC, n.d. (1923?), 4 p.
A call for the release of the fifty-three IWW members who are still political prisoners. MiDW-A

3952. *Appeal to Hotel, Restaurant and Domestic Workers.* Chicago: IWW, n.d., 4 p.
Working conditions can be improved only by organizing. MiDW-A

3953. *Appeal to the Nation's Courage.* Chicago: IWW, n.d. (1922?), 4 p.
Appeal for release of Chicago trial prisoners, especially John Panzner, imprisoned because they thought World War I was wrong. Having political prisoners is a disgrace to a free country. MiDW-A

3954. *An Appeal to the Workers in the Electrical Industries from the Schenectady Industrial Council.* Schenectady, NY: IWW, 1906, 4 p.
Early organizing pamphlet, relating to the country's first sit-down strike in Schenectady. MiU

3955. *Are You Going to Stand for It? Note: Only for Discharged Soldiers, Sailors and Marines.* Chicago: IWW, n.d. (1919?), 4 p.
Veterans should not suffer unemployment while war profiteers enrich themselves. MiDW-A

3956. *Are You Inconvenienced by a Strike on the SP Line?* Mountain View, CA: IWW, 1972, 2 p.

The San Pedro railroad would be better operated by the workers. MiDW-A

3957. *Are You Ready?* Buffalo: IWW, n.d. (1935?), 1 p. Westinghouse-Markel, MMWIU #440.
Strike leaflet appealing for solidarity. MiDW-A

3958. *Are You Ready to Defend Your Rights? The Rights Guaranteed to You by the Constitution.* Seattle, IWW, n.d., 4 p.
Call for a general strike. MiDW-A

3959. *Associated Industries of Cleveland, Ohio vs. the Union of Their Slaves.* Cleveland: IWW, 1935, 4 p.
Demands that jailed organizers be freed and that workers have the right to organize. MiDW-A

3960. *Attention Apple Knockr's!* Watsonville, CA: IWW, n.d. (1938?), 1 p.
Apple pickers must organize. MiDW-A

3961. *Attention Coal Mine Workers! The IWW is Coming! Join the One Big Union!* Chicago: IWW Pub. Bureau, n.d. (1917?), 4 p.
The UMWA allows workers to continue mining in one area while another area is on strike, thus creating a scab situation within the union itself. The IWW would strike industry-wide. MiDW-A

3962. *Attention Coal Miners!* CMWIU #220, IWW, 1929, 3 p.
Program and resolutions of CMWIU #220, Collinsville, IL, for industrial organization in coal mines. MiDW-A

3963. *Attention! Direct Mail Workers!* New York: IWW, n.d., 1 p.
Organization leaflet and call to a mass meeting. MiDW-A

3964. *Attention Trade Union Workers.* Chicago: One Big Union Job Committee, IWW, n.d., 4 p.
Craft unionists should join an industrial union and take action "on the job" as well as in the union hall. MiDW-A

3965. Attridge, Elizabeth. *My Findings on the Centralia Case.* Centralia: CPC, 1929, 4 p.
An investigative reporter's summary. MiDW-A

3966. *Auto, Steel, Metal, and Machinery Workers, Shall It Be No Unionism or New Unionism?* Chicago: IWW, n.d. (1930?), 4 p.
Organizing appeal stating that craft unions are outdated. MiDW-A

3967. *Auto Workers! Motor Industry Profits a Half Billion Dollars!* Detroit: IWW, n.d. (1928?), 2 p.
Demand for a seven-hour day and $1.10 an hour. MiDW-A

3968. *Auto Workers: This Is the IWW Way Out.* Detroit: IWW, 1933, 4 p.
Organizing leaflet, pointing to Briggs strikers as an example of what workers must do to share the profits of the "Big Three." MiDW-A

3969. *Be It Resolved: That the Mine Workers of Butte Are Entitled to an Increase in Wages of $1.00 a Day.* Butte: IWW, 1927, 1 p.
Organizing leaflet. MiDW-A

3970. *Better Tactics for a New Problem.* Chicago: IWW, n.d. (1936?), 4 p.
Urges WPA workers to organize. MiDW-A

3971. *Bill To Repeal Syndicalism Offered.* Chicago: IWW, 1923, 1 p.
Some California legislators are attempting to have the Syndicalism law repealed. California has used the law more than any other state. MiDW-A

3972. *Bindle Stiff.* Chicago: IWW, n.d. (1914?), 4 p.
Graphic appeal for migratory lumberworkers to organize and vivid description of lumber camp conditions. MiDW-A

3973. *A Black Page of American History.* Centralia: WA: CPC, n.d. (1920?), 8 p.
The Centralia Massacre. NNU-T

3974. Blossom, Frederick A. *One Enemy, One Union.* Paterson, NJ: TWIU #1000, IWW, n.d. (1919?), 4 p.
Craft unionism delays the solution of working-class problems. MiDW-A

3975. ———. *The Truth about Centralia—Blame the IWW.* Paterson, NJ: CDC, n.d. (1920?), 4 p.
The story of Centralia from the IWW point of view. MiDW-A

3976. *Booklet of Instructions.* Chicago: GDC, IWW, n.d., 11 p.
What to do if arrested. MiDW-A

3977. *The Boss Says No: We Say Yes.* San Francisco: IWW, n.d. (1978?), 2 p.
Workers should join the IWW whether or not the boss agrees. MiDW-A

3978. *Bread Lines or Picket Lines? Take Your Choice.* Chicago: IWW, n.d. (1931?), 4 p.
Militant unionism is the only solution for unemployment. MiDW-A

3979. *Briggs Worker, Here Is What the Murray Strike Means to You.* Detroit: MMWIU #440, IWW, 1933, 4 p.
Organizing leaflet for Briggs workers, referring to the Murray Body strike. MiDW-A

3980. Brissenden, Paul F. *Justice and the I.W.W.* Chicago: GDC, 1918, 32 p.
Protests the unjust arrests and raids on the IWW. NNU-T

3981. *Brothers and Sisters of the ILU, We're with You.* Honolulu: IU #450, IWW, n.d., 2 p.
Support for an ILU strike. MiDW-A

3982. Brown, A. E. *The Case for a Six-Hour Day.* Sydney, Australia: IWW, n.d., 15 p.
Includes St. John's *Industrial Unionism and the IWW* (see no. 4485). MiDW-A

3983. Brown, William Thurston. *The Revolutionary Proletariat.* Chicago: IWW Press, n.d., n.p.

3984. ———. *Will You Have War or Peace? A Plain Question to Modern Capitalist Society.* Chicago: IWW Press, n.d., 32 p.
The "industrial war" between the capitalists and the working class. CSt-H

3985. *Building Construction: A Handbook of the Industry.* Chicago: BCWIU #330, IWW, n.d. (1924?), 40 p.
The "bosses" have "one big union," their association, and the workers need one too, in the form of an industrial union, the IWW. MiDW-A

3986. *Building Workers! Organize Industrially—The Victory Is Certain!* Chicago: BCWIU #330, IWW, n.d. (1922?), 4 p.
The open-shop drive succeeded because the AFL caved in. The shortage of building workers means that this is the time to join the IWW. MiDW-A

3987. *Building Workers We Need a Union: Join the Union of Your Class.* Chicago: BCWIU #330, IWW, n.d., 6 p.
Organizing leaflet. MiDW-A

3988. *Bulletin No. 2. Marine Workers in Philadelphia Appeal to Their Fellow-Workers in Other Ports for Support.* Philadelphia: Publicity Committee, MTWIU #510, IWW, n.d. (1925?), 1 p.
Call for a national general strike of maritime workers to support the Philadelphia union's strike. MiDW-A

3989. *Bulletin No. 5. Appeal to the Seamen.* Philadelphia: Publicity Committee, MTWIU #510, n.d. (1925?), 1 p.
Appeal to seamen of other unions not to scab but to support the strike. MiDW-A

3990. Calese, Robert. *Blackout.* (*Rebel Worker* Pamphlet #2.) New York: IWW, n.d. (1965?), n.p.
Anarchist aspects of the great New York blackout of 1965.

3991. *California in Chains.* California Branch, GDC, n.d. (1923?), 4 p.
California's harsh Syndicalist laws. MiU

3992. *California, the Beautiful and Damned.* Chicago: GDC, IWW, n.d. (1924?), 32 p.
Protests Syndicalist arrests and trials. MiDW-A

3993. *California, Be on Guard!* San Francisco: CDDC, IWW, n.d. (1924?), 4 p.
California will lose its reputation as a decent state because of Syndicalist trials.

3994. *A Call for a Meeting to Protest against the Kidnapping of Moyer, Haywood and Pettybone.* San Francisco: IWW Local 173, 1906, n.p.
Events prior to the Steunenberg trial. (The name of George Pettibone was frequently misspelled.) CU-B

3995. *A Call to Action!* Chicago: IWW, n.d., 2 p.
Organizing leaflet. MiDW-A

3996. *A Call to Action to All Agricultural Workers. Why Work for Gas and Oil for Yourself?* Chicago: IWW, 1936, 4 p.
Organizing leaflet. MiDW-A

3997. *Call to Action—to All Agricultural Workers!* AWIU #110, IWW, n.d., 2 p.
Organizing leaflet with the same text as no. 3996, but with different graphics. MiDW-A

3998. *A Call to Action—Workers of Boulder Dam.* Boulder Dam: IWW, n.d. (1937?), 2 p.
A strike-call leaflet for construction workers.

3999. Callender, Harold. *More Truth about the IWW.* Chicago: IWW, n.d. (1919?), 47 p.
The Chicago trial. MiDW-A

4000. ———. *Truth about the I.W.W.* Chicago: IWW, n.d. (1918?), 16 p.
Describes the forces arrayed against the IWW and the IWW

prisoners' personal decency and innocence. This is a reprint of no. 3635. MiDW-A

4001. Cascaden, Gordon. *Crimes of Capital.* Detroit: IWW, 1917, 8 p.
Everett Massacre and other incidents as efforts to crush the labor movement. MiDW-A

4002. ———. *Lest We Forget.* Chicago: IWW, 1919, 9 p.
The persecution of the IWW was instigated by big business to destroy labor. MiDW-A

4003. ———. *Smash the IWW!* Detroit, IWW, n.d. (1918?), 4 p.
This cry of the IWW's enemies is really intended to destroy unionism. MiDW-A

4004. *The Case of Mike Lindway.* Chicago: GDC, n.d. (1936?), 2 p.
An appeal for a Cleveland worker imprisoned for picket-line violence. MiDW-A

4005. *Centralia Case.* Walla Walla, WA: Friends of Ray Becker, n.d., 2 p.
Plea for all IWWs to support Becker, a Centralia prisoner. MiDW-A

4006. *The Centralia Case: A Chronological Digest.* Seattle: GDC, 1927, 2 p. MiDW-A

4007. *The Centralia Case: A Chronological Digest.* Chicago: GDC, IWW, 1931, 2 p.
Different from no. 4006 only in its addition of later years. MiDW-A

4008. *Centralia Case (by an American Legionnaire.)* Chicago: CPC, n.d. (1930?), 4 p.
Includes a signed statement by Edward P. Coll, a Legionnaire. MiDW-A

4009. *Centralia Case. Speeches by Elmer Smith and Capt. Edward P. Coll.* Centralia, WA: CPC, n.d. (1929?), 15 p. MiDW-A

4010. Chaplin, Ralph. *The Centralia Conspiracy.* Seattle: IWW, 1920, 80 p.
An account of the Centralia affair. Reprinted many times, including in no. 33. MiDW-A

4011. ———. *The Centralia Conspiracy: The Truth about the Armistice Day Tragedy.* Chicago: GDC, 1924, 146 p.
Greatly enlarged revision of no. 4010, with additional poetry and photographs.

4012. Chapman, C. M. *Lessons in Economics: A Textbook for Workers.* Chicago: IWW, n.d., 38 p.
Twenty-eight lessons, consisting of 317 short questions and answers on the economy. MiU, MiDW-A

4013. *The Chicago Indictment.* Chicago: IWW, 1918, 4 p.
Details the indictment and asks financial and moral support for the arrested IWWs.

4014. *Christmas in Prison—Shall We Forget Them?* New York: GDC, 1935, 4 p.
Appeal for money and moral support for all prisoners. MiU

4015. Christensen, Otto. *Statement Submitted to the Attorney General of the United States Concerning the Present Legal Status of the IWW Cases.* Chicago: IWW, 1921, 42 p. NNU-T

4016. Chumley, L. S. *Hotel, Restaurant, and Domestic Workers: How They Work and How They Live.* Chicago: IWW, n.d. (1913?), 38 p. MiDW-A

4017. *Chunks of Wisdom.* Auckland, New Zealand: IWW, n.d., 16 p.
Collected quotations about industrial unionism, working-class militancy, and a people's government.

4018. *Cigar Makers—Draw Up Your Own Code in Your Union Hall.* Detroit: IWW, n.d., 1 p.
Workers should organize, reject the NRA codes, and form their own.

4019. *Cigar Makers Meeting.* Detroit: IWW, n.d., 4 p.
Call to an IWW organization meeting. MiDW-A

4020. *Circulate the Real Industrial Union Idea!* IWW, n.d. (1975?), 1 p.
Organizing leaflet. MiDW-A

4021. *Civilization Before—1919—After.* San Francisco: CDDC, n.d. (1919?), 1 p.
Quotes the national and the California constitutions; in a parallel column, it quotes the California Syndicalist law's provisions, which appear to contradict the constitutions.

4022. *Class War Prisoners' Christmas Fund.* Chicago: GDC, IWW, 1942, 6 p.
A plea for money and moral support for all IWW prisoners. MiU

4023. *Class War Prisoners' Christmas Fund.* Chicago: GDC, IWW, 1936, 4 p.

A plea for money and moral support for all IWW prisoners. MiU

4024. *Coal Mine Workers and Their Industry. An Industrial Handbook Prepared by The Educational Bureau of the IWW, for CMWIU #220.* Chicago: IWW, 1921, 108 p.

A history of mining and the miners' struggle to organize, with an appeal to all miners to join. NN, MiU

4025. *Coal Miners!* Butte: CMIU #220, n.d., 2 p.

Organizing leaflet urging all Butte coal miners to join the IWW. MiDW-A

4026. *Coal Miners Awaken!* Butte: CMIU #220, n.d., 4 p.

Accuses UMWA of scabbing because members in one area remain on the job during strikes in other areas. MiDW-A

4027. Coll, Edward P. *Legion Officer and Overseas Captain Demands Release of Centralia Victims.* Centralia: CPC, 1928, 4 p. NN

4028. *Collective Bargaining Manual.* Chicago: IWW, 1978, 33 p. MiU

4029. *Colored Workers of America: Why You Should Join the IWW.* Chicago: IWW, n.d., 4 p.

The IWW is fully integrated and draws no color lines.

4030. *Communists Back Doyle—GEB Favors General Convention.* Chicago: GEB, IWW, n.d. (1924?), 2 p.

Pamphlet published during the IWW split. MiDW-A

4031. *Comparisons Are Odious to Labor Skates and Grafters.* Aberdeen, WA: LWIU #120, IWW, n.d., 2 p.

The failures of the AFL compared to the IWW's successes in improving the conditions of lumberworkers. MiDW-A

4032. *Conduct and Events of the Cle Elum Strike.* Chicago: GCWIU #310, IWW, 1933, 9 p.

Call for support for the Cle Elum, Washington, construction workers. MiU

4033. *Construction Workers!* Chicago: GCWIU #310, IWW, n.d. (1920?), 2 p.

Organizing leaflet. MiDW-A

4034. *Construction Workers IU #573—Unity.* Chicago: IWW Publishing Bureau, n.d., n.p. MiU

4035. *Construction Workers! Let's Organize Our Job This Summer!* Chicago: GCWIU #310, IWW, n.d., 2 p.
Organization leaflet that includes poetry. MiDW-A

4036. *Constructive Industrialism—The Structure of Industrial Unionism.* Los Angeles: Detroit Branch, IWW, n.d., n.p.

4037. *Constructive Unionism.* Chicago: IWW, n.d., 4 p.
Organization leaflet advocating a shorter work day. MiDW-A

4038. *Contract Work—An Exposé of the Clever Tricks Used by the Capitalist Class To Make Every Man His Own Slave Driver.* Chicago: Education Bureau, IWW, n.d., 4 p.
Classic IWW position against employment contracts. MiDW-A

4039. *The Contrast.* Aberdeen, WA: LWIU #120, IWW, n.d., 1 p.
The ideas of the IWW contrasted with those of the Saw Mill and Timber Workers Union. Some editions of no. 4039 print the title on the verso.

4040. *Copper Kings Have Spoken: Workers, What Is Your Reply?* Salt Lake City: Haywood and Perry, IWW, n.d., 1 p.
Subscription leaflet asking for funds. MiDW-A

4041. Corder, Raymond. *Industrial Unionism in the IWW: The Job Branch.* Chicago: IWW, 1937, 4 p.

4042. *The Cost of the Criminal Syndicalist Law—How $1,000,000 Has Been Wasted.* San Francisco: CBGDC, IWW, n.d. (1925?), 4 p. MiDW-A

4043. Costello, E. J. *Shame that Is Kentucky's: The Story of the Harlan Mine War.* Chicago: GDC, n.d., 38 p.
Printed in several editions. MiDW-A

4044. *Courage, Confidence, and Loyalty to the Cause.* Philadelphia: MTWIU #510, n.d., 1 p.
Marine Transport Workers strike leaflet. MiDW-A

4045. Covami. *Leaders? Where Will They Lead You? A Proletarian's Lament.* Chicago: IWW, n.d., 3 p.
Appeal in verse for fewer leaders and only one union. MiDW-A

4046. *Craft Distinctions or Industrial Unionism—Which Do You Want?* Chicago: IWW, n.d., 4 p.
The AFL compared with the IWW. MiDW-A

4047. *Craft Union Experiences on the Railroads and How To Get Immediate Organization Results.* Chicago: RRWIU #520, IWW, n.d., 16 p.
The problems of numerous railway craft unions compared with one union. MiDW-A

4048. *Craft Unionism—Why It Fails.* Chicago: IWW, n.d., 48 p.
Painstaking explanation of the failure of craft unionism, industry by industry. NN

4049. *Cut Down the Hours of Work!* Chicago: IWW, n.d. (1923?), 4 p.
Solving unemployment by cutting working hours. MiDW-A

4050. *CWIU #573, IWW.* #13 Bulletin, November 15, 1918. Chicago: IWW, 1918, 1 p.
Bulletin distributed as an organizing leaflet for construction workers. MiDW-A

4051. *Danger! Stop! Warning!* Detroit: Downer-Atclieff Defense, IWW, 1919, n.p.
The Flint, Michigan, Criminal Syndicalist trial. MiU

4052. *Dare to Be Different.* Chicago: AWIU #110, IWW, n.d., 4 p.
Organizing leaflet for migratory workers. MiDW-A

4053. Debs, Eugene. *Class Unionism.* Chicago: IWW, 1905, 29 p.
Class unionism is industrial unionism. IU

4054. ———. *From Capitalism to the Industrial Commonwealth, Epitomized by W. E. Trautmann.* Chicago: IWW, n.d. (1908?), 52 p.
The working man must realize that he is involved in a class struggle. MiDW-A

4055. ———. *Revolutionary Unionism.* Chicago: IWW, 1905, 21 p. WHi

4056. *Decentralization vs. Centralization.* Chicago: IWW, n.d. (1924?), 4 p.
Decentralization is the choice of this faction of the IWW. MiDW-A

4057. *Decline and Fall of the Spectacular Commodity Economy: Watts.* n.p., Solidarity Communications, 1967, 14 p.
The Watts Riot.

4058. Delaney, Ed, and M. T. Rice. *The Bloodstained Trail; a History of Militant Labor in the United States.* Seattle: Industrial Worker, 1927, 172 p.
The story of the persecution of labor, with a long list of examples. MiDW-A

4059. *Demand the Repeal of the Criminal Syndicalist Law!* Chicago: IWW Free Speech Committee, n.d. (1922?), 1 p.
Workers urged to speak out against the damaging law. MiDW-A

4060. *Destroying the Home.* Chicago: IWW, n.d., 2 p.
The capitalistic system, not the IWW, destroys the home. MiDW-A

4061. *Direct Action.* Chicago: GRU, IWW, n.d., 20 p. NNU-T

4062. *Direct Action Is the Way to Freedom.* Berkeley, CA: Berkeley Branch, IWW, n.d. (1972?), 1 p. MiDW-A

4063. *Do You Believe in a Square Deal? "Let the People Know the Truth and the Country Will Be Free—Lincoln."* San Francisco: CDDC, IWW, n.d., 4 p.
The Criminal Syndicalism cases. MiDW-A

4064. *Do You Believe in Unionism?* Chicago: IWW Organizing Committee, n.d. (1937?), 1 p.
The CIO and Workers' Alliance seen as hindrances to real industrial unionism. MiDW-A

4065. *Do You Know These Salient Facts about Humboldt County?* San Francisco: California Branch, GDC, IWW, n.d., 1 p.
Many examples of prejudicial actions against unions. MiDW-A

4066. *Do You Know These Truths about Washington?* Seattle: Washington Branch, GDC, n.d. (1927?), 1 p.
An appeal for the Centralia prisoners. MiDW-A

4067. *Do You Want Mob Rule?* Chicago: IWW, n.d. (1918?), 4 p.
The government arrests and raids on IWW halls. DLC

4068. *Do You Work?* Mountainview, CA: IWW, n.d., 6 p.
Office workers' organizing leaflet. MiDW-A

4069. *Does the IWW Preach Violence?* Chicago: IWW, n.d., 2 p.
The IWW has always opposed violence but has often been the victim of the violence of others. MiDW-A

4070. *Dollars and Steel against Humanity: Iron Ore Miners Strike.* Cleveland: Solidarity Pub. Co., n.d. (1917?), 16 p.
The Mesabi Range strike. MiDW-A

4071. *Don't Be Stampeded! The IWW and Injunctions.* Chicago: GEB, IWW, n.d. (1924?), 2 p.
The 1924 split within the IWW. MiDW-A

4072. *Don't Be Too Loudspoken—Somebody Might Wise Up.* Aberdeen, WA: IWW, n.d., 1 p.
Organizing leaflet with humorous dialogue. MiDW-A

4073. Doran, J. T. (Red). *Big Business and Direct Action.* Chicago: LWIU #500, IWW, n.d. (1918?), 4 p.
The worker should "legislate" directly, at the point of production. MiDW-A

4074. ———. *Evidence and Cross-Examination of J. T. (Red) Doran.* Chicago: IWW, n.d. (1918?), 151 p.
Testimony of one of the Chicago trial defendants. NN

4075. ———. *Law and the IWW.* Chicago: IWW Pub. Bur., n.d. (1918?), 4 p.
Illegal actions against the IWW are aimed at all labor. MiDW-A

4076. Dougherty, T. F. G. *How to Overcome the High Cost of Living.* Cleveland: IWW Pub. Bur., n.d., 16 p.
Join the IWW as a solution to the high cost of living. MiDW-A

4077. Doyle, Tom. *Open Letter to Mssrs. Nelson and Hill of Humboldt County, California.* n.p.: IWW, n.d. (1923?), 14 p.
Rebuttal letter to prosecuting attorneys in the Syndicalist case of *Californina* vs. *Henry Powell et al.* MiDW-A

4078. Duff, Harvey. *Silent Defenders: Courts and Capitalism in California. A Brief History of the Uphill Struggle of the Industrial Workers of the World in California, and an Expose of the Sacramento Frame-Up and Convictions.* Chicago: IWW, n.d. (1919?), 112 p.
The famous "silent defense" trial. MiDW-A

4079. *East Coast and Gulf Seamen—Don't Join the ISU.* New York: GOC, MTWIU #510, IWW, n.d., 2 p. MiDW-A

4080. Ebert, Justus. *The A.B.C. of the I.W.W.: What It Is, What It Has Done, What It Aims To Do.* Chicago: IWW Press, n.d., n.p.

4081. ———. *Is the IWW Anti-Political?* New Castle, PA: IWW Pub. Bur., 1913, 4 p.
The IWW is the only really political group in America. MiDW-A

4082. ———. *The IWW in Theory and Practice.* Chicago: IWW, n.d., 124 p.
Printed in numerous editions. MiDW-A

4083. ———. *The Trial of a New Society, Being a Review of the Celebrated Ettor-Giovannitti-Caruso Case, Beginning with the Lawrence Textile Strike That Caused It and Including the General Strike That Grew Out of It.* Cleveland: IWW Pub. Bur., 1913, 160 p.

4084. *An Economic Interpretation of the Job.* Chicago: AWIU #110, IWW, 1922, 61 p.

Economic presentation concluding that a shorter work day is one key to solving unemployment. IdU

4085. *Education and System: The Basis of Organization.* Chicago: IWW, n.d., 4 p.

Organizing leaflet urging workers to join the IWW and work systematically toward industrial unionism. MiDW-A

4086. *Education. Definition and Function of Education.* Chicago: LWIU #120, IWW, n.d., 4 p.

Only workers educated in unionism will succeed in changing the system. MiDW-A

4087. *Education! Organization! Will You Be One of Five Thousand People for Sunday, April 1, 1923?* Centralia: IWW, 1923, 4 p.

Call to a mass meeting where Elmer Smith and George Vanderveer will speak on behalf of the Centralia prisoners.

MiDW-A

4088. *Education! Organization! Emancipation!* Chicago: MMWIU #210, IWW, n.d., 4 p.

Organizing leaflet for metal-mine workers, printed in many editions. MiDW-A

4089. *Educational Meeting.* Portola, CA: LWIU #120, IWW, n.d., 4 p.

Announcement of meeting at which George Holmes will speak to lumberworkers. MiDW-A

4090. Edwards, Forrest. *One Big Union.* Chicago: IWW Pub. Bureau, n.d., 4 p.

Organizing leaflet. NNU-T

4091. ———. *Economic Revolution.* Yellow Springs, OH: IWW, n.d. (1966?), 4 p.

The profit system will result in a revolution.

4092. *Eight Men Buried Alive! The Centralia Case Calls to Every Decent Man and Woman in the State of Washington To Act Quickly.* Chicago: GDC, 1924, 31 p.

Plea for Centralia prisoners. MiDW-A

4093. *Eight Men Buried Alive! Six Centralia Jurors Confess.* n.p., IWW, n.d. (1928?), 4 p.
Some jurors changed their minds and regretted their verdict. MiDW-A

4094. Elliott, James, and Claude Irwin. *California Oil World Teaches Violence and Tries To Cause a Reign of Terror.* San Francisco: IWW, n.d. (1927?), 1 p.
Protests the California Syndicalist law. MiDW-A

4095. *Elmer Smith Pleads for Liberty of Centralia Men.* Centralia: CPC, n.d. (1928?), 4 p.
IWW defense laywer's plea. MiDW-A

4096. *Emergency Program.* Chicago: GEB, IWW, 1924, 2 p.
The IWW split. MiDW-A

4097. *Emma Goldman Rests Now in Historic Waldheim with Haymarket Martyrs.* Chicago: IWW, n.d. (1965?), 1 p. MiDW-A

4098. *Employees of Cedar Valley Coffee House Are on Strike.* San Francisco: IWW, n.d. (1970?), 1 p.
Strike leaflet. MiDW-A

4099. *An Enormous Contrast and the Reason.* Chicago: LWIU #120, IWW, n.d., 4 p.
Working conditions on the Pacific Northwest coast, where the IWW struck for better conditions and the eight-hour day and got them; in other parts of the country lumberworkers are treated badly. MiDW-A

4100. *Ethics and Aims of the I.W.W.* Chicago: IWW Press, 1919, n.p.
Organizing leaflet.

4101. Ettor, Joseph. *Industrial Unionism—The Road to Freedom.* Chicago: IWW Press, 1912, 30 p.
Organizing leaflet, printed in many editions.

4102. *Ettor and Giovannitti before the Jury at Salem, Massachusetts, November 23, 1912.* Chicago: IWW, n.d. (1912?), 80 p. IU

4103. Everett Prisoners' Defense Committee. *Financial Statement of Everett Prisoners' Defense Committee, June, 1917.* Seattle: EPDC, IWW, 1917, 65 p.
The defense of the Everett prisoners. DLC

4104. *Everett's Bloody Sunday—The Tragedy That Horrified the World.* Seattle: EPDC, IWW, 1916, 4 p.
The Everett Massacre. MiDW-A

4105. *Evolution and the IWW.* San Francisco: CBG DC, IWW, n.d., 4 p. NNU-T

4106. *An Explanation.* Chicago: GOC of MCMWIU #210 and #220, IWW, n.d., 1 p.
Organizing leaflet for metal and coal miners. DLC

4107. *Explanation from the Standpoint of IWW History.* New York: E. P. Reorganization Committee, 1924, 8 p.
An interpretation of the IWW split. MiU

4108. *Exposed by the Marine Transport Workers Industrial Union No. 510 of the IWW.* Chicago: IWW, 1923, 28 p. MiDW-A

4109. *Extracts from the Verbatim Report of the 16th General Convention of the Industrial Workers of the World, Dealing with the 1924 General Administration Controversy, October 13–November 10, 1924.* Chicago: IWW, 1924, 232 p.
The IWW split. NN

4110. *Facts for Hankins Container Workers.* Cleveland: MMWIU #440, IWW, n.d. (1934?), 1 p.
Organizing leaflet for metal workers. MiDW-A

4111. *The Farm Laborer.* New Castle, PA: IWW Pub. Bur., n.d., n.p.
Organizing leaflet for farm workers. DL

4112. *Fear.* Chicago: IWW, n.d., n.p.

4113. *Federal Political Prisoners Still in Prison.* Chicago: IWW, 1922, 4 p. MiU

4114. *Fellow Seamen.* Galveston, TX: MTWIU #510, IWW, n.d., 1 p.
Organizing leaflet for seamen. MiU

4115. *Fellow Union Members: Can We Take Union Democracy for Granted?* Tacoma: Tacoma-Olympia IWW, 1975, 4 p. MiDW-A

4116. *Fellow Worker: Are You Fed Up?* Chicago: IWW, n.d. (1950?), 1 p.
Organizing leaflet. MiDW-A

4117. *Fellow Workers.* Oklahoma City, OK: OWIU #230, IWW, n.d., 4 p.
Organizing leaflet for oil workers. MiDW-A

4118. *Fellow Workers: Emergency.* Long Beach, CA: IU #430, IWW, 1972, 1 p.
A circular about the strike at International Wood Products. MiDW-A

4119. *A Few Reasons Why Packard Employees Should Join.* Detroit: IWW, 1933, 4 p.
Organizing leaflet for auto workers. MiDW-A

4120. *The Fight Is On.* Alexandria, LA: IU of Forest and Lumber Workers, BTW, IWW, n.d. (1912?), n.p.
Leaflet of the Southern lumber strikes of 1912.

4121. *The Fight to Establish the IWW in Cleveland.*
Organizing leaflet for metal workers. MiDW-A

4122. *The First of May, a Workingman's Holiday.* n.p.: United Branches of IWW, n.d., 4 p.

4123. Fischer, Eugene. *Address to Hotel and Restaurant Workers.* Chicago: IWW, n.d., 4 p.
Basically the same organizing leaflet as no. 3935. MiDW-A

4124. Flynn, Elizabeth Gurley. *Sabotage: The Conscious Withdrawal of the Workers' Industrial Efficiency.* Cleveland: IWW Pub. Bureau, 1915, 31 p.
The nature and history of sabotage and its present applications. NN, MiDW-A

4125. *Food: Those Who Prepare and Serve It.* Chicago: FWIU #460, IWW, n.d., 8 p.
Organizing leaflet for food workers. MiDW-A

4126. *Food Workers: Build the FWIU of New York.* New York: FWIU #460, IWW, n.d., 4 p.
Organizing leaflet for food workers.

4127. *Four Fighting Years: A Short History of the Marine Workers Industrial Union.* New York: IWW, 1934, n.p. MiU

4128. *4 Watches! Why Not? And No Wage Cuts.* Houston, TX: MTWIU #510, IWW, n.d., 1 p.
Organizing leaflet for marine workers.

4129. Fraina, Louis. *The I.W.W. Trial—A Socialist Viewpoint.* Chicago: GDC, n.d. (1918?), 4 p.
Employers, the national government, and the reactionary AFL are conspiring to put an end to militant labor. MiDW-A

4130. *Free Political Prisoners by Christmas.* Chicago: GDC, IWW, 1923, 2 p.

4131. *Freedom?* Chicago: IWW, n.d., 1 p.
The source of the totalitarian trend in the United States is capitalism. MiDW-A

4132. *From the Ford Men to the Ford Motor Co.* Detroit: Committee of Ford Employees, 1921, 1 p.
Proposes bargaining and a union.

4133. *Fruit Pickers Attention: What Are We Going To Do?* Sunnyvale, CA: AWIU #110, IWW, n.d., 1 p.
Organizing leaflet for migrant farmworkers. MiDW-A

4134. *Fruit Workers Attention!* Chicago: IWW, n.d., 2 p.
Yakima, Washington, organizing leaflet. MiDW-A

4135. *Furniture Workers! of Grand Rapids, Mich.* Cleveland: FWIU #202, IWW, April, 1914, 1 p.
Urges furniture workers to join the union. MiU

4136. Gahan, John A. *"Equality before the Law": Shall American Justice Be Allowed To Die?* Seattle: GDC, n.d., 4 p.
Centralia proved the antilabor biases of the courts. MiDW-A

4137. *Gandy Dancers Set Up IWW Job Committees.* Chicago: RRWIU #520, IWW, n.d., 4 p.
Organizing leaflet for railroad workers.

4138. *General Amnesty or General Strike!* Chicago: GDC, 1923, 4 p.
Threatens a general strike if the political prisoners are not released. MiDW-A

4139. *General Construction Workers, Builders of America.* Chicago: IWW, n.d., 24 p.
Organizing leaflet. MiDW-A

4140. *General Construction Workers Don't Trust to Luck—Join the Union.* Chicago: GCW, IWW, 1933, 40 p.
Organizing leaflet. MiDW-A

4141. *General Defense Committee of the Industrial Workers of the World.* Chicago: GDC, IWW, 1938, 4 p.
Urges members to join the General Defense Committee and explains its work and its history. MiDW-A

4142. *General Strike.* Chicago: IWW, 1946, n.p. WaPS

4143. *General Strike Bulletin—Take the Strike Back on the Job.* Seattle: IWW Strike Committee, 1923, 4 p.
The IWW does not believe in long, drawn-out strikes; workers should strike on the job, at the point of production.

4144. *The General Strike for Industrial Freedom.* Chicago: IWW, 1933, 48 p.
Printed in many editions. MiDW-A

4145. *General Strike of All Lumberjacks in Eastern Washington, Idaho, and Montana.* Spokane: Central Strike Committee, 1919, n.p.
Announces a general strike in the Pacific Northwest.

4146. *General Strike: Release of Class War Prisoners.* Chicago: IWW, n.d. (1925?), 2 p.
Threatens a general strike if the political prisoners are not released. MiU

4147. George, Harrison. *Is Freedom Dead? Sequel to the Suppressed Pamphlet, Shall Freedom Die?* Chicago: IWW, 1918, 24 p.
The raids and the arrests of the IWW. MiDW-A

4148. ———. *The I.W.W. Trial.* Chicago: IWW, n.d. (1918?), 205 p.
The Chicago trial. NN

4149. ———. *The Red Dawn: The Bolsheviki and the IWW.* Chicago: IWW, n.d. (1920?), 26 p.
How the Bolsheviki were able to change the system. The IWW should follow suit. MiDW-A

4150. ———. *Shall Freedom Die? 166 Union Men in Jail for Labor, by One of Them.* Chicago: IWW, 1918, 23 p.
The arrests, the jailings, and the reasons for them. MiDW-A

4151. *Get Acquainted with a Good Labor Paper.* Seattle: *Industrial Worker,* n.d. (1948?), 1 p.
Members and others should read the *Industrial Worker,* sell it, or pass it along.

4152. *Get Behind the General Strike Movement.* Chicago: IWW, n.d. (1925?), 4 p.
Workers should support the movement for the sake of the prisoners.

4153. *Getting an Edge.* Detroit: Detroit-Ann Arbor IWW, n.d. (1978?), 4 p.
Being in the union is the first step toward controlling your job. MiDW-A

4154. *Giant Industry and the IWW. Against the Concentrated Power of Modern Big Business Put the Concentrated Power of the Workers.* Chicago: IWW, n.d. (1921?), 14 p. MH

4155. Glynn, T. *Industrial Efficiency and Its Antidote.* Chicago: IWW, n.d., 12 p.
The antidote is industrial organization.

4156. *Go Slow!* Chicago: IWW, n.d. (1919?), 4 p.

Workers should not work so fast that they cannot do a good job. All workers deserve an occasional time out.

4157. *Gompers vs. Haywood.* Chicago: IWW, n.d. (1919?), 4 p.

Haywood, in jail for labor's principles, compared with Gompers, hobnobbing with the rich. Cover cartoon shows Gompers dining with royalty while Haywood wears a ball and chain. MiDW-A

4158. *Great Conspiracy.* Seattle: John Grady, IWW, n.d. (1919?), 4 p.

Strikes in the Pacific Northwest and the Syndicalist laws. MiDW-A

4159. Hall, Covington. *Fellow Workers, Hear Me!* Chicago: IWW, n.d. (1970?), 2 p.

Poem urging that the workers shake off their chains and stop selling their bodies, brains, and souls. The leaflet also lists the IWW Industrial Code of workers' demands. Verso has a message from the Tacoma, Washington, branch, headed "Let's Dump the Management." MiDW-A

4160. ———. *Why One Big Union?* Chicago: IWW, n.d., 4 p.

Organizing leaflet.

4161. *Hang On To Your Life Belt!* Chicago: AWIU #110, IWW, n.d., 4 p.

The life belt is the IWW, which reminds workers that they are men as well as workingmen. MiDW-A

4162. Hanson, Nils. *Onward Sweep of the Machine Process.* Chicago: IWW, n.d. (1917?), 32 p.

Inventions profit the owners, not the workers, who will suffer unemployment. The pamphlet includes comments by other writers. MiDW-A

4163. *Hard Work Is To Blame.* Chicago: GOC of GRU, IWW, n.d., 7 p.

A four-hour day would solve unemployment. MiDW-A

4164. Hardy, George. *Address to American Workers.* Chicago: IWW, n.d. (1920?), 8 p.

Organizing leaflet stating that it is more important to organize now, in these times of repression, than ever. The worker is being robbed at the point of production. MiDW-A

4165. ———. *Open Letter to American Workmen.* Chicago: IWW, n.d. (1919?), 8 p. MiU

4166. *Harvest Time Is Honey Time.* AWIU #110, IWW, n.d., 2 p.

Organizing leaflet for farmworkers. MiDW-A

4167. *Harvest Workers, Attention!* Chicago: AWIU #110, IWW, n.d., 4 p.
Organizing leaflet for farmworkers. MiDW-A

4168. *Harvest Workers Attention!* Minneapolis: AWIU #110, IWW, n.d., 4 p.
Organizing leaflet for farmworkers. MiDW-A

4169. Harvey, Thomas. *Here Is the Resolution of the United Mine Workers Demanding Fair Play for the IWW.* Chicago: IWW, n.d. (1919?), 1 p.
One of several printings of the supportive motion of UMWA members. MiU

4170. *Has the Constitution of the United States Been "Recalled" in Paterson, N.J.?* Paterson: IWW, n.d. (1913?), 4 p. NNU-T

4171. *Have You Given Any Thought to the Conditions You Will Be Compelled To Work under When the War Ends?* Chicago: IWW, n.d. (1947?), 1 p.
Organizing leaflet. MiDW-A

4172. Haywood, William D. *Break the Conspiracy.* Chicago: GDC, 1919, 4 p.
Urges a militant and unfearing attitude in the face of current troubles. MiDW-A

4173. ———. *Evidence and Cross-Examination of William D. Haywood.* Chicago: GDC, n.d. (1918?), 312 p. MiDW-A

4174. ———. *The General Strike.* New York: Buccafori Defense Committee, Shoe Workers Industrial Union #168, IWW, n.d. (1911?), 20 p. MiDW-A

4175. ———. *On the Inside.* Chicago: IWW, n.d. (1919?), n.p.
The Chicago trial prisoners. MiU

4176. ———. *Raids! Raids! Raids!* Chicago: IWW, n.d. (1919?), 4 p.
The Red Scare raids, which Haywood considers raids on all labor, not just the IWW. DLC

4177. ———. *Speech of Wm. D. Haywood on the Case of Ettor and Giovannitti, Cooper Union, New York.* Lawrence, MA: Ettor-Giovannitti Defense Committee, IWW, 1912, 16 p. MiDW-A

4178. ———. *Testimony before the Industrial Relations Commission.* Chicago: IWW, n.d. (1917?) 70 p.
Haywood's much-praised testimony about the ills done to labor. MiDW-A

4179. ———. *We Never Forget! Organize and Act!* Chicago: IWW, n.d. (1917?), 4 p.

The lynching of Frank Little will not stop the IWW.

4180. ———. *Will You Help Now? What Price Freedom?* Chicago: GDC, n.d. (1919?), 1 p. OrU

4181. ———. *With Drops of Blood.* IWW, n.d. (1920?), 4 p.

The lynchings, beatings, and other persecutions of the IWW. MiDW-A

4182. *He Was Not a Ten Hour Man in 1922.* Chicago: AWIU #110, IWW, n.d., 4 p.

Deplores farmworkers working overtime and suggests six-hour day to reduce unemployment. MiDW-A

4183. *Heads I Win, Tails You Lose.* Chicago: IWW, n.d. (1927?), 7 p.

The system is a capitalist game that workers will never win until they are organized. MiU

4184. *Hear a Militant Labor Unionist Speak: Can Unionism Be a Force for Radical Social Change?* San Francisco: Bay Area General Membership Branch, IWW, n.d. (1980?), 2 p.

Announces a series of speeches by Frank Cedervall and states that militant unionism can benefit students, workers, and the unemployed by showing them how to work together to get their piece of the pie.

4185. *Helen Keller Scores I.W.W. Persecutions.* Chicago: IWW Pub. Bureau, 1918, 4 p.

Deplores the un-American persecution of the IWW. MiU

4186. *Hell in Harlan.* New York: GDC, n.d., 4 p.

Appeal for food, clothes, and money for persecuted Kentucky miners. MiDW-A

4187. *Help Wanted.* Chicago: MMWIU #440, IWW Pub. Bur., n.d., 4 p.

Organizing leaflet for metal-mine workers. DLC

4188. Hervé, Gustave. *Patriotism and the Worker.* Chicago: IWW, 1912, 32 p.

Copy of a speech delivered in 1905 at the trial of the Paris Anti-Militants. Hervé states that capitalists wish only to keep and gain property while workers fight each other to make those wishes come true.

4189. Heslewood, F. W. *Report of the IWW to the International Socialist and Labor Congress at Stuttgart, Germany, 1907*. Chicago: IWW, 1907, 14 p.

Asks international group to recognize that a new force for revolution is awake in America and that Europe send militant unionists as immigrants to America so that worker will not be set against worker. MiDW-A

4190. *Hey! You Mule Conductors!* Chicago: GCWIU #310, IWW, n.d. (1919?), 4 p.

Organizing leaflet stating that ordinary workers will always be bums until they are organized. MiDW-A

4191. *High Cost of Living*. New York, IWW, 1912, n.p. NNU-T

4192. *Hi-Jacks, Boot-Leggers, Holdups, Gamblers, etc., in the Harvest Fields: Warning to You*. Chicago: AWO, IWW, n.d. (1916?), 2 p.

Warns young farmworkers, especially in Kansas, Nebraska, Minnesota, and the Dakotas, to be careful about their associates and keep their minds on their jobs and their union. The IWW will defend them in court only in a labor case and not a case resulting from personal greed or bad actions. MiDW-A

4193. *"Hip" Rip*. Chicago: IWW, n.d. (1972?), 2 p.

Hip Products workers in Chicago are being ripped off. MiDW-A

4194. *Hip Products Dispute*. Chicago: IWW, 1971, 1 p.

Hip warehouse employees decide to join the IWW and consider a possible strike action. MiDW-A

4195. *Historical Catechism of American Unionism*. Chicago: IWW, n.d. (1923), 95 p.

Questions and answers on the IWW. MiDW-A

4196. *History of the IWW—A Discussion of Its Main Features—by a Group of Workmen*. Chicago: IWW, n.d., 32 p.

Organizing leaflet. MiDW-A

4197. *History of the San Diego Free Speech Fight*. Chicago: San Diego Branch, IWW, 1973, 190 p. MiU

4198. *Hoof and Mouth Disease Spreads: Beware of California Products*. Chicago: GDC, 1924, 2 p.

Deplores the California Syndicalist trials and calls for a boycott. NNU-T, MiU

4199. *Hotel, Restaurant, and Domestic Workers, Attention!* Chicago: IWW, n.d., 4 p.
Organizing leaflet. MiU

4200. *Hotel, Restaurant and Domestic Workers: Stewards, Cooks, Waiters, Dishwashers, Busboys and All Other Workers in Hotels, Restaurants and Cafeterias—Both Men and Women.* Los Angeles: IWW, n.d., 2 p.
The New Deal has done nothing to help waiters, housemaids, and some other types of workers. MiDW-A

4201. *Hotel and Restaurant Workers of Los Angeles.* Los Angeles: IWW, n.d., 1 p.
Organizing leaflet.

4202. *Housemaids' Union in Grip of the Boss!* Chicago: HRDWIU #1100, IWW, n.d. (1925?), 4 p.

4203. *How about a Union?* Chicago: IWW, n.d., 1 p.
Organizing leaflet stating that only by joining the union will a worker see wages rise. MiDW-A

4204. *How Much Good Can a Union Do?* Cleveland: IWW, n.d. (1935?), 4 p.
Organized workers are carrying the unorganized on their backs. MiDW-A

4205. *How Would You Like To Live "Approximately Well"?* Chicago: IWW, 1965, 4 p.
Organizing leaflet stating that if $2 an hour is an approximate living wage, as John Galbraith claims, how about those who do not make that much? MiDW-A

4206. *La Huelga General.* Chicago: IWW Strike Comm., n.d. (1923?), 29 p.
Explanation of the general strike.

4207. *Hungry Babies! Hungry Mothers! Hungry Men! Five Months on Strike at Paterson.* Paterson: IWW, n.d. (1913?), 1 p.
The suffering of the Paterson strikers and their families. NNU-T

4208. *The Idea.* Chicago: IWW, n.d., 4 p.
Call for one big union. Employers are organized by industries, so workers should organize industrially. MiDW-A

4209. *If You're Unorganized, Your Pay Is Too Low.* Chicago: IWW, n.d., 4 p.
An organizing leaflet in several editions. MiU

4210. *Immediate Attention, to Labor Men and Taxpayers of San Francisco.* San Francisco: CDC, n.d., 1 p.
Protests the California Syndicalist laws. MiDW-A

4211. *The Immediate Demand: A 40-Hour Week.* Sydney, Australia: IWW, n.d., 1 p.
It may take a while before labor can take over the government, but workers should demand an eight-hour day in the meantime. MiDW-A

4212. *Immediate Demands of Miners of Clear Creek and Gilpin Counties.* Chicago: MMWIU #210, IWW, n.d., 1 p.

4213. *The Immediate Demands of the I.W.W.: The Spirit of the Times.* Chicago: IWW, n.d., 14 p.
Although there are many long-range plans, the IWW wishes to change three things immediately: wages, hours, and working conditions. MiDW-A

4214. *In California, as in Ancient Rome.* Chicago: IWW, 1924, 22 p.
Protests the harsh Criminal Syndicalist law in California. MiDW-A

4215. *In Jail Two Years for What?* Chicago, IWW, n.d. (1921?), 4 p.
How IWW prisoners were held in medieval-style jails for two years awaiting trial in Wichita. MiDW-A

4216. *In Memoriam.* Chicago: GDC, 1919, n.p.
American freedoms no longer exist and should be mourned. MiU

4217. *In Union There is Strength.* Chicago: IWW, n.d., 4 p.
Organizing leaflet. MiDW-A

4218. *Inciting to Riot: The Reply of the Industrial Workers of the World to an Advertisement in the Chicago Journal of August 8, 1919—Those Who Paid for It Were Too Cowardly To Sign It.* Chicago: IWW, 1919, 4 p.
There are both groups and individuals trying to incite the public to hate the IWW. MiDW-A

4219. *Industrial Evolution and the IWW.* San Francisco: CBGDC, n.d. (1928?), 4 p.
The IWW recognizes change and evolution in industry and believes that workers must organize industrially as the one big union of bosses has already done. MiDW-A

4220. *Industrial Unionism. Hand Book No. 2.* Chicago: IWW, 1938, n.p.

4221. *Industrial Unionism, Real and Imitation: An Analysis of the Lewis Program.* Chicago: IWW, n.d. (1937?), 8 p.

The CIO cannot help workers the way the IWW can because John L. Lewis acts as a dictator.

4222. *Industrial Unionism: Real and Imitation. An Analysis of the Lewis Program.* Chicago, IWW, n.d. (1947?), 8 p.

Different from No. 4221. States that the AFL and UMWA are run from the top down, whereas the IWW runs from the bottom up. MiDW-A

4223. *Industrial Unionism Recognizes an Injury to One as an Injury to All Workers.* Chicago: IWW, n.d., n.p.

4224. *Industrial Unionism versus Anarchy and Reform—How the Working Class Can Abolish Wage Slavery.* Chicago: IWW, n.d., 4 p. MiU

4225. *The Industrial Workers of the World.* Portland, OR: IWW, 1934, n.p. NN

4226. *Industrial Workers of the World.* San Francisco: Bay Area Branch, IWW, n.d. (1975?), 10 p.

Organizing leaflet that answers many questions about the IWW.

4227. *Industrial Workers of the World—Extracts from Speeches Delivered at the Chicago Convention.* Chicago: IWW, n.d. (1906?), 4 p. MiU

4228. *The Industrial Workers of the World, Chicago, Replies to Moscow.* Chicago: IWW, n.d. (1945?), 4 p.

4229. *Inflation: A Pamphlet about the Cause, the Cure, Written by Workers.* Tacoma, WA: Tacoma IWW, 1974, 11 p.

Fewer workers are producing useful goods, and it is the non-productive work that is causing inflation. Decentralization of power and more democratic institutions are needed. MiDW-A

4230. *An Instructive Fable for Workers, Employed and Unemployed.* Chicago: IWW, n.d., 6 p.

Organizing leaflet. MiDW-A

4231. *The International Position of the I.W.W.* Chicago: GEB, 1922, 2 p.

The Red Trade Union International is politically controlled by the Communist Party. The IWW cannot submit to a political group. MiDW-A

4232. *Is Any Printing Union Card Worth While? Not Unless It's the Right Kind.* Chicago: Printing and Publishing Workers IU #450, IWW, n.d. (1923?), 4 p.

Comments on the recent printing strike. Had they been IWW members, they would have been more militant and would have won. MiDW-A

4233. *Is It Treason To Strike?* Chicago: GDC, n.d. (1918?), 1 p.
Circular calling for funds to help the arrested union members. DLC

4234. *Isn't It about Time You Considered Joining the IWW?* San Francisco: EWIU #620, IWW, n.d., 1 p.

4235. *It Used to Be That You Rode the Bus to Work; Now You Work To Ride the Bus.* Chicago: IWW, n.d., 2 p.
New bus fares are hurting the worker, and only militant action can help. MiDW-A

4236. *It's Poison.* Chicago: IWW, n.d. (1939?), 4 p.
The prevalent militarism and talk of war is poison for the worker, who never benefits from war. MiDW-A

4237. *It's Time for One Big Union.* Detroit: IWW, 1933, 4 p.
Organizing leaflet.

4238. *IWW.* Chicago: GRU, IWW, n.d., 4 p.
Organizing leaflet. MiDW-A

4239. *IWW.* Seattle: Seattle Joint Branches, IWW, 1955, n.p.
Organizing leaflet. OrU

4240. *The IWW—A Plain Statement of Its Structure and Principles.* Chicago: IWW, 1934, 40 p. MiDW-A

4241. *The IWW—A Statement of Its Principles, Objects and Methods.* Chicago: IWW, 1920, 4 p.
Organizing leaflet. MiDW-A

4242. *The IWW and the Iron Heel.* Chicago: IWW, n.d., n.p.

4243. *The IWW and You.* Glasgow, Scotland: IWW, n.p., 1 p.
Organizing leaflet. MiDW-A

4244. *The IWW as Reorganized under the Emergency Program—The Facts about the Split.* Chicago: IWW, n.d. (1924?), 12 p. MiDW-A

4245. *The IWW Case at Centralia—Montesano Labor Jury Dares To Tell the Truth.* Chicago: GDC, n.d. (1927?), 4 p.
Some Centralia jurors changed their minds about the guilt of the IWW. MiU

4246. *The I.W.W. Common Questions and Their Answers.* Seattle: IWW, n.d., n.p. NNU-T

4247. *IWW Demands in the Lumber Industry.* Duluth: IWW, n.d. (1933?), 1 p.
List of eight demands, including an eight-hour day and conditions comparable to those in the Pacific Northwest. MiDW-A

4248. *IWW in Theory and Practice.* Chicago: IWW, 1937, 124 p.
One of many editions since the first (see no. 4082). Most editions after 1920 are not attributed to Ebert. WHi

4249. *The IWW—It Is the One Real Union.* Detroit: MMWIU #400, IWW, 1934, 1 p.
Organizing leaflet.

4250. *The IWW: Its History.* New Castle, PA: IWW Pub. Bureau, n.d., n.p. DL

4251. *IWW Literature Price List.* Chicago: IWW Pub. Bureau, n.d., 4 p.
Comprehensive list of pamphlets and papers, including foreign-language ones.

4252. *IWW News.* Los Angeles: IWW, 1946, 4 p.
An organizing leaflet that contains a preamble in Spanish.

4253. *The IWW: One Big Union, the Greatest Thing on Earth.* Chicago: CWIU #573, IWW, n.d. (1922?), 4 p.
Organizing leaflet for construction workers.

4254. *IWW Organization Manual.* Chicago: IWW, 1978, 23 p. MiU

4255. *The IWW Program: Education, Organization, Emancipation.* Chicago: IWW, n.d., 4 p.
Organizing leaflet that explains the meaning of the three stars in the IWW logo.

4256. *IWW Reply to the Red Trade Union International.* Chicago: GEB, 1922, 32 p.
Explanation of the IWW's refusal to join the International (see no. 4231). MiDW-A

4257. *IWW Reply to State's Attorneys: An Open Letter to Mssrs. Nelson and Hill of Humboldt County, California.* San Francisco: CBGDC, n.d. (1923?) 14 p.
Expresses outrage at the prosecution of the Syndicalist laws.

4258. IWW Sacco-Vanzetti Defense Committee. The Story of the Sacco-Fanzetti [*sic*] Case. Roxbury, MA: Progress Printing, 1921.

4259. *The IWW Speaks to Workers of All Industries.* Chicago: IWW, 1946, 4 p.
Organizing leaflet pointing out how workers can be misled

by many schemes like the Townsend Plan and the CIO. The only real answer is solidarity and industrial unionism.

4260. *IWW Statement.* San Pedro: IWW Publicity Committee, 1924, 4 p.
The IWW has been falsely accused of planning an explosion. The newspapers even lied about the raids on the IWW, which were perpetrated by the police and the Ku Klux Klan.
MiDW-A

4261. *IWW: The Greatest Thing on Earth.* Chicago: IWW, n.d. (1920?), 32 p.
Organizing leaflet explaining in detail how the IWW works (not to be confused with no. 4253, a different pamphlet).
MiDW-A

4262. *The I.W.W.—The Institution of the Working Class.* Chicago: IWW, n.d.
Organizing leaflet reminding workers that there is no substitute for the IWW. MiDW-A

4263. *IWW—The Last May Day?* New York: IWW, 1949, 2 p.

4264. *IWW: They Don't Want You SDSers To Go To Work.* Chicago: IWW, 1969, 1 p.
J. Edgar Hoover hopes that young people will not radicalize the workers. MiDW-A

4265. *The IWW Welcomes Students.* Chicago: IWW, n.d. (1970?), n.p.

4266. *The IWW: What It Is and What It Is Not.* Chicago: IWW, n.d. (1925?), 39 p.
Organizing leaflet, printed in many editions. MiDW-A

4267. *The IWW: What It Is and What It Stands for.* Detroit: IWW, n.d., n.p.

4268. *Janitors, Secretaries, Painters.* Milwaukee: University of Wisconsin Branch, IWW, n.d. (1975?), 1 p.
Organizing leaflet urges workers to join the student branch. MiDW-A

4269. Jewell, Gary. *The IWW in Canada.* Chicago: IWW, n.d., 12 p.
History and influence of the IWW in Canada. MiU

4270. *A Job for Every Worker: 4-Hour Day. Organize for Class Power.* New York: Unemployed Group #1 of IWW, 1935, 4 p.
Organizing leaflet stating that a four-hour day would solve the unemployment problem. MiU

4271. *Joe Hill Was for Real.* Chicago: IWW, n.d. (1979?), 1 p.
Students and others should join the IWW. MiDW-A

4272. *Joe Hill's Union Lives!* Chicago: IWW, 1971, 1 p.
Circular passed out at a movie about Joe Hill. MiDW-A

4273. *Join a Real Union.* Chicago: IWW, n.d., 1 p.
Organizing leaflet. MiDW-A

4274. *Join the UAW-CIO? If You Want To Be Tied Up in Contracts That Will Leave You at the Mercy of Your Employer and Your Top Union Officials.* Cleveland: MMWIU #440, IWW, n.d., n.p.

4275. *Judicial Murder.* Seattle: Washington Branch, GDC, n.d. (1929?), 4 p.
Unfair prosecutions and sentences and remarks made by law-connected individuals showing the injustices to the IWW. MiDW-A

4276. *Justice for the Negro—How He Can Get It.* Chicago: IWW, n.d., 4 p.
Organizing leaflet stating that by solidarity and organization, Negroes can win justice. MiDW-A

4277. Kirschbaum, P. W. *To All Wage Earners and Friends of Labor.* Paterson, NJ: IWW Relief Committee, 1913, n.p.
Strike funds appeal.

4278. *Knaves and Fools.* Los Angeles: Alfred Kohn, IWW, n.d., 1 p.
Workers Party of Los Angeles should not denigrate the fighting IWW. MiDW-A

4279. Koettgen, Ewald. *One Big Union in the Textile Industry.* Cleveland: IWW Pub. Bur., n.d. (1914?), 15 p.
The successes of textile workers when they are unionized. MiDW-A

4280. Kolontay, Alexandra. *The Workers' Opposition in Russia: The Workers' Opposition in the Communist Party.* Chicago: IWW, 1921, 48 p.
The struggle in Russia, after the revolution, between those advocating workers' management of production and the "nascent bureaucracy." Stresses the importance of working-class power at the point of production. The IWW was the first in the United States to publish this document. Reprinted in 1961 and since. MiDW-A

4281. Kurinsky, Philip. *The IWW, Its Principles and Methods.* Brooklyn: Yiddish IWW Pub. Bureau, 1916, 63 p.
Organizing pamphlet that explains the methods and organization of the IWW. NN

4282. *Labor Fakers Protect the Interest of Capitalism.* Chicago: IWW, n.d., 1 p.

Many union leaders, especially in the AFL, are protecting the interest of the bosses. MiDW-A

4283. *Labor Has Some Liberty.* Buffalo: IWW, n.d. (1934?), 1 p.

Organizing leaflet for Morrison Steel Products workers in Buffalo. MiDW-A

4284. *Lake Marine Workers on Ships and Docks: A Few Words to You.* Cleveland: IWW Pub. Bureau, n.d., 4 p.

Organizing leaflet. WHi

4285. *Lake Seamen Join Now, Wake Up.* Buffalo: IWW, n.d., 1 p.

Organizing leaflet. MiDW-A

4286. Lane, Winthrop D. *Uncle Sam: Jailor.* Chicago: IWW, n.d. (1919?), 40 p.

Evils of the Wichita jail and the treatment of prisoners kept there for almost two years before the Syndicalism trial. MiDW-A

4287. Le Berthon, Ted. *Does This Explain Reason Innocent Men Are Jailed?* Los Angeles: CBGDC, 1924, 1 p.

The San Pedro incident. MiDW-A

4288. *Lest We Forget.* Chicago: IWW, 1919, 8 p.

The IWW was persecuted in an effort to destroy militant labor. See no. 4002. This edition is not attributed to Gordon Cascaden. MiDW-A

4289. *Let Us Have the Truth.* Los Angeles: CDC, n.d. (1924?), 4 p.

The California Syndicalist trials and the San Quentin prisoners. MiDW-A

4290. *Let Us Suppose.* Centralia, WA: CPC, n.d., n.p.

Leaflet about Centralia. NNU-T

4291. *Let's Act Union: What Sort of a Union Is the IWW Asking You To Build?* Chicago: IWW, 1971, 4 p.

Organizing leaflet.

4292. *Let's All Get Rich.* Chicago: MWIU #440, IWW, n.d., 2 p.

Organizing leaflet.

4293. *Let's Not Trade Wars.* Chicago: IWW, 1970, 1 p.

Anti-Vietnam leaflet urging union solidarity. MiDW-A

4294. Lewis, Austin B. *Proletarian and Petit-Bourgeois.* Chicago: IWW Pub. Bur., 1912, 32 p.
Reprinted many times. MiDW-A

4295. *Lindway Fights the Frame-Up Plant.* Chicago: GDC, IWW, n.d. (1937?), 2 p.
The conviction of Mike Lindway in Ohio for picket-line violence was a frame-up. MiDW-A

4296. *Listen to Facts—A Year's Persecution.* San Francisco: California Branch, GDC, 1922, 4 p.
The Criminal Syndicalist trials in California.

4297. *Loggers and Millmen! Join the Rank and File Union.* Chicago: LWIU #120, IWW, n.d., 2 p.
Organizing leaflet. MiDW-A

4298. *Long Talons in California.* Chicago: GOC, n.d. (1924?), 2 p.
The Criminal Syndicalist trials in California and the San Pedro incident. MiDW-A

4299. *Look Out—Danger Ahead!* Chicago: IWW, 1939, 4 p.
Many promises are being made for "after the war," but it will be up to the worker to see that they come true. MiDW-A

4300. Lorton, Bert, et al. *To the Members of the IWW.* n.p.: Bert Lorton, IWW, n.d. (1924?), 4 p.
The views of political prisoners who refused a conditional pardon. MiDW-A

4301. *Los Angeles Garment Workers.* Los Angeles: IWW, n.d., 2 p.
Organizing leaflet. MiDW-A

4302. *Lost, Strayed, Stolen. One Perfectly Good Third International.* Chicago: IWW, n.d. (1932?), 1 p.
Because Russia is bargaining with the capitalists, the only hope for workers is a general strike. MiDW-A

4303. *Low Pay, Erratic Hours, Sudden Layoffs.* San Francisco: IWW, n.d. (1977?), 2 p.
Organizing leaflet for hotel and restaurant workers. MiDW-A

4304. *Lumber Industry and Its Workers.* Chicago: IWW, n.d. (1921?), 91 p.
Gives much information about lumbering and explains IWW organization and many of its victories. MiDW-A

4305. *Lumber Workers Don't Be Fooled.* Spokane: IWW, 1936, 1 p.
Organizing leaflet.

4306. *Lumber Workers of Columbia River.* Chicago: IWW, n.d., 4 p.
Organizing leaflet. MiDW-A

4307. *Lumber Workers of Michigan, Wisconsin and Minnesota: A Review of Conditions in the Camps.* Chicago: LWIU #120, IWW, n.d., 4 p.
Organizing leaflet. MiDW-A

4308. *Lumber Workers Organize!* Chicago: LWIU #120, IWW, n.d., 4 p.
Organizing leaflet. MiDW-A

4309. *Lumberworkers You Need Organization.* Chicago: IWW, (1925?), 4 p.
Organizing leaflet demanding a six-hour day. MiDW-A

4310. McDaniels, Julius F., and Dorice McDaniels. *The Unknown Soldier.* Chicago: IWW, n.d., 42 p.
Same as no. 3781, which was first printed privately. MiDW-A

4311. McDonald, Edward. *The Farm Laborer and the City Worker.* Cleveland: IWW Pub. Bureau, n.d., 13 p.
Organizing leaflet. MiDW-A

4312. McDonald, J. A. *Unemployment and the Machine.* Chicago: IWW, 1923, 50 p.
How mechanization creates unemployment. MiDW-A

4313. *Make the Plunge.* New York: OBU Conference, n.d. (1920?), 2 p.
Urges workers to join the only industrial union. MiDW-A

4314. *Make Your Voice Be Heard.* San Francisco: GDC, n.d., 4 p.
Urges workers to protest Syndicalist trials. MiDW-A

4315. *Management's Most Delicate Operation—Taking the You Out of Union.* Trenton, MI: Detroit-Ann Arbor IWW, n.d. (1975?), n.p.

4316. *Manifesto: Issued to the Marine Workers of the Universe.* Chicago: IWW, 1921, 2 p.
Announces an international seamen's congress in Petrograd. MiDW-A

4317. *Manifesto—To Workers of All the Industries.* New York: GRU, 1919, 2 p. DLC

4318. *March to the Prisons! Set Free Those Who Are There Because They Thirst for Truth.* Detroit: IWW, 1919, 1 p.
Protests the raids and arrests of the IWW all over the country. MiDW-A

4319. Marcy, Mary. *Shop Talks on Economics.* Chicago: IWW, n.d., 40 p.
How economics works in the factories. The author advises industrial socialism. MiDW-A

4320. *Marine Workers Join the O.B.U. for Action against Wage Cuts and Unemployment.* New York: IWW, n.d., n.p.
Organizing leaflet. MiU

4321. *Martyrs of Texas, Rangel, Cline, Etc.* Oakland, CA: CDC, n.d., 4 p.
Appeal for release of Mexican revolutionaries imprisoned in Texas. MiDW-A

4322. *Masters of the West. The Scene We Must Prevent from Being Enacted.* Salt Lake City: Joe Hill Defense Fund, n.d. (1916?), 4 p.
Asks workers to hold protest meetings and to write letters to save Joe Hill from execution. MiDW-A

4323. *The Meaning of This May Day.* New York: IWW, n.d., 4 p.
May Day's real meaning is international solidarity of the workers. MiDW-A

4324. *Medieval California, Land of Orange Groves and Jails.* Chicago: GDC, n.d. (1924?), 8 p.
Protests the harsh California Syndicalist laws. MiDW-A

4325. *Members of the Draper Shop Branch of the I.W.W. Who Have Joined the United States Army, Navy, or Coast Guard.* n.p.: IWW, n.d. (1942?), 1 p. NNU-T

4326. *Men of the Army—Farewell.* Chicago: IWW, n.d. (1919?), 4 p.
Veterans must think of themselves not as men of the army but as men of the working class who will help build the union. MiDW-A

4327. *Message from the City Jail of Centralia, Washington. Has Patriotism in Centralia Become the Last Refuge of Centralia's Scoundrels?* Seattle: Equity Printing, n.d. (1920?), 4 p.
Pleads for an end to the anti-IWW hysteria. MiDW-A

4328. *Message from the Sacramento County Jail.* n.p., The Ten Defenders, IWW, n.d. (1923?), 4 p.
Urges the public to realize the undemocratic treatment that the IWW prisoners have received.

4329. *A Message to All Seamen.* Glasgow: IWW, n.d., 1 p.
Asks seamen of all countries to back their strike. MiDW-A

4330. *A Message to Coal Miners.* Chicago: WIES, IWW, n.d., 2 p.
Organizing leaflet. MiDW-A

4331. *A Message to the Members of the Industrial Workers of the World and to the Working Class in General.* Chicago: IWW, n.d., n.p. DL

4332. *Metal and Machinery Workers of Toledo.* Toledo: MMWIU #440, IWW, n.d., 2 p.
Organizing leaflet.

4333. *Metal and Machinery Workers, Organize!* Chicago: MMWIU #440, IWW, n.d., 4 p.
Organizing leaflet.

4334. *Metal Mine Workers! A Few Words Addressed to Mine Workers, from Mine Workers.* Butte: IWW, n.d., 4 p.
Organizing leaflet. MiDW-A

4335. *A Metal Worker's Guide: Health and Safety on the Job.* Chicago: General Production Workers Organizing Committee of the IWW, 1976, 22 p. MiU

4336. *Metal Workers of America! Unite!* Chicago: MMWIU #440, IWW, n.d., 4 p.
Organizing leaflet. DLC

4337. *Mike Lindway's Fight Is Your Fight!* Chicago: GDC, 1936, 4 p.
Asks support for Lindway, imprisoned for picket-line violence. MiDW-A

4338. *Miners!* MMWIU #210, IWW, n.d. (1927?), 1 p.
The nine demands of IWW miners in Utah. MiDW-A

4339. *Miners, Attention!* Butte: IWW, n.d. (1928?), 1 p.
Call to a mass meeting of copper miners to protest lay-offs. MiDW-A

4340. *Miners of Illinois.* Chicago: IWW, n.d., 2 p.
Organizing leaflet signed by Forrest Edwards. MiDW-A

4341. *Misconceptions of the I.W.W.; One Aim, One Union, One Enemy.* New York: IWW, n.d. (1918?), 4 p.
The IWW is the victim not only of severe criticism and systematic persecution but also of charges that are totally false. MiDW-A

4342. Mitchell, "Rusty." *Address to Railroad Graders.* Chicago: IWW Pub. Bur., n.d., 4 p.

4343. *Mob Rules Yakima* (GRU Bulletin #4). n.p.: GRU, IWW, 1933, n.p.
The Yakima, Washington, migratory fruit-pickers' strikes.

4344. *Mob Scalds Children: Workers Tarred and Feathered.* San Pedro, CA: Relief Committee, IWW, n.d. (1924?), 4 p.
The San Pedro incident. MiDW-A

4345. *Mob Violence in San Pedro: I.W.W. Statement Supported by Photographs.* San Pedro, CA: IWW, 1926, 9 p.
The San Pedro incident. NN

4346. *A Modern Union for a Modern Industry.* Chicago: RRWIU #520, IWW, n.d., 4 p.
Organizing leaflet.

4347. *Mods, Rockers, and the Revolution.* Chicago: IWW, 1965, 10 p.
Pamphlet with several contributions by young IWWs about the youth revolution, the Beatles, and similar concerns. MiDW-A

4348. Monoldi, P. *Why Building Workers Must Organize in the One Big Union!* Chicago: IWW, n.d., 16 p.
Organizing leaflet. MiDW-A

4349. *More Money for Your Hard Work.* Buffalo: IWW, n.d., 1 p.
Organizing leaflet. MiDW-A

4350. *More Power to You.* Los Angeles: General Membership IWW Reorganization Movement, 1924, 46 p. MiDW-A

4351. *More Truth about the IWW; Facts in Relation to the Trial at Chicago by Competent Industrial Investigators and Noted Economists.* Chicago: IWW, n.d., 48 p. DLC

4352. *Mr. Daugherty Is Mistaken! There Are Political Prisoners in the United States.* Chicago: GDC, n.d. (1922?), 4 p.
A reply to the Attorney General's statement that there are no political prisoners. MiDW-A

4353. *Mugged and Fingerprinted and Sentenced to the Hole.* Boulder Dam: IWW, 1934, n.p.
Leaflet from the Boulder Dam strike.

4354. *Murder on a Picket Line.* Chicago: IWW, 1978, 1 p.
Protest leaflet about the death of a picket-line striker who was run over by a supervisor while picketing in Tracy, California. MiDW-A

4355. *Murphy Cook & Co.* Philadelphia: MTWIU #510, IWW, n.d., 1 p.
Urges transport workers of Philadelphia to boycott the Murphy Cooke Co. MiDW-A

4356. Nearing, Scott. *Those Who Possess and Those Who Produce.* Chicago: IWW, n.d., n.p.

4357. *Negroes—Defend Yourselves! Free Yourselves From Wage Slavery and from Persecution! By Joining the IWW.* Chicago: IWW, 1924, 4 p.

4358. *Neither the Electric Chair—Nor a Living Death! But Freedom for Sacco and Vanzetti!* Washington Branch, GDC, n.d, 1 p. MiDW-A

4359. Nelson, E. S. *Appeal to Wage Workers, Men and Women.* Cleveland: IWW Pub. Bur., n.d., 4 p.
Organizing leaflet. DL

4360. *New Idea: Why Union Men Are Persecuted in California.* San Francisco: California Branch, GDC, n.d., 4 p.
The persecutions are aimed at the whole labor movement. MiDW-A

4361. *New Way To Pay Union Dues Starts Next Week.* Cleveland: MMWIU #440, IWW, n.d., 1 p.
A union representative will stand near the time clock and take dues personally. MiDW-A

4362. *New York Defense Committee of the IWW.* New York: Defense Committee, IWW, 1919, 1 p.
Appeal for funds for IWW prisoners.

4363. *No Conscription, No Slavery.* n.p.: IWW, n.d. (1970?), 1 p.
Antidraft leaflet, parts of which are taken from a Seattle leaflet of 1919. MiDW-A

4364. *No Debeis Comprar in Trabajo! (Restaurant Workers! Don't Buy a Job!* on verso). New York: IWW, n.d., 2 p.
Organizing leaflet for restaurant workers. MiDW-A

4365. *No Room for Race Discrimination—on the Campus—in Industry—in Our Personal Lives.* New York: IWW, n.d. (1968?), 1 p.
Pleas for integration and racial harmony.

4366. *No Surrender!* Casper, CA: Education Department of the Fishing Workers IU, IWW, n.d. (1972?), 1 p.
Protests the announced wage freeze.

4367. *Nothing in Common.* Chicago: IWW, n.d., 4 p.
The IWW Preamble is still true. MiDW-A

4368. *Now's the Time for a Real Building Construction Workers' Union.* Chicago: BCWIU #330, IWW, n.d., 2 p.
Organizing leaflet. MiDW-A

4369. *Off the N.L.R.B. Ballot—Why?* Chicago: MMWIU #440, IWW, n.d. (1949?), 2 p.

4370. *Oil Field Workers Unite!* Chicago: IWW, n.d. (1917?), 8 p.
Organizing leaflet. MiDW-A

4371. *Oil Workers!* Oklahoma City, OK: OWIU #230, IWW, n.d., 4 p.
Organizing leaflet. MiDW-A

4372. *On for the Six Hour Day!* Chicago: LWIU #120, IWW, n.d. (1920?), 4 p.
Urges institution of the six-hour day for lumberworkers and others. Different editions have different graphics.

4373. *On Rubber or on Steel.* Chicago: AWIU #120, IWW, n.d., 4 p.
Organizing leaflet stating that whether a migrant worker drives a car or hops a train to the harvest fields he needs organizing. MiDW-A

4374. *On the Firing Line.* Spokane: *Industrial Worker,* 1912, 46 p.
An account of the McNamara case, the Lawrence strike, the Ettor and Giovannitti case, and the methods and organization of the IWW. MiDW-A

4375. *One Aim, One Union, One Enemy.* New York: IWW, 1918, n.p.
Organizing leaflet. NjP

4376. *One Big Industrial Union in the Textile Industry.* Chicago: TWIU #410, IWW, n.d., 24 p.
The IWW is the best union to meet the problems of the textile workers. Similar to no. 4279. MiDW-A

4377. *One Big Key That Unlocks All Jail Doors for the Centralia Victims of the Criminal Lumber Trust.* Seattle: CPC, n.d., 4 p.
Organizing is the key to freeing the Centralia prisoners. MiDW-A

4378. *One Big Union.* Chicago: IWW, n.d., 32 p.
Organizing leaflet. MiDW-A

4379. One Big Union Club (NY). *AWO—A Story of a Union in the Making.* New York: OBU Club, 1939, 2 p. MiDW-A

4380. ———. *Contracts or No Contracts.* New York: OBU Club, 1939, 4 p.
Contracts are for sectional unions; the IWW does not need them. MiDW-A

4381. ———. *Cooperation and Coordination—the Basic Principles of Union Organization.* New York: OBU Club, 1935, 2 p.
Only one big union can truly coordinate labor's efforts. MiDW-A

4382. ———. *History of "400"—AWO, the One Big Union Idea in Action.* New York: OBU Club, 1939, 23 p.

The history of the Agricultural Workers Organization from its beginning in 1915. MiDW-A

4383. ———. *Hodson's Relief Racket: Thugs on Duty.* New York: OBU Club, n.d., n.p.

4384. ———. *A Labor Union—A Union of Labor Power.* New York: OBU Club, n.d., 6 p. MiU

4385. ———. *Marine Workers: Revolt against False Form of Organization.* New York: OBU Club, n.d. (1939?), 4 p. MiDW-A

4386. ———. *Organization and Strike Strategy.* New York: OBU Club, 1937, 15 p.

4387. ———. *Surplus Value and the Union Road to Power.* New York: OBU Club, n.d., 6 p.

How workers are exploited and how they can remedy the situation by joining into one big union. MiDW-A

4388. ———. *Why One Big Union?* New York: OBU Club, 1936, 12 p.

One big union rather than many diversified ones will allow the workers to reach their goals. MiDW-A

4389. ———. *Why the One Big Union Club?* New York: OBU Club, 1935, 2 p.

Craft and class unions cannot succeed because only with one big union will the workers have the strength to win their battle. MiDW-A

4390. *One Big Union for Railroad Workers.* Chicago: RRWIU #520, IWW, n.d. (1948?), 1 p.

Organizing leaflet. MiDW-A

4391. *One Big Union—Industrial Workers of the World—Where Do You Fit In? Think It Over, Join the IWW.* Chicago: IWW, 1917, n.p.

Organizing leaflet. DLC

4392. *One Big Union of All Railroad Workers.* Chicago: RRWIU #520, IWW, n.d., 2 p.

Organizing leaflet warning railroad workers that they have too many unions and that it would serve them well to belong to one. MiDW-A

4393. *One Big Union of All the Workers.* Chicago: IWW, 1933, 13 p.

Organizing leaflet. MiDW-A

4394. *One Big Union of All the Workers—IWW.* Chicago: IWW, 1944, 30 p.

Organizing leaflet, printed in many editions. NN

4395. *One Big Union of All the Workers—the Greatest Thing on Earth.* Chicago: IWW, n.d., 31 p.
Organizing leaflet. DLC

4396. *One Big Union of the Industrial Workers of the World.* Chicago: IWW, 1944, 30 p.
Organizing leaflet. NN

4397. *One Big Union of the IWW. Chart Included.* Chicago: IWW, 1915, 26 p.
Organizing leaflet, printed in many editions. RPB

4398. *One Big Union Structure of the Industrial Workers of the World.* Chicago: IWW, 1972, 16 p.
Organizing leaflet. MiDW-A

4399. *One Big Union Today—IWW.* San Diego: IWW, n.d. (1975?), 1 p.
Organizing leaflet. MiDW-A

4400. *The Only Real Agitator Is Injustice.* San Francisco: CBGDC, n.d., n.p.

4401. *Open Letter.* Chicago: RRWIU #600, IWW, n.d. (1922?), 4 p.
Urges railroad workers to abandon the AFL and organize industrially. The rank-and-file worker is the most important to the IWW. MiDW-A

4402. *Open Letter from the IWW to the State's Attorneys of California.* San Francisco: California Branch, GDC, 1924, 15 p.
Denies the frequent assertions in the Syndicalist trials that the IWW advocates violence. MiDW-A

4403. *Open Letter to Briggs Employees.* Detroit: IWW, 1933, 4 p.
Urges all workers to participate in the strike. MiDW-A

4404. *Open Letter to President Harding from 52 Members.* Chicago: GDC, IWW, 1922, 28 p.
Prisoners state that they are not criminals and that they deserve unconditional pardons. MiDW-A

4405. *The Open Shop.* Chicago: IWW, 1919, 2 p.
The drive for open shops must be resisted. MiDW-A

4406. *The Open Shop: An Appeal of the IWW to the Craft Unions of Salt Lake City.* Salt Lake City, UT: Propaganda Committee, IWW, n.d. (1922?), 1 p.
Invitation to all craft unionists to come down to IWW headquarters and pick up some literature so they can learn why industrial unions are the only workable kind.

4407. *Open the Iron Gates in Idaho!* Chicago: GDC, n.d. (1924?), 2 p.
Urges release of Syndicalist prisoners, naming A. S. Embree, H. E. Herd, and Joseph Doyle. MiDW-A

4408. *Open the Jails! March to the Prisons! Set Free Those Who Are There Because They Thirst for Truth!* Detroit: IWW, n.d. (1922?), 1 p.
Plea for all the prisoners to be set free.

4409. *Open the Prison Doors.* Chicago: IWW, n.d. (1924?), 4 p.
Plea for the many prisoners still incarcerated. MiDW-A

4410. *Open the Prison Gates, Mr. and Mrs. Citizen.* San Francisco: CBGDC, IWW, n.d. (1923?), 4 p.
Plea for the public to realize how unjust the prisoners' situation is. MiDW-A

4411. *Open Up the Open House!* n.p.: EWIU #620, IWW, n.d. (1975?), 2 p.
Possibly a Madison, Wisconsin, appeal to student workers to join the IWW. MiDW-A

4412. *Opening Statement of Geo. F. Vanderveer.* Chicago: IWW Pub. Bur., n.d. (1918?), 102 p.
Statement at the Chicago trial by the defense attorney. MiDW-A

4413. *Opportunity of the General Construction Workers.* Chicago: GCWIU #310, IWW, n.d., 24 p.
Organizing leaflet printed in several editions. MiDW-A

4414. *Organization Is the Mother of Security.* AWIU #110, IWW, n.d., 4 p.
Organizing leaflet for farmworkers. MiDW-A

4415. *Organization Leaflet: Detroit, Mich—The Secret Document.* Detroit: IWW, 1918, 4 p.
Quotes a document from the Wayne County War Board, showing the board's plan to make workers content by giving them patriotic medals. MiDW-A

4416. *Organization—the Road to Freedom.* Chicago: LWIU #120, IWW, n.d., 4 p.
Organizing leaflet for lumberworkers. MiDW-A

4417. *Organization versus Disruption.* GCWIU #310, IWW, n.d., 2 p.
Organizing leaflet for construction workers. MiDW-A

4418. *Organize, Cafe Employees.* n.p.: EWIU #620, IWW, n.d. (1974?), 1 p.
Organizing leaflet for restaurant workers.

4419. *Organize for Security.* Minneapolis: IWW, n.d., 2 p.
Organizing leaflet. MiDW-A

4420. *Organize Industrially, Railroad Maintenance Men!* Chicago: RRWIU #520, IWW, n.d., 4 p.
Organizing leaflet for railroad workers. MiDW-A

4421. *Organize Together! The Way You Work.* Philadelphia: TWIU #420, IWW, n.d., 2 p.
Organizing leaflet for textile workers. MiDW-A

4422. *Out of a Job! The Fate of Millions.* Chicago: GRU, n.d. (1935?), 2 p.
Organizing leaflet aimed at the unemployed. MiDW-A

4423. *Out of Their Own Mouths.* San Francisco: GDC, n.d. (1924?), 4 p.
About the Criminal Syndicalist trials in California. MiDW-A

4424. *Overalls Brigade to 1972 Convention.* Santa Rosa, CA: IWW, 1972, 1 p.
Plans to reenact the 1908 "Overalls Brigade" at the convention.

4425. *Pastor Scores IWW Enemies.* Chicago: GDC, 1923, 4 p.
Many citizens are forgetting about civil rights.

4426. Payne, C. E. *That Federal Subversive List.* Vancouver: IWW, 1956, 1 p.
The federal subversive list is backed by no federal law. MiDW-A

4427. Pease, Frank Chester. *Revolution and the IWW.* Sydney, Australia: IWW, n.d., 16 p.
The real revolution will be the end of exploitation through the wage system.

4428. *The Penalty of Progress.* San Francisco: CBGDC, n.d. (1925?), 4 p.
The bosses are united, but not the workers. MiDW-A

4429. Perry, Grover H. *The Revolutionary IWW.* Cleveland: IWW, n.d., 24 p.
The method and beliefs of the IWW. MiDW-A

4430. *Persecution of Solidarity—Shall the Master Class Destroy the Labor Press of Pennsylvania?* New Castle: Solidarity, 1910, 1 p.
Protests the jailing of IWW newspapermen.

4431. *Persecution of Union Men in California.* Los Angeles: California Branch, GDC, IWW, n.d. (1924?), 6 p.
The Syndicalist trials and prisoners in California. MiDW-A

4432. *Philadelphia Controversy.* Philadelphia: MTWIU #510, IWW, 35 p.
History of the 1920 controversy among union members.
MiDW-A

4433. *Philadelphia Longshoremen Locked Out.* Philadelphia: MTWIU #510, IWW, n.d. (1921?), 1 p.
Protest about the actions of the ILA, which is trying to lure away members.

4434. *Pie-Card Gang Raids IWW Headquarters with Guns and Drives the GEB into the Street.* Chicago: IWW, 1924, n.p.
Leaflet about the IWW split. MiU

4435. *Piece Work and the Tank Builder.* Chicago: IWW, n.d., 4 p.
The pay rate at plants building tanks is unfair. MiDW-A

4436. *A Plain Statement of Facts to the Union Men of America.* Chicago: GDC, 1918, 1 p.
All union men are in danger of being engulfed by patriotic union-busters. MiDW-A

4437. *Playing with Dynamite.* Chicago: IWW, 1918, 4 p.
Arresting so many IWWs and common workmen will reduce and demoralize the country's work force. MiDW-A

4438. *Poison versus Dynamite.* Chicago: IWW, n.d., 4 p.
Public newspapers cannot be trusted, while IWW newspapers, are truthful and powerful. MiDW-A

4439. *Practical Suggestions for General Construction Workers.* Chicago: GCWIU #310, IWW, n.d., 4 p.
Organizing leaflet. MiDW-A

4440. *Preamble and Constitution, as Adopted and Amended.* Chicago: IWW, 1921, 44 p.

4441. *Preamble and Constitution of the Industrial Workers of the World, Organized July 7, 1905.* Chicago: IWW Pub. Bur., 1911, n.p. WaPS

4442. *Press and Detectives Start New Outrages against the Workers.* Chicago: IWW, n.d., 1 p.
The many raids and arrests of IWWs. WaPS

4443. *Prisoners Should Not Help Prisons Operate.* New York: IWW, 1965, 1 p.
Reasons put forth by prisoners at Hart Island (New York) Workhouse. MiDW-A

4444. *Proclamation: Addressed to All Marine Workers.* n.p.: MTWIU #510, IWW, n.d. (1923?), 2 p.
Call for a strike of all seamen for higher wages and to protest the arrests of many union men. MiDW-A

4445. *Progress Means Change, and How.* Detroit: IWW, 1934, 4 p.
Organizing leaflet for Cadillac Motor Company employees. MiDW-A

4446. *Prosecution or Persecution?* San Francisco: California Branch, GDC, 1925, 4 p.
Protests Syndicalist trials. MiDW-A

4447. *Prosecution or Persecution?* San Francisco: Ford Defense Committee, n.d. (1926?) 4 p.
Urges release of Wheatland prisoners. MiDW-A

4448. *Public Opinion: Where Does It Stand on the Question of Amnesty and Political Prisoners?*
Call for amnesty for wartime political prisoners. MiDW-A

4449. *Put the Boss in Overalls!* Chicago: IWW, n.d. (1922?), 2 p.
Organizing leaflet questioning why the many who work have nothing while a few own everything. MiDW-A

4450. *Put the Boss in Overalls!* Chicago: IWW, n.d., 4 p.
Organizing leaflet stating that workers must control industry and there must be no parasites.

4451. Pycard, John. *Rank and File vs. the Labor Skates.* Vancouver: CDC, 1919, 40 p.
Organizing leaflet explaining the IWW method and organization, as compared with the Canadian One Big Union and the Communists. MiDW-A

4452. Quinlan, James, and Bert Lorton. *An Open Reply to an Underhanded Attack, to Forest Edwards.* n.p.: Quinlan and Lorton, IWW, n.d. (1924?), 4 p.
Accuses Edwards of betraying the IWW and its prisoners. MiDW-A

4453. *Railroad Development Shows Need for New Unionism.* Chicago: RRWIU #520, IWW, n.d., 4 p.
Organizing leaflet for railroad workers. MiDW-A

4454. *Railroad Workers: Do You Want Power?* Chicago: RRWIU #600, IWW, n.d. (1918?), 2 p.
Organizing leaflet for railroad workers.

4455. *Railroad Workers—Don't Take It Lying Down.* Chicago: RRWIU #520, IWW, n.d. (1948?), 1 p.
Railroad workers should be more militant in the face of "featherbedding" accusations. MiDW-A

4456. *Railroad Workers: One Big Union or Unemployment.* Detroit: RRWIU #520, IWW, 1934, 6 p.
Urges workers to solve unemployment by organizing. MiDW-A

4457. *Railroad Workers—One Big Union—Strike While the Iron is Hot.* Pittsburgh: Railroad Workers, IWW, n.d. (1922?), 1 p.
This is the time for a railroad strike and all railroad workers of all unions should join it. MiDW-A

4458. *Railroad Workers—Organize Industrially.* Chicago: RRWIU #520, IWW, n.d. (1923?), 4 p.
Organizing leaflet with humorous cartoon, urging workers to join up. MiDW-A

4459. *Railroad Workers Think This Over—Then Act.* Chicago: RRWIU #520, IWW, n.d., 6 p.
Organizing leaflet, a thoughtful argument for an industrial union.

4460. *Railroad Workers: Unionism or Unemployment.* Chicago: RRWIU #520, IWW, 1925, 4 p.
Railroads may not always be prosperous, and the workers had better organize. DLC

4461. *Railroad Workers You Are Sold Out.* Chicago: IWW, n.d., 2 p.
Warren S. Stone, president of the BLE, has sold out the railroad workers; they should now join a real union, the IWW. MiDW-A

4462. *Railwaymen and Port Workers.* Pittsburgh: Railroad Workers One Big Union, n.d. (1922?), 2 p.
Organizing leaflet. MiDW-A

4463. *Rank and File or Dictatorship?* Chicago: IWW, 1924, 2 p.
Pamphlet on the 1924 split in the IWW. MiDW-A

4464. *Referendum to the Membership of the IWW.* Chicago: IWW, 1908, n.p.
A split is threatening. DL

4465. *Remedy for California's Misery.* Chicago: AWO, IWW, 1924, 4 p.
Protests the Syndicalist cases; the remedy is organization. OO

4466. *Reorganization or Abandonment of Principles.* Everett: Everett Branch, IWW, n.d. (1924?), 4 p.
Leaflet from IWWs who wish to split from the organization. MiDW-A

4467. *Request IWW Delegates To Visit Gandy Gangs.* Tacoma: IWW, n.d., 4 p.
Organizing leaflet for railroad workers. MiDW-A

4468. *Resolutions on Intervention in Russia.* Butte: Workers Council, IWW, n.d. (1919?), 1 p.
Proposes a strike to protest U.S. intervention in Russia. MiDW-A

4469. *Respetad Esta Piquete!* Reversible leaflet, other title: *Respect This Picket Line!* New York: IWW, n.d., 2 p.
Strike leaflet. MiDW-A

4470. *Restaurant Workers: Let's Talk Union.* n.p.: IWW, n.d. (1980?), 1 p.
Organizing leaflet for any kind of restaurant worker, with information about the IWW organization and beliefs.

4471. *Revolutionary Consciousness.* New York: IWW, n.d. (1976?), n.p.
Urges workers to maintain a revolutionary spirit.

4472. *Revolutionary Industrial Unionism.* Chicago: IWW, n.d., 6 p.
Organizing leaflet says the world is upside down and the IWW wants to set it right. MiDW-A

4473. *Revolutionary IWW.* Chicago: IWW, n.d. (1915?), 15 p.
A solution to the social problems of the country: the IWW. NcD

4474. *The Right Union Idea.* Chicago: Chicago Branch, IWW, n.d., 1 p.
Organizing leaflet. MiDW-A

4475. *Right Will Win—Might of Labor Killing Criminal Syndicalism Act.* San Francisco: GDC, n.d. (1920?), 4 p.
The labor protests will stop the Syndicalist trials. MiDW-A

4476. *The Roll Call—Labor Victims of the Criminal Syndicalism Act of California.* San Francisco: CBGDC, n.d. (1923?), 6 p.
Protests the harsh California Syndicalist law. MiDW-A

4477. Rowan, James. *IWW in the Lumber Industry.* Seattle: IWW, n.d. (1915?), 64 p. WaPS

4478. *RR Brothers Headed for the Rip Track.* Chicago: RRWIU #520, IWW, n.d. (1929?), 2 p.
Because railways are declining, the gandies better organize.

4479. *RR Workers Attention! Call for Organization.* Chicago: IWW, n.d. (1920?), 4 p.
Organizing leaflet. MiDW-A

4480. *Russia in America! Bloody Sunday in Everett, Washington.* Seattle: Everett PDC, n.d. (1917?), 2 p.
Protests the Everett Massacre. MiU

4481. *Sabotage Anthology.* New York: IWW, n.d. (1976?), n.p.

4482. *Sacramento 'Cutor Breaks the Law To Make Large Reputation.* San Francisco: GDC, IWW, n.d. (1923?), n.p.
The prosecutor is acting illegally at the Syndicalist trial.

4483. St. John, Vincent. *The I.W.W. and Political Parties.*
Energy should be put into organizing and education rather than wasted on politics. MiDW-A

4484. ———. *The I.W.W.: Its History, Structure and Methods.* Cleveland: IWW Pub. Bureau, 1913, 27 p.
Pamphlet explaining the IWW, printed in many editions. MiDW-A

4485. ———. *Industrial Unionism and the I.W.W.* Cleveland: IWW Pub. Bureau, 1913, 15 p.
The advantages of industrial unions over craft unions. MiDW-A

4486. ———. *Industrial Unionism and the I.W.W.* Chicago: IWW, 1919, 47 p.
A greatly expanded revision of no. 4485.

4487. ———. *Political Parties and the I.W.W.* Chicago: IWW Press Bureau, n.d., 4 p.
Urges unionists to stay out of politics.

4488. ———. *Why the American Federation of Labor Cannot Become an Industrial Union.* Cleveland: IWW Pub. Bureau, n.d. (1920?), 4 p.
Five arguments to prove that the AFL will never change. MiDW-A

4489. *San Pedro Calls!* Los Angeles: IWW, n.d., 1 p.
The San Pedro incident. MiDW-A

4490. *Science,* n.p.: IWW, n.d., 1 p.
No matter how many laws have been passed making it legal to persecute the IWW, it still has a scientific program to educate and organize the workers. MiDW-A

4491. Scott, Jack. *In and of the Civil Power: The Use of the Militia against the People of B.C.* Vancouver, BC: Vancouver Industrial District Council, IWW, n.d. (1970?), n.p.
Historical account of militia use during strikes. MiU

4492. *Scratch a Liberal Businessman and You'll Find a Capitalist Boss!* San Francisco: IU #640, IWW, n.d. (1968?), 2 p.

4493. *Seamen and Dock Workers of the Great Lakes.* Cleveland: IWW, 1916, 2 p.
Organizing leaflet.

4494. *Seamen Beware!* Glasgow, Scotland: Seaman's Rank and File Committee (IWW), n.d., 1 p.
Urges men of the British merchant navy to boycott the establishment scheme that forces seamen to pay for a license to work. MiDW-A

4495. *Seamen—Longshoremen.* New York: MTWIU #510, IWW, n.d., 1 p.

4496. *Security for All.* Buffalo: IWW, 1935, 1 p.
Organizing leaflet for machine workers. MiDW-A

4497. *Shall Joe Hill Be Murdered?* Salt Lake City: Hill Defense Fund, n.d. (1916?), 4 p.
Protests the sentence given Joe Hill.

4498. *Shall Mob Law Tactics Crush Detroit Labor?* Detroit: IWW, 1920, 1 p.
Protests the raids on IWW and radical meetings.

4499. *Shall Our Brothers Be Murdered?* Chicago: IWW, 1906, 1 p.
The arrests of Haywood, Moyer, and Pettibone before the first Haywood trial. NNU-T

4500. *Shall Sacco and Vanzetti Die?* Seattle: Washington Branch GDC, n.d. (1927?), 1 p.
Urges a general strike to save Sacco and Vanzetti from death. MiDW-A

4501. *The Shame of California.* San Francisco: CBGDC, n.d. (1923?), 4 p.
The California Syndicalist cases, with quotations from distinguished persons who oppose the persecutions. MiDW-A

4502. *The Shame of Centralia: A Travesty on Justice.* Seattle: CPC, n.d. (1927?), 4 p.
The Centralia trial and the long imprisonment of the innocent IWW prisoners. MiDW-A

4503. *The Shame of Spokane.* Spokane: IWW, 1910, n.p.
The brutality of the authorities who broke up the Spokane Free Speech Fight. MiU

4504. Shapiro, Shelby. *Unions and Racism.* Oldham, Lancs., England: IWW, 1980, 33 p.
Racism has no place in a good union. MiU

4505. *Shipbuilders' Industrial Unity Caucus.* San Francisco: IWW, n.d. (1970?), 1 p.
Protests the speed-up tactics at the Bethlehem Shipbuilding Co. MiDW-A

4506. *Shoe Workers Industrial Union No. 168 Appeals to All Who Yearn for a Better Day.* Brooklyn: Strikers' General Committee, IWW, 1910, n.p.

4507. *Shorten the Workday!* Chicago: IWW, n.d. (1921?), 2 p.
Urges workers to strike for an eight-hour day to relieve unemployment. MiDW-A

4508. Silbert, Jacob. *What Is Industrial Unionism?* Chicago: IWW, n.d. (1914?), 4 p.
Organizing leaflet intended for any kind of worker. MiDW-A

4509. *The Silent Defense: A Story of the Remarkable Trial of Members of the Industrial Workers of the World, Held at Sacramento, California.* Chicago: IWW, n.d. (1919?), 47 p.
The Sacramento Syndicalist trial in 1918. MiDW-A

4510. Slim, T-Bone. *The Power of These Two Hands.* Chicago: GCWIU #310, IWW, n.d., 12 p.
Organizing leaflet for construction workers, with description of work camps. MiDW-A

4511. ———. *Starving amidst Too Much.* Chicago: FWIU #460, n.d., 40 p.
Organizing leaflet for foodworkers covering the whole industry, with a humorous approach and a cartoon. MiDW-A

4512. *Slow Down and Live—IWW.* Chicago: IWW, 1975, 4 p.
Urges workers to take it easy and not work themselves to death. MiDW-A

4513. *Smash the IWW.* Chicago: IWW, n.d. (1919?), 8 p.
The nationwide raids and arrests. MiDW-A

4514. Smith, Elmer, and Capt. Edward Coll. *Speeches on the Centralia Case.* Centralia, WA: CPC, 1928, 16 p.
Various speeches pleading for the Centralia prisoners. MiDW-A

4515. Smith, Walker C. *The Everett Massacre: A History of Class Struggle in the Lumber Industry.* Chicago: IWW Pub. Bureau, 1918, 302 p.
A history and the causes of the Everett Massacre. MiDW-A

4516. ———. *Sabotage: Its History, Philosophy and Function.* Chicago: IWW, 1913, 32 p. MiDW-A

4517. ———. *Their Court and Our Class.* Seattle: published by the author, 1917, 16 p.
Play about the Everett Massacre, distributed as a pamphlet; the same as no. 4957.

4518. ———. *War and the Workers: General Sherman Said "War Is Hell." Don't Go to Hell in Order to Give Capitalists a Better Slice of Heaven.* New Castle, PA: IWW Pub. Bureau, 1912, 1 p.
Those who own everything should do the fighting. Printed in at least two editions. MiDW-A

4519. ———. *Was It Murder? The Truth about Centralia.* Seatte: CPC, 1922, 48 p.
The Centralia affair.

4520. *So You Need a Job?* San Francisco: IWW, n.d. (1958?), 4 p.
Organizing leaflet. MiDW-A

4521. *So, You're Out of a Job! Wake Up!* Chicago: IWW, 1933, 16 p.
Urges workers to unite in the IWW and work for a four-hour day to relieve unemployment. MiDW-A

4522. *Socialists.* Chicago: IWW Pub. Bureau, n.d., 4 p. MiU

4523. *Some Tips for Railroad Workers.* Hammond, IN: RWIU, IWW, n.d. (1920?), 3 p.
The old craft unions will no longer do the job for railroad workers, who should belong to an industrial union. MiDW-A

4524. *Something Must Be Done!* Chicago: GEB, n.d. (1920?), 2 p.
Suggests a general strike protesting the IWW imprisonments and the suppression of free speech. MiDW-A

4525. Souchy, Agustín [Augustine Souchy, Augustin Souchy]. *The Workers and Peasants of Russia and Ukraine: How Do They Live?* Chicago: IWW, 1922, 144 p.
The problems of the Russians under revolutionary government; politicization is spoiling the revolution. MiDW-A

4526. *Souvenir Program: May Day, 1936. Celebration at Verhovay Hall.* Cleveland: IWW, 1936, 4 p. MiU

4527. Spielman, Jean E. *The Tramp as Home Guard.* New Castle, PA: IWW Pub. Bureau, n.d., 4 p.

4528. *Stand Firm!* Butte, MT: Butte Branch, MMWIU #880, IWW, 1917, n.p. DLC

4529. *The Startling Story of the Minnesota Miners' Strike on the Mesabi Range, 1916.* New York: Minnesota Iron Range Strikers' Defense Committee, n.d. (1916?), 16 p.

4530. Stern, Max. *Political Beliefs Keep Ninety-Six Workers behind Bars in California Prisons.* San Francisco: CBGDC, IWW, 1923, 2 p.
Protests the Criminal Syndicalist trials and asks freedom for the political prisoners. MiDW-A

4531. Stirton, A. M. *Getting Recognition: What It Means to a Union.* Chicago: IWW, n.d. (1916?), 4 p.
The IWW is now recognized very well by the bosses. MiDW-A

4532. *Stop: In Union There Is Strength.* Chicago: GRU, n.d., 4 p.
Organizing leaflet. MiDW-A

4533. *Stop! Look and Listen! The Story of a Revolutionary Strike and How One Big Union Won.* Chicago: IWW, n.d., 4 p.
Leaflet advertising a lecture about the IWW.

4534. *Stop! Recognize Yourself?* Mountain View, CA: IWW, n.d. (1978?), 3 p.
A big university is like a factory; students should organize and join the IWW. MiDW-A

4535. *Stop! This Means You!* Chicago: GRU, n.d., 4 p.
In union there is strength and in organization there is power. NNU-T

4536. *Stop: You Ought to Know.* Centralia, WA: CPC, n.d. (1920?), 4 p.
The many injustices of the Centralia case. MiDW-A

4537. *Story of the Sea: Marine Transport Workers' Handbook.* Chicago: IWW, n.d. (1924?), 80 p.
A lengthy history of seafaring and an admonition for seamen to organize. MiDW-A

4538. *Strike!* Grand Junction, MI: AWIU #110, IWW, n.d. (1964?), 1 p.
Blueberry pickers' strike leaflet. MiDW-A

4539. *Strike at Hetch Hetchy and UC Camps.* Hetch Hetchy, CA: GCWIU #310, IWW, 1922, 1 p.

4540. *Strike at the Bond Plant.* Buffalo: IWW, n.d. (1935?), 1 p.
Strike leaflet for metal workers. MiDW-A

4541. *A Strike Call.* San Francisco: MTWIU #510, IWW, n.d., 1 p.

4542. *The Strike Call for April 25, 1923. General Strike.* n.p.: Strike Committee of the IWW, n.d., 1 p.

4543. *Strike: Natron Cut-Off.* n.p.: Strike Committee, GCWIU #310, IWW, n.d., 1 p.
Construction workers' strike leaflet. MiDW-A

4544. *Strike on the Job.* n.p.: IWW, n.d. (1918?), 1 p.
Suggests that workers work hard for eight hours and then go home, as a way of winning an eight-hour day. MiDW-A

4545. *Strike! Strike! Proclamation.* New York: MTWIU #510, IWW, n.d., 1 p.
Urges a sympathy strike to support British seamen. MiDW-A

4546. *Strike! Strike! Strike!* San Francisco: IWW, n.d. (1924?), 1 p.
Asks workers to come to a mass meeting to support 20,000 Canadian lumberworkers on strike. MiDW-A

4547. *Strikes: Methods, Tactics, and Suggestions.* Chicago: CWIU #310, IWW, n.d., 16 p.
Offers suggestions for potential strikers. MiDW-A

4548. *The Strikers Are Lost.* New Castle, PA: IWW Pub. Bureau, n.d., n.p. DL

4549. *Strikers Deported!* Chicago: IWW, n.d., 4 p. NNU-T

4550. Strong, Sydney. *Industry and Fraternity: Address Delivered at the "Labor Session" of the National Council of Congregational Churches, Columbus, Ohio, Sunday Afternoon, October 14, 1917.* Chicago: IWW Pub. Bureau, 1918, 16 p.
Speech in strong support of industrial unionism and asking for a broader understanding of the IWW. MiDW-A

4551. *The Struck Job vs. the Job Strike.* Seattle: General Strike Committee, n.d. (1925?), 4 p.
Suggests strikes on the job rather than a continuation of the general strike. MiDW-A

4552. *Students! Comrades! We Appeal to You!* n.p.: IWW, n.d. (1970?), 4 p. MiU

4553. *Supplementary Issue, General Office Bulletin.* Chicago: IWW, 1924, 4 p.
Statement by editors about the 1924 split. MiDW-A

4554. *Support the Striking Kentucky Miners.* Berkeley: IWW, n.d., 2 p.
Asks financial support. MiDW-A

4555. *Suppressed Evidence in the Centralia Case. Why Didn't Judge Wilson Admit All the Testimony Offered by the IWW Defense?* Chicago: GDC, n.d. (1927?), 4 p.
The judge did not allow most of the defense evidence, and several jurors have changed their minds about their verdict. MiDW-A

4556. Swift, Morrison I. *Americanism vs. Radicalism.* Chicago: IWW, n.d. (1920?), 1 p.
The IWW is particularly "American." MiDW-A

"T-Bone Slim." See Slim, T-Bone.

4557. *Talking Union,* n.p.: IWW, n.d. (Milwaukee, 1973?), 1 p.
Calls for a strike at the ShopRite market. MiDW-A

4558. *Technocracy and the IWW.* Philadelphia: IWW, n.d. (1933?), 2 p.
The IWW as "practical technocracy." MiDW-A

4559. *Ten IWW Go to Jail in Sacramento Singing.* Chicago: GOC, n.d. (1920?), 4 p.
The Sacramento Syndicalist prisoners.

4560. *Terrorism or Sabotage?* n.p.: IWW, n.d. (1974?), 1 p.
Terrorism cannot help build a better world, but sabotage might. MiDW-A

4561. *That Message from the Boss.* Trenton, MI: Detroit-Ann Arbor IWW, n.d. (1975?), 4 p.
Organizing leaflet.

4562. *That "Victory" of the Coal Miners, Analyzed by the I.W.W.* Chicago: IWW, n.d. (1923?), 15 p.
The settlement agreed upon by UMWA was a Pyrrhic victory and did no good for the miners. MiDW-A

4563. *These Are the Facts! The Truth about the Attempted Mob Outrage in Centralia.* Chicago: IWW, n.d. (1919?), 14 p.
The Centralia Massacre. CSt

4564. *These Two Men in the Boat Have Something To Tell You.* Chicago: IWW, n.d., 4 p.
Organizing leaflet; men rowing the same boat in different directions demonstrate that if workers don't row in the same direction they will have problems. MiDW-A

4565. *This is the Universal Cigar Label of the Industrial Workers of the World.* Chicago: IWW, n.d., n.p.

4566. *This War Is Not for Workers.* Chicago: IWW, n.d. (1971?), 1 p.
Only profiteers will win the Vietnam War. MiDW-A

4567. Thompson, Fred. *World Labor Needs a Union.* Chicago: IWW, 1969, 22 p.
The system of national unionism is out of date now that there are so many multinational companies. We need worldwide unionism. MiDW-A

4568. Thompson, Fred, and Dean Nolan. *Joe Hill, IWW Songwriter.* San Diego: IWW, 1971, 20 p.
The story of Joe Hill and some of his songs. MiDW-A

4569. Thompson, J. P. *Revolutionary Class Union.* Chicago: IWW, n.d., 12 p.
Explains the IWW and states that it is a union for the working class. MiDW-A

4570. *Thousands of Workers Are Now on Strike in the US.* Chicago: IWW, n.d. (1925?), 2 p.
Urges a general strike for the release of political prisoners and lists respectable groups and individuals who are working for amnesty for them. MiDW-A

4571. *Three Criminal Syndicalism Laws—In Old Russia, in Germany, in Washington.* Chicago: IWW, n.d. (1923?), 1 p.
The U.S. is no different from Russia and Germany in regard to such laws. Printed in several editions. MiDW-A

4572. *Three Kinds of Strikes.* Chicago: LWIU #120, n.d. (1927?), 4 p.
Industrial strikes, intermittent strikes, and on-the-job strikes. MiDW-A

4573. *Three New Witnesses of Centralia Tragedy. They Saw the IWW Hall Attacked by Uniformed Paraders.* Chicago: GDC, n.d. (1920?), 4 p.
Fresh evidence in the Centralia case. MiDW-A

4574. *Three Penny Operation or Why We're Picketing the Three Penny.* Chicago: IWW, 1971, 1 p.
Strike leaflet for a Chicago cinema ushers' strike. MiDW-A

4575. *To All Building Workers in Los Angeles and Vicinity.* Los Angeles: BCWIU #330, IWW, n.d. (1927?), 4 p.
Organizing leaflet predicting a building boom and urging construction workers to join the industrial union. MiDW-A

4576. *To All Colored Hotel, Restaurant and Domestic Workers.* Detroit: HRDWIU #1100, IWW, 1919, 1 p.
Organizing leaflet inviting workers to join a union that does not practice racial discrimination. MiU

4577. *To All District Organizers.* Chicago: IWW, June 17, 1920, 2 p.

4578. *To All Lumber Workers of the Northwest.* LWIU #500, IWW, July 20, 1917, n.p.
Organizing leaflet.

4579. *To All Marine Transport Workers.* n.p.: MTWIU #510, IWW, n.d. (1937?), 1 p.
Urges support for workers in Spain. MiDW-A

4580. *To All Marine Transport Workers.* n.p.: Progressive Rank and File Committee, MTWIU #510, IWW, n.d. (1926?), 1 p.
Joe O'Hagan, national secretary, is the victim of lies. MiDW-A

4581. *To All Metal and Machinery Workers.* Newark, NJ: MMWIU #300, IWW, n.d. (1920?), 4 p.
Asks workers to join the IWW to fight the war profiteers, who are now laying off their loyal workers. MiDW-A

4582. *To All Metal Mine Workers: The I.W.W. Is Coming. Join the One Big Union.* Chicago: IWW, n.d., n.p. DLC

4583. *To All the Workers on the Railroads.* Chicago: RRWIU #520, IWW, n.d., 4 p.
Organizing leaflet stating that craft unionism will not work for railwaymen. MiDW-A

4584. *To All Wage Earners and Friends of Labor.* Paterson, NJ: Relief Committee, IWW, 1913, n.p. NNU-T

4585. *To Colored Workingmen and Workingwomen.* Chicago: IWW, n.d., 4 p.
Organizing leaflet. DLC

4586. *To Everyone Working in the Building Construction Industry.* Chicago: IWW, n.d. (1922?), 4 p.
Graft investigations into the building industry prove what the workers are up against. MiDW-A

4587. *To Harvest Workers: Attention!* Chicago: AWIU #110, IWW, n.d., 4 p.
Organizing leaflet for farmworkers. MiDW-A

4588. *To Make the Masters and the Undertakers Smile, Is that the Purpose of Your Lives, You Slaves?* Chicago: HRDWIU, IWW, n.d., 4 p.
Organizing leaflet for hotel and restaurant workers.

4589. *To Organized Labor of Butte.* San Francisco: CBGDC, n.d. (1923?), 2 p.
Syndicalism laws are everyone's business. MiDW-A

4590. *To Railway Men, the Transp. Dept. of the Industrial Workers of the World.* Chicago: IWW, n.d., 6 p.
Organizing leaflet for railway workers.

4591. *'To the Beasts'—in California as in Ancient Rome.* San Francisco: GDC, 1924, 30 p.
The victims of Syndicalist laws compared to gladiators facing animals. MiDW-A

4592. *To the Citizens of Sacramento County.* San Francisco: California Branch, GDC, n.d., 4 p.
Urges action against the Syndicalist trials. MiDW-A

4593. *To the Hotel & Restaurant Workers of Greater New York.* New York: IWW, n.d., 8 p.
Organizing leaflet for restaurant workers.

4594. *To the Iron Workers.* Chicago: BCWIU #330, n.d. (1926?), 2 p.
Organizing leaflet for iron workers asking them to form active committees and get into an industrial union. MiDW-A

4595. *To the Lumber Workers of British Columbia.* n.p.: IWW, n.d., 4 p.
Urges Canadian lumbermen to join the IWW. MiDW-A

4596. *To the Lumber Workers of Michigan, Wisconsin and Minnesota.* Chicago: LWIU #120, IWW, n.d. (1925?), 4 p.
Organizing leaflet for Great Lakes area lumberworkers that compares their wretched camps to the good ones in the Pacific Northwest, which were attained by the IWW by the 1917 lumber strikes. MiDW-A

4597. *To the Paterson Silk Workers!* Paterson, NJ: IWIU #1000, IWW, n.d. (1913?), 1 p.
Reminds workers that the goal is to stop piece work and start receiving wages. MiDW-A

4598. *To the People of Bishop.* Bishop, California: MMIU #210, IWW, n.d. (1941?), 1 p.
The people of Bishop should not believe the citizens who are talking of tarring and feathering American unionists. The IWW is wholly American; lynchers are not. MiDW-A

4599. *To the Producers and Distributors of Food.* Chicago: IWW, n.d. (1920?), 2 p.
Organizing leaflet for food workers, reminding them to demand decent and clean working conditions as well as better wages by organizing industrially. MiDW-A

4600. *To the Public from the Striking Charwomen.* n.p.: IWW, n.d., 1 p.
Expresses outrage that some of the pickets were arrested while peacefully walking. The police would not even let the women use the telephone. (The area is not stated; possibly New York.) MiDW-A

4601. *To The Silk Workers of Paterson.* Paterson: IWW Local #152, 1912, 1 p.
Organizing leaflet. NNU-T

4602. *To the Wage Working Class Everywhere, by Chas O. Sherman, Pres.* Chicago: IWW, n.d., 4 p.
Organizing leaflet. MiU

4603. *To the Workers in the Lumbering Industry.* Chicago: IWW, n.d., 2 p.
Organizing leaflet. MiDW-A

4604. *To the Workers of the World: Manifesto Issued by Conference of Trade Unionists at Chicago, January 2, 3, and 4, 1905.* Chicago: IWW, 1905, 7 p.
Contains the manifesto and the organizational chart. MiDW-A

4605. *To the Workers Who Clothe the World.* Chicago: IWW, n.d., 4 p.
Organizing leaflet that states that textile workers are having difficulty in all areas; joining an industrial union might help improve the situation. MiDW-A

4606. *To the Workers Who Feed the World.* Chicago: FWIU #460, IWW, n.d., 8 p.
Organizing leaflet for food workers. MiDW-A

4607. *To You Who Dare.* AWIU #110, n.d., 2 p.
Organizing leaflet for California fruit pickers, stating that they are the equivalent of slaves. MiDW-A

4608. *Tourists Beware of California!* San Francisco: CBGDC, n.d., 1 p.
Asks tourists to boycott California because of the harsh Syndicalist laws.

4609. *Trades Unionism in Decay.* Glasgow: IWW, n.d., 1 p.
The coming union must be the industrial union. MiDW-A

4610. *Trail to Truth.* San Pedro: San Pedro Publicity Committee, n.d. (1924?), 9 p.
Protests the violent raid in San Pedro. MiDW-A

4611. Trautmann, William E. *Handbook of Industrial Unionism.* Chicago: IWW Press, n.d., 32 p.
How the IWW is organized. NN, MiU

4612. ———. *Industrial Unionism Handbook No. 2. Means and Methods.* Chicago: IWW Press, n.d., n.p.
Same as no. 4220, but with author's name. NN, MiU

4613. ———. *To the Workers of the World: Manifesto (1905).* Cincinnati: Secretary of the Executive Committee, IWW, n.d. (1906?), 6 p.
Probably the same as no. 4604.

4614. ———. *Why Strikes Are Lost: How To Win!* New Castle, PA: IWW Pub. Bureau, 1912, 23 p.
Explains the history of several strikes and analyzes why they were not successful. Strong industrial unionism will help to win strikes. MiDW-A

4615. Trotter, H. E. *Railroad Workers IU #520. IWW Bulletin.* n.p.: IWW, 1921, n.p.

4616. Trotter, H. E., and John Grady. *Railroad Workers Industrial Union No. 520 of the IWW: A Call to Action.* Chicago: IWW, n.d. (1921?), 2 p.
Urges workers to remain steady under persecution and to attend the coming convention. MiDW-A

4617. *True Americans Called On To Protect Liberties.* Detroit: IWW, 1919, 1 p.
Announces a coming visit and speech by William Haywood and discusses Centralia. MiDW-A

4618. Tulin, Lee. *Digest of California Criminal Syndicalism Cases.* Chicago: IWW, n.d. (1926?), n.p.
Lists and information. MiU

4619. *Twenty-Five Years of Industrial Unionism.* Chicago: IWW, 1930, 79 p.
An early history of the IWW. IdU

4620. *The Two I.W.W.'s.* Detroit: Detroit Branch, IWW, n.d., n.p.

4621. *Two Kinds of Unionism.* n.p.: IWW, n.d. (1912?), n.p.
Compares craft and industrial unions.

4622. *The Two Triple Alliances to Trim the Workers on the Job and Off the Job, Going and Coming.* Chicago: AWIU #110, IWW, n.d., 4 p.
The gambler, the bootlegger, and the hijacker, as well as the workers' bosses, are all threats to the workers. Migrant workers especially should beware. MiDW-A

4623. *UAW Pay Cut—GM.* Cleveland: IWW, n.d. (1949?), 2 p.
Urges General Motors workers to join the IWW. MiDW-A

4624. *Un-American and Useless.* n.p.: IWW, 1923, 1 p.
The Syndicalism laws should be repealed. MiDW-A

4625. *Unemployed Soldiers Listen! Veterans of the World War, Why Are We Idle Today?* Chicago: IWW, n.d. (1920?), 2 p.
Veterans will have to work as hard to find a job as they did to fight the Germans. A new set of lyrics to the song "John Brown's Body" entitled "The Unemployed Soldier" is given to put vets in a militant mood. MiDW-A

4626. *The Unemployed—What Shall They Do?* Chicago: IWW, n.d. (1923?), 4 p.
The causes of unemployment are inherent in the capitalist system. Workers should join the IWW and fight the system. MiDW-A

4627. *Unemployment—Why?* Chicago: IWW, n.d. (1921?), 2 p.
Unemployment is the result of the economic system. The only solution is for workers to be in control of industry. MiDW-A

4628. *Unfair! Hip Products, Inc., 1500 W. Monroe, Refuses To Bargain with Organized Labor!* Chicago: IWW, n.d. (1971?), 1 p.
Strike leaflet for Chicago's Hip Products Strike. MiDW-A

4629. *A Union for All Railroad Workers.* Chicago: IWW, n.d. (1949?), 32 p.
Organizing leaflet explains the principles and structure of the IWW and tells railroad workers that they in particular need an industrially organized union. MiDW-A

4630. *A Union for Farm Wage Workers.* Chicago: IWW, n.d. (1933?), 4 p.
Organizing leaflet for migrant farmworkers. MiDW-A

4631. *Union Men Being Used as Strike Breakers.* Chicago: Executive Committee, Haywood Local #300, Sheet Metal Workers and Roofers, n.d., n.p. MiU

4632. *Union Men! If the IWW Can Be Convicted for Demanding "Stated Wages and Certain Terms" from an Employer, So Can You!* Chicago: IWW Pub. Bureau, n.d. (1919?), 1 p.
Asks support for men on trial in California. MiDW-A

4633. *The Union Slant: Fellow Workers, Don't Scab! Don't Kill!* Chicago: IWW, n.d. (1971?), 1 p.
With multinational companies it is easier for employers to find scab labor. MiDW-A

4634. *The Union Wants to Talk to You—Tune in on WEXL.* Detroit: IWW, n.d. (1933?), 1 p.
Reminds listeners to tune into the IWW radio program daily. MiDW-A

4635. *Unionism—Man's Best Bet.* Chicago: IWW, n.d. (1972?), 1 p.
Organizing leaflet stating that some of the indirect benefits of unionism are often overlooked. MiDW-A

4636. *Unions and Racism.* Chicago: IWW, n.d., n.p.

4637. *Unions Fight for the Right To Strike.* Chicago: GDC, n.d. (1918?), 4 p.
Even craft unionists are helping with the defense fund of the Chicago trial because they want to keep the right to strike. MiDW-A

4638. *Unite! Workers in the Metal Industry Organize! Act Today!* Chicago: MMWIU #440, IWW, n.d., 4 p.
Organizing leaflet for metal workers.

4639. *Unity for Action in the IWW.* San Francisco: Ways and Means Committee, 1927, 4 p.
Emergency program leaflet printing letters from various IWW members.

4640. *Unity—Unity of Labor.* Minneapolis: IWW Pub. Bureau, n.d., 4 p. MiU

4641. *The Unskilled Labor Problem.* Chicago: IWW, n.d. (1918?), 4 p.
The IWW prosecutions may turn out to be a blessing if they inform the public about the poor working conditions in industry. MiDW-A

4642. *U.S. Army Officers Protest against the Injustice of the IWW Conviction.* Chicago: GDC, n.d. (1920?), 4 p.

4643. *Using the Espionage Act To Terrorize Labor: Some Judicial Atrocities.* New York: Workers Defense Union, IWW, n.d. (1918?), 4 p.

Lists either 23, 25, or 26 different trials going on in which labor people or those friendly to labor are being prosecuted. There are at least three different versions of this leaflet. MiDW-A

4644. Vanderveer, George. *Opening Statement of George Vanderveer in the Case of the U.S.A. vs. Wm. D. Haywood et al.* Chicago: IWW Pub. Bureau, n.d. (1918?), 102 p.
Opening statement of the defense counsel and other trial excerpts. MiDW-A

4645. Varney, Harold Lord. *Industrial Communism: The I.W.W.* n.p.: IWW, n.d. (1920?), 24 p.
The similarities and differences between the beliefs of the IWW and those of the Bolsheviks and the Soviet government. MiDW-A

4646. ———. *The Truth about the IWW.* Chicago: IWW Pub. Bureau, n.d. (1919?), 4 p.
The accusations against the IWW and responses to them. MiDW-A

4647. *Vegetable and Fruit Workers!* Chicago: AWIU #110, n.d., n.p.
Organizing leaflet for migratory farmworkers. MiDW-A

4648. *Vermin: The Employment Agencies.* Chicago: IWW, n.d. (1914?), 4 p.
Employment agencies are cheating the workers. MiDW-A

4649. *Very Important for All Members and Supporters of the Industrial Workers of the World.* Chicago: IWW, 1910, n.p. WU

4650. *Wake Up! Hotel, Restaurant, and Cafeteria Workers.* Chicago: FWIU #460, n.d., 2 p.
Organizing leaflet. MiDW-A

4651. Walklin, Frank. *A Fair Trial?* Chicago: IWW, 1920, 16 p.
The Centralia trial was totally unfair. MiDW-A

4652. Walquist, August. *The Eight-Hour Day: Its Benefits and How It Can Be Gained.* Chicago: IWW, 1912, n.p. DLC

4653. ———. *The Eight-Hour Work Day: What It Will Mean and How to Get It.* Cleveland: IWW Pub. Bureau, n.d. (1912?), 4 p.
Lists the benefits of working fewer hours and urges the workers to take action to get the eight-hour day. MiDW-A

4654. *Wanted—One Big Union.* Chicago: IWW, n.d. (1937?), 2 p.
The CIO cannot produce real industrial unionism. MiDW-A

4655. *Warning: The Deadly Parallel.* n.p.: IWW, n.d. (1917?), 1 p.
AFL and IWW statements about the war and the reasons for the IWW's opposition to it. MiDW-A

4656. *Warning to Seamen and Longshoremen.* Chicago: MTWIU #510, IWW, 1922, 1 p.
IWW members will not unload British coal to break the American coal strike.

4657. *Washington's Gory History, Page by Page.* Seattle: Washington Branch, GDC, n.d. (1927?), 1 p.
Incidents of violence against the IWW. MiDW-A

4658. *Washington's Judicial Mockery.* Seattle: Centralia Release Committee, 1929, 4 p.
The opinions and contrary verdict of members of the Washington Labor Council, who believe the defendants were innocent. MiDW-A

4659. *Washington's Legal Mockery.* Seattle: Washington Branch, GDC, n.d. (1927?), 4 p.
The Centralia trial mocked justice. MiDW-A

4660. *Watch for Call of General Strike to Free All Class War Prisoners.* Klamath Falls, OR: IWW Strike Committee, LWIU #120, 1923, n.p. n.p.

4661. *Watch Out! Sell Out! Walter "Armored Car" Reuther Has Called Us to Three Meetings.* Cleveland: IWW, n.d. (1937?), 1 p.
At the meetings the IWW Committee was told what to ask for. Members should watch out for the CIO, as it is not a rank-and-file union. MiDW-A

4662. *We Appeal to You.* Detroit: GDC, 1933, 1 p.
Asks support for Yakima, Washington, strike prisoners.

4663. West, George P. *After Liberalism Had Failed.* Chicago: GDC, 1923, 1 p.
The primary purpose of the Syndicalist trials was to keep the port of Los Angeles open and free of labor trouble. The 1924 longshoremen's strike was so effective that it brought on repression. MiDW-A

4664. *What about the Woman Who Works?* Chicago: IWW, n.d. (1915?), 4 p.
The time for women to be the pets and slaves of men is past. Women are needed in the IWW as equal workers. MiDW-A

4665. *What Do the Industrial Workers of the World Called in Short the I.W.W. Officially Stand For?* Los Angeles: CDC, n.d. (1924?), 4 p.

The beliefs of the IWW, the resolution about sabotage, and the unwarranted persecutions suffered by IWW members. MiDW-A

4666. *What Do You Think of This?* Chicago: GDC, IWW, n.d. (1918?), 4 p.

The lynchings of IWW oilworker organizers in Oklahoma. MiU

4667. *What Is Power?* Chicago: GRU, IWW, n.d., 4 p.

Organizing leaflet stating that the greatest power on earth is organized labor power. MiDW-A

4668. *What Is Rank and File Rule: Is It the Rule of Individuals or Is It Rule by Principles upon which the IWW Is Built?* Chicago: IWW, 1925, 11 p.

Organizing leaflet. NN

4669. *What Is the IWW? A Candid Statement of Its Principles, Objects, and Methods.* 3rd. Rev. Edition. Chicago: IWW, n.d. (1920?), 30 p.

Organizing pamphlet telling in detail how the IWW works. MiDW-A

4670. *What Is the IWW? The IWW Is a Union.* Chicago: IWW, n.d. (1945?), 4 p.

Organizing leaflet. MiDW-A

4671. *What Is the IWW Preamble? A Dialogue.* Chicago: Dept. of Education, AWIU #110, IWW, 1922, 40 p.

Organizing leaflet in the form of a dialogue between two workers. MiDW-A

4672. *What Lumber Workers Want.* Chicago: LWIU #120, IWW, n.d. (1925?), 4 p.

Workers demand the release of class war prisoners, the abolition of piece work, an eight-hour day everywhere, and better working camps. MiDW-A

4673. *What Sort of a Union Is the IWW Asking You to Build?* Chicago: IWW, 1965, n.p.

Organizing leaflet. WU

4674. *What We Want You To Help the IWW Do.* Chicago: IWW, n.d. (1975?), 1 p.

Invites all people to join the IWW, regardless of earning power or job. MiDW-A

4675. *What's Going On Here?* Detroit: Detroit-Ann Arbor Branch, IWW, n.d. (1975?), 1 p.
Organizing leaflet. MiDW-A

4676. *What's What in Spain.* Chicago, IWW, n.d. (1937?), 2 p.
Asks workers to support the CNT against the Fascists in Spain. MiDW-A

4677. *What's Your Answer? Do You Sleep as Well as Chessie in Your Bunk Car?* n.p.: IWW, n.d. (1944?), 1 p.
Tells gandies on the Chesapeake & Ohio Railway, as well as others, to improve their working conditions by joining the IWW. MiDW-A

4678. *Where Did That Get Us?* London, England: IWW, 1947, 2 p.
The hotel strike would have succeeded but for trade unionists. Workers are urged to join the IWW. MiDW-A

4679. *Where Do We Go from Here?* Chicago: GRU, n.d. (1937?), 4 p.
Organizing leaflet deploring the Depression and advising workers to get into the union. MiDW-A

4680. *Which Union? A Name Alone Is Not a Union.* Los Angeles, IWW, n.d. (1937?), 4 p.
Warns members to be careful about the attractions of the AFL and CIO, for neither of them is as democratically run as the IWW. MiDW-A

4681. *While Mr. Harding Reviews the Case of the Politicals: Some Comment for the American People To Think About.* Chicago: GDC, n.d. (1922?), 7 p.
Many quotations from respectable persons and newspapers favoring amnesty for the political prisoners. MiDW-A

4682. White, W. W. *Open Letter to the Workers of America.* CWIU #573, IWW, n.d. (1920?), 4 p.
Organizing leaflet reminding workers that it is their turn to share some of the profits their work produces. That can happen only if they organize. MiDW-A

4683. *Who Are The Conspirators?* San Francisco: C. D. D., n.d. (1918?), 4 p.
The raids prove that the government and the employers who really run it are conspiring to stop labor's progress. MiDW-A

4684. *Who Has Paterson by the Throat?* Paterson: Local 1521, IWW, 1913, 1 p. NNU-T

4685. *Who Is Guilty of Conspiracy?* San Francisco: CBGDC, n.d. (1921?), 4 p.
There are land frauds and cheating in Humboldt County and elsewhere by the people who instigated the Syndicalist trials.

4686. *Why Are So Many Workers Out of a Job? With Over 2,000,000 Wage-Earners Unemployed, the Answer to This Question Becomes Important and Necessary.* Chicago: IWW, 1924, 6 p.
Periodic recessions are a feature of the capitalistic system, and workers should become organized to fight for their rights. MiDW-A

4687. *Why? How? When?* Chicago: IWW Pub. Bur., n.d., 4 p.
Urges a drive for the eight-hour day. DL

4688. *Why Join 300?* Chicago: MMWIU #300, IWW, 1920, 4 p.
Organizing leaflet for metal-mine workers.

4689. *Why Mill Workers Must Organize.* n.p.: LWIU #120, n.d. (1919?), 4 p.
Asks workers to join the union and get their share of the profits. MiDW-A

4690. *Why the Criminal Syndicalism Law Should Be Repealed.* San Francisco: GDC, n.d. (1922?), 4 p.
The law is wasteful, vicious, and inhuman. MiDW-A

4691. *Why This Picket Line?* San Francisco: IWW Branch No. 1, n.d. (1972?), 1 p.
Strike leaflet for Hip Products Strike, Chicago and San Francisco. MiDW-A

4692. *Why: To the Workers of Los Angeles and Vicinity.* Los Angeles: GRU, IWW, n.d., 2 p.
The cure for unemployment is organizing. MiDW-A

4693. *Why Unemployment? What Is the Solution?* San Francisco: IWW Branch No. 1, n.d. (1965?), 1 p.
The only solution is to cut working hours and let the unemployed share in the work. MiDW-A

4694. *Why We Are on Strike.* San Francisco: IWW, n.d. (1964?), 3 p.
Leaflet explaining the Cedar Alley Coffee House strike in San Francisco. MiDW-A

4695. *Why We Need a Union: A Message to Apartment Workers . . .* New York: BMWIU #640, n.d., 2 p.
The worker has no power until he is organized. MiDW-A

4696. *Why We're Picketing the Three Penny.* Chicago: IWW, n.d. (1971?), 1 p.
Leaflet for Chicago cinema strike. MiDW-A

4697. *Why You Should Join the IWW.* Chicago: IWW, n.d., 4 p.
Organizing leaflet explaining the methods of the IWW. MiDW-A

4698. *Why You Should Join the IWW—Don't Be a Mr. Block.* Minneapolis: AWO, IWW, n.d., n.p.
Organizing leaflet.

4699. *Why You Will Always Need One Big Union: Attention All Murray Workers!* Detroit: IWW, 1933, 4 p.
Strike leaflet for Detroit's Murray Body strike. MiDW-A

4700. *The Will of the People Says: "Let Them Go Free!"* Chicago: GDC, n.d., 4 p. NNU-T

4701. *Will You Help Now?* Chicago: GDC, 1913, 1 p.

4702. *Will You Join Today?* Chicago: IWW, n.d., 2 p.
Organizing leaflet stating that the IWW is both an idea and an ideal. MiDW-A

4703. Williams, Ben H. *The Constructive Program of the I.W.W., Together with Grover H. Perry's "How Scabs Are Bred."* London, England: IWW, 1915, n.p.
Organizing leaflet.

4704. ———. *Eleven Blind Leaders, or "Practical Socialism" and "Revolutionary Tactics" from an I.W.W. Standpoint.* New Castle, PA: IWW Pub. Bureau, 1909, 29 p.
Quotes leaders who say they speak for the working class and shows how only IWW members can speak for themselves. MiDW-A

4705. Williams, George. *The First Congress of the Red Trade Union International at Moscow, 1921: A Report of the Proceedings by Geo. Williams, Delegate from the I.W.W.* Chicago: IWW, 1921, 68 p.
A full report followed by an IWW statement that the IWW will not affiliate with the Communist group because they are political in character. MiDW-A

4706. Wilson, James. *As to the I.W.W.* Spokane: IWW, 1910, 12 p.

4707. *A Wise Man Learns Till the Day of His Death, While a Fool's Education Is Always Complete.* Chicago: IU #460, IWW, n.d., 4 p.
Men and women of the food industry must think where their best interests lie, with the boss or in solidarity with fellow workers. MiDW-A

4708. *Women! Stand Behind the Family! Join the One Big Union!* Chicago: IWW, n.d. (1920?), 2 p.
Asks women to support their husbands' union activities and, if possible, to join the union themselves. Housewives are directed to the Hotel, Restaurant, and Domestic Workers' Industrial Union #1100. MiDW-A

4709. Woodruff, Abner E. *The Advancing Proletariat.* Chicago: IWW, 1919, 32 p.
Traces the history of the working class from "wage slavery" to "freedom," urging active participation in IWW activities to achieve the latter. MiDW-A

4710. ———. *Evolution of American Agriculture.* Chicago: AWIU #400, IWW, 1919, 17 p.
Traces agricultural work from primitive times, focusing on the changes brought by machinery. Farmworkers are advised to increase their power by joining the IWW. MiDW-A

4711. ———. *The Evolution of Industrial Democracy.* Chicago: IWW, n.d. (1920?), 45 p.
Foretells a future of industrial democracy, with universal participation in production. MiDW-A

4712. *A Word to the Miner.* Chicago: IWW, n.d. (1926?), 4 p.
Organizing leaflet asking miners to think about hours of work and safety in the mines as well as wages. MiDW-A

4713. *A Word to You Lumber Workers.* Chicago: IWW, n.d., 4 p.
Organizing leaflet. DLC

4714. *Work: And How It Gets that Way.* Oldham, England: IWW, n.d., n.p.

4715. *Work or Fight!* Chicago: MMWIU #440, IWW Pub. Bureau, n.d., n.p. DLC

4716. *Work People's College: A Residential School for Rebellious Workers, A Place to Live and Learn.* Duluth: Work People's College, n.d. (1935?), 4 p.
The IWW college and some of its courses. MiDW-A

4717. *Work Peoples College: A Residential School for Rebellious Workers. Why a Workers' School?* Duluth, Work Peoples College, n.d. (1925?), 4 p.

The college has been managed since 1916 either by members or by friends of the IWW; the school is described. MiDW-A

4718. *Workers All!* Butte, MT: MMWIU #210 (800), IWW, n.d. (1920?), 1 p.

Organizing leaflet urging miners to keep up the fighting spirit despite the persecutions. MiDW-A

4719. *Workers, Celebrate. Today Is Your Day and Here Are the Reasons for This Get-Together.* n.p.: IWW, n.d. (1934?), 1 p.

Leaflet for a May Day event. MiDW-A

4720. *Workers Cannot Be United on the Basis of Departmental Craft Autonomy and Hollow Professions.* Chicago: IWW, 1908, n.p. CSt

4721. *Workers' Contempt of Court: IWW Defendants Voice Their Scorn of Capitalist "Justice."* New York: Rebel Workers, n.d. (1920?), 2 p. MiU

4722. *Workers' Education: Work People's College.* Duluth: Work Peoples College, n.d., 4 p.

How workers' education brings working-class power. MiDW-A

4723. *Workers! Employed and Unemployed, Read, Think, Act!* Detroit: MMWIU #440, IWW, n.d. (1933?), 4 p.

Organizing leaflet for auto and machinery workers. MiDW-A

4724. *A Worker's Guide to Direct Action.* Chicago: IWW, 1975, 16 p.

All types of worker actions defined, from slow-downs to strikes. MiDW-A

4725. *Workers in the Lumbering Industry.* Chicago: LWIU #120, IWW, n.d., n.p.

Organizing leaflet. MiU

4726. *Workers in the Metal and Machine Industry.* Bronx, NY: MMIU #440, IWW, n.d., 2 p.

Organizing leaflet.

4727. *Workers, Judge for Yourselves about Centralia.* Butte, MT: NWDDC, 1919, 4 p.

The Centralia Massacre. OrUN

4728. *Workers of the Coal Mines.* Chicago: IWW, n.d. (1927?), 4 p.
Organizing leaflet. MiDW-A

4729. *Workers of the World Unite! Comrades and Fellow Workers.* Chicago: IWW, 1919, 1 p. MiU

4730. *Workers of the World, Unite! One Strike, All Strike!* n.p.: MTWIU #510, IWW, 1919, 1 p.

4731. *Workers of Utah: Awaken!* Chicago: IWW Pub. Bureau, n.d., 2 p. DLC

4732. *Workers, Will You Stand for More Bloodshed?* Chicago: IWW, 1906, 4 p.
The scuffle between IWW factions after the second convention. MiDW-A

4733. *Working People Need the 4 Hour Day: End Unemployment.* Tacoma: IWW, 1972, 4 p.
Urges workers to work toward shorter hours. MiDW-A

4734. *World Wide Strike in the Marine Industry: Strike!* Seattle: MTWIU #510, IWW, n.d. (1926?), 1 p.
Urges support for the striking British transport workers. MiDW-A

4735. *WPA Workers: Where Do We Go from Here?* Los Angeles: IWW, n.d. (1936?), 1 p.
Urges WPA workers to join the IWW to improve their working conditions. MiDW-A

4736. *A Year's Persecution of Industrial Unionists in California under the Syndicalism Law.* San Francisco: IWW, n.d. (1924?), 4 p.
The year 1923 saw the worst series of persecutions in U.S. history. MiDW-A

4737. *You and I.* Chicago: GDC, IWW, 1918, 4 p.
Urges even stronger solidarity among workers during these stressful times. MiDW-A

4738. *You Are Making a Fortune.* Buffalo: IWW, n.d. (1936?), 1 p.
Organizing leaflet saying that the fortune you are making is for the boss. MiDW-A

4739. *You Are Wondering—AFL? CIO? IWW?* Cleveland: IWW, n.d. (1936?), 1 p.
Organizing leaflet.

4740. *You Must Help!* Chicago: IWW Pub. Bureau, n.d. (1919?), 4 p.
Now that so many workers have been imprisoned, workers must show their solidarity and help work for their release.
MiDW-A

4741. *You Need Industrial Unionism.* Chicago: AWIU #110, IWW, n.d. (1930?), 4 p.
Organizing leaflet for agricultural workers. MiDW-A

4742. *You Ought To Know.* Centralia, WA: CPC, n.d. (1927?), 4 p.
Includes facts and new developments in the Centralia affair. MiDW-A

4743. *Young People! The Strike of the Automobile Workers of Detroit.* Detroit: Council of Labor Youth Groups, IWW, 1933, 1 p.
Information on several current strikes and appeal for support. MiU

4744. *Your Boss and You.* Chicago: IWW, 1919, 2 p.

4745. *Your Union Meeting.* Chicago: IWW, 1944, 4 p. MiU

4746. *You've Asked the Question We're Proud to Answer about the IWW.* Chicago: Joint Branches, IWW, n.d. (1949?), 8 p.
Organizing leaflet. MiDW-A

"–TO BREAK THE HEART OF
THIS OLD CROOK
–A SMASHING BLOW TO
THE POCKET-BOOK"

ECONOMIC
POWER

BOSS

JOIN
the I.W.W. for
MORE POWER!

EBA-CES

IWW Newspapers and Magazines

LISTING IWW serial publications is not a simple chore, and a definitive list may be impossible. Not only are there irregularities in the publishing of such publications but there are few full runs of any of them held at any library. Periodic suppression by the U.S. Government; issues that were at least partially seized; and funds that were also seized and not returned, making publishing precarious on financial grounds alone, are only a few of the reasons for the irregularity of these papers.

A newspaper's publication frequently went from one city to another, one state to another; and the arrests of 1917–1923, during the Red Scare, occasioned many abrupt changes of editors as well. IWW editors were favorite targets, and while they were in jail or on trial, temporary substitutes had to be found. Finding experienced editors who would risk imprisonment was not easy. Sometimes volumes were numbered anew when an editor or location changed, and frequently volume numbers were omitted altogether or put down incorrectly. Many issues were confiscated, often before they reached the bookstalls. The perseverance of the IWW under these circumstances was truly astounding.

Because I could not visit every location and determine the dates for myself, I have had to accept what I found in serial lists, often including no more detailed information than the year. In some cases several locations are listed for the papers when it was apparent that no one location was likely to have a full run. Additional locations may be found in union lists.

Foreign-language newspapers are listed after English-language papers (many foreign-language papers are doubtless yet to be discovered in attics and archives). They demonstrate that during some periods the IWW maintained a vast newspaper publishing empire, with newspapers published in many languages.

The work of publishers such as Greenwood Press and Arno Press, which are reprinting old radical papers (many of them IWW papers), is a wonderful advantage to IWW scholars. Once the old relics were difficult to find, were rarely all in the same place, and were crumbling into fragments. Now many of them are easily available and comfortable to read.

In the following list, the titles of the serials are followed by the special agency (such as defense committee), if there is one, and the place of publication, both of these in parentheses. The known dates and the frequency, where known, follow that, as does other information such as changes of place, title, or sponsorship. For foreign-language papers, the language is given preceding the date. Locations are listed last, on the right, unless the paper is widely available; if so, that fact is noted. "Widely available" includes papers on microfilm or in a reprint.

4747. *American International Musical and Theatrical Union Bulletin* (New York).
September, 1906, to August, 1912. Quarterly. IWW only for the first two years. MiU

4748. *Bulletin* (GDC, Chicago).
April, 1927, to June, 1933. Frequency varies. Title varies. *Press Service Release* from August 26, 1931, to June, 1933. IU, NN

4749. *California Defense Bulletin* (San Francisco).
December 7, 1916, to November, 1918. Frequency varies, weekly or semi-weekly. Suppressed in 1918. Five issues prior to December 7, 1916, not located. MiU, MiDW-A

4750. *Daily Bulletin* (Chicago).
February 2 to August 10, 1918. Daily, when court was held during the Chicago trial (April 2 to August 10); otherwise frequency varies, usually semi-weekly. Title varies. *Jail Bulletin* from February 2 to March 23; *Daily Bulletin* from April 1 to April 26; *Trial Bulletin* from May 1 to June 6; *IWW Trial Bulletin* from June 10 to August 10, 1918. MiDW-A

4751. *Defense Bulletin of the Seattle District* (Seattle).
1918. Weekly. NNU-T, NN, MiDW-A

4752. *Defense News Bulletin* (GDC, Chicago).
November 3, 1917, to November 9, 1918. Weekly. Superseded *Solidarity* (no. 4784); was itself superseded by *New Solidarity* (no. 4773). IU

4753. *Defense News Bulletin* (GDC, Chicago).
July to September, 1931. Monthly. Superseded by *Workers Defense* (no. 4788). Not the same as no. 4752. CtY, NN

4754. *Defense News Service* (Chicago).
1922–1925. Frequency unknown. Scattered issues on Microfilm No. 1409 at Tamiment Library. NNU-T

4755. *Fellow Worker* (New York District Council, IWW).
January 1 to August 7, 1920. Semi-monthly. Some issues suppressed. Superseded by *Industrial Unionist* (no. 4761). DL

4756. *Industrial Pioneer* (GEB of the IWW, Chicago).
February, 1921, to January, 1922; May, 1923, to September, 1926. Monthly magazine. Publication suspended from February, 1922, to April, 1923. Issued during the suspension of *One Big Union Monthly* (no. 4778). Reprinted by Greenwood Press. Widely available

4757. *Industrial Solidarity* (New Castle, PA, Cleveland, and Chicago).
December 18, 1909, to present. Frequency varies. Weekly until 1951; frequency varies through September, 1954; semi-monthly October 1, 1954, to April 15, 1965; monthly since March, 1965. New Castle from December 18, 1909, to March 29, 1913; Cleveland from April 19, 1913, to December 25, 1913; Chicago from December, 1913. Title varies. *Solidarity* (no. 4784) from December 18, 1909, to October 27, 1917; *Defense News Bulletin* (no. 4752) from November 3, 1917, to November 9, 1918; *New Solidarity* (no. 4773) from November 16, 1918, to March 6, 1920; *Solidarity* (no. 4784) from March 16, 1920, to September 3, 1921; *Industrial Solidarity* from September 10, 1921, to December 1, 1931. In December, 1931, merged with *Industrial Worker* (no. 4767). Widely available

4758. *Industrial Union Bulletin* (Chicago).
March 2, 1907, to March 6, 1909. Weekly; semi-monthly between August 8 and December 12, 1908. Reprinted by Greenwood Press. Widely available

4759. *Industrial Union Bulletin* (Seattle).
1919. Frequency unknown. Some issues on Microfilm No. R380 at Tamiment Library. NNU-T

4760. *Industrial Union News* (Detroit faction "IWW," WIIU, Detroit, MI, and Troy, NY).
January, 1912, to May, 1924. Frequency varies. Monthly to April, 1919; weekly from May 10, 1919, to October 8, 1921; monthly from November, 1921, to June, 1923; semi-monthly from July, 1923, to January, 1924, then monthly. "IWW" (De-

troit faction) from January, 1912, to December, 1915; WIIU from January, 1916, to May, 1924. From Detroit until May, 1922; from Troy from June, 1922, to May, 1924. Not a "genuine" IWW paper, but the faction called it IWW until the faction's name changed in 1915 to Workers International Industrial Union. DL, MiDW-A

4761. *Industrial Unionist* (New York District Council, IWW).

October 20, 1920, to March 10, 1922. Semi-monthly. Several issues suppressed. First issue titled *Workers' Opposition*. Superseded *Fellow Worker* (no. 4755). DL, MH, NNC

4762. *Industrial Unionist* (Seattle).

1918. Frequency varies. Subtitled "Organ of Western Branches." Some issues suppressed. Location unknown

4763. *Industrial Unionist* ("Emergency Program" faction branches, Portland, OR).

April 11, 1925, to June 16, 1926. Weekly. Reprinted by Greenwood Press. Widely available

Note: Industrial Unionist (New York). May, 1932 to May, 1941. Monthly. Published by the Industrial Union Party (earlier known as the Industrial Union League), a splinter group from the Socialist Labor Party. Not related to the IWW.

4764. *Industrial Worker* (Joliet, IL).

January to September, 1906; January to June, 1907. Monthly. Reprinted by Greenwood Press. Widely available

4765. *Industrial Worker* (Spokane).

March 18, 1909, to September 4, 1913. Weekly. From Seattle, February 5, 1910, to May 21, 1910. Microfilmed by Micro-Records, Inc. Widely available

4766. *Industrial Worker* (Seattle).

April 1, 1916, to May 4, 1918; May 7, 1919, to November 21, 1931, then absorbed by *Industrial Worker* (Chicago), December 1, 1931. Weekly except the first three issues, which were semi-monthly. Suppressed after May 4 issue, until May 7, 1919. Occasionally included, from 1919, a weekly supplement, *Lumberjack Bulletin* (no. 4771). Widely available

4767. *Industrial Worker* (Chicago).

April 4, 1917, to present. Frequency varies. Weekly from April 4 to July 23, 1917; semi-weekly from July 30 to October 6, 1917; weekly from October 13, 1917, to May 11, 1918, when it was suspended. Resumed May 7, 1919, as New Series, vol. 1. Frequency of New Series varies, mostly weekly through 1941, then weekly until October 1, 1954. Semi-monthly until March, 1965. Monthly to present. Absorbed *Industrial Solidarity* (no. 4757) and *Industrial Worker* (Seattle) no. 4766, on December 1, 1931. Widely available

Note: The *Nome Industrial Worker,* although it gave some IWW news, was a WFM paper. The *Allied Industrial Worker,* published in Milwaukee by the Allied Industrial Workers of America, is sometimes designated an IWW paper, but it is not.

4768. *International* (San Diego).

1914. Frequency unknown. Two issues on Microfilm No. 380 at Tamiment Library. NNU-T

IWW Trial Bulletin. See *Daily Bulletin (no.4750).*

Jail Bulletin. See *Daily Bulletin* (no. 4750).

4769. *Labor Defender* (New York).

February 16 to November 15, 1918. Semi-monthly. Superseded by *Rebel Worker* (no. 4779). DLC, DL, WHi

Note: A different and unconnected *Labor Defender* was later published by the ILD (1926–1937).

Lodestar. See *Rebellion* (no. 4781).

4770. *Lumber Jack* (New Orleans).

January 9, 1913, to July 10, 1913. Weekly. Title changed to *Voice of the People* on July 17, 1913. See no. 4786. New Orleans from January 9, 1913, to July 21, 1914; Portland (as *Voice of the People*) from July 30, 1914, to December 3, 1914. Sometimes spelled *Lumberjack.* WHi, DL

Note: Lumberjack (Seattle), December, 1917, to March, 1919, published by L. C. Ward, was not an IWW paper. It merged in 1919 with the *Four L Bulletin,* later titled *Four L Lumber News,* Portland, 1919 to 1935. This paper was an organ of the Loyal Legion of Loggers and Lumbermen, a government-sponsored group opposed to the IWW.

4771. *Lumberjack Bulletin* (Seattle).

Between 1919 and 1931, an occasional supplement to the *Industrial Worker.* See no. 4766. Widely available, with no. 4766

4772. *Machine Age* (GRU, Chicago).

February to March, 1929. Frequency unknown. NN

4773. *New Solidarity* (Chicago).

November 16, 1918, to March 6, 1920. Weekly. See *Industrial Solidarity* (no. 4757). Superseded *Defense News Bulletin* (no. 4752); was superseded by *Solidarity* (no. 4784).

4774. *New Unionist* (Los Angeles).

July 6, 1918, to ?; May 7, 1927, to January 9, 1932. Semi-monthly until 1930, then monthly. CSt-H, MiU, NN

Note: Other *New Unionists* have been mentioned in the literature: one that was published weekly in Seattle, from July 6, 1918, until suppressed, is mentioned by Brissenden on p. 398 of *The IWW: A Study of American Syndicalism* (no. 18). There was also a monthly published in New York; it could not be located.

4775. *One Big Union Advocate* (One Big Union Club, New York).

April, 1939, to January, 1940. Monthly. The One Big Union Club during this time was unofficially IWW. MiDW-A

4776. *One Big Union Bulletin* (MMWIU #440, IWW, Cleveland).

August, 1935, to 1937. Frequency unknown. Not located

4777. *One Big Union Bulletin* (Northern District Organizing Committee, IWW, Tacoma).

1939–1940. Frequency unknown. Not located.

4778. *One Big Union Monthly* (Chicago).

March, 1919, to January, 1921. Monthly. Suspended after January, 1921. Superseded by *Industrial Pioneer* (no. 4756). New Series of *One Big Union Monthly* published from January, 1937, to June, 1938. Reprinted by Greenwood Press. Widely available

Press Service Release. See *Bulletin* (no. 4748).

4779. *Rebel Worker* (GDC, IWW, and others, New York).

February 1, 1919, to December 15, 1919. Semi-monthly. Published by a succession of variously named IWW defense committees. Superseded *Labor Defender* (no.4769). CSt-H, DL

4780. *Rebel Worker* (GRU, Chicago).

Spring, 1964, to January, 1967. Frequency varies. MiU

4781. *Rebellion: Made Up of Dreams and Dynamite* (New Orleans).

March, 1915, to June, 1916. Monthly. First issue titled *Lodestar.* NN, LNHT, CtY

4782. *Recruit* (GRU, Chicago).

1926 to 1930. Frequency varies. NN

4783. *Shingle Weaver* (Everett and Seattle, WA).
January, 1903, to February, 1913. Frequency varies, usually monthly. Superseded by *Timber Worker* (no. 4785). Before 1906 and occasionally afterwards (no certain times) not sympathetic to or connected with IWW. NN, WHi, CU

4784. *Solidarity* (New Castle, PA, Cleveland, and Chicago).
December 1, 1909, to October 27, 1917; March 16, 1920, to September 3, 1921. Weekly. Merged with *Industrial Solidarity* on March 16, 1920, with the name retained until September 3, 1921. See *Industrial Solidarity* (no. 4757). Widely available

4785. *Timber Worker* (Everett and Seattle).
March, 1913, to February 15, 1915. Frequency varies, monthly or semi-monthly. Superseded *Shingle Weaver* (no. 4783). CU, NN, MdBJ

Trial Bulletin. See *Daily Bulletin* (no. 4750).

4786. *Voice of the People* (New Orleans and Portland, OR).
January 9, 1913, to December 3, 1914. Weekly. Titled *Lumber Jack* from January 9, 1913, to July 10, 1913. From New Orleans January 9, 1913, to July 21, 1914; from Portland July 30, 1914, to December 3, 1914. WHi, DL, MiDW-A

4787. *Wooden Shoe* (Los Angeles).
August, 1912, to 1914. Weekly. NN

4788. *Workers Defense* (Chicago).
October, 1931, to December, 1932. Monthly. Superseded *Defense News Bulletin* (no. 4753). CtY, NN, IU

Workers' Opposition. See *Industrial Unionist* (no. 4761).

4789. *Young Recruit* (Chicago).
May, 1930, to November, 1931; December, 1932, to August, 1933. Monthly. MiDW-A

Note: This was a mimeographed magazine for children. From time to time parents or youth groups such as local "Junior Wobblies" clubs published such items, most of which are lost, so that the frequency is not certain. A few scattered issues of such serials are known: *Junior Recruit,* November 1, 1933; *Wobbly,* March 1962, and October, 1963; *Young Libertarian,* December, 1962; and *Young Rebel,* Christmas, 1929 (Workers Socialist Publishing Company).

Other Serial Publications

Various serial publications, such as *Minutes, General Office Bulletin, General Organization Bulletin,* monthly financial reports, and the like, have been omitted here. Among other places, they may be found at the Reuther Library in the IWW Collection, where they are treated as archival material. Individual unions issued periodicals also, but they are too numerous, irregular, and localized to list completely in this bibliography. Among such publications are *Labor Bulletin* (various Portland locals); *Lumber Workers Bulletin* (LWIU #120); *Boulder Dam Worker* (GCWIU #310); *Building and Construction Workers Bulletin* (BCWIU #320); *General Construction Workers Industrial Union #310 Bulletin; Metal Mine Workers Industrial Union #210 Bulletin* (MMWIU #300); *The Boomer* (MMWIU #300); *IWW Seaman* (MTWIU #510); and *Marine Worker* (MTWIU #510). The bulk of these and similar serials came out between 1916 and 1940. They can be found at the Reuther Library and elsewhere, but there are probably no complete runs. NN, MiU, MiDW-A

Foreign-Language Newspapers

This list of foreign-language papers is added to round out the picture of the complicated IWW publishing network. A few were published by groups that were not always IWW (they were often foreign-language–speaking Socialists). Some papers joined the IWW only for short periods. These foreign-language papers were usually direct translations of the English-language papers and were often printed at the same time. Some were partially in English.

The first list (nos. 4790–4806) is comprised of papers that can still be found, either in union lists of serials or in archives. The second list (not numbered) includes papers that appear in older bibliographies or on publishers' lists but that do not appear in common union serial lists. Probably neither of the two lists is complete. Dates are cited as exactly as possible.

4790. *A Bérmunkás* (The wage worker) (Chicago, New York, and Cleveland).

Hungarian. November 15, 1912, to April 7, 1917; November 17, 1923, to December 28, 1946. Weekly. Suppressed April 8, 1917, to November 17, 1923, during which time *Felzsabadulas* was published. See no. 4791. DL, MnHi, MiDW-A

4791. *Felzsabadulas* (Emancipation) (Chicago).
Hungarian. December 7, 1918, to November 26, 1921. Weekly. Published during the suppression of *A Bérmunkás* (no. 4790). DL, MnHi, MiDW-A

4792. *Golos Truzhenika* (Voice of the worker) (Chicago).
Russian. 1918 to May 17, 1924; November, 1924, to 1927. Frequency varies, usually monthly. Not always affiliated with the IWW. MiU

4793. *Huelga General* (General strike) (Los Angeles).
Spanish. August 23, 1913, to September 12, 1914. Weekly. DL

4794. *Industrialisti* (The industrialist) (Workers Socialist Publishing Company, Duluth, Minnesota).
Finnish. March 19, 1917, to October 21, 1975. Daily. MnHi

4795. *Ipari Munkás* (Industrial worker) (Chicago).
Hungarian. August 11 to September 29, 1917. Weekly. Superseded *Uj Tarsadalom* (no. 4806). DL

4796. *Jedna Velka Unie* (One big union) (Chicago).
Czechoslovakian. 1927 to 1931. Frequency varies. WHi

4797. *Nueva Solidaridad* (New solidarity) (Chicago and Brooklyn).
Spanish. January, 1918, to 1919. Frequency unknown. Superseded by *Solidaridad* (no. 4803). DLC, MH

4798. *Nuovo Proletario* (New proletariat) (Chicago).
Italian. November 30, 1918, to November 29, 1919. Weekly. Issued during the suspension of *Il Proletario* (no. 4800). NN

4799. *Nya Varlden* (New world) (Chicago).
Swedish. January 25 to November 22, 1919. Weekly. IU, NN

4800. *Il Proletario* (The proletariat) (Italian Socialist Federation and IWW, New York and Philadelphia).
Italian. 1897 to present. Weekly. Suspended from November, 1918, to November, 1919, during which time *Nuovo Proletario* (no. 4798) was published. From time to time between 1905 and 1919, it was affiliated with the IWW. NN, DL, MiU

4801. *Průmyslový Delník* (Factory workers' daily) (Chicago).
Bohemian. December, 1914, to March 15, 1915. Semimonthly. NN

4802. *El Rebelde* (The rebel) (Los Angeles).
Spanish. February, 1915, to September, 1917. Semi-monthly. DL

4803. *Solidaridad* (Solidarity) (Chicago, Brooklyn, and New York).
Spanish. January, 1918, to May 24, 1930. Frequency varies, usually semi-monthly. Superseded *Nueva Solidaridad* (no. 4797). From Chicago, as *Nueva Solidaridad,* from January, 1918, to 1919; from Brooklyn, as *Solidaridad,* June 14, 1919, to April, 1927; from New York April, 1927, to May 24, 1930. Suspended from January 25, 1930, to February, 1930. Possibly suspended in Chicago, mid-1919. DLC, MH, NN

4804. *Solidárność* (Solidarity) (Chicago).
Polish. August 21, 1913, to September 15, 1917. Semi-monthly. DL

4805. *Tie Vapauteen* (Road to freedom) (New York).
Finnish. May, 1919, to ?. Monthly. NN

4806. *Uj Tarsadalom* (New society) (Chicago).
Hungarian. May 12 to July 21, 1917. Weekly. Superseded by *Ipari Munkás* (no. 4795). DL

Other Foreign-language Papers (current locations unknown; dates often unknown)

Alarm (Minneapolis).
Swedish-Norwegian-Danish. Monthly.

Buoreviestnik (Chicago).
Bulgarian. April 15, 1917, to ?. Weekly.

Darbininku Balsas (Baltimore).
Lithuanian. Weekly.

L'Emancipation (Olneyville, RI).
French. Monthly.

Glas Radnika (Chicago).
Croatian. 1919 to ?. Semi-monthly.

Der Industrialer Arbeiter (Chicago).
Yiddish. February, 1919, to ?. Monthly.

Industrialen Rabotnik (Chicago).
Finnish. 1924. Frequency unknown.

Industrijalni Radnik (Duluth).
Slavonian. Frequency unknown.

Het Licht (Lawrence, MA).
Flemish. Monthly.

Loukkataistelu (New York).
Finnish. 1919 to ?. Frequency unknown.

A Luz (New Bedford, MA).
Portuguese. Semi-monthly.

Muncitorul (Chicago).
Romanian. Frequency unknown.

Probuda (Chicago).
Bulgarian. Frequency unknown.

Prolataras (Chicago).
Lithuanian. Frequency unknown.

Rabochaya Rech (Chicago).
Russian. Weekly.

Rabotnceska Mysl (Chicago).
Bulgarian. Frequency unknown.

Ragione Nuova (Providence, RI).
Italian. Monthly.

Snaga Radnika (Chicago).
Croatian. Frequency unknown.

Solidaridet (Seattle).
Swedish. Monthly.

Teollisuustyo Lainen (Duluth).
Finnish. Frequency varies, usually daily.

La Union Industrial (Phoenix).
Spanish. Frequency unknown.

Der Weckruf (Chicago).
German. 1912–1915? Weekly.

Der Yacker (Brooklyn).
Yiddish. May 1, 1915, to ?. Monthly.

WEBSTER

Government Documents and Publications

A variety of government documents and government-sponsored publications may be useful in studying the IWW. The following is a selected list of some government studies and reports that IWW historians have frequently used and that deal with major incidents, ideas, and issues in IWW history. Locations are given only for those documents that are hard to find.

Selected Chronological List of Publications by the U.S. Congress

4807. U.S. Congress, House. *Coeur d'Alene Labor Troubles.* House Reports No. 1949 and No. 1999, including report from the Committee on Military Affairs, directing Committee to investigate conduct of U.S. Army and Officers in Idaho, with views of minority. 56th Cong., 1st sess. June 5, 1900.

4808. ———. *Report from the Committee on Labor, Calling for Information Relative to Labor Troubles at Goldfield; Report of J. J. Gardner.* House Report No. 285. 60th Cong., 1st sess. January 20, 1908.

4809. ———. *Papers Relative to the Labor Troubles at Goldfield, Nevada.* Message from the President of the United States, transmitting report of Special Commission on Labor Troubles at Goldfield, Nevada, and papers relating thereto. House Document No. 607. 60th Cong., 1st sess. February 3, 1908.

4810. ———. *Peonage in Western Pennsylvania.* Hearings before the Committee on Labor of the House of Representatives, authorizing the Committee to investigate the Taylor System and other systems of shop management. 62nd Cong., 1st sess. August 1, 1911.

4811. ———. *The Strike at Lawrence, Massachusetts.* House Document No. 671. 62nd Cong., 2nd sess. April 4, 1912.

4812. ———. *Miners' Strike in the Bituminous Coal Fields in Westmoreland County, Pa. in 1910–1911,* by Walter B. Palmer. House Document No. 847. 62nd Cong., 2nd sess. June 22, 1912.

4813. ———. *Industrial Disputes in Colorado and Michigan.* Hearings on House Resolutions No. 290 and No. 313, December 10 and 17, 1913, before the House Committee on Rules. 63rd Cong., 2nd sess. December, 1913.

4814. ———. *Michigan Copper District Strike.* With reports by John A. Moffett and John B. Densmore on their efforts to arbitrate. House Document No. 741, Conciliation and Arbitration Series 3. 63rd Cong., 2nd sess. February 7, 1914.

4815. ———. *Report on Colorado Strike Investigation.* House Document No. 1630. 63rd Cong., 3rd sess. March 2, 1915.

4816. ———. *Wages and Hours of Labor in Cotton, Woolen and Silk Industries, 1907–1914.* Bulletin No. 190, Wage and Hours Series 21. House Document No. 847. 64th Cong., 1st sess. May, 1916.

4817. ———. *To Punish Espionage and Acts of Interference with Foreign Relations, Neutrality, and Foreign Commerce.* Hearings before the Committee on the Judiciary. House Reports No. 1033 and No. 1591, Serial 53. 64th Cong., 2nd sess. February 22 and 28, 1917.

4818. ———. *IWW Deportation Cases.* Hearings before a Subcommittee of the Committee on Immigration and Naturalization. Statement of W. A. Blackwood. Reports in the cases of various aliens tranferred from Seattle, Washington, and other points, to Ellis Island for deportation and thereafter released. 66th Cong., 2nd sess. April 27 to 30, 1920.

4819. ———. *Attorney General A. Mitchell Palmer on Charges of Illegal Practices of the Department of Justice, Made by Louis F. Post and Others.* Hearings before the House Rules Committee. 66th Cong., 2nd sess. 1920–1921.

4820. ———. *Investigation of the Administration of Louis F. Post, Assistant Secretary of Labor, in Matter of Deportation of Aliens.* House Rules Committee, Hearings, 1920.

4821. ———. *Amnesty for Political Prisoners.* Hearings before the Committee on the Judiciary, House of Representatives, on House Resolution No. 60. 67th Cong., 2nd sess. March 16, 1922.

4822. U.S. Congress. Senate. *Labor Troubles in Idaho. Crime of the Century; Account of Idaho Infamy,* by Edward Boyce. Senate Document No. 25. Includes reply by Kennedy to charges made against him. Senate Document No. 42. 56th Cong., 1st sess. December 14, 1899.

4823. ———. *Coeur d'Alene Mining Troubles.* Report of H. C. Merriam on miners' riots in Idaho, presented by Mr. Chandler. Further report of H. C. Merriam on miners' riots. Senate Documents No. 24 and No. 142. 56th Cong., 1st sess. February 5, 1900.

4824. ———. *Federal Aid in Domestic Disturbances, 1787–1903.* Report by Frederick T. Wilson. Senate Document No. 209. 57th Cong., 2nd sess. March 2, 1903.

4825. ———. *Statement of the Western Federation of Miners in Answer to the Statement of Mine Owners in Colorado.* Senate Document No. 86. 58th Cong., 2nd sess. February 20, 1904.

4826. ———. *Transmission through the Mails of Anarchistic Publications.* Senate Document No. 426, Series 5265. 60th Cong., 1st sess. April 9, 1908.

4827. ———. *Report on the Strike of the Textile Workers in Lawrence, Mass., in 1912,* by C. P. Neil and Fred Coxton. Senate Document No. 870. 62nd Cong., 2nd sess. Hearings March 2 to 7, and April 5, 1912.

4828. ———. *Conditions in the Paint Creek District, West Virginia.* Hearings before a Subcommittee of the Committee on Education and Labor, pursuant to Senate Resolution No. 37. 63rd Cong., 1st sess. Hearings during March, April and May, 1913.

4829. ———. *Strike in the Copper Mining District of Michigan.* Senate Document No. 381. 63rd Cong., 2nd sess. January 30, 1914.

4830. ———. Committee on the Judiciary. *Hearings before a Subcommittee on Bolshevik Propaganda.* 65th Cong., 3rd sess., and thereafter. Later published as Senate Document No. 62. 66th Cong., 1st sess. February 11 to March 10, 1919.

4831. ———. Committee on Education and Labor. Report of *Investigation of Strike in Steel Industry.* Senate Report No. 289. 66th Cong., 1st sess. November 8, 1919.

4832. ———. *Investigation of the Activities of the Department of Justice, a Report on the Activities of the Bureau of Investigation, Department of*

Justice, against Persons Advising Anarchy, Sedition, and Forcible Overthrow of the Government. Senate Document No. 153. 66th Cong., 1st sess., 1919.

4833. ———. Subcommittee on the Judiciary. *Hearings on Charges of Illegal Practices of the Department of Justice.* Includes report by F. R. Barkley, "Jailing Radicals in Detroit." 66th Cong., 1st sess. January 19 to March 3, 1921.

4834. ———. *Federal Aid in Domestic Disturbances, 1903–1922,* prepared by the Office of the Judge Advocate General, U.S. Army. (Supplemental to Senate Document No. 209, *Federal Aid in Domestic Disturbances, 1787–1903,* prepared by Frederick T. Wilson, Adjutant General's Office, which is reprinted as part of this document.) Senate Document No. 263. 67th Cong., 2nd sess. 1922.

4835. ———. *Conditions in the Coal Fields of Harlan and Bell Counties, Kentucky.* Hearings on Senate Resolution No. 178, Senate Subcommittee on Manufacture. 72nd Cong., 1st sess. May 11 to 19, 1932.

Selected Articles in Government Serial Publications

4836. Ashhurst, F. F. "The I. W. W. Menace." *Congressional Record* 55 (August 17, 1917):6687.

4837. Bryan, J. W. "Seattle Riots." *Congressional Record* 1 (1913):2900; 2902–3; 4400; 4410–13; 5980–83.

4838. Cary, W. J. "Shall the Declaration of Independence and the Bill of Rights Be Deleted by a Censor?" *Congressional Record* 55 (May 5, 1917):1949–52.

4839. Covert, D. W. C. "Story of a Six Weeks' Tour on the 'Spruce Front.'" *Monthly Bulletin,* Spruce Production Division, U.S. Army (October, 1918):7–9.

4840. "Decision on the Application of the Kansas Criminal Syndicalism Act." *Congressional Digest* 6 (June, 1927):212.

4841. "Deportation of Aliens for Membership in Unlawful Organizations." *Monthly Labor Review* 11 (October, 1920):818–25.

4842. "Development of Collective Bargaining in Metal Mines." *Monthly Labor Review* 47 (September, 1938):591–98.

4843. Gadsby, Mrs. M. A. G. "The Steel Strike of 1919." *Monthly Labor Review* 1 (December, 1919):1743–58.

4844. Green, W. R. "I.W.W. Organization; Powers of the Postmaster General." *Congressional Record* 56 (May 9, 1918):6799–800.

4845. Gregory, T. W., Attorney General. "Stronger Espionage Laws Are Needed." *Official Bulletin* 2 (April 16, 1918):102.

4846. ———."What the Department of Justice Is Doing To Curb Espionage, Summarized by A-G Gregory in a Statement Showing Results as Accomplished under Limitations of Laws." *Official Bulletin* 2 (April 19, 1918):6–7.

4847. Humphrey, W. E. "Riots in Seattle, Washington in July, 1913 between Industrial Workers of the World and United States Soldiers and Sailors." *Congressional Record* 1 (September 4, 1914): 4679–93.

4848. Jamieson, Stuart. "Labor Unionism in American Agriculture." *Monthly Labor Review* 62 (January, 1946):25–36.

4849. Johnson, Albert. "The Preaching of Treason and the Breeding of Sedition Must Stop." *Congressional Record* 4 (June 25, 1917): 8037.

4850. King, W. H. "Postal Censorship." *Congressional Record* 56 (May 3, 1918):5978–80.

4851. ———. "Remarks on IWW." *Congressional Record* 56 (May 6, 1918): 6565–66.

4852. "Labor Camps in California." *Monthly Labor Review* 11 (October, 1920):222–24.

4853. Magnusson, Leifur. "Agricultural Camp Housing." *Monthly Labor Review* 6(May, 1918): 277–87.

4854. "Membership in the I.W.W. a Criminal Offense under California Statute." *Monthly Labor Review* 16 (February, 1923):471–73.

4855. Myers, H. L. "The IWW with Special Reference to Butte." *Congressional Record* 55 (August 23, 1917):6869–71.

4856. "Report of the President's Mediation Commission, Condemning Deportations from Warren District of Arizona." *Monthly Labor Review* 6 (January, 1918):13–17.

4857. Sherman, Lawrence Y. "The IWW and the War." *Congressional Record* 56 (June 20, 1918):6566–69.

Chronological List of Books, Monographs, and Pamphlets by the U.S. Government

4858. Albrecht, Arthur E. *International Seamen's Union of America.* U.S. Bureau of Labor Statistics Bulletin No. 342. Washington, DC: G.P.O., 1913.

4859. U.S. Commission on Industrial Relations. *Final Report and Testimony,* 11 vols. Document 415, 64th Cong., 1st sess. Washington, DC: GPO, 1916.

The original, including unpublished reports, is in the Department of Labor Records, RG 174, at the National Archives. Some records were deposited at the State Historical Society of Wisconsin in Madison.

4860. U.S. Library of Congress. Division of Bibliography. *List of References on the Industrial Workers of the World.* Select List No. 291. Washington, DC, July 24, 1917.

4861. President's Mediation Commission. *Report on Bisbee Deportations Made by the President's Mediation Commission to the President of the United States, November 6, 1917.* Washington, DC: Labor Department, 1918. Also printed in the *Official Bulletin of the Public Information Committee,* November 27, 1918.

4862. National Industrial Conference Board. *Strikes in American Industry in War Time.* Research Report No.3. Washington, DC: National Industrial Conference Board, 1918.

4863. U.S. Department of War. Militia Bureau. *Military Protection, US Guards. The Use of Organized Bodies in Protection and Defense of Property during Riots, Strikes, and Civil Disturbances.* War Department, War Plans Division, Document No. 882. Washington, DC: GPO, 1918.

4864. U.S. Department of the Navy. Office of Naval Intelligence. "Investigation of the Marine Transport Workers and the Alleged Threatened Combination between Them and the Bolsheviki and Sinn Feiner." Mimeographed report. Washington, DC, December 23, 1918. National Archives Record Group 174.

4865. U.S. Department of War. *Report of the Activities of the War Department in the Field of Industrial Relations during the War.* Washington, DC: GPO, 1919.

U.S. Department of War. *History of the Spruce Production Division.* Portland, OR, 1920.

Often cited as a government document, this is not an official government document, according to Harold Hyman in *Soldiers and Spruce* (no. 112), page 3. He states that it is a document assembled by Major Cuthbert Stearn and the LLLL as a defense against Congressional criticism.

4866. Baker, Oliver. *Seed Time and Harvest.* U.S. Department of Agriculture Bulletin No. 183. Washington, DC: GPO, 1922.

4867. Harrington, Daniel. *Lessons from the Granite Mountain Shaft Fire, Butte.* U.S. Department of the Interior, Bureau of Mines Bulletin No. 188. Washington, DC: GPO, 1922.

4868. Harrington, Daniel. *Underground Ventilation at Butte.* U.S. Department of the Interior, Bureau of Mines Bulletin No. 204. Washington, DC: GPO, 1923.

4869. Howd, Cloice B. *Industrial Relations in the West Coast Lumber Industry.* U.S. Bureau of Labor Statistics Bulletin No. 349. Washington, DC: GPO, 1924.

4870. Lescohier, D. D. *Conditions Affecting the Demand for Harvest Labor in the Wheat Belt.* U.S. Department of Agriculture Bulletin No. 1230. Washington, DC: GPO, 1924.

4871. Poblete Troncoso, Moisés. *Labor Organizations in Chile.* U.S. Bureau of Labor Statistics Bulletin No. 461. Washington, DC: GPO, 1928.

4872. Oppenheimer, Reuben. *The Enforcement of the Deportation Laws of the United States: Report to the National Commission on Law Observance and Enforcement.* Washington, DC: GPO, 1931.

4873. U.S. Federal Writers' Project, State of California. "Industrial Workers of the World in California Agriculture." 1936? Microfilmed by University of California Photographic Service. Reel No. 67–677. CU, MiDWA

4874. ———. "Toilers of the World." 1919. Microfilmed by University of California Photographic Service. Reel No. 67–579. CU, MiDWA

4875. Peterson, Florence. *Strikes in the US, 1880–1936.* U.S. Bureau of Labor Statistics Bulletin No. 651. Washington, DC: GPO, 1938.

4876. U.S. Department of Justice. Immigration and Naturalization Service. *In the Matter of Harry Benton Bridges. Memorandum of Decision.* Charles B. Sears, Presiding Inspector. Washington, DC: GPO, 1941.

4877. U.S. Federal Writers' Project, State of Montana. *Copper Camp Stories of the World's Greatest Mining Town, Butte, Montana.* New York: Hastings House, 1943.

4878. National Commission on the Causes and Prevention of Violence. *Violence in America: Historical and Comparative Perspectives. Report of the Task Force on Historical and Comparative Perspectives.* Washington, DC: GPO, 1969.

State and Local Documents

4879. California. Commissioner to Investigate Disturbances in San Diego. *Report of Harris Weinstock, Commissioner to Investigate the Recent Disturbances in the City of San Diego.* Sacramento: Supt. of State Printing, 1912.

4880. ———. Commission of Immigration and Housing. *Annual Report, 1913.* Sacramento: State Printers, 1913.

4881. Colorado. *Industrial Disputes: the Northern Coal Fields Strike.* Biennial Report of the Bureau of Labor Statistics, 1911–1912. Denver, 1913.

4882. Commonwealth of Massachusetts. *Annual Report of the State Board of Conciliation and Arbitration for the Year Ending December 31, 1912.*

4883. ———. Bureau of Statistics. *Labor Bibliography, July 15, 1913.* Boston: State Printers, 1913.

4884. ———. *Thirteenth Annual Report on Strikes and Lockouts, 1912. Part 3 of Forty-Second Annual Report on the Statistics of Labor, 1912.* Boston: Massachusetts Bureau of Statistics, 1913.

4885. Lawrence, Massachusetts. *Annual Report of the Director of the Department of Public Health and Charities for the Year 1912.*

4886. Minnesota. House of Representatives. Committee of Labor and Labor Legislation Hearings. "Labor Troubles in Northern Minnesota, Jan. 30, 1917." MnHi

4887. Montana. "Testimony of Hearings Held at the State Capitol, Helena, Montana, May 31, June 1, June 2, 1918, by Montana Council of Defense." Reporter's typed manuscript. MtHiLH

4888. Nebraska. *Industrial Survey of the Wage Earners; Labor Unions; Occupational Diseases; Industrial Accidents; Cost of Living; General La-*

bor Conditions of Nebraska. Bulletin No. 25. Bureau of Labor and Industrial Statistics, 1912.

4889. New Jersey. Bureau of Statistics of Labor and Industry of New Jersey. *Annual Report,* for 1911, 1912, 1913, 1914. Camden: S. Chey and Sons.

4890. New York. Legislature. Joint Legislative Committee Investigating Seditious Activities. *Revolutionary Radicalism: Its History, Purposes, and Tactics.* 4 vols. Albany, 1920.

4891. New York. Department of Labor. *Industrial Relations in New York. Bulletin of the New York Department of Labor* 14 (March–December, 1912).

4892. Ohio. 80th General Assembly. Appendix of "Reports of Committee Investigating Akron Rubber Industries." *Journal,* 1918.

4893. Washington. State Council of Defense. *Report of the State Council of Defense to the Governor of Washington Covering Its Activities during the War, June 16, 1917 to January 9, 1919.* Olympia, 1919.

4894. Spokane, Washington. "Ordinance Relating to the Public Peace and Good Order of the City, Defining the Crime of Criminal Syndicalism, Providing a Punishment Therefore, and Declaring an Emergency." Ordinance No. C2321, passed Council April 22, 1918. (Spokane) *Official Gazette* 8 (May 1, 1918):4595.

4895. West Virginia. West Virginia Mining Investigation Commission Report. Appendix to *Regular Biennial Message of Governor Glasscock to the Legislature for the Period October 1, 1910, to September 30, 1912.*

I.W.W.

TO FAN THE FLAMES of DISCONTENT

SONGS

40 Cents

Printed in U.S.A.

Miscellaneous Writings: Historical, Dramatic, Poetic, and Fictional

SOME materials do not fit the usual categories, yet may be very useful and of great interest. The following section includes a group of such bibliographic leftovers and misfits.

Historical Writings

This list includes written reminiscences of people who were members of the IWW or had a special knowledge about it. There are also some unpublished historical accounts and bibliographic and academic studies. Some of the unpublished writings, notably those of Covington Hall, Ben Williams, and Agnes Inglis, are often cited in footnotes. This list must be considered incomplete and preliminary, for the number of unpublished manuscripts other than student dissertations and theses relating to the IWW must be large. Some of these items lack dates.

4896. Abramson, Paul. "The Industrial Workers of the World in the Northwest Lumber Industry." Senior thesis, 1952. OrPR

4897. Ault, E. B. (Harry). "Thirty Years of Saving the World." Reminiscences. WaU

4898. Barnett, Eugene. "Centralia." MiU

4899. Beffel, John N. "Concerning the Lynching of Wesley Everest and Frank Little." NNU-T

4900. Berman, Hyman. "Education for Work and Labor Solidarity: The Immigrant Miners and Radicalism on the Mesabi Range." Conference Paper, 1963. MnHi

4901. Bogard, Thomas. "Recollections." MiDW-A

4902. Brazier, Dick. "Looking Backward to the Spokane Free Speech Fight." MiDW-A

4903. Briggs Striker. "A Brief History of the Briggs Strike." MiDW-A

4904. Brown, Joseph L. "Technocracy and the I.W.W." 1933. MiU

4905. Casey, Joseph. "The IWW in Relation to the Lawrence Strike." Honors thesis, Harvard University, 1958. MH-Pu

4906. Cedervall, Frank. "IWW Radio Broadcasts from the 1930's." MiDW-A

4907. Corder, Minnie. "You Will Never Go Hungry." Reminiscences. MiDW-A

4908. De Shazo, Peter, and Robert J. Halsted. "Los Wobblies del Sur: The Industrial Workers of the World in Chile and Mexico." MiDW-A

4909. Edwards, Hagburt ("Herb"). "Reminiscences." MiDW-A

4910. Evans, Martha Ann. "Kuzbas Colony, 1921–1927." MnHi

4911. Fry, E. C. "Tom Barker and the IWW." NNU-T

4912. Gallagher, Mary. "Notes." MiU

4913. Garrity, Donald A. "The Frank Little Episode and the Butte Labor Troubles of 1917." Senior thesis, 1957. MtHC

4914. Gedicks, Al. "Isolated from What? Radical Finnish Immigrants in Midwest Mining Communities." 1976. MiDW-A

4915. Gelatly, James R. "Five Dollars for Eight Hours." MiU

4916. Graham, Phillip, Jr. "The Origins of Hysteria: Certain Aspects of the Red Scare of 1919." Honors thesis, Harvard, 1964. MH–Pu

4917. Green, Paul J., and Siegfried A. Vogt. "Sources on the Industrial Workers of the World, IWW." Bibliography, 1978. WaPS

4918. Hall, Covington. "Labor Struggles in the Deep South." MiDW-A, MiU, LNHT

4919. Holland, Allen A. "The Negro and the Industrial Workers of the World." 1942. MiU

4920. IWW Members. "The ABC of Unionism." 1942. MiDW-A

4921. Inglis, Agnes. "Reminiscences." MiU

4922. Kwik, Phillip. "The IWW in Detroit, 1926–1933." MiU, MiDW-A

4923. McGuckin, H. E. "Memoirs." MiDW-A

4924. Martinson, H. R. "Comes the Revolution." Reminiscences of the Socialist movement in North Dakota. NdFA

4925. Morris, James O. "The Dynamite Conspiracy at Lawrence, Massachusetts, in 1912." 1949. MiU

4926. ———. "The Joe Hill Case." 1933. MiU

4927. Morse, Samuel. "The Truth about Bisbee." AzTU-PH

4928. Murphy, Mary, and Bill Walker. "Butte, Montana: A Select Bibliography." Butte Oral History Project, 1980. MtU-M

4929. Ockert, Roy A. "The Wage Structure of the Pacific Northwest Lumber Industry." CU-B

4930. Olilla, Douglas J. "From Socialism to Industrial Unionism (IWW): Social Factors in the Emergence of Left-Labor Radicalism among Finnish Workers on the Mesabi, 1911–1919." MiDW-A

4931. Pinkham, Harold. "IWW's." MiU

4932. Robbins, Matilda. "Memoirs." MiDW-A

4933. Sheetz, R. B. "The I.W.W. in Hawaii." 1975. MiDW-A

4934. Tenney, James B. "History of Mining in Arizona." AzTeS

4935. Trautmann, William E. "The Power of Folded Arms and Thinking Bayonets." 1937. MiDW-A

4936. Van Horn, Schuyler. "The Little Falls Textile Strike of 1912." Independent study project, 1968. NGHWS

4937. Vogel, Virgil J. "The Historians and the Industrial Workers of the World." MiDW-A

4938. Walters, J. A., and W. R. Odule. "The I.W.W.: Do You Want It?" DLC

4939. Wells, Hulet M. "I Wanted To Work." Reminiscences. WaU

4940. Williams, Ben H. "American Labor in the Jungle: The Saga of the One Big Union." MiDW-A

Drama and Dramatic Forms

The following list spans more than seventy years of plays and movies about the IWW. They vary in nature and no doubt in quality, but they represent a sampling of the ways in which the dramatic nature of the IWW has been seen by imaginative playwrights.

4941. Babe, Thomas. *Salt Lake City Skyline.* New York: Dramatists Play Service, 1980.

A play dramatizing the story of Joe Hill.

4942. Beatty, Warren, and Trevor Griffiths. *Reds.* Issued by Paramount. Produced by Warren Beatty. 1981.

A movie about John Reed, once an IWW, who became obsessively involved in Communist radicalism and its in-fighting.

4943. Bird, Stewart, and Deborah Raffin. *The Wobblies.* Produced by the authors. 1979.

A movie about the IWW. It includes interviews with old-timers, including Fred Thompson.

4944. ———. *The Wobblies: US vs. Haywood et al.* Performed in New York, 1980.

A play with the dramatic IWW Chicago trial as its theme.

4945. Davis, Mary, and Joanna Sampson. *Columbine.* 1973.

An opera about Colorado's Columbine mine disaster, an IWW episode. *Columbine* was produced in 1973 by the Boulder Civic Opera Association.

4946. Engledrum, John T. *The O. B. U.: A Drama in One Act and Two Scenes.* Los Angeles: J. Engledrum, 1924.

A play about union solidarity. It was performed frequently in the 1930s before labor groups. MiU

4947. di Gaetano, Nick. *Quo Vadis Domine?* Detroit: Italian IWW, 1914.

A one-act play in Italian that centers on the problem of divided loyalties. MiDW-A

4948. Giovannitti, Arturo. *Come era nel principio, tenebre rosse.* Brooklyn, NY: Italian IWW Publishing Bureau, 1918.

A play in Italian about the need for greater radicalism. NN

4949. Illinois Labor History Society. *The IWW.* Chicago, 1980.

A film that includes IWW music and interviews. Available on TV cassette.

4950. ———. *Joe Hill.* Chicago, 1979.

A film about Joe Hill that includes interviews and comment by William Adelman.

4951. Jonas, Tony. *Boulder Dam.* (Title is tentative.)

A forthcoming play about the part of the IWW in a strike at the Boulder Dam project. A Hollywood production.

4952. Latin American Film Project. *The Libertarians.* 1980.

Brazilian-made film, distributed in the U.S., about Anarcho-Syndicalism in Brazil. It recalls the "revolutionary IWW" in the United States as an example of anticapitalism.

4953. O'Neill, Eugene. *The Hairy Ape.* New York: Boni & Liveright, 1922.

A famous play that includes a scene in a waterfront IWW hall.

4954. Pritchard, Barry. *Centralia, 1919. Minnesota Review* (New Series, Spring, 1977):71–118.

A play about the famous IWW tragedy. It includes combinations of live actors, film, slides, and music. Produced in 1976 by the University of Washington School of Drama.

4955. C. D. Workshop, Roxbury, MA. *The Shape of an Era.* 1973.

A movie in which older miners recall their earlier days of union struggle and younger miners are urged to become more rebellious.

4956. Sinclair, Upton. *The Singing Jailbirds.* Pasadena: published by the author, 1924.

A play about injustices to the IWW, discomforts of the workers, and their ability to sing through their troubles, even in jail.

4957. Smith, Walker C. *Their Court and Our Class: A One-Act Sketch.* n.p.: published by the author, 1917.

A highly satirical one-act play about the trial of the Everett Massacre prisoners. Enacted at IWW meetings. MiU

4958. Stavis, Barrie. *The Man Who Never Died: A Play about Joe Hill.* New York: Haven Press, 1954. Reprint: Cranbury, NJ: A. S. Barnes, 1972.

A popular play about the IWW martyr that has been in production somewhere every year since it was written.

4959. Tippett, Tom. *Mill Shadows: A Drama of Social Forces in Four Acts.* Katonah, NY: Brookwood Labor College, 1932.

A play about drudgery in the textile mills and the importance of strikes.

4960. Zilber, Jake. *How To Make a Decent Revolution: A Full-Length Entertainment.* Vancouver, BC: Mother Earth Publishers, n.d. (1965?).

A play about revolution, taking the IWW and OBU as examples.

Poetry and Songs

The IWW's *Little Red Songbook* must rank as one of the century's greatest publishing and propaganda successes, even though its contents are more artful than artistic. The clever parodies, based at first on familiar hymns and popular songs, and the stirring, heartfelt labor songs appealed to all workers, not just the zealous. To some, the irreverent or shocking element simply added zest. Since 1909, when the first one was printed, the little book has gone through many editions; it is still available. In the "Articles" section earlier in this bibliography there are histories and explanations of the songbook by Archie Green (no. 1352) and by Richard Brazier (no. 496). The John Neuhaus Collection of Wobbly Songs was microfilmed in 1966 and is available from University Microfilms, Inc. Several records of the songs are commercially available.

Of all the IWW poets, Joe Hill was the most popular, but others were appreciated and successful. Some who did not publish volumes but whose writings appeared in IWW publications over the years include Robert Whitaker, Matilda Robbins (Matilda Rabinowitz), Richard Brazier, Louis Burcar (Louis Carrick), Carlos Cortez, Vera Moller, Jim Seymour, W. O. Blee, John Forbes, Lee Fisher, and others too numerous to mention.

The following is a list of some published volumes. Joyce Kornbluh's *Rebel Voices* (no. 132) is the best source for many of these and other imaginative creations from the IWW.

4961. Chaplin, Ralph. *Bars and Shadows: The Prison Poems of Ralph Chaplin.* New York: Leonard Press, 1922.

4962. ———. *Only the Drums Remembered.* Tacoma: Dammeier Printing Co., 1960.

4963. ———. *The Red Feast.* Chicago: Rebel Press, 1935.

4964. ———. *When the Leaves Come Out.* Chicago: IWW, 1917.

Chaplin was both an artist and a poet. He wrote the famous labor song "Solidarity Forever," which is still sung today in union halls all over the world. For his biography and more information, see no. 32.

4965. Cole, James Kelly. *The Poems and Prose Writings of James Kelly Cole.* Chicago: IWW, 1918.

Cole was killed at an early age while trying to hop a freight train on his way to the Spokane Free Speech Fight. He had been particularly loved and was noted for his affability, good looks, and youth; he was memorialized by the publication of his complete works.

4966. Giovannitti, Arturo. *Collected Poems of Arturo Giovannitti.* Chicago: E. Clemente, 1962. Reprint: Salem, NH: Ayer, 1975.

Included in this volume is his particularly popular "When the Cock Crows," a poem about war.

4967. Hall, Covington. *Battle Hymns of Toil.* Oklahoma City: General Welfare Reporter, n.d. DLC

4968. ———. *Rhymes of a Rebel.* Newllano, LA: Llano Cooperative Colony Printery, 1931.

4969. ———. *Songs of Rebellion.* New Orleans: John J. Weiling, 1915.

Hall's fervent poems appeared in IWW publications for more than fifty years. He is the author of an admired history of labor in the South (no. 4918) and was the editor of several newspapers. DLC

4970. *IWW Songs To Fan the Flames of Discontent.* Chicago: IWW, 1980.

This is the 34th edition, available at IWW headquarters. Since 1909, the book has come out with varying titles and subtitles. Songs are added and subtracted in the various editions. Some of the older editions may be found at many archives. Subtitles include, among others, "On the Road, in the Jungles, and in the Shops" (15th ed., 1919); "Songs of Life"; and "Take out the Words, If So Must Be, But Leave, Oh Leave the Melody!" (20th ed., 1924); "Songs of Life—from the Mine, Mill, Factory, and Shop" (21st ed., 1925); "Songs of the Workers, To Fan the Flames of Discontent" (23rd ed., 1927); and "IWW Workers' Sing-Along Book" (IU#630, IWW, 1972).

4971. Patterson, Charles, ed. *Paint Creek Miner: Famous Labor Songs from Appalachia by Ralph Chaplin and Elmer Rumbaugh.* Huntington, WV: Appalachian Movement Press, 1972.

Miners and other workmen and their problems are the themes for these ballads and songs.

4972. Stavis, Barrie, and Frank Harmon, eds. *Songs of Joe Hill.* New York: Oak Publications, 1960.

4973. Weiss, H. G. *The Shame of California and Other Poems.* Chicago: GDC, n.d.

Includes poems about the San Quentin IWW prisoners, the California Syndicalist trials, and the San Pedro strike incident of 1924.

Fiction

Fiction, like all art, depends on the subjective reactions of people and touches on feelings, nuance, pleasure, and pain, apart from mere information. The real texture of IWW history—the lives of individuals, the battles fought for righteous causes, and the hardships and injustices—is reflected in imaginative stories. Novels are therefore included here. The connection with the IWW in many of them may be tenuous, often only inferential: a strike that is only *like* the Lawrence strike, a raid that is only an imaginative simulation of the Palmer Raids. The shame that many felt after the Red Scare and the pain of some memories limited the flowering of such political novels as had earlier been popular. Yet it is surprising how often the IWW has appeared in fiction in the last decade alone. I do not guarantee a "good read" from these books, but I believe that some people will enjoy a fictional dip into the IWW past, as I have. For an expert introduction to the world of fictional special-interest books, the following three writers may be useful.

Blake, Fay M. *The Strike in the American Novel.* Metuchen, NJ: Scarecrow Press, 1972.

Fay Blake points out that five of the authors she studied drew on the life of William D. Haywood in creating some of their characters: Max Eastman (no. 4991); Idwal Jones (no. 5002); Ernest Poole (no. 5006); Carl Van Vechten (no. 5020); and Clement Wood (no. 5024).

Blotner, Joseph. *The Modern American Political Novel, 1900–1960.* Austin: University of Texas Press, 1966.

The author shows how novels reflect the political changes of their times.

Rideout, Walter B. *The Radical Novel in the United States, 1900–1954: Some Interrelations of Literature and Society.* Cambridge: Harvard University Press, 1956. Reprint: New York: Hill & Wang, 1966.

Rideout traces many novels to political and radical movements. He finds that the only books fully involving the IWW are those of Charles Ashleigh and Harold Varney. Since his book was published, several others may be added to the list.

4974. Adamic, Louis. *Grandsons: A Story of American Lives.* New York: Harper, 1935. Reprint: New York: AMS, 1974.

One son's membership in the IWW causes tension in an immigrant family.

4975. Anderson, Nels [Dean Stiff, pseud.]. *The Milk and Honey Route.* New York: Vanguard Press, 1931.
The life of the hobo, described as frequently pleasant.

4976. Ashleigh, Charles. *The Rambling Kid.* London: Faber, 1930.
Days in the life of migratory workers as seen through the eyes of the IWW hero. The story is perhaps autobiographical, as the author was a popular and prominent Wobbly.

4977. Binns, Archie. *The Timber Beast.* New York: Scribner's, 1944.
A tale about lumberjacks in the Pacific Northwest.

4978. Bullard, Arthur. [Arthur Evans, pseud.] *Comrade Yetta.* New York: Macmillan, 1913. Reprints: Boston: Gregg Press, 1968; New York: Irvington, 1968.
Sweatshop worker and trade unionist Yetta, deciding whether to be a Socialist or to join the IWW.

4979. Cantwell, Robert. *The Land of Plenty.* New York: Farrar & Rinehart, 1934. Reprint: Carbondale: Southern Illinois University Press, 1971.
Poverty amidst plenty, as dramatized in a strike at a Northwest lumber mill.

4980. Chidester, Ann. *The Long Year.* New York: Scribners, 1946. Reprint: New York: AMS, 1976 (Labor Movement in Fiction and Non-Fiction Series).
A story about the radical "Bolsheviki" of Boston and an attractive woman from Russia.

4981. Churchill, Thomas. *Centralia Dead March.* Willimantic, CT: Curbstone Press, 1980.
A somber re-creation of the Centralia tragedy.

4982. Churchill, Winston. *The Dwelling Place of Light.* New York: Macmillan, 1917.
The conflict between changing moral values and a desire to maintain the old ones. Janet Bumpus, secretary to the boss of a New England mill, is torn between Syndicalist strikers and her pinchpenny employer.

4983. Colman, Louis. *Lumber.* Boston: Little, Brown, 1931. Reprint: New York: AMS, 1974 (Labor Movement in Fiction and Non-Fiction Series).
Northwest lumberworkers involved in a militant strike.

4984. Conroy, Jack. *The Disinherited.* New York: Covici-Friede, 1933. Reprint: Cambridge, MA: Robert Bentley, 1978.

The hero is a constant victim of the economy who drifts from job to job until he becomes an organizer of farmworkers.

4985. Davis, H. L. *Honey in the Horn.* New York: Harper, 1935. Reprint: Dunwoody, GA: Norman S. Berg, 1976.

A Pulitzer Prize-winning novel in which a young man in Oregon encounters many types of working people and has some adventures during the years 1906 to 1908.

4986. Dell, Floyd. *Love in Greenwich Village.* New York: Doran, 1926. Reprint: New York: Arno Press, 1973 (Short Story Index Reprint Series).

Short stories with a common theme, the psychology of "radicals" in love.

4987. ———. *Moon-Calf.* New York: Knopf, 1920.

A young radical journalist in Chicago becomes one of the "lost generation."

4988. Dos Passos, John. *The 42nd Parallel.* New York: Harper, 1930. Reprint: New York: American Library, 1969.

Novelistic portrayal of real events in the U.S. before World War I, including those involving radicals and Wobblies. This is the first novel in the *USA* trilogy.

4989. ———. *Nineteen Nineteen.* New York: Random House, 1932. Reprint: New York: Washington Square Press, 1978.

Appearances by Joe Hill, John Reed, and other IWWs as part of the montage in this second novel in the *USA* trilogy.

4990. Duffy, Joseph H. *Butte Was Like That.* Butte, MT: Tom Greenfield, 1941.

Sympathetic story of miners and their families.

4991. Eastman, Max. *Venture.* New York: Albert and Charles Boni, 1927.

Tale of a young man immersed in IWW activities, including a strike similar to the Paterson strike. He is patterned after both William Haywood and John Reed.

4992. Foote, Mary H. *Coeur d'Alene.* Boston: Houghton Mifflin, 1894. Reprint: New York: AMS, 1974 (Labor Movement in Fiction and Non-Fiction Series).

A novel of the Far West that re-creates the mining wars of Coeur d'Alene.

4993. Gambino, Richard. *Bread and Roses.* New York: Seaview, 1981.

A novel of clashing beliefs and personal anguish that uses the

Lawrence strike as a pivotal event in the plot. The strike, however, is dated much later than the actual one, which was in 1912.

4994. Garland, Hamlin. *Hesper.* New York: Harper, 1903. Reprint: St. Clair Shores, MI: Scholarly Press, 1974.
A story set against a background of the WFM's struggles in the Colorado mines.

4995. Grey, Zane. *Desert of Wheat.* New York: Grosset & Dunlap, 1919. Reprint: Evansville, IN: Unigraphic, 1975.
The IWWs in the Northwest are the villains in this Western novel.

4996. Hart, Alan. *In the Lives of Men.* New York: Norton, 1937.
A story of lumberjacks and their strikes.

4997. Hedges, Marion H. *Dan Minturn.* New York: Vanguard, 1927.
The life of a young radical politician in Minneapolis, who gradually succumbs to prosperity and the pleasure of power.

4998. ———. *Iron City.* New York: Boni & Liveright, 1919. Reprint: New York: AMS, 1974 (Labor Movement in Fiction and Non-Fiction Series).
Unionism in New England is the theme and background in this novel.

4999. Herbst, Josephine. *The Executioner Waits.* New York: Harcourt, Brace, 1934. Reprint: New York: AMS, 1974 (Labor Movement in Fiction and Non-Fiction Series).
Recounts part of the story of the Wendels, using the rise and fall of the IWW as a background. This is the second volume of a trilogy.

5000. Houghton, Elgar. *The Intruders.* Seattle: Northwest Labor History Assn., 1981.
A novel based on the episodes surrounding the Everett Massacre.

5001. Houston, Robert. *Bisbee '17: A Novel.* New York: Pantheon, 1979.
A lively novel about the Bisbee deportation. Purists will not like the author's reworking of historical facts.

5002. Jones, Idwal. *Steel Chips.* New York: Knopf, 1929.
The powerful grip of a huge steel mill on its workers, as felt by a young apprentice.

5003. London, Jack. *The Iron Heel.* New York: Grosset & Dunlap, 1907. Reprint: Westport, CT: Lawrence Hill, 1980.

Early "science fiction" depicting the future of the U.S. in 1932, showing the final conflict between the "people of the abyss" and the Fascist capitalists. The hero and heroine are linked to both sides.

5004. McCaig, Donald. *Butte Polka.* New York: Rawson, Wade, 1980.

Recent novel using Butte labor history for its background.

5005. Parker, Edwin Stone. *Timber: A Historical Novel of the Pacific Northwest.* Hicksville, NY: Exploitation Press, 1963.

Days of the lumberjacks are recalled in this novel about the working class.

5006. Poole, Ernest. *The Harbor.* New York: Macmillan, 1915. Reprint: Laurel, NY: Lightyear Press, 1976.

The life story of Billy, who is bound for life to the New York waterfront. Includes a big, bitter waterfront strike.

5007. Rodney, George B. *Jim Lofton, American.* New York: James A. McCann, 1920.

A typical "Western," by a prolific author of that genre, that includes some anti-IWW sentiments.

5008. Saxton, Alexander P. *The Great Midland.* New York: Appleton-Century Crofts, 1948.

The daily life of a young railroad worker, ex-IWW, whose growing absorption in Communist activities and labor organizing affects his marriage.

5009. Sinclair, Upton. *Boston.* New York: Albert and Charles Boni, 1928. Reprint: St. Clair Shores, MI: Scholarly Press, 1970.

The radicalization of an upper-class grandmother. The Ettor-Giovannitti trial, which took place after the Lawrence strike, and the Sacco-Vanzetti trial are woven into the plot.

5010. ———. *Oil.* La Jolla, CA: published by the author, 1927. Reprint: Cambridge, MA: Robert Bentley, 1981.

The radicalization of a young oil capitalist in a novel that describes the persecution of the IWW and the California "class war." (Sinclair's *King Coal* (1917) and *The Jungle* (1906) are also notable for portraying the "class war.")

5011. Smedley, Agnes. *Daughter of Earth.* New York: Coward-McCann, 1929. Reprint: Old Westbury, CT: Feminist Press, 1973.

The life and education of a rebellious woman who joins the IWW.

5012. Stegner, Wallace. *The Preacher and the Slave.* Garden City, NY: Doubleday, 1945. Reissued as *Joe Hill: A Biographical Novel.* Reprint: Lincoln, NB: University of Nebraska Press, 1980.
The Joe Hill story novelized, with the implication that he was guilty as charged.

5013. Stevens, James. *Big Jim Turner.* Garden City, NY: Doubleday, 1945. Reprint: Albuquerque: University of New Mexico Press, 1975.
Sympathetic treatment of an IWW character in this novel.

5014. Stone, Irving. *Adversary in the House.* Garden City, NY: Doubleday, 1947. Reprint: New York: New American Library, 1972.
A fictionalized biography of Eugene Debs.

5015. Thorseth, Matthea. *The Color of Ripening.* Seattle: Superior Publishers, 1949.
The story of Norwegian-Americans in the Pacific Northwest, in which the IWW gets kindly treatment.

5016. Tobenkin, Elias. *The Road.* New York: Harcourt, Brace, 1922.
The effect that new ideas and attitudes have on American workers' behavior, with some background on life in Russia just after the revolution.

5017. Traven, Bruno. *The Cotton Pickers.* New York: Hill & Wang, 1969. First published in Berlin as *Der Wobbly* (Buchmeister-Verlag, 1926), then as *Die Baumwollpflückers* (1929).
Story of an ex-sailor who first works for an American farmer in Mexico, then in the Mexican oil fields. Strikes break out wherever he goes; he and his fellow workers often seem like Wobblies.

5018. ———. *The Death Ship.* New York: Lawrence Hill, 1934. First published in Berlin as *Das Totenschiff* (Gutenberg Book Guild, 1926).
Further life of the same sailor as in no. 5017, captured in an adventure novel that condemns capitalism, nationalism, and "the system." For information about the elusive, mysterious author, see the article by Charles Miller (no. 2102).

5019. Turner, George Kibbe. "The Possibilist." *Saturday Evening Post* 192 (January 31, 1920 and subsequent issues through March 13, 1920).

A once-popular magazine serial about a man in love whose flirtation with the IWW nearly ruined the romance.

5020. Van Vechten, Carl. *Peter Whiffle: His Life and Works.* Reprint: New York, AMS, 1977.

A novelized version of the life story of William D. Haywood.

5021. Varney, Harold Lord. *Revolt.* New York: Irving Kaye Davis, 1919.

Story about a young bourgeois man who becomes an enthusiastic IWW but who then turns conservative, just as the author did in real life.

5022. Weatherwax, Clara. *Marching! Marching!* New York: John Day, 1935. Reprint: New York: AMS, 1974 (Labor Movement in Fiction and Non-Fiction Series).

A strike in Aberdeen, Washington, ending in a big, doomed demonstration march, with workers marching straight into the gunbarrels of the National Guard.

5023. Winstead, Ralph. "Johnson the Gyppo." *Industrial Pioneer* 1 (September, 1921). 41–43.

Typical, entertaining short story by an IWW who wrote many charming stories, mainly for IWW publications. This story and another are included in Joyce Kornbluh's *Rebel Voices* (no. 132).

5024. Wood, Clement. *Mountain.* New York: E. P. Dutton, 1920.

A young mining engineer's conversion to socialism by his radical sweetheart. He helps the striking miners in a losing labor battle against his own father.

FRANK P. WALSH, Chairman U. S. Industrial Relations Commission, Writes On,
"My Impressions of the Witnesses and Their Testimony"

Unclassified Addenda

5025. Bracher, Frederick. "How it Was Then: The Pacific Northwest in the Twenties." *Oregon Historical Quarterly* 84 (Winter, 1983): 341–63.
Describes Emil Kowalski, an IWW organizer at Tilton Spur.

5026. Bruns, Roger. "Hobo: For America's Knights of the Road, the Good Old Days Are Gone Forever." *American History Illustrated* 16 (January, 1982):9–15.

5027. Cain, F. "The Industrial Workers of the World: Aspects of Its Suppression in Australia, 1916–1919." *Labour History* 42 (May, 1982):54–62. (Australian journal.)

5028. Cornford, Daniel. "Lumber, Labor, and Community in Humboldt County, California, 1850–1920." Diss., University of California, Santa Barbara, 1983.

5029. Crampton, Frank A. *Deep Enough: A Working Stiff in the Western Mine Camps.* Norman, OK: University of Oklahoma Press, 1982. A reprint of the 1956 edition.
Memoirs of an ex-Wobbly who worked in the Western states.

5030. Dubofsky, Melvyn. Review of *The Radical Persuasion,* by Aileen S. Kraditor (see no 133). *Labor History* 24 (Fall, 1983):588–94.

5031. Ferrell, Geoffrey. "The Brotherhood of Timber Workers and the Southern Lumber Trust, 1910–1914." Diss., University of Texas, Austin, 1982.

5032. Fishbein, Leslie. "Dress Rehearsal in Race Relations: Pre–World War I American Radicals and the Black Question." *Afro-Americans in New York Life and History* 6 (January, 1982):7–15.
The racial attitudes of Debs, Haywood, and others.

5033. Ghetti, Sandra. "Dall'azione Diretta All' 'Organizing To Go Back To Work'" *Movimento Operaio e Socialista* 51 (1982):147–63.
Explains the decline of the IWW as due to new technologies and new labor-handling techniques that made it unnecessary.

5034. Guerin, Daniel. *100 Years of Labor in the USA.* Translated by Alan Adler. London: Ink Links/Pluto Press, 1984.

A French historian finds the IWW more in the American tradition than most other U.S. organizations.

5035. Lee, Art. "Hometown Hysteria: Bemidji at the Start of World War I." *Minnesota History* 49 (Summer, 1984):65–75.

Describes the real Red Scare trouble given such IWWs as Archie Sinclair and a local liberal merchant, Morris Kaplan, by the citizens of this Minnesota town.

5036. McBride, James D. "Gaining a Foothold in the Paradise of Capitalism: The Western Federation of Miners and the Unionization of Bisbee." *Journal of Arizona History* 23 (No. 3, 1982):299–316.

5037. Maffi, Mario. *La Giungla e il Grattacielo: Gli Scrittori e il Sogno Americano, 1865–1920* (The Jungle and the Skyscraper: Writers and the American dream, 1865–1920). Bari: Laterza, 1981.

Explores labor literature and history amid the American jungles and skyscrapers.

5038. Massachusetts Historical Workshop. *Life and Times in Immigrant City: Memories of a Textile Town.*

Pamphlet about the labor history of Lawrence, published in 1982.

5039. Munch, Eric, and Guthrie, Woody. "The 1913 Massacre at Italian Hall." *Chronicle* 19 (Winter, 1983–84):20–21.

Includes a photoessay and a poem about the Calumet-Hecla strike disaster.

5040. Noel, Thomas J. "William D. Haywood: The Most Hated and Feared Figure in America." *Colorado Heritage* (No. 2, 1984): 2–12.

5041. Salvatore, Nick. *Eugene V. Debs: Citizen and Socialist.* Urbana, IL: University of Illinois Press, 1982.

Prize-winning biography.

5042. Seager, Allen. "Nineteen Nineteen: Year of Revolt." *Journal of the West* 23 (October, 1984):40–48.

Describes the Canadian One Big Union and notes various connections and influences of the IWW.

5043. Shapiro, Herbert. "Lincoln Steffens and the McNamara Case: A Progressive Response to Class Conflict." *American Journal of Eco-*

nomics and Sociology 39 (October, 1980):397–412.

Not about the IWW, but an analysis of contemporary attitudes of both hard-liners and liberals.

5044. Van Valen, Nelson. "Cleaning up the Harbor: The Suppression of the I.W.W. at San Pedro, 1922–1925." *Southern California Quarterly* 66 (Summer, 1984):147–72.

Recounts in detail police and vigilante actions, official and unofficial, against the IWW.

5045. Wilentz, Sam. "Against Exceptionalism: Class Consciousness and the American Labor Movement." *International Labor and Working Class History* 26 (Fall, 1984):1–24.

Sees the IWW as one of three divergent strategies of the working class in facing changing problems of capitalism.

5046. Woirol, Gregory R. "Notes and Documents: Observing the IWW in California, May–July, 1914." *Labor History* 25 (Summer, 1984):437–47.

5047. ———. "Rustling Oranges in Lindsay." *California History* 62 (Summer, 1983):82–97.

Describes the diary of Frederick C. Mills, a student of Carleton Parker, who went undercover into the California fruit pickers' world for the Wheatland investigation.

5048. Zanjani, Sally S. "Notes and Documents: The Mike Smith Case, a Note on High Grading in Goldfield, Nevada, 1910." *Labor History* 24 (Fall, 1983):580–87.

Describes unionizing in Goldfield.

Note: Since this bibliography was finished, several more books and many articles have appeared in print. I regret the omission of Donald E. Winters, Jr., *The Soul of the Wobblies: The I.W.W.;* Stewart Bird, Dan Georgakis, and Deborah Shaffer, *Solidarity Forever? An Oral History of the I.W.W.;* and Stewart Bird and Peter Robilotta, *The Wobblies,* as well as recent articles by those authors and by Joseph Conlin, Michael Ervin, Steve Golin, A. Ross McCormack, Jay M. Pawa, and Ann Schofield; there are, undoubtedly, many others as well.

Index

Authors and Subjects

Note: the numbers cited in this index are those of items in this bibliography.

Mark Twain. *See* Clemens, Samuel.

Dione Miles is the Reference Archivist at the Archives of Labor and Urban Affairs of the Walter P. Reuther Library, Wayne State University. She has a degree in Library Science from Wayne State University. As IWW archivist, she processed the IWW papers and wrote the guide to the IWW collection. She compiled a bibliography for Joseph R. Conlin's *At the Point of Production: The Local History of the IWW,* published in 1981.

The Archives of Labor and Urban Affairs at Wayne State University was established in 1960 to collect and preserve records of the American labor movement, with special emphasis upon industrial unionism and related social, economic, and political reform movements in the United States. A second broad theme was workers, working conditions, and the nature of work. Later, the theme of urban affairs was added to the collecting scope. Over 40,000 linear feet of correspondence, minutes, proceedings, newspapers, photographs, tape recordings, personal papers of members, and other items have been gathered from major unions in the United States, making the Archives one of the world's prominent research collections on labor history.

The book was designed by Gary Gore. The typeface for the text and the display is Baskerville, based on the original design by John Baskerville in the eighteenth century.
Manufactured in the United States of America.